Transformations

Transformations

Identity Construction in Contemporary Culture

Grant McCracken

Indiana University Press   •   Bloomington and Indianapolis

This book is a publication of

Indiana University Press
601 North Morton Street
Bloomington, IN 47404-3797 USA

http://iupress.indiana.edu

Telephone orders   800-842-6796
Fax orders   812-855-7931
Orders by e-mail   iuporder@indiana.edu

Manufactured in the United States of America

Library of Congress Cataloging-in-Publication Data

McCracken, Grant David, date
   Transformations : identity construction in contemporary culture / Grant McCracken.
     p. cm.
   Includes bibliographical references and index.
   ISBN-13: 978-0-253-35072-5 (cloth)
   ISBN-13: 978-0-253-21957-2 (pbk.)
   1. Self-perception—Social aspects.   2. Identity (Psychology)—Social aspects.   3. Self-actualization
(Psychology)—Social aspects.   4. Popular culture.   I. Title.
   HM1051. M33 2008
   306—dc22   2007035717

1 2 3 4 5 13 12 11 10 09 08

to the memory of
Hargurchet Bhabra

Contents

Sightings

If one looks back at one life's life, it's like seeing a series of different people.   Anne Meara, playwright and actress[1]

Your life is yours to create.   Richard Linklater, director[2]

I have reinvented myself every 10 years and I recommend that everyone else should do the same.   Nora Ephron, writer[3]

[Asked] if she ever—when she was young—dreamed of being in *Vogue*. "Dreamed to be in *Vogue*? I'm a black woman from Mississippi. Why would I be thinking I was gonna be in *Vogue*?"
        Oprah Winfrey, in *Vogue*[4]

[I am a] transsexual lesbian whose female lover is becoming a man.   Kate Bornstein, writer[5]

When I'm on-line, I'm 37, tall, blond and raring to go.
        Ilene Weinberg, 68, retired social worker
        with Parkinson's disease[6]

A ruler wages . . . warfare against spontaneous and uncontrolled transformation.   Elias Canetti, writer[7]

[T]he post-modernist temper demands that what was previously played out in fantasy and imagination must be acted out in life as well. Anything permitted in art is permitted in life.
        Daniel Bell, American sociologist[8]

I scarcely know without a good deal of recollection whether I am a Landed Gentleman, an Engineer or a Potter, for indeed I am all three and many other characters by turns.
        Josiah Wedgwood, early English industrialist[9]

Ain't no going back. You can't get unfamous. You can get infamous. But you can't get unfamous.
        Dave Chappelle, comedian[10]

It just depends on which me you get.
        Farrah Fawcett, TV star[11]

Preface: Entertainment Is Dead, Long Live Transformation

Entertainment is a mainstay of our culture and economy. As I write this, the television show *American Idol* is drawing 40 million votes a week. Las Vegas is drawing 2.5 million visitors a month. Movie theaters sell 565 million tickets a year.[1]

If we take all forms together—movies, television, radio, music, spectator sports, theme parks, casinos, websites, magazines, newspapers, children's toys, night clubs, theater, and gaming software—entertainment is a $480 billion industry.[2]

And that's just the economics. Culturally, we are preoccupied with the stars. As I write this, the media are wondering what Brad and Angelina will name the baby. (I assume you know who "Brad" and "Angelina" are, and that's telling.) *Entertainment Tonight*, *Entertainment Weekly*, *US Weekly*, and Gawker.com are inexhaustible sources of celebrity and movie news.[3]

Entertainment is alive and well. Right? No, actually; entertainment is dead. It walks, it talks, but it is now merely a zombie in our midst. The concept with which we talk and think about our world is now in forfeit. We still use it, to be sure, but it is now merely a marker. "Entertainment" marks the place where once there was a useful idea.

If entertainment is dead, what will take its place? Almost certainly we will see a variety of ideas emerge to compete for this hallowed space. This book looks at one of them: self-transformation.

Entertainment: Humble Origins

In the medieval period, entertainment was one of the "mechanical arts." Its purpose was to delight, divert, refresh. None of these goals were noble, and entertainment ranked well below the liberal arts in prestige and cultural influence.[4] Metaphorically, we might think of entertainment as a madcap eight-year-old at a family wedding: rambunctious and delightful, but oblivious to the import and solemnity of the occasion, and allowed to interfere with it only in the most marginal way.

In the early modern period, entertainment remained a minor player in both commerce and culture. In the event it got too big for its britches, it was subject to the interference of church and state. Shakespeare's Globe Theatre suffered closure. Entertainment remained a dubious pleasure, both ignoble and obscure.

Academics to the rescue! Contemporary academics have rushed to discover a significance that would have surprised and probably horrified Elizabethan churchmen and perhaps even Shakespeare himself. Johan Huizinga might treat entertainment as play. Arnold van Gennep might treat it as liminality. Mikhail Bakhtin described a "carnival culture" that mocked received convention, hierarchical distinction, and political authority. But entertainment remained "contents under pressure." With social constraint and political intervention in place, it could never be more than a licensed act of departure.[5]

Wishful thinking by twentieth-century scholars aside, entertainment was mostly what medieval thinkers said it was: a relief from economic and cultural tedium. At best, it was a matter of boundary testing, an act of minor mischief, a case of rule infringement. Entertainment might play the fool, it might beard the king, it might play at anarchy, but finally it remained a cultural force no more dangerous than an eight-year-old.

Entertainment might offer minor category reformation, but it was incapable of category innovation. There could be no genre busting, no genre splicing. With the great and truly exceptional exception of the genius from Stratford and some few others, entertainment was incapable of real cultural innovation. Creativity was well contained, all departure strictly liminal.

The Monster That Ate Chicago

If we travel by seven-league boots to the twenty-first century, we find there an entertainment that has changed beyond recognition. By this time, it is active, ubiquitous, and voracious, changing much of what it touches.

Entertainment manages even to work its way into language, and now it is usual to hear the terms "infotainment," "edutainment," and, most alarmingly, "eatertainment." Infotainment is entertainment that informs. Edutainment is entertainment that educates. What is eatertainment? Eatertainment is what happens, apparently, at Chuck E. Cheese and the Hard Rock Cafe.

Entertainment began to colonize domestic space. Living rooms and dens made space for radios, then televisions. Most recently, we have seen the arrival of the "home entertainment center," with its giant screen and five-speaker sound system. Entertainment now had a room of its own.

Entertainment began to consume public space, with large portions of New York City being reserved for its exclusive use. Times Square, the Great White Way, Radio City Music Hall, Madison Square Garden, the off Broadways, Coney Island, Yankee Stadium: all of these existed to serve entertainment. But entertainment's greatest urban achievement may be Las Vegas, a city Neil Postman says is "entirely devoted to the idea of entertainment." Indeed, Postman wishes to go further still, saying,

> Our politics, our religion, news, athletics, education & commerce have been transformed into congenial adjuncts of show business, largely without protest or even much popular notice.[6]

Certainly, this goes too far. Otherwise, why would marketing gurus be urging us to install entertainment in more parts of the consumer society?[7] More to the point, Postman gives his argument that tell-tale eagerness. He deeply wants it to be true, for a larger ideological critique would then be set in train. And what's an intellectual for, if not to offer searing social criticism?

But this is not the real problem. Just at the moment that Postman was mounting his attack on the power and ubiquity of entertainment, entertainment began to die. (Thus does the owl of Minerva take wing at dusk.) Searing social criticism is diverting, even ideologically titillating, but it frequently turns out to be sloppy social science, leaving us unprepared to reckon with some of the changes now upon us. (Postman's argument is one of the reasons this book was not written twenty years ago.)

Entertainment Is Dead, Long Live Transformation

So what happened? Well, the latter half of the twentieth century happened. We have seen the rise of irreverent youth cultures that took power away from cultural elites and put it in the hands of commercial forces and, increasingly, the hands of individual teens. One of these cultures, punk, was dedicated to a DIY (do-it-yourself) philosophy, according to which anyone could pick up a guitar and have at it. Rock stardom was not just for rock stars anymore.

As Henry Jenkins has demonstrated, fans, once fawning, were now participatory.[8] It is unlikely that fans were ever the "dupes" and the "drones" that theory said they were, but now they were active in their relationship to their favorite shows, sometimes hyperactive.

> Some in the X-Files fan community were disturbed by what they saw as significant characterization and continuity problems in season eight [of *The X-Files*]. They are now addressing this issue by rewriting the episodes to correct the problems.[9]

The asymmetries of old were falling away. The notion that an audience should sit in rapt and passive admiration of the work of actors and playwrights was now in jeopardy. The new audience had a new sense of agency. It entertained a new wish to participate. There was no deference left in this audience, and no willingness merely to be "entertained."

New technologies have lowered the barriers to entry. Almost anyone can afford a recording studio. The new technologies were perhaps most spectacularly transformative of the kind of amateur publication called a "zine." The zine was itself a mark of a growing wish to participate in contemporary culture. Instead of merely subscribing to magazines, consumers were now prepared to create their own. The best they could do before the advent of the Internet was to type, copy, staple, and distribute their zines by hand, perhaps by mail. A typical zine might find an audience of thirty people. The Internet and the rise of the Web log, or blog, vastly diminished the cost of production and increased the potential readership. The zine writer became a blogger and, as a blogger, could move much closer to center stage.

But new technologies also allow the establishment of new, more participatory online experience. It was now more possible for people to "become someone else" on line. This was true in the simple chat line, where identity cloaking, borrowing, swapping are commonplace. Second Life multiplied the richness, the definitional markers, and the interactivity of this experience remarkably. Those of you who have wandered Second Life and spoken to people who issue from flaming crowds or manifest as adorable rabbits know what I am talking about.[10] Xbox 360 technology so augments and transforms the gamer that even the life of a "Master Chief" engaged in intergalactic battle (as in the Microsoft game Halo 3) becomes a little more plausible and engaging. The technology puts new transformational options at our disposal.

It is tempting to suppose that this new passion for transformation is the enthusiasm of the young. According to the Fantasy Sports Trade Association, more than 15 million people spend about $1.5 billion annually to play fantasy sports. Real fans have always been deeply engaged in the game. But this is something more than engagement. This is presumption. A player of fantasy baseball says, "Watching from the stands is no longer enough for me. I have to coach and manage, too." This is a transformational reformation of America's game, pursued, mostly, by men of middle age.[11]

Women of middle age have transformational enthusiasms of their own. Indeed this theme is now the mainstay of cable TV. *What Not to Wear, Trading Spaces, While You Were Out* and *Surprise by Design* are now successful shows on The Learning Channel (TLC). *What Not to Wear* offers someone a makeover and in the process plays out a tension between clothing as an expression of the authentic self and clothing as something dictated from on high by fashionistas. We will have to answer many questions as we leave an entertainment culture for a transformational one, and one is particularly vexing: To whom does the transformation belong?[12]

The transformational turn is driven by rising sophistication in the industry and in the fan. Sometime in the last quarter of the twentieth century, popular culture began to use itself as a creative resource. Self-repudiation gave way to self-discovery. Shows like *The Simpsons, Buffy the Vampire Slayer,* and *The X-Files* began unashamedly to draw upon pop culture. A virtuous cycle was set in train. The more self-referential pop culture became, the richer it got; the richer it got, the better it got; the better it got, the easier it was to recruit more talented writers and producers; and the more talented the writers and producers were, the richer pop culture became. Now Stephen Johnson felt it possible to write a book called *Everything Bad Is Good for You: How Today's Popular Culture Is Actually Making Us Smarter.*[13] It is worth pointing out that this improvement of popular culture ran entirely against expectation. The intellectuals and the academics insisted that pop culture was "dumbing itself down," that it would become ever more stupid, ever more craven.[14] I believe recantations are in order.

As producers got better, so did consumers. Andrew Zolli observes that the Internet sensation "All Your Base Are Belong to Us" is, among other things, a display of how formidable are the editing skills of the youthful producers who created it.[15] This display is now everywhere in evidence. When Converse and the advertising agency BSSP decided to ask ordinary people to make ads for the Converse All-Star, they were astonished at the skill that was forthcoming. It was as if everyone had gone "behind the curtain" (to use a metaphor from *The Wizard of Oz*) and returned with impressive production skills. Indeed, in new marketing circles, it is customary to think of the consumer as a "cocreator" of goods and communications. Some people have even gone so far as to suggest that it makes more sense to call the consumer a "multiplier."[16]

A shift is taking place. Individuals who once submitted to the blandishments of entertainment are now interested in something more active. They have mastered the codes of cultural production. They have refused the asymmetries of the old regime. They have collapsed the distance between fan and celebrity. They have made themselves cocreators in the culture they consume. To use the language of industry, the new media consumer is a "lean-forward" participator, no longer a "laid-back" couch potato.

For our purposes, these new creatures are transformational. They may make themselves into a TV producer, a ball club manager, a "whole new me," a rock star, a Master Chief, a video creator, a blogger, a flaming cloud in Second Life. When consumers begin to exercise the new liberties and resources at their disposal, the range of definitional possibilities proves to be quite large. Or, better, when consumers become producers, one of the objectives of their creative activity is the construction and multiplication of new selves.

And this spells trouble for the old standbys of entertainment. The original Disney proposition was, after all, to strap people into conveyances and make them passive witnesses to Disneyland. It is not even remotely possible that the young authors of All Your Base Are Belong to Us would find much joy in a trip to Disney. And what about Las Vegas, the town that Postman says was built entirely of and for entertainment? This is, I think, now struggling. The floor shows, those demonstrations of generic feeling, have been supplanted by Cirque du Soleil. And the Cirque du Soleil performances are, of course, an exercise in the most spectacular of spectacles, the hyperbole of which seems designed to conceal the fact that the audience is still just sitting there. Not even soaring bodies and exploding lights can conceal the fact that the audience is merely auditing. The old regime of entertainment looks more and more like the Hard Rock Cafe: celebrity detritus under glass.

Popular culture has become culture. It is something we understand, produce, participate in, and manufacture, and only then consume. And now that we are more fully endowed with this interest, sophistication, and ability, it turns out that what we want to do with it is to invent and explore new selves. If this is so, if transformation is now one of the great inventive regimes of our culture, the time has come to think about what it is and how it works.

Is this more than an anthropologist's curiosity? Does it matter if entertainment gives way to transformation? I think it must. If the best entertainment can hope for is boundary testing and minor mischief, transformation is another beast altogether. Already, it drives cultural reformation and innovation of which most entertainment cannot dream. Already, it drives the "long tail" markets that are transforming new capitalism.[17] Individuals interested in transformational opportunity will produce and consume startling cultural departures. Entertainment bent us back toward the center of our culture. Transformation will take us away from it.

Introduction

Ovid, let's say, returns to walk among us. He becomes, inevitably, a figure of controversy. The talk show circuit demands his presence and, as a matter of course, sensationalizes his past. (Today on *Jerry:* Ovid! Literary genius or sexpot pornographer? You be the judge!) Almost certainly, Ovid irritates the production assistants. Ignore him for a second and you find him standing in front of a rack of magazines, bursting with questions. "You're telling me that instructions for metamorphosis come every few months from Paris, Milan, and Tokyo? You call this what? 'Fashion'? That's a good name for it. May I get copies, please? Lots of copies, if you please."[1]

But he is not completely astonished by the contemporary world. Parts of it are consistent with the world he sought to capture in *Metamorphoses.*[2] He probably wouldn't blink at a retired and disabled social worker who becomes thirtysomething and blond on the Internet.[3] He might be a little surprised that Nora Ephron transformed herself every ten years. ("Why just once a decade, do you think?")[4]

This Roman *expected* the world to be a fluid place. This is perhaps why he combed classical myth and folklore for instances of transformation. It was a theme of his age. Not only was his world as various as Plato's ("all that can be imagined must be"), it was changeable as well. Both expected fecundity: Plato from new species, Ovid from dynamic ones. What *could* exist, both believed, would exist. Ovid's *Metamorphoses* had a single purpose: "to tell of bodies . . . transformed into shapes of a different kind."[5]

There are differences, of course, between his transformations and ours. Ovid's transformations are mostly divine interventions: gods working on humans, flora, fauna, and other gods. Our transformations, on the other hand, are performed mostly by humans on themselves.[6]

Differences aside, Ovid's view of transformation might prove useful. At a stroke it lets us embrace one of the most vexing properties of the contemporary world—the endlessly liquid character of people. We talk a good deal about "reinvention" and "transformation," but we're frustrated. We are, most of us, the products of a static, continuous world. We expect continuity, sameness, consistency. We think of "identity" as something that comes from things that remain "identical"—from continuities of self, family, home, and work. But we could be wrong. Perhaps it comes from transformation.

We are a little astonished to see how various lives can be. A single self can be a crowded house—sometimes a veritable township—of diversity. What are we to make of the '60s revolutionary, Manhattan stockbroker, and New Age healer when all of them prove to be (Jerry Rubin–like) the same man?[7] How are we to understand the art historian, anti-feminist, and bisexual activist when they are (Camille Paglia–like) the same woman?[8] How are we to understand selves pressed into service on several voyages and now scattered across several ports of call when they are . . . well, ourselves? Ovid would perhaps be interested to see how much of his mythological world has found its way into the one we take for granted and struggle to inhabit day in and day out.

Popular culture shows evidence that we are mobilizing to contend with new imperatives. There is something makeshift about it all, to be sure, but we are further along here than we are on issues of diversity, where moral panic and incomprehension are pretty much the order of the day.

Sometimes, we appear infatuated with transformation. The TV host Joan Lunden advises, "No one can change your life for you. Go for it."[9] The astrologer Sally Brompton says, "Don't be afraid of change—welcome it. Things are changing in your life because you're growing and maturing, not because you have done something wrong. The world is changing, too."[10] Others are more impatient. Sam McKnight, counselor to the stars, says, "You've got to start paying attention. When people don't change, they become caricatures of themselves."[11]

The call for transformation comes even from on high. Carl Rogers, a particularly influential wise man, described the good patient as someone who "move[s] forward in the process of becoming [until] he finds that he is at last free to change."[12] Jeffrey Deitch, the artist, says it's "normal to reinvent oneself."[13] Academics, journalists, and business leaders supply the chorus.[14] Our political leaders used to plead for office by promising to uphold tradition. Now they offer to transform everything from the world economy to the national park system. Phil Knight says that Nike (the shoe maker, not the goddess) starts over every six months.[15]

It is in some ways an Ovidian age. A fashion model says, "My portfolio kills everybody's. Every time you turn the page, it's a different person."[16] A songwriter says, "I take on different characters. I mean, why should I be me?"[17] A player of fantasy games says, "Why be yourself, when you can have the fun, and the risk, of being someone else?"[18] A writer says, "People nowadays can experiment with their lives."[19] Once an extraordinary event for extraordinary creatures, transformation has become more routine and accessible. Many people are taking on "shapes of a different kind." But, again, there is that difference. Transformation used to be what gods did to one another. Now it's what we do to ourselves.

Our transformation has many motives, and seeks many outcomes. Sometimes, it has an uneasy, almost obsessive sound to it:

> I tend to just glom onto someone and adapt their personality, penmanship, speaking style, everything, and I keep moving through a set of individuals I admire. . . . If I spend five days with Salman [Rushdie], I end up looking like him. If I spend two hours with Martin [Amis], I look like a Martin doll that evening.[20]

Sometimes, it is not an individual but a collective undertaking:

> As a writer, my literary agenda begins by acknowledging that America has transformed me. It does not end until I show that I (along with hundreds of thousands of immigrants like me) am minute by minute transforming America.[21]

Sometimes, it is part of a larger social change:

> As a gay person, you are re-creating and reinventing institutions like marriage and family holidays. You see through institutions, and tweak them, and co-opt them and use them for what you want.[22]

Transformation can be a source of creativity. The mystery writer Ruth Rendell, who also writes as Barbara Vine, says,

> Once I was Barbara Vine, I could do something else.[23]

It can be a source of innovation. The basketball star Hakeem Olajuwon says,

> I used to play the low post the way everyone does. . . . Then I started to watch the small forwards and the guards.[24]

It can be a release from disability. The sixty-eight-year-old victim of Parkinson's disease says,

> When I'm on-line, I'm 37, tall, blond and raring to go.[25]

It can be a release from constraints of one kind or several:

> Michelle Shocked never hesitates to escape . . . from her Mormon past . . . from the categories of race, gender and music . . . from her paternalistic record company.[26]

It can be a matter of curiosity:

> You know, sometimes I'd like to get inside that body of [Dennis Rodman's] and look at the world through his eyes.[27]

or simple opportunism:

> I was in advertising for a while, and I'm very good at negotiating my public persona so it doesn't get too closely attached to any temporary phenomenon.[28]

Sometimes, it's the revelation of long-kept secrets. A surgeon who had operated on Britain's Queen Mother announced,

> I am known to everyone professionally as Mr. William Muirhead-Allwood—but for years I have called myself Sarah.[29]

But it would be wrong to think that this enthusiasm for transformation is peculiar to the present day. All humans have the ability to assume "shapes of a different kind." Self-transformation is the native gift of every member of the species.

As it turned out, this was one of the challenges of the present book: how to show transformation as a property of all human communities *and* the special preoccupation of our present one. Could I create a scheme that showed the peculiar approach, the "transformational routine" of each community? Could I "lump" where possible and "split" where necessary?

By "transformational routine," I mean the set of conventions by which an individual is changed. (There are many transformational routines at work in Western cultures. Institutions, industries, governments use them constantly. I am interested in the ones available to individuals.) These conventions specify what one is before, and after, the transformation. They also specify how the change will take place. In sum, these rules specify the point of departure, the destination, and the path in between. In Ovid's language, transformational routines are the processes by which people take on social "shapes of a different kind."

Transformational routines are what we might call, with Anthony Giddens, "mechanisms of identity."[30] They are processes by which the individual takes on private and public selves. I will use the term "self" freely. But it is to be understood that it is precisely this term that is at issue as transformational routines emerge and accumulate. Each routine produces its own social creature.

I will talk about four transformational routines: traditional, premodern or status, modern, and postmodern. Traditional routines are the traditional rites of passage with which anthropology has been preoccupied. Rites of passage are used, for instance, to turn children into adults. Status routines are the processes by which individuals change their social standing. The cult of the English gentleman would qualify here. Modernist routines are used to make the self mobile in both personal and public space. They were devised to pursue new kinds of authenticity and instrumentality. Postmodernist routines open up new kinds of multiplicity and fluidity to the individual.

I propose we treat these four routines additively. In the beginning, all transformational routines are traditional. Premodern or status transformational routines eventually appear, but they do not supplant the traditional routines. These live on. We now have both. When modern routines emerge, the pattern holds. For a moment, these new routines appear to win the day, but eventually they prove merely to be an addition to the standing set. Now there are three. Enter the postmodern routines, and we have four. (Some of the intensity and dynamism of the present world comes from the fact that all these engines of change are running at once.) The problem of how to lump and split caused me some difficulty until I remembered the sumptuary legislation of Elizabethan England, which uses precisely this structure for a different purpose.[31] The additive model looks like the figure shown here (where the rectangle on the far right is us, heir to all the previous transformational routines and adding a class of our own).

Solving one problem creates another. My model appears to claim too much. First, it is not meant to be exhaustive. I have not captured all the transformational activities of the human community. It is also true that

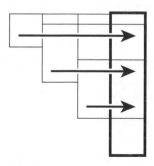

Figure 1. An additive model

there is nothing evolutionary about this scheme. Later stages do not grow out of earlier ones. There is nothing inevitable about each new stage. It merely happened to be the one that happened next. Later stages are not better, more sophisticated, or more advanced than earlier ones. This scheme is driven by no imperative. It could have happened differently (and it probably did). This is merely a way of showing that the transformational routines at work in contemporary culture have diverse origins and histories.

We might think about this model as we do the map of the London Underground. We know that this map achieves clarity by reducing the complexities and confusions of a vast subway system. (For instance, the Circle line is not really a circle and its stations are not at perfectly equal intervals.) My model of transformational routines works the same way. Some of its implications are false, some of its clarities are illusory, but most of its important claims are, I think, true.

The overriding objective of this book is clear and probably too ambitious: to discover an idea that can help us think comprehensively about what is happening to our culture. Plainly, some people have simply given up. No idea, they argue, is broad and supple enough to allow us to see Martha Stewart, New Age spirituality, best business practice, Robin Williams, plastic surgery, the invention of radio, and Ani DiFranco in a single view. Of course, in a very general sense they are right: a unified theory is too much to hope for. What about more modest objectives? Is it possible to establish a single observation platform for the study of this complexity and dynamism? Can we construct a vista?

Most people solve the problem by making some part of it go away. They begin with an act of reduction. The world becomes smaller, simpler, more intelligible. Certain parties (David Frum comes to mind) mock popular culture as our fall from grace.[32] When the ponderable world is diminished in this way, explanation *is* easier—but the cheat is in. Claims to illumination are compromised, vitiated by this first act of reduction.

Another favorite explanatory strategy (and its enthusiasts are legion) is to dismiss all things commercial as the operation of self-interest, opportunism, and manipulation, as non- or anti-cultural. Remove all of these from the problem set, and a solution is more readily achievable. But, again, the game is up before it can begin. The trick is to find a theory, or least a concept, that can comprehend some of the bewildering complexity of the present day, one that lets us find the Burning Man festival and the town of Celebration, Florida, on the same explanatory field.

Some postmodernists have an ingenious solution: they make the problem the solution. They argue that we are a world of maximal heterogeneity, that we are a world of episodes without continuity, that we are a world of solipsistic communities without shared understandings, that we are constructed out of discontinuous generative principles, that the terms of one community contradict and, were we not so successfully solipsistic, would eclipse the terms of another. For the postmodernists, there are no "laws of perspective." Vistas are impossible. There can be no single field of vision. We can see only by leaping from one set of assumptions to another.

This issue, the embracing view of contemporary culture, is surrounded by every kind of intellectual wreckage and arrest. But what are the costs of an abandoned search? If we stop looking for an embracing view we enable our worst suspicions. It may be entirely wrong to suppose that there is no embracing view, but if we cease searching for one, we ensure its nonexistence. We help construct the world we're afraid we see before us.

I want to propose a vista, a concept of transformation that can help clarify. I understand that vistas are out of fashion. As Angela McRobbie put it, "Postmodernism deflects attention away from the singular scrutinizing gaze . . . and asks that this be replaced by a multiplicity of fragmented, and frequently interrupted, 'looks.' "[33] But only a vista will help us see how Ani DiFranco and Martha Stewart are members of the same culture, what art and business have in common, and that Salman Rushdie and his Zelig-like agent engage in the same undertaking. I am not claiming to make full sense of these diverse parties or of anything like the entirety of contemporary culture. I am saying merely that there are commonalities, and that transformation may be one of them.

Transformations

Section 1

Self-Transformation in a Popular Culture

Here are several stories about people or places in the contemporary world, each showing a different aspect of transformation. They show transformation as a theme of comedy, television, Broadway theater, popular music, alternative music, Hollywood, the art world, toys, sports, business, and the Internet. They show transformation at work in the mainstream and the margin, in our ideas of status and gender, in the fine details of everyday speech and the trends shaping our culture. Transformation is a diverse and complicated phenomenon not only across cultures, but also within our own contemporary one. Here is the full range of things a theory of transformation must be able to explain.

These stories are mainly descriptive. I stop from time to time to offer first-level analysis, but most of this will wait for the last section of the book. Think of this section as an anthropologist's workbench, a review of some of the things that characterize a culture we are still struggling to understand.

ROBIN WILLIAMS

In his sixty-five-minute improv routine at the Metropolitan Opera in 1986, Robin Williams transformed into "shapes of a different kind" some 178 times. He became Robin Leach, the elephant man in a car wash, Babe Ruth on cocaine, God on drugs, Kurt Waldheim, a penis, the Three Wise Men, Leon Spinks, Dr. Ruth, his pregnant wife, and—in almost the same breath—his father, himself, and his son. In a hypertransformational mode, he became creatures within creatures: Sylvester Stallone as Hamlet, Ronald Reagan as a Wild West marshal, Ed Koch as Tweety Bird ("Thewr is no cowwuption on Wiker's Iwand"), Dr. Ruth as an African American woman, a penis as Marlon Brando in *On the Waterfront*, his wife as Ralph Cramden, and, finally, Moammar Gadhafi as Omar Sharif, Charles Manson, *and* Colonel Sanders ("come on down, it's a bomb in a bucket").[1]

In an *Esquire* interview, Lisa Grunwald told Williams his act reminded her of the Mozart of *Amadeus*—as if he were taking dictation from God. Williams demurred. "No, I'm channeling," he suggested: listening to several voices. Later, he suggested he had "call waiting," with a new persona always ready to break in.

This does not resemble traditional comedy very much. Generally, comedians look for triumph, to tell jokes so funny the audience surrenders self-control. "The audience was giving it up. Their lungs were coming out of their mouths. I slayed them."[2]

One of the things old-style comedians were after was power. When things went well, the audience became their subjects. When things went badly, power reverted to the audience, which grew lordly and disdainful.[3] Williams does not seem to care about imperial comedy. He practices something else, something more concerned with becoming people than controlling them.

There are a lot of comedic styles in our culture: in most of them, the comedian assumes a single persona. He or she becomes the spirit of frenetic, innocent abandon (Jerry Lewis begets Soupy Sales begets Howie Mandel), the voice of rage (Lenny Bruce begets Sam Kinison begets Bobcat Goldthwait), the courtly, cunning observer of contemporary life (Shelley Berman begets Carl Reiner and Carol Burnett, who beget Steve Martin, Mark Curry, Jerry Seinfeld, and Paula Poundstone), the voice of insinuation (Groucho Marx and Mae West beget Milton Berle begets Benny Hill), the voice of "wise guy" insincerity (Phil Silver begets Bill Murray begets Janeane Garofalo), the voice of taunting anti-hypocrisy (Lenny Bruce begets Denis Leary, Dennis Miller begets Chris Rock), and so on. These are vivid personae, but relatively static. For Robin Williams (who descends from Richard Pryor, who descends from Jonathan Winters), the object is to occupy many personae. This comedic style is deliberately multiple.

Williams departs particularly from conventional impersonation. Rich Little and Frank Gorshin operated according to very different conventions. They repeated the "set-up" until it was clear to the dimmest drunk in the house. Turning his back to the audience for a few moments, the impersonator wheels around with his collar up and his face contorted. The audience howls with recognition. The likeness is, they say, "uncanny." Red Skelton repeated Freddie the Freeloader and Clem Kadiddlehopper so often his audiences came to regard them as old friends.

Robin Williams comes with a routine, but what everyone wants is the improv. In these solos, Williams leaves vaudevillian architecture behind and creates as he goes. Premises are ventured, abandoned, returned to in a swallow's flight. The comedic field is large, multidimensional, shifting. The jokes are unpredictable.

In the place of impersonations, there are visitations. Without rhyme or reason, Williams is a Jewish mother, William F. Buckley, Arnold Schwarzenegger, a gang member, Barbra Streisand, a fashion designer, Bart Simpson. The movement from persona to persona is liquid, more metaphor than simile, a statement of identity ("here's Frank Sinatra") more than comparison ("here's Robin Williams as Frank Sinatra").

Williams departs, too, from the comedy of Peter Sellers (1925–1980). In his early and middle films and especially *The Mouse That Roared* (1959, dir. Jack Arnold) and *Dr. Strangelove* (1964, dir. Stanley Kubrick), Sellers plays multiple characters, but in none of these is he shown to "morph" between them. His stop-motion pattern is also evidenced by Tracey Ullman. Her several personae are discrete, unconnected by an improv bridge. Ullman and Sellers disappear between characters. Williams shows the bridge between the differences, the player in transition. The performance is, among other things, a performance of change. Sellers and

Ullman take out the transformation and give us merely the new destination. Williams makes us watch.

There are other oddities here. Williams's comedic style consists of huge leaps from one character to another. Some of the laughs come from precisely the fact that Williams has managed to vault from Barbra Streisand to Bart Simpson. And these leaps are not just huge, but frequent, speedy. Williams is traveling at something like two hundred characters an hour. Some of this is sheer virtuosity: he's doing it because he can. But it is perhaps also true that he is doing it because this is what we want of him.

The last oddity is the role of the viewer. There is something like participant observation going on here. In her *Esquire* article, Grunwald says that, after a performance, Williams's audience is suddenly reticent. "They adjust their clothes and sip their wine and light their cigarettes as if they've been caught naked. They look at each other tentatively." It is, perhaps, natural that people are discomposed. They have been a great many people in a very few minutes. They've been a large, maniacal man as he has been Elvis, Barbara Walters, and Larry Storch.[4] *They've* been channeling . . . with call waiting. They reach for cigarettes and fiddle with clothing to reassemble a self scattered over dozens of personae. It's as if the only way to keep up with Williams is to take part, to follow him as he moves from one creature to the next. Or perhaps our shadowing of him is not something he demands of us, but something we demand of him. Are we watching transformation, or undergoing it?

If we wanted hints that our culture doesn't always grasp how transformational it is becoming, we couldn't ask for better evidence than Robin Williams's career. How else to explain his perplexing choices? He sometimes insists on playing a single self—as he did in *Popeye* (1980), *Hook* (1991), *Toys* (1992), *Jumanji* (1995), *Bicentennial Man* (1999). His audience comes away disappointed. Watching Williams play a single character seems somehow to miss the point. This is not what they came for. This is not what Williams does. It's perhaps not what we want to do.[5]

Our interest returns when Robin Williams plays several personae at once. And we are particularly charmed when he does this in behalf of others. This is the power of *Good Morning, Vietnam* (1987, dir. Barry Levinson), in which Robin Williams is transformational in service of a purpose, making himself an alter ego(s) for thousands of young soldiers stuffed into a single, uniform self of military service. This is the power of *Dead Poets Society* (1989, dir. Peter Weir), in which he is transformational in aid of a classroom of young men stuffed into the uniform self of the American prep school. And this is the power of the best parts of *Mrs. Doubtfire* (1993, dir. Chris Columbus). When Robin Williams is confined to the persona of a Scottish nanny, the film creeps along. When the film gives him free rein to be a succession of applicants for the nanny position, it bursts into life. Again, these transformations are most touching when they are deployed in behalf of three children who are held captive by an unimaginative mother and stuffed into the self of the American middle-class family. In *Patch Adams* (1998, dir. Tom Shadyac) Williams inflicts havoc on the starched precision of the medical persona in behalf of patients stripped of their individuality and stuffed into the American health care system.

After Williams, a deluge and Jim Carrey.[6] After Carry, Sacha Baron Cohen.

THE LEBRONS

LeBron James is the basketball sensation who moved straight from high school to the NBA. When Mr. James decided to forego a college education, the chattering classes took him to task. You know, the usual: "Here's a child trading away intellectual development for fame and fortune. What is wrong with a culture in which this can happen?"

So when Mr. James showed up in an unusual ad campaign for Nike, the world was surprised. Recently, for instance, we saw Mr. James play four characters. In the space of thirty seconds, he was "Business," "Wise," "Kid," and an athlete very like the NBA player named LeBron James.

Whoa, Nelly. The performances were not just better than the average b-ball celebrity endorsement. They were interesting, daring, dramatic, almost—gasp—artistic! Clearly, the chattering classes had misjudged the kid. Clearly, LeBron James has his wits about him. Apparently, the chattering classes were wrong. (And that never happens.)

To be sure, contemporary culture has moved well beyond the "dumb jock" endorsement. Peyton Manning is doing ads that are funny and engaging. ESPN does exemplary ads for itself, often roping in the athlete at hand.

Some athletes have used ads to escape the "spam in a can" status that is otherwise thrust upon them. They treat the ad as an opportunity for meaning making, as when Maria Sharapova did a fiercely ironic "I feel pretty" spot for Nike, the better to fight the imputation that she was really a pin-up girl who just happened to play championship tennis. But the Le-Bron ad is much better than any of these. And it comes from a kid who is twenty-one years old, working without the "benefit" of a college education. Hmmm. Chattering classes, wrong again.

The campaign is the work of Nike, widely known for the courage of its marketing, and the advertising agency Weiden + Kennedy, widely known for the brilliance of its work. But these are merely the necessary conditions of the "LeBrons" campaign. We do not have anything like a sufficient explanation of this inspired piece of risk-taking.

I have scoured the biographic info available online for illumination. This material is detailed and well researched (sports journalism has got better, too!). But none gives much insight into what Mr. James thinks he is doing.

One possibility, and it is merely a possibility, is that Mr. James has found a way to reproduce the foursome with whom he grew up. Mr. James took a "Four Musketeers" kind of oath with Dru Joyce III, Sian Cotton, and William McGee, with whom he attended St. Vincent–St. Mary High School in Akron. The idea for the LeBrons might, just might, have sprung from this foursome.

Another possibility: Mr. James is famous for his teamwork. Unlike many big stars, he actually passes the ball. His passing game is, in fact, part of his genius as a player, demonstrating his Wayne Gretzky–like ability to see exactly what the court is going to look like before anyone else. Mr. James has no difficulty seeing himself as a member of a team. And now the self has taken on a new diversity; the teamwork continues.

There may be something Sharapova-like going on here. The tag line for this campaign is "You think you know LeBron James, but you don't." Ah, did Mr. James feel himself painted into a corner by all the hype that surrounded his remarkable rise to the NBA? Was this ad a way to take his leave of the identity being constructed for him by the sports journalists and the chattering classes?

But why these characters: Business, Wise, and Kid? Business is a creature so extraordinarily vain, he gets on the intercom during a commercial shoot to tell everyone, "Please be quiet while I am dressing." This is the gigantic ego that awaits every NBA star, and it may serve Mr. James to externalize Business early and publicly before Business internalizes him. Wise is a retired, elderly NBA all-star, cranky, opinionated, and still in possession of a towering sky hook. Wise is the most talkative of these characters, and it's as if LeBron James wants to hear from this man, even as he wants to keep him in his place. Kid is a child, a creature of simple pleasures. And it is clear that LeBron James is living a life that threatens to absolutely extinguish childish things. He may believe it's nice to take Kid with you while you go. It is not impossible that Mr. James constructed the "LeBrons" in order to divide the labor of stardom and make more manageable the life of an NBA superstar.

We can imagine many sources of inspiration for this. Mike Myers plays many parts in the Austin Powers series. So does Eddie Murphy in the two Nutty Professor films and *Norbit*. But the deeper inspiration may be a generational one. Mr. James may be engaged in a new individualism, according to which any individual may claim many selves. I understand that some will be surprised at this. They will ask why an athlete so talented that he threatens to eclipse Kobe Bryant, perhaps even rival Michael Jordan, would not find one self to be quite enough, and perhaps more than his share. Well, finally, Mr. James is a child of his generation. One self is interesting, and certainly the present self is mighty, but it can never be enough.[7]

ANI DIFRANCO

Ani DiFranco is a phenomenon: largely self-taught, almost entirely self-invented, the creator of a genre of music, the founder of her own record company, and probably the most gifted feminist performer at work in the United States today.[8]

To say that she is transformational is to acknowledge that many rock stars are transformational. Madonna made a substantial career out of her movement from one persona to the next.[9] Peter Gabriel is famous for ground-breaking videos that play on the transformational theme. Michael Jackson pursued the transformation of personal gender and race into a plastic surgeon's cul-de-sac, but not before he offered us several interesting mediations on the theme (notably the videos for "Black and White" and "Thriller"). Courtney Love astonished audiences with her transitions from stripper to movie star, from alternative diva to a sometimes swan-like celebrity.[10] Transformation is what rock stars do.

In the old days, they had a simpler time of it. In a sense, the band was a brand. Once they'd done *Dick Clark's American Bandstand* or the *Ed Sullivan Show*, they had "name recognition" and "mind share." The secret to stardom was to stay the same as long as possible—until advancing years forced them to Las Vegas or still more ignominious venues. Thus spake the agent, and Bobby Vinton, Wayne Newton, Abba, and Huey Lewis and the News obliged. Las Vegas became a Shangri-la, a place where hits never aged, where the audience never had to shout, "play 'I Want a New Drug,'" because Huey knew that was what he was there to do.

But the postmodern rock star comes from a more liquid tradition, one in which the rock star changes substantially and often. There are many heroes here. One of the most conspicuous was David Bowie. Bowie's most startling transformation was Ziggy Stardust, a defining figure of Britain's glitter-rock of the early '70s. He was deliberately flamboyant, theatrical, elaborate, and, in gender matters, decidedly vague. Depending on your point of view, he was male become female, or both male and female, or neither male nor female. Ziggy was an experiment in gender.

Bowie now looks back on this creation with some wonder. He says he was a "closet heterosexual," drawn more to the "twilight" of the gay world in London than its sexuality. "I was really only adopting the situation of being bisexual."[11] His Ziggy offered an opportunity to explore the potentialities of a world unconstrained by middle-class mores. Ziggy was a shape for the moment.

Bowie's next persona was Aladdin Sane. This time he appeared on stage with lighting bolts on his face. Bowie now regards this as a transitional self, a way of "getting out" of Ziggy.[12] This self was ephemeral and, once it had served its purpose, it disappeared. On the next album, *Diamond Dogs*, Bowie's head appeared attached to a dog's body.

In the middle '80s, Bowie lost his nerve. After the great success of the album *Let's Dance*, change was risk. He began to wonder whether he had more to lose than gain. "Should I try and duplicate the success of *Let's Dance*, or should I try to change with every album?"[13]

And then, in a surprising gesture, Bowie sought anonymity behind the band *Tin Machine*. For many fans this had all the charm of being forced to watch Robin Williams play the same character for an entire movie. They reacted with scorn and confusion. *Black Tie, White Noise* was Bowie's return to grace. But the persona this time was cooler, more elegant. David Bowie, once the scourge of middle-class convention, had become a gentleman, one of the best defined and most ancient personae in the British envelope of possible selves. But even this persona was short-lived. On the jacket of his 1999 album, *Hours*, we see Bowie holding his own corpse and mourning the passing of yet another self.[14]

Later stars crafted new rules of transformation. First, Bowie did his inventing backstage and between albums. The present generation of rock stars does it live. Courtney Love, for instance, mourned the loss of Kurt Cobain on stage before her fans.[15] Second, Bowie's persona was sometimes merely a stage creation, one he would happily repudiate. The new generation takes the persona home.[16] The private Courtney Love is, by all accounts, the public Courtney Love.[17] Third, Bowie changed by careful stages. The new players are more experimental and more messy.[18] Finally, the present generation of rock stars look upon transformation with more ambivalence than is apparent in Bowie's case. They are particularly unhappy with the standing transformational regimes at work in middle-class America and the music industry. This generation is transformative but not always happily so. Their transformations have an interestingly oppositional, contested quality.[19]

To say that Ani DiFranco is transformational does not say enough. For she is transformational in ways most musicians have not guessed. She is working not only on the persona but on the culture than defines the persona. But first things first. DiFranco has created "DiFranco" without the help of, indeed in the teeth of, the music industry.[20]

In "The Next Big Thing" (on the album *Not So Soft*), she equates corporate exploitation and sexual abuse.[21] Her own label flourishes, but the executives from the major labels still woo her . . . only to find themselves ridiculed on the next album.

DiFranco's approach to self-creation is expansionary. As she says, "There's a crowd of people harbored in every person."[22] Once a lesbian, she identifies herself now as bisexual. More exactly (and tellingly), she says what she is not: "I'm not a straight girl, and I'm not a dyke."[23] DiFranco wants breadth in music and sexuality—as if the transformation were a perpetual opening up, and fixity the threat of closing down.

Her recent excursions into the world of heterosexuality (detailed on the album *Dilate*) have met with controversy. Some members of the lesbian community expressed a sense of betrayal. But DiFranco says this misses the point. Her relationship with a man is one more exercise in the investigation of possibility.

[M]e and Mr. Dilate have an almost ungendered love. It's so funny that I'm now seen as being the straight girl of the universe, whereas with this guy I get more of a girl than any of the women I ever hung out with. Because we sort of take turns.[24]

DiFranco is unhappy with fans who demand that she fashion a single identity and stick with it. "I feel like I'm being reduced to . . . a stereotype of myself."[25] But she knows that her transformation will serve as inspiration and instruction for the transformation of others—and that fans demand constancy for this reason.

[P]art of my job is letting everyone project things onto me. I symbolize their own self-empowerment or possibilities. . . . Uh, that sounds so trite, sorry.[26]

The media are worse than fans. They have set about knocking off the "rough edges," preparing her for the mainstream.[27] Here's what *Spin* had to say about one of the genuinely revolutionary creatures in rock and roll:

[She] has an essential brattiness that's the key to her appeal. When she says, "Fuck you," it's with a big toothy smile splashed across her face.[28]

What is *Spin* up to? Calling DiFranco "bratty" makes her sound like a mischievous little sister. Calling her smile "big" and "toothy" suggests the "fuck you" doesn't matter. Perhaps this is meant to be cultural damage control, something like "Don't worry, America. She's only kidding. Let the gender pageant continue."[29]

DiFranco's transformation is contested by record executives, by fans, by industry, by the press. The machinery of rock and roll may yet consume her.

NEW AGE, BRITISH COLUMBIA

Hollyhock is a faraway place. It sits "on the edge of one of the last great green places on the planet, . . . a vast landscape, barely populated with humans, still intact ecologically."[30] Hollyhock might be called a resort. It consists of forty-eight acres on an island off the coast of British Columbia. It offers accommodation; kayaking, sailing, and hiking; yoga, meditation, and massage; workshops, therapies, and contemplation. It is the kind of place people go to rest and recuperate.

"Resort" is, of course, a bad word, conjuring up the Palm Springs of the 1950s and a riot of behaviors injurious to mind, body, and soul. Too much sun, alcohol, salt, sugar, fat, gambling, and noise. Add cigarettes and cigars, floor shows, exploited sexuality, racist and sexist humor, tasteless décor and color schemes, polyester clothing, neon skywriting, motorboats, and waterskiing pageants, and we approach the decade's idea of recreational perfection, a notion of the "resort" still current in some places.

Hollyhock isn't like this.

It's . . . a pilgrimage by land and sea to a place of healing. Once here, as our many returning guests know, you are embraced by the magic of the land, the surrounding wilderness, and our warm and welcoming staff.

This means no floor show, no groaning smorgasbord, no importuning waitresses.

> Located at the edge of British Columbia's vast pristine coastal wilderness, Hollyhock provides a warm, supportive environment for relaxing holidays, experiential learning, and creative self-expression. The remote setting affords an intimate encounter with the natural world that is both rejuvenating and healing.

Guests do not come to "unwind." This is the mechanistic language of the 1950s, and it betrays a failure to grasp the needs of the soul and the real opportunities of "recreation." In the words of a Hollyhock workshop participant,

> My first visit to Hollyhock has exceeded every expectation. It has been the most healing, rest-filled, transforming, and enjoyable experience in my adult life.

Hollyhock embraces and acts upon several straightforward principles. Several of these are revealed by the way it defines itself as a corporation. Once more, the term is wrong for Hollyhock, but the concept "corporation" is exactly right. Hollyhock is a "body."

The Hollyhock body extends in all directions. Its twenty-five investors think of themselves as "co-stewards" privileged to care for a "geographic, botanical, biological, and atmospheric" entity for a brief moment in its ancient career. They seek nothing so crass or uncomprehending as "ownership." They believe that grave responsibilities accompany the great gift of use.

Hollyhock believes in the body of the enterprise because this idea is everywhere. In the face of the endlessly distinguishable, measurable categories of a rational, scientific, disenchanted instrumentalism, there is a feeling for things that run together, unsuspected harmonies, subterranean continuities, a world in which everything is somehow connected. It is there in the notion of Gaea, of "six degrees of separation," in the 1960s conviction that change in the world must begin as change in the self, in the notion from complexity theory that a butterfly in one place can cause a hurricane in another, in movies like *Pay It Forward* (2000, dir. Mimi Leder) in which it suddenly makes sense to practice "random acts of kindness," in the new international continuities that pollution creates for the planet, in the popularity of Eastern philosophies that insist that everything is connected to everything else.[31] One of the reasons for the loose boundaries of contemporary culture is the conviction that all distinctions are undergirded in this way.[32]

Think globally, act locally. Hollyhock believes itself responsible to the community around it, a place where jobs are scarce, seasonal, and tied to the declining logging and fishing industries. Hollyhock wants something more than occasional labor from its neighbors. According to Joel Solomon, president of Hollyhock,

> Our core business is a form of tourism, with an emphasis on connection to land, learning, rejuvenating, strengthening, and the growth of consciousness. We are attempting to redefine forms of structure and governance which, with trust, relationship building, and a passion for consensus, may enable us to design for a 50-year impact, towards a 500-year vision.[33]

Hollyhock is not a business but a "precious experiment exploring the nexus of service, economy, community, ecology, and land."

Hollyhock visitors find themselves "retuned." The rhythms of movement, speech, emotion, activity, and consciousness all change. Life is still a system of cycles within cycles, of durations within durations, but all of these expand so that the visitor moves away from the staccato timing of city life toward something more ancient, contemplative, and grave, the calm of the deep forest and ocean floor. The senses are retuned as well. It is a Hollyhock commonplace that visitors arrive in a state of sensory crisis. Their senses are so overwhelmed by, so armored against, the din of city life that they arrive frightened, as if cringing. Gradually, they learn to trust their new surroundings, to "open up," to hear and see "as if for the first time."

Two goals in particular bring visitors to Hollyhock: to learn new ways of interacting with others and new ways of interacting with themselves. Hollyhock is dedicated to the idea that competition is a bad thing, something that forces people to obscure the things they share. Individualism, and particularly the notion that the individual is the seat of consciousness, choice, and action, is isolating. Almost everything in our society, from the Hollyhock point of view, discourages open, honest engagement and support. Hollyhock seeks to draw people out of well-defended citadels and into new kinds of interaction and solidarity.

But if the individual is alienated from other people, she is also alienated from herself. The demands of urban, industrial, competitive life discourage self-knowledge. Distracted, frightened, conflicted, she cannot see who she is. The Hollyhock mission is to calm and support the visitor until she can begin again, and then to aid her as she searches out aspects of the self that are forgotten or unsuspected. Hollyhock is about "self-discovery."

Transition is a time of passage and initiation when we bid farewell to old identities and lay the groundwork for a new sense of self. As we dance through the "in between," we are often confronted with the sadness of letting go, the difficulty of living with uncertainty and disorientation, and the excitement of uncovering new possibilities. This workshop, led by spiritual teaching and transpersonal psychologist Thomas Atum O'Kane, offers the opportunity to gather meaning and integrate the many phases of transition.

Hollyhock promises a substantial transformation of the visitor that is simultaneously physiological, sensual, emotional, social, and spiritual. When all of this proceeds to plan, something extraordinary is seen to happen. In the language of Hollyhock, individuals begin to "heal." They become "whole." They "open up." They "return" to the things that "really matter."

Hollyhock has its own mission in all of this, arising from its belief that personal change can result in something larger.

The Hollyhock circle generates continuous ripples, making new circles and linking to other similarly intentioned circles throughout this region, and around the world. Hollyhock offers itself as a touchstone for the larger Pacific Northwest bioregion.

MARTHA STEWART

Martha Stewart is usually alone in photographs. A friend pointed this out to me. "Look," she said, "you never see her with anyone else. That's because she's immaculate. She exists in her own perfect world, the one she made. There's no one else in any of her pictures because none of us are good enough. She's perfect. We're not."[34]

This is one of the ways we think about Martha Stewart. And it is striking how many and how passionate are the ways we think about her. Martha Stewart draws comment—even, perhaps especially, from those who claim to dislike her. Normally, we ignore what we dislike. Not here. When it comes to disliking Martha Stewart, people do go on.

By her own account, Martha Stewart is self-invented. She comes from New Jersey and a struggling Polish-Catholic family. She was one of six kids. She put herself through Barnard with a modeling career. Upon graduation she was a stockbroker and then a caterer. She was very good at catering. The man who was to become her publisher was impressed: "She created the most amazing ambience and food I'd ever seen." He suggested she record her transformational abilities on paper.[35]

The result was *Entertaining*, a book that has sold more than a half million copies. This book demonstrates a mastery of the detailed codes that govern food preparation and presentation in our culture. It's hard not to wonder at this display of cultural knowledge. It's a performance worthy of Joseph Conrad, who came to England with little English and within a few years was writing better prose than all but a few of the natives. Stewart came from hardship and New Jersey to similar accomplishment.

Stewart has made herself a master of material culture. After all, she can turn empty bleach bottles into centerpieces for the dining room table. This is not the bricolage Lévi-Strauss found so interesting. When French handymen make new objects out of old ones, the old ones remain visible. In Stewart's case, the foundational object disappears. Bricoleurs recycle; Stewart transforms.

But bleach bottles are simply the first moment and the phonemic level of the transformational grammar at work here. Her creations become rooms, rooms become households, households become homes, and these become families. Stewart has been called the Goddess of Lifestyle, and Ovid might accept this title as apt. She began by turning the daughter of immigrants into the doyenne of polite society. And then she created an empire predicated on the notion that others might wish to follow the same transformational path.[36]

Our reactions are various but somehow consistent. Some people would emulate Stewart in every detail. At first blush, this imitation looks like madness or hubris, at least. How to copy someone so formidably talented, especially when this talent is now amplified by some 160 assistants?[37] But some people do try, and some of them, I expect, succeed. In the course of research, I have seen several households that approached perfection occupied by householders relatively untaxed by their achievement. There are people who can keep up with Stewart and some of them, no doubt, do.

There is a still larger group who are content with the reproduction of a small corner of the aesthetic enterprise. Once a week, month, or quarter, they redo a bedroom in Stewart's paint, linens, and color schemes. Or they apply themselves to turning a turkey carcass into a card holder. The card holder becomes a synecdoche. It may be a slender or imperfect part of the whole, but it works well enough to stand as a sign of it. Even an occasional card holder helps us claim membership in the world Stewart has wrought.[38]

And what is this world, exactly? Homes and domestic arts are, normally, performances of particular ideas of domesticity, gender, parenthood, and childhood. Which ones apply in Stewart's case? It is not clear. The Stewart world shows just one woman, engaged in furious construction of a world of one. (Is this why she is portrayed alone?) It's as if Stewart can't or won't specify what exists at the center of her perfect creations. That's for the rest of us to specify. Stewart will supply the transformational tools. It's up to us to decide how these will be deployed. And we oblige. As it turns out, people seem comfortable constructing "My Martha" for themselves. Some people embrace her as a paragon of high society. For others, her appeal lies in the fact that she is upwardly mobile. Some, like Camille Paglia, praise her for her homoerotic qualities while others see her as the embodiment of the most conventional notions of sex and gender.[39] That's many Marthas. For a woman widely described as a "control freak," she is surprisingly accommodating of diverse readings.[40]

Still others make no attempt, large or small, to imitate Stewart. They never buy or reproduce a single thing from the magazine, website, or TV program. In a time-poor culture, this is not surprising. People are busy. Lives are hectic. The idea of re-creating even a small part of Stewart's perfection must seem implausible. But, oddly, they still tune in. Many of them *must* watch without participating. How strange this is. Why watch a show about doing—and never do? What is the point of extremely applied knowledge if not to apply it? The answer from some of these viewers is that they *are* applying this knowledge, or at least inhabiting it. For those thirty minutes, Stewart is a virtual self. For those thirty minutes, the viewer is Martha Stewart, masterful, formidable, relentless, a compelling icon for a combination of ideas and ideals that mix the prefeminist, feminist, and postfeminist—not as bricolage, with bits and pieces in evidence, but somehow seamlessly.[41]

And finally there are those who look on Stewart with hostility. For these people, Stewart is an outrage, someone who creates a standard against which everyone else must fail. "Who does she think she is?" is not an uncommon reaction. The satiric response cannot decide between disbelief (*Is Martha Stewart Living?*) and indignation (*Martha Stewart's Better Than You at Entertaining*).[42] The naysayers have created an "anti-Martha," a creature who is monstrously supercilious and insensitive.

But it is not just a matter of personal affront. For Stewart is a cultural artifact shot through with complexity, conflict, and paradox. It is precisely this that allows her to speak powerfully to so many different groups. But since she contains, as she must, a bundle of interpretive possibilities, there are moments when the structure does not hold, and we see through to discordance, tension, or contradiction. It is this that provokes some of the most pointed instances of ridicule, satire, and rejection.

Take the notion of "home." We think of the home as having two faces: perfection on the one side, comfort on the other. It is this fundamental distinction that explains the differences between the living room and den. The former is often a showpiece, roped off to remain pristine. The latter is deliberately cozy, cosseting, casual—in a word, "homey."[43] The trouble with Martha Stewart is that sometimes her creations are too perfect. They offer no purchase for emotion, no room for the occupant. And in these moments she appears that most alarming creature, someone who peddles an empty, status-anxious, inauthentic perfection in which no one can or would want to live. In these moments, the anti-Martha is merely pro-motherhood.

But there is perhaps something more at work. Here is an abbreviated version of the "Martha Stewart Holiday Calendar" that circulated by e-mail in December 1997.[44]

December 1
Blanch Carcass from Thanksgiving turkey. Spray paint gold, turn upside down and use as a sleigh to hold Christmas Cards.

December 2
Have Mormon Tabernacle Choir record outgoing Christmas message for answering machine.

December 4
Repaint Cistine [sic] Chapel ceiling in ecru, with mocha trim.

December 7
Debug Windows '95

December 11
Lay Fabrege [sic] egg.

December 12
Take Dog apart. Disinfect. Reassemble.

December 21
Drain city reservoir; refill with mulled cider, orange slices and cinnamon sticks.

This is harmless satire but interesting stuff. To suggest that Martha Stewart might use the carcass of a Thanksgiving turkey in this way is to suggest that she is a trickster who mixes the sacred and the profane, the everyday and the ceremonial. To suggest that she might have the Mormon Tabernacle Choir on her answering machine, repaint the Sistine Chapel, or drain a reservoir is not only to mock her prodigious energy and ambition but also to impute to her the ability to work on a Gulliver-like scale. To suggest that she *could* debug Windows 95 or *would* disassemble the dog is to impute extraordinary powers to her. This satire may ridicule but it does not diminish. Indeed, it makes exaggerated claims that Martha would not dare make for herself. Ovid would surely approve.

The Christmas e-mail is tepid compared to what happens to Martha Stewart on the Internet.[45] It is now apparently common for fans to take images of Stewart and rework them so that her head appears on the body of a weight lifter, a rural banjo player, and an S&M dominatrix. She appears as a party-goer in a Jell-O hat, a character in the many Star Trek series, and a Greek statue. The range and oddity of the images is striking. If they have anything in common, it's that they are all extravagant transformations of Stewart. And, like the holiday calendar, these impute to her properties (scale, strength, intelligence, and creativity—that Fabergé egg) that are larger than life. Satire is compliment. It acknowledges Stewart's creative powers even as it vents the suspicion and discomfort they must provoke in us. (Goddess of lifestyle, indeed.)

In the spring and summer of 2005, I expected to see the start of Martha Stewart's rehabilitation. Ms. Stewart was out of jail and available for interviews, photo ops, and other revelations of how prison life has changed her.

One of the first of these, a cover story in *Vanity Fair*, appeared not to grasp the opportunity at hand.[46] We were told that Ms. Stewart was "shell-shocked," that she felt the constraints of house arrest, that this empire and empress were diminished. But there was no indication that Martha Stewart was more interesting or complex.

Perhaps, I thought, she just isn't so inclined. Perhaps she was too busy making sure that prison did not "break her" to use it as an opportunity to think about who she is and what she wants. Or it might be that *Vanity Fair* was not listening with sufficient care or intelligence to glimpse a more nuanced subject. (*Vanity Fair* is so celebratory of celebrity, it routinely leaves nuance to others.)

C'est dommage, ça. Here's what Steve Jobs had to say about one of his career dislocations:

> [G]etting fired from Apple was the best thing that could have ever happened to me. The heaviness of being successful was replaced by the lightness of being a beginner

again, less sure about everything. It freed me to enter one of the most creative periods of my life.[47]

Surely, this is the opportunity offered by a cataclysmic change in personal circumstances. It forces us to give up tangible accomplishment for mere promise, something we could never bring ourselves otherwise to do. In any case, even if we do somehow, against the odds, re-create this lost world, we are likely to appear (cliché advisory in effect) "mere shadows of our former selves."

But then Stewart was always an agent, never the object, of transformation. She turned ordinary things into glittering prizes and middle-class lives into status spectaculars. There was no sense that Stewart would ever be acted on, ever allow herself to be transformed.

No, this is wrong. As long as Martha was both the object and agent of transformation, she was more than willing. She began as a Polish-American girl from a small town in New Jersey. She made herself a doyenne of Connecticut grandeur. And perhaps this is the real crux of the problem. When your model of perfection comes from the Connecticut playbook, there is only one set of objectives, only one set of things to aspire to, only one path to greatness.

Thank god for the real transformational options of a contemporary culture. For most of us, they mean that even quite disastrous episodes merely wipe the slate of the present transformation option. They do not foreclose the possibility of becoming someone new. When the fates intervene, we can begin again.

As I considered further, however, I decided that the Martha Stewart puzzle can be parsed more deftly. Martha Stewart is a transformational creature. She has transformed herself from a child of middle-class New Jersey to a doyenne of upper-class Connecticut. She knows the status code cold. Indeed, she has helped to refine and augment this code.

But the transformation is incomplete. By several accounts, Ms. Stewart sometimes treats friends, colleagues, and employees with small regard for courtesy. She is, to put it more bluntly, disagreeable.

It is as if Martha has mastered every detail of Connecticut grace . . . except the grace. And grace turns out to be an essential property of the polite classes, the opportunity for real wealth, the evidence of a virtually Asian detachment from the world (especially useful for women who have NOCD ["Not our class, dear"] husbands who must be patiently suffered), proof of what the humanists said was the real condition of high standing, and finally the only real emotion the WASP is obliged to show in public.

Let me put this another way: those who wish to be, or to pass as, members of polite society should not treat social interaction as a high-contact sport and conflict resolution as a survivalist enterprise.

How do I know this? I'm an anthropologist. I looked it up. (Which makes you wonder why Ms. Stewart didn't do the same. It's not as if the humanists are banned or burned.)

This could have been the understanding that Ms. Stewart brought back from prison with her. Now that would have been both interesting and consistent with the status metamorphosis that is, apparently, Ms. Stewart's only transformational objective.

CANDICE CARPENTER

There are two Candice Carpenters. One appeared in a *New Yorker* article.[48] The other appeared at the "Women Enriching Business" conference at the Harvard Business School in 2000. Carpenter is one or the other. She can't be both.

Candice Carpenter is iVillage's cofounder, and held the positions of CEO and co-chairperson of the board. The iVillage website is designed to help women form communities online. They can use it to find other women struggling with divorce, pregnancy, miscarriage, and breast cancer, or workaday things like careers, homes, kitchens, pets, and gardens. In its day, iVillage was one of the most successful e-commerce start-ups. It began selling common stock on March 19, 1999, with the share price set at $24.00. Trading opened at $95.88. Suddenly, iVillage was worth two billion dollars and Candice Carpenter was a multimillionaire. But the price later plunged to around a dollar. In May 2006, NBC acquired iVillage for $8.50 per share.

What preoccupied the *New Yorker* writer, Erik Larson, were the inconsistencies in the story he was trying to tell. How could a company as "ethereal as air" be worth, at the writing of his article, so much money? Should a company that is building a "village" be trying to monetize it? How could a feminist company be created by a nonfeminist?

Larson appears to want to demonstrate that Carpenter is an unlikely community builder or feminist. He accuses her of having been a teenage beauty "whose idea of ambition was to prevent the chlorine in the pool at the local club from destroying her hair." He describes Carpenter as tough on subordinates, firing a succession of young employees and vice-presidents, and eventually displacing poor, sweet, democratic Robert Levitan, the company's "rainmaker." He shows her to have betrayed her supporter and confidant Mary Meeker, the research analyst at Morgan Stanley Dean Witter.

Some of Larson's vitriol is reserved for Carpenter's style. She wears a see-through blouse, engages in "self-branding," and admires "larger than life" people with "cowboy energy." She builds content on her website by letting companies participate in its construction. The photographs accompanying the article help clarify these points. Carpenter is shown wearing big hair, big jewelry, big attitude and looking altogether too pleased with herself. I came away from the article, as I think I was meant to, repelled. Carpenter was depicted as a person without shame, subtlety, or much intelligence. She was, apparently, a relentless, self-promoting, opportunistic bully.

The Carpenter I saw speak at the Harvard Business School conference was someone quite different. As an HBS grad, Carpenter had returned to tell students what they could expect in the world. She took the stage and the Canadian within me braced for an unbecoming display of self-congratulation. Instead we got plain speech and matter-of-fact talk, with no hint that Carpenter believed herself especially accomplished or glamorous. This Carpenter could not have been more forthright.

She was a little discouraging. When she left the world of old media for the Internet, "everyone acted like I'd gone to Siberia. They stopped inviting me to dinner." And things, she warned, can go steadily from bad to worse.

> There will be hard times. Things will dry up. You will almost fail. It will become unglamorous. Everyone will think you're an idiot. You have to live with Monday morning quarterbacks, people second-guessing you, the venture capital sheep running left and right.[49]

There is, of course, a tradition of winners talking about failure. It makes them look so much more heroic. But Carpenter did not appear to be congratulating herself. Once more she was matter-of-fact:

> I've been afraid a fair amount of the time I've been doing this and it hasn't really mattered. I've been able to lead people when I'm afraid and to get out of bed when I was afraid and not to lose a lot of sleep because I'm afraid. I've had to go against Disney and [other] competitors and it takes courage to know you can do that. . . . Courage does not mean not being afraid. It means being used to being afraid.

This is an interesting refusal of the male approach to fear. Where she might have showed us how stern-jawed and unflinching she was, what we got instead was candor.

Carpenter talked about coming to feminism late. She said she did not get it at first. Now she does.

> As long as children are shooting children, it's hard to say we've gotten it right. Women have got a tremendous amount of freedom and when we reorganize the entire social system around that change, including our children, our whole families, and the organization of work, we'll be done. But we're not done yet. We're not done just because *we* have freedom.

In place of ego is the kind of thing that supplants the possibility of ego: the particular intensity I see in many HBS students. These students are surprisingly little invested in the "performance" of the self. They want to be attractive in a mainstream, Eddie Bauer sort of way. But mostly they appear to be who they are: unadorned, unaffected, ambitious, intense, clear, smart, driven, present.

Students wanted to know the secrets to her success. The first, as the *New Yorker* has told us, is Outward Bound. Carpenter suggested we read *The 7 Habits of Highly Effective People* and *Creating*, by Stephen Covey and Robert Fritz, respectively. She said that she reworks her Covey "mission statement" every year and that it has clarified and enabled her career. She made herself a disciple of Fritz's, using his ideas to find her way in life and business. Carpenter appeared to be struggling to refuse the usual treatment of a captain of industry, someone who rises inevitably to the top because they are exceptional. "I am," she appeared to be telling this audience, "merely the product of good advice, assiduously followed." She was here to pass this advice along.

Had I misread the *New Yorker* or Carpenter? I ran into a student from my MBA class after the talk. She was indignant. In class, we had suggested that the *New Yorker* was giving Carpenter the "treatment," that it was vilifying her for qualities it would have praised in men. But this "due diligence" prepared neither of us for the woman we saw on stage. Carpenter was not only honest and forthright, but apparently incapable of self-aggrandizement. It looked as if the *New Yorker* had done this woman wrong.[50]

"They have handlers, you know," a friend said, "Public relations people who set it all up." And this was not unthinkable. The woman on the HBS stage may have been an illusion, created opportunistically to fight the damage created by hard-hitting journalism. Certainly, it looked as if certain matters of style had changed. The Carpenter of the *New Yorker* photographs had big hair, big jewelry, and big attitude. The one on the stage was sleek and stylish in a Lisa Loeb kind of way, a lot less dame and a little more grrrl.[51]

One transformation or the other? Either Carpenter was falsely constructed by the *New Yorker* in a journalistic double standard that awaits women who distinguish themselves, or she had taken one look at this revelation of her private self and decided on a makeover.

"LIKE" TALKING AND OTHER ACTS OF SPEECH

Terrie: OK, so Robert comes up to me and he's, like, "So where were you last night?" And I go, "I was with Cheryl. Where were you?" And he's all like mad and stuff and walking around and everything. [*struts in a hip hop manner, arms straight, fingers rigid and pointing downward, upper body rolling back and forth*]

Jean: What is the *matter* with him? [*struts too*] "Oh, I'm so tough." What*ever*. He's such a *lo*ser.

Terrie: So he goes, "I thought you were going to be at Jimmie's. You *said* you were." Now he's a little boy, right? "Ew, you said, you said."

Jean: [*in the voice of a child*] "Mommie, Terrie said she was going to be at Jimmie's and she wasn't." [*with a pouting face and voice*]

Terrie: So I go, "Robert, you make me sick."

Jean: [*cutting in, singing in the manner of the song by Pink, with full melodrama*] "You make me sick." [*Terrie joins her for the second chorus*]

Terrie: There is something seriously wrong with that guy.

Jean: Yeah, but you knew that. You said, "Oh, Robert's such a little boy, but he's cute." Now it's totally "Robert is an idiot." We *told* you.

[*Robert enters*]

Robert: [*looking at Terrie, not Jean*] Hey, Terrie.

Jean: [*with irony and emphasis*] Hi, Robert.

Robert: [*still looking at Terrie*] Whatever, Jean.

Jean: Robert?

Robert: [*still looking at Terrie*] What?

Jean: Terrie has something she wants to tell you. [*steps now completely out of Robert's view and gestures with eyes and mouth open, head nodding, hands imploring, as if to say, "Go on!"*][52]

TURTLE ISLAND

As a boy on vacation in the interior of British Columbia, I decided one summer to christen Turtle Island. Turtle Island wasn't truly an island. It was a deadhead, a log submerged and floating on Lake Kalamalka not far from the cottage my family rented for two weeks every year. Turtle Island was home to a couple of turtles who used it as a place to sun themselves. My idea, if a seven-year-old boy can be said to have ideas, was to row out to the deadhead, break a bottle over it, and say, "I declare this Turtle Island."[53]

There were several things wrong with my plan. First of all, it crossed two forms of ritual: christening a ship and claiming land. I was christening land. Rituals are particular about the details and I had got them wrong. Second, it wasn't clear who my audience was. For some reason, I wanted to stage my ritual very early in the morning while everyone slept. Normally, a ritual has observers who validate the proceedings by bearing witness to them. My ritual would be seen by no one. Third, it wasn't clear who the beneficiaries would be: Blue Water Lodge? My family and me? Turtles everywhere? Normally, rituals speak for someone. Mine appeared to carry on a conversation with itself.[54]

My mother, acting as an uninvited ritual officer, suggested one small modification: that in deference to the turtles, it might be better merely to fill the bottle with lake water and drop it in the vicinity of the "island." This was disappointing because much of the point of the exercise was to give a small boy an excuse to break something. But I agreed to accommodate the turtle point of view. More difficulty! Now the ritual wasn't even going to proceed according to my dubious plan.

But things went forward. Very early one morning, I rowed out into the perfect stillness of Lake Kalamalka. I heard two silvery plops as islanders took refuge. I coasted up to the deadhead, filled the bottle with water, tapped it on the "island" twice, and let go. As the dark green Seagram's bottle descended to the lake floor, I intoned, in a piping voice, "I declare this Turtle Island."

I was generally pleased with the event. I hadn't got to break anything but I felt I had participated in something, if not grand, at least worthy. But I cannot claim "ritual efficacy" for my little ceremony. My sisters and mother, with some prompting, are prepared now to say they remember "that, um, island" and, under duress of badgering ("you could at least *try*"), even the name "Turtle Island."

But that was it. Nothing changed, really. The island remained a dead-head. "Turtle Island" failed to make it into the registry of local place names. I think it's safe to assume the turtles were unimpressed. (That summer I gave them significant looks as I rowed past. They would return that reptilian blink that is, I think, unreadable.) My ritual left no trace in memory. It had no transformative effect.

ORLAN AND WILDENSTEIN

The artist called Orlan was born in 1947 in France, the daughter of a housewife and an electrician. We do not know what she was named at birth. This is now concealed. We know only that she decided as a teenager to re-create herself. At fifteen she became Orlan. At twenty-four she canonized herself. Now Saint-Orlan, she began to array herself in the attributes of the female saints.

At forty-three, Orlan struck upon a new way to pursue this career. She began a series of surgical operations to change her physical appearance. Linda Weintraub says,

> Eventually, Orlan will possess the chin of Botticelli's Venus, the nose of Gerome's Psyche, the lips of Francois Boucher's Europa, and the eyes of Diana from a sixteenth-century French School of Fontainebleau painting. In addition, she aspires to the forehead of Leonardo da Vinci's Mona Lisa.[55]

Orlan says the choices were deliberate: Venus for her creativity, Europa as the giver of law, and Diana "because she refuses to submit to gods or to men." But people were skeptical. "Isn't this about vanity? Aren't you," they asked, "merely making yourself more beautiful?"[56] Orlan answered this skepticism by having silicon cheek implants installed in her forehead, a surgical intervention that took her away from beauty. But the point is still moot. The bumps turned out to be attractive. They gave her forehead the cloud-like contours of the "fu dogs" of Chinese statuary.[57]

Orlan says her art is an act of resistance designed to "upset our assumptions, overwhelm our thoughts [and put us] outside norms and outside of the law."[58] She says, "My body has become a site of public debate that poses crucial questions for our time." She says her work is "a struggle against the innate, the inexorable, the programmed nature, DNA (which is our direct rival as artists of representation) and God! My work is blasphemous." Not so much a saint, then, as a fallen angel, cast out of the body for her hubris and her sins.

Jocelyn Wildenstein was born in Lausanne, Switzerland, in 1946. She became a hunter and a pilot and these skills brought her to the Wildenstein estate in Kenya, where she met Alec Wildenstein, an American art connoisseur, collector, and merchant. Alec treated the estate as a place to escape the demands of family, profession, and society. Jocelyn is said to have served on the estate as a "lion hunter." Jocelyn and Alec eloped in 1978 and thereafter lived together in New York City. It was here that Ms. Wildenstein made an uncommon decision.

> Jocelyne realized that Alec loved his jungle estate, and the cats that inhabited it, more than anything else in life. So armed with this information, she returned to her plastic surgeon with an unusual request: She wanted to be transformed into one of the giant cats that Alec loved so much. Though surprised at this unorthodox request, the surgeon did his best to comply.[59]

This outcome was striking.[60] Alec Wildenstein screamed when he saw his wife, we are told. The New York press, always eager to mix it up with a high-society celebrity, dubbed Wildenstein "Bride of Wildenstein" and a "scalpel junky."[61] Like Orlan, Wildenstein had engaged in an extravagant, destructive creativity.[62] But where Orlan sought transformational opportunity by moving upward in the Renaissance hierarchy, toward saints and angels, Wildenstein moved downward, toward animals. To make matters somewhat more complicated, the transformations take an unexpected turn in both cases. Orlan aims at becoming a saint and ends up a rebel angel. Wildenstein begins as a lion hunter and ends up as a lion.

It is not clear whether Orlan and Wildenstein are outliers or precursors. Thirty years ago, we regarded plastic surgery as a shameful secret and a minority interest. According to the American Society for Aesthetic Plastic Surgery, 2.1 million procedures were performed in 1997.[63] If we pretend that this was the first year of plastic surgery in the United States, and that the number of procedures held steady (and did not increase, as it surely has), there are now roughly 11 million people in the United States who have had plastic surgery.[64] This is almost 5 percent of the population. The "shameful secret" is no longer shameful or secret. The question remains, what will we use this surgery to do to ourselves? Orlan and Wildenstein suggest two possibilities.[65]

CHER AND MADONNA

Cher has been called the "poster girl" of plastic surgery. "I am," she says, "the equivalent of a counterfeit twenty-dollar bill."[66] She admits to rhinoplasty and breast surgery, but ridicules the idea that she has had ribs taken out or cheekbones put in. The story of her plastic surgery is part of a larger story of transformation. She was born Cherilyn Sarkisian in California in 1946. She left high school at sixteen and went to Los Angeles to become an actress. She found work singing backup at Phil Spector's Gold Star Studios. Singing together as "Caesar and Cleo," Sarkisian and her boyfriend Sonny Bono found only modest success, but in 1965, using the names Sonny and Cher, they released "I Got You, Babe" and by the fall of 1965, they had six singles in the Top 40. As the counter-culture took hold, Sonny and Cher fell out of step with the times, and by the late 1960s they were reduced to touring the far reaches of the lounge circuit.[67]

By the end of the decade, the act was better and times had changed. Sonny and Cher were invited to play Las Vegas and, in 1971, CBS launched *The Sonny and Cher Comedy Hour* as a summer replacement series. This combined Bob Mackie bombast and Cher's own acerbic humor, and eventually it found a place in prime time. This helped return Cher to popular radio and she had several hits in the early 1970s.

By the end of the 1970s, Cher was again badly out of fashion. Her music career ended and she sought work as an actor. Against the odds, she was given starring roles in *Come Back to the Five and Dime, Jimmy Dean, Jimmy Dean* (1982, dir. Robert Altman), *Silkwood* (1983, dir. Mike Nichols), *Mask* (1985, dir. Peter Bogdanovich), *The Witches of Eastwick* (1987, dir. George Miller), *Suspect* (1987, dir. Peter Yates), and *Moonstruck* (1987, dir. Norman Jewison). This last brought her an Academy Award for best actress in 1988.

Predictably, disaster followed. Cher began to promote her own hair care products and home furnishings on television "infomercials." The world was aghast. She was demoted in the Hollywood hierarchy. She became the butt of "what was she thinking?" comedy routines. The talk shows stopped calling. The fall was steep, and the decade hard. And then, miraculously, Cher was once again reborn. In 1998, she released an album called *Believe*, a collection of dance tracks, and she was, in middle age, once more returned to the Top 10. The title track ranked first in *Billboard*'s Top 100 for 1999.

Without the benefit of training, good advice, or, possibly, native good sense, Cher has managed to move ceaselessly around the world of entertainment, to radio, to variety television, to lounge entertainment, to comedy television, to Hollywood films, to commercial television, to disco. The term "reinvention" is now often used to talk about the careers of American celebrities. But in Cher's case, it is particularly apt. She has remade herself once a decade over forty years.

Cher and Madonna are both transformational, but they represent different strategies.[68] Madonna has demonstrated a gift for playing the currents of the diffusion stream and she is routinely cited as the defining token of a transformational culture. (Salon.com calls her "pop's most irresistible changeling.")[69] She picks up a new fashion just as it is hitting the radar of her fans, and she abandons it as it is about to gain mass appeal and lose its currency. Where Madonna is deft, Cher is inclined to lock on to each new fashion wave. This reckless over-commitment means she is swept violently down the diffusion stream and out of fashion. Only substantial re-creation permits her to return to stardom.

To give Madonna her due, it is exceedingly difficult to play the diffusion wave as well as she does. Thousands of artists try each year, and only a relative few succeed. And no one has succeeded as well as Madonna over the two decades of her career. But Cher's challenge is greater still. She must re-create herself in the face of the repudiation she has brought on herself. It is not clear Madonna could do this.

There is no public record of when, in this remarkable career, Cher chose to have her plastic surgery. But it does seem more or less consistent with the rest of her transformational career. Her plastic surgery is not merely cosmetic. It is hyperbolic, extreme, over the top. More to the point, it is surgery. Where Madonna has managed most of her transitions with changes in clothing, music, and movement, Cher has engaged in a transformational technology that is dramatic and irreversible. Like the rest of her career, what is done must in some cases be undone. Recently, we have seen her experiment with less punishing, less permanent transformations, particularly the vocoder effects in the song "Believe." It remains to see if she is prepared to embrace this more Madonna-like strategy.

But even Madonna was not fully the master of the transformational game. In her 2004 tour, she broke two of its rules.

The first rule is that artists (and the rest of us) should do transformations, not talk about them. Madonna chose to call her new show "Reinvention." This was unnecessary. (Kelefa Sanneh of the *New York Times* compared it to John Kerry calling his cross-country tour "lots of speeches.")[70]

The interest of live performances of transformation is that they come at us in the real time of the real world. This is what we admire about our transformational exemplars. (In the language of linguistics: we want the direct comparison of metaphor, not the proposed comparison of simile.)

The second rule is that the transformer should keep moving. Madonna is now repeating herself. As Sanneh puts it, the new show finds her "shadowboxing with her own past lives." Apparently, Madonna has retired from the diffusion stream. Now she is reprising, not popular culture, but herself. "There were times when Madonna seemed somehow oppressed by the weight of all her old selves, times when it seemed that she just wanted to wipe the slate clean and start over," says Sanneh. Indeed, this is what she used to do and this is what we want our transformers to do. Keep moving.

Maybe she's tired. Living in a transformational society, remaking ourselves with such frequency, leads inevitably to exhaustion. Staying ahead of the diffusion curve in a dynamic society, as Madonna does—or did—must be even more difficult.

Or maybe she is dropping out of the transformational game altogether. She appears to have taken to a gentrified life in England with some enthusiasm. (Though surely that new English accent is one of her very worst impersonations.) New religious enthusiasms also appear to have won her heart. Perhaps the two together, not to mention motherhood and all that wealth, make it more difficult for a girl to follow, or to care about, the diffusion curve.

Poor Madonna. Her concerts were staging areas for the next restless self. They sprinted out ahead of contemporary culture, sending back new intelligence. Now they are more like a high school reunion, with all the old Madonnas turning up, unbidden, unwelcome, and, more often than not, uninteresting. Somewhere in the life of this changeling, the transformation stopped. As Sanneh says, "Having created all those old selves, she can't now disown them, she can only play with them."

CINDY AND BARBIE

Cindy Jackson is the "Human Barbie," as she was recently called by ABC television. She grew up in a farming community in Ohio. She was a painfully self-conscious child with a stutter. She felt herself a "complete misfit." She could hear the call of other places: "I always knew there was another life waiting for me far away from the cornfields of the Midwest."

Jackson tells us that it was the doll she received as a little girl of six that helped shape her idea of this other life. "Through Barbie I could glimpse an alternative destiny."[71]

Ms. Jackson went to art college in Ohio and moved to London in her twenties. She sang in a punk band in the 1980s. It is not clear that Cindy Jackson grasped punk entirely. She says, for instance, "It did not seem to matter that I had no musical training. I was told that I looked the part and just to wing it." (For many punk artists, lack of training is a badge of authenticity.) She remembers Joey Ramone as a "gentle" soul who "didn't need to shout his message, it was all there in his music and the way he lived." (I think it's fair to say Joey Ramone did need to shout his message. Shouting was his message and the way he lived.)

In 1988, on receiving an inheritance from her father, she determined to transform herself. "Little did I know at the time that this was to be the turning point that would ultimately make all my childhood dreams come true and change my life forever." Some twenty-two operations and $100,000 later, the transformation was complete. Ms. Jackson does look a little like Barbie. In 1990, she founded the Cosmetic Surgery Network and she is the author of a book called *Cindy Jackson's Image and Cosmetic Surgery Secrets.*

Interviewing her on the television show *20/20,* Bob Brown worked hard to shake Ms. Jackson's evident aplomb. At first she would say only that she could see nothing wrong with being beautiful when it brings so many advantages. Mr. Brown persevered. Isn't there something wrong, he asked, with making yourself beautiful to please men?

I didn't do it to please men. I did it to taunt them. Beauty is the best revenge.[72]

But as Ms. Jackson was approaching her idea of perfection, the idea itself was changing. Barbie, the doll, was being reinvented. Mattel was feeling the pressure of mothers who wondered why this exemplar for young girls needed to have impossible physical proportions. Did Barbie have to be the equivalent of 38-18-34?[73] Mattel was unable to muster a convincing response and Barbie was now a candidate for plastic surgery (no pun intended). The surgery was a complete success. Some dolls in the Barbie line now had more human proportions. If Ms. Jackson felt abandoned by her heroine, she did not let on.

Then came more bad news for Ms. Jackson. Mattel decided that Barbie was insufficiently hip and gave some models a butterfly tattoo and a nose ring. "Barbie just isn't as cool as she used to be," explained Marianne

Szymanski, editor of *Toy Tips* magazine.[74] Ms. Jackson may have had her punk moment, but the sleek, polished friend to the British royal family, film stars, and Ivana Trump does not appear to be a nose-ring kind of girl. Once again the girl from Ohio was betrayed by her heroine.

As Ms. Jackson struggled to become more like Barbie, Barbie became more like her. It can't be comfortable to pass oneself in the hallway, as it were. But this is one indication of the sheer scale and difficulty of a transformational society: that the modalities of transformation are themselves transformational. The grammars of change are changing and unpredictable. No sooner do they inscribe us than they move on.

VOICE-OVER BASKETBALL

I was playing basketball by myself one day a couple of years ago. It's a solitary business, but it has, for me, several distinct pleasures: the weight of the ball, that ringing sound it makes on the asphalt, the way it rolls through the blue summer sky, and the clang it makes as it bangs against the rim and bounces away. It wasn't long before I was demonstrating I could sink three balls out of ten at will. There is something splendid about being out there on the court by yourself.

Thanks to the influential essay by Robert Putnam, bowling alone has become a sign of the collapse of community and the decay of America's social capital.[75] I believe voice-over basketball represents another, not unrelated, challenge.

On the day in question, I was approaching contemplative joy when, all of a sudden, a station wagon came tearing down the hill, did a wide circle across the court, and came to a head-snapping halt at its far end. Kids issued from the station wagon like Keystone cops and, with noisy enthusiasm, commenced a game of three on three.

The most vocal of the players, a kid of about twelve, was calling the "play by play" as if he were a professional sportscaster. He was rehearsing a victory by the Boston Celtics over the Los Angeles Lakers. He had also taken the role of the star of the game.

It's Larry Bird at the free throw line. It all comes down . . . to this. Sink this basket and the championship belongs to Boston. Sink this basket, and Larry Bird's name will live in the Gardens . . . in history . . . forever.

The kid stepped up to the free-throw line. And in a hushed voice he said, "Bird prepares to take his shot. He's at the line. He dribbles twice. He shoots!"

In sports movies, the world falls silent. The ball moves in slow motion through the heavens. It enters the net and real time simultaneously. The crowd roars. Joy and pandemonium are unleashed. Not here. Here behind the high school, in front of seven not very gifted athletes, the ball bounced away. I waited for an embarrassed silence, the flood of disbelief, the agony of defeat. I did not understand voice-over basketball. The kid caught the rebound, and drove toward the basket. "There's still one second left . . . Bird has the ball . . . he has the lane . . . he has the height . . ."

This time the ball went in. The fan went wild. "He scores! Larry Bird has won it all. The place is bedlam, ladies and gentleman. The crowd is going ab-so-*lute*-ly *mental*." And here he made a rushing sound which sounded surprisingly like forty thousand fans on the verge of riot. The twelve-year-old was dancing around the court with his hands in the air, trading high fives with his team mates. "Larry Bird has done it again. The man is a genius! *Bird is a god!*"

MIKE NICHOLS

Mike Nichols is an American director of plays and movies, the latter including *The Graduate* (1967), *Silkwood* (1983), and *The Birdcage* (1996). He is married to Diane Sawyer, a journalist. He was feted at Lincoln Center's Avery Fisher Hall, where his lifetime achievement in film was celebrated by three thousand people, including Richard Avedon, Itzhak Perlman, and Barbara Walters. If popular culture in America has an aristocracy, Mike Nichols belongs to it. Three thousand people came to celebrate, but most were there in homage.

Nichols came to America as Igor Peschkowsky. He arrived from Berlin in 1939. He was seven, his brother was three. They made the journey alone, by sea. His father preceded him to New York City; his mother would follow eighteen months later. In New York City, Mr. Peschkowsky turned the boys over to the uneven kindness of an English family. Nichols was now bereft of his native country, his native language, the company of his mother and father, and his family's standing in Europe. "I was a zero. . . . In every way that mattered, I was powerless."[76]

Nichols endured the pains of adjustment. His advantage, an eye for detail and ear for nuance, was itself a torment. "The refugee ear is a sort of seismograph for how one is doing. . . . A thousand tiny victories and defeats in an ordinary conversation." To make matters worse, a medical intervention in childhood had left him hairless, so that he was obliged to wear a hat, or a wig, everywhere. Buck Henry, a childhood friend, remembers him as being "as far outside as an outsider can get."[77]

Nichols was obliged to engage in immigrant improv, that essential shield with which newcomers protect themselves from the endless embarrassments of a new world. Any native knucklehead could needle and vex him at whim. "*Saratoga*," says the knucklehead, with that "but of course you must know this" air. Judging from the speaker, the conversation, and the tone of the challenge, "Saratoga" is a literary journal, a cherished brand of American root beer, or the train that travels between Los Angeles and San Francisco. (It is probably not an aboriginal place name. That would be too easy.)

The family established itself. His father was a doctor. In time, a modest prosperity and standing were restored. Then more tragedy. His father died, his mother suffered chronic emotional difficulty, and the family descended into poverty and sometimes squalor. Nichols fashioned his own system of education (chiefly, popular theater and classical literature) and found his way to the University of Chicago, where, at seventeen, he made a happy discovery. "Oh my God, look, there are others like me. There are other weirdoes."[78]

Nichols took to the theater. The University of Chicago was loaded with talent: Paul Sills, Ed Asner, Severn Darden, Barbara Harris. He directed his first play and performed in several more. In one of them, his disguise was pierced. He was Jean the valet in a production of Strindberg's *Miss Julie*. His role called for a working-class man, one of the few adaptations this Russian-German Jewish aristocratic American weirdo could not manage. He was found out by a woman in the audience, an "evil, hostile girl" staring at him from the front row. "[S]he knew it was shit."[79]

What happened next is one of the origin myths of American culture. One day, Nichols saw his inquisitor waiting for a train in a railway station in Chicago. He approached her and asked, in a German accent, "May I sit down?" Elaine May replied, also with an accent, "If you wish." The rest is, as they say, history. Nichols and May made a spy scenario out of thin air. Without benefit of introduction or social ceremony, and in spite of disastrous first impressions, they were now friends. It felt to them both,

Nichols said later, that "we were safe from everyone else when we were with each other."[80]

Certainly, it has the compactness, the telescopic redundancy, of an origin myth. The origin of American improv is an act of improv, first of the moment, then of the stage, then of popular culture. What Nichols and May did in the train station, they repeated at the University of Chicago, and then on the *Dupont Show of the Month* to an astonished America. The captive of *Miss Julie* and fixed theater was released into the sheer creativity that was in any case his immigrant experience. And with improv, America finds its way into opportunities for new dynamism. The path to assimilation proves to be the steep upward ascent to wealth, glory, and fame. Two people give themselves over to this single act of spontaneity and everything changes: the interaction, their relationship, their careers, and an important part of the development of contemporary culture.

In the middle moment, the world is charmed. Nichols and May are perfect, blinding. Touched by this creature, Nichols discovers new talent and the possibility of fame staggeringly beyond the acceptance he had courted, a boy in a wig, a couple of years before. Elaine May is adored, pursued, protean in her creativity, charismatic on stage and off, larger than every occasion and every other companion, impatient with mortals, and terrible in her anger when it is provoked. (Pursued by two men making kissing sounds, May says, "Tired of one another?" and when one of them responds, "Fuck you!" she turns on him and asks, "With what?"[81] Ovid would surely have wanted this for his compendium of transformations.)

And then, in the manner of some myths, it ended. Improv became formula. May wanted to keep inventing but, as Nichols tells us (in an act of greatness), he could not keep up with her and he began to lose the courage to take risks on stage. The improv, the act, and the relationship die in succession. The actors are estranged. Nichols returns to the theater, not to act but, in the ultimate retreat from improv, to direct. He has a period of madness in which he seeks to destroy the art that reflects his wealth and taste. He resurrects himself to make one or two good films but keeps his distance from sheer, untrammeled creativity, falling back on fixed and commercial theater. Elaine May suffers a more spectacular destruction. She falls under the influence of a man manifestly her lesser, and directs him in a disastrously unsuccessful film: *Ishtar* (1987). *This* is shit: overscripted, underdirected, wooden, Beatty-ish, and just not funny. The first creatures to enter Chicago improv had fallen back to earth.[82]

Section 2

Traditional Transformations

In a BBC documentary, the interviewer wanted to know what it was "really" like to be an "African tribesman."[1]

"What," she asked her unsuspecting respondent, "is your life like right now?"

"Well," said the tribesman, "I recently married, acquired cattle, and I'm hoping to be a father soon."

"Yes," pressed the interviewer, "but where are you in the larger scheme of things? What's it like to be *you* right now?"

"Ah," said the tribesman, understanding, "in a few years, if things work out, I'll be an elder."

Patiently, the interviewer rephrased. "But what do you *want* from life. Where are you actually, you know, *going*?"

The tribesman gave the interviewer a long look and said, "In a few years, I hope to be an elder."

RITUAL

A good deal of fieldwork consists of watching people mill around, engaged in activities so ill defined, it's hard to tell where one event ends and the other begins. Ritual, on the other hand, is, in the usual case, unmistakable. It occurs on sacred ground in sacred time. It is enacted with extra-ordinary language, gesture, clothing, objects, music, and care.[2] It creates dramatic tension and extraordinary outcomes. It is unambiguously a center of a community's attention.[3] No milling or muddling. Not even the dimmest observer is likely to miss this grand event. "This is going to be great!" exclaims the anthropologist, clasping his Tilley Endurable and rushing into the village square.[4]

The *what* of the ritual is clear, but not always the *why*. Even a learned anthropologist must sometimes ask, "um, what just happened?" This wins withering looks as the locals stoop to explain the obvious:

> That girl? She's a woman. Those two people? Partners for life. The little man with the cape? He's a god.
>
> Oh! OK! Whew! I could have missed something!
>
> I believe that's true. You are, of course, welcome any time. But, look, the hat . . . um . . . no one wears those anymore.

The power of ritual is various. It can assert the fundamental things a community cares about. Monica Wilson says, "Rituals reveal values at their deepest level."[5] And this is one of the things that make them so useful. A tidal wave decimates a village, and cultural convictions (e.g., that the sea god is benign) are thrown into question. Ritual can restore meaning and confidence. As Sally Moore and Barbara Myerhoff put it,

> [Ritual] banishes from consideration the basic questions raised by the made-upness of culture, its malleability and alterability. Every ceremony is par excellence a dramatic statement against indeterminacy in some field of human affairs. . . . Ritual is a declaration of form *against* indeterminacy.[6]

But the crisis is sometimes more individual than collective. It is sometimes only one man or woman who wonders—with the loss of a child, for instance—whether his or her system of beliefs is not perhaps suspect. Can the culture that fails to explain such a catastrophe be taken at its word in anything else? Nancy Munn observes that ritual can "reorganize the actor's experience of the situation [and] affirm a coherent symmetrical relationship between individual subjectivity and the objective societal order."[7] Ritual is good at restoring a house to order.

Ritual's work is not always as fundamental as this. As we've noted, it has more workaday activities: turning children into adults, adults into elders, or elders into ancestors. It can create solidarity in families, rock fans, towns, sports fans, nations, the faithful, and the revolutionary.[8] It can serve in the curing process, the harvest season, the launching of ships, the slaughter of calves. Ritual can help a nation claim a continent: "I claim this land in the name of her Majesty the Queen." Ritual can do a range of cultural work, from the majestic to the merely urgent.

Anthropologists have concentrated particularly on the "rite of passage," that species of ritual dedicated to the transformation of individuals. Their guide is Arnold van Gennep (1873–1957).[9] Van Gennep was a child of three countries (French mother, Dutch father, German birth), master of several languages, and student of many cultures. He worked largely outside the academic community and in 1909 published his classic *Les rites de passage*, a text still read by anthropology undergraduates and consulted by social and cultural anthropologists.

For van Gennep, transformation is transport. It is the carefully orchestrated movement of the individual down a well-marked path from one life-stage to the next. The classic instance is the "coming of age" ritual. Van Gennep suggests that this, like every rite of passage, has three stages. In the first stage, the individual is removed from the status of "boy," in an act of *separation*. In this second stage, he is in transit, no longer a "boy" and not yet a "man." He is without definition, and now *liminal*. Finally, this creature is delivered to his new social identity, "man," in the ritual's last stage, that of *aggregation*.[10]

The runny-nosed kid inclined to pranks, tantrums, and inexplicable giggling is now someone of substance, standing, and credibility, capable of marriage, parenthood and cattle ownership. Ritual makes this extraordinary change visible, and, more important, it makes it plausible. People who just yesterday despaired over the tantrums are now prepared to consider this fellow as a potential son-in-law. More astonishingly, the giggling is over. Even the boy's persuaded he's a man.[11] The transformational powers of this event are remarkable.

There has been a revolution in ritual studies in recent years. Jack Goody complained that we have used the concept of ritual to distinguish between "us" and "them." We, the West, have ceremony; they, the developing other, have ritual. Others argue we have made ritual too separate, too special, too formal, too sacred. This camp argues that ritual is everywhere in social and secular life. Food preparation, casual greetings, garden work: all of these, they say, are ritualized, although they do not demand their own space or time, ceremonial objects, special incantations, or formalized actions. They are the unexceptional, all but indistinguishable, moments of everyday life.[12]

A particular question has arisen in this revolution: where is the individual in the ritual? Does she have any control over it? Can she change what the ritual is, how it works, what it does? Our individualistic culture now clamors to know whether the ritual is for the individual, or the individual for the ritual. Is ritual a straitjacket? Is there no freedom here?[13]

The answer is "No, actually, not much freedom at all." The individual does not choose whether to participate in the ritual, how to participate, or what the ritual will be. The ritual is a collective act that comes from a collective agenda and works toward a collective outcome. It is not open to the discretionary choice or influence of its participants. In the words of David Parkin,

> [T]hat the ritual *is* a ritual and is supposed to follow some time-hallowed precedent in order to be effective or simply to be a proper performance is not in question.[14]

There appear to be good technical reasons why this should be so. In an influential paper, Maurice Bloch argued that ritual is *necessarily* closed to individual control and manipulation.[15] Ritual takes its emotional force precisely from the fact that it has stripped words and actions of their everyday character and removed them from the realm of individual choice. The English anthropologist Gilbert Lewis, taking up Bloch's argument in his study of ritual in Papua New Guinea, speaks of the ritual as "frozen." It is, he says, "detached from those possibilities of choosing" that characterize normal communication.[16]

Stanley Tambiah disputes Block's argument but not entirely his conclusion. He says, "Rituals . . . are not designed or meant to express the intentions, emotions and states of mind of individuals in a direct, spontaneous, and 'natural' way." Instead, they are sensitive to the "social positions and powers" particular participants have outside the ritual. He notes that in exceptional circumstances, the individual may reshape the ritual, as did King Mongkut in the tonsure ceremony of his son, Prince Chulalongkorn, in 1866, when Mongkut acted out the part of Shiva. But restraints remain in place.

> Although he stretches or transforms or even violates particular customs or norms, the innovator is not attempting and is not viewed as acting to upset the overall framework of customs. King Mongkut was enlarging the institution of kingship, not wrecking it. At the next round they become conventional customs.[17]

Working on the "nonce" ritual of a Jewish senior citizens' center in contemporary California, Myerhoff notes that the great challenge of these rituals is precisely that they are "blatantly made-up . . . laboring under obvious contrivance." Here is a ritual that necessarily allows (indeed, demands) the contribution of the individual. Improvisation and particularization are everywhere.[18] But even in this, the most innovative case, Myerhoff says, the ritual is laboring to make the experience of its audience "tradition-like."[19] It strains toward the appearance of having existed since "time out of mind" that is the trademark of ritual.[20] Even this creation of the individual is seeking to take on the appearance of something not created by the individual.

In sum, the ritual enterprise is taken out of the hands of the individual. No room is left for choice in the making or in the saying. Indeed, individual creativity usually means the ritual means less, not more. When we depart from the rules of ritual, at least in the traditional case, we interfere with something fundamental in the nature of the beast. We put in jeopardy the extraordinary outcomes of which the ritual is capable: the transformation of people and places and things. Options, it turns out, are not optional. As a seven-year-old, this was not clear to me.

MYTH

> When he was a boy Japasa knew frogs and foxes and wind. He knew their songs. He entered the myths that are told about them. He obtained power by joining his own life force to theirs. He knew them in the bush away from the society of other humans. He knew them in the searing transformation of his vision quest. He became their child, one of their kind. He saw them clothed in a culture like his own. He carried them through to the end of his life, and then he let them go.[21]

In a mythic transformation, individuals become creatures of both the natural and supernatural worlds. Japasa's transformation has scale and completeness. He is not merely *like* frogs, foxes, and the wind. In the mythic transformation, he is "one of their kind."

Sometimes, it's a mutual transformation.

The wind came to [Japasa] as a person, the foxes wore clothes and spoke in a language he could understand, the frogs gathered to drum and gamble.[22]

In ritual, transformations relocate us in the human scheme of things. In myth, they relocate us in the cosmic scheme of things.[23]

There are a breathtaking variety of theories of myth.[24] For my purposes, it is enough to think of myths as special metaphors. Every metaphor suggests an equation between two terms. "Mr. Ledingham is a toad." We transfer what we know about "toad" to the teacher named Mr. Ledingham. What we dislike about the teacher is shaped in particular, amusing ways, and he is demoted (and marginalized) in the hierarchy of all creatures. The metaphoric equation, teacher=toad, takes the natural and cultural properties of toadness (e.g., small, slimy, swampy, in the first case; dangerous, malevolent, anomalous in the second) and makes them resident in the teacher. Mr. Ledingham stands before you, the metaphor now vocalizing, concretizing, extending, and vilifying his qualities.

To talk about myth as metaphor is to separate it from the cultural context in which it occurs. It is worth emphasizing that myth is always a part of what Nietzsche calls a "mobile army of metaphors, metonyms, and anthropomorphisms—in short, a sum of human relations, which have been enhanced rhetorically, and which after long use seem firm, canonical, and obligatory to a people."[25] I separate it here for the sake of clarity.

New metaphors occur constantly. "That guy, I'm telling you, he's harder to catch than a weasel on crack." Even those of us with no acquaintance with weasels or crack gain a vivid image and a clearer understanding of how evasive the person in question must be.[26] "It's like herding cats" made the rounds as a way of expressing the difficulty of getting people (especially academics) back into a room after a conference coffee break. Or, at our least inventive, "He's as stubborn as a mule."[27]

New metaphors have a "head-snapping" quality to them. There is a small "whoosh" as things as distinct as teachers and toads are shown to have common properties. What our culture declares distant in the larger scheme of things, metaphors "arc" together. Meaning passes suddenly, unexpectedly, and unprecedentedly in an act of sudden closure. Metaphors surprise and delight for reasons that are both cognitive and cultural.[28]

Three fates await the new metaphor. Most burn up on entry. They appear, illuminate conversation, and then pass from memory. Some stay a little longer, perhaps the duration of a school term. ("Oh, my God, he touched me. The Toad touched me!") But most metaphors come and go. The next time someone thinks to call Mr. Ledingham a toad, it will have the pleasure (and power) of invention. Luckily for Mr. Ledingham, students move on and metaphors die out.

But some metaphors live on. The first time we heard the phrase "herding cats," we laughed. People in conversation *are* like cats: distracted, contrary, and, when provoked, disobedient. We're amused by unsuspected similarity. But the phrase has been used often enough that it no longer "plays" in our head. "Herding cats" is on the way to becoming a "dead metaphor" on the order of "stubborn as a mule," a metaphor with no powers of transformation. It does not incite us to transfer the properties of muleness to a human being. We merely think, "oh, right, really stubborn."[29]

But there is a happier, more glorious fate for a metaphor. It can move upward in the great scheme of things. It can be seized upon as a mythic metaphor.

Like dead metaphors, mythic ones also take on a certain fixity. But this is not because they have been worked to death (sorry). It is because they have undergone an apotheosis and risen to greatness. Here is a metaphor that has been elevated to the status of a truth. "We are the Raven" becomes

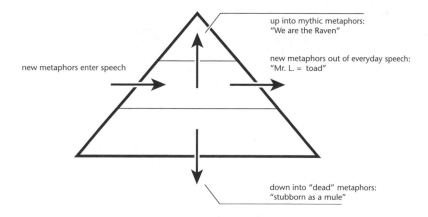

Figure 2. New metaphors

a permanent, fixed, and profound assertion of group identity. Unlike the everyday metaphor, mythic metaphor defines the world essentially and permanently.[30]

This may be a simple process of selection. Metaphors pour through the community all the time. Every so often, one of them is too good to let slip away.

"Say that again," someone demands.

The speaker, startled, backpedals. "I said we're sort of like, you know, um, the Raven."

"Of course, we are. That's exactly right. We *are* the Raven."

The casual comparison becomes a fundamental truth. Of all the metaphors that come and go, one emerges to change fundamental terms of thought and action.[31]

"We are the Raven" says something endlessly telling about us. It says something deeply defining of Japasa that he should say he's a frog. Once metaphor is myth, once it has been told and retold, and fixed itself into cognition and culture, it is covered in glory. It is so deeply felt, so habitual in its associative power, so profound in its transfer of meaning, and so sincere in its intentions that, in fact, it doesn't have to work very hard. It's traded away its powers to link things together in consciousness for the right to take up residence there. It is now a permanent way of thinking. Of course; we are the Raven and Japasa is a frog. We know this in our bones.

The myth insists on the equation, it insists on transformation. In Northwest Coast communities, family crests *show* the mythic equation between humans and animals, and the transformation that myth makes possible. On the family crests,

> human and animal forms [mingle] in ways which show that the two are manifestations of each other, locked in an inextricable mesh of . . . shared identities and destinies. Through the display of crests, . . . humans [are linked] to . . . the vital forces of the cosmos.[32]

The Haida clan hat has this character. It shows a human face below and a bear above, allowing the wearer to proclaim, as it were, "*sumus ursi, ergo sum;* We are bears, therefore I am."[33] In Siberia, the shaman wears a representation of antlers on his hat. Myth, specifically metaphor in myth, has transformed him.[34]

It is, of course, a scam. Myth cannot find a metaphor in nature until culture puts it there. Culture has to invest frogs with a special significance and properties. It has to insist that they are, say, mediators between water and sky before they are useful for metaphorical, mythic purposes. The scam is usually successful and pretty well concealed. We pretend that the metaphor is "found meaning," extant in nature before culture did a thing. It's our version of the Easter egg hunt. We secrete certain meanings in the world and then turn around and say, "why, I declare, what a useful notion! Oh, Japasa."

Myths catch anthropologists' attention quite as much as rituals do. They, too, are unmistakably important. They are set apart as special, they are told with reverence, often by specialists, and often they commandeer ritual as their production company, demanding yearly or seasonal enactments and a large piece of the ritual calendar. The anthropologist rushes into the village square because *stories are being told*.

Myths capture attention but resist interpretation. The anthropologist still has to ask, "So, what was that story about, exactly?" Often, the explanation of a myth is less illuminating than that of a ritual. "Japasa is a frog, you see," someone says. "Ah," says the anthropologist, looking at Japasa with new regard, "a frog." "In a manner of speaking," Japasa concedes, unhappy with this scrutiny, and asks, "Where's your stupid hat?" Frequently the anthropologist doesn't bother with questions and retires to the office to build the most astonishing analytical machines to make the myths make sense. Lévi-Strauss actually used a formula:[35]

$$f_x(a) : f_y(b) \cong f_x(b) : f_a{-}1(y)$$

Anthropology has spent a good deal of energy trying to explain how myths establish the essential equations that define the traditional society.

And this fact makes my discussion here a particularly pallid and partial treatment of the topic. I have neglected, abbreviated, and contorted this intellectual tradition even more than that of ritual. The "metaphor" approach is but one of twelve ways Doty supposes ritual and myth can serve the community of which they are a part.[36]

And certainly there are several competing traditions. Some theorists have treated myths as "messages in a bottle" that a culture sends to itself: myths are a set of instructions to persuade the group to do what they might otherwise not. Frazer's famous *Golden Bough* was one of the first to propose this approach. Malinowski and his students liked to try to guess the "real" purpose (i.e., the "latent function") of cultural phenomena, an approach now widely regarded as patronizing and wrong. Rappaport treats myth and ritual as a secret, unwitting system for the regulation of protein supply and ecological balance. By this reading, myth is adaptive and practical, a way to help a community to organize its affairs.[37]

Jungian theory has inspired a quite different approach. This view, evident particularly in the work of Northrop Frye and Joseph Campbell, has not won widespread support in the anthropological community because it insists that "archetypes" are everywhere the same, across historical time and cultural space. The myth-as-metaphor approach looks for an explanation that is more particular. Every myth, and every transformation it makes possible, serves a community because it is so perfectly crafted and exquisitely chosen.

In the Jungian view, metaphors register because they tap something universal and pan-cultural. In the anthropological view, they do so because they deftly, unexpectedly organize and articulate a field of beliefs and understandings in a particular way. The universality assumed by Jung, Frye, and Campbell is the very thing that makes their accounts suspect. The trouble with the archetype approach is that, when one size fits all, how can it be said to *fit* at all?[38]

The anthropological view has the additional virtue of helping us see a second way in which traditional cultures can be transformational. In them, individuals can try on and take on properties of other creatures around him. They can take on some of the frog's aspects, as these have been defined by their culture. They can try on earth, wind, or fire. The boundaries between the human and natural communities are porous. Passage back and forth is possible and, in these cultures, frequent. Human beings can participate in a vast world of imaginative possibilities, transforming themselves into birds, songs, rivers, bears, stories, rocks, ancestors, or elements.

But this transformation is constrained. The members of the traditional society can transform intensively. Japasa can become a fox, a frog, or the wind with real power and completion. He can become one of their kind. But this is all he can become. Traditional societies transform intensively, not extensively. It's "birds, songs, rivers, bears, stories, rocks, ancestors, *or* elements," not "birds, songs, rivers, bears, stories, rocks, ancestors, *and* elements."

The contrast between traditional and postmodernist worlds shows clearly in the way in which the two treat tattoos. A friend of mine has a tattoo that she says was designed by Scandinavian witches sometime in the medieval period. She sees this tattoo as having several kinds of cultural, and particularly feminist, significance. She got it after some considerable thought, the advice of friends, and the counsel of the tattoo artist. But the choice was hers. That she was going to get a tattoo, when she was going to get it, who was going to do it, what pattern she would get, and what, finally, this pattern means were largely matters of her own choosing. Certainly, a mythic tradition was evoked for transformational purposes, but the tattoo that resulted was almost entirely personal.

Compare the Plains Cree. According to David Mandelbaum and his correspondent Fine-day, tattoos begin as a vision in someone's dream. In the words of Fine-day,

> A man has a dream which gives him the power to do tattooing. . . . Much food is prepared and a large lodge set up. All the medicine bundles in camp are brought in. Then an old man goes around the camp and calls out, "Come early in the morning. When you are tattooed, you will be all dressed up. At a dance all you will have to do is to take off your robe." They coax the boys to be tattooed. . . . The man who received the power to tattoo in a vision begins to pray. He asks that the boys may wear the tattooing to an old age. Then he begins to sing.[39]

In this case, the tattooee must be coaxed and cajoled ("You will be all dressed up"). He can refuse the tattoo, but that is the limit of his discretionary power. I was thinking about the Cree case while walking home one night in Toronto. I wasn't far from a local tattoo parlor, Way Cool Tattoos, so I dropped in. The Cree appear to have access to one basic tattoo pattern. It took some time for the staff and me to work out the number contained in Way Cool. Counting patterns on walls, books, posters, and the bodies of staff members, we figured, finally, that Way Cool has around fourteen thousand patterns.[40]

The difference between the two cultural traditions shows also in the way in which they treat change. Some anthropologists stand accused of insisting that myths do not change. Dennis Tedlock accuses them of "hankering" after pristine forms in the face of obvious dynamism. Zuni storytellers, he notes, routinely offer their own interpretations of the Kyaklo myth, and they are expected to do so. This might make the Kyaklo more like contemporary myth makers, except Tedlock also notes that the person who would "wear Kyaklo's mask . . . must devote his whole life, for one year, to study for the part."[41]

Similarly, Th. P. Van Baaren says, "I should like to posit that changeability is one of the specific characteristics of myth." But he is still obliged to acknowledge that myth and its transformations are publicly certified and collectively established. They are stories that contain the "authority of the entire community." Van Baaren also notes in passing and without further comments that in precontact Tahiti, "priest[s] who made a mistake in reciting [a myth] could be executed."[42]

Kenelm Burridge studied the circumstances of the cargo cult. Here was a culture engaged in spectacular acts of mythic invention, as it struggled to contend with the ravages of Western contact and, especially, World War II. Burridge tells us that innovation in myth making is a collective act. The storyteller listens carefully. He is prepared to venture innovations, but he will repeat and expand upon them only when the audience approves them. As Burridge puts it, "New truths, or rather, statements that are becoming truths . . . are extremely vulnerable to consent."

> Myths in general have the attributes of objective truth largely because, perhaps, they are stories having a weight of common consent. This does not mean that storytellers cannot make their own additions to a particular myth; but it does mean that the additions they make have to obtain popular consent if they are to remain parts of the myth. Myths are stories stamped large with social approval.[43]

It looks as if mythic transformation is collective and constrained in something like the way ritual was. That you participate in the myth, how you participate, whether and how you can change the myth: these are not normally open to individual choice. Apparently, the Cree could choose not to have tattoos, but that was the extent of their choice. We may call upon a Scandinavian mythic tradition to transform ourselves with a tattoo, but when we do so almost everything about the exercise is optional.

In the traditional case, there is a breadth of transformational opportunity.[44] The boundaries between the human, natural, and supernatural worlds are porous. Humans can become birds, rivers, lightning, the wind. But it is almost as if there is a trade-off. This extraordinary movement across boundaries, this fluidity of identity, is predicated on the fact that only certain movements and fluidities are allowed. It is, perhaps, precisely because Japasa cannot enter a tattooing salon with fourteen thousand options that he can become a frog so powerfully and completely.

Let us resist the recitation of Western self-reproach that is usual at this point. (Please feel free to sing along with me.) We are poorer for the fact that we cannot undergo Japasa's transformation. We have lost the habit of transformation. We have destroyed the mythological creatures we could once become. Scandinavian tattoos are merely fad and fashion, no real transformation at all. Isn't this precisely what's wrong with kids today? We have no myths. We have no transformations. Myth made Japasa a wealthy man. It made his world resonate with the wisdom of the ages, the majesty of nature, the real rhythms of the universe.

We take pleasure in this self-reproach. We use it, actually, to define who we are. But, to anticipate later discussion, I would like to entertain the possibility that Japasa might envy us. None of the many transformations noted in the quotations that opened this book were open to him.

Japasa could not become a series of different people over the course of a lifetime. He could not go, as Oprah did, from Mississippi poverty to being an authoritative voice for millions of Americans. He could not follow Nora Ephron and reinvent himself every ten years. He cannot contemplate the transformational liberties we have observed in the lives of Robin Williams and Ani DiFranco. These things were closed to him. Actually, they were beyond the pale. These would almost certainly have been regarded as illicit, illegal, wrong, and provocative and brought Japasa the punishment of banishment.

Too often we observe Japasa's opportunity and envy him. We berate ourselves for having destroyed these rich and powerful mythic worlds. We treat them as a "world we have lost."[45] I think such treatment may be premature.

ANTI-TRANSFORMATION

Traditional society embraces ritual and mythic transformation, but it refuses many other kinds of change. In the practice of everyday life, it is deeply conservative. It devotes much of its energy to keeping things the same. When these things go out of kilter, the response is forceful. Extraordinary efforts are made to restore the world to order. In a postmodernist society, we have grown more or less accustomed to change as a constant. In traditional societies, it's the constant that's constant.

The anthropologist Robert Redfield had valuable insights into this theme. He saw traditional societies as inclined to make the world conform to "a single central vision." As the captives of heterogeneity and plenitude, it is hard for us to imagine such a place. But the "ruling" ideas of a traditional society are truly sovereign. They discourage criticism, originality, and the "disposition to change."[46] They discourage the very "concept of reform."[47] As J. S. La Fontaine puts it, these societies "base their concept of society on the idea of tradition, established once and for all. Society is the projection over time of the original founders, heroes or ancestors."[48]

E. P. Evans-Pritchard put it more forcefully:

> In this web of belief every strand depends on every other strand and a Zande cannot get outside its meshes because this is the only world he knows. The web is not an external structure in which he is enclosed. It is the texture of his thought and he cannot think that his thought is wrong.[49]

We do not need to go as far as this to observe that traditional societies are shot through with inclinations toward and powers of conservation.

Certainly, these societies cannot protect themselves from the person, event, or idea that "comes out of nowhere" to wreak havoc on the ideas, the practices, the world. They cannot protect themselves against people who have new ideas. But they have a way of containing inspirations and accidents so that they prove, finally, not so inspirational or destructive after all. We are quite prepared to surrender to new ideas and to accept most, if not all, of the structural effects they thrust upon us. Thus do we accept the personal computer, Tony Robbins, or "reengineering." But in traditional societies, inspirations of this kind are sealed away from the realm of the thinkable and the practicable. They are forced to fall, as Stanley Diamond puts it, "outside history," the world that is allowed to count. What does not serve the "traditional forms" of a society is not allowed to matter.[50]

For many of these societies, it isn't *wisdom* unless it's received.

> When questioned as to why a particular ceremonial activity is carried out in a particular way, Navaho singers will most often say, "because the kiyin dine—the Holy People—did it that way in the first place." The ultima ratio of non-literates tends to be "that is what our fathers said it was."[51]

The anti-transformational impulse is so powerful it can wrestle change to a standstill. The traditional Tambin rite of passage was put at risk by the rise of plantation labor. The Gnau of Papua New Guinea responded by insisting that plantation labor *was* a rite of passage. In this case the system undoes challenge by co-opting it.[52]

New Guinea islanders were challenged by the introduction of soccer and Western ideas of competitive sports. It was a troubling innovation. Chasing an inflated sphere around an open plain was strange enough. But worse, this activity insisted on declaring a winner. It turned symmetrical parties (the participants) into asymmetrical ones (winners or losers). It made the equal unequal.

This troubles modern and postmodern societies not at all. We thrive on the production of difference. We want outcomes, asymmetries, the unpredictable and imponderable, the unforeseen and uncontrolled. We look forward to political elections, *Monday Night Football*, stock markets, dean's lists, Indy 500s, sorority rushes, Nobel prizes, Las Vegas, serial television, Lotto drawings, game shows, moon landings, Top 10 lists, movie gunfights and car chases, cola wars, and the Olympics. We expect to live in a world of "nexts" that cannot be predicted with certainty from the "now." We are driven by suspense and the need to discover what happened. There may once have been a "shock of the new," but now it's merely the caffeinated buzz of contemporary life. Traditional societies *know* what's going to happen (hence the term "traditional") and they don't like it when they're wrong. There is no such thing as dramatic suspense. Engage in activity until someone wins and someone loses? New Guinea soccer was going to be a problem.

The islanders found a solution. They played to a tie even when this meant playing "several days running [and] as many matches as necessary for both sides to reach the same score."[53] The islanders choose to challenge the game's ability to produce difference, to refuse its ability to create winners and losers. The New Guinea idea was to play the game *against* the game. Thus does a traditional society protect itself from the voracious Western appetite for the new. This is a culture that, in Tambiah's words, prefers to "specify in advance not only the procedural rules but also the sequences of events." This is a culture that, given a choice, will refuse "the unpredictable and unequal outcomes" of competition.[54]

This is not to say traditional societies are anti-transformational. As we have seen, they engage in extraordinary acts of invention. In the moment of initiation, individuals can become animals, gods, or ancestors. But only for this moment. Once the initiation is complete, the initiate is delivered into a single constrained identity. For as Pierre Clastres puts it, somewhat tartly,

> [T]he initiatory [rite] . . . is [not] a matter of individual adventure. . . . [R]ites of passage . . . are intended to communicate to the young . . . a knowledge of the society that is preparing to welcome them. . . . [They communicate] the knowledge of what [society] is, what constitutes it, institutes it as itself: the universe of its laws and standards, the ethico-political universe of its law.[55]

There are two very different impulses at work in the traditional society: transformational liberty in myth and ritual, and its refusal in the workaday world.

A traditional society is a fluid world so effortlessly endowed with transformational opportunity that we are not surprised to encounter the Trickster in the North American aboriginal mythic world. The Trickster makes his right arm fight his left arm, eats his own intestines, changes into a woman and marries the chief's son, gets caught in an elk's skull, pretends to be a snipe, a woodpecker, and a polecat, and turns ice into lilies of the valley.[56] He is the very "spirit of disorder, the enemy of boundaries." He is, in Karl Kerenyi's words, "an exponent and personification of the life of the body: never wholly subdued, ruled by lust and hunger, forever running into pain and injury, cunning and stupid in action," and, we must add, relentlessly transformational.[57]

Why should there be a transformational hero like the Trickster in what is otherwise "all-controlling social order?"[58] Kerenyi believed there was a dialectical relationship between them. The rule of received wisdom, continuity, and stasis demanded such a creature. Order of this order could not exist without mischief.

Societies that are relatively anti-transformational enjoy another advantage. They're disinclined to give individuality, agency, and efficacy to the individual as an individual. In these societies the individual remains submerged within the group. "Submerged" is perhaps the wrong word, for it presupposes an individual who is distinct but somehow contained within the group.[59] Anti-transformational societies do not presuppose this. The individual is not individuated. Still more exactly, the individual isn't.[60]

This is a characteristic of both tribal and traditional societies (with the important difference that in traditional societies the individual is, but is not individuated). As the writer Bharati Mukherjee puts it,

> In Calcutta in the '50s, I heard no talk of "identity crisis"—communal or individual. The concept itself—of a person not knowing who he or she is—was unimaginable in our hierarchical, classification-obsessed society. One's identity was fixed, derived from religion, caste, patrimony, and mother tongue.[61]

It is chiefly modern and postmodern societies that construct a distinct individual and then insist on this construction as the first order of social organization.

> The liberated individual, not the social group, must therefore become the basic cultural unit. Although many people continue to be members of and identify with groups, they believe their group identities to be matters of individual choice, which can be changed without stigma. Group membership thus becomes voluntary, contingent, and fluid, not "given," fixed, or rigid.[62]

Richard Shweder and Edmund Bourne, like Louis Dumont, call our society "egocentric," and suggest that we imagine it to be something "created to serve the interests of some idealized autonomous, abstract individual existing free of society yet living in society."[63] Traditional societies are constructed according to principles that elevate the group and the collectivity above such considerations.

We take our individualism for granted, but, as Clifford Geertz points out, in the larger scheme of things, we are the odd ones out.

The Western conception of the person as a bounded, unique, more or less integrated motivational and cognitive universe, a dynamic center of awareness, emotion, judgment, and action organized into a distinctive whole and set contrastively
both against other such wholes and against its social and natural background, is,
however incorrigible it may seem to us, a rather peculiar idea within the context of
the world's cultures.[64]

There is a deeper, more fundamental reason why the species should
harbor such a powerful anti-transformational tendency.[65] It may be that it
is in the nature of the human animal to cleave to convention and refuse
the innovation we now take so much for granted. Members of the genus
Homo (including our own species, *Homo sapiens sapiens*) have inhabited the
planet for about 2 million years. For most of that time they lived as
hunters and gatherers. This earliest lifestyle was uncomplicated and predictable, mostly a matter of following food around: herds of animals,
schools of fish, wild foodstuffs as they ripened here and there. For the
better part of 2 million years, we repeated ourselves endlessly, trudging
back and forth across Asian steppes and the African savanna, well-
intentioned beings but not, perhaps, especially promising ones.[66]

Someone looking in from another planet could be forgiven a simple
conclusion: these brave little bands might be peripatetic but they didn't
actually appear to be getting anywhere. In the larger, interplanetary
scheme of things, they (we) were the slow kids on the block. We may look
back upon these beginnings with embarrassment (as upwardly mobile
families always do), but there's no disguising our humble beginnings. For
2 million years we were the definition of monotony, intelligent but habit-
bound. There was no sign of new ideas here.[67]

It's been argued that the early passion for habit was forced upon us.
Surely we were up against the wall, obliged to devote all our thoughts
and energies just to survival. But this is probably wrong. There is now a
persuasive body of argument and evidence that says that hunters and
gatherers lived lives of relative plenty. It's even been suggested that they
worked little more than "banker's hours." So there *was* plenty of time
for reflection, creativity, and experiment. Apparently, this time was devoted to the transformational wonders of myth and ritual. Just as
plainly, it was not given to the reformation of their hunting and gathering ways.[68]

The implication is a little startling. If we've spent most of our career
on the planet as the captives of a static world, it's not because we had no
choice. It's because hunting and gathering was enough. It's because we
embraced a cultural system that had a way of bending innovative people,

events, and ideas to its will. The thoughtful interplanetary observer might be forgiven a second conclusion: members of *Homo sapiens* repeat themselves because that is what they like to do. No doubt she would refrain from saying so in a formal report, but over drinks with friends she will speak frankly: it's a poky little species with a numbing taste for sameness.

Then something happened. A dead-end species came alive. We can think of this change as a fragile plume lifting off from a vast rectangle. The rectangle is the roughly 72 billion human beings who lived over 2 million years as hunters and gatherers. The plume is the rest of us, the 8 billion human beings who embarked, many of them involuntarily, upon a radical new experiment: a career of change in just twenty thousand years.

In retrospect, the plume may look inevitable. Our present world seems to us so necessary; surely the species eagerly awaited the opportunity to abandon its origins and get on with development. But the evidence says otherwise. For 72 *billion* members of the species a career of change was unwanted. We spent almost 2 million years on the planet until it occurred to anyone at all.[69] The real question is *not* how 72 billion members of the species could have been so conservative. The question is *what happened to the rest of us?* Who let the genie get out of the bottle? How did the trickster get out of myth and into the world?

Our taste for change came so late and developed so fast, it looks almost like the work of a virus from outer space, the dramatic, dubious theme of *2001: A Space Odyssey*. But only those who believe in cold fusion and the immortality of Elvis are likely to accept this argument. More probably, it was the species working out latent, long-concealed potentialities by itself. Somehow, the old dog taught itself a new trick.

What a trick it was. The transformational habit came late but took well. Our species spent 2 million years mastering the subtleties of the digging stick. (This is what it sounds like, a stick for digging.) And it took us fewer than twenty thousand years to invent reusable spacecraft. Once the old dog learned a new trick, it became eagerly, effortlessly, endlessly inventive. When Fernand Braudel taunts us with a paradox, that we are "as profoundly innovative as [we are] enslaved by habit," the surest solution is to observe that these are the two stages to this evolutionary career: the first in which habit prevails over innovation, the second in which the reverse is true.[70]

What we resisted so steadily for 2 million years is now second nature to us. What used to be called the "accidents" of history are now built in. Commotion and hurly-burly are necessary features of our world. Change is a structural feature, perhaps the very signature of our culture. Our interplanetary observer, looking in at twenty-thousand-year intervals, so little rewarded over her vast lifespan that she now really resents the assignment, will be startled. She turns away for a few thousand years and, presto, all hell breaks lose. Hunters and gatherers go from digging sticks to spacecraft? Sluggo turns into Robin Williams? Her report will be hopeful and alarmed. (Over drinks, she will again be more candid: "I'm telling you, I think they're *on* something.")

We have moved away from our anti-transformational past with astonishing speed, but in all of this the anti-transformational impulse persevered. We have resisted all of the change that has got us here. Every inventor, every artist, every revolutionary has been met with nay-sayers, people who stalled and mocked. Domesticating plants and animals? Wheels? Cities? Voting? Arches? Moveable type? Newspapers? Voting for women? Electricity? Department stores? Flight? Electronic mail? Every invention that has transformed the human community was met with incredulity.[71] All of the things we take for granted, all the things we could not live without, were met with resistance. To judge from our long career on the planet, this resistance may be deeply in the nature of the beast.

When change was embraced it was often papered over. Historians have come to realize how many Western institutions are gussied up to exhibit an antiquity they do not have. For instance, Scottish clan tartans are a latter-day invention.[72] The nation-building that so preoccupied the nineteenth century depended on invented traditions of this kind.[73] These and other discoveries move one historian to note that we have met "the constant change and innovation of the modern world" with "an attempt to structure . . . some parts of social life within it as unchanging and invariant."[74] The practice of "inventing tradition" allowed us to pretend that change was not happening even as it proved unavoidable.[75] In sum, the forces of anti-transformation continued robust. The transformational inclination of a traditional society was balanced by something that looks in retrospect like a passion for stasis and continuity.

Section 3

Status Transformations

UPWARD TRANSFORMATION

"Upward transformation" is what individuals do to (and for) themselves to change their social standing. They cultivate exteriors (e.g., clothing, speech, and deportment), interiors (e.g., thought, emotion, and outlook) and possessions (e.g., belongings, large and small).[1]

When these cultivations are internally and externally persuasive, individuals become, in Ovid's language, creatures of another kind, or at least another degree. They move upward in the social scheme of things. Upward transformation has a double character; it is all the little changes undertaken in the creation of this larger change.

The directionality, the upwardness, of this form of transformation comes from the way status is imagined in Western societies. Status is usually seen as a location in social space, and *this* is seen as vertically oriented. Desirable status is seen, usually, as higher. Desirable movement is therefore upward.[2] Good transformations are upward ones.

Upward transformation is a structural necessity for the collectivity. Every individual born to high standing must learn to act as if this high standing were, in a sense, "natural," inevitable and therefore legitimate. So each new generation must be transformed. Accents must, in certain status systems, be given the right nasality. Emotions must be bound and trimmed with topiarian care. Conversational skills must be brought to perfection and kept there, because conversation offers the best opportunity to detect pretenders. Taste must be cultivated so that, as Bourdieu has pointed out, every choice thereafter affirms both the individual and the class. Transformation is the fount of legitimacy for both.[3]

It is not only those of high standing who must be made ready for their status claims. The upper middle and middle communities also have codes children must learn and perform. These codes may be faint imitations of the codes of higher-ups, but they require the same assiduous parenting and practice. (Communities of lower standing will have codes as well, in which still fainter imitation mixes with parody, transgression, and outright refusal.) "Status anxiety," as the sociologists call it, plays a role here. The further the group is from the social apex, the more anxious is the training in and the performance of status markers. (Indeed, the transformation performed on high-standing children is designed to remove any trace of status anxiety. "Never apologize. Never explain," as the class slogan has it.) For less exalted groups, every status performance is haunted by the possibility of error. Status anxiety is now, as it were, built in. The child cannot take on status without detecting, and taking on, anxiety.

This is a way of saying that the socialization of *every* child in a hierarchical society devotes itself to transforming the child for status purposes. A case in point is the scene in the documentary *Seven Up* (1964, dir. Paul Almond) in which public school students are shown, at the age of seven, still struggling to master both ludicrously overdetermined accents (or so they seem to us now, in the era of Estuary English) and evidence an already robust (and already somewhat defensive) insouciance they will need to defend this presentation of self.[4] We know that in a couple of years these children will feel these accents to be perfectly natural, forgetting the fact and the difficulty of acquisition.[5] By this time, the transformation of speech will have transformed the individual utterly and invisibly. So will all children eventually forget the transformational efforts brought to bear upon them. Now only therapy or a cultural revolution can return these to consciousness.

But some transformations come late. Every status hierarchy must find some way to advance and "retrofit" individuals to replace those lost to accident, disease, madness, commercial failure, or political miscalculation. Ruling classes and other elites would like to seal themselves away, trading, marrying, socializing among themselves, shutting out the lesser world. But they can't. Some method of exogamous recruitment must be found.[6] Backups must be recruited and made ready. Belated transformation is difficult. It begins late and has much to undo. Nonetheless, gifted creatures present themselves and they are taken up.

Social mobility supplies another cause for status transformation that comes late in the individual's life. As individuals work their way up the hierarchy, they must unlearn old status markers and learn the ones appropriate to their new standing. More exactly, status mobility cannot occur without the mastery of new status markers. Whether and how well markers are mastered will decide whether and how high the individual can rise. Here, too, the belatedness of the transformation makes it more difficult and more accessible to consciousness. The individual sometimes catches a glimpse of his or her former self, and sometimes comes to mourn the passing of this former self. This is a theme of a good deal of pulp fiction and television (perhaps designed to reassure the reader/viewer that upward mobility is a "mug's game," after all). Such metamorphs are shown sur-rounded by new status markers, suddenly unpersuaded by their preten-sions, and regretful of what they have done to themselves. They have won the world but sacrificed the "authentic self."

In dynamic Western societies, transformation becomes a life-long ob-ligation. This is because, especially from the eighteenth century onward, everyone has lived in a diffusion stream. Status markers in language, body language, material culture, built form, and entertainment continually flow through the social world. We will discuss this in some detail below, but for these purposes it is enough to observe Georg Simmel's treatment of late Western status hierarchies as a system that engages two shifting par-ties, superordinate and subordinate, driven by two shifting motives, dif-ferentiation and imitation.[7] As a result of this diffusion of status markers, every group in the hierarchy is obliged to master innovations that descend to it from on high, and to do so continually as these innovations flow through. Status diffusion means that all individuals are having to take on, master, and then repudiate a stream of status markers. To be sure, some of these are superficial, things of the surface: a change of colors, perhaps. This is mere change, change that is not in any way transformational. But the diffusion stream sometimes carries things that are more demanding. Buildings are torn down, accents reworked, manners changed, literary tastes redirected, the eye itself reeducated by new "scopic regimes"; some of these changes are thoroughgoing and transformational.

The transformational undertaking is extraordinarily detailed and thoroughgoing. Almost all those who live in a status hierarchy find some of their emotional life organized by it. Without much conscious choice in the matter, they are inclined to admire those above and disdain those be-low. Status also organizes their powers of observation and attention. Al-most everyone somehow manages to notice fine details of manner, speech, and ownership, and to correctly identify who ranks high and low. (We may imagine a range of understanding that extends only partway up and down the hierarchy. Everything beyond one's "place," everything well above and well below oneself in the hierarchy, is perceived less ex-actly, but not, for all that, less powerfully.)

To live in a status hierarchy is to be instructed daily in what status is and why one should care about it. The advantages of status are manifest. It makes life easier. Those with it live better. They are sought out as friends. Real and titular resources come to them more easily.

Its disadvantages are equally clear. To live in a status hierarchy is to become its object. Every individual is daily constructed by the estimation of others. But to live in a status hierarchy is also to be its agent. Individuals are daily called upon to give deference, regard, priority to the high and withhold them from the low. Elizabethans were constantly obliged to acknowledge the rank of passers-by. But even in this most active moment of participation in the hierarchy, even when it is the individual who has apportioned regard and disregard, there can be no real doubt that these acts are fully formed by social convention. What to admire in someone and whom to admire in the world are not open to individual choice.

All of this encourages an impulse toward upward transformation. Individuals can see clearly how, and how much, their own lives would change if they were to rise even a notch or two. This imagining soon establishes a right of way for fantasy. It is easy and sometimes irresistible to imagine what one's life would look like if only . . . And if the imaginative powers are poor, there is always someone in the community who can serve as an inspiration and a model.

What is played out in fantasy or glimpsed in life does not stay there. With a fine eye for detail and the daily practice of giving and getting recognition, it isn't long before the individual is "trying on" some of the markers of status. The individual can change his or her manner, speech, and possessions, by tiny degrees so as not to trigger an alarm, until they read as "higher." The change is big enough to be evident but not yet so big as to be punishable. Really good performances can supply their own warrant, but most people hope for the good fortune of rising wealth and influence. Once the ground is secured, the process can begin again. There may come a day of reckoning when someone says, effectively, "Enough, you are now signaling more status than you possess and claiming more status than you are allowed." But until that day, there is room for maneuver and the opportunity to transform oneself.

Some individuals are insatiable. No sooner have they captured higher ground than they begin to consider it their due and to maneuver once again. The upward movement that was anticipated, dared, accomplished, and savored becomes ordinary and the least the individual can expect of the world. Aspiration renews itself and a new transformational routine is set in train. There are some hierarchies, and some people in all hierarchies, who resist this pattern of relentless aspiration. But most hierarchies indulge or endure it. Some individuals are happy just where they are in the world. But many others can't help thinking that they are fit for better things.

To live in a status society is also to be vulnerable to unhappy moments when the sheer hypocrisy of the exercise is unavoidably clear. Courtiers, especially, were exasperated by the stream of small gestures, verbal and nonverbal, they were obliged to supply in acknowledging the statuses of superordinate and subordinate.[8] But everyone in a hierarchical society can see that the performance of a role does not represent the authentic person but demands instead a constant stream of insincerities. The interior person is not visible here. Indeed, the interior person is suppressed.[9]

The larger point here is that people can see what they are doing. They can wish it were otherwise, but much of this status seeking happens invisibly, as a matter of habitus, as the way one lives. We might play them a tape, and they would be astonished to hear how much an accent has changed or see what has become of their wardrobe (and we have this experience when revisiting photo albums or high school yearbooks). Status has claimed them.

Upward transformation, that wheel of small changes in the wheel of a much larger social change, is driven by several motives and imperatives.

THE MEDIEVAL MERCHANT

Medieval merchants were anomalous creatures, not quite fish of the marketplace, not quite fowl of the countryside. Buying and selling, importing and exporting, all in dynamic urban centers, they could amass great fortunes. But working in these noisy, vulgar cities, uncomfortably near manual labor and the exertions of the marketplace, they were, in the eyes of polite society, dubious candidates for high social standing. Princely wealth was one thing, princely rank another.

But they tried. Merchants made a show of their wealth. Older, established families might struggle to keep up appearances, enduring the discomforts of what a later age would call "genteel poverty." But the successful merchant could lay it on: the house, the horses, the retinue, the wardrobe, the furnishings, the country home. Some of this was bumptious, in our phrase, and overweening, in theirs. But it was, as Sylvia Thrupp points out, carefully crafted consumption: conspicuous, to be sure, but only sometimes ridiculous. Merchants skillfully adopted the lifestyle of those above them in the hierarchy.[10]

The path to becoming a gentleman was living and acting like one.

[T]he possession of a country house could set a city merchant on the way to changing his class status. If, as many of the wealthier men are known to have done, he then assumed the social role of a gentleman in his county.[11]

Merchants were keen to acquire a particular marker of social standing, a family coat of arms. This was a necessary gesture, required of everyone who would join the upper reaches of the social triangle. The herald would pretend to search the records for some precedent and then "discover" that the family in question was merely renewing its gentle standing. This was a particularly transparent fiction for most merchants. Thrupp notes one case in which the herald didn't bother with the pretense. There was no concealing that fact that this particular family was new to high status.[12]

Merchants might style themselves gentlemen and they might be so received, but there was always a shadow of disapproval, the sense that these men were pretenders who had bought their way into a world they could not have entered by any other means. The period had some weapons with which to defend itself against the pretender. Sumptuary legislation specified punishments for the most egregious pretenders. And even the more systematic and acceptable representations of the merchant won the practiced scorn of society's gatekeepers. In this time of hypersensitivity, we can be sure these slights must have stung.

The merchant must have felt a mixture of emotions in all of this. No doubt, he accepted that members of the gentry and nobility were his betters. Yes, he understood that if he wanted to join this world and enjoy the benefits of elevation, he would have to defer to them. But it would not be surprising if the merchant did not harbor some small sense that, really, he was remarkable precisely because his standing in the world was due not to birth, but to hard-won achievement. Of course, he would consent to the self-effacements demanded of him, and the needling humiliations inflicted by social competitors with more standing and less money. But it's not clear that the hegemony of this ruling class overwhelmed every other evaluative point of view.

Truly, this merchant lived in a transformational world quite unlike Japasa's. First, Japasa's transformations took place in a mythical world; the merchant's, very much in the "here and now." The merchant's transformation was a worldly one that changed him both as a social creature and as a brute, empirical presence in the world.

Second, the merchant's transformation was contested. He undertook it in the teeth of skepticism and hostility. He was scorned as "jumped-up." Some rituals, as we noted in the last section, demand the willing participation (or at least credulity) of the mass of men and women. This was missing here. Some members of the hierarchy openly disputed the transformation and its "celebrant."

Third, the transformation was individualized. If the traditional transformation was a collective venture, open to all, supervised by all, confirmed
by all, the merchant's change was something else. Who would undertake
the transformation? It was left for the individual to muster the courage to
try. When was the right time for the transformation? Was it marked by the
cycle of the seasons, a physiological event, the collective will of the community? No, this, too, was an individual choice.

Traditional rituals do their work in the course of the ritual. Upward
transformation was a more protracted affair, driven by the skill and determination of the merchant's performance, and the outcome was judged in
the court of public opinion. Finally, for many families, it would be impossible to say that the transformation was ever over. The merchant's social
standing was still "in play" years after the fact, which gave rise to a continual series of acknowledgments and snubs, invitations and rejections.
Even successful families could see their status shift over several generations. Approval, when it did come, would come in the round, as something understood in retrospect. What kind of ritual takes three generations, sixty years, and ends in surmise?

Finally, the transformation was accomplished not by ritual per se but
by a process of imitation. The merchant styled himself a gentleman in
clothing, housing, and conduct, all fixed by convention but open to a
choice of quality and quantity, and, of course, to the possibility of error.
Imitation took place in a thousand little purchases and choices and over a
very long term. The merchant's transformation was not so much a rite of
passage as the strategic but uncertain process of "living well."[13]

Oddest of all, it worked; in some cases, as Thrupp tells us, it worked
superbly well.

THE ELIZABETHAN YEOMAN

In the Elizabethan era, England was a mobile place. Upward
transformation was both more common and less contested. The courtesy
literature of the time discussed this mobility with the usual misgivings.
Could something "in the blood" begin as a theatrical or performative gesture? Could a family's nature begin with its culture? The answer was a
grudging yes. But, the writers warned, rules would be insisted upon. The
reader who presumed to embark upon an upward journey must understand that it would take five generations for the process to complete itself.

Only over such a long period could he hope to wash away the taint of commonality.

Unofficially, Elizabethan families were making the transition in three generations, and sometimes fewer. Lawrence Stone shows Elizabethans hurtling both upward and downward in a state of status transport. This is one of the things that make the Elizabethan world so vibrant, that men and women could rise (and fall) so quickly and so far. (Come to that [and we must say this *sotto voce*], the Tudors were themselves not a very ancient family and they had risen very fast indeed.) A seventeenth-century writer wondered whether the English might not have a particular genius for this mobility.[14] And Lawrence Stone suggests that, in any event, the English had a gift for "chameleon-like adaptability."[15]

Yeomen worked the land. They were farmers. They were pleased to think of themselves as deeply sensible people and to present themselves as creatures of the "plain style."[16] Not for them the affectations of city and court. Not for them England's growing fascination with fashion.[17] Such things, in the contemporary phrase, "smell[ed] too much of beyond the seas." Some of the trappings of the gentleman were, in the yeoman's view, foreign importations, the work of "musical-headed Frenchmen"[18] and other outsiders.

Still, yeomen were near the minor gentry in the hierarchy. Movement across the social boundary between the two groups was frequent and relatively unexceptional. Some would protest that a yeoman had no place assuming the airs, let alone the standing, of a gentleman. One critic ridiculed the "peacock's feathers cocked upon a raven." The yeoman's gentility, he said, was "bought gentility."[19] But another critic took mobility for granted. Yeomen, Thomas Fuller said, are "gentleman in ore, whom the next age may see refined, and is the wax capable of a gentle impression when the prince shall stamp it."[20] Apparently, yeomen were more welcome to climb upward in the hierarchy than the merchants of the period.

But yeomen didn't always want to. Some disliked the idea of leaving their class and refused to budge. Thus were the literary tables turned. Contemporaries no longer attacked or mocked the merchant who refused to know his place. Now they wondered at the yeoman's reluctance to take up his responsibilities. Now they pelted him with encouragement to get on with it.

Certainly, many yeomen made the transition. All who did, it is worth noting, chose the method that had been followed by merchants. The way to become a gentleman was to live like one. And this was precisely what was expected of them, to give up the plain style and adopt the country home, the clothing, the manner, the speech, and the coat of arms that identified the gentleman.[21] Eventually, culture would turn to nature. Claims to standing would become more plausible the more often and more vividly they were made. And, for one's children, and especially one's children's children, they would cease to be claims. Eventually, they would be accidents of birth—things that just happened to be true. Eventually, gentle conduct would work its way into the family's dispositional and even, apparently, its genetic gift.[22]

Once more, we are worlds away from Japasa. As in the merchant's case, transformation was the work not of ritual but of imitation. Once more, its participants, timing, content, efficacy, and outcome were, relatively speaking, indeterminate. Who should participate, within limits, was unclear. When the transformation should take place was unclear. What should happen, although again restricted, was unclear. And when the transformation was complete and successful was unclear. Once more, the transformation was contested, but, remarkably, now the voice of contestation comes from *inside* the transformational exercise, from the very creature who is supposed to be its beneficiary. Japasa's transformation is collective, fixed, universal, optionless, and clear—fully ritualized. In this Western one, it is individual, dynamic, particular, optionful, and indeterminate—relatively performative.

Still, it would be wrong to go too far. In this Western, modern case, transformation is allowed, but, for social purposes, only one form is tolerated. It is only when the individual is moving upward in social space, it is only when he is changing his social attributions and his class standing as we have seen here, that transformation is possible. This essentially modernist approach to transformation will be the subject of the remainder of this section.

UPWARD TRANSFORMATION: MECHANICS

Upward transformation, as we have seen, is the process by which individuals change their social standing by cultivating exteriors, interiors, and possessions. These small changes lead to a larger change. The individual moves upward in the social scheme of things. A transformational routine of this kind raises mechanical questions. How does the routine work? What are its tolerances and conditions? What follows is a draughtsman's treatment, a sketch that shows its basic structure and no more.

Small changes begin with imitation.[23] The subordinate must get a fix on the characteristics of a superordinate. This can come from direct observation or through novels, plays, movies, or instruction manuals. To be sure, the appropriation is not always fully conscious. Some imitation is "naturally occurring." Suddenly, the subordinate discovers a new laugh, a surprising but welcome addition to the repertoire of behaviors. Sometimes the imitation is more self-conscious. Time is spent before the mirror as practice makes perfect. "Is this me?" "Have I got it right?" "Will anyone 'buy' this?" Every social performance, as Goffman told us, is haunted by the possibility of skepticism and even ridicule.[24]

The small changes must now be debuted, performed before an audience. This performance will go well or badly. It will prove plausible or implausible. What Goffman called the "presentation of self in everyday life" is rich with "trial" gestures of this kind. Frances Trollope spotted one during her travels in eighteenth-century America:

> The lady I now visited . . . greatly surpassed my quondam [i.e., former] friends in the refinement of her conversation. She ambled through the whole time the visit lasted, in a sort of elegantly mincing familiar style of gossip, which, I think, she was imitating from some novel, for I was told she was a great novel reader, and left all household occupations to be performed by her slaves. To say she addressed us in a tone of equality, will give no adequate idea of her manner; I am persuaded that no misgiving on the subject ever entered her head.[25]

Here imitation isn't much more than affectation. This is transformation in its earliest, most experimental moment. Its future is unclear. Done badly and implausibly, it will remain affectation. (And in this case it will actually cost more status than it gains.) Performed well and convincingly, imitation begins to "take" and eventually becomes "second nature."

The performance has several audiences. When Trollope's lady was performing for her neighbors, she may have been successful in offering her pretensions as legitimate status claims. Trollope herself was a harder sell—those of higher standing are. Performances have to be calibrated accordingly. The very worst situation is to have one's status performance refused by a high-standing party while a low-standing party is looking on. Now even they withdraw their consent and the player suffers instantaneous demotion. In usual hierarchical practice, players play to audiences with care.

So far we have talked as if this status performance needed to persuade only external audiences. But symbols are not merely badges. They cannot speak *for* individuals unless they also speak *to* them. Indeed, if they are not internally persuasive they cannot hope to be externally so. So the performance must persuade the performer, too. Even as it works toward a purpose, it must "feel right" and "ring true."[26]

The dynamics are interesting. When a performance is internally persuasive, it fuels itself. The individual can proceed with greater confidence, turn in a better performance, and prove to be still more internally (and externally) persuasive. These dynamics hold for all small changes; the internally successful performance of one feature helps fuel the performance of other features. When the individual succeeds in her performance of an "elegantly mincing familiar style of gossip," she is more likely to succeed in her performance of greeting rituals. Success begets confidence and this begets success.

Even brilliant performances, however, are not in and of themselves enough. Certain external matters—J. L. Austin calls them "felicity conditions"—must be in place.[27] Typically, these are matters of birth, education, accomplishment, or association. Without these additional credentials, the performer cannot qualify for advancement. (Beau Brummell and Disraeli are perhaps exceptions that prove the rule.) This is another way of saying that certain deficits are insurmountable. This is why the status imposter, even the one who gives a note-perfect performance and rises high in the world, is, when discovered, cast down.[28]

The small changes were numerous. The title of a nineteenth-century manual made this tauntingly clear: *Perfect Etiquette: or, How to Behave in Society. A Complete Manual for Ladies and Gentlemen, Embracing Hints on Introduction, Salutation, Conversation, Friendly Visits, Social Parties, on the Street, in Public Places, in Traveling, Driving, and Riding, Letter Writing, at the Table, Making and Receiving Presents, Courtship, Wedding Etiquette, Christening, Funerals, Etc., with Suggestions How to Dress Tastefully.*[29]

All small changes are not created equal. Possessions are the fastest and easiest status markers to acquire—and to counterfeit. And of these, clothing is the most expressive and therefore, within this class, the most fraught with the possibility of error. Deportment—the art and discipline of the body—is less marked by class now than it was in the earlier, hierarchical West. (We are now more interested in cultivating the athletic body than the social one.) In the hierarchical period, it took years to master posture, gait, and motion. And the costs of error were higher still.

There are also the rituals of greeting and interaction. (This is the disciplined body in action, employed to social effect.) These rituals take training and practice. Certain kinds of social interaction are impossible without them. Without these rituals, the individual gives too much or too little deference to superordinates, and exacts too much or too little deference from subordinates. In the inimitable words of a seventeenth-century Englishman,

> You shall never see one new stept into Honour but he expects more observance than an Ancient: for though he be but new come from the Mint, he knows how to looke bigge and shew a storme in his Brow.[30]

Hierarchical societies demand the constant and skillful exchange of status tokens. It is impossible to rise in such a society unless one trades these tokens well.[31]

But the toughest change to master was, and is, that of language. Unlike clothing choices, the subtler linguistic markers of status are difficult for the subordinate to detect and to learn. Unlike forms of deportment, they are almost limitless in number. Unlike rituals, they must be crafted to an extraordinary range of interactions. Most of all, the linguistic markers of status must be produced on demand and under duress. The suspicious superordinate can interrogate and test the unlucky subordinate until the performance begins to come undone.

Learning how to make careful distinctions in the object world, the expressive body, interactive rituals, and language helped individuals to rework themselves. But there was a larger lesson, the importance of discrimination. Whatever the training accomplished in little, such individuals were now in possession of the first rule of status transformation. They could see and mark differences that were invisible to others. Discrimination of the social kind begins with discrimination of the semiotic kind.

> [The] proliferation of highly specialized artefacts [that tea preparation and serving demanded] offered new opportunities for consumption and display, but, more importantly, these objects turned tea drinking into a ritual. As participants moved and conversed, they evaluated potential business partners, potential marriage partners, and possible political allies. Through their participation in these ceremonies they also convinced others, and themselves, of their own gentility and status.[32]

There is a hierarchy of accomplishment. Possessions are the easiest status markers to acquire and the lowest rung of the hierarchy. Deportment is more difficult and more expensive to learn. Nonverbal rituals of greeting are still more difficult and demanding. And language, the apex of the hierarchy, is most difficult and delicate of all. As in Abraham Maslow's hierarchy of needs, each level presumes mastery of the last.[33] Upward transformation begins here.

Climbing this hierarchy has its own transformational implications. Each level introduces the individual to new categories, distinctions, and rules. The individual necessarily becomes more discriminating. This is the learning within the learning. Whatever the individual learns at each level, he or she also learns about the idea of noticing and mastering subtleties in the world—and this is itself an important lesson in upward mobility.

Many of these aspects of upward transformation appear in a story in the diary of Alexander Hamilton, a Scottish physician who lived in Annapolis in the middle of the eighteenth century. Hamilton was traveling in Delaware when he encountered an extraordinary scene. A man called Morison was offered cold scraps for breakfast and flew into a rage. Morison insisted that he was a gentleman, and that he would not be fed as a commoner. To substantiate his claim, he clapped a linen nightcap on his head and began to itemize the contents of his luggage, drawing the crowd's attention to silver buckles and holland shirts. He concluded with a flourish: his wife, he said, drank tea twice a day.[34] Look here, he was saying; I have made myself a gentleman and you must treat me as one.

Morison had merely mastered the lowest stage of the hierarchy of effects that transformation demanded. He had purchased several of the possessions that were the markers of high status, but Hamilton, our Scottish-American observer, could not help noticing that Morison had failed to master other details. In particular, Hamilton tells us, Morison's behavior was clownish, his language coarse, and his conversation inept. (This far down the hierarchy of accomplishment, the aspirant has yet to learn the larger lesson of status: that there are things he does not yet know.)

Richard Bushman's *The Refinement of America: Persons, Houses, Cities* reads like a catalogue of the hierarchy of accomplishment poor Morison had yet to ascend. He could not complete his status transformation until a dance master had given him "aristocratic carriage." He needed to master the highly ritualized show of deference to betters and acknowledgment to inferiors. He needed control of his emotions. (Uncontrolled laughter and yawning were, for instance, forbidden. So were the exclamations and swearwords with which Morison protested his breakfast.) Morison especially lacked "conversation": the proper control of topic, tone, and pace in the navigation of complex social interaction. Upward transformation demanded skill and discipline. It was not enough, it turned out, to slap a linen nightcap on one's head and itemize the objects in one's luggage.[35]

A man like Morison *might* master all of the elements required of him. But one final, particularly subtle, test awaited him. As Karin Calvert notes, it was precisely by his mastery of upward transformation that he could give himself away.

> Ironically, the very zeal of the middling sort to learn the rules of genteel behavior, and the seriousness with which they approached their own self-improvement, set them apart from the elite, who had absorbed the intricacies of genteel behavior from childhood.[36]

What was called for was *sprezzatura*, the art of concealing art with art.[37] Morison would have to learn the last rule of upward transformation, that bad poets borrow and good poets steal.[38]

Upward transformation, with its several demands, rising standards, and trick questions, would almost certainly prove to outwit poor linen-capped Morison. But what he could not do, his children might. They might be more credible (or at least less ludicrous) in their status claims. Starting higher, they could climb further. If the family's luck and prosperity held, Morison's grandchildren might do better still. Upward transformation was a difficult, complicated undertaking, but not an impossible one. There was no doubt that the Morison family would keep trying, for upward transformation was for many people a *raison d'être*, even for this nation of individualists, even in its republican moment.

Every cultural moment specifies its own logic. Tudor England made liberality a way to define relative standing.[39] This was disputed by Renaissance humanists, who preferred to insist that the key to status was reason.[40] In the nineteenth century, Matthew Arnold insisted it was fineness.[41] It would help a good deal if we could agree that there is no such thing as "status." For this is always culturally constituted, not only by relative location, but by the possession of some characteristic or good.[42] And there is no such thing as a simple mechanics. Sometimes upward transformation will be accomplished by exercises of reciprocity, sometimes by demonstrations of emotional control, and sometimes by the exhibition of discernment. In short, the "what" and the "how" of this process are always specified by historical precedent, cultural convention, and local standards. (I have ignored these last to make the mechanics plainer.) Each social world will decide the form, details, ideology, and cultural logic of the transformational process.

Cultures vary in their openness about transformation. As we noted above, there are societies that insist it never happens. Usually, these are either hierarchical worlds in which the social scale is supposed to be too steep to be traversed or egalitarian ones in which it is supposed that there are no gradations of status to move between. Some societies are relatively tolerant and open to mobility. Early modern England, as we have seen, called the yeoman a "gentleman in ore." Still others assume that transformation will be the goal of everyone and a reality for many. Modernist and American cultures are germane here.

Upward transformation has been talked about with a variety of terms, including "social emulation," "status competition," "conspicuous consumption," and "status mobility." If there is something distinctive about the concept as it is discussed here, it is the notion that the social transformation begins with self-transformation. The trouble with notions of social mobility is that, too often, self-transformation is absent from them. Social actors are imagined to be so many boats in the harbor, for which social reclassification is merely a matter of a change of moorage. To be sure, some movement is precisely this, and in it nothing changes but the status of the individuals concerned. They continue to think and act as before. But for others the larger social transformation demands observation, effort, and mastery that is open to risk, error, and reproach.[43]

Self-transformation is sometimes undertaken in groups. To some extent, this is what schools and clubs are for. Groups help specify the transformational routines on which upward transformation depends. (Hence the saying that Eton is not for the sons of gentleman but for their fathers.)[44] But even when self-transformation demands a collective vehicle, it remains a personal accomplishment. Some members of a group or a school will fail to seize the advantage of association, and their upward transformation will be incomplete or unsuccessful.

LATERAL

There is a nice moment in a documentary about the Canadian author Robertson Davies. The interviewer asks a difficult question.

> Mr. Davies, it has been suggested that you do not sound as if you came from a small town in rural Ontario. You sound, well, a little grand.

Davies looks up with surprise,

> Precisely, dear boy. I *do* come from a small town in Ontario. If it weren't for my affectations, I wouldn't have anything at all.[45]

Individuals assume "shapes of a different kind" by moving from the margin to the center of society. In this case, they are moving not upward in social space but across it. The objective is to expunge the markers that identify them as "outsiders" and to take on the appearance of "insiders." Doing so demands thoroughgoing change in speech, gesture, posture, dress, and material culture and in patterns of thinking, feeling, and acting.

There is a joke that makes much the same point. Three kids call up to the window of a friend. In thick accents, they say, "Hey, Jimmy, come on, we're going to the ball game." The friend replies in the same heavy accent, "You go. I'm studying for my citizenship exam." The kids return a week later. The invitation, and the refusal, are repeated. They return a week later, and this time Jimmy replies, in a standard American accent, "Say, would you fellows stop bothering me."[46]

This is a lateral transformation—both of nationality and of manner of speech. Jimmy is prepared to throw off his old friends, and even, the joke implies, his ethnicity. In the modernist scheme, this was the immigrant's usual transformation. Jimmy forsakes the things that create difference, exclusion, and even shame. And he takes on new ones without "accent."

This transformation depends on the hegemony of a mainstream that has the power to define the difference between the accented and the standard and to declare some people outsiders. This is interesting from the anthropological point of view because there is no necessary difference between English spoken with an accent and without. More exactly, Jimmy has an "accent" before his exam and he has one after it. It takes cultural effort to declare an immigrant's behavior peculiar, still more to insist that it marks him as *essentially* peculiar ("Italians!"), and still more to use it as grounds for discriminatory treatment. Such declarations are arbitrary but customary. Most communities are prepared to create a center and a periphery. Everyone knows who's in and who's out.

There is usually an incentive for the individual to throw off the markers of difference and take on the markers of belonging. Whether people undertake a lateral transformation will help decide how they will be educated, employed, advanced, and interred. How well they perform the transformation can decide how much they are paid, whether they are promoted at work, what clubs they will belong to, and even the life chances of their children. In the modernist case, lateral transformation can be the way around systematic discrimination, not to mention the internal punishments of self-doubt.

How apt it is to call it "discrimination." It begins with the possibility of detecting the finest variation. It is precisely because there are so many ways of wearing a hat, saying "hello," or furnishing a room that this hegemony is possible. Even the simplest member of a culture becomes, in these matters, a virtuoso. Any idiot can play the savant: "Say, mister, you're not from around here, are you?"

Lateral transformation often has an element of risk and daring. There is so much to learn, so much, as in Morison's case, to get wrong. The alien may enter the mainstream and pass as a native. But there is no telling when the ability to discriminate between will provoke the urge to discriminate against. People notice things. Even stupid people notice things. Mistakes happen. The pretender is revealed. People then do things. Even, and especially, stupid people do things. (This is their chance to relieve the unhappiness that comes to stupid people.) Lateral transformation is fraught with tension and danger.

One of the chief occasions for lateral transformation is the move from countryside to city.[47] This migration is one of the themes of Western life in the twentieth century as millions of people left farms, hamlets, and small towns for larger urban centers. What made these centers so attractive was the relative ease and prosperity of paid labor and the entertainments and diversions of city life. But people also moved for the glittering prizes of a more sophisticated style of life. Arthur Vidich and Joseph Bensman demonstrated in 1958 that the town of Candor (pseudonymized as "Springdale"), a small community in upstate New York, was thoroughly penetrated by mass media and mass advertising.[48] Prior to television and national magazines, the temptations of city life were communicated by radio and the Sears catalogue. The siren call grew ever louder and more compelling. These sources were instructive, but the best students learned the first lesson: you had to be there.

Lateral transformation figures in *Sister Carrie*, a novel by Theodore Dreiser published in 1900. This tells the story of a young woman, Caroline Meeber, who comes from the little town of Columbia City in rural Illinois. The novel begins as eighteen-year-old Caroline boards the train for Chicago. There are only a few hundred miles between her village and the big city, but the cultural distance is, Meeber fears, rather more. Still, the city's interest is irresistible. "Columbia City, what was there for her? She knew its dull, little rounds by heart. Here was the great, mysterious city . . . a magnet for her."[49]

Generically, *Sister Carrie* is the "fallen woman" story. In the formula, young women trade their innocence and virtue for the excitement of life in the city's demi-monde, and are punished with moral diminishment, from which they are only sometimes rescued by a return to grace. But Dreiser set himself a more interesting inquiry. His novel does not presume to judge. *Sister Carrie* is dispassionately observational, almost anthropologi-cal. As one of the early naturalists in American fiction, Dreiser has large objectives.

Dreiser is particularly concerned with Carrie's appearance, her posses-sions, her posture and facial gestures. He begins with a description of her appearance as she boards the train in Columbia City.

> [H]er total outfit consisted of a small trunk, a cheap imitation alligator-skin satchel, a small lunch in a paper box, and a yellow leather snap purse. (2)[50]

Carrie begins city life in misery. She lives in crowded circumstances with her sister, competes with other girls for miserable factory jobs, suffers the humorless reproach of her brother-in-law, and dreams constantly of something better. This comes to her, eventually, in the form of the affec-tions of a young rake and practiced womanizer named Drouet, who buys her clothing, fine meals, and eventually a pleasant set of rooms where they live under the not very convincing pretense of husband and wife.

Carrie is ambivalent. She feels acutely the shame of her "kept" cir-cumstances and the surrender of her virtue. She reproaches herself for al-lowing objects and ease of life to mean so much more to her than her moral standing. But this internal dialogue is sometimes interrupted by what Dreiser calls "voice of the so-called inanimate."

> "Ah, such little feet," said the leather of the soft new shoes, "how effectively I cover them. What a pity they should ever want my aid." (136)

This is the conventional struggle of the "fallen woman" novel, but Dreiser sees other opportunities. Carrie is shown mastering the large body of semiotic and definitional signs of city life. Some of her instruc-tion comes from Drouet, who turns out to be most informative when least sensitive. He is given to commenting on the dress and demeanor of other women in public. Carrie begins to see how she might present herself and begins to change her speech, dress, posture, facial expression.

No sooner has she mastered what Drouet has to offer than she sees be-yond it. For instance, she can't help noticing the cravat and shoes worn by Drouet's friend Hurstwood.

> What he wore did not strike the eye so forcibly as that which Drouet had on, but Carrie could see the elegance of the material. Hurstwood's shoes were of soft, black calf, polished only to a dull shine. Drouet wore patent leather, but Carrie could not help feeling that there was a distinction in favour of the soft leather. (131)

As Dreiser shows, it is this mastery of detail that allows Carrie to wow Drouet, and then to wow Hurstwood. Here again Dreiser avoids the glib interpretation. He wants to show us Carrie seizing the mechanisms that allow her to move from the margin of city life to its center.

Carrie moves by her own hand. But she is also moved by the city's ability to establish new perspectives and sudden shifts in scale. It is the theater that lets her see her companion with new eyes. "By the end of the third act [Carrie] was sure that Drouet was only a kindly soul, but otherwise defective. He sank every moment in her estimation" (149). It is a drive past the fine houses on Chicago's North Shore Drive that allows Carrie to see that she is living in "but three small rooms in a moderately well-furnished boarding-house" (156).[51]

After a few months, Carrie is changed.

> Her awkwardness had all but passed, leaving, if anything, a quaint residue which was as pleasing as perfect grace. Her little shoes now fitted her smartly and had high heels. She had learned much about laces and those little neck-pieces which add so much to a woman's appearance. Her form had filled out until it was admirably plump and well-rounded. (195–96)

Carrie's progress is not status advancement. After all, Dreiser is sufficiently the captive of turn-of-the-century morality to treat Carrie as a creature of compromise. Upward movement is impossible for her. (Fallen women are moving in the wrong direction, as it were.) What is changing is the mastery of codes that give access to the mainstream. This is the essence of the lateral transformation.

It is not very difficult for Dreiser to persuade us of Carrie's next manifestation, her transition to a life in the theater. After all, readers have seen her training and come to admire her native ability.

> On several occasions, when Drouet had caught her admiring herself, as he imagined, in the mirror, she was doing nothing more than recalling some little grace of the mouth or the eyes which she had witnessed in another. (209–10)

Drouet comes home one night and proposes that Carrie participate in the amateur play being staged by his lodge brothers. Carrie consents, and, to no one's surprise (except of course poor, witless Drouet's), she flourishes. Carrie moves to the stage what she has undertaken in life. In the place of a nineteenth-century morality tale, we are treated to a study of transformation that shows Carrie's cunning and agency. More important, we can see how deep the transformation goes. This is no fall from grace but a rise of the stage, no destruction of the social actor but her recreation.

Carrie's story is, of course, not typical. Most of those who moved from the countryside to the city did not live so well. But most of them underwent changes that were demanding and substantial. City life changed the kit of consumer goods, the manner of speech, the routines of facial expression and bodily posture, the sensibility, and the view of life. Lateral transformation was in some ways as thorough as upward transformation. Dreiser helps make this plain.

There is another kind of lateral transformation: the experience of the immigrant.

I understand Italians can live in Boston for thirty years and not learn more than a handful of English words. (Walking along Hanover Street in Boston's North End some mornings, I could believe this is so.) But almost all immigrants are transformed by the new world around them. And almost all immigrants engage in deliberate acts of self-transformation—even when they persevere with their native language, and especially when they don't. In postwar America, most did not.

Writing in the early 1960s, Milton Gordon referred to the "identificational assimilation" at work in communities governed by what he called "anglo-conformity." In this case, the immigrant does not merely wish to erase difference for strategic reasons. He or she wishes to *become* a creature of the mainstream, to give up one identity and take on another. Gordon notes the novel *Remember Me to God*, about a student who wants to join the Harvard Club because he believes it will teach him the manners he needs to become "one of them." In these cases, transformation is thoroughgoing.[52]

Clubs were one institution that could aid in immigrant transformation. The movie house was another. In the earliest days of the American cinema, patrons went two or three times a week, soaking up instruction in language and culture. "Say, would you fellows stop bothering me." An immigrant audience took notes on how to become an American. Television served this function for some of the viewers of the *Dick Van Dyke Show*.[53] The *Saturday Evening Post* and the Sears catalogue were instructional manuals of a similar kind.[54] All helped supply the cultural materials out of which one could construct a facsimile of belonging and what we might call, after Goffman, the American "identikit."[55]

This form of transformation is usually called "assimilation." It suggests that the objective was to enter into the new culture so completely as to be absorbed by it, to become indistinguishable from the native, to pass without the possibility of detection, to enjoy the full fruits of membership because no one could tell.

Lateral transformation was shot through with ambivalence. In the worst case, individuals would find themselves caught between the culture they had left and the one they had yet fully to join. But even if assimilation was a success, there were moments of deep regret, jolting returns to former selves, and occasional flawed performances of the new self. In the language of another old joke, the only way for us to know someone's "real accent" is to awaken them from a deep sleep.

Upward transformation always complicated the relationship between parent and child. Even when the parents were successful in their own assimilation, it was always possible, indeed likely, that kids might take things too far. With their head start, their hypersensitivity, and their hunger for belonging, teens were almost sure to overdo it, obliterating the last, but crucial, marks of preassimilation origin. Add to this the fact that teens define their difference from parents in the same media now being used to negotiate transformation, and conflict and unhappiness became perhaps inevitable.

Plastic surgery is one of the devices people turned to for purposes of lateral transformation. A relatively simple surgical procedure could close the distance. It could erase the last difference that made assimilation impossible. I am told there are Jewish communities in the United States where plastic surgery is not so much a dilemma as a routine, given, sometimes, as a graduation gift.

Much of what I am describing has passed from practice, but I will report ethnographic data that came to me through recent, personal contact. I was walking through a museum restaurant with a friend of mine, a man in his forties, a member of a Jewish family that had been in North America for three generations, thoroughly knowledgeable in all of its cultural practices and effortless in his enactment of them. As we got to our table, he said to me, "When I walk through a room like this, there is something inside of me screaming, 'I don't belong here and I know you know I don't.'"

The most effective systems work this way. They create rules so multifarious and complicated that only observant gifted outsiders are likely to master them. All the rest are made to participate in their own marginalization. They do not know the insider's code, but they do sense the moments when they have run afoul of it. In these moments, it is customary for the outsider to feel too large, too noisy, conspicuous and unworthy. In these moments, the mainstream has succeeded in turning the outsider into the illegal alien and the border cop all at once. The mainstream has a simple rule: marginalize when you can, stigmatize when you have to.

The most effective systems are also dynamic. When any part of the code of manners and objects is deciphered by an outsider, it can be changed. This is a classic diffusion pattern. When outsiders begin to use insider slang, the insiders cultivate something new. Diffusion of this kind creates the wake of a status society. At the top of the wake are the insiders, innovating. Right behind them are the keenest of the outsiders, adopting innovations almost immediately upon their invention. Further behind are the outsiders who are prepared to wait for innovations to work their way downstream. They are current, but vulnerable to the contempt of the insiders and the faster outsiders. And so it goes in, to use another version of this metaphor, trickle-down diffusion.[56]

There is an odd version of lateral transformation on the dimensions of both sexuality and race. For African Americans, racism made true assimilation both impossible and repellent. There was so much hostility from the mainstream that the possibility of entry was closed off. For this and for other reasons, the African American community created cultures of its own, well clear of the center.[57] But a tiny portion of the community could contemplate lateral transformation, were able to "pass."[58] This group was superficially indistinguishable from white Americans. Now the challenge was to summon an exquisite performance of "whiteness."

In Nella Larsen's novel *Passing* (1929), Irene Westover is having tea on the roof of a Chicago hotel. A woman is staring at her. Westover wonders,

> Did that woman, could that woman, somehow know that here before her very eyes on the roof of the Drayton sat a Negro? Absurd! Impossible! White people were so stupid about such things.

As it turns out, the woman staring is passing too and, when they eventually talk, she remarks, "It's such a frightfully easy thing to do. If one's the type, all that's needed is a little nerve."[59] The apparent consensus here, that passing is merely a matter of nerve, concealed the dramatic perfection need to sustain this nerve.

As F. James Davis points out, passing as a cultural phenomenon is shaped largely by the so-called "one-drop rule," which says an individual with *any* African American blood is to be considered African American.[60] This is the reason that we do not (or did not, for passing has largely disappeared) say that white people are passing when they appear to be African American. (Though, as we shall see below, this has changed in the era of hip hop.) And it is why we do not say that white people in whiteface are passing. Like all lateral transformations, passing is always a movement from the margin to the center.[61]

The jeopardy of passing shows us that transformation is internally differentiated. In the case of upward transformation, living like a gentleman could, with the fulfillment of other conditions, eventually allow the individual to become a gentleman. But there is no performative opportunity here. People may pass as white for the whole of their lives, but, by the rules of the game, they will never cease to be African American. This does not make lateral transformation any less transformational. But it does indicate that, in Western cultures, matters of status are more fluid, more negotiable than those of race.[62]

There is ambivalence here too. The African American is caught first in one and then another strategic difficulty. For passing to succeed, the performance of whiteness must be very good. Any consistent pattern of error and the game is up. But the better the facsimile, the more fully the passer must internalize the transformation. To perfect this thing of the surface, it must be made to go a long way down. But now passing threatens to obscure, perhaps even to dislodge, the passer's "essential" identity. The best solution is a trade-off: the passer wants to go deep enough to perfect the lie, without going so far as to risk the "real" self.

There is ambivalence. The African American community is by some accounts uncomfortable with individuals who forsake their "real" communities for that of whites. The move looks something like collaboration, acquiescence, or at least opportunism. Judith Berzon notes that most of the novels of passing written by African Americans have the passer eventually return to his or her birth community. Charles Chesnutt, an African American writer who chose not to pass, called himself a "voluntary negro."[63] Passing opens up the possibility of transformational choice, and choice in these circumstances must be fraught with political and cultural uneasiness.

On the other hand, the passer may be trapped outside, as it were, forbidden the possibility of return. In Faulkner's *Light in August*, Joe Christmas tries to undo what passing has done to him.

> [H]e would lie in bed . . . sleepless, beginning to breathe deep and hard . . . trying to breathe into himself the dark odor, the dark and inscrutable thinking and being of negroes, with each suspiration trying to expel from himself the white blood and the white thinking and being.[64]

In the case of sexuality and sexual orientation, there is something quite different at work. Gay passing in the pre-Stonewall era was not so much a choice as a necessity.[65] This lateral transformation, this movement from the margin to the center, was a thing of the surface and a matter of concealment. It left the "essential" gay persona unchanged. The bearer of this self could now participate in the life of the center without the same likelihood of discovery or punishment.

Some gay men and women, especially in the pre-Stonewall era, chose to leave some trace of their sexual identity visible in the straight performance. Which trace and how much was a delicate question. If the trace was so discreet as to avoid the possibility of detection, an internal and external penalty was exacted. Internally, the individual was estranged from his or her sexual identity. Externally, it was now impossible to communicate that identity, either to other gays or to nonhostile straights. If, on the other hand, the individual made the trace more substantial, the chance of hostile treatment soared. It may have been a trade-off: the benefits of revelation against the risks of detection. Often the best trace was one communicated in something, such as manner of speech, that could be modulated according to the moment.

This transformational exercise encouraged a sensitivity to whether and what sexual statement was being made, and to all the expressive media at an individual's disposal. This sensitivity is the famous "gaydar," a term that perhaps diminishes its complexity and the skill it involved.[66]

> Surviving as a queer meant mastering appearances, knowing how to manipulate clothes, mannerisms and lifestyle so as to be able to pass for straight and also to signal that we weren't. To stay alive and unharmed we had to handle the codes of heterosexuality with consummate skill; to have any erotic and sentimental life we had to find ways of conveying our otherwise invisible desires.[67]

There is a shift in emphasis here. Passing as straight was perhaps less likely to claim the individual or antagonize the community than passing as white. It is, after all, being done by virtually every member of the community, not just some suspect few. Second, it was perhaps (and I am much less confident here) less thoroughgoing. The gay passer was able to let more show than the racial passer. Note-perfect performance was necessary for some but not for all. If the racial passer was obliged to adopt a disguise "all the way down" to increase the chances of success, the sexuality passer was able to keep it on the surface, like a Mardi Gras mask, separate, discrete, less likely to steal into the soul. Such a mask is not, or not usually, a self by which individuals are tempted, something they want. It is merely a strategic means of concealing what they do.[68]

Should drag be considered an instance of lateral transformation? Probably not. There is no interest here in becoming the creature whose shape is assumed. Indeed, some of the point of drag appears to be to demonstrate that the performer and the performed are not one. Accord-ing to the documentary *Paris Is Burning* (1990, dir. Jennifer Livingston), drag is compensatory. It is precisely because these men are unable to move from the margin to the center that they engage in drag. Drag be-comes, in this dubious and certainly patronizing analysis, what you do *in-stead* of lateral transformation. But another view of drag says it is about what Roberta Best calls the "fluidity of gender."[69] In this view, drag is a way to contemplate the construction of gender. There is no talk of pass-ing here. Some small parts of the drag king's and queen's performances may find their way into their everyday lives and their private personae, but drag is more a performance than a transformation.

Lateral transformation is not always voluntary. It is sometimes co-erced. The Canadian government once made it a matter of policy to transform aboriginal Canadians. In 1857, it passed an act to "encourage the gradual civilization of the Indian tribes." The government was pre-pared to declare carefully groomed candidates to be non-Indians. They were then invited "to join Canadian society." In the annual report of the Department of the Interior in 1876 the government declared it its "wis-dom and duty" to encourage aboriginals to assume what the government called "the privileges and responsibilities of full citizenship."[70]

As part of this "civilizing mission," children were removed from their parents' care and from their communities and made to live in residential schools, often run by the Anglican Church. There they were forbidden to speak their language, retell their myths, or observe their rituals. It now appears that they were also subject to sexual abuse so endemic that it al-most looks like a matter of policy. The government and the Church are only now struggling to put things right. In 1994, the primate, Archbishop Michael Peers, apologized on behalf of the Anglican Church to aborigi-nal peoples for trying to "remake you in our image."[71]

Lateral Transformation Now

Lateral transformation has largely disappeared from view. The postmod-ernist would no doubt say this is because immigrants no longer wish to expunge their ethnicity in return for the doubtful pleasures of a pallid mainstream Americanness. This may be. I believe it is more likely that the work of lateral transformation is largely done. We have all moved toward the mainstream; we have thrown off difference and taken on a main-stream culture. Ethnicity, as Mary Waters demonstrates, is an increas-ingly optional matter.[72] It is something we choose to have (or foreswear).

And it is something we choose to have to the degree and in the ways we particularly prefer. But this ethnic choosing is one of the important modalities of postmodernist transformation, and we will have more to say on the topic in the next section.

The center is no longer quite so magnetic. The costs of exclusion are not so high. In *The Accidental Asian*, Eric Liu explains how he constructed his "Asianness" with art and care, very much as Waters describes. In his youth, he was engaged in a thoroughgoing assimilation that brought him close to being a "banana," or "white-identified." But this lateral transformation was, he notes, due to the influence of his college days at Yale. Plainly, the mainstream has lost the gravitational powers it once possessed. This is evidenced by the fact that Liu is able and willing to write a book about whether, and how much of, his identity will be shaped by it. As Liu puts it, "The meaning of 'American' has undergone a revolution in the twenty-nine years I have been alive, a revolution of color, class, and culture."[73]

But certainly there is still enough antipathy and outright racism that there are other ways to fashion one's sense of self. Ray Chang demonstrates one of these when he turns himself into "punkman," a creature constructed in opposition to all of the stereotypes once used to marginalize Asians. "First thing I did was list all of the stereotypes Asian American males endure. Bowl hair cut, thick glasses, slitty eyes, broken English, computer/math whiz, not artistic, pants too short (and in general, fashion hazards), introverts, nerd/geek-a-zoid etc. From this list I then choose opposing characteristics and formed the antithesis being."[74]

This is a now customary technique of identity formation, in which the marginal group appropriates the stereotype and makes it their own. This is Madonna calling herself a "material girl," African Americans calling themselves "nigger," gays calling themselves "queer." It's cultural smash and grab. The marginal group breaks into the armory of the racist and makes off with several of the best epithets. It then wears them as badges of courage, in acts of defiance. They are sometimes worn to show their wearers' marginality. But from an anthropological point of view, something odd is happening. When marginal groups can appropriate the language of stigma in this way, the battle, if not the war, is over. When you can challenge marginality in this way, you are no longer very marginal. For these groups are now engaged in what Waters might call an act of choice. But this is a contentious point, and more vulnerable than the one I wish to make. More relevant to this discussion of lateral transformation is the fact that something fundamental appears to have happened to the very cultural architecture of Western society. The very notion of a society with an outside and an inside, a margin and a mainstream, is in question. When these groups behave in this way, they tell us at the very least that they care so little about inclusion they are now prepared to celebrate their exclusion.

We may conclude with a word on passing, as one measure of changes here. Things have changed so much that it is hard to imagine an African American choosing to pass. Everyone is a "voluntary Negro" now, including a great many white kids, about whom we shall have a lot to say in the next section. Passing, though not racial passing, supplied a bit of dramatic tension in a TV show called *The Pretender* (NBC, 1998–2000). But in point of fact, the hero was almost never found out, and was at little risk of being found out. Indeed, we are more likely to see the theme made fun of, as it is when Bill Murray is thrust into the world of espionage in *The Man Who Knew Too Little* (1997, dir. Jon Amiel). The world thinks he is a dashing man of action. He believes he is the manager of a Blockbuster in Des Moines, Iowa, involved in a theatrical event. In this case, the hero can pass as a spy only because he has no idea that he is doing so.

ANTI-TRANSFORMATION

Upward and lateral transformation were not free. Every individual was surrounded by a community that said, "What? All of a sudden you're too good for us? You're ashamed of where you came from?" And this fundamental hostility to transformation was accompanied, and enforced, by a fine scrutiny that mocked the individual for any departure from existing patterns of speech, dress, decorum. "Oh, very grand, I'm sure." Some English pubs were once hypervigilant, so that the joys of companionship came with the requirement of conformity. Societies that encourage transformation also harbor forces that work constantly against it.

But in this post-traditional context of the early modern era, transformational liberties existed that were undreamed of in the traditional case. Transformation was now possible outside the world of myth. An individual could embark upon changes in the world almost as extraordinary as those accomplished by Japasa in myth. The individual who came into the world as a commoner could metamorphose into a gentleman or gentlewoman. This transformation might not have Ovidian proportions, but it was, nevertheless, a very large change indeed, one that altered every aspect of the individual's private life.

The ends had changed, and so had the means. The narrow path of ritual was no longer the only way to transformation. In the place of the traditional meanings of transformation (highly conventionalized, public, consensual, and constrained as they are), there was something more fluid, optional, private, and contingent. Perhaps most spectacularly, individuals (the yeomen discussed above, for instance) could even refuse the ritual, something impossible in the traditional case except in the most extraordinary circumstances. Now there were several options. Individuals, within certain constraints, were free to decide whether they would take up a transformation. They were free to decide when and how they would undertake it. Finally, they were free to decide whether and when they had reached their goal.

But anti-transformational forces were not entirely in eclipse. The freedoms of the modernist and postmodernist eras are not in evidence in this period. There were really only two options: up the ladder or in toward the mainstream. Everything else was forbidden, sometimes by law and certainly by convention. The transformations we take for granted in a postmodern era were literally difficult to think. It is as if individuals had won transformation for their private use, but the ends remained in public hands. Or, to put it another way, as if many people had access to a new means of transport, but there were only two roads on which to drive.

What is particularly missing in this period is a downward or outward transformation. This is taken for granted in modernist and postmodernist societies. Individuals frequently choose to slide downward in any cultural hierarchy—of class, age, or gender—that presents itself, or to move, if only momentarily, from the center to the margin. The most individual freedom in evidence in the early modern period is status counterfeiting, the manufacture of false status claims. Outlaw aesthetics and terminology are not cultivated. Even the rule-breakers are captives of the conventional transformational world.[75] There is no evidence that marginalizing language is being reappropriated. No one is moving from the top down. No one is moving from the mainstream out. This is not to suggest that there are no marginal communities, only that they do not get many visitors out their way. More to the point, they remain tiny communities, often under deep cover, incapable of recruiting larger numbers or exerting the cultural influence we take for granted these days.

There is very little substantial innovation in this period, either by individuals or by groups. It is rare to see the invention of new identities.

Line dancing, or breakdancing, or ballroom dancing, cultural innovations that provide new identities, simply do not appear. There are many reasons for this, obviously, but the most interesting for present purposes is that they are hindered by the prevailing values of the collectivity.

We roll our eyes when we hear that someone recently presented herself in a public forum as "Princess Dux," "a 267-year-old ambassador from a subterranean city called Telos, which is in turn part of the ancient underground kingdom of Lemuria, sister civilization to Atlantis and Mu."[76] But we are not struck speechless. This particular species of self-invention, while outlandish and implausible, is not unheard of. In status transformation societies, I believe, it would be looked on with greater astonishment. To survive at all, it would have to claim religious authority, and thus the majesty of an exceedingly public and consensual institution. I would be very surprised if Princess Dux makes any reference to any of the world's great religions. I believe it is more likely that she calls for legitimacy on the grounds that she had a dream and she just "knows" it must be true. This willingness to claim intuition and personal experience as foundation for inventions is one of the characteristics of our day. I do not think it is very much in evidence in traditional or status transformation societies.

And this brings us to another anti-transformational condition. The transformational destinations are socially agreed upon and desired by nearly everyone, even though the possible groups and possible selves may vary. At the very least, there is nothing opaque about this variation. Everyone understands the variations in question. In the modern and postmodern cases, a dizzying number of transformational objectives exist, almost all of which are provocative or mystifying for someone. (I quite often heard music being played in the Harvard Square subway station in Cambridge that I didn't understand. As an anthropologist, I take it for granted that this probably speaks for some social group. But many people do not make this assumption. For them the music will remain a mystery or an outrage.)

Section 4

Modern Transformations

Modernism has many definitions and, by each of these definitions, several properties. There appears to be consensus on one or two points. Modernism, it is widely accepted, redefines the individual in relationship to the group, and creates a more robust individualism. Those institutions that would define the individual, especially the church, state, ethnicity, gender, and class, are diminished in their influence, and the individual is given over to unprecedented freedom and alienation. This is not merely freedom from the power of the group or a superordinate. This is not merely an assertion of equality. It is the right of the individual to define the self by his or her own efforts.[1]

> The liberated individual, not the social group, must therefore become the basic cultural unit. Although many people continue to be members of and identify with groups, they believe their group identities to be matters of individual choice, which can be changed without stigma.[2]

Saul Bellow puts the matter in a more personal way.

> For a Midwesterner, the son of immigrant parents, I recognized at an early age that I was called upon to decide for myself to what extent my Jewish origins, my surroundings (the accidental circumstances of Chicago), my schooling, were to be allowed to determine the course of my life. I did not intend to be wholly dependent on history and culture.[3]

An extreme statement comes from Virginia Satir. Here is her credo, as I scribbled it from a poster in a mall in Oak Park, Illinois.

> I am me: In all the world, there is no one else exactly like me. Everything that comes out of me is authentically mine. Because I alone choose it—I own everything about me. My body, my feelings, my mouth, my voice, all my actions, whether they be to others or myself. I own my fantasies. My dreams, my hopes, my fears. I own all my triumphs and successes, all my failures and mistakes. Because I own all of me, I can become intimately acquainted with me. By so doing I can live me and be friendly and loving to myself in all my parts.[4]

As Richard Shweder and Edmund Bourne reproduce the myth, the modernist individual lives in a society that "[has] been created to serve the interests of some idealized autonomous, abstract individual existing free of society yet living in society."[5] Individuals are both free and forced to construct themselves. The individual must be individuated. If not before this act of self-construction, certainly after it, the modernist individual is supposed to be unique. Frederic Jameson says,

> The great Modernisms were, as we have said, predicated on the invention of a personal, private style, as unmistakable as your fingerprint, as incomparable as your own body. But this means that the modernist aesthetic is in some way organically linked to the concept of the unique self and private identity, a unique personality and individuality, which can be expected to generate its own unique vision of the world and to forge its own unique, unmistakable style.[6]

The individual defined by status transformation focuses on what Lionel Trilling calls "sincerity": the note-perfect performances of the social self and the careful observation of its roles, responsibilities, and obligations in the theater of social life. Indeed, only a creature exquisitely attuned to the demands of the group would undertake (or care about) upward transformation. The modernist individual is more concerned with self-discovery, autonomy, authenticity, and a "real self," even when this means defying the social world.[7] It is this shift from a concern for sincerity of role to a concern for authenticity of self that marks one of the essential differences between a society centered on status transformation and one centered on modernist transformations.

The modernist gift to this individual is the right of self-invention. He or she is free of the definitional tyranny of family, ethnicity, community, religion, even state. Here is John Cawelti speaking of a premodernist time (Benjamin Franklin's America) but in a language and an ideology influenced by the modernist view.

[M]en were beginning to think of themselves not as members of a traditionally defined group with an established social role but as individuals with the capacity to choose between social roles, or to create new ones; [this world] meant that the individual was no longer given an identity by birth, but that he had to create one for himself.[8]

This is the radical individualism that modernism helped install in Western cultures. It comes to us in language exhausted by the polemical exertions of sociologists, existentialists, social critics, and others.[9] And cast in these overarching, politicized terms, it is almost impossible to see as a way of life. An ideological scrum discourages us from imagining that anyone ever thought these ideas, and makes it still more difficult to imagine that they lived them.

For instance, we are accustomed to thinking of the suburb as a place of stifling conformity and some bleakness. To be sure, the accusations of alienation and anomie are modernist favorites, but their constant recitation makes it hard to see that the suburb looks, in some ways, purpose-built to accommodate the new individual. As M. P. Baumgartner points out, suburbanites "experience substantial independence and individuation." The suburb is a place in which social connections are characterized by "comparatively weak ties," there are "no ties of dependency between neighbours," and people avoid one another, especially in moments of conflict.[10]

There is a new temporal orientation. Modernist societies are inclined to regard the present as a way station on the road to the future and to treat the past with scant regard. Modernist societies, like modernist individuals, insist on the right and the freedom to invent themselves. The cultural hero is the avant-garde artist living in defiance of middle-class standards, who rushes out of what is known into the pursuit of what is new. Modernist societies practice a willed and collective amnesia. Not only are they not rooted in the past, but for several purposes they disdain an active memory of the past. Time flows through the modernist world at a terrible rate, each moment almost instantaneously repudiated to make way for the new.

Modernism keeps old myths alive and creates new ones of its own. One of these is the notion that the individual is free to define the self for the self. This is an anthropological impossibility, and nothing if not mythic. But as it helped transform Western societies, it was always more an idea than a reality. Ritual was also present in abundance. Ancient forms like citizenship and marriage formalities continued robust. And new rituals emerged, including a rite of passage called the "driver's exam."

The status transformation devices of upward and lateral transformation were active, too. People still wished to climb upward. The films of

Preston Sturges, for instance, seem obsessed with the theme. The prosperity of the period following World War II made upward mobility a reasonable expectation for many families. A succession of jobs, houses, and cars all marked the upward or inward movement of the period. Immigrants still wished to make themselves over into Americans, and in the modernist period this could mean a thoroughgoing transformation in language, appearance, attitude, and outlook.

But modernism threw old routines into question. The avant-garde artist believed that upward and lateral transformations were a defacement of selfhood, a struggle that took the individual into hypocrisy and artifice, and away from self-exploration. For other modernists, these transformation routines were earnest and slavish. What counted was the enabling of the individual. What counted, as we shall see, was not tradition, stasis, and hierarchy but mobilities undreamed of in the status transformation regime.

It is clear that my approach to modernism departs a little from the conventional view. A few words of clarification are in order.[11] First, scholars have presented modernism in art and literature in the period 1890–1930 as a duality:

> Modernism was in most countries an extraordinary compound of the futuristic and the nihilistic. . . . It was a celebration of the technological age and a condemnation of it; an excited acceptance of the belief that the old regimes of culture were over, and a deep despairing in the face of that fear.[12]

In the common view, however, this duality often disappears, and the modernist individual, and especially the modernist artist, is represented as a creature of crisis defined only by nihilism, alienation, and disorder. Celebration is obscured by condemnation. Indeed, this would seem to be the burden of the usual distinction between modernism and modernity. The latter is made to stand for the machine age and all its social, technical, and commercial changes—inchoate forces that the modernist artist struggles to define, if only so as to repudiate them.[13]

Certainly, this description seems appropriate for the American writers of the 1950s known as the beats, though, as we shall see, it obscures certain of their defining poetic activities, especially the cross-country drive. But it is altogether misleading as a way to think about brightwork, a stylistic innovation that was produced by Detroit's automakers in the same period. Brightwork celebrates progress, science and technology, and an individual mobilized in geographical and cultural space. It is precisely a celebration of the futuristic and the technological age. But "celebration" suggests dumb admiration, when, in fact, brightwork is engaged in something much more constructive and deliberate. No doubt, I have created an imbalance on the other side, ignoring the nihilism and despair that haunted the brightwork enterprise. But I believe this enterprise is a modernist one as much as the beats are, and room must be made for it in the definitional envelope.

Second, I am not interested in the modernism that is said to be defined by difficulty. "The Modernist poets in New York . . . were committed to the idea of poetry which was astringent, uncompromising and difficult. . . . The obvious, the sentimental, the lyrical . . . were suspect, and a new vocabulary (irony, complexity, tension, structure, ambiguity, toughness) enters the lexicon of modern critics."[14] Once more, the beats would have accepted this notion, though we must acknowledge the possibility that they sought an "accessible difficulty." Brightwork, on the other hand, was nothing if not the product of a cultural world that wished to amuse, attract, and delight. Renato Poggioli suggests that the "cult of novelty" that drove modernism and the avant-garde was the basis of its "substantive and not accidental unpopularity."[15] But I hope to show that, in some venues, the cult of novelty was precisely what gave modernism its great popularity.

Third, I am interested in a modernism that plays itself out in the mainstream of contemporary culture. Modernism has been seen as the creation of artistic elites occupying the bohemian margin of society and an avant-garde.[16] This description also applies well enough to the beats—though I believe some of the beats were media-savvy creatures who were aware of their role in mainstream culture. (It is, perhaps, not because we are well read that we can summon so readily the images and attitudes of Ginsberg, Kerouac, and Burroughs. It is because they have been an unexceptional, relatively ubiquitous feature of the media stream for some decades. *Time* and *Life* have done at least as much to publicize the movement as the City Lights underworld of poetry readings and publications, and they did this, I believe, at the bidding, or at least with the ready compliance, of the beats themselves.)

Again, the avant-garde notion is precisely wrong when it comes to brightwork and the constellation of cultural materials that centered on the 1950s automobile. For these mainstream purposes, the avant-garde was located in time, not social space. It was the future rushing on. I am prepared to entertain the possibility that there is a serial relationship here, that brightwork is diffused or democratized modernism. I am even prepared to use the term "mid-century modernism" to mark a difference.

But I believe brightwork is a modernist enterprise, even when it is embraced by (and embracing of) non-artists, the mainstream, and the middle class.[17]

Modernism and modernity are, surely, both force and form. It is easy enough to dismiss modernity as the dark side of the twosome, as the triumph of science and technology, of industry and the marketplace, of instrumental logic and practical reason, of social reform and city renovation, all of which overwhelmed the individual, human scale, tradition, social connection, and cultural continuity. In this reading, modernity is uninhabited by agency, design, concept, or choice. It is neatly excised from the world of intention, and becomes, in the usual phrase, something brute, perhaps even the favorite cliché, a "brute force." Modernism is what people thought, wrote, felt, expressed. Modernity is what merely, recklessly, thoughtlessly, relentlessly happened to the world.

There is a mirror inclination to suppose that modernism is all idea. This excises, too. Now modernism cannot be a set of ideas at work in the world, with its own dynamism and unpredictability, finding its way into the world to unsettle and transform before alighting in the world of concept again . . . or perhaps not returning but disappearing into the world, as a an idea/event/inclination, a way to see and to act. In the excised reading, modernism is all cultural form, and never brute. I am looking for a treatment of modernism and modernity that says that the former is as much force as form, and the latter as much form as force.[18]

Finally, and now to summon a different debate, I am not interested in the "modernity" that figures in the literature of the development of world economies. Charles Taylor calls this an "acultural" theory of modernity and says that it characterizes modernity as a "set of transformations which any and every culture can go through."[19] I believe this discussion will show how profoundly particular are the cultural impulses and materials that figure in the world of the beat and brightwork. The chances that these can be replicated by "any and every" culture are, manifestly, zero. I do not go so far as to say that this must mean that other cultures cannot modernize. I mean merely that Western cultures and economies were in possession of their own momentum, to use the apposite metaphor. Other cultures can achieve development, but they will do so without these cultural routines.[20]

In sum, this approach to modernism proceeds on the assumption, and with the wish to show, that modernism and modernity are both cultural and historical matters. In the sections that follow, then, I want to explore two transformational routines. One of these was invented by the beats, and the second is brightwork. There is no mistaking how different these movements are. On first blush, it is hard to imagine that they can have anything in common. But I think they do, and that their study can show us something about how the transformational palette took shape in the modernist period. I do *not* mean to suggest that beats and brightwork are the only transformational routines. I am committed by my larger argument to suggest that traditional and status routines are still at work. And I believe there are other modernist routines at work as well. Beats and brightwork are merely two.

BEATS

The beats were American writers who took shape as a group in the 1940s and came to prominence in the 1950s. Their senior inspiration, advisor, and participant was the heroin-addicted, Harvard-graduated, wife-murdering William Burroughs: trust-fund kid, mordant wit, dandy, and pederast. The most conspicuous of the beats were Allen Ginsberg, author of *Howl*, and Jack Kerouac, author of *On the Road*.[21] Supporting characters included Edie Parker, Lucien Carr, Herbert Huncke, Vicki Russell, Carl Solomon, Neal Cassady, Joan Vollmer, Carolyn Robinson, and Gregory Corso, and, after Ginsberg's move to San Francisco, Robert Creeley, Gary Snyder, Lawrence Ferlinghetti, and Kenneth Rexroth.

In *The Birth of the Beat Generation*, Steven Watson says the term "beat" comes from circus argot, where it stood for the privations of life on the road, and from the drug world, where it meant "cheated" or "robbed." It found its way to Burroughs, Ginsberg, and Kerouac courtesy of Herbert Huncke, a man who ran away from home at twelve, riding the rails and hitchhiking across America, dividing his time between jail, freak shows, and the street, until he ended up in Times Square in 1940, a place that began increasingly to attract what Ginsberg called "apocalyptic hipsters."[22]

The term "beat" resonated nicely with "beatific," evoking the hipster feeling for the visionary, and, metaphorically, it captured the notion that wisdom was to be got by self-impoverishment, by breaking down the conventional categories of seeing and being. Psychic impoverishment, cultural displacement, these were the road to illumination. The term took on new meaning as part of "beatnik," a term invented by Herb Caen of the *San Francisco Chronicle* in 1957. This invention, suggests

Watson, helps mark the transition from poetic movement to popular culture.

The beats attacked bourgeois standards both from the vantage point of the anti-hero and from that of the willful schoolboy. (Ginsberg's college motto was "Do what you want to when you want to.") There was a third position, that of the inspired goof—Neal Cassady is, for instance, remembered in a biography called *The Holy Goof*. There was more to be learned from the marginal and maladroit than from the learned or accomplished. Burroughs said that his Harvard degree "didn't mean a fuckin' thing."[23]

There was ambivalence in Burroughs's case. He was prepared to mock his degree, but he did choose to enroll at Harvard and to finish his degree there. As Watson demonstrates, he was not above trading on the association with Harvard when it suited him. Burroughs dressed in a formal manner and his emotional style was controlled and self-restrained. His speech was, at least in tone, cultivated. And we know he possessed several tell-tale markers of the WASP style. Introduced to morphine in 1944, he responded with that signature of the Protestant self, the production of understatement where overstatement would have been forgiven.

> Burroughs averted his head as the morphine was injected. Pins and needles pulsed through his system in waves, from the back of his legs to the back of his neck; his face flushed, and he seemed to float, without discernible corporeal outline. Burroughs looked around and coolly observed, "Well, that's quite a sensation."[24]

Several of the beats were children of privilege. Not Ginsberg or Kerouac, to be sure, but the circle that moved in and out of Joan Vollmer's apartment near Columbia in the 1940s included the son of a Philadelphia banker and the daughter of a Detroit Judge. Burroughs was sustained by a monthly stipend from the Burroughs adding machine fortune.[25]

Beats were determined to explode the conventions of middle- and upper-class life. Burroughs was drawn to Chicago's North Side, described by Huncke as a place of "dikes, faggots, a certain so-called hip element, the swish places and the she-she places." Burroughs styled himself a criminal and found his most sustained and satisfying employment as a bug exterminator. The boy from upper-class St. Louis had found a home.[26]

The beats liked to talk like street-toughened cynics. Joan Vollmer responded to Ginsberg's news of an epiphany in the summer of 1948:

I've been claiming for three years that anyone who doesn't blow his top once is no damn good. When I refer to it as top-blowing, I'm sure you know what I mean. No percentage in talking about visions or super-reality or any such lay terms.[27]

This is ostentatiously populist language. Even as she shows a disdain for "lay terms," Vollmer indulges in "no percentage," "blowing his top," "no damn good." Language of this kind represented for the beats another way out of middle-class convention. But it is borrowed, dare we say appropriated, language, and not the sort of thing Vollmer learned at Barnard or Ginsberg at Columbia. More to the point, it was precisely the kind of thing that the upwardly and laterally mobile wished to put behind them. Language that closed one transformational door opened another.

The aspiring middle class, when not tempted by the "swank" and the "suave," was cultivating the "pleasant" and the "gracious," an aesthetic conducive to promotion in the larger social scheme of things. They were trying to avoid things that gave offense. For the beats, such avoidance was the path to blindness. Striving upward must impoverish the seeker. Kerouac and Ginsberg both disdained Franklin's self-made man, "tyrannized" as he was by what the latter contemptuously called the "normative American stereotype."[28]

But the beats did not break rules merely to scandalize the middle class (as hippies were accused of doing in the 1960s). The beats were at odds with every kind of constraint: social, legal, and cultural. They believed that illumination would come to them when they were least culturally constrained and least self-censoring. In particular, they believed in what Rimbaud called the "derangement of the senses."[29] Ginsberg, looking back, said, "The new vision assumed the death of square morality and replaced that meaning with belief in creativity."[30]

The conflict between square and beat turned, to some extent, on each group's understanding of imperfection. Squares treated it as failure, as a definite barrier to bourgeois acceptance and advancement. For beats, it was the one true path to illumination. Beats sought out imperfection eagerly, taking it from its best producers: the mentally ill, street hustlers, addicts, criminals, the sexually or racially marginalized. Beats came to understand that if they were to break out of received understandings, they had to follow any "holy goof" who could lead the way.

To this extent, the beats were like other avant-garde artists.

It is because the artist is spontaneous in the face of an environment asking him to conform to it that he is able to sense reality in all its presentational immediacy. To put this in Whiteheadian language, it is because the artist does not accept society's symbol systems that he is able to sense with unusual directness what is fundamental. He is more alive, as it were, or rather more sensitive to his aliveness, than the rest of us, which is why he is ecstatically alive to sense presentations.[31]

The beats were always trying to get out from under the symbol systems of postwar America. Kerouac worked endlessly in pursuit of a method that would give him access to direct experience. He wanted the world *before* it was constituted by culture. Or, better, he believed that if he waited till his experience was constituted by culture, he was left with something systematically diminished—beat, as it were, in the wrong sense of the term. Kerouac believed that it was his responsibility to experience and communicate as directly as he could.

And this was hard. Kerouac could feel the dead hand of culture constraining his experience and writing both. In his early experiments with method, he looked for spontaneity in Benzedrine, jazz, and trances. Later, after the completion of *On the Road*, he mastered a technique he called "wild form" prose.[32] He and William Carlos Williams criticized Ginsberg for being too intent on rule-bound poetry. Make poetry, they urged him, according to what the eye sees.[33]

The beats began with the advantage of living in a loosely bounded world. As a child, Kerouac "saw things" and this, says Watson, persuaded him "the line between the emblematic and the actual . . . was permeable."[34] When Ginsberg admitted to a ghost-filled childhood, Kerouac replied, "Gee, I have thoughts like that all the time."[35] Much later, living in Tangiers, Burroughs was to say he lived in a world with "no line between 'real world' and 'world of myth and symbol.' Objects, sensations, hit with the impact of hallucination. Of course I see now with the child's eyes."[36] What did not come to them disaggregated by their own sensory inclinations and dispositions was made so through drugs, travel, sex, music, and the company of fools.

Naturally, beats were accused of posing. This accusation was to be expected, perhaps, when it came from Herbert Gold in *The Nation*, and Norman Podhoretz in *The Partisan Review*.[37] But it was more troubling from the distinguished West Coast poet Kenneth Rexroth, who declared Kerouac's Buddha a "dimestore incense burner, glowing and glowering sinisterly in the dark corner of a Beatnik pad and just thrilling the wits out of bad little girls."[38] Certainly, beats cultivated a public image. Certainly, they broke rules for the sensation of doing so. One of them was prepared to mock even the pose of the rebel. In what may be the beats' best comic moment, Carl Solomon stole a peanut butter sandwich in the Brooklyn College cafeteria and immediately surrendered himself to the police.[39]

The beats sought out new personae often and publicly. This theme is everywhere in the life of Burroughs, from his childhood on. It may even have helped encourage the circumstances in which he shot and killed his wife, Joan Vollmer. In the course of early psychoanalysis, he claimed to have several personalities, including

> [a] simpering lesbian English governess, . . . sharecropper tobacco farmer named Luke who cherished his shotgun and possessed the charm and menace of a psychotic redneck sheriff [and a] Chinese man sitting and starving on the banks of the Yangtze, revealing neither ideas nor feelings, a chilling and utter blank.[40]

Carr and Ginsberg found occasion to dub themselves Claude de Maubris and Gillette. Carr and Kerouac dubbed themselves Arthur Rimbaud and Paul Verlaine. Ginsberg, Kerouac, and Burroughs engaged in theatrics designed to allow them to "charade spontaneously."[41] The fluidity extended to everyday life. Ginsberg informed his diary,

> I will be sweet to Trilling; sharp & unfathomable to Bill, cute & annoying & superficial & profound & overrational to Joan; insignificant to Jack.[42]

They were even tempted by Matthew Arnold's pursuit of perfection. Burroughs said of his extraordinary efforts to complete *Naked Lunch*, "I am shitting out my educated Middlewest background once and for all. By the time I finish this book I'll be pure as an angel, my dear."[43]

In the late '50s, beats became "beatniks" and a new part of popular culture. This change may be observed particularly in the enormous success of *Bonjour Tristesse*, a novel that captured the existential angst of the café dweller and a place on the best-seller list.[44] The movie *Funny Face* (1957, dir. Stanley Donen) shows Audrey Hepburn plunged into a beatnik world. In *Bell, Book and Candle* (1958, dir. Richard Quine), Jack Lemon takes a turn as a kooky bongo player at a Manhattan jazz club. *Rebel without a Cause* (1955, dir. Nicholas Ray) presents James Dean as a hoodlum or greaser, but his character draws heavily on the beat movement.[45] The TV series *The Many Lives of Dobie Gillis* featured a character called Maynard G. Krebs who wore black clothes and a goatee, played the bongos, and used coffee-house argot to comic effect.

One eight-year-old identified closely with the Krebs character. "Maynard had . . . a profound effect on my personal development. In 1967, I

read Ginsberg's *Howl* for the first time. Now six or seven years after Maynard's caricature, I had 'real' contact."[46] In this case, popular culture was
derivative, on the one hand, but a first mover, on the other.

In the 1961 film version of *Lolita* (dir. Stanley Kubrick), the character
of Charlotte, played by Shelley Winters, is a study of middle-class preten-
sion that is defined precisely by her pursuit of the mysteries of the poetry
reading, the jazz solo, and the African mask. Apparently, some middle-
class homes stretched to accommodate beat values.[47] Whether this was
mere fashion, respite from suburban rigidity, or, finally, something more
genuine and thoroughgoing, it is hard now to say. But what we see here is
probably the influence of the highly publicized beat.[48]

Dylan and the Beats

In the documentary *Don't Look Back* (1999, dir. D. A. Pennebaker), Bob
Dylan is captured on tour in England.[49] It was 1965. Dylan was touring
London, Manchester, and Birmingham. It was a small tour by rock standards. No gleaming buses, no swarm of roadies. In fact, the whole group—
Joan Baez, Albert Grossman, Bob Neuwirth, and occasional others—
appear to have fit into a single taxi, and this is where the documentary
often finds them. "Subterranean Homesick Blues" was making its way up
the English charts. The tour was selling out. Teens were gathering in small
numbers outside the hotels. English artists and entertainers, particularly,
were turning out to see the new phenom from America. This was an
acoustic Dylan: one man on the stage with his guitar and harmonica.

In each city, between performances, Dylan sat in his hotel room, spar-
ring with the press. His mood was, by turns, listless, ironic, incredulous,
impassioned, ridiculing, and coy.

All of these moods show in an interview with a reporter from *Time* included in the documentary. But Dylan is particularly patronizing on this occasion. He warns the reporter (mild, thoughtful, restrained, observant, curious, English), that there will be parts of the concert he, the reporter, will
not understand. "It's going to happen fast and you're not going to get it all
and you might even hear the wrong words." There will be no post-show explanation of the lyrics because, Dylan explains, "I don't write 'em for any
reason. There's no great message." Dylan says he doesn't care how the reporter will tell the story—and that he doesn't have to care. "I've never been
in *Time Magazine* and this hall [the Albert Hall] has filled twice."

Dylan then begins a detailed critique of *Time* and the reporter. "If I
want to find out something, I'm not going to read *Time Magazine*," he says

scornfully. "*Time* has too much to lose by printing the truth. You know that." "What is really the truth?" asks the reporter, eager to have a chance to clarify, or perhaps just pleased to have something to ask. Dylan pauses for some time, and then replies. "A plain picture . . . let's say a tramp vomiting, man, into a sewer." *Time* should create a collage, Dylan says, and show the tramp together with a picture of Mr. Rockefeller. But they won't, he says, because "there are no ideas in *Time Magazine*, just facts."

"Don't you see," Dylan implores, "this can't be a good article." It can't be good because it will be assembled by someone in New York City who never leaves his office. More important, the reporter can't ever know Dylan. "I know more about what *you* do—and you don't even have to ask me how or anything, just by looking—than you will ever know about me, *ever*. I could tell you I'm not a folk singer and explain it but you wouldn't really understand." Dylan then proceeds to talk somewhat cryptically about the "big letter" and the "small letter" versions of a word. He argues, "each of us really 'knows' nothing." He concludes with the observation that both he and the reporter will someday die (or, as he puts it, "go off the earth"), and that both of them must live in the world with this knowledge.

Pennebaker's camera swings around to capture the reporter's reaction. He is caught unprepared and struggles for a moment to find his question. Finally, he asks, "Do you care about what you sing?" It is asked flatly, with evident sincerity and without any sign of rancor. Dylan erupts. He has suggested just moments before that he and the reporter, faced with the sheer scale of the universe and their insignificance before it, cannot possibly offend one another. But now he takes offense mightily. "You've got a lot of nerve asking me that! Do you ask the Beatles that?"

The Pennebaker documentary *is* a study of journalistic incompetence. Over and over, poor Dylan is asked questions that demonstrate the reporter's lack of fitness to cover the tour. People keep asking Dylan for his "message," and why he is so "angry," and whether fans "really" understand what he represents. They are clumsy, clueless, and manifestly out of their depth. But it's not clear that the *Time* reporter is one of them. "Do you care about what you sing?" might have been the first smart question of the tour.

To ask "Do you care about what you sing?" is, or may have been, to enter into the spirit of Dylan's tour. It acknowledges the possibility that Dylan did not come to England to claim the mantle of the artist, rock star, or moral exemplar. It invites Dylan to elaborate on things he has been saying to the press and in this interview—that the universe is much too cryptic and allusive to be captured by his music. It invites Dylan to explain why he is not a folk singer (a claim that the journalists find particularly puzzling). If folk singers speak for the wisdom of the ages (and the folk), Dylan was interested in more difficult truths. "Do you care about what you sing?" was Dylan's chance to say, "No, caring about what you're singing would be to presume authorship in a world that is not in fact intelligible."[50]

In a word, the reporter's question was, or may have been, beat. And it is germane because Dylan was, in some ways, beat. The Pennebaker documentary begins with "Subterranean Homesick Blues," a song about drug use, marginal people, and street life. This shows Allen Ginsberg in one corner of the frame, while in the other stands Dylan with a handful of cue cards. It as if the two of them are saying, "You already know this, you just need a little prompting." In "It's All Over Now, Baby Blue," Dylan encourages us, "Take what you have gathered from coincidence."

Dylan was, in his protean way, beat and an important agent of beat's diffusion. Working his own syncretic miracle, combining beat with folk with popular music and eventually with rock, he found a way to bring beat sentiments into the counter-culture of the 1960s. There is no doubt that they were already there. For many people, this cultural revolution began with a reading of Kerouac's *On the Road.* But the revolution was crowded with other influences, from the pop vacuities of Carnaby Street and Southern California to the folk-poet pain of a Donovan, not to mention political programs without poetic inclinations or spiritual objectives.[51]

We can hear Dylan constructing a generation gap. All the principles are there, all the things that countless children were to say to their bewildered, affronted parents: I can understand you, but you can't understand me. Your world is bankrupt because it is dedicated to competitive individualism and a pragmatic rationality; my world is rich because it is dedicated to social solidarity and a consciousness that is open to the unmanaged and the unfathomable. You live in a world of facts; I live in a world of ideas. You have constructed a prison house of suburban conformity; I live in the diversity and eccentricities of the city. I have plumbed the depths. You are lost on the surface. The 1960s generational schism took quite a lot from the beat understanding of the world.

With Dylan's appearance, the beat heritage found a residence in something more profound and influential than TV beatniks and daringly "primitive" home decoration schemes. Thanks to Dylan, the beat heritage found a way into the counter-culture, and, thanks to the counter-culture, a way into contemporary culture. The beat and the counter-culture were many things, but they represented a transformation routine deeply at odds with upward transformation. The idea that the individual should be rational, integrated, purposeful, economistic, and most of all mobile in the constant pursuit of status resources and upward advancement was anathema. The idea that the individual should throw off imperfection and randomness as threats to a finished, presentable social self was ludicrous. The idea that life is a game of advantage and advancement, that other people are status competitors, failed to impress. Dylan and the beats believed themselves engaged in a larger, richer, more difficult mission. From the point of view of the dharma bum, the *Time* reporter was a hack sent to examine something he could not understand on behalf of an institution that was obliged, in any case, to lie.

Beats scorned upward transformation and the conviction that the individual must rise by mastering a social code in pursuit of a cultural capital called "status." They sought the imperfect. They bid the self run wild. And they scorned the idea of lateral transformation. To conceal the self beneath ethnic and racial impersonations was manifestly wrong. Both upward and lateral transformational impulses forced a sacrifice of illumination and authenticity in exchange for the thin, misleading corruptions of a mainstream, middle-class, bourgeois style of life. Most of all, upward and lateral transformation forced the obliteration of the very things that beats believed could get them out from under culture and onto the path of wisdom.

BRIGHTWORK

Another transformational routine was at work in the postwar period. Even as Ginsberg, Kerouac, and Burroughs were hammering away at the bourgeois values of a middle-class society, something odd and interesting was emerging there. It was, I think, a creation of modernism, just as much as the beats were. No doubt the beats were aware of it, and no doubt they regarded it with disdain. This is predictable but unfortunate. For brightwork was, in its way, as deliriously inventive as anything the beats could imagine. Indeed, it is unlikely the beats could ever have ingested enough drugs, befriended enough marginals, or written enough pell-mell prose to have invented it themselves.

What emerged from and for the middle class was the "forward look" in automobile design and a theme of flight in the advertising for the new cars of the middle 1950s. Both the cars and the advertising carried traces of an "unofficial modernism," a constellation of ideas and values that we will draw out by stages.[52] The reader's patience is requested. But before we go looking for this little-studied variety of cultural meaning, let's acknowledge the presence, in cars and their ads, of the more usual kinds of meaning.[53]

Status, the thing that Vance Packard believed to be the obsession of this period, was in evidence.[54] Ads often showed doormen of swank hotels and resorts looking with open-mouthed admiration at the arrival of the new Buick, Cadillac, or Dodge. But this was a diminished theme. In spite of Packard's ravings, status meanings were no longer the most potent kind of meanings to invest in cars. So said Pierre Martineau, one of the marketing authorities on status, to the readers of *Advertising Age* in 1954.[55]

Fashion was in evidence, too. Several advertisements took the form of an invitation to visit the "spring fashion show" of automobiles. Ads begin to dwell on interior details of color, shape, and texture as if they were fashion accessories. A Fisher body advertisement featured clothing fashions by the designer Schiaparelli. Plymouth presented its visuals in the manner of a fashion sketch. Studebaker announced that Raymond Loewy had won a gold medal from the New York School of Fashion for his design of the 1954 Studebaker. It claimed that "in the style department," Studebaker was "50 miles ahead of any other American car." The most patronizing of these efforts appeared in a Chrysler ad which asked, "What kind of 'hat' does your horsepower wear?" The Chrysler V-8 engine is shown wearing a spring bonnet.[56]

A variety of other cultural approaches were being ventured. Pontiac, for instance, offered automobiles with a special affinity for the "moon-lit drive." Hudson treated an urbanizing America to an idealized country landscape. In a culture struggling with career, social, and residential mobility, and with the demands of postwar parenting, Ford presented its new model together with a father and his son walking through a farm field. Chevrolet showed a father (looking like Bing Crosby) taking his daughter on a fishing expedition.[57]

Modernism of the official kind, from the world of built form (lack of ornamentation, clean lines, geometrical shapes, an exercise in aesthetic order and clarity), is very much in evidence. Since it was enthusiastically embraced by the consumer in clothing fashion and built form, it's not surprising that Detroit regarded it as a promising promotional opportunity. The advertisements show how eagerly car manufacturers pressed it into service. Cars were parked in front of conspicuously modern houses and International Style office buildings. Lincoln promised to make "your driving as modern as your living." Its car was free, the company said, of "old fashioned touches" and "useless brightwork." As we have seen, Studebaker hired Raymond Loewy, the preeminent American designer of mass-market modernism. Its ads show a somewhat forlorn Loewy standing in front of his 1954 Studebaker. Above him is the slogan "The only really modern cars in America."[58]

As it turned out, official modernism was not what Americans wanted in their cars. They embraced it in their homes and offices. They embraced it, with somewhat less enthusiasm, in their clothing styles. But in their cars, it turned out, what they wanted was "useless brightwork." What they took to were "cruel-looking tail fins, grinning front grilles, tensed wrap-around windshields, and splendid bodies lashed with chrome high-lights."[59] This was a new transformational motif of which the beats could not have dreamed.

"Sales Acceleration Leaves Detroit Auto Men Breathless" reads the headline in *Advertising Age*. The new approach to brightwork was a sensation. It was introduced by Cadillac, Buick, and Oldsmobile, which had been planning it since 1950, and it was largely the work of Ned F. Nickles and Harley Earl at General Motors. The new look took the nation by storm. An astonished Knoxville dealer received 10,000 visitors on the first day of the new season. In Los Angeles, 750,000 people visited Ford dealerships alone. By the following year, demand was so great Detroit was obliged to produce 8,000,000 vehicles to satisfy it.[60]

One of the reasons Americans liked the new look was that it suggested flight. Nickles and Earl had discovered airplane imagery, especially that of fighter jets. The names of new models were telling: "Pontiac Strato Star," "Hudson Jet," "Oldsmobile Rocket." Buick, Pontiac, Oldsmobile, and Ford hood ornaments took the shape of planes. Even the Packard Clipper now had a plane on its hood. Many Americans were driving with a tiny airplane tucked into the base of their peripheral vision. Introduced in 1954, brightwork began to colonize the industry rapidly. *Time Magazine* observed of the 1956 models, "[M]any new cars borrowed from the shape of swept-wing aircraft to give autos a jet-propelled look."[61]

As the sheer force of the new look became apparent, Detroit responded accordingly. Features were redesigned and renamed. Oldsmobile's ads refer to "new Jetaway hydra-matic," "starfire styling," and a "rocket engine." All of this beneath a picture of a plane streaking through the heavens. In a moment of candor, a Buick ad admitted, "True, this Buick won't fly—but it does have variable pitch propellers in its Dynaflow Drive." Another Buick ad, entitled "Flight into Anywhere," promised the "untroubled soaring ecstasy of graceful flight." Plymouth showed its 1956 model against the profile of a fighter plane.[62]

The General Motors "Motorama" auto show introduced the 1955 models by making them soar through clouds of flash powder over a large pool of water. Lincoln introduced the experimental Futura, which featured a roof canopy indistinguishable from the Plexiglas canopy of a jet. The General Motors "dreamcar," the Firebird designed by Harley Earl and shown as early as 1954, was perhaps the most exaggerated instance of the trend. It looked remarkably like a fighter jet, wings, cockpit, and all. Only the thoroughly incongruous wheels in evidence gave any indication of its true vehicular nature.[63]

Studebaker got into the swing of things, finally. Having lost $29 million on their 1954 models, the company gave up on official modernism. It renounced Loewy at a press conference. It redesigned the car, stuck a plane on the hood, and introduced that fabled technological advance, "flightomatic" transmission. It spent $8 million telling the world that the Studebaker now had "take off torque."[64]

It is customary to look back with amused astonishment at these acts of aesthetic extravagance. They have been declared "vulgar," "crude," "gaudy," "childlike," and "grandiose."[65] What really offended was the suspicion that "most of the trappings were purely for show and had nothing to do with improving the vehicle's qualities as a medium of transportation."[66] But it helps to see that these objects were also a medium of communication; material culture, as it were, with which culture was made material.

America at mid-century believed in the modernist version of progress. People spoke about America "forging ahead," "moving upward," and "advancing to meet its destiny." The future "belonged" to America.[67] In anthropological terms, this is an unusual way of defining and valuing time. Many cultures, and most traditional ones, see time as repetitive, circular, and conservative; they suppose the future will reproduce the present.[68] Modernist cultures, as we have noted, are inclined to think of time as open-ended, and the future as something necessarily discontinuous with the present. Often, in this view, the future glistens with promise. Western cultures, with due ambivalence and some uncertainty, imagined the future with a certain breathless anticipation. Many cultures would find this approach odd, even unimaginable. Forty years after the fact, we're inclined to think so, too.[69]

In the case of American postwar modernism, a constellation of values, institutions, and objects gave the future substance and presence. Indeed, a cascade joined progress on high to domestic life below. Science was the incomprehensible domain of the "egghead."[70] No one doubted that progress would be made through better science. Knowledge and know-how were the secret. MIT "brains" (and other people with tape holding their glasses together) would pave the way. It was as technology that science came down out of the heady, incomprehensible realms of the new physics and made a practical difference to peoples' lives. ("Progress," said GE, "is our most important product.") Technology was changing most of the details of domestic life, with a stream of inventions that included televisions, stoves, dishwashers, washing machines, and, most particularly, blenders. The most desirable of these devices came equipped with "push buttons," the mark of absolute convenience and a measure of scientific solicitude. It was, finally, often as gadgets that progress finally appeared in the individual's life. Americans of this period have been called "gadget-crazy." Gadgets were progress writ small; they were science made possessable. To own a gadget was to participate in one of the great cultural enterprises of the moment. It was to embrace the future.[71]

This combination of progress, science, and technology was sharpened by a sense of international responsibility and the presence of a foreign challenger. Soviet ideology and arms threatened the American agenda. Progress was not merely the responsibility of civilization, it was now a cause of the "free world." And science was not merely a disinterested inquiry into nature. It was the demonstration of America's "just cause" and its resource in the struggle with the Soviets. Technology was not merely the gadgetry of better toasters and telephones. It was now the machinery of international competition and the very instrument of war.

This cultural constellation found particular expression in a piece of 1950s material culture: the fighter jet. Horn calls the jet a "fitting symbol of the 1950s" and notes that the decade is actually sometimes called the "jet decade."[72] This extraordinary machine was simultaneously an affirmation of America's command of science, a glorious example of its technology, and the deadly apparatus by which the Soviet threat would be subdued. The F-series fighter plane became a media star in the mid-fifties. In March 1956 the readers of *Time Magazine* were treated to passionate studies of its military abilities. *Life Magazine* called these planes "wondrous weapons" and spoke with pride and awe of the "billions" that were being spent on their development and production.[73] Flyboys like Chuck Yeager were the heroes of the day. For many Americans, the fighter plane represented the essential American accomplishment. It was the triumph of progress, science, and technology and now the great hope of international competition. It was the very symbol of a resonant constellation of values.

The car design that captured the mass infatuation with the idea of progress writ large also captured the idea of mobility writ small. Planes were about a national struggle for progress. Cars as planes were about a personal struggle for advancement.[74] And in both cases there was a cunning act of metaphor, one that is still so prevalent in our culture it is hard to see plainly. The movement created by planes and cars in physical space mattered because it played out the theme of movement in social or cultural space. Here was a way of making manifest the movement of nations up the ladder of civilization and of individuals up the ladder of a hierarchical society. When Detroit presented a car charged with the meanings of progress and mobility, the consumer saw a car that might serve the personal struggle for advancement. Lashed with status-enhancing chrome and the heroic symbolism of flight, here was a device that let the consumer "move ahead" in every sense of the phrase.

Raymond Loewy understood none of this. The year after his departure from Studebaker, he wrote an article for the *Atlantic Monthly* in which he railed against the "bulk," the "flash," and the "wastefulness" of Detroit's new "chrome gadget rat race." The "sad parade of the 1955 models" was, he said, an act of "vulgarity and blatancy." Worse, it was an "orgiastic chrome-plated brawl." The industry argued that it was merely giving the public what it wanted, but Loewy demurred.

> [I]sn't it the company's cultural responsibility to choose a high standard instead of a low one? I realize that I am setting myself up as an arbiter of taste, but I have helped develop a profession in this country that sells taste.

One transformational routine meets another. Upward transformation relied on careful distinctions between high and low and on gatekeeping by "arbiters of taste" like Loewy. Modernism, with its "clean-cut expression of mechanical excellence," managed at least to preserve these hierarchical distinctions and the authority of Loewy's office. But it stood aghast and astonished by the work of another, a new, transformational regime.[75]

Brightwork transformation used chrome and other details as an act of metaphor. To be sure, the result was noisy and extravagant. After all, this brightwork was the very definition of daring design. It was laboring to turn ugly, earth-bound objects into planes. To suppose that these cars should conform to Loewy's notion of design, especially the impoverishment exacted by the ideology that form should follow function, was to miss the point altogether. This brightwork and these cars had much larger cultural responsibilities. They were supposed to speak for a culture obsessed with forward motion, progress, Cold War preparedness, and the heady accomplishments with which science, technology, and gadgets routinely improved the collective and individual condition.

And the metaphor was used not only for collective purposes, but also for more personal ones. Cars counted because they passed the meanings along. They endowed the owner, the driver, with new definitions. Surrounded by the exoskeleton of Detroit design, the individual was now light-bearing, sleek, aerodynamic, powerful, formidable, and mobile. In this transformational exercise, individuals were now prepared to participate in the acts of mobility that preoccupied a modernist culture.

Cars were capable of several kinds of movement. In them, individuals could imagine that their movement through space was the modernist movement through time. They could imagine themselves outdistancing the present. They could see themselves "moving ahead." As Warren Susman later put it, "To many Americans, movement in space was the equivalent of social mobility."[76] Cars outfitted them with real and aspirational status meanings, articulating their movement in a social space. To the extent that families used the car in the classic Sunday drive, visiting neighborhoods in which they hoped someday to live, the car opened access to modernism's private destination. Motion now served as a symbol for mobility. To the extent that it allowed individuals to imagine themselves the masters of their destiny, the act of driving became an enactment of the promise of modernism.

Driving was an enactment of mobility. It does not now seem altogether strange that individuals should have been eager to embrace cars that evoked the preeminent technology for this mobility, the fighter plane. Ahead, forward, advanced, new, tomorrow, the future. This was where modernism located the most desirable condition of the individual and the state. It was hard to resist the vehicle of transport that seemed to make such movement possible. It is easy for us to mock the "useless brightwork" of the period, but doing so prevents us from seeing that indeed this chrome was used to a purpose, to trick cars out in the symbolism generated by the preeminent ideologies of progress.

Progress as planes, planes as cars, cars as people. It is a transformation not very different in some respects from Japasa's turning himself into a raven. Culture designates "ravenness" or "planeness" and then draws on this quality to constitute some part of the social actor. But it is worth pointing out that the brightwork look was an act of transformation that issued from a somewhat less certain act of consensus, production, and consumption. The car as plane may have been an irresistible creation of a culture with the temporal orientation of modernism. But it came from Detroit designers and Madison Avenue consultants who, I think it's safe to assume, never guessed that they were aiding in the invention of a culture, or that they had assumed this extraordinary responsibility. This mythic metaphor came from commerce, not from the wisdom of the ages. It was then nominated by the individual, not by any religious or political figure. It became the transformational gesture of the individual, his or her opportunity to participate in the cult of the 1950s version of modernism and progress, as an act of choice.

We have called this a "modernist act of transformation" in the face of three potential difficulties. First, what about the grillwork? Surely this violates one of the tenets of modernism: the feeling for simplicity, clarity, integrity, the prohibition of ornament and decoration that so defines the modernist tradition in architecture. Those little planes on the hood, all the brightwork round the side, surely these are nothing if not decorative and tacked on. Doesn't this prevent us calling this constellation of objects and ideas modernist? Isn't it true that the advertising and automotive industries repudiated the prince of commercial modernist design, Raymond Loewy?

I believe there is room in the modernist dogma for the car-plane equations of the 1950s. After all, if we are prepared to call Louis Sullivan a modernist, the case against ornament apparently admits of some very important contradictions. Sullivan's ornamentation is forgiven, because it is not decoration for the sake of decoration.[77] He was playing out an organic metaphor, which is to say the decoration came from somewhere . . . and was going somewhere. And this is precisely what I want to argue in the case of brightwork. When this decoration is an act of metaphor, intended to construct a similarity between cars and planes, it is not decoration for the sake of decoration. It is merely culture working itself out in the material world.[78]

Second, the argument that brightwork is a modernist enterprise depends upon the claim that modernism has a temporal orientation. Does modernism lean, as I suggest here, toward the future? Does it prize the future over the present, and the present over the past? Does it encourage an amnesia that makes the present narrow and disposable, and the past a mere junkyard of irrelevancies?

Something like this leaning can be found in Jean Baudrillard's book on America and his treatment of highway driving as a metaphor for America. A car traveling at speed on the highway moves in space as America moves in time: constantly leaving the moment and entering the future, the world streaming past it, receding in the rear-view mirror, the nation defining itself by successively repudiating the place it finds itself in right now.[79] Jurgen Habermas calls modernity a "changed consciousness of time," an "anticipation of an undefined future and the cult of the new." It revolts against the "normalizing functions of tradition," giving new importance to "the transitory, the elusive, and the ephemeral."[80] Matei Calinescu says, "[M]odernity came about as a commitment to otherness and change, and . . . its entire strategy was shaped by an 'antitraditional tradition.' "[81] In another place, he says, "the revelation of the new is always there in the art of the modernist."[82] Peter Osborne calls modernity "a form of historical time which valorizes the new as the product of a constantly self-negating temporal dynamic."[83] Frederic Jameson claims to have discovered the very processes by which amnesia is induced. "One is tempted to say that the very function of the news media is to relegate such recent historical experiences as rapidly as possible into the past. The information function of the media would thus be to help us forget, to serve as the very agents and mechanisms for our historical amnesia."[84]

Third, the argument that the decoration of the cars of the 1950s is about the temporal orientation of the modernist is, I think, incontrovertible. "If tomorrow is in your thinking—if bold new styling stimulates your senses—if fashion of true modernity is important in your motoring—you belong in a Buick." General Motors claimed to be making the "car of the future." Lincoln called its test car of 1955 the Futura. Buick claimed to be making the "car of tomorrow." And Oldsmobile was offering a car it called "forward looking and forward thinking."[85]

The language of the future, of modernity's notion of the future, is in evidence in automotive styling and marketing. I believe that it had so effectively colonized popular culture in this period that it was everywhere.[86] As we have seen, it took some time for the industry to get a fix on it. Other design and marketing themes were attempted and then forsaken. And there was, as we have seen, the red herring of official modernism. It was only after Detroit managed to get at the ideological content, and beyond the stylistic form, of this modernism that it was able to make the necessary connection. And it is worth pointing out that it needed only to make a small connection in order to let the marketplace respond. With the sales figures for 1954 in hand, the further and expanded use of modernism was no real risk at all.

Perhaps the most interesting difficulty is in the apparent contradiction between the beat and the car buyer. How could such perfectly antithetical creatures both be the product of modernism? It is possible here to see the two as creatures engaged in a comparable exercise. I think they shared the modernist sense of time and culture. Both of them insisted on a world that was open-ended. Both insisted that the individual (and the collectivity) is best oriented in this world when cantilevered out over the future.

To be sure, the differences between them are striking. The beats sought a world that was raw, unconstituted, chaotic. This was where creativity and truth were to be found. The beats sought to get out from under culture. They accepted, with Rousseau, that culture can only have corrupted these possibilities. Only if you could outrun culture through the deliberate use of mind-altering drugs, company, and technique could you enter the null space. The individual posited by this cultural undertaking was ragged, confused, self-destructive, and fecund.

Brightwork was a very different cultural exercise. It propelled the individual into the future, but into a space that was brilliantly illuminated. This is the social space of modernism. Its world was free of constraints, constantly opening to empowering opportunities, bright with promise, thrillingly without horizons, endlessly expansive, clarified by reason. And the individual who entered this space had distinctly aerodynamic or autodynamic properties. He or she was sleek, powerful, swift, relentless, capable of upward and lateral movement, moving steadily away from the limitations and restraints of the group, convention, prejudice. This was mobility for the group and the individual.

Beats and the brightworkers shared a point of departure. Both believed that the only truly sensible cultural move was to vacate the present for the future. Both accepted that they should be suspended over the present, in a constant state of forgetting the present and becoming the future. Brightworkers moved up into a glorious, brilliant, mobile world, beats down into a darker, richer, creative one. We are inclined to accept the beats' point of view. In that ideological battle, they emerged triumphant. Intellectuals have accepted their view of the brightworkers and the '50s. But this acceptance obscures the fact that beats and brightworkers had quite a lot in common. (And this makes me wonder what else the "culture of containment" argument has obscured from view.)

Brightwork suggests that the individual lives in a social space that has the classic aesthetic properties of modernism: clearness, openness, lack of ornamentation, abundant light, the absence of distractions, geometricality—the perfect opposite of Victorian clutter and fussiness. This space shares some of the properties of a living room in those split-level houses with which North Americans filled their postwar suburbs. It has all of the properties of the modern office building. This social world was conceived to be uncluttered, brilliantly illuminated, effortlessly navigable.[87]

Individuals move through this space effortlessly. They have thrown off everything that is old-fashioned and out of date. They have repudiated anything that does not come from the modernist regime. It is a thoroughly rational world, where things don't happen unless they spring from the brow of the time-and-motion engineer. They live in a society that honors initiative and ability, and propels people to their proper stations in life. They live in a society in which people change houses three times a decade. They are freed of constraints. They are, in another key modernist term, streamlined.

In this vision of the social world there is not much left of the body politic. The social world owes little to organic connections, long-standing ties of family, locality, ethnicity, and profession. In the American South, it is perhaps true that, as Faulkner said, "the past is not dead, it is not past." The modernist future demands a different aphorism: "the present is not present, it's just over there." In short, there isn't much body in the body politic.

Modernist Transformation Now

We've been largely abandoned by our notion of progress. This was a grand narrative that made many other stories, grand and small, make sense. But we are now deeply suspicious of what progress, science, and technology can do for us. Aren't they how we managed to do such damage to the environment? Some of us are now persuaded that science's "disenchantment" of the world and the installation of a market rationality have flattened and desiccated our worlds. New Age experiences and therapies thumb their noses at the very notions of objectivity, dispassion, rationality, and empiricism. Doctors and scientists have lost their standing as the wise men and women of the community. Yes, we still admire them, for they have learning, income, and status. But they no longer have "wise man" status. We are still mad for gadgets, especially the Palm Pilot, the cell phone, and the laptop. But then, prosthetic extensions of the body spring from postmodernist motives just as easily as from modernist ones.

Section 5

Postmodern Transformations

The following essays explore some of the transformational abilities we have cultivated in the postmodern period. We will consider them discretely for the moment and then return to characterize postmodern transformation as a whole.

TURTLE ISLAND (THE DIMINISHMENT OF RITUAL IN THE POSTMODERN WORLD)

Ritual has escaped from the temple. It was once a sacred trust in the possession of special officers, reserved for collective purposes and enacted on great, solemn occasions. It had ballast, ceremony, and sacrality. It was charged with solemn transformational responsibilities. But it stole into the world, into the profane and ordinary affairs of everyday life. It has fallen into many hands and is being used for many purposes. In the process, it assumes many new forms. The results are interesting, odd, unpredictable, tragic, and even ludicrous. But they are no longer particularly majestic. Once the most powerful device for transformation, ritual is a shadow of its former self.

In *Sacred Space: Clearing and Enhancing the Energy of Your Home*, Denise Linn offers advice on rituals to remove spirits and summon "house angels." This is what she says about timing:

> Some people make a study of just when the time is exactly right to do a ritual. However, I prefer to use intuition to determine when to do a ritual. I usually choose a time when it just feels right.[1]

This is evidence of a new regime. When the ritual "authority" is something as variable as intuition, things have opened up considerably. Now ritual can be as various as the people practicing it.[2]

Some communities are more scrupulous. Marion Weinstein offers this cautionary note:

> Everyone who participates in a ritual should understand every tiny detail of it. Every word should be understood, and that goes for other languages, too. Remember the ritual at the end of the film, *Raiders of the Lost Ark*? When the ancient secret words were said over the ritual object, what happened? Nazi demons were unleashed! Or demons who liked Nazis, that part wasn't clear. But the point is, they were hideous, noisy, uncontrollable, and full of special effects. Nothing you would want in your living room.[3]

This essay is a companion to the essay called "Turtle Island" in section 1.

In this case, one does *not* proceed when things "just feel right." Something more exacting is called for. Furthermore, detail counts, as Weinstein puzzles out the possibilities ("that part wasn't clear"). But is this a return to ritual in its traditional form? Well, no. Steven Spielberg is a successful filmmaker, but it is probably wrong to think of him as a ritual authority.[4]

Carole Kammen and Jodie Gold recommend ritual as a good way of "bringing sacred tribal values into modern life." But their idea of ritual has an oddly optional quality about it. They advise the would-be celebrant, for instance, to bring along "any objects and materials you will need," an indeterminacy that I think would bewilder most ritual officials.

> Before you begin the actual ritual, you may want to prepare yourself in some way. This might include fasting, bathing, wearing a special amulet or a certain kind of clothing. Depending on the ritual, you might want to prepare yourself for several days, or for just a few minutes.[5]

"Prepare yourself *in some way*"! These rituals have a certain DIY (do-it-yourself) quality about them.

But ritual is not changing merely to accommodate kooky new purposes such as clearing a house of spirits. Even wedding services are being reformed. Vows are changed to include songs, sonnets, and even passages from the Bible. A poem from Kahlil Gibran's *The Prophet* has become particularly popular. The Reverend Don Fallon thinks this may be because Gibran's poem emphasizes that "although we [the couple] are one, we have our own individual growth and our own sense of worth."[6] It is precisely this sort of individuality that ritual has had to learn to accommodate—and it is precisely this that runs so at odds with the traditional ritual agenda. Accommodating individual growth, allowing for a personal sense of self-worth, these are at odds with what ritual is. There is no evidence that people are being cavalier in their choices or adaptations. But there was a time when it was supposed that the *only* way to do something as solemn, difficult, and important as getting married was through the most scrupulous observation of ritual detail. Indeed, for many people, *any* departure from a wedding ceremony was enough to put the validity of the marriage in doubt.

In the newly popular "vow renewal," couples reaffirm their commitment to one another by repeating the wedding ceremony (or some variation thereof), sometimes several times in the course of their relationship. This is a mark of our postmodernity. Traditional marriage vows establish a relationship that is supposed to endure "till death do you part." Renewal actually blunts the effect of the original ceremony. If something is going to need renewal, it's not really a solemn, terrible promise in the first place. If weddings need renewal, what kind of ritual have they become?

Kath Weston reports on rituals of marriage in the gay community. One of her correspondents, Al Collins, describes his experience this way:

> We bought rings after we had been together about six months and we said vows to each other and it was just like . . . to us it was a formal commitment and bond and marriage, although it wasn't sacramental by law of the church. But to the two of us, it's law.[7]

There is a confidence here that the *ad hoc* ritual can create bonds as robust and binding as those of the state or church. In Collins's words, "it's law." This is a mark of the new confidence that many share. What the collectivity (church or state) once reserved to itself, we feel free to claim for ourselves. As this confidence spreads, a key condition discouraging the creation of *ad hoc* rituals is removed. The state and church are no longer the locus of ritual authority.

But let us take an example at the far edge of possibility. Here is an *ad hoc* ritual from *Boogie Nights* (1997, dir. Paul Thomas Anderson), one that, sensationally, presumes to create ties of blood.

Amber: I miss my sons—my little Andrew and my Dirk. I miss them both so much. I always felt like Dirk was my baby, my new baby. Don't you miss Dirk?

Rollergirl: Yeah.

Amber: He's so fucking talented, the little bastard. I love him, Rollergirl. I mean, I really love the little jerk.

Rollergirl: I love you, Mom. I want you to be my mother, Amber. Are you my Mom? Just . . . I'll ask you if you're my mother and you say, "yes." OK? Are you my mother?

Amber: Yes, honey. Yes. Yes.[8]

This is an extreme case, one that is perhaps intended by Anderson to show the effects of cocaine and the desperation of his characters. And it does violate our cultural rule that says ties of marriage are matters of choice, while those of blood are matters of nature.[9] But Rollergirl believes that she can access the powers of ritual with a phrase . . . and with this gesture create a blood tie. We blink but we do not goggle. We are surprised but not incredulous. Under the new rules of ritual, perhaps even this is now possible.[10]

Other rituals of the Western world, especially the political ones, are hedged by skepticism. Some of us believe that political ritual is more likely to conceal the real factors and forces at work in the political arena than to shape them. (For example, it is not unusual to hear people say that it's the oil industry that decides a presidential election, and that the swearing-in ceremony is a mere duplicitous after-thought.) Some thought the funeral of Diana, Princess of Wales showed the opportunistic hand of a member of the royal family. The opening ceremonies of the Olympics, we sometimes think, celebrate an American style more than an international one.[11]

Christmas rituals, we suppose, have been tainted by commerce.[12] Gift giving, the very stuff of social connection, is seen to be driven by marketing. Ritual celebrants are manipulated by big business into buying presents that they then use to manipulate others. The icons of Christmas, especially Santa Claus, are themselves seen to be commercial artifacts shaped by a commercial artist in the employ of the Coca-Cola Company.[13]

Thanksgiving rituals are spoiled less by commerce than by the chronic inability of some families to perform them without coming to blows. *Home for the Holidays* (1995, dir. Jodie Foster) is a well-observed study of how demanding and perilous these family events can be. In one scene, two members of the family are reduced to trading punches on the front lawn, and cease only when a senior member of the household turns the garden hose on them. When neighbors gather to watch this spectacle, he snarls, "Go back to your own goddamned holidays."[14] This may or may not be a new ritual in the making.

Halloween continues robust.[15] It flourishes in the face of our general skepticism and even in the face of its own razor-blade scares.[16] But the spirit of innovation and individualism is ferociously active here. Halloween has been adopted and transformed by a gay community for a parade that is held each year in Greenwich Village.[17] Adults of every sexuality go to parties dressed as a variety of characters, including American presidents, Stuart Smalley, Hunter S. Thompson, Ted Koppel, and Barbara Walters. So dressed, people are called upon to entertain with a set piece that then gives way to improv. Individuality and innovation are prized. Thus does Halloween march steadily beyond the traditional array of ghosts, goblins, and vampires. Of all the contemporary rituals, this one has best succeeded in accommodating postmodern inclinations.[18]

What is the source of our hostility to old rituals? What is the cause of our liberality with new ones? Why is there so much Turtle Island variation and departure in ritual? What has displaced ritual as our chief transformer?

Our hostility to old ritual is not surprising. Ritual has been on several "hit lists" for some time now. Enlightenment and Reformation thinkers mocked ritual as an affront against reason in the first instance and as indicating a too-mediated relationship with God in the second.[19] Modernism scorned ritual as a dumb, rote show. Some lifestyles have taken particular aim at ritual: Hippies and Travelers scorn traditional rituals as the oppressive constraints of a bourgeois society, and create their own. Ritual has been diminished by our several commitments to what Charles Taylor calls the "affirmation of ordinary life."[20]

The "adversary intention," as Lionel Trilling called it, was hostile to ritual. Trilling asked writers to detach "the reader from the habits of thought and feeling that the larger culture imposes, [and give] him a ground and a vantage point from which to judge and condemn, and perhaps revise, the culture that produced him."[21] This new skepticism transformed popular culture. Filmmakers, artists, writers, and intellectuals driven by the "adversary intention" devoted themselves to showing the vacuity and falsehoods of "bourgeois society" and especially the insincerities of its marriages, graduations, Christmases, and Thanksgivings. The modernist commitment to dismantling ritual was very strong.[22]

But part of our hostility to ritual also comes from what Michèle Lamont calls the "cultural sovereignty of the individual."[23] We bridle at the idea that our graduation from college *requires* a ceremony. And we make no distinction between those who took their degree from the hand of the college president and those who got it sent them in the mail. (In some societies, this would matter.) We are dubious about any agency that presumes to define the individual. In our society, rights of authorship are jealously guarded. No one wants anyone, least of all society, deciding who they are.[24] No one wants to be "processed" by ritual. We are inclined to mock rites of passage, and any military, fraternal, or Girl Guide organization that insists on them. We turn ornery when people propose themselves as the authorities who decide who we are. When ritual is imposed upon us, we react badly. We respond with anti-ritual. Graduating students show up with no socks, no shoes, shaved heads, funny walks, angry outbursts, outrageous outfits, militant salutes, stupid faces, "kick me" stickers, or rabbit ears. At the beginning of *Say Anything* (1989, dir. Cameron Crowe), a celebrant offers an impromptu, alcohol-assisted, deeply ironic version of "The Greatest Love of All."

Teens are chronically hostile to ritual induction. They prefer to choose for themselves the timing and nature of their maturation. Typically, they press for early enactment, the use of their own ritual implements and symbols, and an identity that can seem to parents not so much a social designation as a creature beyond the pale. Most of all, they dispute, and fiercely resist, the exercise of a larger authority. "Who do you think you are?" is one of the favorite slogans of this resistance. The power and ubiquity of this phrase is one useful marker of how far we have moved from being a "ritual society."

Things are not simpler at the other end of the age spectrum. Adults are increasingly reluctant to accept the rituals that deliver them to the designation "elderly." Part of the problem is that, as Elizabeth Colson suggests, we do not have a "full-blown age-grade system" or "a full set of . . . transition rituals."[25] But the problem is deeper than this. Ritual candidates simply do not wish to go where the rituals would take them. And they doubt the authority of any ritual that might apply to them.[26]

New groups are necessarily hostile to existing rituals. After all, they don't wish to go any of the places these rituals can take them. They must therefore fashion their own rituals. Otherwise, in van Gennep's terms, they have created a destination but no way of getting there—a paradox no community will tolerate for long.

> As a gay person, you are re-creating and reinventing institutions like marriage and family holidays. You see through institutions, and tweak them, and co-opt them and use them for what you want. That's what *Martha Stewart Living* does.[27]

What is the ritual to be? When should it take place? Who will make it up? These are all now imponderables for us. But the key question is, finally, the political one. By whose authority will ritual participation and outcomes be decided? No one, not society, parents, husbands, wives, union bosses, church leaders, magazine editors, book reviewers, politicians, rock stars, government bureaucrats, or community leaders, is going to tell us who we are.

This is a technical problem that stems from the cultural problem. There are many and various destinations, so many identities, on the developmental path. Our ritual would have to have as many stops as the London Underground to accommodate all the places we want to go. How could any one rite of passage serve us?[28]

It is not clear that this technical problem is widely understood. Robert Bly calls for initiations that will create "Wild Man" masculinity. He believes that this will solve the difficulty our society now has "leading boys toward manhood."[29] But how can there be a single ritual destination, persona, or wild man in a society as pluralistic and individualistic as our own? We have a great many ideas of what manhood is, including those of Robert Bly, Anthony Robbins, Andy Dyck, Michael Stipe, and the Backstreet Boys, to name a few.[30]

Here is Joseph Campbell discussing ritual with Bill Moyers:

Moyers: Society has provided [teens] no rituals by which they become members of the tribe, of the community . . .

Campbell: That's exactly it. That's the significance of the puberty rites.

Moyers: Where do the kids growing up in the city . . . Where do these kids get their myths?

Campbell: They make them up themselves.[31]

Campbell thought this was the problem: that young men were making up their own rituals. Supply these, and the world is put right. But in fact, we cannot create and insist upon a single coming-of-age puberty rite. There is no single identity awaiting boys becoming teens, or teens becoming adults. But, worse, teens have claimed rights of self-authorship, and they will not give them back. To call for the restoration of traditional myth and ritual in postmodern Western societies may be a little naïve.

It is also true that ritual has been replaced by sport, and our concern with sport is a place where ritual can flourish. The Rose Bowl Parade is covered in tradition. Superbowl Sunday is formulaic. The tailgate party that precedes the college football game is formalized. Fans prepare to watch a game with the attention to detail we associate with high ritual. Everything—sandwiches, chair, libations, lighting—must be "just so." Even soccer hooligans observe ritual.[32] Sports teams, especially in hockey and baseball, are famous for arcane and elaborate preparations.[33]

> On each pitching day for the first three months of a winning season, Dennis Grossini, a pitcher on a Detroit Tiger farm team, arose from bed at exactly 10 AM. At 1 PM he went to the nearest restaurant for two glasses of iced tea and a tuna fish sandwich. Although the afternoon was free, he changed into the sweat shirt and supporter he wore during his last winning game, and one hour before the game he chewed a wad of Beech-Nut chewing tobacco. During the game he touched his letters [the team name on his uniform] after each pitch and straightened his cap after each ball. Before the start of each inning he replaced the pitcher's rosin bag next to the spot where it was the inning before. And after every inning in which he gave up a run he would wash his hands.[34]

But sports themselves are anti-ritualistic. They make the world an arrow where ritual wishes to make it a circle. They produce outcomes. They create events. They shuffle the order of the world. In the immortal words of Lévi-Strauss,

> Games [in the Western competitive tradition] thus appear to have a disjunctive effect: they end in the establishment of a difference between individual players or teams where originally there was no indication of inequality. And at the end of the game they are distinguished into winners and losers. Ritual, on the other hand, is the exact inverse.[35]

Sports are, in certain respects, unpredictable and uncontrolled. They destroy the order and predictability that ritual is designed, in most cases, to create. That we as a society care so about sports says, to some extent, that we must be a society that does not care about ritual.

The other great institution that displaces ritual is Hollywood. There are, at any given moment, perhaps ten credible, potentially definitional movies in circulation. Over the course of a year there are perhaps a hundred movies that have the power to inspire individuals and assist them in changing how they think about themselves. Joseph Campbell saw movies as our substitute for myth and ritual. But he believed that movies were a corrupted form of ritual. After all, rituals are made by priests and movies are made for money.[36] Our construction and presentation of a public persona draws heavily upon the definitional resources that movies make available. Movies help us make selves the way rituals do, with the important and inevitable postmodern difference that the selves are more multiple, more changeable, more optional, and more customizable.[37]

In face-to-face society, of the kind the tribesman interviewed by the BBC in the opening to section 2 may or may not occupy, ritual is an intricate and powerful piece of social machinery. It is the earliest form of public transit. It is the way individuals get through life, moving in the social system from one status or role to the next. It is the way society gives out identities and the way individuals take them on.

No more—or at least, less and less. In the place of ritual, we have daring, flimsy inventions in the Turtle Island tradition. Referring to the modern practice of inventing traditions, Eric Hobsbawm says,

> One marked difference between old and invented practices may be observed. The former were specific and strongly binding social practices, the latter tended to be quite unspecific and vague as to the nature of the values, rights and obligations of the group membership they inculcate.[38]

The tribesman had no doubt. We have lots of freedom. Two more different transformational traditions cannot be imagined.

"Turtle Island" rituals are missing many, if not all, of the conditions of the traditional ritual. They tend to have little or no *mass:* no participants, no ritual officers, no audience, and they speak neither for nor to a collectivity. They are undertaken for and by an individual. They have no *calendar:* they can be evoked capriciously and sometimes never enacted again. They have no *ballast:* they neither come from nor issue in tradition. They are invented and performed at the discretion of the individual. They have little *ceremony:* it doesn't much matter how they are performed. We make things up as we go along, using ideas and objects that happen to be at hand. They have little *sacrality:* there is often nothing especially grave or solemn, and usually nothing at all sacred, about our rituals.

Myth Now

Myth has lost standing for much of our world, that much is clear. Sheldon Wolin says it has been supplanted by "technological reason." It has become, in his words,

> the consolation of marginal minds who savor its traces precisely because they appear anachronistically in a world that is progressively being shaped by technological reason and interpreted by social-scientific methods and conceptions. Myth occupies the status of a residual category that justifies whatever intuitive, nonrational, poetic, religious, or other fugitive experiences we happen upon in a world orchestrated by postmythic powers.

Wolin says contemporary myth is a "premeditated act of fabrication." The politics of the modern and postmodern world are myth-free.[39]

This argument has something to recommend it, but it is, of course, wrong. It is true that the rise of scientific inquiry discredited the metaphoric impulse on which myth depends. Sometime in the early modern period, Marjorie Nicolson notes, the new science began to destroy myth and metaphor together.[40] The fecundity and pliability of the world, and many of its transformational powers, were diminished. The world, to use Weber's term again, was disenchanted.[41]

But it is also true that Wolin is perpetuating one of our most fervent myths: that we have no myths.[42] This myth says that we believe things only when they have been divested of falsehood, surmise, and prejudice. We believe only "facts" that survive dispassionate inquiry. It was with this authority that experts like Margaret Mead, Masters and Johnson, and Dr. Spock helped change cultural ideals and practices. These were scientists, not moral leaders. But they spoke as if mythically, inscribing what we can see now were quite arbitrary first principles in belief and practice. Myth was not dead. It had merely found a powerful new source of authority.

We might also say that myth had taken up residence in the "great ideas" of the Western tradition. Individualism is shot through with ideological assumptions and the imagery of frontiers and free markets.[43] It was also there in the conviction of the chattering classes that we were on the verge of a cultural catastrophe as a result of television, Hollywood, talk shows, materialism, advertising, narcissism, incivility, the death of the liberal arts. Intellectuals found many guilty parties. Whether this was a new contribution to the mythic tradition or merely a new way to tell the myth of the fall was never clear. But we may say at least that we are not quite as myth-free as Wolin believes.

But the most troubling thing about Wolin's argument is the remarkable rehabilitation myth has enjoyed in the fourteen years since he described its death. Our enthusiasm for "nonrational, poetic, religious, or other fugitive experiences" has grown remarkably. The key indicators—health care practices, spiritual patterns, Hollywood movies, and network television—are awash with these experiences, as I think the previous section shows. Myth could now tear away the veil. It was not necessary to dress up in the authority of another discourse. Indeed, myth could now actually trade on its strengths, the inarticulate, the ineffable and the unprovable. These were now good things, evidence that the wisdom of the ages had somehow been tapped.[44]

Myth is caught somewhere between its violent demotion at the hands of science and its rehabilitation thanks to New Age practices. But if it is regaining some of its influence, we are obliged to note that this mythic impulse is not much like the one that Japasa believed in. Our myths have been opened up to the creative efforts, ceaseless innovation, and now apparently endless diversification that characterize several aspects of the contemporary world. Our myth is changeable, negotiable, transformable in a way that Japasa's was not. Most of all, it is optional. We have made the individual the arbiter of the myths that she believes in. And if she doesn't like these myths, we have made her free to create new ones. It is easy to call this "supermarket spirituality," another measure of our disorder as a culture. But doing so would be inaccurate.

CANDICE CARPENTER (AND SWIFT SELVES)

In the world of rock climbing, there is "zooming out" and "zooming in." Zooming out is what the climber does when she has a chance to rest on a mountain face. Zooming in is what she does when she is moving methodically across it. Zooming in demands concentration and constant movement. The climber is held to the rock face as if by surface tension. The hand is set in motion with no clear knowledge of where it will come to rest. But it must eventually come to rest. Momentum is everything.[45]

Zooming in is characteristic of extreme sports, generally.[46] They require a thoroughgoing investment in the moment, something deeper and more profound than what Mihaly Csikszentmihalyi calls "flow."[47] The players are not merely absorbed by the task at hand, they must struggle constantly and self-consciously to remain coincident with it. As one enthusiast told me, "you have to go to the edge of what you can do . . . and see if you can stay there."[48] Zooming in is open and open-ended. The athlete is not contained by the experience but constantly being poured out of it into what will happen next. This is less "flow" than "flood."

Extreme sports have moved with surprising ease from the margin of contemporary culture into the mainstream. What began as a minority interest cultivated by bad-tempered surfers now informs the enthusiasms of millions of teenagers, a small but growing part of the economy, and a substantial piece of contemporary culture. In a key migratory development, extreme sports have been embraced as a guiding metaphor in the New Economy. Extreme sports became a model for extreme business.[49]

In *The New New Thing*, Michael Lewis tells about an afternoon in the life of Jim Clark, creator of Netscape and one of the key figures in the development of Silicon Valley and the New Economy. Clark was learning how to fly his latest acquisition, a McDonnell Douglas helicopter. Some way through the flight, Clark turned to his instructor, a large Vietnam veteran.

> "Were you controlling it?"
> "That was all you, Jim."
> "I felt you controlling it."
> "No, no, it's been all you."
> "This really pisses me off."[50]

This essay is a companion to the essay called "Candice Carpenter" in section 1.

There were a couple of reasons for his irritation. Clark is one of the princes of the new capitalism. He is unaccustomed to being controlled or corrected, especially when he is demonstrating his formidable powers of adaptation. But it is also true that he was engaging, or trying to engage, in extreme flying, trying to be absolutely present in the moment, to establish a boundaryless connection between himself and the machine, to create a frictionless exchange of data in and adjustment out. And there's this guy in the way.

Larry Ellison is the chief executive officer of Oracle.[51] He competed in the 1999 Sydney-Hobart sailboat race that went disastrously wrong. Ellison and his crew sailed into a hurricane and were lucky to escape with their lives. Interestingly, Ellison does not see sailing through a hurricane as extreme sport. With thirty-foot waves and wind speeds of eighty miles an hour, we might think it would qualify. But as Ellison sees it, the essential balance of control and chaos was missing. The crew were not at the edge of their competence but far beyond it. Ellison and his crew returned to port in tears. They asked their wives to forgive them for having put themselves at risk. They did not come away with a sense of athletic accomplishment or bragging rights. Ellison looks at the experience in retrospect merely as a "stupid way to die."[52]

Extreme sports are, I believe, the latest manifestation (and perhaps an intensification) of a long-standing cultural project, one that has been in our midst, in one form or another, for a long time. In this project, individuals define themselves as creatures in process. They see the self as something in motion.[53] Some cultures treat the self as something that can define itself best by removing itself from the world. The swift self offers a different orientation, a self that defines itself by rushing into the world, which is itself relatively inchoate and emergent (and doing some rushing of its own). This is the way of, and the rationale for, zooming in. The extreme climber finds definition by rushing away from definition into . . . something else. She must give herself to the moment(um). She must hope the "surface tension" holds.

The mobility of the swift self comes partly from our individualism, from a stripping away of the connections, contexts, and constraints that surround the traditional and status transformation self. Individuals are now capable of extraordinary mobility, in part because they have been released from certain domestic, social, and other constraints.[54] Like Saul Bellow, they refuse or revise the definitions imposed by history and culture, especially those of ethnicity, gender, and class. These definitions both complete the self and slow it down. Swift selves throw them off and rush into the world to find new ones.

The mobility of the swift self comes also from its instrumentality.[55] The swift self is driven by purpose. It makes itself a means to an end. This instrumentality stands in opposition to the powerful tradition that says that the individual must cultivate the self for the self, that the most noble creation of a self *is* the self. The swift self is cultivated only to make it more effective in the world, upon the world. This means that swift selves are often not particular about the self itself. It matters as a means. Swift selves suspend internal accomplishments for external ones. They endure difficulty, they suspend satisfaction, they forego cultivation of the self for cultivation of the world. And this makes the world still more nervous. The swift self is unbound and determined to put its mark upon the world. Surely mischief, and something more substantial than mischief, must follow.

Swift selves flock well. For all their voracious individualism, they are prepared to enter into associations if these will aid them in the world. Indeed, swift selves delight in strapping on the instrumentalities and powers that corporations put at their disposal. Institutional augmentation is generally regarded as a good thing. But the swift individuals are unsentimental about their ties to the corporation. They do not expect to give or receive thoroughgoing loyalty. The corporation uses them; they use the corporation.[56] Something is accomplished beyond the trade of salary for services. Both selves and corporations get swifter.

Swift selves, especially the business versions, are prepared to be treated as modular. This offense against the supposed uniqueness of the radiant self is acceptable to the swift self. This is one reason they serve so well in the corporate world. They are happy to fulfill a fixed set of responsibilities, to adapt themselves to the demands of a position. And they are not surprised or affronted when the corporation decides to put someone else in their place. They do not believe that their value comes from their uniqueness as individuals or the distinctness of the self. They are prepared to conform to the demands of the role. They are prepared to be seen as substitutable.[57]

The swift self comes, in part, from the marketplace, from an Adam Smithian understanding of human behavior as gain-seeking and the rise of capitalism that so inspires and rewards this particular performance of the self. The swift self springs from what Daniel Bell calls instrumental individualism. It is responsive to the demands of competition, to the inducements of opportunity. Indeed, marketplaces and swift selves are mirrors of one another. Both define themselves through their responsiveness. Both are not very particular about form and are pleased to go with what works. Swift selves and marketplaces flourish together. The difference is that markets, in their dismal way, do not care what becomes of them, whereas, of course, individuals do. The triumph of capitalism, over two hundred years, has created a test case. What can selves endure? How fast can they be made to go? Following up on Candice Carpenter's remarks in section 1, how much fear can they take? To some extent, the structural properties of the market and the self are now the same. But, at some point, those of the first begin to test those of the second.

But it would be wrong to associate the swift self only with Smith's economic man. The mobility of the swift self comes, finally, from the willingness to give the self over to what happens next. This is the fundamental orientation at work. Certainly, many swift selves prefer markets, but not all of them do. Swiftness does not need a free market.[58] It merely needs indeterminacy. The bicyclist racing down a mountainside has abandoned a "command" modality for the moment, and has become a stream of data in and decisions out. It would be reckless to stop to reconnoiter and contemplate her options. The soccer hooligan pieces his mischief together on the go. The jazz saxophonist steps off into the solo. Good teachers proceed as much by improv as by plan. Economic man is merely one version of the swift self.

Indeed, the extreme version of the swift self may someday eclipse the economic man. This will come as a surprise to those who believe that the latter is the ne plus ultra of social development. The trouble is that the rationality of the economic man is in fact unadaptive in the emerging marketplace. In a world ruled by disruptive technologies and steady change, in a context that penalizes conventional kinds of risk avoidance, the creature who calculates advantage too narrowly is out of place and uncompetitive.[59]

This is the great paradox of the new managerial literature. Once a champion of economic caution, it now routinely argues that only reckless risk-taking can hope to succeed. Tom Peters, in particular, says that those who wait must lose.[60] Managers are told that they must act without the benefit of full information, without a clear idea of their exposure, and without anything like the "due diligence" that business school and executive education are supposed to instill in them. Extreme selves are particularly well positioned as the rules of business change.

Another way to think about the swift self is to contrast it with the tribesman quoted at the beginning of section 2. This man entertains a self that has very clear destinations along a ritual path. The BBC interviewer finds him puzzling because she is a modernist Westerner. She believes, without thinking about it much, that everyone, even the culturally conservative, is in a state of becoming. She is asking the tribesman for his particular hopes and wishes, not the shared and traditional objectives of collective life. More particularly, she is asking for the results of a personal struggle to find the "real self."

But the tribesman has, as they say, other ideas. He does not live in an emergent world or an individualistic one. He is not pursuing uniqueness. His world is designed to turn in toward the familiar, not out toward the new. He does not believe his self will somehow emerge out of the play of accident, purpose, fate, and the direction he's been able to give his life. Indeed this idea of a life, had the BBC interviewer made it explicit, would almost certainly have struck him as bizarre. This individual moves through life along a well-marked path. He believes he has the benefit of perspective, that he can see things coming from a long way off, that he can know more or less clearly what the future has in store for him. For this man, dynamism in general, and swiftness in particular, are not a source of transformation; they are for him the failure of transformation.

Thrilling but . . .

Inhabiting a swift self is thrilling, but difficult. Popular culture is cluttered with survival strategies. The most radical is simple repudiation. Hollywood likes this theme particularly, and frequently declares the swift self bad and the slow self good.[61] Swift selves, it insists, are inauthentic, ungrounded, and opportunistic. Another survival strategy is to distinguish between the demands of Christ and Caesar: swift selves for the marketplace, something else for the home, Internet, family, lifestyle, church, and community. This strategy has taken on a new intensity as some individuals now treble and quadruple their selves, to give the swift self new companions. (This is a theme to which we will return.) A third strategy is to do selves in sequence. We caught a glimpse of this as Generations X and Y took to the New Economy, some of them choosing start-up over selfhood. It was common to hear members of the dot.com world say that they would figure out who they were when they had made their fortune. In the meantime, swift selves.

Swift selves have a special feeling for optimism. They are exhorted, especially by self-help authors, to refuse criticism from without and discouragement from within. Their "mission" (swift selves love to have missions) is to "go for it" in the first instance and to keep going "no matter what" in the second. They would defy George Herbert Mead and the conviction that the meaning of the self comes from without. This optimistic defiance is the point of the Hollywood movie *Rudy* (1993, dir. David Anspaugh), in which a young man without any of the requisite qualities succeeds in making the Notre Dame University football squad. Rudy triumphs despite the fact that everyone is persuaded of his insufficiency. This sort of thing appeals to the scriptwriter in all of us. Yes, of course, we should refuse the nay-saying a cruel and conservative world heaps upon us. But, in the real world, this refusal may mean isolation. Some of the world's messages must be taken seriously, if we are to avoid a perfect solipsism. Otherwise, we are not so much courageous as obtuse and out of touch.

Many people with swift selves believe that their suspension of the self is temporary, that the swift self is a means to an end. Eventually, they believe, the enterprise will pay off, the career will mature, rewards will come. But sometimes, perhaps often, this is not the full truth of the matter. Many swift individuals fear stasis. They are happiest when in motion. They don't want ever to "arrive." They prefer to be a means; they fear becoming an end. The pleasure of this self is precisely its swiftness and momentum, the bracing sense of power and safety that comes from being on the move.

The swift self is, to use a favorite phrase, a "high-risk proposition." Swift selves are so dedicated to action and an exterior world that they are not very contemplative or self-aware. This can mean, for instance, that they do not see emotional difficulty coming until it is upon them, and they are disinclined to study their own complexity. The trope here is movement, and swift selves solve many problems by just "getting on with it." This works well enough for some purposes. But when it does not work, there can be no outcome but crisis. Swift selves often have a hard time slowing down in late middle age. The American lifecycle posits the possibility of maturity and the contemplative pleasures of a more sedentary way of life. But many swift selves are forced to remain in motion. After all, their swiftness has cost them alternatives. Except at work, they are relatively friendless and relatively disconnected from family and community. They have no real homes to go home to. And they are also deeply attached to the power and exhilaration of their swiftness. Everything else, everything more rooted, can seem ordinary and pallid by comparison.

And this is why swift selves are brought low by illness, the departure of a spouse who is tired of waiting, a sudden collapse of an enterprise or change in the economy, or, not infrequently, alcohol or drugs that they've been using as braking devices. Now they must figure out what their life could be besides forward motion. It is a difficult transition, a movement between modalities so different that they might as well be separate cultures. In the new, relatively still world, people and moments count more than outcomes and processes. It is an enormous change, and for some, though I don't wish to be melodramatic about it, self-destruction or renunciation of the world seems an easier course.

Swift selves learn odd strategies to deal with their condition. In a recent study of people living in Silicon Valley, I noticed that almost all the swift selves I talked to had elaborate "exit strategies": detailed plans to buy a little farm in Montana or a place in small-town California. In most cases, these second homes were places of emotional respite only, never actually to be purchased and lived in. They existed to allow the swift self to solve one of its most pressing contradictions, to give relief from mobility without actually compromising this mobility. There were sad moments in several interviews, when I could see respondents seeing the lie: that they had created an exit strategy they would not, could not, use. The respite had to feel real and remain virtual.[62]

There is something tragic, in the classical definition of tragedy, about the swift self. Its contradictions mean that, left to their own devices, things will end badly. The last moments of the arc are particularly unhappy. The swift self knows it can't keep moving indefinitely. It is neglecting its needs and exhausting its resources. But it also knows that it cannot stop without crashing. Without forward motion, there is no surface tension. At worst, the swift self suspects there is no stopping, only falling. Swift selves rarely end with grace.[63]

Origins

The swift self has several antecedents and origins. The most obvious of these is modernism, whose temporal orientation treats the present as a mere antechamber to the future.[64] Paul de Man calls the act of "ruthless forgetting" that propels a self into action "lightened of all previous experience" an expression of the "authentic spirit of modernity."[65] Capitalism has made a contribution, not least through its instrumental individualism. But the swift self comes also from expressive individualism. Swift selves find themselves in work and express themselves through work.

We can also see versions of the swift self in the individual, whom the Reformation made a locus of new responsibility and agency. The swift self has captured a great deal of contemporary culture. It is the modality of the self that comes close to satisfying the Western mythological notion that the social world "has been created to serve the interests of some idealized autonomous, abstract individual existing free of society yet living in society."[66]

Brightwork and the streamlining of the 1954 automobile played up an essential aspect of the swift self, its love of prosthetic extension. Swift selves delight in extending their mechanical powers.[67] They are happy to claim these powers as their own, to blur the distinction between the self and the device. As we have seen, in the 1950s this blurring took the form of flattering comparisons (and confusions) with cars and fighter planes. More recently, the prosthetic device has been the computer and the wireless PDA (personal digital assistant). These devices provide individuals with a constant stream of information and opportunities to act upon the world. Swift selves look forward to this prosthetic enhancement. The ability to act on anything through the Net, from anywhere in the world, driven by anything in the moment, offers opportunities for swiftness they have not dreamed of.[68]

One of the great sources of the swift self in this century is the so-called "self-help" literature. Western societies have an inexhaustible appetite for this literature. The tribesman interviewed by the BBC would find this one of the oddest things about us. To read a book to see how one might transform oneself, rooting out some characteristics and installing others, with a view to making oneself more capable, more productive, more aggressive . . . all of this would seem a mystery. But a good deal of the self-help literature reads like design specifications for the swift self.[69] I examine it cautiously, because it is a favorite whipping boy of the chattering classes. Nothing gives so much comfort to so many intellectuals as a verbal thrashing administered to the likes of Anthony Robbins in the pages of a rigorous magazine.[70] Let us see if we can restrain ourselves.

Self-Help

Let's begin with the work of Norman Vincent Peale. This was filled with an argument for self-creation. Peale's work makes the radical claim that an individual can become an author of the self. Peale believed that the individual need only care enough and work hard enough to strip down the self and build anew.

What becomes of the self so constructed? In Peale's view, the self becomes machinery, the purpose of which is to act, with ever greater efficiency, upon the world. Comparisons with machines are everywhere in his work.

On a roadside billboard I saw an advertisement of a certain brand of motor oil. The slogan read, "A clean engine always delivers power." So will a mind free of negatives produce positives, that is to say, a clean mind will deliver power. Therefore flush out your thoughts, give yourself a clean mental engine.[71]

Three things are visible in this advice. First, Peale believes that the individual has extraordinary control of self and destiny, that wishing makes it so. He recommends a kind of anticipatory transformation:

The "as if" principle works. Act "as if" you were not afraid and you will become courageous, "as if" you could and you'll find that you can. Act "as if" you like a person and you'll find a friendship.[72]

"Surely," a little voice within us says, "the world is less accommodating than this. Surely acting 'as if' is not, in itself, enough to transform the world." To which, of course, the Pealean enthusiast replies with a variation on Augustinian wisdom: "Act that you may understand, don't understand that you may act."[73]

Second, Peale's self makes the individual "aerodynamic" by removing anything that creates resistance. Too often this means giving up subtlety and self-reflection. By the time the self is ready for "takeoff," many of the things that make it unusual, interesting, and creative have been polished away. If this is the cost of swiftness, we say, it's a bad bargain.

Third, Peale invites the creation of a self that seems almost to exist *sui generis*, taking its reference points from the furious acts of self-scrutiny and self-exhortation rather than from the community outside. When Peale invites us to refuse "negative thoughts," we may be forgiven for wondering whether such thoughts are not the very foundation of self-scrutiny and perhaps even the interior voice of the community.[74]

We are inclined to dislike Peale's ceaseless optimism, with its refusal of subtlety and its insufficient connection to the world. But these traditional dislikes are the usual caviling and they must not be allowed to prevent us from seeing how deeply rooted the Pealean project is in our culture. Yes, it was installed there without expert supervision or permission. But this doesn't matter at all. (When will intellectuals cease to be surprised by how easily contemporary culture proceeds without them?) The swift self is a DIY enterprise, invented often by solitary individuals and embraced by local enthusiasts, one book at a time. This swift self springs from the efforts of "kooky" outsiders speaking to a struggling non-elite. This swift self has been given almost no support from on high, from the pulpit, the press, government, the academy. It has found

its place in the world through a spontaneous supply and demand of inspiration. Intellectuals may sneer at Peale's ideas, but these ideas represent something very like a populist movement.

What can we say about a man who compares himself to "the celebrated quarterback who sprints onto the field in the last quarter of the
game, confers in the huddle, confidently strides out to the line of scrim-
mage, and throws the perfect spiral pass fifty yards downfield into the
end zone to score the winning touchdown"?[75] There is something so relentlessly self-congratulatory (and exclamatory!) about Anthony Robbins that just a few pages of his *Awaken the Giant Within* brought this
reader to the screaming point. (And, no, that is not the sound of the giant within.) The title itself is a good example of Robbinsian arrogance.
Robbins is very, very tall. His title hints, with a characteristic lack of
subtlety, that the giant within is Mr. Robbins himself. This arrogance is
enough to discourage all efforts at self-examination.

The Pealean trinity is visible in Robbins's work. Robbins believes in
the power of positive thinking, in the importance of stripping the self
of doubt, and in the self as something that exists *sui generis*. He is so relentlessly enthusiastic that, reading the book, I wondered what it must
be like for Robbins, or one of his disciples, to have a bad day. In Robbins's world there really are no acceptable reasons why each individual
shouldn't rise to extraordinary accomplishments *all the time*. All performances must be, oxymoronically, "peak performances." Robbins em-
powers but, as he does so, he broadens the Protestant plain that makes
failure obvious and responsibility inescapable. But this is an outsider's
quibble. Insiders are not troubled by these contradictions, at least in the
short term.

But Robbins moves away from the mechanistic models that came so
easily to Peale in the 1950s. Robbins appears to believe in the uniqueness of the individual. "We all want to believe deep down in our souls
that we have a special gift, that we can make a difference, that we can
touch others in a special way, and that we can make the world a better
place."[76] This is not quite the same as encouraging us to examine the interior life for secret signs of individuality, but it is very different from
Peale's advice to embrace efficacy and damn the particulars. Robbins
points the swift self toward the endlessly divisible realm of a full individualism. If Peale's selves were being made ready for competitive success, Robbins's selves are opening up to a florescence of self-discovery.
Certainly, the promise of competitive success is still part of the appeal
here. (The foreword to *Awakening* calls Robbins "a great coach in the

game of life.") But the giants in Robbins's world are all, somewhat alarmingly, different giants.[77]

Robbins's work marks a shift of emphasis. The self is now as much an end as a means. Robbins offers strategies for discovering the conflicts that frustrate peak performance. And for Peale this would have been enough. But the point of the exercise for Robbins is, in part anyway, the discovery of what the self is and what the self wants. Certainly there are moments in Robbins when we can hear the voice of Peale. "You'll be sending your brain a new message *commanding* new results."[78] This is the classic language of self as instrument. But Robbins also uses the language of a more expressive individuality.[79]

Robbins goes a step further. He makes the self not merely an agent, but an arbiter. In the Pealean scheme, the individual acts in and upon the world . . . and is judged by it. Success and fulfillment are determined and defined by the world. In Robbins's scheme, the self can be its own judge.[80] This suggests a change in the very nature of swiftness. For at the end of this arc lies a daunting possibility: a relativist's self that has so internalized the right and power to decide who it is that it no longer needs the world. This swift self risks making itself the captive of a new contradiction in a tradition already riddled with them.

But this is speculation. It is enough to say that the self-help literature (and this part of the human potential movement) can be read as a scheme to make swift selves swifter. It encourages individuals to root out anything that might keep them from realizing their potential, that diminishes their effectiveness or efficiency. This is particularly vivid in the time management literature, which brings time and motion studies to the individual herself, that the "plant" may run with ever greater efficiency. Individuals sometimes experience this as a joyful opportunity to take charge of their lives. But many swift selves are coerced selves and their devotion to this literature is tinged by desperation. Some read Peale and Robbins not to succeed, but to survive.

The extreme swift self is a break from the self-help tradition. It does not represent yet another pragmatic routine, a new efficiency, a further domestication of the self. It helps the individual to rise to the occasion, always a self-help desideratum, but here the rising is a matter of falling, as it were, of giving oneself over to the event. The self-help tradition believes the world responds to technique and strategy. The extreme tradition believes these are old tools, too clumsy for the new realities. The extreme swift self demands new rules which will test the self-help tradition to its limit.

Ambivalence Inside and Out

Swift selves experience their mobility as release, as freedom, as the opportunity to define themselves by their own efforts. They are held up as the heroes of self-creation, as people who point the way for the rest of us. But they also experience mobility as a separation from the community and from family, as alienation and anomie. The swift self asks, "Am I rooted?" The answer to this question is often "no," and under the influence of the right Hollywood movie or current therapy, the swift self will make a brave, sometimes tearful, effort to "put down roots" and "reconnect" to the world. This lasts two and a half weeks, usually. The moment the swift selves catch their breath, they are off again, indifferent to the comforts and securities of stasis.

Partisans, boosters, the can-do enthusiasts, the go-getters, the self-help writers, the Regis Philbins of the world all celebrate the swift self. They insist that many extraordinary members of society are, or have, swift selves. They argue that it is nearly impossible to be a productive academic, lawyer, engineer, doctor, or civil servant without being relentless, adaptable, durable, self-monitoring, and creative in just the way that swift selves are. These qualities, they say, are the source of the achievers' constant motion. They are what makes them essential to a society undergoing constant change and adaptation.

There are those who wish to temper and enrich the swift self. This desire is at the heart of the Stephen Covey revolution, in which the classic swift technology of time management meets a careful and constant determination of long-term goals and moral responsibilities.[81] Covey moves in both directions. He further domesticates the self with ever greater acts of discipline and scrutiny. But he also releases it from the furious activity of the moment that sometimes obscures the values that give it purpose. It is impossible, on balance, to know whether this improves the swift self or further constrains it. Likely, it does both.

The community of opinion that took shape during and after the protests against the 1999 World Trade Organization meetings in Seattle deeply distrusts the swift self.[82] The WTO protest regards swift selves as the storm troopers of capitalism. Its members fear that swift selves, made great by the corporation, will rule everything. They wonder whether the purpose of WTO agreements is not, finally, to make the world safe for the swift self, with disastrous consequences for local culture, local government, and the environment.

The WTO protests were in part a response to the "devolved" governance established by the governments of the United States, Great Britain, and Canada. The supports and the safety nets once supplied by the public sector were rolled back under Reagan in the United States, Thatcher in Great Britain, and Mulroney in Canada. This forced the individual to become more swift, independent, and aerodynamic at the very moment that the marketplace was itself becoming swift and aggressive. In effect, individuals have been forced to take on swiftness, to focus their concerns more on the marketplace and the readiness to succeed there; in sum, to rob Christ to pay Caesar. Some experience this pressure as coercion, others as decentering. (It means, to choose one example, that the individual who works to make time for playing, attending, or collecting chamber music is now obliged to work longer and to concentrate much harder on "this-worldly" concerns.) It marks a cultural shift and the imposition of American values (under the cover that they are merely economic ones). It is quite possible that the recent European protests against Disney, Coca-Cola, McDonald's, and genetically engineered foods represent a moral panic and a sub rosa protest at this exportation of the swift self as the new template.

On the other side, ideologically, there are political scientists and political leaders who see the swift self as the first condition of a new form of sociality. Individuals, freestanding, self-directed, their own agents, their own arbiters, will, acting in their own interests, do whatever they will. Out of this will emerge a social world. Government, we are told, will wither away. This is a radical individualism, but it holds sway in several circles in the Republican Party, and it makes its influence increasingly felt in Western democracies. A diminished state demands the installation of new powers of self-scrutiny and self-creation in the individual. (Similarly, in the Reformation it was believed that the diminishment of the church would allow, and require, the individual to assume some of the church's former functions.)

This may be a workable vision of the body politic, but it assumes that everyone, or almost everyone, will have access to a swift self. This is a rash assumption. It also assumes we will want to live in a world in which swift selves are the "operator" out of which the rest of the world emerges. What does a world look like that depends upon the presence of a polity in which everyone is self-directing, self-motivating, and self-constrained? We do not have a theory of complexity that can answer this question. But it may be that social capital and a public life are so diminished in such a polity that the proposition fails even before it begins.

Perhaps each of us will discover the giant within. But do we have room for this many Gullivers? What becomes of a leviathan filled with leviathans? It is an alarming prospect, especially when we add what Robbins adds to Peale. Or perhaps the swift self will be one in a portfolio of selves, one way to satisfy Caesar even as we pursue other, more personal possibilities. It may be that the swift self is the simplest, most productive, and most transparent self and therefore the best one to ask of each of us. But the swift self demands more and more of the resources and the time that we need to cultivate and inhabit the other selves. We may find ourselves to have made a bad bargain, stuck with a self that is extraordinary in its demands and modest in its returns.

The skeptics are numerous. Academics tend to see them as thoughtless, unreflective, and self-aggrandizing.[83] Environmentalists see them as a danger to the planet, so relentless in the pursuit of short-term opportunity they cannot see long-term costs. Those with New Age sympathies see swift selves as worldly and opportunistic, the humans most likely to offend against the natural rhythms, larger verities, secret forces, higher unities in which the world consists. Religious leaders see swift selves as too much persuaded of their agency, and therefore guilty of hubris. Individuals concerned with community development and social capital ask, "Is the swift self a member of the community—or freestanding and irresponsible? Is the swift self constrained by anything?"

We regard swift selves with ambivalence. They make us nervous and a little despairing. We look on them as the English looked on Americans at the end of World War II—as creatures without finesse or understanding, but manifestly the new custodians of empire. Too often, swift selves and societies have forsaken some of the things that give richness and subtlety, trading away nuance for power. Our culture is so ambivalent about the swift self that our attitude looks sometimes like a classic double-mindedness. We cannot, collectively, decide what we think, even when in the middle '60s this self was in bad odor, or in the 1980s when it was celebrated as a compelling shape of personhood. In an act of intellectual agility not characteristic of us, we are inclined to hold both ideas at once (practicing amnesia, in between).

Transformational Properties

The swift self is a transformational self. In its pragmatism, it is prepared to change just about anything about itself to improve its effectiveness in the world. And the changes are astonishing. As we have seen, swift selves are prepared to strip away the supports of family, community, and anything else that stands in the way of performance. The self-help literature says, "Say 'no' to those who refuse to let you be you. Say 'no' to your internal 'no.'" The most extreme example is perhaps athletic training that encourages the individual to brutalize herself in order to develop toughness. But this transformation is not undertaken merely on the playing field. Competition of every kind is regarded as something the individual cannot succeed in unless he hardens himself. Swift selves do not hesitate to tear out and replace large tracts of the self, as if it were just so much psychic landscaping to be refurbished at will. Or, to use a more apt figure of speech, they are prepared to do anything to the self to improve its aerodynamics, even hack away the contradictions, attachments, and encumbrances of the self, pulling it in and making it smooth, as opposed to those who tuft, trail, and pink the self.[84]

Swift selves will change the body as much as they do the self. Some part of the regime of physical health that has held sway since the 1980s in North America may be attributed to this effort to make the self more capable, more resourceful, more mobile. Running, which was recently such a fad (though it has become less popular), was undertaken not for its own sake but in the pursuit of improved performance. (Movement of one kind enables movement of another.) Swift selves will be the first to install cyber technologies in their bodies. Among them, the confusion of human and machine is no secret fear but a not-so-secret hope.

Swift selves repudiate some of the most powerful and interesting transformational instruments. They sometimes harbor the suspicion that art and design are distractions from the pragmatic task at hand. Their method of problem solving is always to break through appearances and to get to grips with the "real" facts of the matter. Art and design, by this reckoning, are epiphenomenal and misleading. They are more exteriors to be seen through. The enemies of the swift self delight in treating this approach as evidence of a lack of imagination, courage, or subtlety, but sometimes they are wrong. Some swift selves offer outward conformity merely for convenience: another instrumentality, as it were. Beneath this conformity, there is sometimes an originality or eccentricity that would make them the envy of the avant-garde. (I sometimes encountered such originality while teaching at Harvard Business School. I could find myself in the middle of a conversation with a student and realize that I was staring into the eyes of someone who might as well be Martian for all they knew or cared about the conventional arrangements of mainstream society.)

Swift selves embrace the transformative powers of language, but rarely with the self-consciousness that appeals to the intellectual. They prefer language that is forthright, muscular, dramatic, and punchy. This "action language" is supposed to signal that the speaker is competent, enthusiastic, engaged, and, of course, swift. It bothers no one that this language is sometimes redundant. Thus, "action plan" is preferred to "plan." It is sometimes unreflective. Thus, "ground zero" is used to mean "the place things start," when in fact its original meaning, deriving from bombings in World War II, is grisly, tragic, and just the opposite. There is a preference for anything that evokes mastery of sports, especially football ("end run," "three minute drill," and "take the hit").[85] Swift speakers like to refer to themselves as machines, and particularly as computers ("off line," "bandwidth," "granular," "baud rate," "chip speed").[86]

I spotted a swift self while I was doing research on teens at the end of the 1980s.[87] The cultural moment had just turned. (Swift selves come in and out of fashion, enjoying moments of particular currency in the 1950s, 1980s, and late 1990s.) The preppie regime was just ending. Most of the teens were putting some distance between themselves and the swift, instrumental selves that had been cultivated in the 1980s.[88] They were now embracing cynicism, irony, distance, detachment. Swiftness was now for idiots. The classic preppie look, consisting of polo shirts, chinos, and Top-Siders, that had been the fashion for much of the 1980s was now, to borrow a phrase from Jean Cocteau, the "insignia of feeblemindedness."[89] But there was one teen who hadn't got the news. He appeared before us in preppie mufti and enthusiastically announced his plan to become a lawyer. His attitude toward the world captured some part of the essence of the swift self. He said, "Just tell me what the rules are, and I'll learn them right away." This is an instrumental self at work. And this is what it is to live in a culture of commotion. Unlike the tribesman interviewed by the BBC, he has no well-marked path. History can drive the prevailing norm, in this case the swift self, from fashion—and suddenly we are ridiculous.

But these internal and external changes are the least interesting of the swift self's transformational accomplishments. Its great strength is apparent when it begins to act upon the world. Here it is driven by two things:[90] a brute curiosity that asks, "What is possible?" and a brute urge that asks, "Can I do it?"[91] The quintessential swift self, I sometimes think, belongs to the Army Corps of Engineers. These clear-eyed zealots redirect rivers, level mountains, bridge chasms, and pave continents. (NASA would qualify as well, as would its successors, the engineers of Silicon Valley.) These swift selves manage to be both world-embracing and world-renouncing. They work their will on the world without ever taking an interest in their surroundings. This is why the engineering offices of IBM in North Carolina are a warren of white boxes without a shred of color or imagery.

This is why the world's great programmers eat the world's worst food. This is why one Cambridge physicist drools on his shirt front.[92]

What counts is the idea and the mark it leaves upon the world. This version of the swift self defines (and defends) itself in terms of usefulness. It cares about nothing that does not advance the task of problem solving. This is the warrant for what swift selves do. This is the test that lets them decide whether something is worth doing or not. It is an astonishingly effective discipline. It has given us the industrial revolution and now the computer revolution. It reshapes the world relentlessly. Driven by the brute forces of curiosity and drive, these selves have changed the world beyond recognition. Nothing, they like to say, is impossible. And, over the long term, this claim appears to be something more than hyperbole or self-promotion.

This is, of course, precisely what alarms us about the transformations of the swift self. The swift transformation of the world, in its economic or technological form, is relentless and apparently without guidance. It is always an evacuation of the present for an investigation of the possible. But the present is where we keep our collective understandings of what the world should be. To engage in this swift movement into the future is to constantly suspend our larger understandings and goals. It requires us to be shaped more by brute curiosity and drive than by judgment. The swift transformation is heartless, inexorable, and automatic. It is precisely Lévi-Strauss's scientists searching after that "other message," any other message.[93]

Candice Carpenter

We begin with a young woman who, as a teen, is chiefly concerned with the effects of chlorine on her hair. Through her brother, she attends Outward Bound. The problem is now not chlorine, it's white water. She attends Harvard Business School, the West Point of capitalism. She enters the empire of self-help, guided by the advice of Covey, Robbins, and Fritz. Carpenter's transformational arc takes her steadily away from the state of ornamental teenager.

Carpenter enters the world of business. Many of her classmates become investment bankers or corporate executives. She decides on the media, and works for Time Life Video and Television. She runs Q2 for Barry Diller and then she leaves for iVillage.[94] She's not sure why, exactly. But it has something to do with zooming in. The old media are fashionable, profitable, powerful, and glorious—and, in a sense, over. The new media are risky, emergent, extraordinary . . . and little more than an idea in process. In her transformational arc, Carpenter is working her way out of the early, easy stages of swiftness into a more demanding one. She is no longer merely pragmatic, individual, and driven. She is now prepared to work by zooming in, to survive by surface tension, to embrace the extreme model of business.

> In climbing, you have to make high-stakes decisions that affect a lot of people, and you have to act quickly or you're in trouble. Managing an Internet firm is just like that. . . . The speed at which companies are made or destroyed is incredible. If you don't like taking risks, you won't really like this sort of thing. The only reward is getting to the top. Being able to build value quickly is unbelievably exciting.[95]

As it turns out, iVillage is a mixed success. The Web is an experiment. Everyone talks about the glory of new constellations of interest and participation that the Web makes possible, but no one is quite sure how to create them. Venture capital pours in, and in the heady days of the late 1990s many IPOs, including iVillage's, go up like Roman candles. But there is no clear business model, and most people understand that, unless the industry can find a way to pay for itself, many dot.coms will return to earth as so much damp, incinerated cardboard.

In the early days, things go well. Carpenter is one of the few women in e-commerce and she finds a place in the media sun immediately. The iVillage IPO makes her wealthy and famous. But even before the stock price begins to waver, the world begins to ask questions. "Can a woman run a corporation; can she be a swift self?" The *Wall Street Journal* says Carpenter has a "brash and hard-charging management style."[96] This would be praise for a male CEO, who is expected to be short on finesse and long on aggression. But applied to Carpenter it appears to mean something else. Swiftness is still gendered.

But under the sexism are the contradictions of a transformational culture. Carpenter comes to iVillage as a swift self only to discover that she is at odds with the task at hand. iVillage is, after all, about women, about creating community for women. It is not about streamlining the competitive self to make it more mobile, more aggressive, more efficient.[97] Sexism aside, the *New Yorker* and the *Wall Street Journal* are raising routine cautions. Can a swift self dedicated to transcending community serve a business dedicated to creating community?

Carpenter hears this criticism and the transformation begins again. Her version of swiftness becomes still less Pealean and more Robbinsian. She embraces feminism and sees it as a platform for larger social change.

"Women have got a tremendous amount of freedom and when we reorganize the entire social system around that change, including our children, our whole families, and the organization of work, we'll be done. But we're not done yet. We're not done just because *we* have freedom."[98] And there is a stylistic change. The big hair, jewelry, and attitude of the *New Yorker* photographs are replaced by something more stylish, more grrrl.

Carpenter is reinventing the self. She is following the transformational arc that took her from pool-side dolly, to swift self, to extreme self, and now she is looking for something a little more radiant. "They have handlers, you know, public relations people who set it all up." And this is possible. It may be that the new Carpenter is a PR fiction. But it is very hard to listen to the woman giving a speech at Harvard Business School and think this is so. Carpenter comes to feminism at a time when it is itself still trying to think how to claim swiftness without having to inherit its soul-destroying efficiencies. To this extent, she is in distinguished company.

The thing about postmodern transformation is that there are now many transformational routines. They may work in consort or they may conflict with one another. They can make exhaustive claims on the individual or they may work on a group. And, as we have seen, it is no easy matter to move from one transformational routine to another. We do not have any clear idea of what these meta-transformational arcs look like, or how they work. It would be wrong to think that Carpenter is driven merely by pragmatism or self-interest. She moves from one transformational modality to the next according to a great many little factors and one great big one: the American right and responsibility to make oneself up.

In 2000, Candice Carpenter was brought low. She stepped down as the CEO of iVillage, though she remained chairperson and the company's strategist, alliance builder, and public speaker. This was a tough time for iVillage, as it was for many dot.coms. Share price was down to under a dollar. Dot.com companies suffer defections in these situations, and iVillage had recently lost its chief financial officer and its chief operations officer. The *Wall Street Journal* referred darkly to Carpenter's "brash and hard-charging management style," as if this might somehow be responsible. But we have seen this criticism before.[99] The real challenge for her now was not to develop a new management style, but to continue the transformational arc in a manner that satisfied the many problems and possibilities before her. Or, better, the problem was not only corporate but transformational management. How was she to continue the project of self-invention, capture new transformational modalities, and make her way in a world filled with sexist journalists, venture capital, and Wall Street sheep, and the challenges of a world that changes almost constantly? As we have seen, Carpenter has something like a genius for moving from one transformational modality to another. What would be next?

NEW AGE, BRITISH COLUMBIA (AND RADIANT SELVES)

Matt Field is a notable skateboarder. It is hard to imagine him at Hollyhock, which is likely too middle-aged for him, but he has the radiant self that prevails there. He has abandoned his birth culture and the persona of a white, middle-class teenager. He has adopted reggae and a Caribbean style of life. He worships Bob Marley. He wears dreadlocks because they "reflect the divinity within me." He eats a Caribbean diet of rice and beans, because "they are the sun, you are eating the sun."[100]

In an interview with *Thrasher Magazine*, Field was asked why he moved away from the spiritual options of his Euro-American upbringing.

> I look at the language almost like an English connotation like Queen Elizabeth language and then the Rasta language [*sic*]. I'll give you one example. When we say we're dedicated skateboarders, we don't dead-icate ourselves to the dead, it's time to live-icate ourselves. It's easy, man. Look at the things you say: "I'm going back home." Naw, man. It's time to say "I'm going forward home" 'cause you're never moving backwards. It's always forward position. 360°, God, Jah, Yahweh, Buddha, Brahma, Jesus Christ, it all comes in one time frame. It's all multitude in oneness.

Matt Field, let's be fair, sounds like an idiot.[101] But he is not a "big fat idiot," to use the useful distinction suggested by Al Franken.[102] And this means, among other things, that his self-indulgence is an opportunity for ethnographic observation.

Field exhibits a radiant self, porous and expansive, designed to let the world in and the self out. It is existentially promiscuous and culturally mobile. This means embracing reggae and a Caribbean style of life despite the fact that Field is not black, not poor, not a native of the third

---

This essay is a companion to the essay called "New Age, British Columbia" in section 1.

world, not a member of a folk culture, not a victim of poverty or racial discrimination, not in any way, except by personal declaration, Caribbean. Radiant selves are unapologetically mobile, slipping the moorage of the present self and the present coordinates of time and space for new definitional possibilities. They do not all "live-icate" themselves as Field does, but it is not uncommon for them to claim equally ambitious rights of passage.

The radiant self is a porous self. Deepak Chopra, New Age doctor and best-selling author, says we are not "disconnected, self-contained entities."

> Although each person seems separate and independent, all of us are connected to patterns of intelligence that govern the whole cosmos. Our bodies are part of a universal body, our minds an aspect of a universal mind.[103]

This claim is one way to show the porous, mobile self. But not all radiant selves open up to a universal body and mind. Some believe they escape the bounded territory of the individual by reaching across ethnographic space or historical (and mythical) time. For Field, this means making a connection to the Caribbean. For others, it means reaching out to ancient Egypt or eighteenth-century France. All these radiant selves depart from what Clifford Geertz calls "the Western conception of the person as a bounded, unique, more or less integrated motivational and cognitive universe."[104] These selves are relatively unbounded, relatively unguarded, and often not very integrated. In Field's language, they are "360°." They have discovered new transformational resources and they give themselves license in the use of these resources. The radiant self is a florid, changeable, and voluptuous presence in postmodern society.

Hollyhock offers a course called Way of the Shaman, which teaches students how to "enter non-ordinary reality" through "shamanic journeying." This is "an ancient technique for awakening dormant spiritual abilities and connections with Nature" that may be used "in contemporary daily life to heal yourself, others, and the planet." All radiant selves have this shamanic quality. They all claim the ability to leave the present self for new destinations, to cross cultural boundaries at will. That Hollyhock offers this course reveals an additional presumption: that it is possible not only to travel across time or space, but actually to enter a profession that does so routinely. This is an extraordinary claim to mobility, but it is consistent with the radiant approach to things.

New Age

Mythic accounts of the world once appeared in popular culture only as a conceit. W. P. Kinsella's use of one to describe American baseball, in his 1982 novel *Shoeless Joe*, was unexpected and a little daring.[105] By the time the film version of the book appeared seven years later (*Field of Dreams*, 1989, dir. Phil Alden Robinson), it was less conceited and less surprising. A decade later, American television and movies were making frequent and sustained references to the supernatural.[106] We are told that 20 percent of Americans believe some part of the so-called "New Age philosophy."[107]

The typical North American eight-year-old has never known a world that did not treat angels, vampires, and goblins as ordinary features of prime time entertainment.[108] A new genre of film is called "magical comedy" (e.g., *Big*, 1988, dir. Gary Ross; *Phenomenon*, 1996, dir. Jon Turteltaub).[109] The 1998 television season included shows about the devil's helper (*Brimstone*), angels (*Touched by an Angel*), a god (*Cupid*), witches (*Charmed*), and vampires (*Buffy the Vampire Slayer*).[110] The 1999 season brought a show in which the protagonist routinely talked to her deceased mother (*Providence*). Successive seasons have brought still more shows, including *Supernatural*, *Medium*, *Heroes*, and *Ghost Whisperer*. Whether this represents the creation of a new age may be debated, but it is clear that certain notions of authority and credulity are changing.

Plenty of New Age references appear in everyday life. It is not unusual to hear well-educated, sober-minded people say things like "everything happens for a reason" and "there's no such thing as an accident." It is not unusual for them to speak of forces and agencies for which there is no secure scientific explanation: feng shui, auras, past lives, chakras, goddesses, witchcraft, Ayurvedic cooking, ki, the life force, fairies, to name a few. What would have been dismissed a few years ago as superstition is creeping into common usage. Until twenty years ago, *The Celestine Prophecy* would have been regarded as a literary crank call.[111]

This increase in New Age attitudes may be a response to Max Weber's disenchantment of the world.[112] Simplifying a good deal (as one sometimes must with Weber), the notion of disenchantment is this: the rationalism of Western culture made reason the test of every other kind of authority.[113] Some social, folk, medical, technical, and religious beliefs and practices failed the test and were driven out of use—or underground. The results were intellectually exhilarating. The light of reason was brilliant, making new kinds of knowledge and progress possible. But the results were emotionally difficult. Certain matters, especially those of the heart, of faith, of fundamental belief, were put at risk. The "great vehicle of human emancipation" left some feeling spiritually impoverished and endangered.[114]

The New Age seeks to put the world back together again. It restores alternative authorities and the systems of meaning they sponsored. Ancient ways of knowing, such as witchcraft and astrology, have regained a certain currency. New explanatory schemes, such as iridology, have been introduced.[115] Reenchantment creates a world in which feeling, intuition, drama, art are newly credible ways of knowing, and reason and science are for some purposes declared untrustworthy. Even magic, reason's earliest prey and first triumph, has been allowed back in.

But New Age reenchantment faced two challenges. The first was the great rush and fecundity with which the nonrational regime came back. The reenchantment of the world was no simple restoration. It encouraged (or perhaps merely forgave) a fluorescence of practice and authority. None of the beliefs that returned had "time out of mind" authority, and none made exclusive or even competitive demands on the believer.[116] In a more perfect world, one system would have been restored: the Catholic church, for instance, with its presumption of an embracing view and its breadth of advice. Instead we saw the creation of a spiritual smorgasbord. The New Age was prepared to give the Catholic church a supporting role, as the best haven against the new ghouls. But no more. No sooner did organized religion escape the playground bully than it found itself having to deal with notions like magic and witchcraft that it had, itself, supplanted.[117] After reason, a flood of possibility.

The second challenge was the new believer. Reenchantment was able to restore beliefs and practices, but not the authority that had made them binding. It was obliged to contend with an "overmighty subject" who refused to enter into the old bargain. In the old bargain, the individual supplied enthusiasm, credulity, and obedience in exchange for access to the wisdom, clarities, and comforts of the ages. This believer was a vessel, to be filled by convention with convention. Reenchanted, radiant individuals demand a different bargain. They have the freedom to refuse authority. They will not make themselves a medium for someone's else message. They will not consent to serve as a mere member of the body politic. They decide, mostly by their own intuition, what to believe and how to believe it. They choose their beliefs, jettisoning what does not appeal to them, mixing and matching ideological materials without regard for their origins or consistency. Now individuals are arbiters, creatures who presume to fashion their own enlightenment.[118] In Georg Simmel's words, "What characterizes the modern age is the tendency to live and interpret the world according to the reactions of our inner life."[119]

The radiant self responds well to reenchantment and both of its challenges. On the one hand, it is open to the great breadth of materials now available. It is curious and catholic enough to search out the new options, credulous enough to try them on, mobile enough to adopt apparently unlikely definitional opportunities, and adroit enough to embrace several at once and, when necessary, move on. On the other, the radiant self is robust and self-confident, overweening enough to claim the right of self-invention, clever enough to exercise it with relative success, dramatically gifted enough to display the result with conviction, and enduring enough to live with the ideational and emotional turbulence that must ensue. The radiant self is a presumptuous self. It is inclined to see itself as master of its own fate, author of its own circumstances, rightful inventor of the self. The radiant self is well adapted to the world reenchantment has wrought.

Hollyhock also offers a course called Transition.

> Transition is a time of passage and initiation when we bid farewell to old identities and lay the groundwork for a new sense of self. As we dance through the "in between," we are often confronted with the sadness of letting go, the difficulty of living with uncertainty and disorientation, and the excitement of uncovering new possibilities. This workshop, led by spiritual teaching and transpersonal psychologist Thomas Atum O'Kane, offers the opportunity to gather meaning and integrate the many phases of transition.[120]

This, too, is characteristic of radiance. The course is grounded in the assumption that transitions are necessary, difficult, unpredictable, and a matter of personal choice. I believe this course would be difficult to explain to the tribesman interviewed by the BBC. For him there is one cause for departure, one path to move along, and one destination to move toward. There will be ritual officers in attendance. But they will not "offer the opportunity to gather meaning." For him, meaning is clear, fixed, public, and shared, and does not need gathering.

Radiant selves, as mobile selves, move across emotional space. In the early experiments of est and Lifespring, of Fritz Pearl and R. D. Laing, participants were encouraged to move through psychic space, entering previously uncharted territories of the self, breaking through barriers they had spent lifetimes constructing. These radiant selves opened themselves up to their most terrifying fears and debilitating insecurities. They excavated aspects of the self, however odd, unflattering, or reprehensible.

Radiant selves are courageous. They go where they believe the truth is resident. They have discovered and staked out territories within that our culture would otherwise happily ignore. This assault on what Trilling called "sincerity" was simultaneously a search for the authentic, the true, the real that lay buried beneath the falsifications of polite society and rote performance.

Radiant selves, as mobile selves, also range across cultures and epochs. In Matt Field's case, this means relocation to the Caribbean. Other radiant selves take up "residence" amongst North, Middle, or South American aboriginals, or in ancient Egypt, medieval Europe, aristocratic Russia, Maoist China, or mythical Atlantis. Radiant selves wear seven-league boots. As we shall see, there are many cultures and epochs they don't seem to wish to investigate. But few cultures appear closed to them.[121]

Radiance is not curio hunting or thrill seeking. In most cases, it is a search for meaning. Field finds in the Caribbean an alternative spirituality, material culture, and style of life. And he takes them up precisely because they are more expressive, sensual, homemade, anti-instrumental, and natural than the tradition in which he was raised. North American aboriginals offer a somewhat different body of meanings. These aboriginals are typically cast as guardians of nature, mediators of the spirit world, advocates of a world in harmony, and a gateway to natural and spiritual forces radiant selves cannot find in their own culture.[122]

John Stuart Mill would likely disapprove. Radiant participation in other cultures is not an exercise in empathy. There is no liberal compassion in evidence or prospect. Radiant individuals engage in this evacuation of the here and now for their own sake. Something is learned in the process—Field is almost certainly better informed about the Caribbean than most of us. And this is no doubt a good thing. The Caribbean is fortunate in having a champion like Field. But radiance is self-centered, in the exact sense of the term. It is both more selfish and less patronizing than the project Mill had in mind.

Radiant selves move also across species. Seizing upon animals for their totemic or metaphorical value is common in Western cultures. But the radiant approach pursues something more than mere metaphor. Substantial claims of similarity and identity are being made.

Hollywood has toyed with the theme in human-wolf transformations.[123] Siegfried and Roy believe themselves to have a special connection to tigers, with the latter claiming to be descended from them.[124] In *Women Who Run with the Wolves*, Clarissa Estés supposes that a woman's wholeness depends on a return to her instinctual nature and her "feral" roots.[125] Lord Baden-Powell, founder of the Scout movement, encouraged children to think of themselves as jungle animals. The TV show *Beauty and the Beast* (1987–1990) presented "the adventures and romance of a sensitive and cultured lion-man and a crusading District Attorney."[126] In the TV show *Animorphs* (1998–1999), five teenagers were able to turn themselves into any animal they touched.[127] Matthew Barney has explored human-animal transformations in his extravagantly appointed works of art that explore, among other things, the theme of problematical maleness.[128] Erik Sprague has undertaken extensive surgery and tattooing to become the Lizard Man.[129] In all these cases, humans define themselves by characteristics they find in an imagined animal world.[130]

In the case of wolf-human transformation, the radiant self avails herself of whatever "wolfness" means, or can be made to mean, in our culture. Transformation gives "ferality" in a simple metaphoric transfer: the properties of the wolf in nature become the properties of a woman in culture. In the case of the "sensitive and cultured lion-man," the meaning chain is more circuitous. Lions are made noble by long-standing cultural convention; this nobility is recovered for definitional purposes, and then topped up with notions of the natural man and, oddly, the pet. Add to this notions of unrequited love from the chivalric tradition, and the "lion man" captures and organizes several disparate cultural meanings. The animal world makes available many meanings, and many cultural residences.

It is wrong to suggest that human-animal transformation happens only in the radiant tradition. In the video for the song "Hunter," Björk appears both to welcome and to resist a transformation into a polar bear. This, while singing the refrain "I'm the hunter" and the lyric "I thought I could organize freedom, how Scandinavian of me."[131] Snoop Dogg has pushed the human-canine comparison too far for some.[132] In the movie *The Animal* (2001, dir. Luke Greenfield) a man (Rob Schneider) takes on the traits of animals from which he has received transplanted organs. Predictably, this transformation is played only for laughs.

If the human-animal comparison is being made across contemporary culture (and not only in radiant circles), it is perhaps because something fundamental has happened to the way we think about animals. Donna Haraway has pointed out a change in the basic terms of our understanding.

> By the late twentieth century in United States scientific culture, the boundary between human and animal is thoroughly breached. The last beachheads of uniqueness have been polluted if not turned into amusement parks—language, tool use,

social behavior, mental events, nothing really convincingly settles the separation of human and animal. And many people no longer feel the need for such a separation; indeed, many branches of feminist culture affirm the pleasure of connection of human and other living creatures. Movements for animal rights are not irrational denials of human uniqueness; they are a clear-sighted recognition of connection across the discredited breach of nature and culture.[133]

A classical hierarchy arrayed creatures according to relative intelligence: gods, angels, humans, animals, in that order.[134] In this view, any confusion of humans and animals threatened humans with a demotion in the larger scheme of things.[135] But this demotion is precisely what is sought by the radiant self. Some members of the radiant community entertain the post-Renaissance suspicion that civilization amounts to a kind of spiritual domestication. Animals, it is said, know things without having to think about them. Animals do things spontaneously, without the interference of filters or self-consciousness. To those who believe they have lost touch with nature, animal transformation promises a return.[136]

Here and in my earlier discussions I am describing a Romantic contention that "advanced," developed, and especially first-world cultures are corrupt. Traditional and folk cultures are supposed to have a purity and authenticity first-world cultures have lost. There is, however, a second camp of radiant selves who are prepared to investigate post-traditional developments, including European witchcraft and vampire traditions. It is worth noting, perhaps, that the first camp often seeks identities characterized by a certain innocence, while the second seeks something less benign. In both cases, the native Western civilized tradition is vilified. As we noted, neither Japasa nor the tribesman interviewed by the BBC is ever tempted by this counter-cultural exercise.

The useful enemies of the radiant self are several. Reason and civilization are targets, as we have seen, but more often the enemy is capitalism. Many radiant selves believe their mission is to throw off the deformations visited upon them by the instrumental, economistic logic of the marketplace. They make themselves agents of reenchantment and opponents of the swift self without and within. They champion the very affectation, eccentricity, and quirks that swift selves jettison for the sake of improved efficacy. They treat as sources of illumination the very blurring, imprecision, indeterminacy that are, for swift selves, anathema. In another Weberian phrase, radiant selves intend their other-worldliness as refusal of those who are this-worldly.

Hollyhock, in particular, sees itself as fighting the damage capitalism inflicts upon the planet and its inhabitants. It hopes to be the prime mover of a particular chain of events: Hollyhock (and other radiant centers) takes in people damaged by capitalism. It repairs them by the infusion of radiant ideas and practices. Returned to the world (it is hoped), these individuals will carry radiant ideas (sometimes called "viruses," in an oddly threatening parlance) into the world and correct or at least diminish the "business as usual" on which capitalism relies. This "catch and release" program makes spiritual and ecological repair mutually presupposing, and it creates the hope of a virtuous cycle in which what is done for the individual works to the benefit of the collectivity.

Radiant selves particularly loathe the "consumer culture" that is supposed to spring from late capitalism. In this culture, people are invested with a "false consciousness," persuaded to want things that must distract them from spiritual objectives. Radiant selves pursue simplicity for its own sake, but also as a blow against a system that clutters the mind, poisons the environment, and distorts people's understanding of what really matters. People come to Hollyhock for "deprogramming," to be freed from the cult created by marketing.

But it would be wrong to think that radiant selves are merely reactive, that they are driven only by their opposition to reason, civilization, capitalism, and consumer culture. Sometimes the motive for radiance is simple curiosity, sometimes it is playfulness, sometimes it is a kind of nineteenth-century passion to discover and catalogue the experiential world. Sometimes radiance is driven by the conviction that there is more out there than is dreamed of in the present philosophy. One of the consequences of a smaller planet, a better educated world, and the diminishment of the fear of difference is that some people wander from culture to culture just because they are now able to.

It is also true that radiant selves believe that they are special, perhaps unique. This conviction is a product of our robust individualism, an ideological force that persuades us of difference even when none exists.[137] And it is fair to say that most members of Western societies share this conviction. It can best be detected in the life story each of us has prepared—internally, in order to make our life make sense, and externally, in case of examination (or perhaps intimacy). In these cases, it is usual for people to emphasize (with studied casualness) that there was a university president in the family, that they are $\frac{1}{32}$ Choctaw, or even that they come from a family that included idiot savants or the mentally ill.

Some of these are simple status claims—and to this extent the narrative is about upward transformation. Claiming aboriginal ancestry is something else, and in some cases it is merely an exoticism. But the reference to descending from idiot savants makes no obvious status claim and, if it is exoticism, its pragmatic force appears to be more to differentiate than to distinguish. At least one of the inspirations that sends the individual in the direction of radiance is the effort to find and claim specialness. The discovery that one is an Egyptian pharaoh incarnate or the victim of childhood horror is particularly useful.[138]

Ambivalence Inside and Out

There are many things to dislike, even to mock, about the radiant self. There is something facile about it, too little evidence of effort or discipline, not enough that is dedicated or earnest. In the Hollyhock case, students take a week-long course to achieve a shamanic status that in traditional societies is open only to exceptional individuals and only after methods of induction somewhat more demanding than the payment of a registration fee. The radiant community appears to be trying on spiritualities as if they were so many party hats. We are tempted to ask whether the efficacy of an ancient ritual does not depend, to some extent, on the care and respect with which it is enacted. Denise Linn gives no hint of solemnity.

> I have driven a few hotel managers to distraction by coming in to a hotel room before a seminar, and beginning to clear the energy in the room using ancient techniques such as waving a feather in the air and chanting Native American chants.[139]

There is something so unapologetically glib about this, it is hard to believe that the charge of triviality is entertained only by the enemies of the radiant self.

Radiant discourse can be suspiciously hackneyed. One wants to know why imitated selves so often come from ancient Egypt, medieval Europe, aristocratic Russia, and mythical Atlantis, and not from places untouched by Barnum and Bailey allure. It is rare, for instance, to find someone claiming spiritual resonance with an illiterate, tubercular, cruel, and stupid charwoman struggling to raise five children in eighteenth-century Montreal. The hidden agenda here, the criticism goes, is self-dramatization. Unless the participant is made more glorious, interesting, or remarkable, there is no interest.

Radiant selves are vulnerable to the charge of "spiritual tourism." This might be wrong in Field's case. He has made an effort to learn something about his adopted culture. (Certainly he appears to have changed his native language almost beyond recognition.) But he is not exhaustively imitative. It would surprise us to learn that he has deprived himself of nutrition, health care, dental care, or education, for instance. He is entitled to reply that these are not choices made by the reggae community, but unhappy necessities that have been forced upon it. And not all radiant selves are fair-weather friends.[140]

A woman called Sazacha Red Sky identifies herself as the daughter of Chief Dan George and Haida princess Minnie Croft. But some claim she is really Nancy Nash of Vancouver and Los Angeles. Ms. Sky clarified things by noting that while Chief George is not her biological father, he is, in fact, her biological father. "I have never said he was my biological father. I know that he was my biological father lives ago."[141] Once on New Age territory, the reaffirmation of family and ethnic connections often takes on this epic, breathless quality. Almost no one seems to rediscover a connection to the illiterate, impoverished, or itinerant. There is often a celebrity of some kind in the picture.

Radiant selves open themselves to the charge of Orientalism. The radiant self appears to imitate other cultures particularly when they supply liberties the individual cannot find at home. The radiant selves seek not what the new culture is, but what their own culture is not. The ethnographic or historical other is deliberately misconstrued, an inspiration of convenience, as it were. Both Jim Jarmusch's film *Dead Man* (1995) and Kevin Costner's *Dances with Wolves* (1990) show a European male recreated as an aboriginal, less Western and more wise.[142] Not surprisingly, some members of aboriginal communities were offended. James Luna responds with a transformation of his own.

> Everybody wants to be an Indian so they can say they have a culture.
> Everybody wants to be an Indian so they can be spiritual.
> Everybody wants to be an Indian so they can be funded.
> Everybody wants to be an Indian so they can be a victim.
> Everybody wants to be an Indian so they can be multicultural.
> . . .
> I don't want to be an Indian anymore.[143]

Some years ago, a friend of mine attended a wedding that brought together elites from diverse parts of American life. An aboriginal was asked to participate in the service to bless the occasion. In the Western tradition, these remarks run usually around two minutes, sometimes five. But this man, it turned out, came from a cultural tradition that believed in oratory. Two minutes into his talk, people still had the look of liberal self-congratulation, the one that says, "Is this hip, or what?" Eight minutes into the oration, little bubbles began forming over heads that read, "Casting!" And twenty minutes in, the bubbles appeared to read, "OK, you know, I haven't actually *had* any cocaine for at least, well, like a couple of hours, plus . . . hey, what language is this guy speaking, anyway?" Their impatience demonstrated the cosmetic or decorative nature of the radiant impulse. Contact with the other must never be allowed to become laborious, because, in fact, true contact is not desired. Some other point is being made, too often "Is this hip, or what?"

Radiant individuals are seen to be fuzzy, easily distracted, a bit out of touch. This blurriness is a feature of their radiance, their ability to comb the heavens for new frequencies, to hear what is not well formed by existing cultural expectation. It is also what makes them so annoying to nonradiant, and especially to swift, selves, who prefer the individual to be a little better focused and more clearly defined. The radiant self was affectionately documented and lampooned by the *New Yorker* cartoonist Edward Benjamin Koren, whose objects of satire always appeared slightly wooly and out of focus, so as to represent their cluelessness.

The radiant world of possibilities has been accused of making itself a kind of smorgasbord.[144] Individuals tend to graze upon possibilities, wandering from one persona to the next. In the worst case, this wandering becomes a recitation of failure and a demonstration of the capriciousness that caused it.

> So I was really interested in alien abduction, but then I realized it was all probably due to sexual abuse I suffered as a child . . . my uncle, right . . . and it seemed at first rolfing might work but finally I settled on a combo of astral projection and that Shaman thing. You know, but who knows? A lot can happen. Like, i.e., whatever.[145]

Radiance can have a "slash and burn" quality. Individuals move on because they have exhausted the nutrients of the extant self, and they are incapable of entering into a sustainable ecology. And this movement in its turn encourages people to level all the charges noted so far: lack of discipline, glibness, opportunism, and self-aggrandizement.

Radiant selves are open to the charge of fatuity. Take, for instance, their insistence that the individual must be open to the "harmonics" of the universe, forces and powers uncomprehended by a rational, scientific view of the world, and unspeakable in our usual Western vocabulary of sensation and understanding. Hollyhock's Roger Housden leads a "silent walking retreat" in Death Valley.

> The purpose of this retreat is to allow the vastness and majesty of Great Nature to pour through our senses; to regain the intimacy of our belonging in the natural

world. . . . On this contemplative journey, the land is the teacher. In the silence, the great wilderness can speak to us, and we may begin to realize why so much of the wisdom of Christianity, Judaism, and Islam was born of the desert.

The idea that the wilderness can "pour through" us is a radiant sentiment, but the experience is, oddly, not considered dangerous. It is assumed that experience can only be, as Martha Stewart would say, a good thing. The nineteenth-century notion of the sublime emphasized the sheer physical and conceptual power of this experience. The sublime was supposed to work upon consciousness, threatening the integrity of the categories of perception. The radiant tradition imputes great power to the sublime, but it does not acknowledge the danger this power implies. (I am not saying that this danger is real, only that it's telling that it is never contemplated.) It is simply (and perhaps fatuously) asserted that a walking retreat will reestablish the "intimacy of our belonging in the natural world."

I attended a conference on the New Age.[146] It was held, perhaps mischievously, in a conference facility pinned to a mountain above Boulder, Colorado. As one of the speakers described the importance of finding our way back to nature, all eyes turned wistfully to the serenity of the mountains outside. Ah, nature. There was a snort of derision from someone at the back of the room. "Nature isn't a *good* place; it's not a *kind* place." We wheeled around to identify the speaker and it proved to be a surprisingly mild-looking man in a checked sweater. "Nature doesn't care about us at all. What's that phrase: red of tooth and claw? That's what nature is. We wouldn't last more than two or three days out there," he sneered. And we stared out at the mountains once more and, obligingly, they stared back with a menacing cast.[147]

Radiant nature is almost always a benign nature: gentle, forgiving, and wise, the repository of things that are true, elemental, and universal. (This is a widely shared view, and a mainstay of the Disney view of the universe, for instance.) Ironically, Western cultures appear to want to treat nature as the gold standard that underwrites other meanings. How good, how true, how real is a meaning? It depends on how natural it is. And to deepen the irony, this notion of nature, on which our culture now depends, is itself highly selective.[148]

There is much to dislike. A fundamental criticism comes from the distinguished political scientist Sheldon Wolin. From his point of view, the disenchantment of the world cannot be undone. For Wolin, reenchantment and radiance are for the weak-headed and indiscriminant.

They are the "consolation of marginal minds," offering a chance to take refuge in "intuitive, nonrational, poetic, religious, or other fugitive experiences."[149]

But the disaffection comes not just from without. Radiant individuals have their own doubts about the enterprise and they have voiced all of the criticisms we have noted here.[150] And there are still deeper anxieties. What, for example, if the individual loses control of radiance? What if the self rushes out and the world rushes in without mediation, without the individual being able to choose from it? It will annoy radiance advocates that I use such an example—too coarse, too commercial—but something of this fear is captured in the movie *The Mask* (1994, dir. Charles Russell), in which an ordinary man finds himself in possession of a formidable transformational device, a mask. Stanley Ipkiss (Jim Carrey) finds himself only marginally in control of the mask's transformations. Usually, he is pulled helplessly along behind them. This is a stock comedic device (man controlled by natural, emotional, or magical forces larger than himself), but it is also plays out, perhaps, a fear that the mobility of the self might expose the self to ridicule or worse (harm, illegality, immorality). This is radiance that puts the self at risk, that lets things rush in and take over.

Still more frightening is the prospect suggested by the film *Being John Malkovich* (1999, dir. Spike Jonze). In this film's view, the self is open to foreign occupation. Anyone can drop into the theater of consciousness to observe the world through the eyes of John Malkovich, whose porous self is so vulnerable it remains unaware of occupation. This porous self, it turns out, cannot be locked, guarded, or even closed. But there are things worse than occupation, such as the surrender of control. Skillful visitors begin to operate the self. John Malkovich becomes a thrashing puppet as other people play out their desires and conflicts through him.[151] *Being John Malkovich* and *The Mask* turn on the suspicion of a new vulnerability: that in a transformational culture, the self is alienable, able to be scooped up and carried off, or broken open and taken possession of. And from a radiant point of view, this anxiety appears rational. If the self is porous, movable, accessible inside and out, why should it not be vulnerable to theft and occupation?[152]

Radiant selves are open to suggestion. The radiant self works on a mix of curiosity and credulity. It is mobile and questing. It is open to discovering, for instance, that the individual suffered trauma at birth or sexual molestation as a child. Radiant selves are so open, so sensitive, they can detect trace quantities and weak signals. They may even detect what is not there. Things that arrive over the transom do not have a provenance that establishes their authenticity. Radiant inspirations, as we shall see, are necessarily inchoate and hard to discern. It is easy to be wrong.

But radiant selves are thoroughly tested selves. It is not long before the exuberant, triumphant self begins to feel the effect of all of this mobility. Exhaustion, confusion, unhappiness are common. Now the radiant self will clutch at palliatives as it once seized inspiration. Now it will believe anything to get the guy wire back in place. And with this effort at recovery, all of the existing problems grow apace. Now the self is even more credulous, prone to imagining things, quick to move on, and subject to the charge of insincerity. Sensitivity compounds itself.

Radiance is not an unmixed blessing. If the self can get out, disorder, mischief, and malevolence can get in. The radiant self is open to the control of new agents. It can be hijacked by addictions to drugs, love, sex, food, shopping, gambling, or religion, and it can be freed only by twelve-step programs. These laborious transformational exercises are often de-transformational, an attempt to talk people off a ledge of their own making, a way to protect them from the rough air of their transformational excesses. In sum, an unhappy progression is waiting to claim the radiant self: when it makes itself porous, it opens itself to misunderstanding and imagined mischief, and thus to the loss of self-control, responsibility, and, perhaps, agency, and these losses open it to reactive measures that sometimes make matters worse.

Radiance creates, as we have noted, a mobile, relentlessly curious self, and this means that there is usually, at the end of the day, an accumulation of selves. As Irving Howe puts it, "The self turns out to consist of many selves, as Walt Whitman happily noted: partial and fragmented, released through the liberty of experiment and introspection."[153] The radiant self can manage this multiplicity in a variety of ways. The self can be a noisy, crowded bus driven by Otto of *The Simpsons*.[154] Or it may be serene and orderly. But the risk of "civil unrest" is always present as one self conflicts with another—and objectives, agency, and responsibility begin to blur.

A Closer View

Some, like Wendy Kaminer and Melanie McGrath,[155] have made a sport of catching radiant selves out, of spotting their contractions and vulnerabilities. But the radiant self is perhaps not well judged from the outside, nor by its anxieties. It is easy (not to mention facile) to judge radiance by standards it does not care about. But doing so makes it impossible to see the radiant self as one of the new modalities of a transformational culture.

It would be easier, of course, if radiant selves would simply treat what they are doing as an artistic or poetic undertaking. (It is not as if they do not have a gift for this; see, for instance, Field's suggestion that he is "eating the sun.") If they made woman-wolf and man-lion comparisons as metaphors, and not claims to identity, we would be less bad-tempered in response. If Matt Field were saying he was *like* a Caribbean, instead of actually Caribbean, we would be less likely to hunt for contradictions and insincerities. But of course radiant selves won't present themselves in this manner, and they can't. They are, after all, essentialists. They believe they have crossed the ice flows of cultural space and historical time, discovered a new and compelling self, and brought it home. They believe they have a deeper, more thoroughgoing connection to the new self than a mere comparison would allow. They believe they return from abroad essentially changed.

It is better to judge the radiant self on its own grounds, by its own standard. From this point of view, two questions pertain. The first is whether the radiant self left off its cultural assumptions and actually achieved transit. Did mobility occur? Did the radiant self actually radiate? The second question is whether radiant selves occupy in any substantial way the identities they take on. This is what they claim to care about—and these are the criteria on which to judge them.

On the first question, it is clear that sometimes radiance has not actually been achieved, and when it has not, the radiant self is guilty as charged. It is merely traipsing through cultural space, treating the world like a tourist shop filled with dream catchers, mood rings, desktop waterfalls, Buddha-shaped incense burners. But more often there is evidence of movement. Matt Field, for all of his linguistic indulgences, gives proof that he has moved away from his culture and made a real, even when imagined, contact with another culture. Matt Field has transformed himself. His radiance may be dubious on certain counts of essentialness. He may not seem very Caribbean, by Caribbean standards. But he is fully Caribbean by another, radiant one. He has moved away from the culture of his birth in a deep and thorough way. He has taken on a body of ideas and practices that have some of the power, coherence, inconsistency, and holistic nature we take to be the signature characteristics of culture.

The radiant point of view delights in leaping from one set of assumptions to another. It is perhaps not surprising that it is drawn to stories and verbal sleights of hand that lay these assumptions bare.

There was a fisherman in China who was using a straight needle to fish with for forty years. When someone asked him, "Why don't you use a bent hook?" he replied, "You can catch ordinary fish with a bent hook, but I will catch a great fish with my straight needle." Word of this came to the ear of the Emperor, and he came to see this fool of a fisherman for himself. The Emperor asked the fisherman, "What are you fishing for?" The fisherman replied, "I was fishing for you, Emperor."[156]

Whoa! "Whoa"? Sorry. I lapsed into the hippie version of radiant language.[157] "Whoa" is a way of observing a sudden shift of assumptions. (It comes, I think, from a drug culture in which the user is sensitive to the presence of meanings at work beneath discourse, and feels any shifting of these as a movement underfoot. "Whoa" is a remark on the abruptly, briefly vertiginous.) Invisible when assumed, the understanding presents itself to consciousness with force. And it is precisely the ability to observe the unobservable that the radiant self prizes. Wisdom is often, for the radiant self, a matter of seeing the lens through which the world is seen. Radiant selves like little stories of this kind because they catch us (and an emperor) making assumptions.

Radiant selves are constantly on the lookout for another logic at work in the world. This is why they are susceptible to fads, something we particularly disapprove of in those who claim to be questing after the truth. But it makes sense that radiant selves should sometimes travel in packs. After all, the truth comes as a glimmer, and it is possible for all radiant selves, working together like an array of radio telescopes, to pick up what one individual can not. We have observed cultural traditions that are hostile to anything that confounds the assumptions in place. Radiant selves thrill to such confounding. After all, they are open and in retraining. They are engaged in deprogramming themselves, trying to find a way out of the culture that came to them, as it were, "factory-installed."

The second question is whether radiant selves live the meanings they have claimed. Robust and—dare I use the word?—*authentic* radiant meanings are serviceable, habitable meanings. A correspondent recently wrote to tell me that in the first year of her relationship with her present boyfriend, she "went out" with him always in character and always on line. Sustained, elaborate dramatic performances have been played out in the streets of San Francisco by the Goth community. The community attends in costume and in character. "Real" events take place, and the "real" (i.e., nondramatic, non-Goth) world is changed as a result.[158] There are historical precedents that make these performances something more than the froth of a contemporary popular culture. The defunct tradition of fancy-dress parties and masquerades might qualify as such a precedent.[159] So might Richard Payne Knight, an Englishman of the late eighteenth and early nineteenth centuries, who lived as an ancient Greek in a simple cottage beside his ancestral home.[160]

Habitation is not imprisonment. Radiant selves make us suspicious because too often they appear to be migratory when what we want is evidence of commitment. We accuse Field of ignoring the pain and privations of a Caribbean childhood. But are these essential to what Caribbeanness is? Do all claims to identity, to connection, to participation depend upon complete immersion? I think there is good inferential evidence that we do not believe this. Isn't it true that we can believe ourselves genuinely touched by a dramatic story that takes an hour on the stage or two hours in the reading? We do not claim now to be the characters with whom we suffered, but we do claim to have suffered with them, to have made a real connection. Field has done much better than this; he has devoted years to contact, and his performance is thoroughgoing and sometimes remarkable. Movies, novels, and plays give us intellectual and emotional access to the experience of another. To be sure, we would think it odd if someone claimed to identify with Ada McGrath (the character played by Holly Hunter in the film *The Piano*, 1993, dir. Jane Campion) a week after seeing the film. But we would not be surprised to find them moved to tears in the immediate aftermath—not because they felt bad for McGrath but because they felt as bad as McGrath. Matt Field plays out his identification over a longer, more sustained period.

Let us think of this identification in terms of the living history museum. Plimoth Plantation, Upper Canada Village, and Colonial Williamsburg are designed to re-create communities that existed in seventeenth- and eighteenth-century North America.[161] They are staffed by people who dress, speak, and conduct themselves as villagers of the period (and then go home to twenty-first-century diets, central heating, and dentistry). They are attended by tourists who wander in and out of these people's "homes," asking tentative, where-do-I-begin questions as they go. I believe visitors can claim to have made some experiential connection with the original villagers. They can say, "For a moment I knew what it must have been like." In this moment, they feel their assumptions shift beneath them and they gain a deeper knowledge of what this life was like. This is a legitimate claim to radiant knowledge, I would argue. But Matt Field is making a stronger claim, closer to that a staff member at such a living history museum might make. We should be no more unhappy with his claims to identity than we are with theirs.[162]

Matt Field may look like a spiritual tourist, but to see him as one is to judge the radiant self by the wrong standard. It is true that he is not black, not poor, not a member of the third world, not a product of a folk culture, not the victim of poverty or racial discrimination, not in any way, except by personal declaration, Caribbean. But this personal declaration is more than an empty, rhetorical gesture. It goes deep and changes him as it goes. Radiant selves are exploratory selves. They are let loose in a culture where boundaries are down and license is up. Yes, they are guilty of appropriation and Orientalism, but they do come back profoundly changed.[163]

A Broader View

But what about the radiant contribution to the collectivity? Radiant selves are sometimes an advance party. They help to dismantle the authority, clarity, inevitability of existing cultural definitions and to test new ones. They are engaged in a lowlands exercise, reclaiming something from the watery world of mere possibility. Someone else will inhabit this world, and in our culture it is surprising how quickly someone does. (To this extent, radiant selves assume the significance of a playwright, as we will use this term.) Goth was a daft, daring, improbable exercise, until it became a permanent fixture of the social world. It is hard now to find someone whose ideas of radiance, medicine, and relaxation have not been substantially changed by the New Age movement. Jerome Bruner saw the literary figures of the middle twentieth century playing a similar role. He calls it "mythmaking," the creation of transformational resources for the rest of the world.

> James Dean and Kerouac, Kingsley Amis and John Osborne, the Teddy Boys and the hipsters . . . represent mythmaking in process as surely as Hemingway's characters did in their time, Scott Fitzgerald's in theirs. What is ultimately clear is that even the attempted myth must be a model for imitating, a programmatic drama to be tried on for fit. One sees the identities of a group of young men being "packaged" in terms of the unbaked myth. It is a mold, a prescription of characters, a plot. Whether the myth will be viable, whether it will fit the internal plight, we do not know.[164]

The forms for transformation are now supplied by many smaller parties, and radiance is everywhere at work among them.

But there is a more general contribution, the creation of simple license. If it is true that we are all credulous, more mobile, less alarmed by passage, less inclined to take on or maintain prejudice, these qualities are partly due to the radiant selves among us. In those moments when we believe our culture to be in peril, we are inclined to point an accusing finger at the radiant community. But I believe none of us could endure a return to the old regime, when the world of possibility was defined by hard-headed science and the orthodoxies of mainline religions, when the gate to imagination, fantasy, and self-invention was kept by tough-minded experts. Would anyone wish to live in Wolin's world, where the "intuitive, nonrational, poetic, religious" is considered "fugitive experience" in flight from the omniscient god of reason? Surely even the most hard-headed of us would revolt at the prospect of this imaginative impoverishment.

A little radiance has found itself into many lives. It is often the best respite from swiftness, and the way we can recover from the exhaustion and privations that swiftness brings. Radiance appears to demand our complete participation, but, as it turns out, it remains spiritually effective even with occasional use. Swiftness and radiance have an ecological relationship. They are very different creatures who have come to depend on one another. Without radiance, swiftness would consume its carriers. Without swiftness, radiance would prove unendurably earnest, good-hearted, and woolly-headed. But the deal is deeper than this. Every year the great driving machines of the American upper class pour into Santa Fe bearing the sick, the wounded, and the merely stressed. They have come from a mainstream world, spiritually and physically damaged by its demands, and they come in the hopes of recovery, of saving a marriage, of discovering the self, or of dying well.[165]

Radiance is most transformational when it serves as an inspiration and an encouragement that helps people break away from their culture, experiment with expressive possibilities, give up untenable selves and search out new ones. Such breaking away looks self-dramatizing, and it is often accompanied by innovations that make us uncomfortable: Matt Field's Elizabethan English, Hollyhock's week-long schooling in shamanic wisdom. But we would be better off using the language the radiant self prefers. These are self-actualizing creatures inventing themselves by their own efforts and the peculiar ways and means of the radiant approach to things.[166]

Transformational Logic in Review

Radiance begins often with a hunch. Something is wrong. Somehow the world is malformed or askew. Restoring the world is not a collective or institutional undertaking, but an individual one. "Change comes from within." Finally, it is believed that the self that is restored is an essential, "really real" condition, not merely some better arrangement.

What begins with hunches proceeds by hunches. Individuals find their way along the path of enlightenment by detecting barely audible signals, by following will-o'-the-wisp intuitions, by listening to their gut. And arrival, once achieved, is still a little mysterious. New authorities and proofs apply. "It just feels right." So much of the search is nonverbal and intuitive, it is hard to report what happened or how certainty was achieved. The claim that "it just felt right" makes Wolin suspect addle-headedness—but, from a radiant point of view, anything more forthcoming would provoke suspicions of another kind. This is why Wolin's point of view is so inadequate as an account of how the mythic regime operates. What comes to us through reason must disqualify itself, from the radiant point of view, in the process.

There are barriers. Often these are the falsifications put in place by the mainstream culture, as amplified by our socialization and the mental habits of a lifetime. There can be many villains here: organized religion, science, big business, popular culture, Ron Popeil.[167] This is where conspiracy theories flourish to explain how the truth, now so obvious, was obfuscated. And vigilance is necessary: the world can be relied upon to jam the spiritual signals.

When knowledge comes, it comes paradigmatically. Everything we knew was wrong. We were blind and now we see. The world reveals itself. And now entire ways of life must change. What we eat, how we dress, how we speak, all must change. Do we look ridiculous in any of this? We do not care. The radiant self cares about the authentic demands of the inner life, and it scorns the very idea of impression management and social conformity. Some radiant selves proselytize, but some leave us to our wretchedness—after all, those who criticize help define. Often the new persona has been discovered by someone gifted with powers of sight, and then brought forward by the extraordinary efforts of the initiate. Discovery and self-discovery are always difficult because, it turns out, conventional culture doesn't merely obscure the new transformation. It actively resists it.

The radiant self does not care about social status. Indeed, it mocks those who transform themselves to move upward in the world. From a radiant point of view, such a transformation is ludicrously confining and deforming. Radiant selves are also anti-aerodynamic, designed to be open where brightwork and modernist selves are closed. They have much in common with the beats, but they will endure a multiplicity that beats would have found dizzying.

Radiant selves are curious, courageous, and relentless. They are prepared to investigate and express themselves in any number of ways. They embrace the new freedom to invent the self. But they are also driven to escape the chilly alienations created by the regime of reason and the great disenchantment. Good motives aside, there is a ludic element here, a simple joy in exploring the possible because it *is* possible.[168]

The influence of radiant selves comes and goes. Todd Gitlin remembers the moment in December 1966 when the crowd gave up "Solidarity Forever" for "Yellow Submarine."[169] Cultural experimentation and a long period of experimentation in radiance were to follow. I remember someone telling me that drugs were OK because, after all, our bodies consisted of chemicals, and they were merely tinkering with the balance. Regimes of every kind were undertaken to "cleanse the doors of perception" and open the self to new experiences and identities. The influence of radiance continued into the 1970s, but it could not withstand the conservative moment of the 1980s. *Animal House* (1978, dir. John Landis) defines its decade when John Belushi (as Bluto) seizes a folk singer's acoustic guitar and smashes it against the wall. This movie celebrates the insensitivity of the fraternity male, a creature who in the voices of Letterman and O'Rourke scorned the romantic, the sensitive, the questing. The 1980s were virulently anti-radiant, using new slogans ("Nuke the gay whales") to make way for that least radiant of objects, the Filofax.

VOICE-OVER BASKETBALL (AND MALE TRANSFORMATIONS)

A colleague of mine used to be a "soccer Dad" on Saturday mornings. He'd go and watch his son, Tim, a preschooler, play defense. When his team took the ball up the field, Tim would "lose focus" a little. If the ball stayed at the far end of the field long enough, he would put on his invisible magic cape and begin swooping around the field in small circles, increasingly oblivious to the world around him. As the ball came back down the field, his father says, Tim would be caught between the magic cape fantasy and his responsibilities as a defenseman. Eventually he would return to soccer, but he usually did so with an air of reluctance and obligation. The sport was, apparently, less engaging than the fantasy.[170]

This essay is a companion to the essay called "Voice-over Basketball" in section 1.

I played touch football throughout childhood and on and off again in adulthood. When a player makes a particularly good catch, it is not usual for someone of my generation to shout, "Biletnikoff lives!" This makes perfect sense to me at the moment. But I know that someone from another culture would want an explanation. Even after they had learned that Biletnikoff was a gifted receiver for the Oakland Raiders in the 1960s and '70s, they'd still be puzzled. "Yes, but why do you say 'Biletnikoff lives' when one of *you* makes a catch?"[171]

Biletnikoff was an athlete among athletes. That we should see a similarity between his accomplishments and our own is hubris. We are slow, earth-bound, ham-handed, engaged in an event far below the standards of professional sports. Indeed, in the "real world" we are tough-minded professionals who routinely refuse outlandish comparisons. But here on the playing field, no one blinks an eye at "Biletnikoff lives."

In the first case, a little boy treats sports as a distraction from transformation. In the second, it is a source of transformation, so potent it can survive even the most implausible claims upon it. Or we might put this more plainly: very young boys run away from organized sport. Older ones run toward it. We might even put it telegraphically. As a result of some deep cultural transposition, "fantasy yes, sports no," becomes "sports yes, fantasy no."

I do not intend to solve this mystery. (Nor do I intend to mourn it.)[172] I mark it because it contains a smaller mystery important to our theme. By the time a male has embraced the transformational routine contained in sports, he thinks ill of transformation. By a cultural sleight of hand, he insists that he is not transformational at all, that transformation is the preoccupation of the non-male: women, artists, gays, intellectuals, academics, and marginals.[173] Some men believe that all expressive pursuits, even practical ones, fall into a feminine domain. Thus, art, design, theater, literature, poetry, architecture, dance are suspect.[174] In this view of the world, men see transformation as a threat to their gender claims. It is a founding paradox of our culture that men should engage in transformation but treat it as something hostile to their sex.[175]

But there is a simple truth to be reckoned with. In the case of voice-over basketball, an overweight kid with no detectable athletic ability has turned an outdoor court badly in need of weeding into the brightly lit hardwood of the Boston Garden, and himself into one of the great basketball players of all time. The truth of the matter is that men engage in transformation of this kind all the time, using movies, cars, music, played sports, watched sports, and, in this case, performed sports. It is probably not too much to say that the male identity in Western cultures actually requires these activities. Voice-over basketball is a triumph of the voice over the phenomenal world. Attention is focused, emotions mobilized, participation engaged, meanings transferred, and a teenager assumes, in Ovid's phrase, a "shape of a different kind."[176]

So why is it that men should be hostile to the idea of transformation? What cultural logic permits or obliges them to suppose that they do not care about transformation even as they engage in it? One of our culture's enabling assumptions is that men are elemental. By this reckoning, men cannot be agents of transformation because they are never really the objects of transformation. The myth has it that men are a force of nature. They are socialized and civilized only under protest and only provisionally.[177]

This helps explain many of the creatures men find admirable: Sylvester Stallone, Arnold Schwarzenegger, Russell Crowe. And it helps explain an odd episode during the Reagan presidency. It took place in a Washington stateroom filled with dignitaries, luminaries, and celebrities, one of the grand fetes designed to celebrate the imperial presidency and the new Reagan era. This was Washington at its most sumptuous. The president himself was about to speak. The crowd fell silent.

Almost silent. From a far corner of the room came a rumbling sound, almost as if someone were snoring. As it turned out, someone *was* snoring. Someone had fallen asleep in front of the president of the United States on one of the great social events of the season. The ceremonial order of Washington had been breached. The new imperial presidency had been wounded.

People were outraged. Who dared affront the president? Eyes searched the room for the author of this impertinence. Where was the poor schmo who had conked out in his salad? He will be made to rue this day. The crowd would like to set upon him . . . but they are on their best behavior. They'll have to settle for hounding him from Washington into a life of bureaucratic insignificance on the far reaches of empire—in Wilmington, say.

Two legs stuck out from beneath rich linen folds to mark the culprit's lair. Here the snorer lay. A group gathered to look on in astonishment and indignation. Someone peered under the table. He was first puzzled, and then he smiled. The word spread, and now everyone was smiling. The snorer, it turned out, was John Riggins, running back for the local football team, the Washington Redskins.

The diplomatic incident de-escalated as suddenly as it had arisen. Everyone suddenly stopped recoiling in horror and sniffing in disapproval.

No one leapt to restore the honor of the president. Security personnel wondered whether they shouldn't remove this stupid, vulgar man. But everyone just looked at them, as if to say, "What, are you kidding? Let him sleep. He's probably really tired or something." In the blink of an eye, everyone went from high indignation to wry amusement, as if to say, "Well, that's John Riggins for you. Riggins fell asleep listening to the president? Wait till I tell the kids."

What protected Riggins from punishment? Partly, it was the old joke, "Where does an elephant sleep?" (Answer: anywhere it wants to.) But there was something else. Riggins's gesture tapped the way Americans define maleness. Confronted by ceremony, formality, and politesse, the Riggins male is supposed to crawl under a table and go to sleep.

Football players, the theory goes, are works of nature untouched by civilization. They are men who do not know and do not care for the niceties of polite society. Football is, after all, the practice of barely mediated violence. It is an exertion of a primitive kind. Off the gridiron, out of violent male company, obliged to present a social self, these men are bored witless. Remove the elemental man from his elements, and a nap is inevitable.[178]

Almost every group of males includes a Riggins male, and almost all such groups regard him with ambivalence. He is essential even as he is there on sufferance. He will often react without thinking. He will often engage in reckless behavior. He will precipitate misadventure, fights, and commotion. He is gives new meaning to the cliché "an accident waiting to happen." He is tolerated by the group precisely because he is like Riggins, because he keeps the flame for the group; he is an elemental male.

The classic representation of this character in popular culture was John Belushi, an actor who made the cultural form his part both on screen and, tragically, off.[179] A somewhat more nuanced portrayal was given by Steve Zahn, who played the part in *SubUrbia* (1997, dir. Richard Linklater). He plays Buff, a maniacal teenager who plays triumphant air guitar and taunts the world with mock but vivid threats of sex and violence. He is exuberant, good-hearted, red-necked, and clueless. Buff is never really sure what is going on around him, but he is quick to surrender to the impulse of the moment, whatever that might be. His group of friends indulges him even when his behavior reflects poorly on them. He is a cherished member of the group even when at odds with it.[180]

In *Out of Sight* (1998, dir. Steven Soderbergh), Zahn (as Glenn Michaels) plays the role again, but Soderbergh, in his characteristically brilliant way, finds a way to undo the myth.[181] Glenn is another thoughtless force, but it isn't long before he finds himself out of his depth. In a key scene, he is called upon to participate in a savage act of murder, and he is thoroughly undone. The remaining scenes show him wandering catatonically in a blood-stained sweater, still at a remove from the world around him, but no longer because he is a vital, primitive force at odds with it.

This version of the American male is not exclusively the domain of teenagers and filmmakers. The forty-second president of the United States, William Jefferson Clinton, evoked it to good effect on the campaign trail. The cameras caught him in his jogging shorts wandering through fast food outlets. *Saturday Night Live* obliged by treating him as a politician who solicited votes only to get more fries. ("You going to eat all those? Do you mind if I have a couple?")[182] It was a good strategy. Who could dislike a man who was so transparent, so helpless in his appetites? In an era when politicians and Hollywood stars were obliged to present themselves as "just folks," who would begrudge this big, harmless goof his bid for power?

By contrast, poor Hilary Rodham Clinton looked like a self-important, stuck-up know-it-all at the White House. The contrast grew more strained when the president got himself a dog called Buddy. Buddy was photographed doing puppyish things like jumping up on people on the White House lawn. ("He can't help himself. He's a puppy.") The comparison was clear. Clinton was Buddy ("He can't help himself. He's the president") and America was the buddy politic. Naturally, the big, harmless guy routine began to wear a little thin when it became clear that the president was "jumping up" on interns. But it may have been one of things that allowed Clinton to survive the nation's outrage.

Most men live an uncertain, contested relationship with the Riggins male. Certain crucial practices are dedicated to helping them get in touch with this aspect of their character. One of these is alcohol consumption, more particularly beer consumption. In drinking, it is supposed, a certain devolution takes place. Men are given license to throw off their manners and engage in behavior that is gross and disgusting. They are seen to return to their essential condition and make contact with the natural man. Men lose their social skills in unison, moving as a group toward grossness. (This paradox tells us that the descent into vulgarity is, in fact, rule-bound and culturally constituted.) Intoxication helps, but the culture of beer is crowded with rituals and devices for the initiation and management of a downward journey.

The Steve Zahn male is especially useful here. He is the first off the mark. He is the least constrained by politesse. He leads the group into the wilderness and works to engage them there. It is incumbent on the group, and especially the leader of the group, to carefully manage these departures into the wilderness. The Zahn male, or someone in a Zahnian moment, can run out of control. This possibility must be both prevented and kept alive. The evening that is not kept on point will slide into boredom, and a disappointing performance of the maleness these guys have come to renew. Or it may slide into disaster. Unless such a disaster ends in permanent injury or criminal records, it enters the oral tradition of the group, to be retold endlessly and with affection. (Indeed, the retelling of these events aids in the descent into a "natural" condition on future nights out.)

This theme is in evidence elsewhere in popular culture. Tim Allen built a comedic career by discussing the "essential" differences between men and women, and he frequently made a primate sound to identify the male animal within. His television program, *Home Improvement*, frequently turns on the image of the home as a dangerous place for "real men." The show saves itself from sheer stupidity by making Allen's character often incapable of the things with which men usually declare their masculinity. Thus does the show reify what it mocks.

The theme is present in recent attempts to rehabilitate maleness. In his book *Iron John* Robert Bly says,

> every modern male has, lying at the bottom of his psyche, a large, primitive being covered with hair down to his feet. . . . [This] Wild Man is not opposed to civilization; but he's not completely contained by it either.[183]

Bly believes it is because they are alienated from their "interior warrior" that men have lost their way. This message proved inspirational for some. Men took to the forest to daub themselves with smudge sticks, dance around an open fire, and chant to the moon. This from men raised to ration their words, control their emotions, and otherwise "snap out of it." The old model will do anything, even contradict itself, to persevere.

To sum up, men engage in transformation. They use it to perform, to play out, to construct their sense of themselves as males. But only one kind of transformation serves them: the one that aids them in an apparent devolution from a relatively civilized condition to a relatively naturalized one. Other kinds of transformation are looked on with some suspicion. These transformative activities are self-conscious or contrived. They move away from the natural to the cultural. They are therefore seen to be a threat to the performance of maleness. They are the pursuits of the non-male.

So speaks the old regime. But something interesting is afoot. Men are employing new devices to construct gender. The movie director Quentin Tarantino appeared some time ago on the Keenan Ivory Wayans show, according to one press account,

> sporting a Kangol cap—favored by all the best-dressed rappers—[and] pepper[ing] his speech with expressions such as "M'boy!" "Y'knowhudahmsayin?" "Whassup wit' dat?" and other bad approximations of African-American slang complete with appropriate hand gestures.

Spike Lee took exception. He asked whether Tarantino wanted to be "an honorary black man," and compared him to "my daughter's little hip-hop friends . . . basically African-American kids in white skin."[184]

But this gesture is not just the prerogative of celebrities. Here is a passage from a Web page. It represents an act of transformation Spike Lee would recognize.

> yo wuddup, yo this is DJ [name of person removed] from Strong island, im representin [name of town removed], i dunno if you ever heard of it but its a little rich white town on long islan in ny. i was just wonderin if this shits for real or you guys just fukin round, cause if you for real i give you niggaz propz. i am also white but my ass is deeply into the hip-hop rap scene. me and muh boyz from [name of town removed] always been true to this shit and all i gotta say to all tha punk asses out there tryin to diss wiggaz or white boys who represent rap and hip-hop FUCK YOU cause you nuttin more than some tight ass white boys drivin mommys car round, fukin dissin on tha kids who wear the baggy ass clothes and get all the fly hunnies cause you stuck wit some hoe who shops at the gap and don't even suck dick good. i said my peace
> werd ta da wiggerz
> DEATH TO THA MUTHA FUKIN KKK SHIT YOU DUMB REDNECK HONKEYS
> Peace, DJ [name removed][185]

Here a white supremacist uses a turn of phrase from the African American community to declare her racist sympathies:

> That's why I hate Spike Lee. Because he's a racist. And that's when I started thinking, If black kids can wear "X" caps, and Malcolm is calling us all 'white devils,' what's wrong with *being down with* white power?[186]

At this writing, the white appropriation of black style is endemic.[187]

When DMX—who, more than most popular rappers before him, orients his music toward a strictly black audience—came on stage, the almost entirely white crowd pumped its collective fist in the air and sang along with every word, drowning out DMX himself as they shouted the lyrics to "My Niggas." Then our brave troops watched the most popular white rock bands of today—Kid Rock, Limp Bizkit, Insane Clown Posse, Everlast, Korn, Rage against the Machine—shamelessly plunder every trick in the hip-hop book without ever trying to display (with the sole exception of Everlast) any hip-hop credentials.[188]

Tarantino's appropriation of the hip hop style is an uncomplicated act of cultural imitation. And his motives are not mysterious. The African American community has enjoyed stylistic hegemony in matters of music, dance, athletics, body language, and rituals of greeting for some time now. This community is indisputably the master of the cultural form called "cool."[189] This form has appeal outside the African American community because it seems to confer street credibility and the mastery of popular culture this implies.[190] (That Tarantino, boys from Long Island, and Korn fans do not wish to *entirely* obscure the difference between themselves and African Americans is, I think, a safe assumption. As the comedian Chris Rock put it before a house of admiring fans, "No white person in this room would trade places with me, and I got a lot of money."[191])[192]

No descent is intended or implied. Tarantino has not relocated himself in the larger order of things. There is no evidence of devolution. And there is no question but that Tarantino was self-conscious about his choices. (No one is less entitled to a "what, this old thing?" rationale than a Hollywood director.) This was contrivance, plain and simple. In this instance, we see a male engaging in a transformational activity with scant regard for its traditional objectives or constraints. Tarantino was engaged in dress-up. Spike Lee and journalists objected to his helping himself to the cultural symbolism of a community to which he does not belong. But no one accused him of betraying his sex or compromising his masculinity.

Teens like the one from Long Island presumably have a motive beyond the appropriation of cool. Their "conversion" to hip hop appears to allow a descent in the order of things—at least of a kind. They imagine themselves to be giving up the middle-class niceties of the suburb for something apparently more worldly, formidable, dangerous, and sexually accomplished. The hip hop style helps efface the fact that they are "white boys drivin mommys car round." It allows them to relocate themselves, as our respondent puts it, from Long Island to Strong Island.

This is not a devolution but a desocialization. It sounds a little like the cultural logic of traditional male transformation. It suggests that the individual is giving up the rules and regulations that somehow compromised the claim to maleness. But the difference is clear. This is a movement not from culture to nature, but from culture to culture. Furthermore, the boy's descent is not a repudiation of, but an exercise in, contrivance. One does not master this hip hop style by "coming undone," by regressing from the higher-order disciplines that constrain language and social conduct. Hip hop style requires training and practice. There is no imitation without arduous, explicit, self-conscious study.[193]

What's to be said about Limp Bizkit and their fans?[194] A year living in Boston allowed me to encounter several angry men, all young and white, who were prepared to treat the rules of social interaction as if they were entirely optional.[195] As we have seen, this is an imitation of the African American style. And something, R. J. Smith says, is changed in the process.

> But if hip-hop is "for" everybody, it was created by African-Americans, and when white kids pick it up, they can't help but transform it. Right now, what white artists have taken from hip-hop is a towering sense of resentment. Rap today has a well of aggrievement, and when a black artist is sloppy about his rage, race relations have a way of focusing the issues for him. It doesn't take much thinking to imagine what a black rapper might be mad about. But when white kids start talking that talk, the rage often comes out inchoate; it appears and vanishes like a half-formed thought. And it doesn't take much to release it. A parking ticket, a dirty look, a crossed wire, and a whole mass of young men are ready to act as if a substitute teacher has walked into the classroom. All bets are off. And the easiest targets get flayed the worst: women, of course, and gays.[196]

Truly, this *is* devolution. Smith suggests that it is informed by an African American idiom, but I think we are entitled to suggest that it owes as much to gender as it does to race. This devolution would surprise even the Zahnian male. Mooks have taken the process of finding the animal within to new lengths. They are descending into something vengeful, rancorous, nasty, brutish, and, we must hope, short-lived.

The question is, how much of mook behavior is posturing of the kind that youth have often done to scandalize their elders, and how much of it marks a new decline into a presocial condition? Some cultural critics claim to have seen this decline coming. They believe it is inevitable in a culture that encourages Beavis and Butthead, South Park, the Farrelly brothers, Adam Sandler, *Dumb and Dumber* movies, and other exercises in juvenilia and incivility. The argument that today's teenagers herald the end of civilization as we know it stretches back to at least the 1950s, which means it has been wrong at least five times. But I will not insist that it is wrong here. It is, as they say, an open question.

On November 13, 1995, Bill Murray appeared on the David Letterman show in an ill-fitting tuxedo and too-small bowler hat to reveal, with his trademark "applaud only if you feel you must" false modesty, that he was there to promote "his" new picture, *GoldenEye*.[197] He piously explained to Letterman that *his* interpretation of Bond was a "touchy-feely" version, "because [*pause for dramatic effect, assume look of pained sincerity*] the tough-guy thing is over, Dave." He brought along the inevitable celebrity's clip, in this case, Murray theatrically overbound in hemp ropes being pummeled by a man in a bad leather jacket. Murray is heard complaining—without a whit of courage—"You're hitting me too hard. What are you hitting for? We like the Russians now. Hey, that's too hard."[198]

By itself, this would qualify as a prank from a gifted satirist. But it is worth pointing out how thoroughly it departs from Murray's first persona. Murray began his career playing a man with so much self-confidence that he controlled the situation in which he found himself. In *Ghostbusters* (1984, dir. Ivan Reitman), he plays a man so smooth and self-admiring that Dana (Sigourney Weaver) is moved to remark, "You're not really like a scientist, at all. You're more like a game show host," and in *Stripes* (1981, dir. Ivan Reitman), as John Winger, he has chutzpah enough to subvert the parade-ground conventions of the U.S. military.

But the new Murray is *never* equal to the present situation. He held news conferences to declare his intention to try out for the NBA. The joke was, of course, that "white men can't jump"—especially those who are also old, out of shape, and desperately naïve. In a mock interview, Shaq O'Neal played the joke to perfection: "Look, I'll be honest with you; he doesn't really have a perimeter shot."

Coming as it did within a month or two of Michael Jordan's decision to take up professional baseball, this was plainly intended as a comment on Jordan's very odd transformation. The greatest player of his game, Jordan had suddenly opted for another sport, minor-league status, and the ignominy of cheap hotels and through-the-night bus rides. There is very little even in Ovid's *Metamorphoses* to compete with this. If the best basketball player in the game could turn himself into a baseball player (and a minor one at that), surely new transformational opportunities were available to everyone. Even Bondom for Bill. (And, more gratifyingly, Billdom for Bond.)

But Murray's Letterman appearance also stands as a piece of performance art in which Murray takes up a new self only to discover (and demonstrate) that this self is impossible to occupy. This play on the notion of transformation worked in several ways.

First, it demonstrated that some definitional possibilities, especially a prefeminist male self of the Bondian kind, were now simply improbable. No one could present himself as Bond without a healthy dose of self-ridicule. As it turned out, *GoldenEye* proved successful, and this tells us there still many men out there who wish they had a radio in their shoe and the witless admiration of every woman in an evening gown.[199] But Murray's routine tells us this cultural artifact is perhaps on notice. The once princely icon of Western culture is being reduced to the status of a comic-book hero.[200] Murray put on Bondness only to send it up. Thus does a transformational culture winnow and slough. The Bond persona was once immensely influential in Western culture, a gender compass for millions of men. It is now, a few years later, ridiculous, the ready object of Murray's derision.[201]

But Murray was also making light of the transformational activity itself—especially the improbable case. His appearance on the Letterman show said that he, Murray, was no better at being Bond than Jordan was as a minor-league infielder. Both were attempting transformations that did not fit, that could not work. And at this moment in our transformational culture when so much change is thrust upon us, when we feel ourselves to be more like test subjects than test pilots, we find such attempts both deeply amusing and reassuring. Here's someone else who is struggling with the demands of a transformational world, and failing. It's nice to have company, especially the likes of Murray and Jordan.[202]

While Robin Williams appears not to understand his true comedic talent, as discussed in section 1, Murray appears to understand his own perfectly well. His early roles, as noted above, are all about a certain frat-boy swagger, the one he, Leno, and Letterman made so fashionable in the preppie 1980s. The trouble with this persona is precisely how untransformational it is. It is always the same, the smart aleck elevated by his cynicism. Murray appears to be moving deliberately away from this persona. The smart aleck of *Stripes* (1981, dir., Ivan Reitman) and *Ghostbusters* 1 and 2 (1984, 1989, both dir. Ivan Reitman) is replaced by a character who is *never* going to be a basketball star, a gauche and clueless spy (*The Man Who Knew Too Little*, 1997, dir. Jon Amiel), someone who can rob a bank but not find his way to the airport (*Quick Change*, 1990, dir. Howard Franklin and Bill Murray), a man so craven he would follow his psychiatrist on vacation (*What about Bob?* 1991, dir. Frank Oz).

Murray has moved steadily away from preppie self-assurance to new terrain. He made himself into an object lesson in transformation, by portraying characters who could not inhabit their chosen selves. And by doing so, he opened up a profusion of rich and unlikely possibilities far beyond the reach of the former frat boy. Now Murray could play good-natured gangster Frank Milo in *Mad Dog and Glory* (1993, dir. John McNaughton) and camp queen "Bunny" Breckinridge in *Ed Wood* (1994, dir. Tim Burton). Having taken down certain exhausted personae, he could try others on. If Eminem and company are resurrecting the most preposterous notions of maleness, others are taking them down.[203]

But let us continue for a moment with one or two other less inscrutable and less frightening events in the male experiment. We have seen weightlifting change from an exceptional, and optional, male activity to an ordinary and, in some circles, obligatory one. This effort to change the shape of the male body is interesting on two counts. First, it is unashamed in its contrivance. There was a time when men were supposed to earn their muscles by doing things in the world. Muscles were supposed to be lop-sided as evidence of their accidental nature. Anyone with symmetrical muscles was obviously a gender pretender. (The charge of contrivance was doubled when steroids were added to weightlifting.) Second, this contrivance is designed to augment the secondary sexual characteristics of a male. If contrivance was, in the old order, seen as dubious, contrivance in aid of constructing maleness was a particular abomination.[204]

Men have adopted a new attitude toward fashion. There was a time in this realm too when men, again overanxious, would rather dress badly than *à la mode*. But the evidence of a changed attitude is strong. Calvin Klein's advertising of perfectly formed male torsos presents the male body not as an agent but as an object. *GQ* takes for granted that men will care to learn the latest fashions. The steady increase in the advertising and sales of men's grooming products suggests that some men now cultivate their public appearance—and these are the people who were once uncomfortable with the idea of moisturizers.[205] The anti-contrivance rule is now apparently in a shambles.

We might even see a new approach to transformation in the boy providing a voice-over to his own basketball game, playing at being both the announcer and Larry Bird. In point of fact, Jimmy isn't very good at being Bird. His shots fall short. His rebounds are flawed. He can't jump to save his life. What Jimmy is good at and what he particularly delights in is first the improv and then the *mise en scène*.

When Jimmy misses a shot, which is often, he instantaneously repairs the drama. "There's still one second left . . . Bird has the ball . . . he has the moves . . . he has the height . . ." The historical script breaks down, but the imaginary clock keeps ticking. Jimmy becomes Bird plus the improv. The drama goes best when it goes badly. Jimmy is most engaged when least like Bird. What is Jimmy really good at? In this case, it's finding a way to save sport with theater. (So much for the theories of hero worship, role models, and celebrity identification that turn on abject admiration and the search for perfect imitation.)

Jimmy is also good at being the announcer. In fact, he was so good I thought it would not take a lot of training for him to acquit himself relatively well in the booth. He has managed to combine everyman chumminess with grandeur, the voice of history. He is also surprisingly good at sounding like a crowd. The sound he makes in the back of the throat, the one that sounds like forty thousand people cheering, is uncanny.

This is Jimmy performing Bird's rise to greatness, his passing into immortality. "Sink this basket, and Larry Bird's name will live in the Gardens . . . in history . . . forever." He has made himself the voice of record, the broadcaster who describes and inscribes the moment. And he is the crowd as it registers and responds to the moment, and, most of all, as it viscerally acknowledges it. He does this well enough that some small, but not inconsiderable, part of the performative charge remains in place.

Jimmy is not especially good at being Bird. But he is quite good at simulating, with modest resources, the transformational apparatus by which Bird is elevated to greatness. What he's good at, in his way, is apotheosis—or at least what passes as such in a culture deeply interested in celebrity athletes. I don't doubt that the chief objective of this transformation is a construction of gender. But it is not clear that this gender identification is a simple matter of hero worship. This is no dumb admiration or simple imitation. (This is not a mimetic model, but a transformational one.) In fact, Jimmy has stolen the technology. He has appropriated the official organs of acknowledgment and elevation. Jimmy is engaged in an exercise, a construction of maleness, that is in fact floridly transformational. It is openly contrived. And there is no hint of devolution or desocialization. This is a construction of maleness that breaks all the rules of the old regime.

Plainly, Jimmy is doing many things with his Bird imitation. He is claiming kin. He is hero-worshipping. He is trying to "crash" celebrity. He is trying to coax magic from the heavens. He is trying to improve his free throw. He is trying to puff himself up. He is making a claim to preeminence. He is dressing himself up in Bird's greatness to see if it becomes him . . . and if he can become it. He is stapling his ordinary world to an extraordinary one. He is insisting on parallels by constructing them. He is claiming identity with a "great white hope" of American basketball, maleness, celebrity, and athletic genius.[206] And he is stealing fire from the gods.

We send our male children onto the playing field. At first, they are disoriented. They run in the wrong direction. They panic as the ball flies toward them. And sometimes they slip into a magic cape and steal out of the game. Did John Riggins ever slip into a magic cape? It's hard to imagine. At some point, the game did its work on him. Riggins surrendered the cape to become a force of nature, someone so formidable, so credentialed, he could interfere with the imperial presidency without punishment. Lesser males strive for Riggins's accomplishment through the strategic use of alcohol, friendship, and sports. They negotiate an apparent descent from culture to nature to make contact with the natural man within. This is the transformation through which they achieve their masculinity. And it is the transformation, apparently, by which they swear off transformation. Now that they have the keys to the kingdom, they look with scorn on other devices. Other kinds of transformation are now threats to their masculinity.

But this regime is already behind us. When Tarantino adopts hip hop, he is still in the business of arraying his masculinity but he has broken the noncontrivance rule. Artifice is now acceptable. Many men now engage in weightlifting and personal grooming, activities that are unapologetically contrived. There are some really frightening developments here, as young men entertain new ideas of maleness and a descent into the natural man that pushes the conventional idea further than had been thought possible. Jimmy takes us a step further still. He is so contrived as to be theatrical. (If his performance were in aid of anything but sports, eyebrows would be raised.) But more than that, he is not interested in devolution or desocialization. Yes, he is constructing his maleness, but his logic and objectives are profoundly different. Jimmy is very nearly living in a world in which, to construct his gender, he needs a magic cape.

ANI DIFRANCO (AND FEMALE TRANSFORMATIONS)

[A woman] can get whatever she
wants, not by being forceful,
but by being feminine. A
woman is often like a strip of
film—obliterated,
insignificant—until a man puts
the light behind her.

—George Hamilton, movie star[207]

The song "My Man" was first performed in 1921. One lyric reads "It cost me a lot. But there's one thing that I've got. It's my man." When Billie Holiday offered her version of the song, she added a lyric: "He beats me, too. What can I do?" In "My Man," the singer implies it makes no sense to leave her man because she would eventually come back to him, abject and craven.

Feminism puts in an odd appearance in *The Philadelphia Story* (1940, dir. George Cukor). Tracy "Red" Lord (Katharine Hepburn) is witty and self-possessed. But these qualities stand between this "snooty society beauty" and marriage, and she must forsake them.[208]

Tracy: You seem quite contemptuous of me all of a sudden.

Dexter: No, Red, not of you, never of you. Red, you could be the finest woman on this earth. I'm contemptuous of something inside of you you either can't help, or make no attempt to; your so-called "strength"—your prejudice against weakness—your blank intolerance.

Tracy: Is that all?

Dexter: That's the gist of it; because you'll never be a first-class human being or a first-class woman, until you've learned to have some regard for human frailty. It's a pity your own foot can't slip a little sometime—but your sense of inner divinity wouldn't allow that. This goddess must and shall remain intact.[209]

This essay is a companion to the essay called "Ani DiFranco" in section 1.

Tracy's father takes up the theme.

Mr. Lord: . . . You have a good mind, a pretty face, a disciplined body that does what you tell it to. You have everything it takes to make a lovely woman except the one essential—an understanding heart. And without that, you might just as well be made of bronze.

Tracy is a snob and lacks the emotional generosity a man looks for in a woman. The question of class turns out to be a question of gender. Tracy's superordinate airs of class prevent her from taking on the subordinate's obligations of gender. Tracy consents to her family's criticism, and prepares herself for marriage.

Tracy: (To her father) How do I look?
Mr. Lord: Like a queen—like a goddess.
Tracy: And do you know how I feel?
Mr. Lord: How?
Tracy: Like a human. Like a human being.[210]

The theme was still more marked in *Woman of the Year* (1942, dir. George Stevens). Tess Harding (Katharine Hepburn) is a well-known, well-connected journalist. She calls herself a feminist and she has been celebrated for her accomplishments as a "woman of the year." But she is flawed. Tess Harding has been so preoccupied by her professional responsibilities that she has neglected the domestic world and matters of the heart. Only the firm hand and the patronizing advice of a sportswriter (Spencer Tracy) can bring her to her senses. Eventually, Tess repudiates her role in the world . . . and is rewarded with a husband (the sportswriter).[211] In the Billie Holiday version of "My Man," women live utterly without feminism. In these two movies, a feminist enters popular culture only to be diminished by it.

Ani DiFranco was born in the year of women's liberation, 1970.[212] Four years before, Betty Friedan had founded NOW, the National Organization for Women. Two years before, the "Funeral Oration for the Burial of Traditional Womanhood" had been given a public reading.[213] One year before, Shirley Chisholm had declared before Congress, "As a black person, I am no stranger to race prejudice. But . . . I have been far oftener discriminated against because I am a woman than because I am black."[214] Gloria Steinem called 1970 the "year of women's liberation" because the movement was finally getting mainstream coverage. Feminism was now recruiting beyond the college campus.[215]

By the time DiFranco made her first album in 1990, an astonishing amount had happened. The first battered women's shelters had opened. *Ms. Magazine* began publication. The National Women's Political Caucus was founded. The first rape crisis hotlines were created. Susan Brownmiller published *Against Our Will: Men, Women, and Rape*. Title IX of the Education Amendments was passed. The Supreme Court handed down its decision in *Roe v. Wade*. Women were entering public life in new numbers. The U.S. military academies were opened to women. Germaine Greer published *The Female Eunuch*. The group Women against Violence against Women was founded. In 1978, a hundred thousand people marched in Washington, D.C., to support the ERA. Take Back the Night marches appeared across the continent. Judy Chicago's exhibit "The Dinner Party" opened in San Francisco. Susie Orbach published *Fat Is a Feminist Issue*. Sandra Day O'Conner was appointed to the U.S. Supreme Court. Geraldine Ferraro ran as a vice-presidential candidate. In 1989, three hundred thousand people marched in Washington, D.C., to support women's reproductive rights. The Supreme Court declared sexual harassment a form of illegal job discrimination.[216]

This was the second wave of feminist reform (the first wave having swept through in the late eighteenth and early nineteenth centuries). It represented some of the things that could be accomplished by political organizing and legal efforts. To get at something as deeply rooted as the sexism of *The Philadelphia Story* or "My Man" would take a third wave. The categories of thought and habits of a lifetime would have to change. This movement brought forth rap sessions, consciousness raising, marches on centers of power, and a great deal of music, including that of Ani DiFranco. But in an era that was to be shaped by the likes of Fred Durst and Jenny McCarthy, it is not clear that even this was enough.[217]

The third wave turned on an investigation, an anthropology, of contemporary culture. The asymmetries of privilege and power, it turned out, were everywhere, insinuated into the smallest details of men's and women's interactions and into almost every aspect of the material world.[218] They were there in the way Hollywood portrayed the world. Jean-Luc Godard said that the history of film is "the history of boys photographing girls."[219] Nancy Friday says, "I am a woman who needs to be seen."[220] Even the act and the object of looking were constituted by culture and gender.

The rap session became an excavation. Feminists scrutinized everyday life to see where power was being claimed and where it was being relinquished. Sexism was found not only in the obvious things, such as gestures of courtesy toward the "weaker" sex, but in the interrogative lilt with which some women would end a sentence.[221] It was found in the register in which women spoke. When Jane Fonda embraced feminism in the late sixties, she found her voice suddenly lowered.[222] Women began to pore through television, movies, and advertising, the design of the family, the structure of the workplace, the rituals of interaction, the rules of ornament. Sexism was everywhere here as well. The conclusion was clear: Only an attack on the cultural foundations of sexism held hope of reform.

Ani DiFranco took up the challenge.[223] We get some idea of her approach in the song entitled "My I.Q." on the album *Puddle Dive*.

In a sexist society, menarche is an act of self-betrayal, a bodily transformation that puts the female child at risk. Sexual maturity turns girls into "women," creatures whose attractiveness will mean they are never completely safe from the threat of sexual predation, abuse, and exploitation.[224]

DiFranco also attacks the rules of gender. A nineteenth-century commonplace said that men were energetic but not very subtle.[225] Women would define themselves in other ways.

> Above every other feature which adorns the female character, delicacy stands foremost within the province of good taste. . . . where [this delicacy] does not exist as a natural instinct, it is taught as the first principle of good manners, and considered as the universal passport to good society.[226]

For DiFranco, delicacy was a trap. It forced a trade. Delicacy would impose fineness, worship would cost autonomy. DiFranco responds. DiFranco refuses good manners, because these are a trap.

Culture is rarely so robust as when encoded in the invisible rules that govern the body in everyday life. It is perhaps never so powerful as when written into the individual's muscle memory by the repetitions of a lifetime. What is it to be a woman? For millions of women, some of the surest evidence of identity came from movements of the body, the gestures of the hands, characteristic ways of holding, touching, pointing, emphasizing, including. The discipline of these gestures was a gender template, a constant reminder and performance of who they were. Gestures were gender. When DiFranco wipes her face with the back of her hand, a revolution is set in train. She has found a way out of the cultural captivity that gender, as we define it, imposes on women.[227]

DiFranco takes on beauty. This is still a quality demanded of women, and it will be the greatest determinant of the life choices of some. In the name of beauty, women spend several billion dollars more than men each year on cosmetics, plastic surgery, hair care, perfume, clothing, exercise regimes, diet—and magazines that encourage and direct the spending spree. DiFranco, the woman who at one point chose her least flattering photographs for her album covers, will have none of it.

> If you're female, with long hair and fairly cute, you get plenty of the wrong kind of attention. If a woman is independent, it's not seen as sexy. At one time I remember thinking, "If this is my only option, I'll be ugly."[228]

In another revolutionary gesture, DiFranco made ugliness a moral, political, and aesthetic imperative. Only thus can women free themselves of having to choose between beauty and power. Here, too, culture and tradition are most robust when secreted into our vision of the world. DiFranco's attack on our ideas of beauty takes her deep into culture. She is helping to rewrite the rules of perception.[229]

This is a rare act of cultural innovation. A woman, in the company of many women, is getting "under" culture and changing categories, beliefs, assumptions, and rules. How many cultures will suffer the presumption of someone so motivated? How many of them endure the changes that ensue? It is characteristic of a postmodern society that a DiFranco should emerge and flourish. Only here is it possible for someone to engage in "freelance" transformation and in the process create something as culturally revolutionary as the feminist revolution.

DiFranco does not work alone. Millions of women participate in the revolution. But they are not all revolutionary in the same way. It helps to distinguish between three kinds of transformational players: playwrights, off-Broadway players, and Broadway players.[230] Playwrights, of whom DiFranco is one, engage in an act of personal departure from culture. They are inventing dramatic materials that may not exist in theater and certainly do not in daily life. They may be driven by inklings of cultural developments in the works, but they are traveling alone, driven by their own initiative and inclinations, haunted possibly by their own demons, writing from their own needs to their own specifications. Playwrights like DiFranco are inventing themselves, but in the culture of commotion their creations sometimes recruit avant-garde followers and even mainstream enthusiasts. From their efforts to invent themselves can come substantial changes in the global culture.

The off-Broadway players seize upon the playwrights' work to take their leave from the traditional order of things, to stage a new production of the self. They create lives according to the innovations of people like DiFranco. What they do takes courage and imagination. They utterly change their music, speech, clothing, residence. They invite and suffer the disapproval and sometimes the hostility, even violence, of the mainstream world. But they are somewhat better protected than the playwrights, for they are traveling in a group. Their transformation makes them members of this group. They are not, except as a group, getting "under" culture. They are not, as DiFranco is, reconstructing cultural categories and cultural rules. The collective effort of their community may begin to move a culture's center of gravity. But this is not the achievement of an individual. The off-Broadway player is engaged in a personal transformation. Only the playwright accomplishes cultural transformation.

There is an interesting relationship between the playwright and the off-Broadway player, a relationship of mutual dependence and sometimes hostility. The players take their lead from the playwright. They are inhabiting a world that the playwright has opened up. In the early moments of the relationship, it is not unusual for the off-Broadway player to revere the playwright for her revolutionary accomplishments. But the playwright keeps moving—even if this means abandoning the cultural terrain she has opened up. The player is incensed. This is roughly what happened when DiFranco declared, "I'm not a straight girl, and I'm not a dyke" and took up with Mr. Dilate.[231] For some lesbians, this was betrayal. The lesbian community is sometimes obliged, by ideology and necessity, to pull together in its own construction and representation. And now one of the exemplars of the movement was breaking ranks.

DiFranco feels the hostility of this part of the lesbian community, but because her transformational activity is a matter of continual innovation (as opposed to off-Broadway identification), her choice was clear. She would continue to search out new possibilities.

> [M]e and Mr. Dilate have an almost ungendered love. It's so funny that I'm now seen as being the straight girl of the universe, whereas with this guy I get more of a girl than any of the women I ever hung out with. Because we sort of take turns.[232]

When the players demand that DiFranco remain true to her innovation, she is unhappy. She is being asked to commit to the most recent of her transformational manifestations. And the costs of doing so are clear. "I feel like I'm being reduced to . . . a stereotype of myself."[233] DiFranco is not naïve about her role as a cultural innovator. "[P]art of my job is letting everyone project things onto me. I symbolize their own self-empowerment or possibilities. . . . Uh, that sounds so trite, sorry."[234]

But her transformational routine is, in Michael Silverstein's term, "relatively creative," while that of the off-Broadway players is "relatively presupposing." (The Broadway players are entirely presupposing.) Players transform the self according to a collective pattern. Playwrights transform the self always by breaking with a pattern.[235]

The difference between the playwright and the off-Broadway player goes deeper. The playwright is trying to get into culture while the player is fashioning something new upon its surface. The playwright is taking leave of a community while players are struggling to make themselves part of one.

The two groups are shaped by their agenda. It is precisely because off-Broadway players are struggling to create a community that they are vigilant about who qualifies and what someone has to do to remain a member in good standing. (It is this pressure that accounts, I believe, for the worst abuses of identity politics or, as it is sometimes called, "political correctness.")[236] There are collective objects and pressures at work here that playwrights find intolerable. What the playwright seeks, what the playwright needs, is liminality. She wants and needs to find out what happens once you climb the city wall. The playwright pursues a relentless curiosity, a flitting in and out of possible selves, the liminality of Mardi Gras, Halloween, and New Year's Eve without the rules that constrain these events. She seeks a liminality that is openly at war with orthodoxy, both that of the mainstream and that of the off-Broadway player.

The accomplishments of DiFranco and other third-wave feminists are not yet clear.[237] In the place of the standard view that treats gender as a single, clear distinction between men and women, dictating clear and precise rules for their interaction, there are several competing models, the old flourishing alongside the new. Actually, it's even more complicated than this. There are *many* competing models. But this is not the same as saying that nothing has been accomplished. In the early twentieth century, some women had only the tragic self-effacement of a Billie Holiday to inform their relationships with men. And at mid-century, many were obliged to give up power to fulfill themselves as women.

Gender Separatism

We appear to have entered an era of gender separatism. Some observers appear to have given up hope of a rapprochement between the sexes. The self-help books read like diplomatic briefing manuals, saying, "You will never understand their culture, but here are suggestions that will help make your life with them a little easier." According to one conceit, this is because men are from Mars and women are from Venus. John Gray's book of that title has sold 6 million copies and inspired an institute, a syndicated newspaper column, and a daytime TV show—some indication of how powerful the conceit has proven.[238] Gray's empire turns on the idea that most of the problems in communications between men and women come from the fact that they have forgotten that they might as well come from different planets.

Sometimes men and women are described as differing just as species of animals do. Here is a particularly odd example.

> Men communicate through actions, as a German shepherd does. Non-verbal communication is all you can rely on to understand your dog. It is all you should rely on to understand a man. . . . Your chances of turning your romantic vision of a relationship into a reality improve dramatically once you come to recognize and accept that, in a relationship, men are as different from you as they can possibly be.[239]

Men don't have to be dogs. Laura Zigman's novel *Animal Husbandry* and the film *Someone like You* (2001, dir. Tony Goldwyn) suggest that it makes more sense to think of them as cows. In *The Animal* (2001, dir. Luke Greenfield), the protagonist (Rob Schneider) takes on characteristics of a dog, monkey, dolphin, and goat. These portrayals, coming as they do after a century of effort to break down the notion that men and women are two solitudes, incapable of understanding one another, begin to feel like separatism. They promote reestrangement, emphasizing irreconcilable difference just when rapprochement was coming into view.

Trent (Vince Vaughn), a character in the movie *Swingers* (1996, dir. Doug Liman), calls women "little babies" and treats them as such. This brings us full circle. Trent literally does not see females unless they are dressed in beauty, and he cannot interact with them until they have turned themselves into "women." George Hamilton has found an heir.

Vince Vaughn is famous for being something like Trent in real life. A breathless article in *Premier* magazine describes him as playing "cowboys, loners, fighters—[men who share] an unabashed masculinity that evokes an earlier era, when heroism was still believable." Vaughn indulges himself in strip clubs and "doesn't apologize for any of it." Vaughan has some of Trent's elemental quality, the ancient confidence that the male point of view is really the only point of view. "There's only one truth going on, one reality happening."[240] (Sometimes the comparison with a German Shepherd doesn't seem far-fetched at all.) Vaughn's new definition of maleness began to appear elsewhere. In *L.A. Confidential*, *The Insider*, *Romper Stomper*, and *Gladiator*, Russell Crowe presented a succession of charismatic males, all of whom seemed, as Manohla Dargis put it, "securely out of touch with their feminine side."[241]

Vaughn may represent the attempt to resurrect the old stereotypes. But it is also true that he has been called into being by feminism. Sometime in the last two decades, an odd collaboration took place. Some women decided to chuck feminism and return to the old forms. And Vaughn is well suited to this group; a "real" man for "real" women, so to say. A second group decided that beauty was a source of power for women and that, as long as women were in control, they should use their sexuality to political effect. This appears to be the theme of Madonna's "Material Girl" (1985) video.[242] This was modeled on Marilyn Monroe's performance of the song "Diamonds Are a Girl's Best Friend" in *Gentlemen Prefer Blondes* (1953, dir. Howard Hawks), and it said that as long as the social performance of femaleness was knowing, calculated, and unforced, women could present themselves as "boy toys" and use their sexuality to "play" or control men.[243]

This new regime depended on two cultural developments: the feeling for irony that has found its way into popular culture,[244] and the feeling for camp that had been so successfully cultivated by the gay community.[245] These allowed women to present themselves as sexual creatures without re-creating the old power relations. (Indeed, they could present themselves as sexual creatures as a way of protesting old power relations.)[246] They could be sexual without surrendering what DiFranco calls the "breakable, take-able" body to male consumption. Madonna's strategy allowed women to insist that their sexuality was play and performance. It put a woman's sexuality in quotation marks, and it gave her the right to withdraw the performance when it was read according to the rules of the old regime. In a kind of reversal of Silverstein's rule of diplomatic nonindexicality, Madonna's strategy allowed women to say, "I was just playing."

Having reappropriated their sexuality, women were now prepared to use beauty. And now some of them wanted, not the sensitive males of the early '80s, but someone more robust and forthcoming. The unkind view said, "Of course they want guys like Vaughn. You can 'play' a guy like Vaughn." The more generous view said, "Now that women have returned to their sexuality, they want men to return to theirs." The stuff of intrigue and connection, the argument went, was difference instead of sameness. Forget the Alan Alda routines, and let's get on with it. As long as it is clear that there are new rules in place and that women are not going to trade power for beauty, the sexes can once again interact as profoundly different creatures. A rough equality was now in place, and neither sex was going to pay a higher price than the other. A man like Vaughn wasn't going to be capable of much sensitivity, but, empowered by feminism, women no longer needed sensitivity in a male to protect them from systemic sexism.

Ah, but men were changing too. Let us pull back and see the full context of a Vince Vaughn. The later 1990s saw the rise of single malt whiskies, steak houses, cigar bars, and rat-pack masculinity; this trend was captured and amplified by the movie *Swingers*.[247] There was also an extraordinary rise in the popularity of swing music.[248] Does this represent a new approach to gender? Swing bands were called Big Rude Jake, Cherry Poppin' Daddies, and Sugar Daddy Swing Kings.[249] Men returned to two-fisted drinking, hard liquor, and a conventional "steak and potatoes" cuisine.[250] This was a world in which the men were men and the women were easy . . . or in the formula that was sometimes preferred, men were men and women just had to put up with it. As in the disco fad of the 1970s, men were the marked species, with broad-shouldered suits and wide-brimmed fedoras.[251] It is probably not coincidental that several magazines emerged in this period that include women as estrogen events only, including *Maxim* and *Loaded*.[252]

Men were taking back the high ground. There is no reliable ethnography, but one heard reports of women sitting patiently as men returned to the simplicities of sirloin steaks and Cuban cigars. Vaughn's remark that "There's only one truth going on, one reality happening" turns out to have a rider, something like "and it's a male truth, a male reality." The possibility of a frank, brave equality seemed to break down almost immediately. Madonna femaleness and rat-pack masculinity created two solitudes, a world where men and women retreat to their corners, forget what feminism has taught them, play out the drama of gender in the most hackneyed terms, and return, in effect, to a world in which both sexes repudiate an anthropological view of the other for something more mechanical. This approach says, in effect, "Who knows how men [or women] think? This is what you do to keep them happy." I asked a friend what she thought of the return of swing and rat-pack masculinity and she said, "Let them have their cigar bars and get it out of their systems. I'm grateful if that's all it takes." This returns us to the notion that "men will be men," and to gender separatism.

The Madonna strategy proved too much for some men. It demanded the ability to see quotation marks, irony, and performance, and because many of them were raised in a sexist regime to treat subtlety as a non-male characteristic, they found it confusing. For the Vaughns of the world, a femaleness constructed out of camp and irony was an impossible subtlety. For many, and especially the Zahnian male, things had become very confusing indeed.

We may think of this as a failure of the quotation marks. As it turned out, when men re-created *their* masculinity, they were actually moving away from the possibility of an ironic view. This was a performance of gender, to be sure, but this performance was seen as the recovery of an authentic type. Men wanted us to think of it as a return to the real thing, and to believe that their gender was something natural and precultural. They were disinclined to see female performances as ironic. After all, the last thing a "real man" wants is someone *playing* femaleness.

I listen to some men talk about feminism and it seems to me that they are like cattle who have just discovered an electric fence in the far pasture. They are not entirely clear about what it is, but they have a plan: "don't go over there." To these men, the Madonna video was a kind of all-clear signal that gave them license to revert to old ideas and behaviors, and they did so with relief and gratitude. They know that certain comments and behaviors get them in trouble. But it turns out that if you avoid these, the world pretty much returns to normal. At around this time, figures like Tim Allen offered a stand-up comedy routine which claimed that men were really primates: simple, thoughtless creatures, equipped with appetites and relatively few other faculties. This figure proved so successful that Allen created a television series around it called *Home Improvement*, which proved sensationally successful.[253] America was eager to restore old rules and old roles.

Well, we might expect something like this. Gender is so close to the cultural orientation of the individual that it is difficult for someone raised in one era to fully adapt to a new one. Perhaps, the argument goes, it's just a matter of letting prerevolutionary males die out. Perhaps the next generation will produce a more sensible, sophisticated male. Males are, after all, the creations of a popular culture largely dominated by irony. If anyone can see quotation marks, it should be them.

Eminem (Marshall Mathers) is a rap artist from Detroit. He has been called the "great white hope" of hip hop. His *Marshall Mathers LP* was released in the summer of 2000 and sold almost 2 million copies in its first week of release. As of 2007, it had shipped more than 10 million copies, which is to say that, at one point, it was selling at a clip of a million albums a month.[254] Eminem is, among other things, a measure of the extent to which hip hop has crossed over from an African American audience to a large white audience. The world waited to see if he would be punished for his hubris as Vanilla Ice had been, but talent and Dr. Dre's sponsorship got him through. He is now an extraordinarily influential young man. If the new generation of males is coming to a new understanding of women, we might expect to find it here. In a song called "Kim," a song apparently about his wife, one of the lyrics reads, "Now shut the fuck up and get what's comin' to you."

In a sense, Eminem marks the return of Andrew Dice Clay, *né* Andrew Dice Silverstein. This comedian was driven from the public stage for his homophobia, his racism, and especially his sexism. Feminists, film critics, politicians, experts spoke out in indignation.[255] It is interesting to note that, less than ten years later, there is not enough public outcry to threaten his successor with the same fate.

Eminem claims transformation as his defense. Songs of violence come from his stage persona, Slim Shady, he says, not from the man himself, Marshall Mathers III. Critics of pop music have spoken up in his defense. Eminem is an artist and demands the rights of one. (It is a nice irony that popular artists have given up asking us to give them the dignity of the high artist and now demand that we give them the liberty of the avant-garde one.) But the larger question remains: who is responsible? What is the locus of responsibility? It does not seem to me any defense at all to say, "Slim Shady did it." Slim Shady remains Eminem's creation and his responsibility.[256] And if, for a moment, we accept the right of the artist to exercise especially free speech, that artists have the right to explore culture freely and without constraint, it is not clear that sexism, violence against women, or misogyny is in any way clarified by this music. It is a safe bet that a song like "Kim" has provoked and justified more hostility toward women than it has illuminated. There is no question that Eminem is talented in ways his competitors cannot dream of, but it is not clear that he is an artist in any of the ways that matter.

Two other members of what Steve Dollar aptly calls the neo-cracker elite, Limp Bizkit and Kid Rock, are famous for their misogyny and offer no such defense.[257] In the world of the mook, women are bitches and hos.[258] The term "ho" (an abbreviation of "whore") is such a fixture of rap lyrics, only the most original of lyricists can do without it. By one count, some 4,559 hip hop songs contain the word.[259] In the mook world, women appear to play out the hip hop drama of a pimp and his hos, to supply cigarettes, sexual services, and admiration. Still worse, they are frequently presented as legitimate targets of the mook's hair-trigger violence. This is a campaign of diminishment so at odds with the feminist revolution as to take one's breath away.

This diminishment has not gone unchallenged. Sarah Jones, in a song called "Your Revolution," says, "the real revolution ain't about booty size, or the Versaces you buys."

Queen Latifah opens "U.N.I.T.Y." with the question "Who you calling a bitch?" The chorus is "You gotta let them know, you ain't no a bitch or a ho."

Kandi, in a song called "Don't Think I'm Not," tells the male listener that she will match his indifference to her.[260] Even the hit song by Destiny's Child, "Say My Name," may be read as a refusal of the hip hop inclination to reduce women to sexual opportunities. It is not clear, though, that these acts of resistance have done anything to diminish the mook hostility toward women. *Rockrgrl* editor Carla DeSantis complained recently of how few people have spoken out.[261]

Generally, it looks as if the mooks have won the day. Their notion of gender prevails in high schools and on street corners. Far from coming to appreciate the new subtleties on which feminism depends, these young men are creating a world that makes their elders look like paragons of discernment. Mook masculinity is terrorized and terrorizing. These men are obviously deeply frightened. Hip hop music is an outpouring of their fear, but it is also, and more frighteningly, an attempt to reimpose asymmetries and to regain power. Contemporary teen women might find in Billie Holiday's "My Man" a song that speaks to them.[262]

I have drawn this argument rather too generally and with a tendency toward pessimism. There is evidence of small developments from which we may draw hope. Let us consider the television series *Sex and the City*.[263] Carrie Bradshaw (Sarah Jessica Parker) is a columnist and "sexual anthropologist" for the *New York Star*. She and three friends "vow to stop worrying about finding the perfect male and start having sex like men."[264] Charlotte is keen on relatively conventional gender relations, including courtship and marriage. Samantha is a sexually adventurous public relations executive. To her, men are disposable creatures from whom and to whom commitment would be a bore. Miranda goes out with younger men and is inclined to cynicism. "If a man is over 30 and single, there's something wrong with him, it's Darwinian—they're being weeded out from propagating the species."[265]

Carrie is perhaps the most complex of the characters. There are moments when she is sometimes uncomfortably close to Billie Holiday in her dependence on Mr. Big (Chris Noth). But as the sexual anthropologist, she is more often mulling over a field of possibilities. "Maybe some women aren't meant to be tamed. Maybe they just need to run free til they find someone just as wild to run with them."[266]

Carrie and her three friends represent a range of possibility. The show is not simply following the Spice Girls' strategy of creating enough variety that the viewer can find someone with whom to identity. It seems more likely that it expects viewers to like and identify with all four characters. The show is a bundle of transformational opportunities, a set of options to be moved into and out of.[267]

John Ellis has observed this pattern elsewhere, and he proposes that such multiple identification is one of the ways we consume the movies. When watching, we identify

> with the various positions that are involved in the fictional narration: those of hero and heroine, villain, big-part player, active and passive character. Identification is therefore multiple and fractured, a sense of seeing the constituent parts of the spectator's own psyche paraded before her or him.[268]

This might be the state of gender at the moment. The gender revolution may have made playwrights of us all. There are now many, many options, and, for many people, no clear cultural mandate that makes one of them the compelling choice. More to the point, there is now so much transformational appetite in play that the *Sex and the City* fan might seek out all four opportunities for identification even if one of them *were* culturally mandated.

Here are two images with which to close the essay: Meg Ryan in *You've Got Mail* (1998, dir. Nora Ephron) and Jennifer Lopez in *Out of Sight* (1998, dir. Steven Soderbergh). In the first, Meg Ryan plays Kathleen Kelly, the owner of a little bookstore that trembles on the edge of insolvency, its sales diminished by the arrival of a "big box" bookstore. In an e-mail exchange with an anonymous correspondent, Kelly seeks advice on what to do. Little does she know that her correspondent is Joe Fox (Tom Hanks), the owner of the big store, and, irony of ironies, Fox tells Kelly to fight her opponent with everything she's got. As her bookstore begins to prepare for the contest ahead, we see Kelly in the back, shadow-boxing in an athletic reverie, throwing stylized punches in the air, and wrinkling her nose in a show of toughness. We can hear her repeating something under her breath. We strain to hear. "Float like a butterfly, sting like a bee." She is reciting the Muhammad Ali mantra. Kelly is not actually preparing for physical confrontation. This is clear. She is mustering her resolve. She is preparing for war.

In the second, Jennifer Lopez plays Karen Sisco, a U.S. marshal who is taken hostage by Jack Foley (George Clooney) and Buddy Bragg (Ving Rhames) during a jailbreak. Sisco escapes the two outlaws and joins the FBI manhunt intended to recapture them. We watch Sisco defend Foley's girlfriend with cool efficiency. Later, she talks to Kenneth (Isaiah Washington), the brother-in-law of another prisoner. She identifies him as a fighter and they talk about the sport for a moment. Things get awkward.

Kenneth: You like the fights, you like the rough stuff? Yeah, I bet you do. I bet you like to get down and tussle a little bit. Like my dog Toughie . . . before she got run over. We used to get down on the floor and tussle all the time. I used to say to her, "You're a good bitch, Toughie, here's a treat for ya." And I'd give Toughie what all good bitches like best. And you know what that is? A bone. I give you a good bone, too, girl.

Sisco: You're not my type.

Kenneth: [*laughs*] That shit don't mean nothing to me. I let the [indistinct] out, you going to do what it wants.

Sisco: I gotta go, Kenneth. Maybe we'll see one another sometime.

Kenneth: No, we're going to tussle first.

[*Sisco takes a collapsible metal pole from her handbag. She strikes Kenneth first on the arm and then on the side of the head. He falls onto a sofa, holding his head.*]

Kenneth: Damn it! What the fuck was that?

Sisco: You wanted to tussle, we tussled.[269]

Sisco is peculiarly without bravado in all of this. She responds to Kenneth's threat, as she does to the attack on Foley's girlfriend, without drama. We get none of the stern-jawed impassivity, the willed blankness, with which male action heroes prove they are not afraid. When she dispatches Kenneth, she does so dispassionately and without heroic exertion. She merely knocks him down, forgoing the genre's preferred outcome, which would be to render him prostrate and unconscious. Kenneth is astonished, and asks how the rules of gender could have been so violated. The answer (and here we get a small note from the heroic idiom: steely understatement) is "You wanted to tussle, we tussled," which might be read as "You presumed to call rape 'tussling.' Allow me to diminish this beating the same way."

Sisco foregoes the triumphant language that male cinematic heroes find so irresistible. (Examples are legion: Bruce Willis's "Yippeekieay, motherfucker," Schwarzenegger's "I'll be back," Clint Eastwood's "Make my day.")[270] She does not indulge in the rhetoric of superordination, in which the vanquished is humiliated and finally unmanned. There is just the quiet, almost *sotto voce*, "You wanted to tussle, we tussled." The real work of the phrase is done by quiet implication. As Sisco speaks this line, she closes the collapsible pole, in another undemonstrative, anti-phallic gesture.

These scenes face in two directions, backward to the old regime of femaleness and forward to a new possibility. In *You've Got Mail*, Kathleen Kelly is putting on a persona to prepare herself for the battle with Joe Fox's bookstore. She is turning herself into a prizefighter, into Muhammad Ali on the eve of his triumph over Sonny Liston.[271] This is not the transformation of voice-over basketball. Kelly's enactment of Ali does not, actually, make her anything like him. It serves, instead, to show how little they have in common.

Watching Kelly do her Ali imitation, we are meant to think, "How adorable." And when we do, Kelly (and Ryan, and, of course, Ephron) has succeeded in one of the classic devices by which Western cultures have constructed gender: diminishing through contrast.[272] Shadowboxing allows Kelly to show how small she is, and thus how unthreatening she is. Kelly may be preparing to compete with a big-box bookstore and its male owner, but don't worry, she is still sweet, adorable little Kelly.[273]

Sisco, on the other hand, is engaging in male behavior without apology. Furthermore, she manages to strip this behavior of its gender markers. She foregoes the heroism, the triumphant superordination, the display of courage on which Hollywood normally relies to persuade us of a character's manliness. She and the filmmakers have opened up a space between the two termini of the conventional scheme. Women must either apologize for male behavior or be accused of imitating it. Sisco manages to exercise a power and violence that are not male power and violence.

This seems to me to complete the process that DiFranco begins. If we think of DiFranco as engaged in an archaeology designed to get at the deep construction that genders the world and that marks out certain powers and capacities for men, we may think of the Sisco character as giving us proof that there is a habitable world "on the other side," as it were. She exercises a power that has no trace of apology or appropriation. It is now merely what a woman does. She exercises a power that has no gender.

That this liberates men as well as women is, I think, evident. Now men can imagine power that does not oblige them to engage in ludicrous posturing. They may escape the trade-off that gives them power but forces them to look like idiots. They need no longer declare their masculinity so hyperbolically that the viewer is obliged to ask whether they do not protest too much. Most of all, it gives them the opportunity to escape the exaggerations of a mook masculinity at the very moment that Eminem has made it a fatally injured enterprise.

Gender is itself the object of transformation. In a way that would astonish traditional, hierarchical, and modern societies alike, it is now open to the constructive efforts of diverse parties. The mainstream feminism that began in 1970 has proceeded by two paths, one a matter of law, the other a matter of culture. Following the second, Ani DiFranco breaks into culture to change fundamental notions of the body, grace, and beauty, the deep residence of what and how a woman is. She plays a playwright for players, who play playwrights for the rest of us, as new transformational opportunities open up. But DiFranco feminism meets with another revolutionary force, what we have called the "Madonna strategy." This used the quotation marks of irony and camp to rehabilitate old forms of femaleness. By this strategy, it was hoped, sexual power could be got without paying the price of gender asymmetry.

The male reaction was rat-pack or swing masculinity, a rehabilitation of another kind. But this reaction bore no quotation marks. Men were reasserting a naturalistic claim to power. Our hope that this reaction is confined to a single (and soon irrelevant) generation is dashed by the rise of the mooks, who assert the claim with something like gender terrorism.

There is a little evidence to suggest that all may not be lost. The multiplicity of the viewer's participation in *Sex and the City* suggests that some women are cultivating a portfolio of gender possibilities. And the Sisco character in *Out of Sight* suggests that popular culture may be creating notions of femaleness entirely consistent with the feminist, the DiFranco transformation.

MARTHA STEWART (AND STATUS TRANSFORMATIONS)

Why is Martha Stewart selling things at Kmart?[274] Surely, as a taste maven, she is misplaced there. When Kid Rock wears a Kmart t-shirt, we suppose he's honoring his "hick town" roots.[275] But Martha Stewart? Isn't she the girl who worked so hard to put New Jersey and ethnicity behind her? Isn't she the woman who has made herself an arbiter of taste, the one who lived for the cameras in a great house in Connecticut, the one who wouldn't be caught dead in the company of Kid Rock or a Kmart t-shirt?

The short answer is upward transformation. Stewart is selling status. Clay Timon calls *Martha Stewart Living* "very middle-American, with a slight aspiration—not to reach Rodeo Drive, but to live life a little better."[276] She is instructing Kmart shoppers in the small details of self- and home construction on which certain status transformations depend. She is doing what Lisa Birnbach and Ralph Lauren did in the 1980s. Birnbach and Lauren addressed themselves to the middle class. A decade later, in keeping with the diffusion cascade, Stewart speaks to a lower middle and lower class. Kmart is not so odd a choice for Stewart. It is, after all, the best place for her to reach out to the likes of Kid Rock when he decides to "decorate the place." Ms. Stewart may not like it, but, for status diffusion purposes, Kid Rock is "her people."[277]

Upward Transformation: Recapping

Upward transformation is defined for our purposes as how individuals change themselves to change their social standing. They cultivate exteriors (e.g., clothing, speech, and deportment), interiors (e.g., thought, emotion, and outlook), companions (e.g., neighbors, students, colleagues, club members), and possessions (large and small).[278] Upward transformation takes place in three rounds. The first round is a growing mastery of the distinctions that categorize exteriors, interiors, companions, and possessions, the qualities that sort them into high and low. The second round consists of two changes, one in inward experience and the other in

---

This essay is a companion to the essay called "Martha Stewart" in section 1 and the one called "Upward Transformation" in section 3.

outward performance. In the third round, if experience and performance are persuasive, individuals feel themselves, and are seen to be, creatures of a different kind. They move upward. They have higher status. And with this, they complete their relocation in the social scheme of things. Upward transformation, then, has a treble character; it is many little changes undertaken in the creation of two larger changes in the creation of a still larger change.

The details of the first round of changes are specified by international, national, and local status communities. The individual begins to master differences that were before invisible or unimportant.[279] Speech, clothing, and deportment, to begin with the exteriors, open to reveal a set of distinctions.[280] This can be an obvious difference: does one use a diphthong or not? Or it can be a subtle one: where should the second button on a man's dress shirt fall?[281] These are not distinctions for the sake of distinction. It is precisely the possession of the higher-marked item that creates a sense of being higher. "No, of course, we would never pronounce it that way. One doesn't."[282]

The second round consists, first, in a change in experience. Now that individuals have the ability to observe fine details, they will experience the world in new ways. Social life is attended by a stream of observations. Some are kindly: "What a well-turned phrase!" says an inner voice admiringly. Some are not: "Where in God's name can he have got that tie?"[283] The act of noticing makes a difference. Feminist theory has instructed us in the significance, the politics, and the constituting power of the male gaze.[284] We might adapt this argument to identify the "status gaze," a gaze that powerfully constructs the noticer—whatever it may do to the noticed. The act of noticing has been colonized by many little distinctions and the conviction that their observation counts for something.[285] Increasingly, what the individual notices about the world are status details. These, more than aesthetic, devotional, historical, or ecological matters, are what leap out. Status calculations are the tracks along which surmise tends to move. Eventually, things begin to seem simply natural. To know and to notice are now seen to be acts that identify the best of the world. To know and to notice is to begin to prove that one is better. Increasingly, noticing becomes what one does, what one does well, and manifestly what one ought to do. It becomes who one is.[286]

The second round consists, second, in a change in performance. All of the small differences, those of exteriors, interiors, companions, and possessions, are brought together, tuned, and enacted in what Erving Goffman called "the presentation of self in everyday life." Mrs. Trollope's host and Alexander Hamilton's traveling companion could manage only part of the performance. They could not assemble the whole and they could not animate it with verisimilitude. They could not, in the contemporary phrase, "pull it off."[287]

The details of the third round are structural, too, and still more simple. Do the differences make a difference? Do they persuade the individual that he or she has higher standing? Do they effect an interior change, the blithe understanding (and with this understanding a confidence) that this is "who I am"? In the third round, the individual comes to believe: this is the world in which I belong. These are my markers and rituals, my clubs, my friends, my entitlements, my world. And then this seeing must be repeated from the outside in. Do others look at me and see someone who is one of them? If the transformation has really taken, they look at me and see themselves. Ovidian change, attaining the status of a "creature of a different kind," is not complete unless this internal and external persuasion takes place.[288]

Upward Transformation after World War II

Upward transformation was, as we noted in section 3, the reigning transformational modality in the premodern West. It commandeered aspirations and activities at almost every level of society. We are told that the emerging consumer society of the eighteenth century required that people be taught to want to want.[289] This is nonsense. The "instruction set" for wanting had long been in place, and it came from upward transformation.[290] But by the modern and especially the postmodern period, this transformational modality had been displaced and diminished. It was now crowded by competitors, not least by the rise of a celebrity culture which supplied a new, more populist, transparent, and imitable set of exemplars. And it was hidden from view. Both the middle class and the academic world found it hard to make sense of. This did not prevent it from enjoying a brief, and contested, renaissance in the 1980s, as we shall see. And it does not prevent it from becoming a very lucrative commercial opportunity for Martha Stewart in the present day, as we shall also see.

As we noted in section 3, every hierarchical social system must allow for mobility, if only to replace individuals lost to accident, war, disease, and other actuarial inevitabilities. But some social systems go further and insist on mobility as a structural feature of the social world. Generalizing a good deal, it is possible to say that Western hierarchies allow more mobility than Asian ones,[291] the English are more mobile than the French,[292] and the Americans are more mobile than the English. It is the American system that concerns us here.

Neil Smelser and Seymour Lipset say that upward mobility was available to millions of Americans in the period following World War II.[293] There was new wealth as the economy expanded. There was pent-up demand due to the privations of the war years. There were things to buy, including new and second cars and new homes in the suburbs; new sources of information and entertainment, including radios, high fidelity phonographs, and televisions; and increased leisure options, including vacations, cottages, resorts, night life, cameras, and films. There were new reasons to buy as babies arrived, families grew, and the teenager emerged as a voracious consumer. Not least, there was a new social competition as families with new wealth struggled to establish relative standing. In the language of a more recent riot of consumption, people were "living large."

A friend discovered home movie footage of a barbeque held by her parents in the 1950s. The event was all loud shirts, brush cuts, cigars, and mixed drinks. What impresses in retrospect is the bonhomie of the occasion. These people appear astonished by their good fortune. A similar astonishment has led Kristin Ross to speak of a cargo cult in postwar France.[294] If the French had cause to pinch themselves, Americans were entitled to a delirium of self-congratulation. The standard of living was rising almost visibly. Opportunities for occupational advancement were multiplying at every level of society.[295] The American dream had never been less dreamlike, never more within one's reach. Americans were moving upward *en masse*.

This rise looks like rank consumption, bounty for its own sake, a feeding frenzy. But the people in my friend's home movie were spending fortunes for purposes beyond mere show. They were also buying encyclopedias, magazine subscriptions, china, pianos, silver, music lessons, crystal, art, wine, museum memberships, art lessons, and "Great Books," and these purchases were gestures in the direction of refined taste and high culture. The "cargo cult" at work in 1950s America demanded none of these. For the celebration of postwar prosperity, going to Las Vegas, driving Cadillacs, visiting resorts, wearing minks, and drinking martinis were sufficient. But many others, millions of others, in the lower and middle classes took on additional objects and costs. We will return to this topic below.

Upward mobility is not upward transformation. It is not enough merely to have more money, in the manner of an Elizabethan yeoman and the contemporary self-made man.[296] And it is not enough to move upward from one package of consumer goods to another, more expensive, one. There must also be a change in the style, the performance, of life.[297] The change must be qualitative as much as it is quantitative, or the actor is not transformed.

In the eighteenth century, it was widely understood that social elevation required a substantial, an essential, change in the individual. (It was this change that Morison, the hapless fellow discussed in section 3, failed to achieve; he had acquired silver buckles and other trappings of elevated rank, but remained as boorish as ever.) But as we enter the period following World War II, things are not so clear.[298] The status system exhibited a new indeterminacy. To be sure, some parties played the game according to traditional rules. But others, especially those of the burgeoning middle class, were less clear on how to proceed. The basics of upward mobility were plain enough, but the finer details of upward transformation could be invisible, impracticable, bewildering . . . or simply uninteresting.

Thomas Luckmann and Peter Berger detected the depth of the problem. Things were sufficiently unclear that individuals were forced back upon an "anticipatory socialization." They were forced to imagine and rehearse the steps needed for their upward movement. The classically preferred method, the imitation of local superordinates, was no longer possible. In a "mass society," superordinates were hard to find and sometimes hard even to identify. Instead, individuals resorted to what Luckmann and Berger call "identity-producing agencies," especially movies, television, and advertising.[299]

Celebrities were especially influential.[300] What transformations did they invite, what powers did they promise? The transformation they offered was very different from the one implicit in upward transformation. It was simpler, more accessible, less demanding. Beauty was enough for what we might call "agent apotheosis." Being in the right place at the right time before the right Hollywood executive was a new path to glory. The myth of Lana Turner's discovery at Schwab's Drugstore fired imaginations.[301] Kerouac said the road to Los Angeles was lined with beautiful waitresses and gas jockeys, people who had heard the siren call of Hollywood and failed to make it all the way there, or all the way back. Hollywood looked more open and accessible than polite society (or even the next rung up).

If the classic transformational modality was unforthcoming, others were more clear. Modernism supplied a compelling and coherent view of what social movement might look like. Modernism in the form of split-level homes, delta-shaped coffee tables, plane-like cars (as discussed in section 4), and sunburst clocks was a compelling package, and suburbs filled up with a reasonable facsimile of this good life.[302] Gerry Pratt has actually suggested that newly arrived families preferred modernist style. Codes were for more established families, and because they were *designed* to resist apprehension, they represented a cost, and a risk, the rising middle class was sometimes unprepared to venture.[303]

Beats (also discussed in section 4) supplied a modality deeply at odds with upward transformation. Their goal was to live like a creature of the street and to write like a child of the wilderness. Several of the beats, including Burroughs himself, came from good families preoccupied with upward transformation, and we may suspect that a beat existence was partially motivated by the desire to throw over classical form for romantic authenticity. In any case, when beats engaged in transformation, they steered well clear of anything that looked hierarchical or aspiring.

There were still other idioms. The so-called "Rat Pack" that included Frank Sinatra, Dean Martin, and Sammy Davis, Jr., was inclined to Vegas self-advertisement, high-roller extravagance, and a certain tough-guy bravado. These men were defined by their cynicism, their loyalty to the group, their indifference to status niceties, and the conviction of each that he was entitled to "do it my way."[304] That they were something more than distant heroes is shown by the admiration and passionate identification with which men of this generation still refer to "Frank." The Rat Pack cared not at all for upward transformation. That was for "swells" and "stiffs."

If the middle class was distracted and unclear on upward transformation, artists, academics, and intellectuals were having troubles of their own. Many insisted that the status behavior of the postwar period was driven by the conspicuous consumption described by Thorstein Veblen, seeing it as something thoughtless, mechanical, shaped more by status anxiety than by a status code. The America of the 1950s, they said, was other-directed and conformist.[305] The sociologist David Riesman compared the suburb to "a fraternity house at a small college."[306] It is clear that the observers were, for their own unflattering reasons, deeply invested in a disparaging view of the period.[307] But it is also true that they were hampered by the ideas at their disposal. From the Veblenian perspective, it was impossible to distinguish between thoughtless consumption and consumption shaped by a cultural agenda. From this point of view, all consumption looked the same.[308]

We know the argument was wrong in some of its applications. This much is clear from the well-known study of Forest Hill (called "Crestwood

Heights"), a suburb of Toronto, by Jack Seeley and others. Seeley and his colleagues missed virtually all the strategies of upward transformation in which this upper-middle-class community engaged. In their view,

> Here, in North America, the possession of wealth confers prestige upon its hold-ers. Because there are few strong ties of locality or kinship, a man is judged largely by the number and the quality of the things he owns. . . . In this sense, the com-munity serves the psychological purpose of a super-marketplace, where status may be validated in the acquisition and exhibition of material and nonmaterial "ob-jects": houses, cars, clothes, jewellery, gadgets, furniture, works of art, stocks, bonds, membership in exclusive clubs, attendance at private schools.[309]

These objects were intended to help accomplish upward transforma-tion, but, wearing Veblen's blinkers, Seeley and his colleagues saw them only as evidence of conspicuous consumption. They were particularly un-able to interpret the family home. They called the home a stage, not an unpromising way to start, but then concluded, "the central theme of all the dramas the house supports becomes competition for social status." To their credit, they sum up this dismal science with a confession: "in Crest-wood Heights standards of style and taste shift and change in bewildering complexity."[310] What makes the study particularly odd is that it seeks to tell us about a status community in Upper Canada, a community shaped not a little by a Scottish Presbyterian discomfort with open or aggressive expressions of wealth, a community in which competition, when it was the objective of social behavior, began as an act of self-transformation.[311] Even the actors could tell you that social discrimination was a distant out-come, and never the goal, of the undertaking.[312] So we have proof of how badly the social sciences were misrepresenting status in this period.

Lloyd Warner

We might give up hope of finding evidence of upward transformation al-together were it not for the efforts of a few isolated scholars. The most accomplished of these was Lloyd Warner, and his work on Newburyport, Massachusetts ("Yankee City") has been unjustly neglected. With his col-league Paul Lunt, he noticed the transformational power of the homes of Yankee City. "[A]fter several generations, the 'new people' who live in these homes and who have adopted upper-class behavior will become members of old families and enter the upper-upper class."[313] Here was the truth, evident to someone who was prepared to ask Americans what they were doing rather than rely on Veblen's Martian view.[314]

In *The Living and the Dead*, Warner tells the story of Biggy Muldoon, an extraordinary man ("champion of the people, martyr, traitor, villain, fool and clown") who served as mayor of Yankee City. Muldoon attacked the ruling elite of the city by desecrating the neighborhood that was their seat. Warner is confronted by a mystery: how could Muldoon have created such outrage merely by cutting down a handful of trees and destroying a mansion's garden wall? He answers this question by showing how the houses, gardens, art, and landscaping of the neighborhood "evoke and maintain in people sentiments about who they are and what they must do to retain their superior images of themselves and keep before them an interesting and gratifying vision of the superiority of their world."[315] The answer to the mystery rests in upward transformation.

Warner takes issue with the prevailing argument of the day.

> The purchase of such a house is not only a display of wealth and a public statement of a family's economic position but a demonstration that the family knows how to live according to a code of manners and can conform to the stylized pattern that makes up their way of life. A good house is one of the most important symbols upwardly mobile people can use to transform money into claims of superior behavior.[316]

Then he takes aim at Veblen. "Despite what the theorists say, conspicuous expenditure *per se* is insufficient to achieve this end. The form and manner in which conspicuous expenditure is made determine its efficacy for advancement in status."[317] Ah, well, form and manner, those pesky ethnographic particulars. Consider these, and upward transformation actually appears to have flourished in the postwar period—at least, some people appear to have managed it handily.

But we need not rely entirely on Warner. There are published accounts by insiders. Nelson Aldrich tells us that in his community, status is not a matter of reckless, riotous consumer behavior, but something more programmatic and deliberate. In his community, he says, status

> requires long and intensive training. From dancing class to the varied "lessons" of the country club, the yacht club, and the Grand Tour, from Fay School to St. Paul's School to Harvard, from the Porcellian Club to the Somerset Club and the Knickerbocker Club, from the summer place at Northeast Harbor, Maine, to the winter place in the firm, at the bank, and most important, "on the board"—all these stations of Old Money life appear not only as constitutive of the class but instructive of it. . . . Before it is a status, . . . Old Money is . . . a curriculum.[318]

There is evidence, then, that upward transformation existed in the postwar period, if only as a minority player in the transformational scheme of things. It could be glimpsed from time to time in the novels of Edith Wharton, Henry James, or Louis Auchincloss, the movies of George Cukor or Preston Sturges, and *New York Times* accounts of Upper East Side "rituals, scandals and breedings."[319] And people like Paul Fussell had made a small industry of retailing its secrets to an educated middle class that pretended not to be interested.[320] Occasionally, a member of polite society would have impolite things to say about being a "beacon showing the more successful of those storm-tossed [middle-class] strivers the way to a more gracious, edifying, and socially responsible life."[321] But some substantial part of the middle class ceased to care, their once voracious interest displaced by the factors Luckmann and Berger note: the rise of the Hollywood celebrity, the growing confidence of the middle class, and popular culture's disinclination to take its orientation from high culture.

Upward transformation did the honorable thing. It retired to diminished influence and straitened circumstances on the eastern seaboard, a mystery to most Americans and all economists. Upward transformation was now a local enthusiasm, a tribal oddity. It was known to the middle class that some families gave their children first names that sounded like last names, entrusted them to private schools, and sent them finally into the far-away worlds of law, finance, and sometimes politics.[322] But from the outside and to the middle class, upward transformation was now manifestly a specialty interest.

And then came the outbreak. Sometime in the late 1970s or the early 1980s, popular culture rediscovered the status code. In an extraordinarily swift and substantial shift of values, Americans were once again prepared to acknowledge hierarchy, to engage in status display, to admire the rich and powerful, and once more to undertake acts of imitation in the hopes of moving up. They were once more prepared to contemplate the treble change of upward transformation.

"Getting a Life"

To understand the release of this virus, we need to observe a number of cultural changes that set the stage. One was the new popularity of phrases like "go for it," "get a life," "get a grip," "snap out of it," and "loser."[323] These slogans were suddenly everywhere in circulation. They were used by BMW drivers stuck behind a VW bus dozing at a stop sign. ("Snap out of it!") They were used to encourage those who were wondering whether law school could be made to square with their '60s values. ("Go for it.")

They were used when someone said something addled at the water cooler. ("Well, everybody's equal, don't you think?" "Oh, get a grip!") There was a cultural revolution going on, and these were its little show trials. Thousands of such comments were offered as quiet, humorous acts of reproach designed to tear people away from the wooly, good-hearted enthusiasms of the 1960s and early 1970s that were still in circulation.

These phrases were also directed at the disco enthusiasms of the later 1970s. In the place of flash and glitter, a new sensibility was established that was buttoned down, turned in, measured, understated. By these new standards, the likes of Studio 54 appeared vulgar, crass, arriviste, and suburban. In this context, "get a grip" meant any number of things: "get over yourself," "stop showing off and get on with your life," but mostly it meant "stop making a spectacle of yourself." This injunction, "never make a spectacle of yourself," is one of the first principles of upward transformation. Its code begins as the Hippocratic oath does: "first, do no harm."

The movie *Animal House* (dir. John Landis) appeared in 1978. This too helped dismantle what was left of the '60s. It managed to be a winning celebration of the vulgar and the crude. ("I think that this situation absolutely requires a really futile and stupid gesture be done on somebody's part. We're just the guys to do it.") A symbolic moment comes early in the film. A long-haired college student (Stephen Bishop) sits on the stairs of Animal House, the eponymous fraternity, playing his guitar and singing a folk song of sappy, hippyish sensitivity. John "Bluto" Blutarsky (John Belushi) wanders by and is transfixed. We cannot tell what he is thinking until suddenly he seizes the guitar and smashes it against the wall. He returns the tangled remains to the owner with a look of "I couldn't help myself" apology. In a few frames of film, popular culture seemed to turn its back on the pieties, and especially the earnestness, of the 1960s cultural revolution. These values, so concerned with notions of honesty, authenticity, openness, were anathema to upward transformation, which, as we have seen, prefers artifice and the management of impressions.

Animal House was written, in part, by Doug Kenney, who cofounded the *National Lampoon* in 1970 with experience, staff, and inspiration taken from the *Harvard Lampoon*.[324] The *National Lampoon* published parodies of *Newsweek* and *Life*, the *1964 High School Yearbook Parody* (1974), and a well-received issue bearing on its cover the warning "Buy this magazine, or we'll shoot this dog." By the end of the 1970s, circulation had reached nearly a million copies per month.[325] The magazine dedicated itself to dismantling the ideological remainders of the 1960s and repudiating the dance-floor self-advertisement of the 1970s. But it had an objective of its own: to make a prep school sensibility national.[326] It captured the voice of the ruthlessly witty Ivy League undergraduate and the self-possessed private school boy, creatures who treated ordinary lives and contemporary culture as an opportunity for sport.[327]

For these people, a high school yearbook was parody for free. The lives of ordinary people (i.e., those without the benefit of good families and exclusive educations) needed no artifice or exaggeration to make them ridiculous; all one had to do was write it all down. These were kids for whom anything earnest was risible. They were contemptuous of anyone who wasn't in on the private school joke. This joke said, in effect, "the world belongs to you; everyone else is a toiling, rule-bound drudge." The voice of the *National Lampoon* was a paradox, a class secret being retailed to the world. But it was also a demonstration piece. This humor offered a point of view, a way of seeing the world, and, most of all, a demonstration that these kids were above the rules. This was humor as class privilege. To master the humor was to take possession of this privilege. Now, paradoxically, anyone could do it.

The *National Lampoon* proved a training ground, a net exporter, as it were, of writers who moved to still more influential venues. Doug Kenney went on to write not just *Animal House*, as we have seen, but also *Caddyshack* (1980, dir. Harold Ramis), which featured the honorary prep, Bill Murray. One of the original contributors, Michael O'Donoghue, left in 1975 to become head writer for *Saturday Night Live*. P. J. O'Rourke left eventually to write for *Rolling Stone*. (O'Rourke specialized in the "snap out of it" clarity with which the '80s batted aside the idealisms of the counterculture and the Left, and has made a career of it since.) Several preps (all of them, it turned out, honorary ones like Murray) began to appear in popular culture—at the movies in the characters of Otter (Tim Matheson) in *Animal House* (1978, dir. John Landis) and Rick Gassko (Tom Hanks) in *Bachelor Party* (1984, dir. Neal Israel), and on late-night television in the person of David Letterman (*Late Night with David Letterman* premiered in 1982).[328] These figures spoke with a voice that combined wit, irony, scorn, smugness, self-possession, and an impatience with anything that sounded highbrow, idealistic, or other-worldly.[329] If ever there were an index of how much things were changing, it was the fate of *Rolling Stone*. What began as a document of social protest and cultural ferment took a decidedly mainstream turn that was to be mirrored by the well-publicized Reaganesque consumption patterns of its publisher, Jann Werner.[330]

Tom Wolfe published *The Right Stuff* in 1979 as a frank celebration of the traditional American can-do spirit. Talk of the "right stuff" ten years before would have met with ridicule. It was such talk as this, after all, that had driven the military industrial complex to abuses, mishaps, and excesses of every kind. *The Right Stuff* was also, and still more surprisingly, a de-demonization of the military and a rehabilitation of the values for which it stood: patriotism, hot-shot competition, and a self-advertising individualism that had been out of fashion for some time. The way was now clear for *An Officer and a Gentleman* (1982, dir. Taylor Hackford) and *Top Gun* (1986, dir. Tony Scott).[331]

Several key events took place in 1980. *Free to Choose: A Personal Statement* by Milton and Rose Friedman took its place on the bestseller list.[332] And Ronald Reagan began his "imperial presidency" in 1980 with inaugural festivities that have been described as "the most extravagant in American history."[333] The Friedmans' book was an ideological warrant for a life of individualistic competition, and the Reagan inauguration was an indication of what the resulting social world might look like. Nancy Reagan surprised the nation by spending $200,000 on a set of gilt-edged Lenox china. This was four times the amount she had been given to refurbish the whole of the White House. Status consumption of a particular kind was back in fashion. Coming as it did after a succession of low-church Protestants in the White House, Presidents Nixon, Johnson, and Carter, the nation was a little taken aback at this grandeur, but impressed enough to begin thinking about china patterns of its own.[334]

Lisa Birnbach published *The Preppy Handbook* in 1980. This was a tongue-in-cheek account of "how to be really top drawer." It was in fact 224 pages of ethnographic detail: what to wear, where to go to school, what sports to play, what sports to watch, what slang to speak, how to be rude to a salesperson, how to mix a Bloody Mary, and the best way to display Daddy's varsity oar. The devil of status is often in the details, and there are thousands of them here.[335] The pragmatic function of all this knowledge is to allow the reader to pass as someone who came from an old family with money, standing, and membership in America's upper class. If the *National Lampoon* had supplied the new voice of the decade, here was lifestyle instruction of a much more detailed kind.

Had it been only a handbook in this very literal sense, it would have been less interesting and probably less influential. But *The Preppy Handbook* proved to be good anthropology. It got at the way preppy clothing managed to keep itself out of, and unsullied by, the diffusion stream—never in fashion, never out. It got at how the blandness of the look was relieved by "go to hell" pants and other systematic but hard-to-predict departures.[336] It noted preppy androgyny and the passion for clothing that obscured secondary sexual characteristics. Preps were shown to be slightly bemused by sex, and generally ill at ease with the body except as a vehicle for sports and a vessel for drink. This was a tough sell to a college crowd that was nothing if not hormonal, and that the sell worked tells us something about the power of the moment and the document.

The preps in the *Handbook* are so persuaded of their standing that they believe themselves entitled to misbehave without consequences and certainly without loss of status. Preppies carouse, drink, moon, gator, and vomit with the conviction that it's all jolly good fun, and that rules are for the nervous middle classes. It is a long-standing Western convention that those at the top of a hierarchy may break its laws with impunity. (Thus do Cambridge dons identify themselves. Only they may walk on college lawns.) But it is hard not to notice that the preppies in the handbook all break the same rules in the same way. This is rule-bound rule breaking.

The *Handbook* celebrates the small, repeating-motif print, a new emblem of class. This is a field of slate grey, green, or blue adorned with a repeated iconic image: sailboats, crossed tennis racquets, golf clubs, whales, lobsters, maps of Nantucket, elephants, or, particularly, ducks. The figures are small (from a distance the fabric appears to bear neat rows of abstract shapes) and function as a synecdoche, each (with the exception of the elephant) a part that evokes the whole, in this case the summer world of the eastern seaboard, Martha's Vineyard, Nantucket, and the coast of Maine.[337] This motif found its way from preppy ties and boxer shorts to wallpaper and upholstery fabric and, from there, into the homes of the middle class. To the contemporary eye, there is something disciplined, uniform, and slavishly referential about this motif, but at the time it was the true and arresting hallmark of the prep.

The *Handbook*, no doubt for satiric effect, makes preps noisy creatures without intelligence or other qualities that might qualify as even faintly patrician.[338] Once the thrill of being passed class secrets has worn off, the book makes for grim reading. These preppies are clubby, self-congratulatory, sexless, and not very bright.[339] It is hard in retrospect to see how such a picture could have mobilized the aspirations of millions of American teenagers. But it did. Suddenly Harvard Yard, never especially presentable in its architecture, appointments, or personnel, filled with glossy children in down vests, Norwegian sweaters, and Top-Siders, all newly minted by L. L. Bean. Some of them were the children of old money following ancestral footsteps into the Ivy League. But more were kids from Boston University who believed that the Yard made a better lifestyle accessory than their own, newer school.

But it was more than a matter of accessories. Ann Stroh recalls her infatuation with the new definitions.

> As a teenager [my mom] was pulling *The Preppy Handbook* out from under my [sleeping] cheek. These were the mid-80's, and I just lapped up all that puppy/yuppie/J. Crew catalogue/Land's End stuff. I didn't want to live in Wisconsin; rather, I wished my parents played tennis and would send me away to Phillips Exeter. In fact, I waged a two-year send-Ann-to-Exeter campaign ("or, hey Choate would be O.K. C'mon, at least consider the University School of Milwaukee!"). I wished we summered on Martha's Vineyard and wore penny loafers without socks. I wanted to ski in Vermont during Christmas vacation like my copy of *The Preppy Handbook* recommended. . . . I wanted to live far away from Wisconsin and my family and come home only at Christmas. As pathetic as it sounds, deep in my soul I wished I owned a navy-blue blazer with my school's crest embroidered on the lapel and wore grosgrain ribbons in my hair. I daydreamed about the day when I would go East to college, and I believed I would.[340]

The preppy revolution swept the code from the eastern seaboard into the mainstream, the middle class, and as far away as, in this case, Milwaukee. Millions of Americans now wanted to appear as if they descended from old money.[341]

Family Ties was a comedy that ran on NBC from 1982 to 1989. Unexpectedly, it proved an ideological beachhead of the decade's neoconservative movement, converting teens to Reaganesque and Republican values. Alex Keaton (a seventeen-year-old played by Michael J. Fox) slept with a picture of William F. Buckley over his bed. Designed as an object of mockery, this character surprised everyone by becoming a champion of the preppy era. Next to his good-hearted, slightly clueless, former hippie parents, Keaton appeared to be the only one on the show prepared to "get on with it." This persona proved influential.

> I was an 80s over-achiever. I rooted for Alex Keaton. I wanted to be Alex Keaton. It was during the 80s that I learned that enough money could iron out any problem and make you happy. Any job was tolerable if it paid well enough. I decided to become a lawyer in the 80s. I espoused a Darwinian winner-take-all philosophy because I always won. I would do anything to win. I wore preppy clothes: topsiders, khaki pants, the whole deal.[342]

Cheers was a comedy that ran on NBC from 1982 to 1993. In the place of career-minded, upwardly mobile, status-sensitive preppies, *Cheers* offered unambitious, unapologetic losers. The character Sam Malone (Ted Danson) had binged his way out of a career in professional sports. Carla (Rhea Perlman) was a single mother with no career expectations. Norm (George Wendt) was an accountant trembling on the edge of unemployment. Cliff (John Ratzenberger) was a self-satisfied mailman. All of them preferred the bar and one another's company to the long hours of self-sacrifice that career mobility demanded of them. It can be argued that *Cheers* flourished precisely because it was a place to take refuge from the demands of the '80s and the arduous tasks of upward transformation. The bar, and the show, were places where "everyone knows your name," where acceptance did not depend upon success in the world, where downward mobility was not only acceptable but somehow becoming. When preps appeared on the show (as the characters, Diane, Frasier, Lillith, and Rebecca), they were mocked for their vanity, effeteness, and self-absorption.[343]

The supplier of goods to the middle class dazzled by this status code was less likely to be the classic purveyor, Brooks Brothers or J. Press, than the retail stores of Ralph Lauren. Once denigrated as "that jumped-up tie salesman,"[344] Ralph Lauren positioned himself to profit from the new trend with a pitch-perfect ear for the change at hand. But, because culture and commerce mix so frequently and so intensely in our culture, Lauren's efforts to cash in on the trend contributed enormously to its shaping and dissemination. His Polo line of clothing was deliberately designed to capture "the preppy heritage of American menswear."[345] Ralph Lauren retail outlets were built into department stores with the express view of evoking the clubhouse of an Ivy League university. Rumor had it that Lauren had hired someone to travel the country buying rugby team pictures, rowing oars, and cricket bats with which to furnish these shops. Finally, Lauren spent a fortune on sumptuous "lifestyle" advertising, buying four-page four-color inserts in the *New York Times Sunday Magazine* that featured impossibly beautiful young people draped about the lawns of ancestral homes. These proved to be "identity-producing agencies" of some force.

Mario Buatta was dubbed the Prince of Chintz, and his contribution to the proceedings was an extraordinary mastery of the English country-house motif. I had the opportunity to talk to him in the middle 1980s, and he described his frustration with a new client.[346] He had just redesigned her Fifth Avenue apartment. There to supervise the last details, he found her earnestly drawing a pattern of a side table to indicate the positions of objects he had scattered there (lighters, ashtrays, art objects). When he asked her what she was doing, she said with a trace of panic, "But, Mr. Buatta, what if somebody moves something?" This is a nice indication of how nervous some people were about their new status statements. The irony is especially cruel in this case, for part of the appeal of the English country-house and old-money motifs was supposed to be their easy, informal grace.

And so we return to the question that haunted status behavior in the 1950s. Was this imitation of the eastern seaboard truly a matter of upward transformation, or was it an example of anxious conspicuous consumption of the very kind Veblen anticipated? Certainly, for some the preppy look was merely a set of surfaces. It was undertaken because it was the fashion, and because it allowed for a credible, competitive presentation of self. And because it was so alienated from its defining cultural meanings, to a few of these people it represented status without further specification. But this group did not construct a new self. Nothing changed. The self remained untouched.

The two ethnographic notes offered above suggest something more substantial than the Veblenian view, but perhaps not enough for them to qualify as anything like "proof of concept." The girl from Milwaukee masters the details. This substantial shift in her enthusiasm surely manifested itself in a change in experience and performance, but she does not confirm this. She gives us no hint that she or others were persuaded that the change had taken place. It is possible that her preppy transformation was entirely a matter of fantasy. I accept John Caughey's argument that imaginary changes are substantial ones, but plainly this testimony is a problem.[347]

The testimony from the Alex Keaton fan is still more problematic. This individual uses the preppy inspiration to warrant behavior that is distinctly "not our class, dear," to use the preppy phrase for a moment. He uses it to make himself an opportunistic bully, violating the preppy prohibition against being seen to try too hard and straying too close to commerce. In the first case, the multidimensional change in which upward transformation consists has no outward manifestation—and may be doubted. In the second, a transformation takes place, but there is nothing upward about it.

In sum, the upward transformation made what we might call a cameo appearance in contemporary culture in the 1980s. For some it was no transformation at all, but merely the latest fashion. This is the first round of the transformation only. For others it was a change that shaped experience but not performance, or performance but not experience, leaving them stalled at the second round of transformation. For still others, it shaped both experience and performance, but failed to persuade internally or externally. They could not complete the third round. For a few, however, it was something very like the robust, embracing, thorough-going transformational routine it was in the hierarchical West and had remained for some of the elites of the twentieth century.[348]

Finally, there is, I believe, a postmodern reason why upward transformation should have reappeared in the 1980s only in these fits and starts.

In its traditional form, it is imperial and preemptive. It demands complete compliance. It brooks no distraction. It cannot be done by halves. This demand does not sit well with a postmodern society that it is characteristically interested in a variety of transformational options. Upward transformation is only one of these, and to remake the self entirely in its image is to preclude several other transformational opportunities that now call out. I believe this is, for instance, the explanation for the bobo, the bourgeois bohemian.[349] In this case, the upward transformation of the bourgeoisie is blunted by the individual's wish to have access to the modernist transformation of the beat. It is also the explanation for the use of a preppie motif in the gay community, where the idiom of upward transformation is blunted by the new sexual and gender definitions it is being used to express. We will return to this in the final section of the book.

"Die Yuppie Scum"

The tide turned again. A repudiation was in the works. My first warning was graffiti on a poster for a Tom Cruise movie that read, "die Yuppie scum."[350] This was followed by a pair of instances of life imitating art: the film *Wall Street* (1987, dir. Oliver Stone), hailed by Ebert as a "radical critique of the capitalist trading mentality,"[351] and the fall of Michael Milken, the junk-bond trader indicted in 1989 for violations of federal securities and racketeering laws. Then came the movie *Heathers* (1989, dir. Michael Lehmann), in which teens excluded by snobbery take a terrible revenge against the preps.[352] The next sign was the publication of Bret Easton Ellis's novel *American Psycho* in 1991. This was, among other things, an extraordinary vilification of the prep as a serial killer in 1980s Manhattan.[353]

I did research amongst teens in 1990 and, almost without exception, they said, "Well, I guess you could say I'm a preppie, but I don't really think I am."[354] Or, still more forcefully, "The last thing I want to be called is a prep." This was coming from kids who appeared before us in button-down shirts and Top-Siders. Other teens were still more forthright on the topic. Better to be anything but a prep. Teens were moving on, some to the emerging subculture of rap, some to the revival of the hippie regime. We do not have access to this data, but we can assume that sales of Ralph Lauren, Rolex, BMW, and the other flagship brands of the 1980s fell sharply. Presumably, furniture and textile stores suddenly found it difficult to move their duck and sailboat motifs. The upward transformation modality was in retreat.

And it would remain in retreat. In the decade to follow we saw the upward transformation motif relieved once more of its influence. The "alternative" revolution that began in the American Pacific Northwest created a cultural impulse deeply hostile to this transformational modality. Kim Deal, a member of the highly influential band the Pixies and the Breeders, noted a statistical oddity that helps capture how far removed one was from the other.[355] Everyone, she observed, was now claiming to have been the most disaffected, troubled, disheveled kid to have graduated from their high school, the one true misfit malcontent.[356] The best-formed self was now an ill-formed self, incompetent, world-renouncing, self-absorbed, tortured, anti-competitive and entirely unpresentable. The "loser" so disdained by the preppies was now an exemplar. In a word, the best-formed self was the anti-prep. America was forsaking Michael J. Fox for Kurt Cobain.

All kinds of anti-preppy things were now in fashion, including tattooing, All-Star Wrestling, rude health, bump-and-grind sexuality, weightlifting, the celebration of "dumb and dumber" tastelessness, disco, casual Fridays, kitsch, self-advertisement, and, of course, Ron Popeil. The mightiest foe of upward transformation, new wealth, was especially active. Boston car-dealer Ernie Boch recently graced Martha's Vineyard, that stronghold of upward transformation, with a 15,000-square-foot summer home accented by 85 skylights, 214 windows, 24-carat-gold-plated fittings for the shower, three kitchens, a lighted dock, and a herd of llamas.[357] Needless to say, the locals were unhappy. But what is more interesting is that Mr. Boch was surprised his neighbors did not embrace him. ("You're not saying I offended them somehow?")[358] By the end of the 1990s, upward transformation was so marginalized that it was unable to inform even the behavior of someone who wanted to achieve it.

But there was one group that was still keen. The revolution was still moving. The status code was cascading downward. The forces of diffusion were carrying it into the lower middle and lower classes. Someone would need to serve as the translator. Someone would have to mediate. Someone was going to have to do for the turn of the twentieth century what Lisa Birnbach and Ralph Lauren had done in the 1980s.

The editor of *Martha Stewart Living* says that Martha Stewart is about "self-reliance." "It's not about attitude. It's about information."[359] This couldn't be more wrong. Stewart is about status symbols: how to choose them, how to use them, and how to make them. Martha Stewart is a latter-day Lady Bountiful, an arbiter of taste, an agent of class diffusion. In the phrase of the day, Stewart's job is to bring "class to mass" by demonstrating the small changes of interior and exterior that assist in the larger change of status mobility.

If there is any doubt, we have a test, a satire performed by TV journalist Bill Geist.[360] Geist offered a parody of the Martha treatment, in each case substituting new objects in the process: Tic Tacs, a Budweiser can, processed cheese, air fresheners, and pizza.[361] The joke worked well enough to make a point. Materials like these, with lower-class associations, cannot supply (or take) the status charge Stewart intends for her creations. When the object under construction is a Budweiser can or pizza box, the Martha transformation failed in small and in large.

Stewart's particular contribution may be the removal of the velvet rope that stands guard in many families, protecting the living room from use. Students of the American home have long remarked on how often the living room is blocked off in this way.[362] This despite the fact that it represents a substantial portion of available space in the home and consumes a substantial portion of its disposable income. Really nervous families will cover furniture with plastic and the tables with drapery. No definitive study has been done, but doubtless this practice reflects a certain status anxiety. For these families, status is so fraught with confusion and uncertainty that roping off is the best strategy. It removes the possibility of error. The family has made its best status statement and sealed it away. The only one who uses the room now is the family dog, who sneaks in when the family is out. ("Mom! Roger's sleeping in the living room again. Bad dog!") It's not that Roger doesn't see the velvet rope. He just doesn't believe in it.

Martha takes the rope away. She promises to make the viewers of her show, and the readers of her magazine, more fully the masters of their own homes. This is habitable status. This is status that does not provoke fear and stiffness. Martha's house is supposed to have the breezy informality of an English country house. Status without the fuss. EZ Status™ for the masses. And this is why viewers watch Martha toil without ever themselves performing the domestic arts she makes look so easy. The point of the endless demonstrations is demystification. Look how easy. Look how simple. Martha reassures us that there's nothing to it after all. All acts of status diffusion give secrets away, but Martha says the secret is that there is no secret, really. More exactly, she manages the difficult task of balancing her message: status matters, but not so much that it should be intimidating.

Typically, polite society makes upward transformation more difficult by putting barriers in the way. In a manner of speaking, superordinates booby-trap their status markers. Inexpert handling and the thing goes off. To make matters worse, they make changes constantly. Things are plucked from fashion so that what was the right choice one month is a dead giveaway the next. Think of *Martha Stewart Living* as instructions in bomb disposal.

She is doing for others what she did for herself. She is, as we have seen, self-invented, one of six children in a struggling Polish-Catholic family in New Jersey. First Barnard, then modeling, stockbroking, catering, writing, and finally performing on TV. Everything she learned for her own upward ascent, she retailed to others. And with each success, she had new resources with which to fund a further excursion into the good life. Martha has been selling upward transformation in order to fund her own upward transformation.

On matters of gender, she is more various. In the essay on Martha Stewart in section 1, we noted how effortlessly Stewart appears to mix the prefeminist, feminist, and postfeminist. Some of her fans find themselves scattered across all three of these cultural terrains. It is entirely possible that Stewart allows all the disparate pieces of a single self to watch her simultaneously. In this case, she has created a multiplicity to help her viewers cope with their multiplicity. I believe it is here that Martha picks up her middle- and upper-middle-class audiences. They don't much need the status advice, but the gender constructions are more useful.

Status at the Moment

Things are a mess. There are too many elites,[363] too many evaluative schemes, a shortage of qualified gatekeepers,[364] and a deep uncertainty about what precisely status is and how it should be apportioned.[365] More important, the centrality of the system is now in question. It is no longer the only system, the great hegemonic power at the center of things. And finally, its ability to recruit our transformational ambitions is now qualified. It exists still, it matters still, it recruits still. But it is merely one of several possibilities.

As we noted, there were many alternatives to upward transformation in the postwar period. But the present day offers still more of them. Upward transformation is one definitional option among many. Youth culture, once home to the preppy virus, is now almost completely indifferent to it. Hip hop culture, like the alternative culture of the 1990s, is at odds with it. Hip hop's gangsta variant manages to break virtually every rule of the code, especially those mandating understatement and self-concealment. Disco and rave cultures are equally hostile to the code.

We are still, as a culture, committed to a long tradition of anti-status. The twentieth century is filled with times when the social location of status has been not "up" but "down." In these conditions, the individual makes himself over with the definitional resources of people who stand beneath him in the status hierarchy. Influence and the pattern of imitation are now turned on their head.[366] "English leftist intellectuals of the Auden group in the 1930s likewise set about proletarianizing themselves. Auden wore a cloth cap, dropped his aitches and ate peas with a knife: Isherwood drank bad tea and ate chocolates to induce worker-style tooth decay."[367] Oxford and Cambridge periodically adorn the children of the middle class with working-class accents. As we have seen, William S. Burroughs took to a demi-monde existence on Chicago's north side, forsaking his privileged upbringing to cultivate new patterns of speech and dress. Tom Wolfe caught Leonard Bernstein in this inverted snobbery in an essay entitled "Radical Chic."[368] In the language of diffusion, we have seen a whole host of social practices "trickle up," invented by low-standing groups and adopted by high-standing ones. This pattern may be detected particularly in the world of beats and punks, who suppose that anything without street credibility is to be regarded with suspicion.

Celebrity culture continues to be difficult. Roseanne Barr built her celebrity partly by flaunting the conventions of polite society. It was not until she butchered the national anthem that anyone took umbrage. There was a time when upward transformation enjoyed this protected status, but no longer. But the important case in point here is Drew Carey. In the television series *The Drew Carey Show* he breaks most of the rules of polite society, but he does not do so daringly or provocatively. Unlike Roseanne, he is not resisting or transgressing. Drew Carey simply doesn't care. He lives in a world independent of and indifferent to the old regime.

There is even a counter-claimant. The tradition of the dandy, of Beau Brummell and Oscar Wilde, claims to be the true locus of the code.[369] The dandy is a perfect status construction. Quentin Crisp, armed against New York City only by his perfect self-possession? Indeed, it is sometimes too artful,[370] or descends (or is deliberately driven) into burlesque, class as camp. But when they are on their game, dandies are a true threat to the code of upward transformation. They are better at every part of the transformational exercise, better at noticing, better at cultivating, better at performing, and finally better at persuading. This is status hijack, as a result of which the authentic bearers of the code appear imperfect, clumsy, and amateur.

All of this is to say that there are now a variety of competitors, challengers, and alternatives that diminish the significance of upward transformation as a transformational modality. And this is what it is to live in a postmodern transformational society. People still care about status. They are still prepared to speak, dress, and conduct themselves in an aspirational manner and to celebrate their status achievement. But upward transformation seems to have lost some of its power and much of its centrality. It is no longer the preoccupation of our social lives. It is now merely one of the options at our disposal.

The multiplicity of options in the general culture is now reflected by a multiplicity of options within the individual. Postmodern selves are often multiple, and the status persona is, for many people, merely one option in a portfolio of selves. People are interested in the code of upper-class life, but no longer obsessed with it. They are keen to learn some of the details, but their self-esteem and life chances no longer depend on how well they do so. It is, I think, more accurate to say that their admiration now runs in all directions. The premodernist and modernist passion for upward transformation has been replaced by a breath of curiosity and ambition. It is a characteristic of the postmodern, I think, to wish to experience several locations on the class continuum, instead of merely one. At one level, people make themselves the passionate students of *Masterpiece Theatre* and *Architectural Digest.* At another, they watch *Martha Stewart* and *Dynasty* reruns. The impulse to continue to draw upon and appropriate status markers from above has not died. It has been joined.[371]

Surely, there are some who would act as gatekeepers, scrutinizing social performances for the status claims they make. Such gatekeepers once had great power. They performed a sorting function, advancing a few, putting the rest in their place. But no one believes they have a place any longer. They are understandably surprised when someone tries to put them in one. There has been a withering of the witherers. The gatekeepers are discovering that almost no one asks for entry.

We look with curiosity on those few who do believe in the status game. We are puzzled. "Why put all your eggs in this one basket?" We are puzzled because we know that their commitment to this transformation costs them the opportunity to explore all others. It is as if the rest of us have, with the help of Martha Stewart and others, decanted class of some of its status anxiety, some of its "But Mr. Buatta, what if somebody moves something?" We engage in upward transformation, but it does not rule the middle class with its tyranny as it once did. In the particularly apt language of Michèle Lamont, we are much too concerned with the "cultural sovereignty of the individual" ever to consent to this tyranny again.[372]

Some of the transformational movement we see on the status highway appears to be motivated as much by curiosity as by admiration. This means that sometimes people seek to move upward in fact or fancy just to see what it is like there. This movement has taken on the character of an ethnographic excursion. What is this? Who are these people? What is it like to be like them? This isn't aping, as it was once so cruelly called. It is something more virtual and experimental. Let me try this self on and see what becomes of me and the world.

But the supplantation of admiration by curiosity also means that we are prepared to move downward, the very movement that was once regarded as dangerous and damaging, or as a form of slumming, as something titillating, a walk on the wild side. Now that the hierarchy's ability to belittle those who rank low has diminished, we are free to visit the lower levels with something like impunity. More to the point, we are simply curious, stigma or not. The same questions prevail. What is this? Who are these people? What is it like to be like them? What happens to me when *they* happen to me? The old motives for downward mobility— the thrill of slumming, the Orientalism of walking on the wild side—are extinguished. We are not visiting touristically, to thrill at how other the others are, to delight in the liberties we gain when we impersonate them. There is something more grave and, again, curious about the encounter. Slumming was all about the thrills and dangers of trespass; our boundaries are so much looser now that slumming is easier and therefore less thrilling.

Upward transformation: to think, it was once monarchical and now it's merely Martha.

FASHION, DESIGNERS, AND TRENDS (AND COLLECTIVE TRANSFORMATIONS)

> Can it have been merely by coincidence that the future was to belong to the societies fickle enough to care about changing the colors, materials and shapes of costume, as well as the social order and the map of the world—societies, that is, which were ready to break with their traditions? There is a connection.
>
> —Fernand Braudel[373]

In the introduction to this book, we pictured Ovid standing in front of a rack of magazines, struggling to grasp a commonplace of our world.

> You are saying . . . what are you saying? I see. These are "magazines." They're about "fashion." Fashion. OK. People buy them and read them and then what? They change their clothes. Not always? OK. Not always. Not usually? Really? OK. What's *Vogue*?

Thoughtful, exuberant, and now a little overwhelmed, the author of *Metamorphoses* is trying to understand the moments when we move more or less *en masse* from one material form to another. As usual, people in the magazine store are in a constant movement of their own, stepping around one another as they browse the shelves. Everyone's staying well clear of the man in the toga. Ovid keeps looking around as if to get his bearings. He's finding the halogen lights bright and the magazines numerous . . . and shiny . . . and numerous. Sometimes he seems to be getting it. Sometimes not.

This essay is a companion to the essay called "Orlan and Wildenstein, Cher and Madonna, Cindy and Barbie" in section 1.

Part of the problem is his getup. He's wearing a standard Roman toga. This is a single woolen cloth draped around his body and over his shoulder. It is flowing and more or less graceful in the Roman manner. Ovid keeps stealing glances at the people around him, and he wants to know how poets dress in the present day. The answer is another puzzle. A "shirt" that encases the torso, "pants" which encase the legs, "socks" that cling to the ankle, and "shoes" that lace up tight. To a man who is not so much dressed as draped, this looks confining.

> This would have been my "fashion"?
>> Well, no, you would have to choose a *particular kind* of shirt and pants.
>> From these magazines?
>> Yes, and from what's going on in the street, movies, TV, things "in the air," as we say. Like, if you were a poet in the 1960s, you'd probably wear long hair, a loose cotton shirt and pants, muted colors, informal, well worn, un-ironed, casual, and not too fashionable. But in the 1970s you might have worn disco stuff, brilliantly colored synthetics, tight-fitting, showy, the latest thing for the dance floor. Or not. I don't think poets really went for disco. Maybe you would have dressed like Kerouac, jeans and a red-checked shirt for the duration. It'd depend.

The idea that there could have been this much change in fashion in the space of ten years is another stunner for Ovid. It is much, much more change than he would have seen in a lifetime. Roman dress changed slowly.[374] That we should, in a decade, move from cotton to rayon, baggy to fitting, informal to stately, casual to showy, dazzles him quite as much as the halogen lights.[375]

If Braudel is to be believed, there's a reason for this. "[T]he sovereign authority of fashion," he says, "was barely enforced in its full rigour before 1700. At that time the word gained a new lease of life and spread everywhere with a new meaning: keeping up with the times."[376]

If fashion, as a sovereign authority, was to gain power, real sovereigns would have to give way.[377] One small but telling episode in the enduring struggle between the rival courts appears in the story of Beau Brummell (1778–1840). Despite his youth and modest origins, Brummell ruled matters of taste and society in London from the time he bought a house there in 1798 until his departure for the continent ahead of his creditors eighteen years later. So great was this power that all London hoped for his approval and all feared even so little as a dismissive glance from him. Brummell ruled with the power of exquisite taste. "Brummell had only to look upon or speak to or walk with a man to make him fashionable, and only to cut another to make him a pariah." The person to whom this power properly belonged, the Prince of Wales (later King George IV), was at

Brummell's mercy just as much as the rest of the capital. As Brummell put it, "I made him what he is and I can unmake him."[378]

The rivalry between the two appeared in a public exchange of insults. They encountered one another in public one day, each in the company of a mutual friend. The prince stopped to talk to Brummell's friend, ignoring Brummell as he did so. When Brummell's turn came to speak, he addressed the prince's companion, casually asking at the end of the conversation, "Who's your fat friend?" It's hard for us to grasp the enormity of this gesture. A monarch so often and inevitably the recipient of deference now insulted, by a commoner, in public, with a comment about his person! It was one measure of Brummell's power that he dared such a thing, and another that he survived it. Brummell's opportunity to rule London in this way was due to many historical developments, but it is probably not wrong to think of him as the ambassador of an emerging power, or, in any case, as someone who could not have risen to power were fashion not rising, too.[379]

Fashion's authority grew steadily. At the close of the nineteenth century, the German sociologist Werner Sombart was alarmed by what Frederic Schwartz calls the "frantic speed of changes in fashion." Schwartz says of this period,

> The instability of taste that so disturbed contemporaries was very real. At the end of the nineteenth century, the historical styles followed one another very quickly indeed, certainly in comparison with what seemed to be the centuries-long development of styles in the historical past. Within twenty-five years, taste in Germany had gone through the phases of late Classical, Romanesque, Gothic, Renaissance, Baroque and Rococo, not to mention neo-Classical, Empire and various Orientalisms.[380]

Fashion was not just changing faster but also moving into new domains. Sometimes this was, as Roland Marchand notes, a simple matter of changing the color of things.[381] But even when the change was as small as this, it was unsettling to see things previously fixed by tradition open to new influences and responding to things in the air. Fashion was becoming an ivy that threatened the house with occupation more than with ornament. It was suddenly everywhere. A social critic writing in the middle of the nineteenth century exclaimed, "I should like to see the thing it does not meddle with."[382]

Fashion was a challenge not only to the authority of monarchical power but to the supposed rationality of the marketplace. It challenged the Smithian idea that individuals were utility-seeking, and therefore predictable, actors. It suggested that the motives of economy were perhaps not so transparent after all. Where was the invisible hand, the emergent order of the marketplace, if men's and women's hearts were ruled by caprice? At the heart of modern societies, there was something that did not make sense.[383]

There were three ways to respond to fashion's increasing power: to dismiss, to accuse, and to cower. At the worst, none of these were much more than intellectual palliatives. None of them made the challenge go away. But they gave comfort. They helped suggest that the upstart fashion that so troubled monarchs and marketplaces was perhaps intellectually containable, at least.

The attempt to dismiss fashion for its superficiality was haunted by circularities. The changes in colors, materials, and shapes did appear gratuitous. After all, they did seem to come from nowhere and to signify nothing at all. But this was a self-created difficulty. As long as the intellectuals refused to take fashion seriously and develop methods of thinking about it, how could fashion appear as anything but a trifle? The superficiality of fashion said more about the theories designed to account for fashion than the phenomenon itself.

The second circularity came from the way the idea of fashion was implicated in the cultural definition of women in modern Western societies. The superficiality of one was taken to be proof of the superficiality of the other. (Women's superficiality was central to the late-nineteenth-century debates over extending the vote to them.) How did we know women were superficial? Because they cared about fashion. How did we know fashion was superficial? Because women cared about it. The superficiality of fashion had found a purpose.[384]

Finally, the superficiality of fashion was a play on the cultural logic of the term. The superficial is by definition a thing of the surface.[385] Fashion is apparently a thing of the surface. (It is even a thing of the surface of surface, as when it amounted to new buttons and bows.) The term and the phenomenon seemed literal and figurative expressions of the same thing. Long-standing cultural conventions were at work here.

The accusatory response was more substantial but not much more penetrating. Fashion, it argued, concealed the operation of something devious. It was a way of creating obsolescence, of removing things from usefulness before their utility had been exhausted. Fashion was a way of training consumers to disdain things they once wanted, moving them on to another purchase. Most of all, by this account, fashion was a way of renewing desire. There are problems with this argument, as well. Was it really enough to change color, line, shape? Was mere change (change, that is to say, without structural or semiotic significance) all it took to train people this way? Was the consumer really as dim, as thoughtless, as jackdaw-like, as this? The dupe theory—and this is what this argument amounts to—has been disavowed in most circles. But in this academic neighborhood, theoretical remainders like this one are still in circulation—still, in fact, quite fashionable.[386]

The fearful response darkened the explanation still further. The shifts in taste and preference that had marked the consumer revolution of the eighteenth century had occasioned suggestions that society was in the clutches of an epidemic. This alarmist rhetoric was still popular two hundred years later. George Bernard Shaw called fashion an "induced epidemic." Northrop Frye referred to a "manic-depressive roller-coaster." The Lynds made lurid reference to "rouged clerks promenading languorously." Others referred to a mysterious "Vatican," ruled by its own arcana and elites. In these analyses fashion is played out as a mystery, incompletely controlled.[387]

The rhetorical cannons of diminishment, reduction, consternation, and condemnation were thus arrayed and were now firing at will. The mystery of fashion had found a way of perpetuating itself. Fashion was fatuous, cunning, or malevolent . . . or possibly, in the kind of contradiction with which cultures often acknowledge the limits of their explanatory power, all three. The suspicions were many and damning. And they remain so in the present day. For all I know, several of these accusations are true. My chief concern is that we have been so eager to bury fashion, we have neglected to look at it. No explanation rooted in these objections can serve as a test of Braudel's question. But what if he is right? What if something essential and defining about Western cultures is caught up in the willingness to change colors, materials, and shapes?[388] What if some of the transformational power of these societies comes precisely from the little transformations that emerge each month from Paris, London, and Tokyo? What if it turns out that our understanding of fashion magazines is no better (though less candid) than that of our imaginary Ovid?

First Question

Fashion may serve the cause of transformation in four ways. First, fashion might help explain why, and how, change happens at all. As we have seen, forces of conservation and reaction are deeply rooted in the human animal, our career on the planet, and the most aggressively innovative of our societies.[389] Bourdieu's extraordinary account of habitus gives us a glimpse of why the past should have such a powerful hold on the world.

> The *habitus*, a product of history, produces individual and collective practices—more history—in accordance with the schemes generated by history. It ensures the active presence of past experiences, which, deposited in each organism in the form of schemes of perception, thought and action, tend to guarantee the "correctness" of practices and their constancy over time, more reliably than all formal rules and explicit terms. This system of dispositions . . . is the principle of the continuity and regularity which objectivism sees in social practices without being able to account for it.[390]

How, with habitus in place, does change happen at all? Part of the answer here is perhaps that fashion helps set in train a set of critical little changes. One of the ways to ask this question is to consider a case study.

Oscar Gets a Haircut

Let us take a hypothetical example, a man we'll call Oscar, a twenty-seven-year-old in the year 1968. Oscar is the product of a middle-class family. He has finished college and is now in his last year of law school. (He took a couple of years off to travel around Europe.) There is a fashion shift in the works. Oscar has noted that people on the street are wearing their hair longer. Some of his classmates have started to do so, too. Oscar's response is to wear his hair a little longer. This means that he is getting his hair cut every three weeks instead of every two. Mostly, nothing happens. His hair is a little longer, that's all. But Oscar likes it, and he lets it go another week. Now in the fourth week he gets comments from his father ("gettin' a little long at the back there, eh, Oscar?") and from his classmates ("looks like someone is getting ready to join the revolution").

Oscar has entered an intermediate zone. His hair is still too short for him to look like anything but a law student when he goes to be-ins and rallies. But at least he is no longer being called a "narc."[391] And it is still short enough for him to attend family get-togethers without provoking suspicion or reproach. He has opened diplomatic relations with one group without forcing another to revoke them. Oscar continues to let his hair grow, going six weeks between haircuts and demanding that the barber "go easy" when he does get a cut. He is testing the boundaries of the zone.

At some point, Oscar may decide to grow his hair "really long." This will win him credibility in, or at least readier access to, radical circles.

And it will cost him the good humor and possibly the emotional and financial support of his family. Or he may choose to give up the "whole long-hair thing" and return to the more usual appearances of his law school classmates. Or he may continue to occupy and test the middle ground. But in all of this, we see Oscar trying on a set of little changes that help to audition a larger change. Thinking about his hair offers a chance to think about who he is, what he believes in, and, most particularly, whether he will join or eschew the counter-culture. Does he want to participate in the revolution that is in the works, how much does he want to participate, what will the costs of participation be, is he prepared to pay these costs? Sorting out what to do with his hair is a way of sorting out larger questions.

But the *how* of this process of discovery is as important as the *what*. The change from haircuts every two weeks to every three is tiny. It can be made without risk. In a sense, only Oscar knows what's going on. But this is enough. He does know. He can have a look. He can see what he thinks. By the time he moves from a three-week to a four-week schedule, the world begins to notice. But the change is still small, and, more important, in our culture, it's "just hair" and "just fashion." Both are mere things of the surface. As Oscar begins to move into the intermediate zone we have described, he can proceed by small changes that are revocable. They can be scaled back to the point of comfort or they can be repudiated altogether, each without consequence. This fashion transformation lets Oscar start small, scale up carefully, scale down at will, and break off without lasting penalty. It allows Oscar to audition change with a minimum of exposure and risk. Were the costs and the risks of change higher, Oscar and other followers of fashion might refuse change altogether.

There is also an inside and an outside at work here. On the inside, Oscar is engaged in a complicated dynamic of emotion and behavior. Now that I look different, how am I received? Now that I am received that way, what behaviors can I engage in, what people can I meet, what events can I take part in? Now that I can engage with new people and events, how do I feel about the creature I am becoming? As Oscar explores his options, as he checks his and others' tolerances, as he auditions this thing called the "counter-culture," he is watching to see what is becoming of him and trying to decide what he thinks. Fashion is one of the ways Oscar can separate himself from what Bourdieu calls the "active presence of past experiences." Fashion is the thin edge of the wedge.

On the outside, there were, in 1968, millions of Oscars, kids who could hear the siren call of new cultural and political ideas. They were growing their hair a little longer in the back, going to the occasional rally, listening to new music. And even as each of them was trying on novelty, the response of the world, and the meaning of the novelty, were changing. Working *en masse*, millions of Oscars created a more receptive, less risky environment for one another. Working *en masse*, millions of Oscars reset the tolerances and moved a culture toward change. The great change of the counter-culture came from millions of little gestures, tiny departures, modest risks brought together into a magnificent aggregate.

It is, then, something more than a question of risk. It is a question of habituation on the one hand and collective movement on the other. What begins, in the words of the famous Frank Zappa song, as hair that's "getting good in the back" allows and spurs personal change, which in its turn allows and spurs collective change.[392] If Bourdieu's notion of stasis turns out to live in the exquisitely fine details of everyday thought and action, this is precisely the residence of what we might call Braudel's notion of transformation. Change starts in the tiniest, most personal, quintessentially superficial gestures. The way to understand his suggestion is to contemplate (and that's all we will do here) the possibility that the counter-culture, anti-war protest, the estrangement of parents and children, a wave of new drug use, new sexual practices, and gender reforms all began with hair that was starting to get "good in the back."[393]

Second Question (the thing about waves)

The second question is how we can change without riding off in all directions at once. How do we change but stay together? The moment that change is allowed, it is technically possible for every individual to embrace his or her own innovation, to rush toward uniqueness. This second question has a second question of its own. When we are all changing in response to fashion, how do we keep our differences intact? The moment that change is allowed, it is possible for individuals all to end up in the same place (rushing away, as it were, from the uniqueness with which they begin). Neither happens. In our usual metaphor, change runs like a wave through the community, as some parties take it on and others leave it off. Change is allowed . . . even as commonality is preserved serially over time. Furthermore, change is allowed . . . even as difference is maintained.[394]

There are three explanations for how change is made to occur without leading to these undesirable outcomes. Each of them helps to show how change takes place, how it moves through the community, how commonality is preserved even as difference is maintained. These accounts are sometimes conflicting, but not always. I review them briskly.

Georg Simmel suggested that innovations were normally made at the top of a status hierarchy.[395] They would then pass down the line by a process of imitation. Hats, let's say, become all the rage among the titular nobility. The second wave, untitled nobility, take note, and take to the hats themselves. Now the third wave, the gentle class, takes note and begins to adopt hats as well. And imitation provokes differentiation. The moment that the second wave starts wearing hats, the first wave thinks better of it. And by the time hats have been adopted by the merely gentle, the second wave are also sneering at the garb they once found so irresistible. By this time, the first wave have adopted a new fashion, and the process begins again.[396]

There is always a trade-off. When the innovation is first introduced, it is new and it appeals to relatively few people. As innovations take, they gain enthusiasts but they lose currency. This is not only literally true, in the sense that the longer they exist in the world, the less novel they are, but it is figuratively true as well. The longer innovations exist in the world, the less they startle. Or, to use the more usual metaphor, the less hot they are. (Next to liquid, heat is the metaphor most frequently used to describe fashion.) The trade-off: adoption for currency. In this sense, every fashion is caught in a tragic exercise. Its adoption will mean, will create, its repudiation.

Examples are everywhere. Until the twentieth century, this was the most important form of diffusion. Josiah Wedgwood scrutinized the aristocratic class for "lines, channels and connections" through which to make contact with the aspiring middle classes. He regarded aristocrats as "legislators in taste" who only needed to smile on his products to send them trickling down the social hierarchy.[397] The records of colonial America are filled with the complaints of high-ranking people about the temerity of those below them. But, as I have suggested in the essay above, it is Simmel's diffusion effect that helps explain what Martha Stewart is doing with her empire of magazines, TV shows, and websites. She is a conduit (a "line, channel, and connection") by which fashion knowledge from the top of contemporary culture is made available to the bottom.

In this model of fashion, we are the recipients of innovations because we all stand somewhere in the diffusion stream. Eventually, things will come to us, charged with the charm of the new. We will adopt one because our betters adopted it before us. We will give it up because they have given it up. That we adopt it will make it attractive to our inferiors. That we give it up will, eventually, prompt them to give it up, too.

Simmel's model is still useful but it is subject to several important modifications. First, this model, in its pure form, assumes that everyone learns of an innovation from the parties immediately above them in a status hierarchy. As Charles King pointed out, the mass media of the twentieth century provided fashion knowledge to everyone more or less at the same time.[398] Those magazines Ovid finds so dazzling disintermediate Simmel's diffusion chain.[399] Courtesy of the pages of *Vogue*, innovations can leap into the lives of people in the Upper East Side, the Upper West Side, the Lower East Side, the Bronx, and Queens simultaneously. No one has a class advantage. The creation of *Fashion Television* (a show and a channel) by Jeannie Beker and Moses Znaimer disintermediated the fashion world even more, diminishing the gatekeeping power even of *Vogue*.[400] Now everyone can see what the fashion press saw.

Second, Simmel's model supposes that people adopt new fashions to gain the status these fashions have as a result of their adoption by people of higher status. The trickle-down system of diffusion invests new fashions with this cultural meaning and this meaning only. The rise of a celebrity-centered culture changed things dramatically. These taste leaders can give new fashions many meanings, among them charisma, sexuality, hypermasculinity, and hyperfemininity. Social status is only sometimes one of them and almost always the least interesting.

There is a second approach. Let's call it the "currency" model.[401] In this case, innovations occur at the margin of the social world and they move, when they move, toward the center. A dance step is invented, say, in a club in Amsterdam. It moves to the latest clubs in London, New York, and L.A. It moves from the hippest kids at the clubs, the ones who seem to be always and effortlessly in the know, to those who are merely cool, to those who are hangers-on, and, finally, to those who stand outside the club without a hope of getting in. It begins to appear in the repertoire of clubs that are more and more mainstream. Eventually, it reaches the dead center, the mainstream. Now parents are doing it, and now, of course, what was the latest thing is utterly over.[402]

What distinguishes the various parties is not their status but their currency. They are now arrayed according to how close they are to the cutting edge of novelty, how long it takes them to learn the latest. Typically, people who are really in the know, the first wave, as we are calling them, devote extraordinary amounts of time and attention to staying in touch with what is going on. It is almost impossible for the person who goes to the clubs once a week to learn enough to sustain this status. Paying scant attention to what's happening, the individual is lucky to win membership in the second wave. Sarah Thornton, following Bourdieu, calls this knowledge "subcultural capital." She says that in these circles, fashion knowledge serves as a good from which individuals can draw power, prestige, standing, and sometimes professional advancement.[403]

Simmel's diffusion is still at work here. The early adopters give currency to the new fashion. They make it attractive to those who rank high on the "hipness" scale. This second wave adopts the fashion, with the two consequences that Simmel predicted: the first wave abandons it and the third wave prepares to adopt it. But something substantial has changed. The relative standing and location of various adopters are not defined by social status. And the worth of the innovation is not status by proximity. It is currency, the new as the new.

This means that King's criticism no longer applies. It is *not* possible for all interested parties to get simultaneous notice of a new innovation. Now the first wave must invest a lot of time to stay current. (Indeed, the first wave must now sometimes choose between being the hippest thing at the club and "getting a life.") The costs of staying current come out of the fund of energies and attentions that one would otherwise spend on training, education, a career. Individuals assess this trade-off according to their own lights. The bourgeois assessment is straightforward: high standing in the clubs in the short term is a bad bet when it interferes with social advancement in the long term.

It is easy to think of this as a youth's game only. But this would be wrong. I know someone in Manhattan who subscribes to a service that keeps her apprised of the latest restaurants. She pays handsomely for the ability to take friends to "an interesting little place I've discovered around the corner." ("That Jane! How does she *know* this stuff?") This is another way of saying that Jane is prepared to turn economic capital into cultural capital . . . and that's because, as Bourdieu would note, the cultural capital will, especially with the right lunch, especially in a place like New York City, return as economic capital. But there is an important difference, something that makes Jane's version of this game different from the clubber's version. It is precisely that the clubber gives value to things that are unknown to, and unanticipated by, the mainstream. Clubbers take a special pleasure, as Thornton observes, in differentiating themselves from commercial and bourgeois circles of influence. (And they consider the bourgeois calculation above the stuffiest, most impoverished calculation possible.)

There is another important difference between Simmel's model and the currency one, and that is that almost anyone can play. The status model gives priority to people who come from the right homes and the right schools, people who were born high or have moved upward in the hierarchy. Club cultures do not care about status. They require a certain physical attractiveness and dancing ability, and some disposable time and income, but otherwise they are relatively inclusive. Many are called, many are chosen.

The inclusive quality of the currency model allows it to explain cultural innovation in a way that the Simmel model could not. Certain innovations cannot be created by high-status groups. To use the now tiresome contemporary phrase, they cannot think outside the box. The innovation that defined the 1990s, for example, was literally unthinkable. The origin myth of the music that came from the Pacific Northwest is that it combined punk and heavy metal as a gesture of defiance of the rock industry that had excluded Seattle from concert tours. This is a perfect example of innovation under the currency model. It comes from players too far outside the mainstream to know better. Or, to put it more accurately, the margin can do things the mainstream is too invested culturally or economically to do. For the mainstream, what emerged from the Northwest was astounding. Nirvana's *Smells like Teen Spirit* was greeted with exclamations of astonishment and a collective acknowledgment of what Foucault once called the "sheer impossibility of thinking that." There is no novelty like this kind of novelty. The ones that come to us by Simmel's diffusion chain seduce, charm, inveigle if need be. In the currency model, innovations astonish. In this case, currency has a current. It overloads the faculties, it ravishes the senses. These innovations change from unthinkable to inevitable in the blink of an eye.

There is one more difference that needs noting. Simmel's diffusion can work quite slowly. It may take a full year for something to work its way from the top to the bottom of the hierarchy. The club scene, on the other hand, changes more quickly, with innovations in dance steps, clothing, and linguistic styles each season and even each week. I am told that we are on the verge of clothing whose color and brightness can be controlled by the wearer. When this is available, we will be able to stand on the balcony and watch styles sweep back and forth across the dance floor like the northern lights.

Commerce is increasingly caught up in the currency game. It is precisely the strategy at work when a restaurateur sells his business as the third wave of diners begin to come the restaurant. Prospective buyers (often dentists who are financially liquid but not well informed) can't believe their eyes.[404] People are lined up out the door. But in fact the restaurant is dead. The first and second waves have come and gone—and it won't take long for the third wave to notice their absence. At the moment of sale, the restaurant is not fashionable. It is merely popular, a very bad thing when sky-high prices have no justification beyond the currency of the place.

Madonna appears to have mastered Simmel's diffusion effect. She keeps a careful eye on innovations both in art and dance circles and on the street. Her strategy has been to adopt and release these innovations at precisely the right moments. She has found a way to tread water in the diffusion stream, not rising so high as to bewilder the mass of fashion-sensitive consumers, nor sinking so low as to seem out of touch and insufficiently hip. And she can change horses in the middle of this stream, deftly releasing the old and picking up the new. As Michelle Goldberg puts it, she has "metamorphic skills [and the] ability to shed personas like snakeskin."[405] Phrased this way, it sounds as if Madonna's secret to remaining a star over almost twenty years was a simple matter of domesticating Simmel's ideas. This is not untrue, but it is worth pointing out that thousands of entertainers have struggled to do what she has done and failed. This despite the fact that there were millions of dollars at stake and they were getting advice from the best agents and advisors in the entertainment industry.

Another commercial development is the one Malcolm Gladwell dubbed the coolhunt.[406] The tastes and preferences of so many consumers are subject to changes in fad and fashion that many industries and brands are obliged to stay constantly on the lookout. They hire consultants who specialize in watching what the first wave is doing and predicting whether and when the second wave will follow. There are some quite good coolhunters. And there are also some very bad ones. I have watched the latter advise industry, and it is not a pretty thing. All these people know about the world is what's hot. The names Simmel, Bourdieu, and Thornton are deeply exotic to them, the notions of diffusion and transformation impossibly foreign. Their specialty is getting "jiggy" with the kids. As they enter middle age, this exercise becomes increasingly far-fetched and ever more embarrassing. The only thing that protects them from discovery is that the corporations know still less.

Simmel's work applies here. Corporations act as third-wave adopters, often destroying what they adopt. Club kids move on abruptly and with some indignation. But as Thornton points out, there is something gratifying about corporate imitation. It confirms a club's place in the universe and, as Simmel would point out, it stimulates innovation. Finally, this is a cat-and-mouse game as corporations continually imitate and kids continually differentiate. Punk was meant to be, among other things, the fashion that could not trickle up. These innovations were "spiked," as environmental protestors spike trees, so that they would never be adopted by the mainstream. Safety pins in noses, slashed clothing, slogans painted on leather jackets, S&M gear, all of these were supposed to defy the assimilative powers of the mainstream. But of course, in a development that still troubles the intellectual and cultural world, the mainstream of fashion adopted punk motifs with a brief, thrilling frisson of daring, and moved on. If we think of contemporary culture as the product of the endless struggle between the inventive powers of marginal groups and the assimilative powers of mainstream ones, it is clear that neither party has found its limit.

There is a third model. We might call it the "critical mass" thesis.[407] This says that the spread of fashion is constrained and directed by our tolerance for novelty. Some people are prepared to adopt a new style upon first seeing it. Their tolerance for novelty is high. Others need to see the new style, say, six times (or over, say, six months) before it is comfortable or familiar enough for them to adopt. Their tolerance is low.

By itself, this model posits the several waves that all diffusion theory depends upon. The first wave needs no prior acquaintance. A new style of sweater? No sooner does something appear on the runway than it enters the world of the first wave. The second wave needs to have seen, say, four of them. The third wave needs to have seen six. Sweaters do their own recruiting. Early instances break down our fear of the new and prepare the way for later ones.

It would be wrong to emphasize the creation of familiarity too much. For the critical mass theory explains the movement of innovations according to the relative balance of familiarity and novelty. The first wave needs no familiarity. The last wave wants no novelty. Everyone in between wants a combination of the two. So it is not the case that the third wave is waiting merely until novelty wears off. It is waiting until there is enough familiarity so that the novelty can now thrill instead of terrify.[408]

Critical mass, or what Gladwell calls the tipping point, is achieved when a small change makes a cataclysmic difference, a quantitative difference with qualitative consequences, as it were.[409] Critical mass theory cares about differences that make a difference. But this is really to say that it is interested in the interface between the second and third waves, or that point when something breaks out of the status of a minority enthusiasm to be embraced by *tout le monde*. It privileges one moment among a series of identical moments: the moment when it appears that everyone is joining in. This is a problem of optics. *All* the differences are making a difference; some merely happen to be more conspicuous than others.

There are several problems with critical mass theory. First, it can be a little mechanical. It seems to suggest a steady, monotonous increase, like program code that increments a variable on each iteration. In fact, adoption is always driven by something more than familiarity. The innovation in question must *mean* something compelling to move toward adoption. Simple increments of one do not suffice. Second, the theory is so enamored of the idea of the tipping point that it often fails to see what Simmel shows so well: that each wave is impelled by the same motives, working according to the same principles, as the last. This is another way of saying that critical mass theory helps obscure Simmel's great insight. Third, it does not show us what we have called the "tragic condition" of fashion innovation (that, in growing, fashion dies). Fourth, critical mass theory, taken as it is from the study of the natural world, does not seem to see that what novelty is and what it means will be decided outside anything posited by the model. Models of contagion or theories of the meme are really not much use when adoption is mediated by ideas and values.[410] Much worse, the cultural forces that *do* decide what novelty is and why novelty counts cannot be thought about from inside the model. The model must always smuggle in other accounts to survive its own inadequacies.

But enough complaints. What critical mass theory does is what all these theories do: show how it is that fashion allows change even as it creates a serial commonality and preserves difference. All of these theories, Simmel's, currency, and critical mass, show how fashion transformation enters on cat's feet, discreetly, without drama, and, most important, without the warning signals that would provoke our vigilance, resistance, or umbrage. Fashion transformations come in small and gentle increments, the better to catch us unawares, to enroll us painlessly. They may be the harbingers and the first moments of a social development as thorough-going as the counter-culture of the 1960s, but they are careful not to stampede the horses. They break us in.

Can we refuse fashion's conscription? Can we step out of the continuous process of transformation? Can we grasp one fashion and stick with it even as it sweeps down the diffusion stream and out of fashion? Well, yes, it turns out we can. This is, for instance, what devotees of the mullet have done. The mullet is a haircut for men that is short on top and long at the back. It is worn by celebrities such as Jeff Foxworthy and Billy Ray Cyrus. It is mocked in newspaper articles and on websites.[411] The same derisive tone is directed at those who wear a "full Milwaukee" (a white leather belt and white leather shoes) or even a "half Milwaukee" (one or the other). Anyone called "bridge and tunnel" by residents of the island of Manhattan has failed in fashion in some way or another, and is being held up to the same ridicule. It is clear that we are, even in this time of heightened sensitivity, not above mocking people who have withdrawn from fashion. This language works with sheepdog efficiency to drive those who are "fashion-nonresponsive" back into the fold.

What these models do not show is how active we have become in this transformational process. They treat us as passive recipients of innovation, waiting for something new to come to us in the diffusion stream. But we are sometimes more aggressive than this . . . Ani DiFranco, as we have seen, is much more aggressive than this. Her first wave does not wait for something to come to it over the transom. It takes the cultural world by storm, reinventing as it goes. And those behind it, those in the second wave, do not passively receive these new ideas of femaleness and self-presentation. They claim them by living them, almost always in the face of external hostility and internal doubt. We are not merely a riverbed for the diffusion stream. The time is surely upon us to rethink Simmel's model by giving the names "playwright," "off-Broadway player," and "Broadway player" to the members of the first, second, and third waves, respectively.

Third Question (how to audition everything)

Fashion might also help explain where transformations come from, and, still more strikingly, how it is these transformations begin as evanescent quirks and whims, how they can be drawn from a great breadth of possibility, how they can be auditioned as powerful directions of larger change, how they can be tweaked up to the very last moment of distribution to fit with a still more powerful stylistic development. So often the whipping child of the nervous intellectual, fashion may actually serve as a way of listening to, sorting, selecting, articulating, and setting in train the trends that routinely shape and direct contemporary culture.

When the sociologist Herbert Blumer looked at fashion, what struck him was how fecund and how wasteful it was.[412] Fashion innovation begins, he noted, in the imagination of the designer, from which spring thousands of ideas, some of them barely formed, some committed to paper in a line or a shape. Hundreds of these ideas end up in fuller sketches and, of these, tens find their way into a finished article of clothing. Only a handful of these will be selected for coverage by the fashion press, and fewer still will be chosen by the buyers from Bergdorf Goodman and Neiman Marcus. Fewer still will be embraced by the consumer. This Cambrian pattern of profusion and reduction happens every season. Forget bewildered Romans. Even a latter-day sociologist was a little overcome.

To make matters worse, this profusion is accompanied by something that begins to look like an oath of nondisclosure. Designers are frustratingly vague about how it is they invent, how they choose, how they know that this or that shape is the one on which to bet the season.[413] "You just know," they say. Further questioning is futile. Pressed, they will sometimes resort to showing you a half-drawing and saying, "Well, it was pretty obvious." They are working by intuition, taking key decisions from unconscious depths. This has the effect of opening up the process of invention to a vast array of possibility and to the identifying and syncretic powers of the unconscious mind. In this way, fashion makes itself sensitive to the faint cultural tremors beyond and the formidable powers of pattern recognition within.

All parties, it turns out—designers, buyers, press, and consumers—proceed this way. They are waiting for the ineffable moment that characterizes so many intuitive and unconscious activities. Everyone is listening for resonance, that whoosh, ping, or click that tells them they are in the presence of . . . something. "I can't really tell you what it is, but I know it when I see it." What they know is the moment that something in them responds to something in the fashion.

This vagueness might be a bad thing, a confirmation that fashion is as superficial as some suspect. But vagueness could also be a mark of what it is fashion is designed to do. If one were to design a cultural SETI program that combed the heavens for intelligible signals, it might well look like the world of fashion. What do designers listen to? It turns out they listen to everything: to the movies, the street, kids in Tokyo, the new music of South Africa, tribal fashions from North Africa. How do they listen? Widely and with great vagueness, as we have noted. What do they produce? In any given season, there are many thousands of ideas in play. What do they insist upon? Almost nothing. The new is maximally underspecified. We are free to make what we will of these ideas. ("That? Oh, that just seemed right.") Who else produces like this? No one, really. The university and industry insist on framing and constructing their innovations quite narrowly, even though these innovations often end up being used in ways their originators couldn't imagine. This unpredictability is taken for granted in the world of fashion.

We might ask (and given the state of the literature, asking is, once more, all we can do) why it is that designers should be charged with this task. (Plainly they are not the only listeners. Most entertainers, artists, journalists would qualify as well, and much of what I am saying here describes them too.) It might be precisely because these individuals are burdened by so little in the way of pragmatic responsibility. It might be precisely because we insist, and they too often agree, that they are "only" fashion designers. It might be precisely because they are listening for will-o'-the-wisps. Far from being good evidence that fashion is insubstantial, these things may be evidence of its ability to listen, capture, sort, combine, and articulate. Designers are open to the arbitrary in a way that Hollywood storytellers and other-worldly artists cannot be. Designers are listening for unintelligent life in the universe, as it were, something too recognizable for the artist and too odd and truly new for the storyteller. Designers are neither mainstream nor independent, to rehearse the current choices. They are someplace near the seams of contemporary culture, which are a favorite haunt of the new.

Fashion listens well. There is something Darwinian about the way it listens, to be sure. It produces lots of everything and then it lets people choose, and it lets lots of people participate in the choosing; the films that are considered for the Oscar have gone through a lot of filters. This is why it must be wasteful. It wants to include anything. This is the only way it can get things out of the heavens into material form and, eventually, public discourse. What starts in the domain of fashion can work its way through. What starts on the sketchpad can enter the world of style. It can live on to make its way into lifestyle.[414] What is variously contemplated, acted on, and acted out here enters subculture. And what is again selected in subculture enters culture itself. Finally, what begins as fashion can become Bourdieu's habitus, something that strikes us as inevitable, obvious, to be taken for granted.

Fourth Question (the flattering lie)

Fashion contains a deliberate lie. It gives almost everyone the right to include themselves in the magic circle. It is one of the mysteries of contemporary culture. Everyone believes that they are truly, really, or authentically Goth (or prep, or rave, or Republican), and anyone less committed is, "like, a total pretender." Thus does the line between the in and the out shift to include the speaker and exclude everyone who is a little less *au courant*. If we were more observant, this might give us pause. We might say, "umm, if he is out of it and I am only a couple of notches more current, it could be that I'm out of it, too." If we were more observant, there would be institutions designed to bring this unhappy truth to our attention. But this is not how it works in our cultural universe. We are as generous here as we are with our pronouns. Anyone can claim to be "me." Anyone can claim to be "hip."

The shifting boundary of fashion means that each person can consider him- or herself the last one in. Each passes through the door and shuts it . . . but no one tells the next in line. That person does the same thing, and now the boundary moves to exclude the next. In this way, fashion can sort without alienating, discriminate without antagonizing. All hierarchies and evaluative schemes are haunted by the possibility that those who rank low will exercise what Albert Hirschman calls the right of exit.[415] Rather than consent to being mocked, they will find a way to leave or to denigrate the system that so judges them.[416] The designations "hip" and "cool" are elastic. There is always room for the speaker. Even a phrase as specific as "bridge and tunnel" can be made to refer to someone else. ("Sure, I'm from New Jersey. But, hey, I'm not the one they mean.")

Conclusion

There is an argument for Braudel. First, fashion helps us remove ourselves from the grip of orthodoxy, convention, and habitus. It allows us to respond by carefully modulated degrees, with a minimum of exposure, always with the ripcord of a costless repudiation near to hand. But more than that, it lets us audition the change, try it out by subtle stages. Both externally and internally, fashion works as the thin edge of transformation's wedge.

Second, fashion lets us all move away from orthodoxy even as it allows us both to stay together and to maintain our differences. There are a variety of ways of thinking about this and it is probably true that Simmel, currency theory, and critical mass theory are all correct, the several facets of fashion's cunning.

Third, fashion is also a listening device, a cultural conning tower, a way of detecting tiny changes and finding the most compelling material form for representing them.

Finally, fashion allows us to include ourselves in the magic circle. Fashion, it turns out, is a shifting category. It allows all of us to claim to be "hipper than thou" while protecting us from this logic when it is exercised by others.

This essay has narrowed its focus to fashion. But I believe that what has been said about fashion applies to trends. (And notice the gender effect of this statement. "Oh, it's trends we're talking about. Whew! I thought this was just about, you know, girl stuff.") Trends are organized by the same diffusion dynamics and serve the same latent functions. We have used clothing as our talking point, but I believe that fashion is constantly drawn upon and shaped by the worlds of music, movies, television. It remains to see how these domains interact with one another, how they divide the labor, how they work together to draw transformations out of the heavens and enroll all of us as participants. I leave this task for someone else or another time.[417]

Fashion pulls us into transformation so subtly that we have no sense of movement. We feel we are the same people we were a decade ago. To suggest otherwise invites an indignant response. "Creature of fashion, me? I don't think so." Fashion is always for other people. But we need only pick up photographs taken a decade ago to start at how much we have changed. Actually, this is not our reaction. We have not changed, we maintain. Evidently, someone has been at our photographs with Photoshop software. But this should be an opportunity to see how tied to the moment (to use a famous phrase by Yves Saint Laurent) even the most conservative of us are.

The moment passes. We would rather not suppose that something crucial to what we are as individuals and a culture has anything to do with fashion. As I will try to show in the next essay, fashion sits somewhere between involuntary improv, the transformation that is forced mercilessly upon us, and Shakespeare in the Park, the transformation that we engage in voluntarily for the ludic pleasure of doing so. Fashion is transformation that invites our participation even as it coerces it. It is the transformation that happens to each of us by happening to all of us . . . and vice versa.

Once Ovid recovered from his admiration for the fashion magazines, once he grasped the way fashion serves us as a means of transformation, I believe he would smile on it. He was accustomed to thinking of transformation as something that gods did to one another, and, occasionally, to mortals. He would be interested, I think, to see that it is something that mortals now do to one another and themselves. He would be interested by how ubiquitous it has become, how it has found its way into the smallest details of everyday life, how it now takes its direction from kids on skateboards almost as much as from the great designers of Paris and Milan. He would be particularly taken, I think, by our ambivalence about fashion, how little we think of fashion designers and ourselves when we answer fashion's siren call.

Ovid would be particularly interested to hear about the artist called Orlan, who now fashions her body according to the most current ideas of the intellectual world of postmodernism. Ovid has a question. What happens when the one who calls the tune here in matters of body transformation is no longer an artist? What happens when it is the designer you call Miyake or the company you call Disney? What happens when it's Martha Stewart? What happens when you don't have to resort to the messy, expensive, and relatively permanent process called "plastic surgery"?

We liked him better when he was a man in a bookstore bewildered by the halogen light. The intellectual embargo against fashion is, these efforts notwithstanding, still in place, some thirty-five years after Braudel's call for an inquiry. And it will remain so. Fashion is one of the best-kept secrets of the transformational society, almost perfectly hidden from view behind our ambivalence.

INVOLUNTARY IMPROV (FORCED TRANSFORMATIONS)

Popular culture engages us from time to time in something we might call "involuntary improv." It does so when we are confronted with something new in the self or the world, and we are obliged to respond speedily without full knowledge of what has happened or how best to proceed. The scripts or routines with which we normally respond are not useful.[418] But a nonresponse is not allowed. In colloquial language, we must "seize the moment," "cobble something together," "give it a try," "see what happens," and "change things as we go along." In more formal language, involuntary improv is urgent, obligatory, experimental, tentative, reflexive, and dynamic.[419]

There is so much variation, discontinuity, and departure in the contemporary world that it is easy to be stampeded into the supposition that we live in a world overwhelmed by change. This is a favorite refrain of the futurist, *Wired Magazine*, and the industry expert. I, for one, am disinclined to

---

This is a companion to the essays called "Robin Williams," and "Mike Nichols" in section 1.

go this far.[420] But there is enough change to oblige us to engage in quite a lot of improv. Indeed improv, especially involuntary improv, is one of the modalities with which we seek to cope with a transformational world. So much of this improv is coerced and unpleasant that we haven't yet acknowledged its existence. As Marshall Sahlins might say, cultural concept has yet to catch up to cultural practice.[421] Henry Adams claimed that "chaos cannot be taught."[422] This may be true, but it is clear that we are obliged to try.

There are three forms of involuntary improv. In the first form, change comes to the self or the world: the loss of a job, a divorce, a change in health, a change in the cultural and social climate, a change in the economy, a change in the industry or field in which one works, a change in political climate, or, more personally, a change that comes from within, a change of values or life goals. With organizations continually expanding and downsizing, with the emergence of new economies and the eclipse of old ones, with people changing marriage partners on average twice, careers three times, and cities five times in a lifetime, with continual change in individual and collective values and goals, the chances that the individual will have faced a substantial change of some kind, and even several such changes, are quite high.

Sometimes change comes with a real or figurative severance package. Notice is given, money is set aside, preparations are made, counseling is provided, transitions are smoothed. More often, and this is the case with involuntary improv, the change is sudden, even precipitous. One moment the world asks for one thing; a week later it demands something different.[423] The individual must respond with improvisation, coming up with new routines and, sometimes, transforming a part or parts of the self on the fly. This first form of improv is exacting. To fail in it is to risk diminished life expectations, perhaps a marginal existence, or, in the extreme case, displacement and homelessness.

In the second form of involuntary improv, individuals are confronted with something extraordinary. The task of responding takes them to the limit of their capability. The inscrutability of the change is striking. It comes, as we say, out of nowhere, and it is even more urgent and coercive. It is necessary to respond straight away and there is still less choice in the matter than there was with the first kind of improv. The stakes have gone up. The individual is forced further from native ground, from familiar parts of the self and the world, and must come up with a performance that has not been supplied by training or experience.

It is perhaps inevitable that popular culture should have taken an interest in improv of this kind. It is, after all, so irresistibly dramatic. But then many things are irresistibly dramatic, and we are required to explain why this particular theme should now be a Hollywood favorite.[424] The action-adventure film, for instance, is equally gripping and more thematically straightforward. But it is involuntary improv that is now ubiquitous. In *The Game* (1997, dir. David Fincher), an investment banker (Michael Douglas) is stripped of wealth and power, and finds himself, inexplicably, without papers in a small town in Mexico. In *Enemy of the State* (1998, dir. Tony Scott), attorney Robert Clayton Dean (Will Smith) finds himself stripped of financial instruments and identity. In *Regarding Henry* (1991, dir. Mike Nichols), a gunshot victim (Harrison Ford) returns from a coma to a life he does not recognize. In *Trading Places* (1983, dir. John Landis), a child of privilege (Dan Aykroyd) and a street hustler (Eddie Murphy) are dropped without warning or explanation into one another's lives. In *Dream Lover* (1994, dir. Nicholas Kazan), Ray Reardon (James Spader) makes the bewildering discovery that his wife has invented herself almost entirely and is in fact a stranger to him. In *While You Were Sleeping* (1995, dir. Jon Turteltaub), a young woman (Sandra Bullock) finds herself called upon by circumstance and a family's wishes to play the fiancée of a man she doesn't know.

In *In & Out* (1997, dir. Frank Oz), Howard Brackett (Kevin Kline) is notified of an unsuspected sexual identity, abruptly and on television. In *House Sitter* (1992, dir. Frank Oz), Davis (Steve Martin) is astonished to find that an almost perfect stranger, Gwen (Goldie Hahn), has taken up residence in his country home and is now treated by everyone, including his parents, as his new wife. In *Pleasantville* (1998, dir. Gary Ross), David (Tobey Maguire) and Jennifer (Reese Witherspoon) find themselves thrown through their television set into a strange town with strange mores. In an episode of *The X-Files* called "Dreamland" (broadcast November 29, 1998), Fox Mulder (David Duchovny) finds himself dropped without warning or explanation into the life and identity of a deeply obnoxious family man (Michael McKean).

In *After Hours* (1985, dir. Martin Scorsese), Paul Hackett (Griffin Dunne) finds the world of New York City growing ever more unrecognizable and uncontrollable. In *The Tenant* (1976, dir. Roman Polanski), Trelsovsky (Polanski) finds himself the captive of a malevolent apartment building and his life begins to come undone. In *Dark City* (1998, dir. Alex Proyas), John Murdoch (Rufus Sewell) gradually realizes that he occupies a fabricated world and that he is surrounded by people whose identities are reinvented every night. In *Total Recall* (1990, dir. Paul Verhoeven), Arnold Schwarzenegger is bewildered by the irruption of a new identity that proves finally to be an old, forgotten one. In *The Long Kiss Goodnight* (1996, dir. Renny Harlin), Samantha Caine (Geena Davis) begins to guess she may not be a suburban housewife after all, as the talents of a trained killer begin suddenly to emerge in her. In *Passion of Mind* (2000, dir. Alain Berliner), the protagonist (Demi Moore) finds herself living two lives in parallel, one as a Manhattan literary agent, the other as a book reviewer living in the south of France. In *Fight Club* (1999, dir. David Fincher), the protagonist (Edward Norton) discovers, belatedly, that he has a second self (played by Brad Pitt), one so disassociated from the first that he experiences it as discrete and autonomous.[425]

To be sure, these are all bizarre occurrences and they are, we are tempted to say, only possible in the hyperreality created by Hollywood. Can anything like this, we wonder, occur in real life? A couple of cases appear to qualify. Consider the case of Julie, an employee of a dot.com startup in Silicon Valley.[426] When she signed on in 1998, Julie was promised wealth and advancement. Jim Clark and other members of the first generation were cashing out spectacularly, and it looked as if the world of e-commerce was just getting started. Venture capital seemed available for the asking. Buy-outs were commonplace. (Julie sometimes went to work chanting her new mantra, "Please let us be bought out today.") Julie was being paid mostly in stock, and, depending on the movements of the NASDAQ, it looked as though her sweat equity would someday be worth millions. Then came the crash of April 2000. Julie watched in horror as her share price slid downward, eventually disappearing below the $10.00 mark, the one that told you whether you were being paid or not. It settled finally, with a great many other dot.com stocks, at under a dollar. Two and half years of labor were gone. Julie was no longer a millionaire in waiting. She was merely older, poorer, and rudely surprised.[427]

But Julie's story might be an exception. Is it not a reflection of the dot.com mirage that came and went so suddenly? It is true, I think, that something like this happened to managers in the public sector, who saw their jobs eliminated in the 1980s by the attacks on "big government" that helped bring to office Prime Ministers Thatcher and Mulroney and President Reagan. Something similar also happened to middle managers in the private sector, who watched their jobs disappear in downsizing and reengineering. These cuts came with stunning suddenness. In May, these employees were valued members of the corporation, highly regarded, frequently promoted, and well paid. Many had made long-term commitments in the expectation of a robust career. By June they had been declared expendable, and by the end of the summer they were gone. The instabilities of wage labor had come to the lives of the management class. We might suppose that this contraction of the private and public sectors was a one-time adjustment. But Jeremy Rifkin suggests that such contractions will be more and more common.[428]

Al had a somewhat different experience, but the outcome was the same. Picture him sitting in the wood-paneled office of his used car lot. It is mid-afternoon. Al's had a big lunch. He's got his feet up on the metal desk in front of him, the chair tilted back. A fly makes a noisy circle on the window sill . . . and then stops. The world's so quiet it feels like it's been hollowed out. Al is used to quiet on a car lot. But this is two and half weeks now. Sales are down so much he had to let his salesman go. Al's beginning to wonder if he's ever going to see a customer again. Al has heard about the Internet, but he believes it's mostly something to help his daughter do her homework. He hasn't yet heard of disintermediation or CarsDirect.com.

But could this dynamism belong to the economic domain only? Perhaps our domestic lives are more stable. Lorraine finally decides in mid-career that her relationship with her husband is insufferable. She is done compromising. She will not fold her life into her husband's life any longer. She will not forego personal aspirations for those of the family. She demands a divorce, things turn hostile, and she gets her own apartment. Declaration to departure took around six weeks. Lorraine now barely recognizes her life. We find her sitting in the laundry room of her apartment building, exhilarated and a little taken aback. She can't escape the thrilling, fearful conviction that she is becoming someone else. Released from the role obligations of domesticity, she discovers a taste for P. D. James novels, Jane Campion films, and her own company, hours of it. Changes of this order are not quite common in our culture, but they are not unheard of.[429]

One more example. Grant, let's call him, is on the verge of finishing a book that has preoccupied him for the last six years. He has changed jobs and cities three times in this period. He has been focused on the book and tried to fit everything else around it, changing anything in his life that threatened his ability to complete it. As they say, he lived and breathed the book. Now he faces the prospect of completion. In the language of the 1980s, he's obliged to get a life. We find him sitting at his keyboard, typing furiously, rushing toward the end of the manuscript. But he knows that hundreds of postponed decisions await him there. Writing the book was an exercise in improv. Finishing it will be much worse. He has several options, but no clear sense of how to choose between them. The temptation to start writing another book will be very strong.

The difference between the first and the second form of involuntary improv is the degree of change and the extent to which the origins of change are apparent. It is, also, the extent to which the response to change can be identified and judged sensible and promising. In the first form, it is relatively clear where a change such as job loss comes from and what needs to be done to put it right. In the second form, change is somewhat more mysterious. (Why should Lorraine's patience with her marriage have run out just then? What became of Julie's industry—why were there five years of explosive growth and then collapse? What, for Al, is the Internet?) And the response to change is also less clear. What, exactly, does one do? Is there a cultural routine or script with which to solve such a problem? In the case of the first form, the answer is often yes. In the second, the answer is often no.

The third, the strong, form of involuntary improv occurs when the improv is continually required. Transformation is now the enduring, apparently endless, order of things. No sooner have people begun to adapt to one world than they are confronted with a new one. In the television series *Quantum Leap* (NBC, 1989–1993), the protagonist found himself propelled from one circumstance to another in just this way. Dr. Sam Beckett (Scott Bakula) is dropped into a house fraught with tension. Medical crisis? Home invasion? Super Bowl Sunday? Dr. Beckett cannot say. He does not know his role, those of the other players, what is expected of him, or the hazards of the moment. Indeed, not until he has a chance to see himself in a mirror can he know his age, gender, race, or appearance. Beckett makes what adjustments he can, only to be pitched into another inscrutable world.[430]

In *Stay Tuned* (1992, dir. Peter Hyams), a husband and wife (John Ritter and Pam Dawber) find themselves sucked into their television and tossed unpredictably from culture to culture: the Wild West, an American city in the 1930s, and a futuristic wrestling match.[431] In *Clean Slate* (1994, dir. Mick Jackson), a private detective (Dana Carvey) wakes up each day to find that he has no memory of the world around him. He does not recognize his apartment or his dog. He does not know his name or profession. This is a world so utterly unrehearsed that everything from finding his toothbrush to greeting the next-door neighbor becomes a catalogue of surprises. What he learns in the course of each day is erased by night and he must leave notes to himself on the bathroom mirror: "your name is Pogue."

In *Memento* (2000, dir. Christopher Nolan), the protagonist suffers a failure of memory so profound that ordinary notes are not enough.

Leonard Shelby (Guy Pearce) has a memory so unreliable it can reset at any second. He may find himself mid-sentence wondering what his topic is and who he's talking to. He records short-term memories on Polaroid pictures and long-term memories by tattooing them on his chest and forearms. In one particularly memorable scene, his memory resets while he is running through a trailer court. We hear him ask himself, "OK, what am I doing?" and when he sees another man running too, he surmises, "I must be chasing him." When the man turns on him and points a gun, he thinks again. "No, he's chasing me."

I listened to a man give a retirement speech several years ago and I wondered if he had not been forced to perform strong-form improv. He was reflecting on forty years of academic teaching, his home life, his experience in the community, what it was like to be a parent. This survey of his life was interrupted here and there by comments on the women's movement. "Well, and, of course, let's not forget to thank the secretaries. Do we call them secretaries, anymore? OK, administrative assistants, hey, hey. Assistants are women, er, people, too, and they don't make coffee anymore [*pause for a moment of self-congratulatory laughter*], no, sir, they keep your life in order. Really. If it weren't for Cheryl here, I think I'd have forgotten to wear my pants to class. Oops, can't talk about pants, can we? Hey, hey."

Everyone was now looking at the ceiling, praying silently for a speedy end to the proceedings. The speaker meant these comments as evidence of how thoroughly he approved of the women's movement, but as the comments began to accumulate, listeners began to understand a) that he had never really understood the women's movement; b) that this movement had, whether he liked it or not, changed fundamentally the way in which he was now interacting with women at work, in the classroom, and, presumably, at home; and c) that because he had never really grasped the nature (or perhaps the legitimacy) of this social change, his world had become a series of surprises. Without this important key to the new social reality, he was forced to fake his way through many interactions. He had learned to make a few of the right noises and to desist from certain behaviors, but somehow, as the English say, the penny had never dropped. His world had just gotten odder and less predictable.[432]

In all three forms of involuntary improv, individuals become a kind of test subject. They are obliged to respond to a sudden, unpredictable prompt, like competitors on *Whose Line Is It Anyway?*[433] Suddenly the future is upon them. In Jeffrey Sweet's phrase, they are called upon to do "something wonderful right away."[434] At its worst, involuntary improv is a study of how much transformation an individual can endure, a study of human tolerance. It is not surprising that Hollywood should take an interest in this peculiar human moment. How could it not? The arc of the story, the tension of the moment, the dramatic possibilities are obvious. But it might be asked whether these movies do not identify a new set of anxieties characteristic of the culture from which they come, our own.

Alfred Hitchcock made three movies that turned on the theme of mistaken identity: *The 39 Steps* (1935), *Vertigo* (1958), and *North by Northwest* (1959). Mistaken for someone else, a character in each must fathom and manage a series of bizarre events. But there was something like a bargain here. Hitchcock's audience could take comfort in the knowledge that the person in danger would eventually be saved, that things would be clarified, that all would turn out in the end. No comfort of this kind awaits the viewer of *After Hours* or even the otherwise undemanding *Clean Slate*. No genre is at work, no outcome is promised. Perhaps more important, in Hitchcock's films, the protagonist is periodically let in on the nature of his or her difficulty. In *North by Northwest*, for example, Alfred A. Thornhill (Cary Grant) is given several moments of clarity, and he seizes these moments to summon wit and courage and to form a plan. The victims of mistaken identity are quite well treated. They live in an orderly world. Not so the citizens of the culture of commotion. Contemporary lives and movies are less forgiving. Change comes swift and cruel. Transformation, when it comes at all, comes by fits and starts and only with difficulty.

Occasionally, the wretched enjoy a moment of triumph. In *Clean Slate*, the confused and disoriented hero is spirited away to a surprise birthday party. His devoted friends look at him with great affection. He returns their gaze without a trace of recognition. He must speak—but he has no idea about what or to whom.

> Seeing all your faces here today brings back such memories . . . it's hard to know where to begin. Sure, I could talk about John and Susan and Mary, Fred and Ethel and little Ricky and all the others whose friendship means so much to me, but that wouldn't be fair. I'm reminded of a story . . . a story about blood and guts and patriotism . . . and *love*, let's not forget about love. [*hugs man beside him*] I think we all know who I'm talking about. [*nods significantly to crowd; some nod back*] . . . I'm sure you have your own stories. Raise your hands if you have your own stories. Come on, put them up. [*members of the crowd shyly oblige*] Yeah, lots of stories, lots of hands [*shot of man in tears*], which is to say [*here his voice breaks*] I have a rare group of friends. [*the crowd responds with sighs, tears, applause*][435]

This is an odd kind of triumph. The test subject saves himself from involuntary improv only with more improv. He contends with peril by compounding it. Some of the members of contemporary culture feel themselves moving steadily from a world characterized by the weak form of improv to one characterized by the middle form, and some feel themselves on the verge of the strong form. For some people, the order of novelty increases steadily. Powers of and opportunities for response diminish. It is not likely that we will find ourselves reduced to leaving notes for ourselves on the mirror. ("Your name is Pogue.") But ours may be a culture in which, even here, life threatens to eventually imitate art.

Responses

If Hollywood is dwelling on the problem of involuntary improv, it is also conjuring responses. In Robin Williams we have a demonstration of versatility. In his Metropolitan Opera performance, he is protean, changing shape nearly two hundred times in an hour. It is unlikely that his audience wishes to be any of the creatures he becomes: Robin Leach, the elephant man, Kurt Waldheim, Leon Spinks, or Dr. Ruth. But it finds something to admire in his navigational skills. To summon response, to negotiate transition, to evidence this range and breadth of possibility, to show this order of ingenuity, speed, and grace in one's reactions is to have precisely the qualities that would remove the sting of involuntary improv. We might now be the equal of weak and middle challenges. We might even survive the strong form.

What Williams has done on stage, Mike Nichols has done in life. He began as an immigrant, awkward, clueless, unattractive, tormented by his ability to see how badly he was doing. ("A thousand tiny victories and defeats in an ordinary conversation.")[436] Certain powers of improv emerge, and Igor Peschkowsky becomes Mike Nichols. The child mystified by Saratoga now knows it's a town in upper New York State and an Indian place name. At the University of Chicago, Nichols finds his way out of organized theater into improv. He meets Elaine May and together they find a way to make a small but substantial change in American comedy, theater, and eventually television. What these children of immigrant America are constructing, besides entertainment, is a way to manage the complexities of a postwar America. ("The only safe thing is to take a chance.")[437] This America had a way of turning locals into immigrants and it was becoming clear that this thing called "improv" had its uses.

As Nichols rose from obscurity and the status of immigrant, he appeared to become a master of improv and no longer vulnerable to its involuntary form. But in the *New Yorker* interview, he gives us a glimpse of how demanding his world can be.

> I couldn't be a person that many hours a day. I needed—still need—a lot of time lying on the bed absolutely blank, the way I assume a dog is in front of the fire. A persona takes energy. I just needed a rest from it. Not to be anything in relation to anyone else.[438]

Williams and Nichols are particularly gifted performers of improv. But their gift is not only inborn. Williams was trained at the Juilliard School of Music and Drama and Nichols got his education at the University of Chicago. (Almost certainly he felt the influence of Paul Sills there, founder of Compass, the improv company, and this made him the beneficiary of the wisdom of Viola Spolin, Sills's mother and one of the founders of improvisation in the United States.)[439] The rest of us must improvise our training for improv. We may look for this training at the movies, in the films of Robin Williams, say. We might draw inspiration from the mercurial cast of *Whose Line Is It Anyway?* But often what we see in such places are virtuoso performances that intimidate as much as they instruct. These actors are appallingly adroit, apparently never at a loss for words, capable of breathtaking invention at the drop of a hat, prepared to accept and advance any premise, however far-fetched. The benefits of training are obvious. The benefits of a self-conscious feeling for improv are too.

It would be a good thing if involuntary improv could be mastered with material learned from voluntary improv. And, indeed, some of what has been learned in the theater, jazz, movies, and brainstorming does appear almost entirely transferable, as we shall see below. But involuntary improv is more difficult than the voluntary version.

First, players often don't know the improv has started. Worse than that, they often don't know that they may not know. All they know is that something's wrong. One spring, customers just stop showing up to Al's used car lot. Al has had droughts before. The thing to do, according to conventional wisdom, is to put your feet up and wait it out. You have built it, they will come. And even after the bad news ("Dad, they're probably going to www.autobytel.com, or something. You know, *on the computer?*") has arrived, clarity has not. Figuring out what has happened to him will require Al to climb a steep learning curve. He will have to grasp the e-commerce revolution. He will have to understand disintermediation. He will have to see that the foundations of his enterprise have changed beyond the hope of restoration. But first he will have to come to know *that* he doesn't know.

The second difference is that in involuntary improv we are looking for something more than an amusing answer to a premise like "your hair is on fire." We are looking in some cases for something as substantial as a recreation of identity or enterprise. Lorraine is trying to imagine life on her own. What does divorce change? What is it to be a mother without a father around the house? Does she join the community theater, buy a dog, or take up yoga? What happens on Sundays now that she's on her own? Julie is trying to think what her career might look like. Maybe she should go back to school, back to the east coast, back to traditional media, or . . . maybe it's time to move on. Al is wondering whether he should chuck the lot and buy into a fast food franchise, or whether this is a good time to retire. Involuntary improv often demands thoroughgoing reinventions. Snappy answers will not do.

The third difference is the high emotional costs of involuntary improv. As people grapple with the fact, and the scale, of change, they endure great stress. Al may well take some of his unhappiness home, and before very long he has put his relationship with his wife and children at risk. At the very moment when he most needs his family's support, he is turning the home into another source of instability. Julie has always had a tendency to procrastinate, to let bills pile up and to let decisions go unmade. Now that so much is uncertain, she finds she is having a hard time making even the simplest decisions. Uncertainty is compounding itself. Lorraine has never slept very well and she is finding that both the exhilaration and the novelty of her situation make things even worse. Her doctor suggested a benzodiazepine as a short-term remedy. But that was four months ago and now she finds she cannot sleep without it. It leaves her groggy in the morning and nervous that she might be adding dependency to the list of things in her life she is struggling to put in order. Lorraine is now having to manage both change and her reaction to change.

All of these people are "playing with pain," as they say in sports. The improv players of *Whose Line Is It Anyway?* are well rested, well trained, animated, engaged, amused, and keen. Involuntary improv players are distracted, confused, anxious, and conflicted. Voluntary improv players have nice clear boundaries—between when to start and when to stop, between what's in and what's out, between who's playing and who's not. The involuntary improv player has no such clarity.

If there are three differences, there are three commonalities, things from voluntary improv that can serve us in the real world. Improv has been an active part of music, theater, and business for about a century, and particularly in the post–World War II period. It is often thought of as an exercise in pure spontaneity, but we have learned quite a lot about how it works and how to teach it. Some of what we have learned is useful as we struggle with the problem of involuntary improv and the status of a test subject. What follows is not a systematic treatment of the problem, but a sketch of some of the things that seem to help.[440]

Involuntary Improv and Free Fall

Involuntary improv cannot work unless the individual gives up what he knows and the ways he conventionally reacts to the world. The trouble is that what he knows is deeply embedded and interconnected in a field of knowing. There is no simple way of swapping out the old and swapping in the new, to use the popular and deeply misleading imagery of the world of computers.

Furthermore, there is no obvious way of preparing for what comes next. The usual model, once so loved by the military and corporate worlds, is to assess the problem, gather intelligence, weigh alternatives, choose a course of action, and reenter the world. But this will not work; these careful steps are now impossible. The speed of change, the urgency of response, require that we step off into the moment. Individuals must trust that they are swift enough, and skilled enough at improvisation, to manage things on the fly. The old system was designed to maximize care and thoughtfulness. One paused and thought of a strategy. The new regime so forces the issue that individuals must trust their instincts, piece things together as they go.

Happily, it turns out that improv has an unexpected cushion. It may seem to demand immediate reactions, but it has a way of stretching out the moment, breaking it up into discrete episodes. There is room here we did not know about. If you will allow me an odd illustration, I see this confidence in my cat, Daz, who at sixteen months likes to wow me by jumping high in the air in pursuit of a bit of cardboard on the end of a wire. He doesn't care how he goes up, or what happens once he gets there. He is perfectly focused on getting the cardboard. He doesn't even care what happens on the way down. As a young cat, he's fit enough to leave that for later. When later comes, 1.5 seconds on, he takes stock of the moment. "OK, missed the cardboard. OK, where am I? OK, in a dive, upside down, two feet off the floor." And he has plenty of time, it turns out, to rotate 180 degrees and land on his feet. It turns out there is something like this room for reaction in our own efforts at improv. As the individual falls into the moment, an unsuspected pocket of freedom opens up. There is time to react, adjust, and make choices. A good deal of improv allows for "just in time" reactions.

What one cannot do is block.[441] In official improv, blocking occurs when one improv player refuses the lead of another. The first player suggests a premise: "Your hair is on fire." There are no obvious cultural scripts for dealing with such a situation, but improv tolerates neither hesitation nor refusal. The second player must say *something*. If she says, "Yes, it's the latest thing in Finland," she has accepted the premise and the improv may proceed. If she says, "No, it isn't," or, worse, "You're wrong," she has blocked and the routine dies.

In the real world, blocking kills more than routines. I saw a moment of involuntary improv one afternoon at the Coca-Cola Company. Sergio Zyman, then a senior vice president,[442] interrupted a meeting without warning and said, "OK, I want to try something else. How about this? You're the Catholic church. What do you do?" It turned out that, without warning or explanation, Zyman was asking us to address the strategic circumstances of the Coca-Cola Company by identifying its similarities to the Catholic church. (The two institutions turn out to have several things in common.) This was a radical departure for everyone because corporations in general, and Coca-Cola in particular, do not often use metaphor in this way. As it was, some rose to the occasion. They said, "fine, metaphor, got it" and proceed to play the game. Other people blocked. They could not or would not use metaphor in this way. They refused Zyman's sudden shift of premise. (Any time someone asks me to defend the value of a liberal arts education, I think of this moment.)

As it turned out, Zyman was pitiless. He went round the room and asked everyone at the table to take up the metaphor. "You are the Catholic Church, what do you do?" To use the current phrase for corporate failure, a couple of his lieutenants flamed out in the most spectacular fashion. One said, "pass," and the other actually said, "um, what he said," pointing to the person beside him who had just spoken. The room braced. Corporate Icaruses plummeted earthward. These were deeply talented administrators, men who can make a spreadsheet do astonishing things. They were men in mid-career, marked for success and advancement. No longer. They had blocked.[443]

There are other kinds of blocking dangerous to involuntary improv. Keith Johnstone says that some players insist on "guarding the gates of consciousness," a self-censoring that makes the free flow of reactions impossible.[444] Smaller forms of blocking, especially indecision and avoidance, can have the same effect. All of these are factors that prevent the involuntary improv player from stepping into the moment. All of them block the moment of abandon on which response demands. Improv training helps to eliminate the cautions, the hesitations, the repressions created by socialization and training.

There are people who censor for us. I have an acquaintance in Toronto who has done this for perhaps thirty years, in every relationship or organization of which he has been a part. In the world of improv, he has been a one-man wrecking machine. He is particularly good at making sure that conversation is never allowed to get to the falling stage. He sabotages proceedings with a variety of techniques: by asking people to define their terms, asking relentlessly for clarification, observing the tiniest inconsistencies, venturing no opinions or possibilities of his own, and generally refusing to accept those suggested by others. He is particularly amusing when confronted by metaphor, which of course requires a little moment of abandon as we allow the meaning of one term to transfer to another. He always reacts as if this were the first time he had ever actually witnessed the rhetorical event called "comparison," and as if he will have to think about it a good long time before going any further.

Involuntary improv demands a willingness to suspend what one believes to be true of the world and to, as it were, fall into the possibilities that are emerging. The paradox here is the safety of risk. (Remember Elaine May's statement that "the only safe thing is to take a chance.") It turns out that there is no real advantage to keeping our distance from involuntary improv. It is almost always better to engage, to close the distance, and to work close up. Of course, this is unexpected. Confronted by involuntary improv, everything in us shouts, "Caution!" But caution removes us from the only place that we can work out the possibilities, what the world demands, and what the world allows. Distance turns difficulty into more difficulty. It is also true that there is more room in engagement than we are inclined to expect. Or to put this more simply, the trick seems to be to move up close with the understanding that, like my cat Daz, we will nonetheless have time to recover from mistakes.

Involuntary Improv and Pattern Recognition

Improv demands a pattern of problem solving characterized by generality and imprecision, messiness and simultaneity. It's as if all the things at hand internally (in one's experience, training, and problem-solving past) are being brought to bear on things at hand externally. Something inside begins to resonate with something outside, and they begin to define each other. Something emerges. This process of invention is not systematic or even orderly. Patterns emerge all of a sudden, as if on their own. We experience ourselves less as the author of the insight and more as the place it chose to happen.

Here is Mike Nichols describing voluntary improv.

> [W]hat happened after some time was that you had access to everything you knew and some things you didn't. You got so that under the stress of performing and improvising for an audience, instead of being crushed by it and made small, as one is to begin with, you could actually become more than yourself and say things you couldn't have thought of and become people you didn't know. Certainly not all the time because for every one of those times there were, let's say, ten when you relied on certain tricks and certain things you'd done before and certain gimmicks you knew always worked. But that tenth or eleventh time when there was a dybbuk, when you suddenly didn't have to think at all, that was the most, the only, exciting thing about it.[445]

Many patterns are called, few are chosen, and almost none is rejected entirely. The problem solvers keep throwing things back into the pool of possibility and fishing out more until they have something that will serve for the task at hand.[446] This is one of the causes of messiness. Nothing (or almost nothing) is useless until the moment of inspiration. Then everything, except the inspiration, is. The trick here is to keep things in play so that the element that works badly in one configuration can return in another. The messiness also helps account for the strange narrative structure of invention. Nothing seems to have been accomplished until the problem is fully solved. There is no patient methodology that lets us know how far we've come and what it is we should do next.

Patterns become propositions, things we try out in and on the world. The improv people call these "offerings," and this term is apt because, like everything in improv, the offering enters the world as a suggestion, to be accepted or refused, and almost certainly reformulated. This is highly self-conscious pattern recognition. We are scanning the world to see whether, how, and how much our offering fits. And we scan to see how it changes the world as it enters it. And it is dynamic pattern recognition. The process of interaction between internal and external worlds is now taking place between our offering and the world out there. Offerings make more data stream in. We have proposed something and the world has responded. The improv is well in train.

Offerings are necessarily an exercise in what Kathleen Foreman and Clem Martini call "naming and framing."[447] An offering helps shape the moment, both negatively and positively. It eliminates certain things from possibility. Some suspicions are confirmed, others are encouraged. Good offerings also supply a pretext, profile, or premise. They give the world something to work with. They give it something to organize itself around. This too is an argument for the safety of risk. The only way we can find out what the world will bear is by trying things out. The only way we can open up options is by trying them out.

Pattern recognition is an iterative process. We keep trying things until one of them appears to fit. There is no very clear or deliberate process of evaluation. It is, as the colloquial phrase has it, a matter of throwing things at the problem and seeing what sticks. Messiness and dynamism reappear. Good offerings are no sooner identified than they are taken up. Taken up, they change the world, and new offerings are now possible . . . and taken up. Experimentation, trial, error, and outcome seem to happen all at once. We are not judicious. We do not parse the world and assay solutions. It is a muddle, sometimes glorious and exhilarating, more often not. It is not that the several steps of rational action cannot be performed; it is that they must now be performed all at once.[448]

And in this circumstance, individuals treat one another as sources of offerings. They do this by building up a number of interpretive possibilities. Each individual suggests a way to respond to the challenge at hand. And eventually, as the group warms up, these come thick and fast. A few offerings are ludicrous, and their presentation is marked by a brief silence, a period of mourning, as it were.[449] Some offerings are immediately identified as useful, and they are embraced and put to use. Whatever else we think, we must think this. And still others are neither accepted nor refused. Instead they are shelved.[450] Presumably, this is one of the logics of the support group, that device with which so many people equip themselves for difficult transformations.[451]

The conventional rules of deliberation appear not to apply. Things are exceedingly messy. There are moments of clarity and consensus, but everything remains in a state of suspension. We are thinking this in this way for these purposes, but we might very well repudiate or refigure both the way and the purposes. Everything is in quotation marks, subject to revision and abandonment. This messiness, so contrary to the rules of grave deliberation, appears to be the very stuff of creative endeavor. It is only when we create a rumpus of possibilities that the really interesting and useful ideas can emerge.

The interesting thing about this muddling is that it requires no executive function. No one sits in judgment of offerings. The group needed to comb through these ideas, judging and sorting. It's enough to grasp the best ideas and go with them. The others will wither from a kind of benign neglect. Somehow the group edits without ever having to exert its collective will in any obvious, explicit, or, inevitably, contentious way. This means, and this is where the muddling comes from, that the group really never knows where it is. There is no sense of development or progress. No one could take minutes of its proceedings. Everything is a perfect muddle, until someone shouts, or more usually enacts, "Eureka!" "What if you put this with this and with that?" Out of a great many offerings emerges something that organizes the best of them into a coherent whole.[452]

Improv and Transformation

We become something new to respond to the challenge of involuntary improv. The creature we become is constructed according to Darwinian principles. It has the characteristics of the world in which it must survive.

It is messy and unstable, continually proposing things to the world and reworking itself as the world responds. This instability allows responsiveness, but at the cost of the calm that once prevailed.

It is tentative. We understand that a behavior that works well for the moment may prevent us from understanding and acting tomorrow. We scrutinize behaviors even as we engage in them.

It is reflexive and self-scrutinizing, keeping behaviors always in the forefront of its consciousness, never allowing them to be taken for granted, become just how one does things. This means that it can't ever achieve the power and ease that comes when behaviors are routinized.

It is spontaneous and freewheeling, getting things out of the self into the world as rapidly and vividly as possible. This means that each of us and all of us live in a world ruled much less by impulse control than was once the norm.

It is dynamic. It has discarded its former stop-and-start pattern, its tendency to see change as a short-term challenge and adaptation as a one-time event. This creature created by involuntary improv is in a continual state of transformation, swapping techniques into and out of its interaction with the world. It is those fountains that stand in front of the Metropolitan Museum of Art in New York City, always the same fountains, constantly renewed in their composition.

The creature that we create to respond to the world of involuntary improv, the transformation we become to be capable of transformation, is lively, self-aware, spontaneous, and in process. But it is also a little frantic, self-conscious, overwrought, ungrounded, and evanescent. We may look a little like Robin Williams in the middle of one of his improv pieces. But in fact we are vastly more tested and, at our best, rather more accomplished.

SHAKESPEARE-IN-THE-PARK TRANSFORMATIONS (FREE TRANSFORMATIONS)

Terrie: OK, so Robert comes up to me and he's, like, "So where were you last night?" And I go, "I was with Cheryl. Where were you?" And he's all like mad and stuff and walking around and everything. [*struts in a hip hop manner, arms straight, fingers rigid and pointing downward, upper body rolling back and forth*]

Jean: What is the *matter* with him? [*struts too*] "Oh, I'm so tough." What*ever*. He's such a *loser*.[453]

Speech like this is sometimes called "Valley Girl talk" or, simply, "Valley talk."[454] Notice the words "like" and "go." "He's, *like*, 'so where were you last night?' And I *go*, 'I was with Cheryl.'" Once this would have been "He said, I said."

The words "like" and "go" alert the listener. Terrie is using them to say, in effect, "I interrupt this conversation to bring you a little drama." Terrie is not reporting what Robert said to her. She is enacting it. For that moment in the conversation, she becomes Robert, attitude and all. And a moment later, she is not telling Jean what she said to Robert. She is performing the person she was last night.

Some will say that we shouldn't be surprised by this kind of dramatization—especially from teenage girls, who are, after all, inclined to take a dramatist's interest in the fine details of everyday interaction, and especially when these concern teenage boys. But mostly they will say Terrie and Jean are just kidding around. This is certainly true. Not all of our transformational activity is involuntary improv. A good deal of it is playful, spontaneous, and dramatic. But should we think of it merely as play?

This essay is a companion to the essay called "'Like' Talking and Other Acts of Speech" in section 1.

I have studied the Elizabethan theater outside London, how people used the symbolisms of the body to participate in and to play out the theater of everyday life, as it were. It seemed to me that what Shakespeare was able to do inside the theater was encouraged in some small way by what the English were able to do outside the theater, that the theater of everyday life was finding its way onto the stage. As I began to survey the sheer range and robustness of the voluntary transformations that are the topic of this section, it occurred to me that the reverse was happening in our time. In "like talking," the theater of popular culture (and by this I mean particularly movies and television) is finding its way into contemporary life. Hence the notion of a Shakespeare freed from the theater, Shakespeare in the park.

An "air guitar" is an invisible or imaginary guitar, or the playing of one. Usually, the player plays a solo on his air guitar while listening to the original music. Tom Cruise (as Joel Goodson) plays an air guitar in *Risky Business* (1983, dir. Paul Brickman), and Mike Myers (as Wayne Campbell) plays one in *Wayne's World* (1992, dir. Penelope Spheeris).[455] In some circles, air guitar is confined to one's bedroom. In others, it is acceptable behavior at parties, and guests will join one another in performance. (A teenage host told me that air guitar is one way to tell if your guests are enjoying themselves.) It is true that there is often something playful, even ironic about air guitar. But it is also true that most practitioners play with a certain intensity. For the moment, they are the soloist.[456]

There is also "air baton," proving that "air" exercises are not the preserve of low culture. Some listeners stand in sock feet in their living rooms and conduct their favorite symphonies. They are apparently untroubled by the fact that they are conducting the prerecorded efforts of professional musicians who cannot see them. The satisfactions are real enough. The air batonist decides for herself whether her performance was good or bad. The recording is both a cheat and a failsafe. In the event of pilot error, the symphony goes on . . . and so may the air batonist.[457]

In lip sync, as in air guitar and air baton, the player insinuates himself into someone else's performance.[458] But lip sync goes a step further. The player commandeers the song in an appropriation of celebrity. He or she becomes the star. And there are a variety of additional motives. Lip sync is a way to claim one or several qualities of the artist. It is a way for kids to claim maturity, for the mature to claim youthfulness. It is a way for a fourteen-year-old to become something she sees in the creature called Britney Spears. It is a way for an account executive to become something she sees in the person, the character or the role of Kathleen Battle. It is a way for a gay man to claim, claim fellowship with, evoke, or ridicule the gender, character, charisma, or circumstances of Cher, Madonna or Judy Garland.[459] It is a way for a lesbian to claim, claim fellowship with, evoke, or ridicule the gender, character, charisma, or circumstances of Tom Jones.[460] Lip sync involves more risk than does air guitar or air baton. Performance counts for much more. Air guitar forgives imperfection. Lip sync often scorns it.

Karaoke is ruder and more honest. In karaoke, the player does not accompany the performer. She replaces her. The voice of Whitney Houston or P. J. Harvey is excised from a song, leaving thousands of dollars of studio production in place. The karaoke singer must carry the song in a way the air guitarist and air batonist don't have to. There is less room for error. In the event of error, the song cannot survive. Performed in front of friends, karaoke gives us a chance to make idiots of ourselves. Performed in a bar or a night club, it must survive the scrutiny of hostile strangers. Karaoke makes a greater claim on celebrity and it risks more ridicule.[461]

Microsoft's Flight Simulator program permits the individual to fly a Cessna or Concorde to the major airports of the world, and renders some of them, including those of London, San Francisco, and New York, in detail. We might well sneer at Flight Simulator as a species of transformational opportunity, but it is widely regarded as the "killer app" that helped sell the first personal computer, and so helped start the revolution in personal computing that changed the last decades of the twentieth century.[462] Millions of people spent thousands of dollars apiece for the simulation of taking off from a runway at Meigs Field in Chicago. (They then proceeded to see how close they could fly to the John Hancock Tower without colliding with it, and then what happened when they flew right into it.) It was a "wire-frame artifact" in the worst sense of the term, not particularly engaging, sophisticated, or lifelike, but Flight Simulator was a killer app nevertheless.

In the computer game Myst, the player finds herself in a place of eerie beauty. There is evidence of human occupation: an unsettling combination of cultivated landscapes and industrial monoliths. Eventually she may find her way into a palazzo. It is empty and she can establish, after poking around for awhile, that it has been overwhelmed by violence and then abandoned. This is no wire-frame experience. No people can be found in the Myst world but there are traces, first, of their tragic fate and, still more eerily, of the formidable intelligence of the game's creators, the brothers Robyn and Rand Miller. The world's sounds and sights are so compelling that it becomes a reality in its own right. After a couple of hours of Myst, I was crossing Toronto's University Boulevard, and, as I looked north to Bloor Street, I thought to myself, "That's really well rendered."[463]

In the game Sim City, the player assumes the role of a city planner, designing, creating, and maintaining parks, city services, public institutions, and highway access. It is, finally, an exercise in trade-offs. Build too many factories and pollution climbs. Build too few and tax revenues fall. I found I could not play this game with any pleasure. No sooner had I laid out my little town, the one I want to live in, the one where nothing bad ever happens and everyone is happy all the time, than I was informed that an earthquake demanded the provision of emergency services. I panicked and ran. This was not my first glimpse of the Woody Allen within, but it was vivid and convincing.[464]

I have seen Sim City played by those who like it. The son of a friend of mine, then a young teen, spent hours constructing his town. His father suggested I ask for a tour. Christopher was pleased with the attention and displayed his creation with pride. One particular feature of Christopolis caught my attention, though. "Um, Christopher, it looks like you've built a prison in the middle of your most expensive suburb." Christopher looked at me coolly and said, "It pleases me to do things like that." Game, set, and match to the teenager. Catching adults making assumptions about cities and sons is a privilege of the teen years, and, in the right hands, it is one of the several things Sim City makes possible.[465]

Will Wright, original designer of Sim City, also created a later game called The Sims.[466] Here the player works on a more intimate scale, creating a family, the Sims, and the environment in which they live. The player chooses the gender, age, astrological sign, career path, job, job performance, and salary of each member of the family. The player is also asked to specify their personalities, but the choices sound like something out of a junior high yearbook: neat, outgoing, active, playful, nice. Skills are categorized oddly: cooking, mechanical, body, logic, creativity.

In spite of the paucity of these choices, players prove inventive. They create thousands of families and appearances. Some players take a perverse pleasure in torturing their Sims by giving them conflicting qualities and putting them in appalling situations. The response to The Sims has been remarkable. Players swap scenarios, identities, hints, and strategies on a profusion of websites.[467] No anthropologist is studying Sims, but this final proof of their place in the world can't be far off.

Sometimes simulations encourage creativity that was never intended. Consider the case of the TV series The X-Files. Fans decided that the show was not enough. An episode would end with Mulder and Scully driving down the usual lonely country road, and fans would keep writing, describing what happened after the episode, developing a new storyline, sometimes creating an entire new season. "Fan fiction" (or "fanfic"), as this writing is called, began as a kind of homage. It was a measure of how passionately fans cared about the show and its characters. But it came eventually to represent fans' proprietary feeling for the show and detailed expectations of what should happen on it. (There is actually a term, "shippers," for those who called for the consummation of the relationship between Mulder and Scully.) Chris Carter, the show's executive producer, suddenly found the world filled with would-be Chris Carters, many of them prepared to doubt and query his every plot and casting choice.[468] On About.com, David Sweeney wrote,

> Some in the X-Files fan community were disturbed by what they saw as significant characterization and continuity problems in season eight [of *The X-Files*]. They are now addressing this issue by rewriting the episodes to correct the problems.[469]

Will Wright is probably thrilled when someone invents something with one of his games. Chris Carter may feel somewhat differently. *The X-Files* has, in effect, been hijacked. When fans make what they believe are better choices, they are prepared to say so: to other fans, to the Internet, to the media, and, when acting in concert, to the Nielsen ratings. This once god-like Hollywood producer has something in common with Tudor monarchs: overmighty subjects. The good news turns out to be bad news. People care deeply about the show and they are, some of them, presumptuous enough to seek power over what happens on it.[470]

It could be worse. "Talking to the screen" is the practice of shouting out dialogue, directing, or giving production advice while watching television.[471] John Caughey tells us there are African American communities in which listeners keep up a withering stream of comments.[472] Colleges have long hosted midnight movies, the express purpose of which is to give the audience a chance to shout out better dialogue. A canned but sometimes still funny version of this exercise was the television show *Mystery Science Theater 3000* (and the 1996 movie based on it, directed by Jim Mallon). The same urge to talk back can be seen in the culture-jammers movement that scrawls dialogue on advertising billboards (e.g., a dialogue bubble beside a high-fashion model that contains the words "feed me") and in the magazine *Adbusters*, where Kalle Lasn and his staff rewrite advertisements.[473] In his most generous moments, Carter can imagine himself caught up in a creative partnership. It could be much worse. He could be the object of an outright assault.

What is it to participate in a simulation? Who does one become? This is not always clear. In Myst, the player is a person who comes after whatever has happened, but whether he or she come from Starfleet Command or a band of gypsy pirates, the game does not specify. In Sim City, the player is a city planner. The kind who bicycles to work with pant legs tucked into socks, or the kind who prefers to pass through the city in a Ford Explorer? Again, the game does not say. Players may choose, or they may choose not to choose. ("It's just me playing the game.") In the case of The Sims, the player is God-like, or, if Sims are being tortured, something more demonic. In the case of fanfic, the "player" is an executive producer and writer . . . or Chris Carter. And, in the latter case, we can't be sure whether the player is a generic executive producer, a generic Chris Carter (i.e., hip, young, alternative Hollywood player), or trying to get closer to the man himself. ("Yeah, I like ambient when I'm writing because I hear it's totally his favorite.")

Matters of identity are clearer in the computer game Blade Runner. The player in this case becomes Rick Deckard, a low-level detective (or "blade runner") charged with tracking down and "retiring" five replicants, androids who look like humans but live like slaves. This character was richly described in Philip K. Dick's 1968 novel *Do Androids Dream of Electric Sheep?* and again in the movie based on the book, *Blade Runner* (1982), directed by Ridley Scott. The player takes on a ready-made persona. But the novel, the movie, and the game all turn on a deliberate uncertainty. Is Deckard a human, or is he, unknowingly, a replicant? As the game unfolds, conflicting evidence emerges. The game ends dramatically, forcing the player to choose.[474] When I reached this dénouement, I was surprised to discover that I had no doubt. I "knew" I was a replicant and, to my further astonishment, I acted on this knowledge by shooting the blade runner who approached me. This game is constructed to allow players to discover to what extent they have taken up residence in the character. In this case, unexpected choices supply hard evidence of a transformation we might not otherwise admit to.[475]

Some of these transformational opportunities depend upon a collectivity of players and real-world events to play themselves out. Camarilla (also known as Vampire: The Masquerade) was a role-playing game enacted in an arts pavilion in San Francisco in the mid-1990s.[476] Seventy-five men and women met there to step into well-developed characters who were members of a long-standing, richly scripted community of vampires.[477] As Douglas Rushkoff shows, Camarilla is equal parts script and circumstance. Some of the drama of the event comes from the scenarios and rules supplied by the game. These are rich enough to put Microsoft Flight Simulator or The Sims to shame.

Everyone present is pretending to be a member of one of several vampire clans, who are all competing for some measure of control over the city of San Francisco. The many different clans of vampires give different personality types the opportunity to express themselves within the game. As Laurenn [a game player] breaks it down, "Malkvanians are exhibitionist, and want to be crazy in real life. People who play Tremere are spooky, and have a mystical spiritual bent. Nosferatus tend to be ugly, or think they are. People who play Ventrue want to be military, mighty, powerful or yuppie. Toreadors want to be beautiful club people, and Brujahs just want to rebel."[478]

But this is only the frame of the game. How it plays out depends on the interactions of the characters Prince Vitosius and Lord Julius, as these reflect the personalities, strengths, and inclinations of the people playing them . . . and, in this particular game, on the behind-the-scenes power struggle between two players, Michael and Craig. In a sense, the game supplies the vector of events, but completion is left to players, whose intentions and actions are only shaped, but not determined, by the narrative arc of the game. This is a transparent—draughty, one could even say—vampiric exercise. Without the participation of many people, it exists only as a ghostly idea. To work as a transformational opportunity, the game needs the world. This makes it very different from, say, the *Rocky Picture Horror Show* ritual, in which individuals engage in impersonation and drama that is exclusively drawn from and mostly addressed to the movie on the screen.

Some will argue that this game is merely dress-up, an exercise for nerds whose only real hope of seduction comes from pretending to be vampires. This is one way to look at it . . . and Rushkoff tries this out. But it is worth pointing out that the game played that evening was one instance of a very large underground of gameplaying activity. Games like Dungeons and Dragons, Magic: The Gathering, Virtual Worlds, and MetaWorlds, and invented worlds such as those of MUDs and MOOs, engage the enthusiasm of millions of people, some of them at formative ages.[479] Some see the transformations in the game as leading to transformations in the world. Rushkoff is among them.

Craig's entire persona seems based on the rejection of hand-me-down conventional values in favor of self-made rules: "For something to be cool for society," he explains, "someone has to come up with something creative so people go 'wow, I never thought of that. I'd like to jump on that train of thought.' Well, in the Elysium, we're inventing whole personas, and make-believe worlds, and giving color to them, and creating alternate lives for ourselves. And that, by my definition anyway, is cool."[480]

There are other events that require the participation of the world. Rotisserie League baseball is one of these. The player assumes the persona of the owner/manager of a major-league baseball team, which includes players from across professional baseball. It is the summing of their performances in the real world that decides the fate of a Rotisserie League team. The *Wall Street Journal* was concerned with what might happen during the baseball strike of 1994. "More addictive than crack cocaine, more consuming than flesh-eating bacteria, Rotisserie is a hobby with a million-odd adherents who, deprived of their fix, could well prove a menace to society." Walter Shapiro, manager of the Nattering Nabobs, was nervous, too, wondering whether, in the event of a strike, "I'll wake up at 3 a.m. on Friday and have to think about death and the meaning of life instead of where to get a decent relief pitcher."[481]

Remarks like these, and names like "Rotisserie" and "Nattering Nabobs," are designed to tell us that the players do not take themselves or Rotisserie League baseball too seriously. But of course the truth is otherwise. This transformational opportunity is a passion, against which distinguished careers, family crises, national events can sometimes pall. This is not entirely surprising. Ours is a culture in which baseball is, for many kids, one of the transformational exercises of childhood. Indeed, voice-over basketball, discussed earlier, has as its original voice-over baseball, and many people can recite the mantra of childhood with which one steps to the sandlot plate: "It's the ninth inning, the bases are loaded, the count is full. . . ." It is precisely the difference between Rotisserie League baseball and Fantasy Camp baseball (to which men of middle age repair to look for the indistinguishable pleasures of the game and their youth) that helps reveal what is at work here. Rotisserie baseball is no hankering after the game that was. It is an earnest engagement with a persona located in the here and now. Unlike that of Fantasy Camp baseball, this engagement is not sealed away from the world, but directed by it.

The Hollywood Stock Exchange (usually called "HSX") works on a similar principle.[482] The player assumes the persona of a stockbroker (or perhaps a producer), and is given two million "HSX dollars" to invest in particular movies, actors, studios, and funds. The value of the portfolio is decided by the performance of movies in the world and by the trading activity of other players. I have made a fortune on Kevin Spacey, buying his stock cheap when the scent of scandal sent the share price plummeting. I have lost a fortune on Don Cheadle . . . and I don't know why.[483] (So much for the "flight to quality.") But here too artifice is sustained by real events and the world outside the game. Indeed, the creators of HSX believe that their game now has a real effect on the way in which Hollywood makes its decisions. And they await the moment when this fantasy stock exchange becomes a real one.[484]

Some transformational events tip the balance of structure and event still further. In the 1980s, young, well-educated professionals living in London began to conduct themselves as inhabitants of the eighteenth century, adopting Georgian patterns of clothing, housing, transportation, and entertainment.[485] Now the persona, whatever else it does, must serve the individual as he or she engages in the practical affairs of a day-to-day world. This was the interesting thing about Severs's version of the undertaking. By forsaking electricity, plumbing, and other "mod cons," he demonstrated an interest in something more difficult than mere playacting and made clear what he was prepared to sacrifice to play the transformation out.

But if these transformational activities depend upon performance, it is clear that they also draw voraciously on preexisting worlds of meaning. The game Blade Runner draws upon a preexisting novel and a movie, but in a more general sense it draws on the conventions of both science fiction and noir detective fiction. Camarilla depends upon the Goth traditions given extraordinary depth by Mary Shelley and detail by Anne Rice, and on films like Holly Dale's *Blood & Donuts* (1995), Abel Ferrara's *The Addiction* (1995), Robert Rodriguez's *From Dusk till Dawn* (1996), and Fran Rubel Kuzui's *Buffy the Vampire Slayer* (1992).[486] Rotisserie League baseball takes advantage of the fact that most players have a life-long acquaintance with the game. And HSX appeals precisely because it gives players a chance to put their knowledge of popular culture to work. Similarly, in *Brady Bunch* evenings people reenact episodes and leverage their knowledge of the show and of situation comedy.[487]

Camarilla draws upon not only these cultural precedents, but also the life of the city around it. It uses San Francisco, and particularly the arts pavilion, as a stage. Both the city and this magnificent building contribute something substantial to the proceedings. (To guess how much, we need only imagine staging Camarilla in an Elks hall in Skokie, Illinois.) Detective fiction buffs attend murder mystery games staged in cities up and down the west coast.[488] One called Murder in May turns Vancouver into the scene of a crime and encourages players dressed in 1930s costume to wander the city in search of clues. (The city is not particularly rich in '30s landmarks, but it accepts the conceit with the distracted grace it gives to everything.) In Tamara, players take over a grand family home in Toronto. (Better to keep it indoors. Toronto has powers of enchantment rivaled only by Skokie, Illinois.) *Tony n' Tina's Wedding* spills into the streets.[489] The player attends as a member of an extended Italian family, the cousin no one quite remembers, and is swept up in family rivalries, solidarities, spats, and celebrations as these are played out on the city stage. Now the transformational exercise has the world's most dramatic city at its disposal.[490]

What about commerce? Camarilla is amateur theater of the truest kind. No one pays or is paid to participate. There are, no doubt, many attempts to find the commercial opportunity that these experiments open up and the business model that will allow for the maximum "extraction of value." But these attempts are only exploratory. The conventional leisure and tourism industries are not much help. Those who go to Vegas are merely gambling, and the extravagant floor shows, architecture, and cityscapes do not invite the visitor to step into a new persona. (The purpose of Vegas design is to make us feel less like our cautious, penny-pinching selves, not more like someone else.)

Club Med styles itself a kind of pagan departure from civilized life, but visitors do not experience any shifting or reworking of the self beyond an exploration of the libidinous.[491] "Pagan," in this case, means "no rules," not "new rules." The outcome is less interesting than the TV series *Survivor*, itself more participatory but still badly crafted. Those who go to Disneyland have long complained that they are too strapped in to enter the new worlds arrayed before them. We may think of Celebration, Florida, the town built by Disney, as a chance to leap to the far end of the passive-participatory continuum. Here the Disney experience was framed by American verities of small-town life and left to see what real life would bring to the proceedings. The results are mixed and, as we might expect, confusing.[492]

But new models are emerging. Starbucks has used store design and music to offer what Joseph Pine and James Gilmore call an "experience."[493] Restoration Hardware uses store design and its catalogue to give consumers a chance to recapture their own or someone else's past.[494] These business strategies demonstrate both that capitalism is mobilizing to incorporate transformation . . . and how far it has to go. The likes of Planet Hollywood and Hard Rock Cafe have discovered that it is not enough to jam celebrity memorabilia into a glass case. This gesture of amateur museology failed because it forced observers out of the celebrity experience when the rest of popular culture conspires to let them in. ("Here's you. OK, here's the celebrity.") Niketown is stranded somewhere between the cold, sanctimonious grey of its interior (who thought this "designer color" would speak to sports fans?) and the daunting challenge of that always empty hardwood court. ("Go ahead, dunk it.")

These exercises break one of the rules of managed transformation—the one that says we must not stand between players and their transformational vehicle. In the Hard Rock Cafe, the fan is forcibly removed from it. He is forced to see that the celebrity is adored by millions, of whom he is very merely one. The restaurant also suffers the problem that haunts almost all amateur museology. The amateur assumes that it's all about the object: Wayne Gretzky's hockey sweater, say. This is wrong because by itself, alienated by Plexiglas, illuminated by halogens, the object begins to lose meaning. Divorced from the larger world from which it comes, the sweater begins to return to its original condition: protective clothing made of cotton. The fan can now glimpse an analogy. He is to hockey what the sweater is to Gretzky: divorced and moving away at speed. Under Plexiglas and halogens at the Hard Rock Cafe, the object loses its significance, and both it and the fan are pushed from hallowed ground.

Niketown is still worse, still more anti-transformational. It manages to heighten the contrast between athlete and fan. That accusing hardwood floor, those giant monolithic images. Fans are reminded of the things that make identification with athletes difficult: that they are slow, out of shape, athletically challenged, insufficiently aggressive, among other things. Niketown has managed to turn itself into the opposite of television. For TV manages to blur the differences and to collapse the distance between a fan and her heroes. It is only when the fan attends a live sporting event, particularly football, hockey, and basketball, that TV's transformation becomes clear. It's all happening so fast! Everyone's so big! These are secrets television helps forge and then keep. Niketown, by contrast, "gives the game away."

The not-for-profit world treats the transformation as an opportunity. The "Rembrandt/Not Rembrandt" show at the Metropolitan Museum of New York asked visitors to assume the role of critics. As Simon Schama put it, this marked a shift in the usual visitor-museum relationship: "usually busy instructing visitors on what to see and how to admire, [the MET] has paid the public the shocking compliment of asking it to exercise its own judgment."[495]

But normally there is confusion in the museum world. This was evidenced by a show called "Sharks! Fact and Fantasy," created by the Natural History Museum of Los Angeles County, that toured North America in the middle 1990s.[496] The show was designed to make a point that is now a cliché of nature TV and museum programming: that sharks have more to fear from humans than humans do from them.

But visitors didn't much care for this message. They came, as one of them put it, "to feel the fear."[497] They came to glimpse the shark's ferocity and danger. Those not-very-convincing papier-mâché models provoked murmurs of admiration and alarm. The museum community was outraged. Murmurs of admiration and alarm! What, this is what you think we do here, provide thrills? You think we'd pander to a Coney Island blood lust? Isn't this what we're supposed to be saving the sharks from? Museums must learn that people come to them to seize a transformational opportunity (and that transformation is the great existential modality of contemporary culture), or they will continue to mount shows that no one much cares about. They must learn not to confuse the transformation they prefer with the one visitors care about (in this case, sharkish power).

Shakespeare-in-the-Park Transformations in Review

Can we generalize about this welter of transformational exercises, conventions, and precedents? Can we work our way up from these particulars toward a general view? Can we begin to construct a theory that helps explain Valley talk, Blade Runner, Camarilla, and Shakespeare in the Park?

In Ovid's language, the question is: Bodies of how *many* different kinds, exactly?

What "bodies of a different kind" do these exercises open up? There is a great range of possibility. These games reach in all directions. They allow players to choose from a range of occupations (museum curators to baseball managers to film producers), literary genres (noir fiction to gothic literature to science fiction), and personae (blade runner to Brady Bunch kid to Lord Vitosius). Their range is remarkable.

There are limits in place. Plainly, there are some things players do not wish to become. There are no games that offer up the experience of an Untouchable in India or a North American child with cancer. But it is not clear that this lack is a necessary condition. The format and conventions of the game appear supple enough to stretch to cover even these. The Untouchable case would ask the player to decipher a culture to survive there. ("That man, the one in white, is always a source of hostility unless you defer to him, in which case things change considerably. The one in Western clothing is helpful but only if you sometimes pretend to read the religious literature he keeps handing out. What about *wearing* Western clothing?") The player of a child with cancer would begin by finding himself in bandages, forced to deduce his circumstances from snippets of conversation. ("Oh, I'm six," "Oh, I'm sick," "Oh, I'm in a hospital.") Plenty of themes could be explored in such a game in the manner of *The X-Files* (i.e., government conspiracy) and *Erin Brockovich* (2000, dir. Steven Soderbergh) (i.e., poisoned suburb), but a straightforward engagement with the body and medicine from a child's point of view would be substance enough.[498]

There is an interesting moment in the computer game Blade Runner that helps illuminate the possibilities. Deckard's apartment has a balcony. Playing the game, I "walked" out onto it several times, but I was unable to find anything playable there—being on the balcony did not make doors spring open, or clues materialize, or anything in this world more clear or manipulable. (Or, if it did, I failed to notice.) But, eventually, I came to like the balcony. It didn't advance the game in any concrete or practical way, but . . . I liked being there. I'm still not sure why. Possibly, it delivered a noir moment, a sense of the detective caught in a morally dubious enterprise, of a city losing its moral compass, of a postnuclear city teetering on the edge of disarray. Or, more to the point, perhaps not. Perhaps its pleasures were less generic than these . . . but still useful within, and productive of, the drama of the game. This suggests that games can deliver odd, opaque, or imponderable transformations and still engage their players. It suggests that these games don't have to be aggressively game-like or to have that slap-happy, addled "old media" feeling to them to serve as transformational opportunities.

But surely there *is* a limit. To use an example we have noted above, no one is likely to create a game that allows us to experience the life of an illiterate, tubercular, cruel, and stupid charwoman struggling to raise five children in eighteenth-century Montreal. (Though no sooner do we deliver ourselves of a statement like this than we begin to wonder. "Like, what if, you know . . .") At the present moment it's impossible to say whether a theme like this is permanently excluded from this transformational world, or whether it is now off limits merely because new media are still shaped by old media, which were too mass-oriented and mechanically good-humored to contemplate such things. It seems to me possible that we will see the new media explore difficult and tragic themes. These technologies and the new media will then come to have more in common with classical and avant-garde traditions of literature and theater than with the mass-market fiction, television, and movies they resemble now. Some transformations are sought out because they are flattering, aggrandizing, self-extending. But players' raw curiosity also makes them look for experiences that do not amuse, flatter, enable, or extend. This is something to come back to.

There is another way to make this argument. It is sufficiently dubious that I have left it until now. I believe it's possible that most of the products of *Saturday Night Live* and *Second City Television* serve us as transformational possibilities. These shows have been stunningly prolific, creating Wayne and Garth (Mike Myers and Dana Carvey), Superstar (Molly Shannon), Stuart Smalley (Al Franken), Hans and Franz (Dana Carvey and Kevin Nealon), the Blues Brothers (Dan Aykroyd and John Belushi), Fernando Lamas (Billy Crystal), the Spartan cheerleaders (Cheri Oteri and Will Ferrell), and Bob and Doug McKenzie (Rick Moranis and Dave Thomas), to name fewer than half of their successful characters.

Our first reaction is to say, "But this is satire. We mock these characters." But if this is true, why do we see them so relentlessly imitated? In its time, the catchphrase of Billy Crystal's character Fernando, "You look marvelous," was repeated everywhere. These days I see perfect imitations of Molly Shannon's clumsy schoolgirl. It is, in some circles, still considered witty to pretend to be Garth, Stuart, or Hans. During the Bob and Doug McKenzie era, people would play out entire skits or pepper their speech with "hoser" and "take off, eh." Isn't this odd? Are we not making ourselves ridiculous? Why would we do this? To cash in on the joke? Do we really buy a few laughs at the cost of making ourselves look like idiots? Nothing in Erving Goffman prepares us for behavior of this kind.[499] Are there not cheaper, safer sources of humor?

I think it's possible that this imitation appeals to us because there is a certain pleasure in becoming someone who doesn't really "get it." There is something endearing about the person who is obsessed with bodybuilding or the complexities of beer. It turns out we have a weakness for idiots—especially ones who are protected from the world by their simplicity. (Why this should be so is not clear. I believe the answer is partly how utterly innocent of transformation these creatures are. But never mind.) And certainly there is the pleasure of the second moment of the exercise. Our imitation is also an act of repudiation. These men and women, we eventually acknowledge, are losers.[500] Who would want to be like this? Well, actually, we did. For a moment, before the repudiation, we quite liked being Molly or Bob. This definitional mobility tells us that we are already taking up residence in characters that are not only not heroic but positively risible. We have already opened up the range of possibility.

Grammars of the Game

If there are several transformational destinations, there are several transformational vehicles to get us there. Some of these, as we have seen, draw on a wide variety of materials. Camarilla draws on five: 1) novels (and the Gothic genre), 2) films (and the vampire genre), 3) the dramatic particulars specified by the game, 4) the extra-dramatic conflicts between actors in and out of character, and, finally, 5) the ambiance of its setting, the real-world place it is played. The Georgian reenactment movement draws upon the English people's knowledge of the eighteenth century and a fondness for public theater as long-lived as the treasured memory of Beau Brummell. Blade Runner draws upon a good novel and a great movie. (There are books to be written about the interrelationships between the Blade Runner game, novel, and movie. This is perhaps not the same "game" in three versions. It is one event spread over three media.) Rotisserie League baseball draws on the individual's lifetime acquaintance with the game and incorporates the competitive play organized by the game. The Hollywood Stock Exchange draws on the actor's knowledge of popular culture, and it incorporates the effects of the marketplace it has created.

We might call such a transformational exercise "glassy." At its simplest, this transformation looks in two directions, back on cultural precedents and resources that will give the transformation richness and veracity, and forward to some part of the world "out there" that will give the game richness and veracity. A transformation qualifies if it "lets light in," if it is porous to cultural precedents *and* practical events. To judge quality, we may ask a second question: "But is it stained glass?" How well does it transform the light it lets in?

But not all games are glassy. Some are opaque. They stay within themselves, neither drawing from nor opening onto the world outside. Microsoft Flight Simulator, The Sims, and Sim City admit almost nothing from the world, fictional or actual. But they still manage to engage. How is this? Flight Simulator gives the illusion of flight. The player can soar over Paris or New York City. This may be a little tedious. It may be a little unconvincing. (We make our way back and forth over Manhattan, but this is not the Manhattan anybody cares about. Indeed it is a place of relative locations, but not the things located.) But even in wire frame, we are as a god. Sim City creates the illusion of control. There are moments of frustration and challenge, but if one chooses, one can put a prison in the middle of the most expensive suburb. This may be an illusion of control, but it is also extraordinary power. An entire city bends to the player's will. In the case of The Sims, individuals exist only if and as the player gives them life. How they live depends on her. That players of The Sims torment their creations is a puzzle, but it indicates the opportunities of the game. All of these games give in power what they lack in dramatic richness. These games exist *sui generis* because they are reflections of, and exercises in, the player's power.

A third category of transformation is a straightforward bid for celebrity, or some property thereof. In "occupancy" games, the player takes up the air guitar and joins Slash on the introductory solo of the Guns N' Roses song "Sweet Child O' Mine,"[501] or wields the air baton and joins Sir Georg Solti in conducting Beethoven's Ninth, or lip-syncs to join Barbra Streisand in a song from *Funny Girl* (or replaces her, in karaoke). In this kind of transformation, the player becomes the celebrity at the moment the celebrity is most celebrated, in that moment in the sun.

Celebrity is a good in and of itself. It is the self made large, conspicuous, attractive (perhaps irresistible), powerful, and, literally, adorable. At least, this is how celebrities appear on the stage. We can only imagine what their private lives are like, strewn, we guess, with private planes, vacation homes, the best tables at the good restaurants, access to anyone they might like to meet, and the constant, adoring attention of a public that always keeps a discreet, devoted distance. Players want to appropriate some or all of this through their performance. They wish to make themselves glorious. The things to be gotten from celebrity here are, manifestly, things that endow the player with power—but they are not merely power.

As we noted, the occupation of a celebrity is often a search for something beyond their celebrity. It is a search for their definition of gender, character, class, charisma, or personhood. The celebrity world is a definitional experiment as stars invent selves, looking for what will differentiate them from other stars and speak to their fans. In the real world, the rest of us, watching the rules of gender, character, class, charisma, and personhood change regularly, wondering how we might define ourselves, pay careful attention. There are tips to living in celebrity. Celebrities are models of what we might look like—after careful acts of self-construction. The game that allows us to step into the identity fashioned by a Cher, Madonna, or Judy Garland has something more than the high voltage of stardom to recommend it.[502]

The appeal of the celebrity and the power of the promise of becoming a celebrity can be explained in another way. Celebrities are not just good at playing out one persona. They are good at playing out a range of them. How comforting and, again, instructive this ability is. Celebrities are proof of the possibilities of change *and* continuity. This is why, incidentally, we dislike them when they change too much, as Meryl Streep does, or too little, as Sylvester Stallone does. We want someone—Julia Roberts, say— who can be a variety of people (prostitute, legal secretary, law student) without obscuring the continuities of stardom from role to role. We want someone who can be a star without overwhelming us with differences between roles. This is perhaps a third way to explain the pleasure and interest we take in occupancy transformations.[503]

A fourth category of transformation appears in Myst. This game does not draw upon the world, it does not give a godlike power, it does not allow for the occupation of celebrity, a celebrity part, or a celebrity competence. It is merely arrestingly interesting and beautiful. It uses its extraordinary management of sights and sounds to make another world, a world distinct from the one we normally occupy. Poor players of the game, of whom I am one, find that some of this beauty disappears beneath the endless number of fiddly exercises. But for good players these exercises are merely another way the game inducts them into the delirium of the event.

Let's name this transformational type for the exemplar of the category. Let's call it the Myst transformation. ("Away games" is another possibility, but I believe this term is taken.) In Myst games, we enter a world that feels as if it exists *sui generis*, in and of itself. To step into this world is to step out of the existing one. It is to discover a world in which any rules could apply, in which we might be obliged to become any kind or number of creatures in response.

Myst transformations are "away" experiences with all the advantages and opportunities thereof. They allow us to enter a world that can be constructed entirely out of displaced meaning, both utopian and dystopian. It can have any of the properties we would wish the real world had. It can have any of the properties we fear that characterize the real world, and wish now to confront in some other shape or form. Myst transformations are a chance to participate in a world we can imagine but never construct.

Motives outside the Game

At some foundational level, Shakespeare in the Park is driven by what we might call the participatory turn that has emerged in contemporary culture. We have seen a steady shift away from the passive to the active voice. Increasingly, members of this culture see themselves as entitled to participate in the worlds around them.

The participatory turn has always been visible in the small circle of aficionados who surround a community of producers. Jazz clubs, Florida training camps, Hollywood insiders, all of these contain people who feel themselves entitled to participate, to comment, to present themselves as people in the know. The best example of this may be the Apollo Theater, that Harlem institution where the audience, no doubt properly, regards itself as something more than an audience. Its members are arbiters, and their message is clear: We decide what counts as entertainment, not the artists. Do not present yourself on our stage unless you are up to our standard. This is roughly the spirit of the anthropology seminar at the University of Chicago. All attendees, even those who are not at the center of the proceedings, regard themselves as players, with rights of criticism and, if need be, censure.

Before the installation of the participatory turn in our culture, the Apollo Theater or the Chicago seminar room marked the far extent of the insider universe. Everyone else was unwashed and unwelcome. They would eventually get to see what was being crafted on the stage and in the seminar, but only when it was finished, fully formed. Before the installation of the participatory turn, passivity was required of anyone outside the magic circle of the insider.

This is not the place (and, evidently, I am not the person) to chronicle the rise of the participatory turn. But four things may be taken as measures and indicators of its development. The first is the rise of punk in the 1970s.[504] Punk was fiercely inclusionary. As Bernard Sumner said of his first exposure to the Sex Pistols, "They were terrible. I thought they were great. I wanted to get up and be terrible too."[505] The standards of punk musicianship were deliberately low. The whole movement had a decidedly DIY quality about it. Partly this quality was a populist attack on the rock industry and its use of musical and production standards to control who could participate. Partly it was a piece of the punk attack on bourgeois notions of training, accomplishment, and excellence. But mostly it was a refusal to pull rank on the audience, to insist that those on the stage were not in any sense more remarkable than those before it.[506]

I encountered the second indicator of the participatory turn when I was doing research for a museum exhibit on contemporary teens. When I asked them to talk about contemporary culture, I saw clearly the same attitude as at the Apollo Theater. Teens talked about television series and Hollywood movies in a way that was proprietary, familiar, presumptuous. As if they could have and would have done better. I realized the last time I had heard anyone talk this way was when working on a film set, and in the presence of *real* insiders.[507] We have heard a good deal of talk about this generation's feeling of irony, and this talk is apt (for irony requires an insider's sophistication) as long as it acknowledges that there is a double motive at work here. These kids had an outsider's pleasure in the story and an insider's pleasure in (or disdain for) the camera angle.[508]

The third indicator of the participatory turn is zines (amateur magazines) and the Internet. Teens have produced zines in great number. The most generous estimate is 50,000. Stephen Duncombe, an expert here, puts the number at 10,000.[509] Multiplying titles by subscriptions by readers, Duncombe estimates a readership for these magazines at around 750,000. Even if we proceed more conservatively (say, 10,000 titles with five subscribers per title and five readers per subscription) we are looking at a parallel universe of some size.

Much of the best of the Internet has been created by volunteers. What has driven them is the sense that they are entitled to participate. The movie reviewers at the Internet Movie Database (http://www.imdb.com) include Roger Ebert and thousands of people who feel comfortable sharing a website with him. Amazon.com invites people to review books and they do. Plastic.com is designed to allow its participants to use one another's efforts to navigate and evaluate current affairs.[510] Hold the Dan Rather. We'll do it. The Internet exhibits a profusion of creative activity, as people write fiction, review films, and otherwise conduct themselves as the creators and proprietors of popular culture.

This sense of ownership is likely the effect of sustained exposure. Almost all of us have seen so much of the old and new media that we have come to see it with more critical eyes.[511] A river runs through us. We have logged thousands of hours. The rhythm of *Law and Order* and the duration of the commercial break are things we know by heart.[512] There is an irony here. The intellectuals of the 1950s were persuaded that popular culture would have a terrible compressive effect, encouraging conformity, simple-mindedness, and, most of all, passivity. It turns out they were wrong. All this exposure has merely encouraged a fine knowledge of chord structures, camera angles, plot devices, comedy hooks, casting choices, and other things that were simply Greek to the first audiences of film and television. Most of all it introduced us to the man behind the curtain and the confidence that we could participate. We now know, or believe we know, what's happening on the inside. Happily, this is an exuberant knowledge. We haven't become jaded and indifferent. No, we are still keen to find out the finer details. Hence the simulations. They give us this more detailed knowledge, or at least we believe that they do.

The overmighty subject is, in a sense, the final moment of the participatory turn. Such a player is not merely prepared to participate.

She believes she can do better than the original creator. It's not clear that anyone is ever going to parlay their experience with Microsoft Flight Simulator into an actual job as a pilot, but we can expect people who were once mere fans to act as if they have rights of participation and even ownership that were previously inconceivable. It is another nice irony that at the moment that the intellectuals are working to persuade us the subject is now dead, it should emerge with such robustness and self-assurance.

Motives inside the Game

One of the reasons we care about this transformational opportunity is that it opens the great range of opportunity we have just examined: we can become a museum curator, baseball manager, or film producer; creator of noir fiction, gothic literature, or science fiction; a blade runner, a Brady Bunch kid, or Lord Vitosius. If my speculations are correct, we will see transformational possibilities widen still further to include, perhaps, even the experiences of people bereft of power, beauty, stability. They might even expand to include the ineffable pleasures of Deckard's balcony, and in doing so the simulated world opens to embrace the full range of possibility that now exists for theater and literature. Such transformations allow us to experience selves and worlds that would otherwise be closed to us.

These transformations allow us to play the idiot (Bob and Doug), to take a moral holiday (The Sims), to assume godlike power. They allow us to become sharks. They allow us to rival a celebrity (such as Chris Carter) or to become one. They allow us to become a celebrity, to assume the celebrity's power, or to assume some new cultural property that the celebrity has helped invent. They allow us to enter a world that has been mapped out by novels, but that was previously closed to us. Now we may see what it is like to act out the character and to respond when the world responds.

In all of this, we are newly fearless. We are not much concerned about the possibility of embarrassment. Norbert Elias reads the increasing civilization of Europe as a rising of the threshold of embarrassment.[513] And we might imagine that this rise is most apparent in what Lionel Trilling calls the culture of sincerity.[514] This is a culture in which what concerns us is not perfect performance of our roles. What we work most assiduously to accomplish is a lifelike performance of mother, daughter, citizen, etc. Parents worked hard at creating children who were presentable in this way. They took pains to discourage them from standing up in public and belting out show tunes. In a transformational culture, we take it for granted that people may do so.

What we care about now is an exploration of the realm of possibility. What, we ask ourselves, would it be like to be like *this*? What if I were an x, y, or z? Raw curiosity is at work. We don't much care if we pursue transformation into lives and experiences that are not joyful, flattering, or dignifying. Indeed, we do not engage in transformation, as we once did, to imitate our betters and become more like them. We engage in it for a brute, dispassionate, almost mechanical empathy. It also brings us a lightness of being. We are transformational for the sheer, entirely evanescent pleasure of being someone else for a moment.

Terrie: OK, so Robert comes up to me and he's, like, "So where were you last night?" And I go, "I was with Cheryl. Where were you?" And he's all like mad and stuff and walking around and everything. [*struts in a hip hop manner, arms straight, fingers rigid and pointing downward, body rolling back and forth*]

Jean: What is the *matter* with him? [*struts too*] "Oh, I'm so tough." What*ever*. He's such a *lo*ser.

POSTMODERN TRANSFORMATIONS (IN REVIEW)

We have released the self from the obligations of full-time residence. It is now mobile and, in some cases, far-ranging. Ovid would recognize this aspect of the postmodern self. The radiant self is prepared to cultivate new, delocalized ideas of the body, self, and soul, and to move freely back and forth across once-strict boundaries between humans and animals, between humans and the plant world, between reason and myth, between rationality and emotionality, between the past, present, and future. Indeed, in many cases, it protests these distinctions and seeks to break them down.

Thus do some of the liberties of what Lévi-Strauss called *la pensée sauvage* return to societies of the first world. It is, actually, liberty plus liberty. Radiant selves are not merely allowed to cross these borders, they may exercise a shamanic liberty in doing so. (They can go where everyone goes, *and* where they themselves choose to go.) They have claimed the privilege of the wildest of the wild thinkers. But it is, in truth, liberty plus liberty plus liberty. For radiant selves may go where no one, even shamans, has gone.[515]

The original transformational power, once the property of gods, elders, and shamans, is now in civilian hands. Once collective, it is now individual, open to everyone, even Princess Dux (see section 3). Once sacred, it is now profane. Once directed by the ceremonial calendar, it can now happen anywhere and anytime. Once strictly bound by tradition, it is now free, or at least freeform. When the power of transformation entered the profane world, it was exuberantly transformed. Once this culture learned how to give itself "bodies of another kind," it did not cease until it was capable of endless range and variety, including Colonel Sanders, Mike Nichols, Chris Carter, Mohammed Ali, and Princess Dux.

The price, of course, was high. Driving ritual from the temple cost us dearly. The punishment was the loss of an enchanted world that submitted to, that resonated with, human designs. The universe became a chilly, alienated, dislocating place. Good thing everyone now had their own powers of self-invention. They were going to need them.

Premodern transformations advance the individual in the status hierarchy. Individuals change themselves to change their social standing. In its original form, this transformation was a jealous god, insisting on a narrow interpretation of the possibilities and marginalizing other transformational projects, especially those that took leave of the existing rules of gender, species, time, space, lifestyle, and, of course, class. All of these belonged to it. You may transform the self, it said, but here is what you must do. There will be no amateur improv or artistic license. Here is the rule book—better, the style sheet—by which you may distinguish good transformation from bad, the winners from the victims. This is why Trollope refused a "quondam lady" her claims to polite society—not because she was upwardly aspiring but because her performance was so badly done, so patently cribbed. Good poets steal, bad ones borrow. Pretending was tolerated. Indeed it was the necessary stuff of transformation, but only when it was humble and discreet—controlled, in other words, by the rules that controlled the self it was creating.

We see upward transformation everywhere still in popular culture. It is the theme of the television show *Frasier*, a story of two status-conscious brothers who are periodically appalled by their father, who cares not at all for upward transformation and prefers dogs, chairs, and drinks that point in another direction.[516] It is the theme of *Dharma and Greg*, a show about two people who spring from very different traditions, one radiant, the other upwardly transformational. Generally, when it appears at all, upward transformation is a laughing-stock, manifestly out of touch with the real possibilities of the self. It carries on, but it is, like a great family reduced to straitened circumstances, obliged to insist on the dignity it once made such an art of taking for granted.

But good news from England? Upward transformation may have won an important convert. Madonna is now being accused of becoming an Anglophile, of putting on aristocratic airs, and forgetting what Camille Paglia calls her "gritty family past in lower-middle-class metropolitan Detroit."[517] (Her husband, Guy Ritchie, director of *Lock, Stock and Two Smoking Barrels* [1998] and *Snatch* [2000], both gangster films, is accused of moving in the opposite direction.) It is odd that the master of postmodern transformation should care about the premodern form. But it may be that she is suffering a kind of transformational exhaustion. We saw David Bowie go through this. In his hour of need, when he had changed shape once too often, he resorted to the form of the English gentleman. Upward transformation could well feel like a safe harbor to those living in the wind tunnel of popular culture. It is, after all, ancient, stable, and, most important, still. What is odd, though these reports may not be trustworthy, is the suggestion that Madonna is doing the transformation badly. This would be unlike her, but it would also create a particularly interesting standoff: a master of transformation versus the form of transformation that is designed to discover bad performances. Upward transformation sets traps for the pretender and it insists that transformation can never be as simple as changing one's exteriors, which is, of course, exactly the postmodern, and Madonna's, game.[518]

Upward transformation remains one of the important motives of the social actor and the consumer, both a narrative of popular culture and an engine of the economy, but it is now merely one of several routines. Once the exclusive object of our affections, upward transformation must now actually compete for our attention. So desperate is it to recover a little of its former glory, it is not above compromise—even with a Ralph Lauren or a Martha Stewart. This must be an especially bitter pill. Once the sport of kings, upward transformation now depends on a second-generation American from New Jersey. This may help explain its ambivalent status, and the fact that we rush toward it in one decade, only to abandon it in the next. The little shrines are still in place: the note-perfect living rooms and dining rooms. But these are often too stuffy to be habitable. More and more, upward transformation is a Procrustean bed. It would have us forsake aspects of the self that come to us through radiant, beat, swift, and gender transformations.[519] We are prepared to keep it as one self among many selves, the way we keep one set of clothes "for best." But sometimes even this seems like more than it deserves.

Beat and brightwork open up new locations. But they begin by challenging the previous transformational regimes. The beats took aim at upward transformation. Bourgeois society was, they said, a trick and a lie, and the sooner it was undone, the better. The status-crafted self was, they said, false, inauthentic, and corrupting, a stranger to itself. When warned about the anarchic creatures that might be found beneath the role performance, they scoffed. Authentic creatures, people in touch with their feelings and essences, would surely be more worthy, honest, and true than those who had been trained to lie to themselves and to others. The object was to break through the upholstered, enameled, adorned surface of bourgeois culture and society, to throw off things Rousseau found so corrupting, and make contact with essential truths. Drugs, holy goof simplicity, the demi-monde, wild prose, even driving made up the new liberation theology.

The beats were democratizing the counter-Enlightenment and the Romantic impulse. Sensation, emotion, idea, event (or whatever these are before they are these) were liberated from the dead hands of culture, competence, and orthodoxy. They become places to discover truth "while it's still true." Naturally, it's impossible to make good on this act of bravery. The possible is eventually sheared of the sheer and then of the possible. Even epiphanies eventually *become* culture, competence, and orthodoxy. But some individuals, for a brief period, opened their senses directly to the world, or came as close to doing so as one can without, as Joan Vollmer put it, "blowing one's top."[520]

Swift selves were at war with upward transformation, refusing role performances and Trilling's "sincerity." The low-church Protestant tradition, the one that treated the self as an instrument, was active here, but it was reworked so that it was now as much an objective as an instrument, as much an end as a means.[521] No sacred purpose contained or directed it. No relationship with God gave it purpose. It was, in the characteristically swift way, peculiarly relationless. This was *homo economicus*, the Smithian creature for whom society is a precipitate of economy. But swift selves are not only economic. They need only the right to construct themselves without the interference and baggage imposed by religious and social authorities. And then they are away.

The '50s version of the swift self took the form of brightwork. In this happy moment, modernism and popular culture conspired together to make science and technology, military and social competition, international and individual mobility work in concert. Our future has darkened sufficiently to discredit these pairings, but the swift transformation continues. This is, after all, enterprise, capitalism's innovative side. It is the engine of the entrepreneur, the adventure of the venture capitalist. The swift self is almost as imperial as the upwardly transformational one. But it discourages other selves, not through scorn but by creating an environment in which all but swift selves are disadvantaged and displaced. We are not sure we want what swiftness does to the rest of us. Increasingly, we have no choice but to accept it anyway.

Brightwork has several futures to look forward to. One is what Christopher Dewdney calls the "fusion of human flesh with machines."[522] We accuse the swift self of being gadget-crazy, of caring too much for cell phones and PDAs, but these are rehearsals for transformations to come. When swift selves can build these into the body, they will. The wireless will give way to the fleshful.[523] Eventually, this could be what we might call, after the novel by William Gibson, the Mona Lisa Overdrive option.[524] This creature is nothing if not swift, no one if not relationless. She has been stripped even of her corporeal form and moves effortlessly through electronic space, with all knowledge as her dominion. Or we might call it the Burning Man option, after the festival that tries to create a virtual world in the desert.[525] Everything is stripped away: the infrastructure of the city, the marketplace, the institutions of learning, the places of habitation, systems of transport, theaters, parks, and stadiums. Burning Man asks all participants to supply their own HTML and XML, as it were. But the desert is merely a stand-in for virtual space. When Burning Man can be held online, it will be. And when individuals can take up residence in the Burning Man, they will. Whatever the means, whatever the destinations, virtual space will be irresistible to the swift self.

The postmodern moment is less ferocious than its modern predecessors. It is more inclusive, but then it is so promiscuous it can afford to be. We can be Goths, Deckard of Blade Runner, Chris Carter of a fanfic X-Files, or Robert, that fourteen-year-old boy Terrie and Jean find so mockable. We can occupy a range of people, professions, and predicaments, among them air batonist, aviator, city planner, and museum curator. We can cultivate several versions of the gendered self. We have cobbled something together in response to one or other moment of involuntary improv. Some of this is make-believe. Some of it is short-lived. But not all of it is insubstantial. We may not take up all the new possibilities, but we have seen them. Some of the integrity and unity of the old self depended on a life buried in the provinces, lived "down on the farm."

The postmodern exercise introduces a self or selves that are newly vulnerable. If the self is so easy to vacate or appropriate, can it be scooped up and carried off? This is the theme of several recent movies: *Single White Female* (1992, dir. Barbet Schroeder), *The Sixth Day* (2000, dir. Roger Spottiswoode), *All of Me* (1984, dir. Carl Reiner), and *Basic Instinct* (1992, dir. Paul Verhoeven). The boundaries of the self are porous for good and porous for bad. They allow relocation, but they create an anxiety. If I can get out, who can get in? All of these movies are about selves that open to others, selves that are incapable of defending themselves against someone's else mobility.

Put these locations together and we begin to see that the postmodernists have probably underestimated the range and intensity of our new mobility. (The postmodernists have constructed an idea of popular culture that relieves them of having to scrutinize it. The details are usually sketchy at best.) To make matters worse, it is not clear to me that the postmodernists have seen that these are not only locations for everyone, but locations for anyone. We have made of the self a crowded house. We are air batonists, Deckard on the balcony, radiant, upwardly aspirational, laterally mobile, swift, and beat, all at once. The new plenitude is within. The real mobility is an interior event.

The postmodern self is heir to the accomplishments of its transformational predecessors and the author of innovations of its own. Let us observe the principles by which this self is constructed. Here are seven properties of the postmodern self, culled as it were from the preceding discussion and offered here in review. I don't make special claims for these properties. They are merely "ideas of opportunity," rough ways to identify what is common to the great variety of things at work in the postmodern era.

1. Selfhood is porous. The individual can swim in and out of the self with the freedom of a goldfish passing through an aquarium castle. The obligations of residence are no longer onerous, not at all what they once were. There are no authorities to notify, registration forms to fill out, or passports to surrender. The postmodern self lives in the new Europe, where border control has been reduced to something like a formality. As we have noted, the new mobility is remarkable. Set it against the Renaissance cosmology, the one that situated man in a hierarchy between angels and animals, with no hope of substantial movement up or down, whatever the humanists might urge. Postmodern selves move in time and space, crossing religious, ethnic, and even species boundaries, claiming kin with angels and animals without so much as a fare-thee-well. As we have noted,

this is the story of Orlan and of Jocelyn Wildenstein. This new mobility would impress the Renaissance. It would wow even Japasa. Postmodern selves are at liberty . . . or at least at large. Permissions are things of the old order. Papers are one of the ideas that the overmighty subjects of the transformational world scorn as unnecessary.

The ability to move in the world at will, to import what one wants in new and spectacular acts of free trade, has created a new sense of vulnerability. If the individual can get out with such ease, what can get in? Might the self be lost, appropriated, distorted from without? The modernists were not troubled with this anxiety. The self was relatively well defined and well guarded. Perhaps too well defined and guarded. The problem was opposite: I am alienated, anomic, alone. The modern self was thin, attenuated, extracted by its individualism and existentialism from the world. The postmodern one is full fraught, as they used to say, troubled by complexities, fluidity, and multiplicity that let us out and the world too freely in.

It is this aspect of the self that seems to beg for postmodern treatment and the notion that selves are more signs in the salad spinner of contemporary culture. In Jean Baudrillard's "culture of the simulacrum," signs endlessly chase signs. They refer increasingly to themselves and lose touch with their originals, authenticity, anything that might be "real" or "true."[526] Tell it to Prince Vitosius and Lord Julius. It turns out that these selves are habitable—and inhabited on and off the Camarilla stage. Someone actually *lives* here. That Camarilla is possible tells us how rich and well organized this Gothness is. That Mike and Jim can play out their antagonism on stage and off, that Gothness can reach so deeply into what and who they think they are, that Gothness can serve, as Craig suggests, as a laboratory for new social selves, all of this provokes in postmodern theory an embarrassed silence. Were we truly living in a culture of the simulacrum, there could be no such thing as Camarilla.[527]

2. The world is porous. If the self can move so far, it is because the world offers so little resistance. As the sociologists now put it, it has loose boundaries. One of the great accomplishments of liberal scholarship and universal education has been a taking down of barriers that were once insurmountable. Difference has been diminished. It is virtually impossible, however much we sometimes try, to attribute the amount and the kind of difference to the other that Victorians, say, took for granted. There are no more "dark" continents. There are no more "oriental" imaginaries. No elites, subcultures, demi-mondes, or netherworlds are forbidden to the well-educated mind or closed to the mobile self.

The world has blurred categories. Cultural categories were once as well defined as a Cambridge college. This is college. This is not college. Precautions were taken against blurring. Walls marked the boundary. Porters kept the gate. Contemporary culture has no such clarity. Its cultural categories are open to several, sometimes conflicting, definitions. What is an "American," a "woman," an "executive," a "mother," a "wife," a "daughter," a "*New Yorker* reader," a dweller in New York City's "Upper West Side," a "Jew," a "P. J. Harvey" follower, a "*Law and Order* fan," a "Starbucks customer," a "long-distance runner"? None of these "mean" with their old clarity. Definitions are multiple, dissenters are many. Even when we know they all apply to "Janice," we can't be sure who "Janice" is.

It is a world of dynamic states. All of the things that define Janice are open to innovation, accidental change, slow, drifting adjustments. The notions "woman," "Jewish," and "*New Yorker* reader" have all changed steadily in the postwar period. Janice changes just by standing still, as the categories beneath her continue to shift. Even when we resort to conservation, restoration, or return, what went before is rarely simply reinstated. More often than not, Hobsbawm and Ranger say, even our traditions are invented.

An example that shows how porous selves and porous worlds interact may be found in the recent experience of Silicon Valley. Homa Bahrami and Stuart Evans discovered that the start-ups of the early 1990s were showing a transformational versatility unanticipated by conventional models. Executives who served as venture capitalists on one project were returning as consulting engineers on another. The CEO would return as the marketing expert. Individuals were changing hats with each new start-up. So many professionals have worked in such close quarters with one another that their skill sets are now largely indistinguishable.[528]

These professionals are mobile. They are prepared to move from one definition of what they do to a rather different one. More important, they are prepared to surrender their professional identity to someone else. This is the death of the spirit of the guilds, the one that insists that the players are profoundly different from one another and defined by impenetrable mysteries. It turns out that the postmodern professional can master and practice a variety of skill sets, and that it's relatively easy for these skill sets to produce a CEO where once they produced a venture capitalist. It is also the death of a traditional division of labor. It's as if we are moving away from Durkheim's organic solidarity, in which each individual takes a distinct part, to a mechanical solidarity in which each individual reproduces the whole.[529]

Something like this pattern appears in the film *Any Given Sunday* (1999, dir. Oliver Stone). There is a good deal of switching of hats. Lawrence Taylor, an accomplished football player, takes the role of Luther Lavay and, against the odds, appears almost as gifted on the screen as he did on the field. (This is to say that his appearance in this film as a football player is a coincidence. With gifts like these, football movies are a small part of his filmic options.) Cameron Diaz (as Christina Pagniacci) was a model before she was an actress. Jamie Foxx (Willie Beamen) was a comedian before becoming an actor, and, less predictably, shows enough athletic talent in his role as a quarterback to make us wonder whether he could not follow Lawrence Taylor's career trajectory in the opposite direction. In the film he takes advantage of his new celebrity as a quarterback to release a record, and, here, shows enough musical talent to make us wonder whether he could not follow LL Cool J's career trajectory in the opposite direction. LL Cool J (Julian Washington) began his career in hip hop, and continues to make music even as he becomes a better-than-cameo actor. Oliver Stone was a screenwriter before he became a director, and, in the film, he puts in a credible performance as the sports commentator, Tug Kowalski. Popular culture shows this pattern of career mobility so routinely we no longer remark upon it. Comedians appear to be the most mobile, and this may be due to their improv training.

But it is not just the porousness of the individuals that makes this fluidity possible. It is also the porousness of the world. The jobs themselves allow for this easy passage of individuals through them. Capitalism has declared war on the "silos" that created specialization and discontinuous expertise. It allows, in fact demands, corporate positions that are knowledgeable of and open to one another. Business roles are porous because executives are struggling to manage a company that must be porous in a world that is porous. Silos, once the first principle of managerial capitalism, are intolerable in the entrepreneurial capitalism that has emerged to contend with what Stanley Davis and Christopher Meyer call "blur."[530] We used to defer to difference. Increasingly, we "see over" it.

3. The individual has been newly enfranchised. Now the individual bears the right to change the self. (This cultural right to choose may well be more precious than the political right to choose. More people appear to exercise it.) Mary Waters has observed that people fashion their ethnic identity, suppressing what might have been the obvious tie, highlighting sometimes obscure connections, and engaging in outright invention when they have to.[531] This fashioning is sometimes driven by the whims of the moment. It is hard to imagine that Americans of the early eighteenth

century were quite so eager to announce, "Did I tell you I'm $\frac{1}{32}$ Choctaw?" But it also represents a pursuit of new definitional materials. Being Choctaw, for instance, is seen to give one access to the natural, the spiritual, and the mysterious. (Whether these materials are well chosen, well deployed, or genuine is a separate question. Too often we let our contempt for bad performances move us to reject all other identity claims.) The freedom that exists in ethnicity extends to gender, class, lifestyle, age. Who Janice is as American, Jewish, and middle-aged, as a mother, wife, and daughter, as someone living on New York's Upper West Side must be specified. Janice has a freedom to choose that her great-great-grandmother could not have imagined.

Lamont treats the "cultural sovereignty of the individual."[532] This is the individual's freedom to define herself in some of the matters of personhood. These are the discreet but defining matters of speech, clothing, emotion, music, reading, entertainment, residence, physical activities, leisure choices. All of these used to be specified by upward transformation. Or they came with identity as specified by ethnicity, gender, lifestyle, or age. Now they are individual decisions to be made discretely. We are accustomed to mocking these as the empty choices of a consumer society, a false liberty that decides nothing. But this mockery has not come to grips with the fact that these small choices have large consequences, that the individual is the sum of hundreds of little choices.

A culture that creates this right creates, inevitably, a responsibility. Individuals are now obliged to engage in this transformational activity. Those who decline, those who step out of the mass transformations we call trend and fashion, those who "spoil their ballots," all suffer a social cost. They become, respectively, pallid, ridiculous, or threatening. A culture that creates a responsibility must also create the resources with which to fulfill it. Contemporary culture courses with these. A river runs through us. Films, novels, current events, trends, emergent groups, nostalgic recovery, all sustain a stream of definitional materials.

Within the right to change the self is a self to ratify the changes. The emergence of this self is in some ways the most counter-intuitive development. In a world that conforms to the theories of George Herbert Mead, identity is ratified by what the individual sees in the mirror of other peoples' reactions. The individual knows herself as she is known by others. This mechanism operates still, but it has been joined by a new inclination on the part of the individual. When is it clear that you have become the person you want to become? As the respondent would likely say, "You just know. There's this pong in your chest." Pong in your chest?

But the informant insists on the ability and the right. "You're the only one who can decide who you are. Only you know you." We don't know what happens to cultures that entertain this degree of solipsism. We are going to find out.

Those who exercise these rights become, as we have seen, overmighty subjects. The postmodern era has seen the end of awe, a refusal to defer, a new taste for presumption. People are prepared to take on identities that another time would have regarded as too good for them. Chris Carter must live with fans who believe that they know better than he what should happen on the last episode of the season. His subjects are restless. They await their Essex. They have found their Brian Eno. But even this is old-world thinking. They no longer need someone to lead them to out of the old regime. Individuals exercise and occupy their own dominions. As Eddie Izzard puts it, they have become their own role models.[533]

As overmighty subjects, they have their own performative powers. A preteen on a basketball court takes possession of the voice-over that belongs to the sports announcer and the color commentator. He uses this to take possession of the pretext, the script, the accomplishment, and the admiration that belong to a celebrity athlete. This is what, in basketball, they call a steal. The preteen has intercepted powers that belong to the meaning makers. It is endemic hubris, a matter-of-fact appropriation of superordinate powers by a subordinate party. The twelve-year-old makes Larry Bird a god and himself Larry Bird. Such subjects are overmighty and increasingly common.

This license is modernist in origin. In the modernist scheme, as we noted above, the individual was free to take leave of the definitions of self routinely supplied by parents, extended family, ethnicity, religion, locality, nationality, and other "identity-producing agencies." The cost of this freedom was, often, alienation and anomie. Individuals were so fully disaggregated, so separated from the group, that they suffered a sense of dislocation.

In the postmodernist case, the license serves another purpose and it comes at another cost. Postmodernism offers something more like "free-dom to" than "freedom from." The postmodernist self takes for granted that it may define itself free of familial, social, and local influences. Liberty is not for the construction of the modernist self, described by Geertz as something "bounded, unique, [and] more or less integrated."[534] Liberty is for the often voracious, typically restless explorations of new experien-tial, existential possibilities, even when these are incompatible and contra-dictory. This is a way of saying that the postmodern liberty very often has consequences that violate the modernist one. Boundedness, uniqueness, and integration are often thrown into question.

4. The individual has been newly enfranchised in another way. Now people have the right to change the categories to which they belong. This is a cultural right that runs in parallel with political ones. It gives the likes of Ani DiFranco the right to redefine cultural notions of gender, the idea of femaleness, even as other feminists are petitioning Congress and marching on Washington. As we have seen, DiFranco went to work on the most basic rules of gender, on the deepest cultural forms of self-presentation and identity.

The reform of categories is a complicated business. Their "taken-for-grantedness" must be shifted, and the extraordinary power of habitus gainsaid. It is probably true that only performers with DiFranco's abilities can hope to accomplish this.[535] New ideas of gender must be fashioned. And in DiFranco's case, it is then necessary to tour for months at a time in a Volkswagen bus, performing for audiences of eight people, and building a following by tiny eddies of word of mouth. If DiFranco is to speak to Janice, all of this will have to be done to perfection in an act that is equal parts individual creativity and consensus. DiFranco plays the playwright for players and they in turn play playwright for Janice in a complicated process we do not yet understand.

Lots of groups now exercise this right of cultural invention, gays, Goths, and Republicans among them. Margo Jefferson observes the invention of "new cultural types" in what she calls "feats of stylistic engineering."[536] As we have noted, every film persona that takes is, potentially, a new social form, part exemplar in the old tradition, part habitable self in the new. Jefferson was talking about the once-conspicuous Dennis Rodman, and it is likely that only a few people have taken up residence in that persona. But Dennis Miller, Frasier Crane, and Diane Sawyer are more accessible, more habitable, and each of them is a feat of stylistic engineering that a celebrity culture creates as a vehicle of transport, an opportunity for transformation. We have spent so much time mocking and decrying the celebrity culture, we have only the most remote idea of how this works. We need to see that it is not just the DiFrancos of the world that rework our ideas of identity.

This is a cultural right with political consequences. As Elias Canetti put it, "A ruler wages . . . warfare against spontaneous and uncontrolled transformation."[537] No politician in recent memory has engaged in this warfare. (Some would argue, though, that Margaret Thatcher declared war on arts funding for this reason.) The culture wars were, among other things, a fight over who had the freedom, the right, and the means to invent new social species or reform old cultural categories.[538] No one won these wars because both parties have now seized the means of production to remake the world. What becomes of a world in which a profusion of different types are engineered, as the cultural logic beneath them is thought and rethought, is not clear.[539] But cultural reinvention must someday issue in political outcome and reform. Canetti's ruler is now an artistic director for a theater obliged to work with ideas and actors from disparate traditions: pantomime, Gilbert and Sullivan, puppetry, Yiddish theater, youth theater, Lithuanian theater, Chekhov, Wilde, Kabuki, Brecht, and several more in the works. Transformation is prolific, various, and noisy. Our political models are not.

5. The individual consists in many selves. We used to call these "roles," but the concept of a role will not stretch to cover the diversity we see in even conventional individuals. Janice, for instance, is not unusually composite, but there are lots of differences within her. If we take a single dimension, gender, this is clear. Janice is operating with at least four different notions of femaleness: the notion bequeathed to her by her very Jewish mother, the one she fashioned in college as a nascent feminist, the one she created for herself as a professional working woman, and the one that emerged in the third wave of feminism, as women returned to some of the markers of a conventional femaleness. Each of these posits its own assumptions, calls for its own performances, encourages its own frame of mind and mood, and results in its own self-concept. On the Venn diagram of gender, these four possibilities overlap very little. But the Venn-diagram approach is not entirely helpful. We need something closer to a Haight-Ashbury light show, in which each self is a different color and viscosity, washing back and forth, sometimes intersecting, more often not.

The problem is implicit in the metaphor. The term "roles" implies that the individual is merely divided across the several characters of a single dramatic enterprise. But Janice is more expansive than this, playing roles from disparate plays and drawing even from disparate traditions: Gilbert and Sullivan, Yiddish theater, and Kabuki. More precisely, the trouble is that several identities within the individual work from, and presuppose, discontinuous or conflicting assumptions. Some of the selves within Janice are as different as different cultures. How she manages to keep these "selves" from internecine interaction, how she manages the transitions between them, is not clear, though plainly some players manage this complexity by practicing a systematic amnesia or perhaps merely a kind of attention deficit disorder. Attention must break off as the individual moves from one discontinuous self to another. This can give the individual a choppy, distracted quality, as he or she struggles to find the self appropriate to the moment. In an attempt to account for one such moment exposed, uncomfortably, to public view, Farrah Fawcett explained, "It just depends on which me you get."[540]

Janice should give us pause. When we add the experiences of Matt Field, Martha Stewart, Ani DiFranco, Larry Bird, Candice Carpenter, Mike Nichols, we are given a glimpse of the postmodern self as something decentered, chaotic, constructed, mobile, loosely bounded, discontinuous, and various. In some circles, this sight was enough to prompt a declaration that the self is dead. (The official certificate gives the date and place of death as 1972, Paris, and names the attending physicians: Drs. Foucault, Derrida, and Lacan.)[541] What is being challenged is the idea that transformation can result in selves that are integrated, authentic, unified, centered, controlled, executive, essential, or true. Certainly many of the Enlightenment adjectives are now dubious . . . and we can see why. There are, as we have seen, so many transformational activities and objectives at work in any individual that unity *is* probably too much to hope for. But a death certificate may exaggerate. To say the self is not centered or unified is, surely, not to say that it is dead. It is to say merely that it has taken on new properties.

We are looking at a creation that is under the influence of every kind of transformative force. We have DiFranco reinventing its possibilities. We have the overmighty subject seeking out new definitional opportunities. We have more extensive space; there is absolutely more definitional range within. We have more intensive depth, as individual selves become better defined and more fully realized. We have less collective determination of how individuals may define themselves. We have a constant pressure from both voluntary and forced improv to invent or embrace new definitions. And, as we have just noted, we have less communication between the selves. We need multiple selves if we are to survive the demands of a postmodern society. We want them if we are to take advantage of the opportunities of a postmodern society.

But there is no question that these new developments create every kind of problem. The personal is profoundly political. How are we to manage a self that is stretched across, and expanded by, this much cultural territory? Is it a cheap hotel, occupied by strangers, transient, unreliable, indifferent to one another when not actively antisocial? Must this collectivity devolve from association to mere aggregation, no longer possessed of integration, unity, or common purpose? Is this a self in which only the most modest rules of public order apply? No spitting in the elevator. Otherwise, it's every self for itself.

Perhaps it is a rooming house. There is acquaintance, some degree of mutual understanding, shared residence making up for the lack of shared purpose. More probably, the individual is a residential college. Within certain limits, Janice's selves share a purpose, agenda, and life stage. The question then is how aware these selves are of one another, how accommodating, how capable of compromise and mutual comprehension. The Blade Runner question discussed above is a real one. What *are* the possibilities we might discover within, and what might follow from them?

But this is too tidy. The working self is a record of its construction, and this has been unpredictable, complicated, and sometimes cataclysmic. There have been abrupt shifts, as existing selves have been abandoned, experimental selves hastily brought forward, bits and pieces cobbled together, issues forced, and mistakes left standing. So much of the postmodern self has been constructed under the pressure of involuntary improv and out of the spontaneities of Shakespeare-in-the-Park transformation that it's all a mess, really. The working self looks like ganglia. It is not hierarchical and stacked, but interconnected and spread. The individual has worked and reworked the self until many things connect to one another. Some of these are active connections, some are reduced to country roads (to mix the metaphor), some are mere reminders. New nodes appear constantly. New pathways spring up between them, growing and shrinking as traffic demands. And there is really no telling where things are headed, where, that it is to say, we should be buying real estate.

So can there be a chief executive in all of this? The best we can hope for may be the boatman of Central Park. The pond south of New York's Metropolitan museum (the "conservatory water," it is called), sometimes has a wooden boat on it.[542] This is about five feet long, painted the blue and white of a Greek fishing boat, with a sail about twelve feet square. At first, the boat appears to have a motor or wireless navigational control. It does not. What keeps it at large on the pond, and what keeps it from smacking into the concrete lip of the pond, is a stately gentleman who dresses like a head gardener and carries a very large stick. He walks around the pond waiting for the boat to drift near the shore, and when it does so, he pushes it back out again. This is an inexact science, and the boatman can't guarantee the boat's next direction or speed. To renew its journey is to renew its haphazardness.

Plainly, we have to do better than this—not in life, but on the page. We can posit an organization of complexity, a division of labor and power. The selves, the forms, within the self are not an utter rabble. Each has its own agenda. And if the larger executive function has the boatman's imprecision, there are nonetheless brief moments of clarity and direction. But doing better is someone else's job. It is enough here to suggest that the declarations of the self's death were perhaps premature and, by clarifying the transformational routines at work within the self, to show some of the things we need to contemplate to do better than this—not only on the page, but in life.[543]

6. There is a triad here, a division of labor in which some players serve as playwrights, some as off-Broadway players, and some as Broadway players. We have treated DiFranco as an example of the playwright. She seeks out new cultural possibilities, new habitable forms. Playwrights seek or at least require fluidity. Playwrights inspire players, who have the difficult job of occupying the ground DiFranco has opened up. In DiFranco's case, the players were a part of the lesbian community, who began to see what DiFranco's creation would look like as a day-to-day creation. In a sense, DiFranco supplies the "artist's concept." Players, to mix my metaphors with abandon, are architects and engineers, the ones who will see what happens when the self is made load-bearing, site-specific, and a creature fit not for four and a half minutes of music but for the rough and tumble of the real world. DiFranco sings and moves on. The off-Broadway players must endure, even in the face of a sometimes hostile community and the costs of novelty.[544]

But players must also endure the perfidy of their leader. While they take up residence, and suffer the hardship of homophobia and the difficulties of making the transformation work as a style of life, DiFranco moves on. And they are outraged. "But you said . . . !" DiFranco looks disingenuous, but she is merely doing what playwrights do. When she takes up with "Mr. Dilate," she is not "betraying the cause," but merely searching for new ground. Players can feel ill treated from two sides.

Broadway players are the rest of us. The playwrights explore, the off-Broadway players define and make habitable, and the rest of us wait and see. Most of what is invented passes overhead. We don't know about it and we don't want to know about it. But some innovations recruit geometrically, until even the most clueless of us have heard about "that disco thing." Before long, most of us have been to a disco. You know, just looking. And before long, our clothing, language, and hairstyles have felt the influence of Saturday night: the occasion, not the movie. And before long, the way men think about themselves as men, the way women think about themselves as women, the way we present ourselves in public, all of these take on a certain Saturday night character as well.

Until it's just *so* over.

"Disco? No, I don't believe I ever got involved in that sort of thing."

"But we have pictures of you . . . on a dance floor . . . in polyester . . . You're actually pointing at something, like John Travolta."

"OK, once. I went once."

The bell sounds. The trend is over. And everyone walks away. We are not kind to playwrights and the off-Broadway players. What we embrace for the short term, we repudiate soon enough. What we embrace for the long term, we claim as our own. In the first case, the playwright takes the blame. In the second, she is denied the credit.

But we need to think of this triad as something that exists within as well as without. The multiplicity of selves within a single individual will contain playwright selves, off-Broadway player selves, and Broadway player selves. The first are created to explore new possibilities. They spring into existence to make certain kinds of experience or experiment possible. They do not know or care that there are other experiments at work. They do not know or care that there is a larger frame, an enduring self, in place. They require almost no order, continuity, or companions. In a sense, they are "bots" built for a narrow purpose, useful but not indispensable, useful even when short-lived.[545] My Sim City form that abandoned the city in a moment of crisis was illuminating, even if it disappeared immediately.

Some selves serve as longer-term projects. They are "pioneers." These are experiments that are maturing into real, permanent aspects of the larger whole. They remain in quotation marks, not quite in, not quite out of the larger whole. They may be resorted to on an occasional, ad hoc basis. This settler form is far enough away to allow for experiment and disaster, and close enough to deliver real insight and experience.

Indwelling selves have the rights and privileges of a long-standing member of the community. In that ambivalent term, they have "been around." They are more inclined to acknowledge the presence of other selves and the objectives of the larger whole—or at least to have made their peace with them. Where antipathy rules, there are long-standing routines that allow them to ignore one another and the whole.

7. Postmodern transformation comes from a variety of motives. There is a triad here as well. As we have seen, some transformations are forced, some are free, and some are both forced and free.

Involuntary improv is transformation performed under duress. The world changes suddenly and without warning, and the individual has no choice but to respond with improv. This means coming up with a facsimile performance, cobbling something together out of the materials at hand, often rooting through gender and status for plausible ways of being. The best response, as we have seen, is often messy, unstable, tentative, reflexive. This transformational modality punishes those who give way to the natural inclination to remove themselves from the source of commotion, those who "block." And it rewards those who step off into the novelty at hand. Involuntary improv is tyrannical. In the worst case, it demands an absolute dislocation of the individual and of characteristic ways of being in the world. Individuals are obliged to abandon what they know, locate themselves wholly in the new, and change themselves continually to stay there.

Shakespeare-in-the-Park transformations are voluntary. They are embraced for the sheer joy of seeing what will happen. What is it like to be a city planner, a detective in a noir novel, a symphony conductor? Sometimes the motive is self-aggrandizement, to be sure: what would it be like to be a maestro, to conduct the great orchestras in the great symphonies? What is it like to be in control of an entire city or a whole family? But there are moments that are closer to pure play. The transformer participates in the decision making of a Hollywood producer, but not to assume the godlike powers that so often animate the Hollywood player. Indeed, such a transformation is an interesting test of the intrinsic vs. extrinsic proposition. It is the activities of the Hollywood producer stripped, as if systematically, of the things producers regard as their due (the cars, homes, tables, starlets, and deference). The play springs from many motives, too.

The transformations that come from trend and fashion are partly willing and partly coerced. Fashion comes so discreetly, it draws us in with such subtlety, that it makes us complicit in these transformations. Oscar joins the counter-culture by carefully modulated stages, and always with the sensation that his choices are voluntary and that he may repudiate the new any time he wishes. Finally, the choice is his. But the costs of not joining are high, not quite as high as the costs of wearing a mullet or a "full Milwaukee," but still substantial. Not to "join the sixties" (a common phrase at the time) was to remove oneself from full participation in the world. It was to declare a certain bankruptcy. To be sure, not all fashions and trends are so embracing, coordinated, and thoroughgoing. Rave culture does not demand much more than conformity to a certain envelope of stylistic possibilities in dress, movement, and social conduct. But the punishment for refusing to stay within this envelope is not inconsiderable. Knowing glances, small smiles, and an extra cushion of space on the dance floor send a message. You are in the group but not of the group. You are, as we say, "out of it." And what one is "out of" is the stream that moves us from innovation to innovation and from one stylistic envelope (often called a "decade") to another.

Each of these seven principles represents both a possibility and a problem. We are thrilled to think that we are porous, that the world is porous, that we are newly enfranchised, multiple, and motivated. But we are, often, also terrified. None of us, except perhaps the very young, were raised to live in a world such as this. We are struggling to make our adjustments, and, as usual, we are having to do so under fire.

But plainly there is a deeper challenge at issue here. Our most fundamental notions of identity, self-creation, self-government, and responsibility are being tested and, routinely, failing. Predictably, we lose our nerve from time to time, as individuals and as groups. We insist that the transformational modality is over, that we are going to return to a simpler, stiller time. But it is clear that these are temporary failures of nerve. We are obliged by our curiosity and by structural necessity to persevere in the transformational experiment. It will not do to cry the crocodile tears of the postmodernist, to intone that all philosophical bets are off, that the ideas of self and society with which we once organized ourselves are now useless. Surely this is why we sustain an intellectual and an academic class: to work out new ideas, not to dance on the graves of old ones. I make no particular claims on behalf of the ideas here. I have no doubt that someone can do better than the image of the boatman of Central Park.

In fact, fundamental notions of the self are changing. Geertz has sketched the usual notion of the Western self, arguing, usefully, that this notion is a culturally specific accomplishment.

> The Western conception of the person as a bounded, unique, more or less integrated motivational and cognitive universe, a dynamic center of awareness, emotion, judgment, and action organized into a distinctive whole and set contrastively

both against other such wholes and against its social and natural background, is, however incorrigible it may seem to us, a rather peculiar idea within the context of the world's cultures.[546]

It turns out this concept is now "rather peculiar" in Western cultures as well. As may be seen in these seven structural characteristics, the very notions of boundedness, uniqueness, integration, and centeredness are at issue and entirely corrigible.

Conclusion

This book suggests one way to think about the transformational foundations and activities of contemporary culture. With an exposition of the four routines, I believed my responsibilities as a writer were more or less complete. Then, a racket in the hallway! A conclusion elbowed its way into the proceedings, like an unwanted, too-boisterous party guest. It is an odd idea, but it appears to belong here even though it is not expected or welcome. It squares with the ethnographic data at hand, and it does help open up the vista this book has struggled to create. And, frankly, just between you and me, reader, I'm now a little nervous about asking it to leave.

It is possible we are witnessing the creation of a global self and an expansionary individualism. The global self is curious and catholic in searching out new definitional options, credulous in trying them on, mobile in its incorporation of diverse and improbable materials, adroit in its embrace of several at once, skillful in managing the portfolio of selves that is the result, and sturdy enough to live with the ideational and emotional turbulence that must ensue. Most of all, it is imperial. The global self is a presumptuous self, seeing itself as master of its own fate, as the author of its own circumstances, as the rightful inventor of the self. It claims all experience as its province, all definitions of the self as its domain. The global self looks like the early modern Dutch, Spanish, or English courts, taking on and using up anything in its reach.

Some of this we have seen before, to be sure. Individuals claim many identities and a certain fluidity of self—this much is accepted by popular consent and postmodern theory. (We now accept that identity has less and less to do with things that remain identical.) But the data also point toward a conclusion that is not entirely anticipated by popular or academic understanding: that there is a global self, an aggressive, ambitious project that claims the right to pursue identities, to invent new options, to control the means of production, and to certify outcomes. The term "global self" seems useful because, at the limit, the new self appears to wish to reproduce the world within itself, to create the outside world inside, to make a universe of the ego. But the global self has more modest forms as well. It is present even when we are talking about a restless, sometimes reckless pursuit of options and an abrogation of rights of self-creation, self-approval, and self-government.

One of the oddest illustrations of an expansionary individualism, the extreme version, is the Payphone Project, created by Mark Thomas. Mr. Thomas has collected the numbers of 300,000 pay phones around the world. This means that he can call a pay phone almost anywhere: outside the Vatican, in the bus station in Los Alamos, in the zoo in Central Park. By itself, this is interesting, but it's no more than an American counterpart to the train-spotting exercises invented by British schoolchildren. Mr. Thomas told *Shift Magazine* that he began the project as a way to make contact with strangers. But then he let slip his expansionary motive:

> [When I call one of the phone numbers in the database and someone answers,] I freeze up. I never really know what to say. Sometimes I just ask for myself. Is Mark Thomas there? A blond guy with glasses?[1]

I do not, at this early stage, have ethnographic data with which to prosecute the argument, but it appears to be the case that popular culture is shot through with evidence of an expansionary individualism. The global self is, for instance, well represented at the movies. It is being played out as the theme of individual movies, individual characters, individual careers. It is the cultural logic of the celebrity and the fan.

The Nutty Professor is a film that has appeared in several versions. In the Jerry Lewis original, released in 1963, a chemistry professor, Julius Kelp, finds a way to transform himself from an unassuming college man into the handsome, obnoxious Buddy Love. In the Eddie Murphy remake

(1996, dir. Tom Shadyak) this transformation reappears, and the Kelp character, now called Sherman Klump, moves back and forth between the college man and Buddy Love. But the burden of the film and its ability to revive Murphy's career after a string of failures come not from this but from another transformational exercise. For in *his* version of *The Nutty Professor*, Murphy plays not only Sherman Klump but also Lance Perkins, Cletus "Papa" Klump, Anna Pearl "Mama" Jensen Klump, Ida Mae "Grandma/Granny" Jensen, and Ernie Klump, Sr. In the inevitable but not discreditable sequel, *The Nutty Professor II: The Klumps* (2000, dir. Peter Segal), Murphy adds Young Cletus Klump. Lewis was two characters. Murphy is eight.[2]

Advances in special effects and makeup over the years *might* have encouraged Jerry Lewis to take up a larger transformational palette. But is it likely he would have attempted eight characters? In Murphy's film, eight Klumps is more than the comedy demands and, in some places, more than the narrative can sustain. But, oddly, this multiplicity remains the centerpiece of the film. In his review of the film for *Rolling Stone*, Peter Travers excoriated Murphy for having failed to make contact with Lewis in his preparation for the project. "Why would I?" a mystified Murphy asked the inquiring Letterman. Why, indeed? With the advent of a cultural project that did not exist forty years ago, the two films are now only superficially similar.[3]

Sometimes it is the characters, not the actors, who are expansionary. As we have seen, Hollywood is warming to this theme. *Sliding Doors* (1998, dir. Peter Howitt), *Multiplicity* (1996, dir. Harold Ramis), *Fight Club* (1999, dir. David Fincher), *eXistenZ* (1999, dir. David Cronenberg), *Passion of the Mind* (2000, dir. Alain Berliner), *The Family Man* (2000, dir. Brett Ratner), *Me Myself I* (1999, dir. Pip Karmel), *Down to Earth* (2001, dir. Chris Weitz and Paul Weitz), *Possible Worlds* (2000, dir. Robert Lepage), *The One* (2001, dir. James Wong), *The Bourne Identity* (2002, Doug Liman), and *Catch Me if You Can* (2002, dir. Steven Spielberg) are recent movies that have engaged with it.[4] These movies represent what is, in effect, a $447 million bet on the theme by Hollywood filmmakers over these few years.[5] From a cultural perspective, we may recall that John Ellis argues that the contemporary audience identifies not only with the hero but also with all the other key players in a film.[6] And if this is so, it may also be true that the audience identifies with all of the roles played by a character. In these films, the audience has watched Gwyneth Paltrow, Michael Keaton, Edward Norton, Brad Pitt, Jennifer Jason Leigh, Jude

Law, Demi Moore, Nicolas Cage, Rachel Griffiths, Chris Rock, Tom McCamus, Jet Li, Matt Damon, Leo DiCaprio, and Tom Hanks assume global selves on the screen.

Sometimes it is the career, not the character, that has a global aspect. Celebrity is, always, a sum of parts. We know each actor by all the roles he or she has played over the course of a career. The celebrity is to this extent a composite of many creatures. Hollywood insists on this overlap between roles.[7] (It is one of the ways stars bring something to the movie. And it is the reason we are not sure whether Meryl Streep is a star in any conventional sense. There is so little overlap in her career.) But the point is this: every celebrity who has made more than a single film exhibits a global self. The creatures we admire so enormously, to whom we give such (sometimes unfounded) esteem, around whom so much of the emulation and admiration of our culture is now organized, these creatures exhibit global selves.

Perhaps we can speak of the celebrity's two bodies as once we spoke of the king's two bodies.[8] In the medieval era, the king was seen to have a physical body and a figurative one. His figurative one was the body politic, all the members of his kingdom. The frontispiece of the first edition of Hobbes's *Leviathan* shows this monarch looming large over his kingdom, his body composed of thousands and thousands of smaller bodies.[9] The celebrity has a second body, we might say, comprising all the creatures he or she has played over a career, and this body is a global self.[10] Whether this is indeed the real object of our admiration may be argued. I wish merely to suggest that it is one of the things we have in our field of vision when we "wish upon a star" and take up residence in that third body—as fans who revere the celebrity and emulate this second body in part or whole.

But the global self may be at work even in the experience of the filmgoer. It is possible that the movie fan now identifies, to some extent, with everyone on the screen. To quote John Ellis again, the filmgoer is identifying

> with the various positions that are involved in the fictional narration: those of hero and heroine, villain, big-part players, active and passive character. Identification is therefore multiple and fractured, a sense of seeing the constituent parts of the spectator's own psyche paraded before him or her.[11]

This is a very global self. If filmgoers were once grateful for the opportunity to identify with the hero on the screen before them, perhaps a little timid about doing so, now they want the experience of everyone they see there.

The expansionary self is evident elsewhere in contemporary culture. Frith is prepared to describe the Rolling Stones as "intellectuals [who] show an acute, almost contemptuous, grasp of their own paradoxes: British makers of American music, white romancers of African-American culture, middle-class triflers with working-class urgencies, adult observers of youth, aesthetes of body music."[12] When the film critic of the *New York Times*, Elvis Mitchell, asked Steven Soderbergh how he prepared for his movie *Out of Sight*, Soderbergh said he warned himself, "If you blow this, you will be doing art-house movies for the rest of your life, and that's as bad as doing big-budget things. I wanted to do both."[13] How easily Soderbergh dismisses the distinction between commerce and art that was the preoccupation and agonized choice of an earlier generation of filmmakers. As a creature of our expansionary individualism, Soderbergh takes these as his due.[14]

The artist Rodney Graham exhibits an expansionary individualism. In *Fishing on the Jetty*, he appears as an artist playing Cary Grant playing John Robie, a character in *To Catch a Thief* (1955, dir. Alfred Hitchcock), who is searching for a man who has stolen his signature style of stealing gems, those identity-producing icons of the very rich, as Luckmann and Berger might call them. In *City Self / Country Self (Paris Street Scene 1865)*, Graham plays two versions of himself, an urban dandy and a provincial rustic. The city self and country self meet, they fight. They exist, as it were, in the same frame. Other artists explore the theme of multiple identities, particularly Cindy Sherman, Yasumasa Morimura, and Iké Udé. This art can be read as an appropriation of filmic role or celebrity, and as a way of allowing the artist to take up residence in a one-off series of persons and personae. Graham's art engages in this identity play, but his approach is expansionary, as several creatures coexist in a single telescope of selves or an uneasy confederation thereof.[15]

Artists are searching out multiple forms. Yo-Yo Ma, a classical cellist, says, "I've spent a lot of time asking myself what it means to be an American musician now. It means finding out everything that's going on in America musically. That's why Cajun music and Texas fiddle are interesting."[16] Brian Eno, one of the inventors of electronica, goes further still: "We feel affinities not only with the past, but also with the futures that didn't materialise, and with the other variations of the present that we suspect run parallel to the one we have agreed to live in."[17] Who would wish to commit their creativity, or selfhood, to captivity in a single genre or convention?

In *Bobos in Paradise*, David Brooks puzzles over the paradox of baby boomers who wish to be both bourgeois and bohemian.[18] Baby boomers are famous for reinventing the world to suit themselves. But the ease with which they combine these usually mutually exclusive and antagonistic categories *is* a little breathtaking. This is perhaps more than boomer self-indulgence. It is characteristic of our cultural players, boomers and not, that they should be restless, inquisitive, mobile, and versatile—and relatively matter-of-fact about it all. This is characteristic of the global self.

It is there in the everyday behavior of the sons of a film critic. The so-called "alphabet generations" ("X," "Y," and "Z")[19] demonstrate a fluidity that would impress (even as they, in this case, alarm) their boomer parents.

> "Whooha! Whooha! It is you, young Skywalker, who are mistaken. Alrightee then! Power and the money, money and the power. Minute after minute, hour after hour. Thank you, come again." . . . Crashing into the kitchen, my sons talk in the private languages they've worked up from exposure [to pop culture] . . . shifting at near-electronic speeds from, say, imitations of Apu, the Kwik-E-Mart manager in "The Simpsons," to Darth Vader, then to Snoop Doggy Dogg and on to jaw-jutting taunts from "Ace Ventura" and other Jim Carrey movies.[20]

In *No Sense of Place*, Joshua Meyrowitz observes what he calls the "blurring" of childhood and adulthood. "In the last thirty years . . . there has been a remarkable change in the image and roles of children. . . . Children speak more like adults, dress more like adults, and behave more like adults than they used to. In fact, the reverse is also true. There are indications that many adults who have come of age within the last twenty years continue to speak, dress, and act much like overgrown children."[21] Meyrowitz offers several plausible explanations, but not the one that concerns us here. It is possible, and I understand that I am pushing the argument a little here, that the global selves entertained by one group will want to take possession of definitional opportunities available to another, even if it means violating the boundary conditions that once enforced the distinction between the two groups. The global self is a selfish self; it wants whatever another self has.

The inclusiveness of the global self is reflected elsewhere in contemporary culture. Popular music has largely abandoned genre for something more pluralistic. This was evident in the summer tour of the 1990s, Lollapalooza, and it is evident in the event organized more recently by Moby. AREA ONE included Outkast, Incubus, New Order, Derrick May, Billy Corgan, Nelly Furtado, Paul Oakenfold, The Orb, Carl Cox, The Roots, and Rinocerose. Some will scoff that this diversity is a simple marketing device: the wider the range a tour can cover, the wider is its audience. But it is now routinely remarked in the rock press that the "tribal" fan base has disappeared. So AREA ONE, we may safely surmise, will not have attracted one audience for Furtado and another for Carl Cox. More usually, the same fan comes to hear both. The diminishment of genre in the music industry reflects, perhaps, the diminishment of a singleness of self, and a wish to pursue bundles of expressive possibility.

I have in this book rehearsed an argument that suggests that, at a minimum, we should expect to find a variety of selves "at home" within any given individual. We should expect to see a radiant self, curious, questing, prepared to cross boundaries of time, space, culture, even species in pursuit of new expressive possibility. We should expect to see a self that engages in acts of self-transformation designed to win advancement in a status hierarchy. The radiant self looks with disdain on the status self, and the feeling is mutual, but the two somehow coexist in a single global self.

But there is still more variety here. We should also expect to find a swift self that makes itself the instrument of instrumental reason, dismissing, in the process, radiance and status as impediments to its mobility. But to add to the complexity and possibility of contradiction, this individual may well cultivate an avant-garde sensibility and seek experience that is relatively raw and unmediated by mainstream cultural conventions. Needless to say, this self looks with horror on the swift self, and the swift self responds without question in kind. But the two somehow coexist, perhaps as the Bobo recently described by Brooks. Finally, we should expect to see a postmodern exercise in which the individual cultivates a sense of self that is multiple, porous, fluid, and extraordinarily mobile. Sometimes under the pressure of involuntary improv, and sometimes simply because they are accessible, this self looks for experiences and expressive opportunities that would once have been avoided as a threat to the integrity and coherence of the self. Selves pile up. The "portfolio" grows ever more crowded, ever less consistent.

This sounds messy because the postmodern composite of selves is messy. There is nothing organic, interdependent, or coherent about the whole. In point of fact, for many people there is no whole. The global self is so ambitious, so imperial, in its pursuit of new possibility that it refuses ever to compromise this pursuit in order to satisfy the ordinary conditions of the self. The global self is, often, a set that makes no conditions of entry, insists on no boundary rules, forsakes the very idea of governing principles, overriding logics, or internal rules of order. At the limit, the internal components of the global self appear to practice a kind of solipsism. Where there is a connection between selves, this connection is so unpredictable and unsystematic as to evoke unexpected metaphors like ganglia. The irony is worth noting. In this case, we resort to an organic image to show how little interconnection exists in the body politic.

The range, complexity, and difficulty of the global self are not entirely consistent with the postmodernist view of the self. Calvin Schrag characterizes the orthodox view:

> For the most part, questions about the self, and particularly questions about the self *as subject*, are deemed anathema. . . . Questions about self-identity, the unity of consciousness, and centralized and goal-directed activity have been displaced in the aftermath of the dissolution of the subject. If one cannot rid oneself of the vocabulary of self, subject, and mind, the most that can be asserted is that the self is multiplicity, heterogeneity, difference, and ceaseless becoming, bereft of origin and purpose. Such is the manifesto of postmodernity on matters of the human subject as self and mind.[22]

Quite so. Global selves are good evidence of the postmodernist argument for "multiplicity, heterogeneity, difference, and ceaseless becoming." But, in another way, these selves present a problem. For the creatures of contemporary culture manage to embrace variousness without altogether forsaking their claims to, or compromising the operation of, selfhood. The postmodern self detailed in this book does not evidence the symptoms that must surely beset the creature Schrag describes. There is no sign of fatal compromise, of systemic instability, of debilitating confusion, self-doubt, or incoherence. On the contrary, the postmodern self is robust, perhaps even bumptious. In its moments of greatest stress, even under the pressure of the worst moments of involuntary improv, it remains surprisingly . . . operational. And even in the face of accumulating difficulties, it makes ever larger claims to variety, authority, and autonomy. As an academic construct, the postmodern self may suffer every kind of difficulty. As a creature of everyday life, it appears to move, if precariously, from strength to strength, from deference to presumption, and from the margin to its own, self-created, burgeoning center. The global self is not only a boisterous party guest here in these pages.

We may put this another way. Strindberg described the characters he had created for the play *Miss Julie* in a particular way.

> Since they are modern characters, living in an age of transition more urgently hysterical at any rate than the age that preceded it, I have drawn them as split and vacillating . . . conglomerations of past and present . . . scraps of books and newspapers.[23]

Modernist creatures were the captives of fragmentation, discontinuity, and transition largely because these had been inflicted on them, if not by a playwright, then by the complex of forces, impulses, and events that make up what we now call modernism. Postmodernist creatures endure these conditions less passively. They experience them as opportunity as much as they do as crisis. Global selves actually sometimes appear to seek out fragmentation, discontinuity, and transition, or at least to endure them as a means to an end. They are their own playwrights, taking up modernist afflictions for the expressive, exploratory, and definitional opportunities these make available.

Modernist creatures sought authenticity with the conviction that they were both free and obliged to search out an essential self hidden beneath the falsehoods of status transformation, bourgeois convention, and received wisdom. The postmodern self appears to have lost confidence in this scheme. These days, it is rare to hear people, except perhaps in radiant circles, speak of an authentic self. We are more likely to hear people speak, somewhat paradoxically, of a pursuit of several authentic selves. Still more unexpectedly, they will identify the "authentic" self as one of the many selves they wish to claim for themselves.

The idea of self-discovery, once the great modernist imperative, is displaced. Where once individuals undertook an archaeological investigation down through the epiphenomenal distractions of self and world to get at the authentic self, now they are more likely to represent their undertaking as a matter of self-definition and to treat it as something that takes them constantly out of the known self into a variety of new experiential and definitional domains. Postmodern individuals care about authenticity, but they are moved by schemes that no longer treat it as the first consideration. Artifice, among other things, is okay. Capturing and claiming experiences that take individuals out of their "native ground" and essential selves is better than okay, it is the very point of the exercise. More tellingly, the postmodern individual is prepared now to sacrifice authenticity to pursue new possibilities. The authenticity documented by Marshall Berman and Charles Taylor no longer appears to be the great object of self-knowledge, self-exploration, and self-definition.[24] Now variousness is.

We have observed many ways in which people are tested, diminished, and even derailed by transformation. But it is also true that many individuals with global selves appear to enjoy robust powers of agency and to pursue Schrag's "goal-directed activity" without hindrance or penalty. They pursue transformational opportunity blithely, even eagerly. We

have observed confusion and misdirection, but not all postmodern creatures find themselves "bereft of origin and purpose." Expansionary
selves do not appear to forego their subjectness in the pursuit of transformational freedom or to be rendered subjectless by transformational
necessity.

Somehow, the tent top holds. Somehow, the players sustain a unity
of consciousness, however much diversity or discontinuity exists within.
Without question we have observed people struggling to find purchase on
the slippery, shapeless, too-various surfaces of the transformational self.
But, on the whole, individuals seem peculiarly undisturbed and not obviously undone by the "dissolution of the subject."

What is daunting (and, happily, a task for someone else) is how to
explain how consciousness has been expanded to accommodate the many
options of a transformational society. On these points, the postmodern
manifesto appears to falter.

It remains to ask where expansionary individualism may have come
from and why it should be flourishing. We have touched on some of its
origins in this book, I hope. The transformative power that escapes the
service of ritual and myth, the creation of status mobility, and the modernist objectives of cultural and temporal mobility, all of these can be
seen as expansionary individualism in training. More practically, we solve
some of our most pressing problems by resorting to multiplicity. The revolution in gender and race has introduced new selves, and many people
appear to have embraced the new without jettisoning the old. We proceed
as cities do, laying down the new on top of the old. Both as individuals
and as collectivities, we admit the innovation without allowing it to supplant the original form. The result is a profusion of possibilities, an interior portfolio in place of the self that is tidy, integrated, and consistent.
To live in a family, business, community filled with creatures who are
both internally and externally various is to see daily evidence of the virtue
of a variousness of one's own. It turns out the old, dubious selves are
sometimes useful, if only because there are some people for whom they
are not so old or dubious. Also, as we have seen, the constant press of
involuntary improv rewards the fluid, multiple personae. It is almost as if
having several definitions of the self creates a state of preparedness.
When the environment is unpredictable, the good gardener has several
plant types on the go.

One of the reasons given for the rise of the big novel was that some
authors believed that they could not create any world unless they created
a large, varied world. In a culture of fragmentary, contested meanings,

only sustained narrative could succeed as narrative. Novels were now obliged to create both the medium and the message. And this was possible only in novels as big as those of Gore Vidal, Norman Mailer, and David Foster Wallace. Perhaps this is true of selves as well, that identity and understanding are for some people possible only when the self contains and describes a substantial, heterogeneous universe of meanings.

There may be other forces at work. Writing this book, examining the variety of transformational activities in which people engage, I was encouraged to think that we are sometimes driven by a sheer curiosity about what is possible, a pure inclination to try things on, a fundamental temptation to rummage through the definitional possibilities now open to the self and . . . see. It's as if what has happened in the culture of plenitude is now taking place in a global self. As Daniel Bell describes the former,

> the post-modernist temper demands that what was previously played out in fantasy and imagination must be acted out in life as well. . . . Anything permitted in art is permitted in life.[25]

In a culture of expansionary individualism, it is almost as if anything permitted in art is now *expected* in life. Aggressively curious selves demand a way into the worlds of, say, television producers, deep-sea princesses, city planners, symphony conductors, and baseball managers. It's as if the force Plato believed to be at work in the universe is now peering into the self, wondering whether this too might be a domain in which to work.

> [T]he universe is a plenum formarum in which the range of conceivable diversity of kinds of living things is exhaustively exemplified. . . . no genuine potentiality of being can remain unfulfilled.[26]

But this is all rather grander than it needs to be. The fact of the matter is that, as I tried to show in *Plenitude*, these days difference is different. Once the thing most likely to provoke hostility and antagonism, difference is now, for some people, provocative of curiosity and the need to imitate, even appropriate. "Really? So a Romulan would be what kind of mother? Like, how would she treat her family? OK, so . . ." Difference is now an opportunity for experience, an invitation to rework the self, and, finally, an opportunity to find out whether what's "out there" can be made to exist "in here."

The larger picture is daunting. The private and public problems that will issue from a global self and expansionary individualism are many and vexing. Durkheim wrestled with the problem roughly a hundred years ago, and his approach saves us from the several chronic errors that plague the humanities and social sciences. He argued that individualism was something *more* than a failure of the collective will or a departure from the common good, that it was not merely the irruption of selfishness or narcissism. He refused the "searing critique" of a "selfish society" that has become the irresistible fixture of the intellectual world of the twentieth century. Durkheim was clear. A lapsarian, the-sky-is-falling argument would not do.

Whatever else it was, Durkheim argued, individualism was an idea.

> One is thus gradually proceeding towards a state of affairs, now almost attained, in which the members of a single social group will no longer have anything in common other than their humanity, that is, the characteristics which constitute the human person in general. This idea of the human person, given different emphases in accordance with the diversity of national temperament, is therefore the sole idea that survives, immutable and impersonal, above the changing tides of particular opinions; and the sentiments which it awakens are the only ones to be found in almost all hearts.[27]

What Durkheim could not anticipate was that the balance would continue to shift until what was true of societies was true of individuals. Here he contemplates the pluralism of the social world. But he might as well be talking about the expansionary self. I ask the reader to substitute the word "individuals" for the word "societies" in the passage that follows.

> As societies become more voluminous and spread over vaster territories, their traditions and practices, in order to adapt to the diversity of situations and constantly changing circumstances, are compelled to maintain a state of plasticity and instability which no longer offers adequate resistance to individual variations. These latter, being less well contained, develop more freely and multiply in number; that is, everyone increasingly follows his own path.[28]

But here Durkheim's intellectual strategy must surely direct us. The expansionary individualism that consumes our culture is not the opposite or the end of culture. It is a fully formed, relatively systematic creature that springs directly from the culture it declares war upon. In Durkheim's terms, expansionary individualism is an idea before it is a condition, a crisis, or an ending. I hope this book will help illuminate what this idea is and what it makes of us.

Appendix: The Argument in Brief

The argument: Contemporary culture has embraced an "expansionary individualism." This consists of four transformational routines.

Traditional transformation: In face-to-face societies, ritual and myth are the chief means of transformation. Individuals use them to move through the lifecycle (from child to adult to elder) and through the great metaphors that define the group ("we are the Raven"). This transformational liberty leaves the individual fluid and the world unbounded. But liberty and movement are constrained. Only some transformations are allowed. Individuals may not choose or invent their transformational routines or their transformational objectives. Traditional transformations limit what individuals may become. A variant of traditional transformations exists in the present day, in the New Age movement, the rave, and the "radiant self."

Status transformation: Hierarchical societies claim to be static, insisting that individuals may not move out of the social station of their birth. But in Western hierarchies, mobility has been an open secret and a structural necessity for several centuries. Individuals routinely changed their social standing through upward or status transformation, cultivating their exteriors (clothing, speech, and deportment) and interiors (thought, emotion, and outlook) and convincingly performing a social self. Many upward transformations take generations. But a gifted individual can accomplish one in a few years. Status transformation is more individual, competitive, and various than traditional transformation. For centuries, it was the key worldly transformation in the West, supplying the underlying logic of status competition, conspicuous consumption, social mobility, and the consumer revolution. Status transformation exists in the present day, most evidently in the preppie trend of the 1980s and the more recent popularity of Martha Stewart.

Modern transformation: The beat poets declared war on upward transformation. They called it a corruption of the essential individual. They called for personal transformation through drugs, writing, the demimonde, the down and out, all to resist the falsehoods of a bourgeois society. They valued self-discovery and expression over social performance.

Brightwork transformation was more mainstream and middle-class, but not so different. It, too, repudiated upward transformation, seeking another kind of mobility, that of the "swift self" and the 1950s automobile. Brightwork engaged a constellation of cultural ideas: progress, science, technology, jets, cars, and gadgets, as well as national and personal competition. Modern transformation and the swift self exist still in self-help literature, the *homo economicus* of the business world, wireless technologies, cyberpunk fiction, and the Burning Man Festival. They also exist in the pursuit of authenticity, self-expression, and the refusal of mainstream society.

Postmodern transformation: There are seven characteristics of postmodern transformation: 1) The self is porous, and encourages excursions in and out. Contemporary culture is preoccupied with the creation of vehicles for these excursions. 2) The world is porous. This porosity marks a return to the fluidness and open boundaries of traditional societies, and the ability to move across categories of time, space, cultures, and species. 3) The individual claims the right of self-authorship. 4) The individual claims the right of cultural creation, the right to change the cultural categories that define him or her. 5) The individual consists of many selves, demoting essence and authenticity in favor of exploration. 6) There is a division of labor in the creation, exploration, and occupation of new selves. 7) Transformation comes from a variety of motives, some free, some forced. Postmodern transformations are visible in Hollywood films, contemporary music, trends and fashion, teen interaction, the arrival of new transformational vehicles, and the emergence of a global self.

Notes

Sightings

1. Quoted in William Harris, "Anne Meara Goes on Stage, as a Playwright," *New York Times*, January 15, 1985: H5.
2. From the director's commentary for *Waking Life* (1991), in a bonus track on the DVD.
3. Ephron said this in a popular journal that appeared in January 1995, but unfortunately I have lost the reference.
4. Jonathan Van Meter, "Oprah's Moment," *Vogue* 188, no. 10 (1998): 329.
5. Kate Bornstein, *Gender Outlaw: On Men, Women and the Rest of Us* (New York: Routledge, 1994), 3. Ms. Bornstein is a woman who was once a man, who when she published this book was living with a man who was once a woman. This was a heterosexual relationship—but only because both parties switched genders.
6. Quoted in Jennifer Abramsohn, "Helping the Homebound," *Wall Street Journal*, June 19, 1995: R19.
7. Elias Canetti, *Crowds and Power*, translated by Carol Stewart (London: Penguin, 1992), 438.
8. Daniel Bell, *The Cultural Contradictions of Capitalism* (New York: Basic Books, 1976), 53–54.
9. Quoted in Margaret C. Jacob, *The Cultural Meaning of the Scientific Revolution* (Philadelphia: Temple University Press, 1988), 136.
10. Dave Chappelle, interview by James Lipton on *Inside the Actors Studio*, rebroadcast on Bravo, December 18, 2006.
11. Farrah Fawcett, interview by Matt Lauer on *The Today Show*, NBC, October 6, 2000, when asked to account for her behavior on the *David Letterman Show*.

Preface

1. According to Paul Dergarabedian, quoted in Reuters, "MI-III to Make the Impossible, Possible," April 28, 2006.
2. Michael Wolf, *The Entertainment Economy* (New York: Three Rivers, 2003), 4.
3. Grant McCracken, "Celebrity Culture: Muddles in the Models," post at This Blog Sits at the Intersection of Anthropology and Economics, October 21, 2005, http://www.cultureby.com/trilogy/2005/10/thanks_to_piers.html.

4. D. H. Green, *The Beginnings of Medieval Romance: Fact and Fiction, 1150–1220* (New York: Cambridge University Press, 2002), 31.

5. Steven Greenblatt, *Will in the World* (New York: W. W. Norton, 2004); Johan Huizinga, *Homo Ludens: A Study of the Play Element in Culture* (Boston: Beacon, 1955); Arnold van Gennep, *Rites of Passage*, translated by Monika B. Vizedom and Gabrielle L. Caffee (Chicago: University of Chicago Press, 1960); and M. M. Bakhtin, *Rabelais and His World* (Bloomington: Indiana University Press, 1984).

6. Neil Postman, *Amusing Ourselves to Death: Public Discourse in the Age of Show Business* (New York: Viking, 1985), 3–4.

7. B. Joseph Pine and James H. Gilmore, *The Experience Economy: Work Is Theatre and Every Business a Stage* (Boston, Mass.: Harvard Business School Press, 1999); and Bernd Schmitt, *Experiential Marketing* (New York: Free Press, 1999).

8. Henry Jenkins, *Textual Poachers: Television Fans and Participatory Culture* (New York: Routledge, 1992). It is almost impossible to exaggerate how important this book was in offering an opportunity for social scientists to escape their self-imposed theoretical captivity. Certainly, it helped me write the first edition of *Plenitude* in 1997.

9. This paragraph appeared on the first page of the *X-Files* About.com website on July 22, 2001 (http://xfiles.about.com/mbody.htm). The website was then run by David Swinney.

10. For more information on Second Life, see its website at http://www.secondlife.com.

11. Alan Schwarz, "Baseball Is a Game of Numbers, but Whose Numbers Are They?" *New York Times*, May 16, 2006.

12. I am indebted to Orit Kuritsky, a graduate student in MIT's Comparative Media Studies Program, who is now working on a thesis entitled "Transformational Tales: American Makeover Shows and Practices of Their Consumption."

13. Stephen Johnson, *Everything Bad Is Good for You: How Today's Popular Culture Is Actually Making Us Smarter* (New York: Riverhead, 2005).

14. The contention that commercial influence makes a wasteland of our culture has sustained a small industry that continues to this day. Vance Packard, *The Hidden Persuaders* (New York: D. McKay, 1957); Dwight Macdonald, *Against the American Grain* (London: Gollancz, 1963); Stuart Ewen, *Captains of Consciousness: Advertising and the Social Roots of the Consumer Culture* (New York: McGraw Hill, 1976); George W. S. Trow, *Within the Context of No Context* (Boston: Little, Brown, 1981); Paul Fussell, *Bad, or the Dumbing of America* (New York: Summit, 1991); Benjamin Barber, *Jihad vs. McWorld* (New York: Random House, 1995); Katharine Washburn and John F. Thornton, *Dumbing Down: Essays on the Strip Mining of American Culture* (New York: W. W. Norton, 1996); and Juliet Shor, *Born to Buy: The Commercialized Child and the New Consumer Culture* (New York: Scribner, 2004).

15. See the All Your Base Are Belong to Us website, at http://allyourbase.planettribes.gamespy.com/. Andrew Zolli is, among other things, the organizer of the PopTech conference.

16. I thank Ed Cotton for a glimpse of the Converse competition he created at BSSP. Grant McCracken, "Chevy Cocreation," post at This Blog Sits at the Intersection of Anthropology and Economics, April 25, 2006, http://www.cultureby.com/

trilogy/2006/04/chevy_cocreatio.html; and Grant McCracken, "'Consumers' or 'Multipliers': A New Language for Marketing?" post at This Blog Sits at the Intersection of Anthropology and Economics, November 10, 2005, http://www .cultureby.com/trilogy/2005/11/consumers_or_mu.html.

17. Chris Anderson, *The Long Tail* (New York: Hyperion, 2006).

Introduction

1. The term "pornographer" refers to the imperial displeasure (and supposed exile) that greeted Ovid's love poetry. (Jerry's production staff miss nothing!) For Ovid's own account of this period of his life, see Ovid (Publius Ovidus Naso), *Poetry of Exile*, translated by David R. Slavitt (Baltimore: Johns Hopkins University Press, 1990). In a manner of speaking, Ovid *has* returned to walk among us. As a contemporary reviewer puts it, he is "back . . . as fresh and contemporary as ever." "Shakespeare's Crib," *The Economist*, April 15, 1995: 82. We have seen a host of new versions and commentaries, some of which are available online. See Ferdy Hanssen's page at http://www.croky.net/ovidius/.

2. *Metamorphoses* was Ovid's great accomplishment, an epic poem of almost twelve thousand lines. It appeared just before he was sent into exile. (There is some question about whether this exile was actual or imagined for poetic purposes.)

3. "When I'm on-line, I'm 37, tall, blond and raring to go." Ilene Weinberg, 68, a retired social worker with Parkinson's disease quoted in Jennifer Abramsohn, "Helping the Homebound," *Wall Street Journal*, June 19, 1995: R19.

4. This is roughly what happened to Tiresias. Ovid (Publius Ovidus Naso), *Metamorphoses*, translated by Mary M. Innes (London: Penguin, 1955), 82.

5. Ibid., line 1.

6. Not that these are always discrete categories. Solomon points out that it is not unusual for the leaders of the new digital revolution, such as Stewart Brand, to compare themselves to gods. Evan Solomon, "The God Complex," *Shift* 4, no. 2 (November–December 1995): 6. For the influence of Ovid, see Charles Martindale, ed., *Ovid Renewed: Ovidian Influences on Literature and Art from the Middle Ages to the Twentieth Century* (Cambridge: Cambridge University Press, 1988). For Ovid's theme through contemporary eyes, see Michael Hotman and James Lasdun, eds., *After Ovid* (London: Faber, 1995). For a review of the revival of the *Metamorphoses*, see Peter Green, "Thou Art Translated," *Times Literary Supplement*, December 30, 1994: 3.

7. Jerry Rubin (1938–1994) came to national attention for his part in the Vietnam War protests that took place in Chicago during the Democratic National Convention of 1968 and for his role as a founder and member of the Yippies. In the 1970s, he joined the "human potential" movement and experimented with yoga, est, and rolfing. During the 1980s he organized networking seminars for young professionals on Wall Street.

8. Camille Paglia (1947–), an outspoken critic of contemporary culture who was trained by Harold Bloom at Yale (Ph.D., 1974), surprised the world with her highly publicized (sometimes self-publicized) attack on feminist politics, her celebration of Madonna, and her alternative sexuality.

9. Quoted in Jane Marion, "Celebrity Chef: Joan Lunden's Recipe for Change," *TV Guide* 21, no. 27 (1997): 18.

10. Sally Brompton, "If Your Birthday Is Today," *Globe and Mail*, December 20, 1996: C18.

11. Quoted in Kathy Healy, "Behind the Scenes with a Virtuoso Stylist," *Allure* 2 (September 9, 1992): 140.

12. Carl R. Rogers, *On Becoming a Person* (Boston: Houghton Mifflin, 1961), 166. The reference to "directions natural to the human organism" is perhaps problematical. Rogers appears to assume that self-transformation is self-*discovery*, that the successful patient is getting to a "real" self buried beneath false ones. Sometimes this is precisely, or relatively, true. But therapist and patient are not always clearing away falsehood, suppression, and mistaken identities. Sometimes they are inventing what they claim to find. (Postmodernists would claim, of course, that this is always true.)

13. Jeffrey Deitch, *Post Human* (New York: Distributed Art Publishers, 1992), 19.

14. Gary Hamel and C. K. Prahalad, *Competing for the Future* (Boston: Harvard Business School Press, 1994), 19; Hal Lancaster, "Quick-Change Artists May Find Fast Route to Executive Positions," *Wall Street Journal*, May 9, 1995: B1; and Michael Hammer and James Champy, *Reengineering the Corporation* (New York: HarperBusiness, 1993), 1.

15. "In this business, every six months is like a new life." Phil Knight in Donald Katz, *Just Do It: The Nike Spirit in the Corporate World* (New York: Random House, 1994), 26.

16. Quoted in David Livingstone, "Model Behavior," *Saturday Night* 107 (March 2, 1992): 75.

17. Toivo Pajo, "Space Proves a Delicious Blend," *The Strand*, February 12, 1997: 9.

18. Quoted in Gary Alan Fine, *Shared Fantasy: Role-Playing Games as Social Worlds* (Chicago: University of Chicago Press, 1983), 212.

19. James G. Ballard in Liam Lacey, "Down 'n' Dirty at Cronenberg's Crash Site," *Globe and Mail*, May 20, 1996: C1.

20. Frank Bruni, "The Literary Agent as Zelig," *New York Times Magazine*, August 11, 1996: 28.

21. Bharati Mukherjee, "American Dreamer," *Mother Jones* 22, no. 1 (1997): 35.

22. Quoted in Barbara Lippert, "Our Martha, Ourselves," *New York Magazine*, May 15, 1995: 32.

23. Ruth Rendell in Sarah Lyall, "Mysteries, of Course, but Ruth Rendell Also Sees Real Evil," *New York Times*, April 10: B2.

24. Hakeem Olajuwon in a halftime interview with Bob Costas, NBC coverage of Indiana Pacers and Orlando Magic game, June 2, 1995.

25. Ilene Weinberg in Abramsohn, "Helping the Homebound," 19.

26. Milo Miles, "Michelle Shocked: Kind Hearted Woman," *Spin*, January 1997: 96.

27. Brendan Malone, former coach of the Toronto Raptors, in Chris Young, "Will Malone Attract Rodman to Raptors?" *Toronto Star*, June 3, 1995: E1.

28. Mark Leyner, comedian, in John Allemang, "Leyner Writes from Eye of Nihilism," *Globe and Mail*, February 17, 1997: C1.

29. Quoted in "Surgeon in Sex Change Shocker," *South China Morning Post*, April 1, 1996: 11.

30. Anthony Giddens, *Modernity and Self-Identity: Self and Society in the Late Modern Age* (Cambridge: Polity, 1991), 2.

31. Grant McCracken, "Rank and Two Aspects of Dress in Elizabethan England," *Culture* 2, no. 2 (1982): 53–62.

32. David Frum, *How We Got Here: The '70's, the Decade That Brought You Modern Life (For Better or Worse)* (New York: Basic Books, 2000).

33. Angela McRobbie, "Postmodernism and Popular Culture," in *Postmodernism*, edited by Lisa Appignanesi (London: Free Association Books, 1989), 165.

Section 1. Self-Transformation in a Popular Culture

1. *Robin Williams Live at the Met* (Mr. Happy Productions/HBO, 1986). Robin Williams (1952–), born in Chicago, Julliard student, participant in San Francisco street theater, came to national prominence in the television show *Mork and Mindy* (1978–1982, ABC).

2. Sandra Shamas, a Canadian comedian, in the documentary *Wisecracks* (City TV/Alliance International, 1994, dir. Gail Singer).

3. A model of political relations is implicit in the comedian's routine. If he or she is successful, the audience surrenders autonomy and self-control. If not, the audience grows restless and impatient. The comedian is monarch one moment, fool the next, with power earned one joke at a time. This power is exceedingly contingent and perishable. It may reflect an essentially male approach to things. On the other hand, Shamas is one of several women who discuss their comedy in essentially imperial terms in *Wisecracks*.

If the transition from the old-style comedian to Williams marks a move away from an old-style political relationship, what is it a move toward? Does this transition mark yet another refusal of hierarchy, deference, and reverence? Does the new style of comedy suggest a new style of politics? Do our audiences want to be insiders, instead of outsiders? Would they rather participate than defer? They want to be Bart Simpson or Barbra Streisand, and they're willing to become Williams to get there? In this modality, celebrities, or at least this celebrity, are a conduit, not an adored, heroic figure. Audiences are not so much looking up as looking out. We will return to this theme in the essay entitled "Shakespeare-in-the-Park Transformations (free transformations)" in section 5.

4. Larry Storch played a character in the TV comedy *F-Troop*, broadcast by ABC from 1965 to 1967. More details on the show's site at the Internet Movie Database (IMDB), at http://us.imdb.com/Title?0058800.

5. There are, I know, two exceptions to this argument: *The Fisher King* (1991, dir. Terry Gilliam) and *Good Will Hunting* (1997, dir. Gus Van Sant). In both of these Williams is compelling but not transformational—though in both cases he figures as a crucial party to the transformational efforts of an other.

6. Jim Carrey (1962–) began his career with stand-up and small parts in films (e.g., *Peggy Sue Got Married*, 1986, dir. Francis Ford Coppola; *Earth Girls Are Easy*,

1989, dir. Julien Temple), and assumed national prominence on Keenan Ivory Wayans's television comedy series *In Living Color* (Fox, 1990–1992). Three films released in 1994 established Carrey's transformational gusto and box office appeal: *Ace Ventura, Pet Detective* (dir. Tom Shadyac), *The Mask* (dir. Charles Russell), and *Dumb and Dumber* (dir. Peter Farrelly).

7. Adam Roth, director for United States advertising at Nike, says, "We're not afraid to try new things. We focus on flying out on the bleeding edge." Stuart Elliott, "Nike Reaches Deeper into New Media to Find Young Buyers," *New York Times*, October 31, 2006. See also "Lebron [*sic*] James Returns in a Second Season of 'The Lebrons' [*sic*] to Debut Zoom Lebron [*sic*] IV Shoe" and "Maria Sharapova Dispels 'Pretty Girl' Image in First Solo Nike Campaign," 2006 press releases from Nike; "LeBron James Biography," *Encyclopedia of World Biography*, http://www.notablebiographies.com/news/Ge-La/James-LeBron.html; Grant McCracken, "Peyton Manning: The Man and the Brand," post at This Blog Sits at the Intersection of Anthropology and Economics, December 12, 2005, http://www.cultureby.com/trilogy/2005/12/peyton_manning_.html; and [Mark Stewart], "LeBron James Biography," http://www.jockbio.com/Bios/James/James_bio.html.

8. For a full biographical treatment of DiFranco, go to http://www.righteousbabe.com/ani/index.asp.

9. I discuss Madonna further below.

10. "I kicked the habit / Shed my skin / This is the new stuff / I go dancing in / Won't you show for me? / I will show for you," from Peter Gabriel's song "Sledgehammer" on his album *So* (Geffen Records, 1986), copyright Peter Gabriel Ltd PRS. On the Michael Jackson video, see Grant McCracken, "Seeing the Future in African-American and White," *Globe and Mail*, November 21, 1991. There are many examples of transformation in popular music. Two more: Annie Lennox in the Eurythmics' 1987 video *I Need a Man* and Carlene Carter in her 1993 video *Every Little Thing*. A last robust, if somewhat alarming, example: Paul Leary, of the Butthole Surfers, explains, "We started out as the Dick Clark Five, then we were the Dick Gas Five, then it was the Ashtray Babyheads, then Nine Foot Worm Makes Own Food, Vodka Family Winstons, Abe Lincoln's Bush, Ed Asner's Gay, the Right to Eat Fred Astaire's Asshole, which was shortened from the Inalienable Right to Eat Fred Astaire's Asshole." Joe Nick Patoski and John Morthland, "Feeding the Fish: An Oral History of the Butthole Surfers," *Spin* 12, no. 8 (November 1996): 64.

11. Quoted in David Sinclair, "Station to Station," *Rolling Stone*, no. 658 (June 10, 1993): 80.

12. "Rock Style, 1967–1987." *Rolling Stone*, April 23, 1987: 82.

13. Quoted in Sinclair, "Station to Station," 63.

14. Thanks to Nicholas Greco, graduate student in the Department of Art History and Communications Studies at McGill University, for keeping me up to date on Bowie's transformational cycle.

15. This approach to stardom makes for some interesting twists and turns. Love was accused of "playing herself" in *The People vs. Larry Flynt* (1996, dir. Milos Forman). But if she is hired because of the self she has created and played out in public life, whom else would she play?

16. "After her brother, playwright Philip-Dimitri Galas, died of AIDS in 1986, Galas began to see that as an artist and intellectual in a world on the brink of a

plague of epidemic proportions, she had no choice but to make her music and live performances platforms for her rage." Erin Hawkins, "Diva in Flames: Diamanda Galas: The Singer as Avenging Angel," *Eye*, October 31, 1996: 16.

17. For an illuminating treatment, see Kevin Sessums, "Love Story: The Long, Strange Trip of Rock Icon Courtney Love," *Vanity Fair*, June 1996: 106–15, 169–71.

18. Prince (or the artist no longer formerly known as Prince) is another important experiment. In the manner of a Michael Jackson, he toyed with existing definitions of gender and race as if determined to escape them. But he has done this without Mr. Jackson's ingenuous earnestness. Instead, there is sometimes something insinuating, almost tawdry and vaudevillian, about the Prince performance.

19. A tradition of transformation has lately taken hold in the rap community, where Fat Boy Slim and Wu Tang have many names. Michael Kramer, "Trying On New Names to Plumb the Mystery of 'I,'" *New York Times*, April 25, 1999. Thanks to Dave Dyment for pointing this phenomenon out to me.

20. This exaggerates a little for effect. DiFranco's liner notes are generous in their acknowledgments, especially of band members and manager Scot Fisher.

21. In the early days, DiFranco met with an "indie" label and was not impressed. "If those are the good guys, we're really fucked." J. Poet, "Ani DiFranco: Independent as She Wants to Be," *Pulse*, September 1996: 4.

22. Ani DiFranco, "Light of Some Kind," *Not a Pretty Girl* (Righteous Babe Records, 1995).

23. Quoted in Poet, "Ani DiFranco," 5.

24. Quoted in Brantley Bardin, "Ani DiFranco: Taking Me Seriously Is a Big Mistake. I Certainly Wouldn't," *Details* 12, no. 2 (1997): 130.

25. Ibid., 130. See Jonathan Van Meter, "Righteous Babe," *Spin* 13, no. 5 (1997): 56 for a dramatic account of DiFranco stopping a concert to take exception to fans who want to tell her who she is and what she believes.

26. Quoted in Lorraine Ali, "Ani DiFranco," *Rolling Stone*, no. 753 (1997): 20.

27. DiFranco has managed to alarm and intimidate. "People thought I'd have fangs and a puppy hanging out of my mouth." Poet, "Ani DiFranco," 1.

28. Van Meter, "Righteous Babe," 60.

29. Spare us the sons of the father. When the article that became this chapter was written, *Spin* was run by Bob Guccione, Jr., son of *Penthouse* owner Bob Guccione.

30. All quotations in this section come from the Hollyhock catalogue entitled "Hollyhock 2000," published in January of 2000, or from the website at http://www.hollyhock.bc.ca. I am indebted to Amy Domini for bringing this catalogue to my attention.

31. "Gaea" or "Gaia" is the "mother earth" of Greek mythology. As adapted by British biochemist James Lovelock, the name invites us to think of the planet as a living, breathing creature. "Six degrees of separation" is sometimes called the "Kevin Bacon game." For treatments of complexity theory, see M. Mitchell Waldrop, *Complexity: The Emerging Science at the Edge of Order and Chaos* (New York: Simon and Schuster, 1992) and Roger Lewin, *Complexity: Life at the Edge of Chaos* (New York: Macmillan, 1992).

32. I use the concept of loose boundaries throughout this book, taking it from several sources. I first came across it in Richard M. Merelman, *Making Something of*

Ourselves: On Culture and Politics in the United States (Berkeley: University of California Press, 1984), 27–69, and then again in Michèle Lamont, *Money, Morals and Manners: The Culture of the French and the American Upper-Middle Class* (Chicago: University of Chicago Press, 1992) and Dick Higgins, *Intermedia* (New York: Something Else, 1969). It is everywhere in Donna Jeanne Haraway, *Simians, Cyborgs, and Women: The Reinvention of Nature* (London: Free Association Books, 1991), especially on page 152, where Haraway refers to "leaky distinctions." Arthur Danto's work is a study in loose boundedness though, to my knowledge, he does not use this term. Arthur Coleman Danto, *Beyond the Brillo Box: The Visual Arts in Post-historical Perspective* (New York: Farrar, Straus and Giroux, 1992).

33. As someone who grew up in British Columbia, I have the feeling that this language will have surprised some of the locals. Some of these people have taken advantage of the fact that they live in a beautiful place to work at jobs where they can be outdoors and as undistracted as possible. This may be why, in some B.C. communities, the chief source of employment, the B.C. Department of Highways, is affectionately referred to as the Department of Holidays. From this point of view, I can't help wondering whether Solomon's pronouncement didn't have a certain Martian quality to it. On the other hand, B.C. has always managed to be a place more Columbian than British, and to take on, in the process, a magic realism in the context of which Mr. Solomon's remarks were perhaps not so out of the ordinary after all.

34. Thanks to Laura Linard, director of historical collections, Baker Library, Harvard Business School, for reminding me of the importance of Martha Stewart, and to Catherine Piggott, then of CBC Radio, for the "immaculate" observation. (This remark is reproduced from memory, and may be inaccurate in some of its details.) Thanks especially to Susan Fournier, Alvin Silk, and Kerry Herman, all of Harvard Business School, for discussion of and readings on Ms. Stewart.

35. Alan Mirken, then president of Crown Publishing Group, in Diane Brady, "Martha: Inside the Growing Empire of America's Lifestyle Queen," *Business Week*, January 17, 2000: 70.

36. The author of the "Goddess of Lifestyle" remark is Barbara Haber, of the Schlesinger Library, Radcliffe Institute for Advanced Study, speaking on the National Public Radio show *The Connection*, hosted by Christopher Leiden, July 7, 1997.

37. I. Jeanne Dugan, "Someone's in the Kitchen with Martha," *Business Week*, July 28, 1997: 58.

38. For Martha Stewart as license for one's imperfection, see comments on the *My Martha Stewart* page at http://www.cjnetworks.com/~jessa/me/love/martha.html.

39. Camille Paglia's remark was offered on the July 7, 1997, episode of *The Connection*.

40. I wonder whether powerful women are sometimes more multivocalic than powerful men—or it may be that sexism makes this vocality a useful strategy. One hesitates to make the comparison, but there are some similarities to the case of Elizabeth I (Roy Strong, *The Cult of Elizabeth: Elizabethan Portraiture and Pageantry* [Los Angeles: University of California Press, 1977], 47).

41. Whether and how Martha Stewart may be considered a feminist is an interesting question. She is formidable and powerful in ways that defy the feminine

stereotype. But she draws much of this power, at least in the first instance, from the practice of domestic arts which have long been considered a bulwark of sexist definitions of the world. The editor-in-chief of *Martha Stewart Living* says that the key theme is self-reliance: "You'll never find articles in the magazine about getting a man, dieting, or fixing your hair." Brady, "Martha," 66. This change developed in the 1980s, when women took conventional looks and supercharged them in order to make them expressive of women's new status in the world of work. Grant McCracken, "Consumer Goods, Gender Construction, and a Rehabilitated Trickle-Down Theory," in *Culture and Consumption: New Approaches to the Symbolic Character of Consumer Goods and Activities* (Bloomington: Indiana University Press, 1988), 93–103.

42. Tom Conner, *Is Martha Stewart Living?* (New York: HarperCollins, 1995); and Tom Conner, Jim Downey, and J. Barry O'Rourke, *Martha Stewart's Better Than You at Entertaining* (New York: HarperCollins, 1996). Some of the satire on the Web gets very nasty indeed: see http://www.members.tripod.com/~MrsMegaByte/links.html.

43. Grant McCracken, "Homeyness: A Cultural Account of One Constellation of Consumer Goods and Meanings," in *Interpretive Consumer Research*, ed. Elizabeth Hirschman (Provo, Utah: Association for Consumer Research, 1989), 168–83.

44. I reproduce this e-mail in part. I have been unable to identify its author. Readers who can are encouraged to let me know so that the author may be acknowledged.

45. See the Ultimate Martha Stewart Collection at http://www.mrsmegabyte.com.

46. Matt Tyrnauer, "The Prisoner of Bedford," *Vanity Fair*, August 2005: 110–18, 176–80.

47. Steve Jobs, commencement address at Stanford University, June 12, 2005, published in the *Stanford Report*, June 14.

48. Erik Larson, "Free Money: The Internet I.P.O That Made Two Women Rich and a Lot of People Furious," *New Yorker*, October 11, 1999, 76–85.

49. These quotations come from a transcript of Carpenter's address to the Harvard Business School Women's Student Association Conference, January 22, 2000. I am grateful to Natalie Zakarian for making the transcription.

50. In the HBS student newspaper, Lisa Gunther, one of the organizers of the event, had this to say about her encounter with Candice Carpenter: "I was prepared to dislike Candice Carpenter. In the research that I had done to prepare an opening for her keynote address, I found a woman who seemed to be narcissistic, impatient, and the queen of self-promotion." After a lunch with Carpenter, Gunther concluded, "It was not an instant friendship, but I decided to throw my preconceptions out the window." Lisa Gunther, "Women Enriching Business Closing Key Note Speaker Candice Carpenter (HBS '83)," *Harbus* (Harvard Business School student newspaper), January 31, 2000. I thank Alice Gugelev (HBS MBA, 2001) for sharing her impressions with me.

51. "Grrrl," a word coined by Bikini Kill singer and activist Kathleen Hanna, is a spontaneous young-feminist reclamation of the word "girl." "Riot Grrl is a loosely affiliated group of young, generally punkish, take-no-prisoners, feminists

who publish zines, play in bands, make art, produce radio shows, maintain mailing lists, create Websites and sometimes just get together and talk about our lives and being women in contemporary society." Ednie Kaeh Garrison, "U.S. Feminism— Grrrl Style! Youth (Sub)Cultures and the Technologics of the Third Wave," *Feminist Studies* 26, no. 1 (spring 2000): 141–70. See also Laurel Gilbert and Crystal Kile, *Surfer Grrrls: Look, Ethel! An Internet Guide for Us!* (New York: Seal, 1996).

52. This is an imaginary conversation and records no particular instance of speech. In one or two places I have taken the advice of Bree Short, one of my consultants in these matters.

53. I understand that I tell this story, potentially, against myself and that some reviewer is going to say, "You know, he's still at it."

54. This was not the end of my problems. "Turtle Island" figures prominently in the origin myths of North American aboriginals. (It is now, for instance, the title of the largest-selling aboriginal newspaper.)

55. Linda Weintraub, *Art on the Edge and Over: Searching for Art's Meaning in Contemporary Society, 1970s–1990s* (Litchfield, Conn.: Art Insights, 1996), 79. Orlan treats her plastic surgery as art activity. Her surgeries are broadcast by live satellite around the world. Surgeons appear in costumes by Issey Miyake, hip hop serves as the "soundtrack," and Orlan quotes from the work of Michel Serres. She throws off "relics" with Christophe's eye for merchandizing. For $1,000 we may buy a collection of fat, flesh, and blood-soaked gauze inscribed "This is my body, this is my software." For a series of billboards for India, she imagined her operations as film productions, herself as Kali, and her body "as a costume to be shed."

56. This sentence is my construction. Ray Conlogue, "The Avant-Garde Extracts Its Pound of Flesh," *Globe and Mail*, September 27, 1997: C10. A detailed treatment of Orlan can be found in Sander L. Gilman, *Making the Body Beautiful: A Cultural History of Aesthetic Surgery* (Princeton, N.J.: Princeton University Press, 1999), 319–24.

57. The jury is actually divided on this one. A friend tells me that Orlan in person is terrifying to look at.

58. See Orlan's website at http://www.orlan.net.

59. This quotation is from an interesting treatment of Jocelyn Wildenstein by Jeff Woloson, which I found at http://www.divasthesite.com/Society_Divas/jocelyne _wildenstein_a.htm. Woloson is the source of the suggestion that Jocelyn Wildenstein served as a lion hunter. This is not confirmed by the *Vanity Fair* article, which has Alec Wildenstein as the lion hunter when he and Jocelyn first met. George Rush, "Jocelyne's Revenge," *Vanity Fair*, March 1998: 244–49. Note to Graydon Carter: Might it be time to join the twenty-first century and get *Vanity Fair* on line?

60. See the photograph of Wildenstein and a cat at the top of Woloson's page: http://www.divasthesite.com/Society_Divas/jocelyne_wildenstein_a.htm.

61. For the *New York Daily News*'s treatment of Wildenstein as a "scalpel junky," see its edition of August 18, 1998. The "Bride of Wildenstein" remark may be found in the *New York Daily News*, March 18, 1998, and in the Wikipedia entry on her at http://en.wikipedia.org/wiki/Jocelyne_Wildenstein.

62. "The Human Face," *The Economist*, July 17, 1999; and Rush, "Jocelyne's Revenge."

63. Joan Kron, *Lift: Wanting, Fearing and Having a Face-Lift* (New York: Viking, 1998), 16.

64. I am making the doubtful assumption that each procedure was performed on a different person. Nonetheless, I am still persuaded that this calculation under-estimates the real figure.

65. Most plastic surgery is undertaken to make the recipient more beautiful. Presumably, relatively few plastic surgeons are being asked to make their patients look like saints or felines. But it is perhaps worth remembering that there was a time when most consumer goods were purchased to allow their owners to show, claim, or prove their social status. They were being used, that is to say, for pur-poses of upward transformation. This motive persists, but it has been joined by a great many others. It is possible that the objectives of plastic surgery may eventu-ally expand in the same way. Lauren Slater recently offered a treatment of Joe Rosen, a plastic surgeon at Dartmouth-Hitchcock Medical Center ("Dr. Daedalus," *Harper's Magazine* 303, no. 1814 [July 2001]: 57–67). Dr. Rosen con-templates new transformational opportunities, including wings for human beings. He asks, "Why are plastic surgeons dedicated only to restoring our current no-tions of the conventional, as opposed to letting people explore, if they want, what the possibilities are?" (58). Slater says, "Everyone I tell about Rosen and his wings, his *fin de siècle* mind, widens his or her eyes, leans forward, and says, 'You're kid-ding.' People want to hear more. *I* want to hear more. His ideas of altering the hu-man form are repugnant and delicious" (61, emphasis in the original). Orlan and Wildenstein could be the future.

66. Quoted in Kron, *Lift*, 51. More information can be founded at http://www.cher.com.

67. This account of Cher's life is highly abbreviated and comes from two sources, both of which are recommended: the biography by Deborah Wilker at http://www.justplaincher.com/bio.htm (unfortunately, the website is defunct) and Cintra Wilson's article "Cher," *Salon*, February 22, 2000, http://archive.salon.com/people/bc/2000/02/22/cher/index.html.

68. There is a more detailed treatment of Madonna's transformational efforts in "Fashion, Designers, and Trends (and collective transformations)" in section 5.

69. "Editor's note" on Strawberry Saroyan and Michelle Goldberg, "What's Up with Madonna?" *Salon*, October 10, 2000, http://www.salon.com/ent/music/feature/2000/10/10/madonna/index.html.

70. Kelefa Sanneh, "Madonna's Latest Self, a Mix of Her Old Ones," *New York Times*, May 26, 2004. See also Saroyan and Goldberg, "What's Up with Madonna?"

71. All quotations are from Ms. Jackson's website, at http://www.cindyjackson.co.uk/.

72. "Cindy Jackson: The Human Barbie," *20/20*, produced by Joe Pfifferling, ABC, December 8, 1995. I am indebted to Jim McKenna for this reference.

73. For the source of these measurements and more on Barbie's physical proportions, see "Barbie Undergoes Plastic Surgery," BBC News, November 18, 1997, http://news.bbc.co.uk/1/hi/business/32312.stm.

74. Rachel Beck, "At 40, Barbie's Having a Midlife Crisis," *Seattle Times*, February 4, 1999, http://archives.seattletimes.nwsource.com/cgi-bin/texis.cgi/web/vortex/display?slug=2942478&date=19990204&query=barbie.

75. Robert Putnam, "Bowling Alone: America's Declining Social Capital," *Journal of Democracy* 6, no. 1 (1995): 65–78. Mr. Putnam has published a book of the same title, adroitly reviewed by Margaret Talbot in the *New York Times Book Review*, June 25, 2000.

76. John Lahr, "Making It Real: Mike Nichols' Improvised Life," *New Yorker*, February 21 and 28, 2000: 198.

77. Ibid., 202.

78. Ibid., 198.

79. Jeffrey Sweet, *Something Wonderful Right Away: An Oral History of the Second City and the Compass Players* (New York: Avon, 1978), 73.

80. Lahr, "Making It Real," 204. There is some confusion in the record about precisely what was said in the train station. In the Sweet interview, Nichols says that he used a German accent. Lahr says nothing of this but suggests that May replied with a Russian accent. This may have been the two sides of the improv, but it seems to me more likely that Nichols spoke, and May replied, in a German accent. This was, after all, their first date.

81. Sweet, *Something Wonderful Right Away*, 71.

82. My account of the beginning of improv indulges itself in a mythic language. A fuller account can be found in the opening essay, "History," in Sweet, *Something Wonderful Right Away*, pp. xv–xxxiii.

Section 2. Traditional Transformations

1. Unfortunately, I do not have a record of the name of this documentary or its producers. It appeared on Canadian television sometime in the fall of 1997. This dialogue is reconstructed from memory and probably not fully accurate.

2. For the material culture of the ritual, see particularly Victor W. Turner, ed., *Celebration: Studies in Festivity and Ritual* (Washington, D.C.: Smithsonian Institution Press, 1982). For the importance of body and gesture, see David Parkin, "Ritual as Spatial Direction and Bodily Division," in *Understanding Rituals*, ed. Daniel de Coppet (London: Routledge, 1992), 11–25.

3. Victor W. Turner, *The Ritual Process: Structure and Anti-structure* (New York: Aldine de Gruyter, 1995).

4. The Tilley Endurable is a floppy cotton hat manufactured in Canada. It is generally worn by tourists who have given up all hope of dignity, and by anthropologists. The manufacturer likes to say that the Tilly Endurable can be eaten by elephants and survive intact. In Canada this counts as a virtue. Hargurchet Bhabra once told me that he had heard Canadians engage in learned, passionate dinner conversation about the relative virtues of the Tilley "A" and the Tilley "B": something to do with brim size, he gathered. See the Tilley website at http://www.tilley.com/.

5. Monica Wilson, "Nyakyusa Ritual and Symbolism," *American Anthropologist* 56, no. 2 (1954), 241.

6. Sally F. Moore and Barbara G. Myerhoff, "Secular Ritual: Forms and Meanings," introduction to *Secular Ritual* (Amsterdam: Van Gorcum, 1977), 16–17.

7. Nancy Munn, "Symbolism in a Ritual Context," in *Handbook of Social and Cultural Anthropology*, ed. John J. Honigmann (Chicago: Rand McNally, 1973), 605–606.

8. Lloyd Warner called Memorial Day a "sacred ceremony" and proposed that we think of it as a device for the unification of a community divided by religious differences. W. Lloyd Warner, *American Life: Dream and Reality* (Chicago: University of Chicago Press, 1953).

9. Nicole Belmont, *Arnold van Gennep: The Creator of French Ethnography*, translated by Derek Coltmann (Chicago: University of Chicago Press, 1979).

10. Arnold van Gennep, *The Rites of Passage*, translated by Monika B. Vizedom and Gabrielle L. Caffee (Chicago: University of Chicago Press, 1960).

11. For a close treatment of van Gennep's model, see Terence Turner, "Transformation, Hierarchy and Transcendence: A Reformulation of Van Gennep's Model of the Structure of Rites de Passage," in Moore and Myerhoff, *Secular Ritual*, 53–72. The great modern-day student of van Gennep's work was Victor Turner.

12. This argument is wrong, in my opinion. It is one thing, and no small thing, to see that some aspect of social life is "patterned" or "rule-bound." It is another, quite unnecessary, thing to insist that this makes it ritual. Let us distinguish between what is patterned and what is ritual, if only because this gives us the opportunity to honor particularly the looseness and spontaneity of the first and the enunciated character of the second.

13. Victor W. Turner, *The Anthropology of Performance* (New York: PAJ Publications, 1986), 22; and Felicia Hughes-Freeland, introduction to *Ritual, Performance, Media* (New York: Routledge, 1998), 1–28.

14. Parkin, "Ritual as Spatial Direction," 15, emphasis in the original.

15. Maurice E. F. Bloch, "Symbols, Song, Dance and Features of Articulation," *Archives européennes de sociologie* 15 (1974): 55–81.

16. Gilbert Lewis, *Day of Shining Red: An Essay on Understanding Ritual* (Cambridge: Cambridge University Press, 1980), 144.

17. Stanley J. Tambiah, "A Performative Approach to Ritual," in *Culture, Thought, and Social Action: An Anthropological Perspective* (Cambridge, Mass.: Harvard University Press, 1985), 132, 161. We might speculate that monarchs may have exceptional powers of innovation precisely because as monarchs they are special agents in the ritual affairs of the community.

18. Barbara G. Myerhoff, "'We Don't Wrap Herring in a Printed Page': Fusion, Fictions, and Continuity in Secular Ritual," in Moore and Myerhoff, *Secular Ritual*, 199–224.

19. Moore and Myerhoff, "Secular Ritual," 9.

20. For more on this aspect of ritual, see Caroline Humphrey and James A. Laidlaw, *The Archetypal Actions of Ritual: A Theory of Ritual Illustrated by the Jain Rite of Worship* (Oxford: Oxford University Press, 1994). There are several exceptions to this general point, but I do not believe that any of them overturn it. First, there is a kind of "freshening" rule at work. Rituals that are forced into a state of super-rigidity lose their ability to involve or persuade. Parkin observes the "sustaining" role of small departures ("Ritual as Spatial Direction," 17). Tambiah also observes the possibility of ritual "tedium," and the "decline of meaning" that must result unless innovation is "let in" ("Performative Approach," 161). These observations are reminiscent of work

on genre in contemporary culture, with the important difference that in the latter case entire social forms run through a creative cycle into tedium. Without "freshening," they must disappear. John G. Cawelti, *Adventure, Mystery, and Romance: Formula Stories as Art and Popular Culture* (Chicago: University of Chicago Press, 1976). A further exception is apparently identified in the work of Susanna Rostas, who observes the "individuality and resourcefulness" of participants in the Conceros vigils and dances. Rostas helps make the present argument, for individuality is exhibited least by dancers who are from the most traditional parts of Mexican culture and most by those who are most urban and participants in an individualistic Western cultural model. Susanna Rostas, "From Ritualization to Performativity: The Conceros of Mexico," in Hughes-Freeland, *Ritual, Performance, Media*, 85–103.

21. Robin Ridington, "Fox and Chickadee," in *The American Indian and the Problem of History*, ed. Martin Calvin (New York: Oxford University Press, 1987), 133. Japasa was a Beaver Indian from what is now the interior of British Columbia. The slightly overwrought quality of this prose makes me nervous. I suspect it is being used to give a sense of how this world feels to Japasa. But it also suggests the possibility that Ridington is romanticizing. On a second matter: I will refer to Japasa in what follows as if he were still alive and as if I had some personal acquaintance with him. Both of these implications are false. I haven't a defense, really, except to say that mischief is not, in these rhetorical traditions, unheard of. I am indebted to Trudy Nicks for this reference.

22. Ridington, "Fox and Chickadee," 134. This mutuality is probably unusual. Crocker observes that social metaphors tend to run in one direction only. "Bororo men compare themselves to macaws, not macaws to themselves." J. C. Crocker, "The Social Functions of Rhetorical Forms," in *The Social Use of Metaphor*, ed. J. D. Sapir and J. Christopher Crocker (Philadelphia: University of Pennsylvania Press, 1977), 54.

23. These are sometimes the same thing, and some people will be unhappy with the way in which I have separated myth and ritual. Myth and ritual are often deeply caught up in one another. One of the most popular theories contends that myth and ritual are mutually presupposing, with ritual being an enactment of myth and myth both the pretext and the context for ritual. For an extended treatment of this idea, see Robert A. Segal, ed., *The Myth and Ritual Theory: An Anthology* (Malden, Mass.: Blackwell, 1998). I have separated them for ease of exposition, and because myth and ritual are not always mutual enterprises.

24. For a usefully synoptic view of the full range of possibilities here, see Thomas J. Sienkewicz, *Theories of Myth: An Annotated Bibliography* (Pasadena, Calif.: Salem, 1997).

25. Quoted in James Clifford, "On Ethnographic Self-Fashioning: Conrad and Malinowski," in *Reconstructing Individualism: Autonomy, Individuality and the Self in Western Thought*, ed. T. C. Heller, M. Sosna, and D. E. Wellbery (Stanford, Calif.: Stanford University Press, 1986), 141.

26. Metaphors are richer than this implies. In this case, the metaphor amuses by unexpectedly combining something completely urban and human (crack) with something completely rural and animal (weasel).

27. I am not distinguishing between metaphors and similes here. Another reader advisory: I will be mixing metaphors. For an interesting account of our

discomfort with the mixed metaphor, see Dale Pesmen's inspired essay "Reasonable and Unreasonable Worlds: Some Expectations of Coherence in Culture Implied by the Prohibition of Mixed Metaphor," in *Beyond Metaphor: The Theory of Tropes in Anthropology*, ed. James W. Fernandez (Stanford, Calif.: Stanford University Press, 1991), 213–43.

28. George Lakoff is best positioned to illuminate the cognitive properties revealed by metaphor (*Women, Fire, and Dangerous Things: What Categories Reveal about the Mind* [Chicago: University of Chicago Press, 1987]), but some anthropologists are unhappy with how little account his approach takes of the cultural context that fashions and arranges the categories in the first place. See Naomi Quinn, "The Cultural Basis of Metaphor," in Fernandez, *Beyond Metaphor*, 56–93.

29. It's interesting to see how many dead metaphors are agricultural ones. And this may tell us that it is not repetition alone that extinguishes a metaphor, but also lack of acquaintance.

30. For this approach to metaphor, see Sapir and Crocker, *Social Use of Metaphor*; and Fernandez's exemplary collection, *Beyond Metaphor*. For a rich anthropological review of myth theory, see William G. Doty, *Mythography: The Study of Myths and Rituals* (University: University of Alabama Press, 1986).

31. There is a danger of creating an origin myth for myths, namely that they come in moments of illumination. This is certainly sometimes true, but it is probably also true that they come to a community like water from the water table, seeping up toward the surface everywhere and gradually until they are just there. I know why I favor the former possibility. Frankly, it makes a better story, and, like every myth maker, I am bound by the rules of narrative. Also, this is the way in which I see crucial discoveries being made in the brainstorming sessions in which I participate for government and industry. More on this in "Involuntary Improv (forced transformations)" in section 5. A final note: I am suggesting that the metaphors that stick do so because they have, once articulated, a compelling logic. There may be something fortuitous about the appearance of the metaphor, but it should be emphasized that there is never anything fortuitous about the metaphor itself. Which metaphor will prove compelling and how it will work its magic has everything to do with the culture from which it comes and to which it speaks. This much has been established by the classic studies of social metaphor by Leach, Bulmer, and Tambiah: Edmund Leach, "Anthropological Aspects of Language: Animal Categories and Verbal Abuse," in *New Directions in the Study of Language*, ed. E. H. Lenneberg (Cambridge: MIT Press, 1964), 23–63; Ralph Bulmer, "Why Is the Cassowary Not a Bird? A Problem of Zoological Taxonomy among the Karam of the New Guinea Highlands," *Man* 2 (1967): 5–25; and Stanley J. Tambiah, "Animals Are Good to Think and Good to Prohibit," *Ethnology* 8 (October 4, 1969): 424–59.

32. Stanley Walens, "The Weight of My Name Is a Mountain of Blankets: Potlatch Ceremonies," in Turner, *Celebration*, 178–88.

33. John J. MacAloon, "Sociation and Sociability in Political Celebrations," in Turner, *Celebration*, 261.

34. S. Ia Serov, "Guardians and Spirit-Masters of Siberia," in *Crossroads of Continents*, ed. William W. Fitzhugh and Aron Crowell (Washington, D.C.: Smithsonian Institution Press, 1988), 241–55. (For the hat of a transformed shaman, see figure 334 on p. 247. For a bird-skin coat, see figure 326 on p. 241.)

35. Mark S. Mosko, "The Canonic Formula of Myth and Nonmyth," *American Ethnologist* 18, no. 1 (1991): 126–51. I am pleased, finally, to have got an equation in the book.

36. Doty, *Mythography*, 104–106.

37. James G. Frazer, *The Golden Bough: A Study in Magic and Religion*, 3rd ed. (New York: Macmillan, 1935); Audrey I. Richard, "The Concept of Culture in Malinowski's Work," in *Man and Culture: An Evaluation of the Work of Bronislaw Malinowski*, ed. Raymond Firth (London: Routledge & Kegan Paul, 1957), 19; and Roy A. Rappaport, *Pigs for the Ancestors: Ritual in the Ecology of a New Guinea People* (New Haven, Conn.: Yale University Press, 1967).

38. Ford Russell, *Northrop Frye on Myth: An Introduction* (New York: Garland, 1998).

39. David G. Mandelbaum, *The Plains Cree* (New York: The American Museum of Natural History, 1940), 210.

40. Yes, it is right to say that this number is high because Way Cool contains a great many variations on a smaller number of themes. But this raises an interesting anthropological question: why should there be so many variations? I thank the owners and staff of Way Cool Tattoos (604 Yonge Street, Toronto) for their patience with my questions and help with the addition. I think it's fair to say that I am not statistically gifted. (Eighty HBS students can attest to this.) I think this probably holds true for Way Cool staff as well. There's a good chance we were off by a couple of thousand.

41. Dennis Tedlock, "The Spoken Word and the Work of Interpretation in American Indian Religion," in *Myth, Symbol, and Reality*, ed. Alan M. Olson (Notre Dame, Ind.: University of Notre Dame Press, 1980), 131.

42. Th. P. Van Baaren, "The Flexibility of Myth," in *Sacred Narrative: Readings in the Theory of Myth*, ed. Alan Dundes (Berkeley: University of California Press, 1984), 222, 223, 218. For another statement of anthropology's "reluctance to treat [myths] as possibly recent or changing items," see Raymond Firth, "The Plasticity of Myth: Cases from Tikopia," in Dundes, *Sacred Narrative*, 209.

43. Kenelm Burridge, *Mambu, a Melanesian Millennium* (London: Methuen, 1960), 250. The first quoted sentence actually follows the excerpt. A similar play of innovation and tradition is observed in Michel Perrin, "The Myth in the Face of Change: An Anthropologist's View," *Social Research* 52, no. 2 (1985): 317.

44. A. I. Hallowell, "Ojibwa Ontology, Behavior and World View," in *Culture in History: Essays in Honor of Paul Radin*, ed. Stanley Diamond (New York: Columbia University Press, 1960), 22, 23

45. To be precise, the phrase "world we have lost" comes most recently from the book by Peter Laslett and refers to one of the several variations of our lapsarian origin myth. Sometimes it is the loss of an "aboriginal" innocence that has cost us so dearly. Sometimes it is the loss of an "agrarian" innocence that has caused the difficulty. Peter Laslett, *The World We Have Lost: England before the Industrial Age* (New York: Charles Scribner's Sons, 1971).

46. Robert Redfield, "Thinker and Intellectual in Primitive Society," in Diamond, *Culture in History*, 15. For a glimpse of the order that results from such a tendency, see Evon Z. Vogt, "Structural and Conceptual Replication in Zinacantan Culture," *American Anthropologist* 67, no. 2 (1965): 342–53. I believe Redfield is

right to accept Radon's argument on "primitive" intellectual activity (that it contained "speculation for its own sake") *and* right to doubt the presence of real skepticism or mold-breaking creativity here. (I make this argument with the understanding that Radin did observe some creativity; see Paul Radin, *Primitive Man as Philosopher* [New York: Dover, 1927], 289.)

47. Robert Redfield, *The Primitive World and Its Transformations* (Ithaca, N.Y.: Cornell University Press, 1953), 120, 123.

48. J. S. La Fontaine, "Person and Individual: Some Anthropological Reflections," in *The Category of the Person: Anthropology, Philosophy, History*, ed. Michael Carrithers, Steven Collins, and Steven Lukes (Cambridge: Cambridge University Press, 1985), 137.

49. E. P. Evans-Pritchard, *Witchcraft, Oracles and Magic among the Zande* (Oxford: Oxford University Press, 1937), 194.

50. Stanley Diamond, introduction to *Primitive Views of the World* (New York: Columbia University Press, 1964), v. Lévi-Strauss makes this same point for *ideas*. As he puts it, both the Bricoleurs and the scientist are on the lookout for messages, but the former is prepared to contend only with those that have "been transmitted in advance, like the commercial codes which . . . allow any new situation to be met economically, provided that it belongs to the same class as some earlier one. The scientist, on the other hand, . . . is always on that look out for *that other message* which might be wrested from an interlocutor in spite of his reticence in pronouncing on questions whose answers have not been rehearsed." Claude Lévi-Strauss, *The Savage Mind* (London: Widened and Nicolson, 1966), 20, emphasis in the original.

I do not mean to suggest that traditional societies did *not* engage in transformational activity. As I have just demonstrated, they evidence traditions of myth and ritual that are precisely that. What I mean to argue is that myth and ritual are the most important places they were transformational. These transformational activities were not performed in or upon the world.

51. Clyde Kluckhohn, "Myths and Rituals: A General Theory," in Segal, *The Myth and Ritual Theory*, 330. Kluckhohn approvingly quotes Harvey Ferguson's assertion that "man dreads both spontaneity and change . . . he is a worshipper of habit in all its forms" (330) and suggests that myth and ritual "represent the maximum of fixity" (332).

52. Lewis, *Day of Shining Red*, 212–15.

53. Lévi-Strauss, *The Savage Mind*, 30–31.

54. Tambiah, "Performative Approach," 128. The original discussion of this aspect of the Gahuku-Gama adoption of soccer appears in Lévi-Strauss, *The Savage Mind*, 30–33. See also the comments of Marshall Sahlins, to which I am indebted: Marshall D. Sahlins, *Culture and Practical Reason* (Chicago: University of Chicago Press, 1976), 50–52. For a remarkable document on what becomes of Western sports in non-Western circumstances, see the Trobiand remaking of cricket as treated in Gary Kildea and Jerry Leach's documentary film *Trobiand Cricket: An Ingenious Response to Colonialism* (1976, dir. Jerry Leach).

55. Pierre Clastres, "Indians of the South American Forest," in *American, African, and Old European Mythologies*, compiled by Yves Bonnefoy and translated by Wendy Doniger (Chicago: University of Chicago Press, 1993), 80.

56. Paul Radin, *The Trickster: A Study in American Indian Mythology* (New York: Philosophical Library, 1956).

57. Karl Kerenyi, "Commentary: The Trickster in Relation to Greek Mythology," in Radin, *The Trickster,* 185.

58. Ibid., 185.

59. Lawrence Stone takes this approach in his treatment of early modern England: Lawrence Stone, *The Family, Sex and Marriage in England, 1500–1800* (New York: Harper & Row, 1977).

60. This counter-intuitive proposition (and anthropological commonplace) is treated in some detail by several authors in Carrithers, Collins, and Lukes, *The Category of the Person.* It is customary for some intellectuals to rail against the rise of individualism because it destroys community and isolates this individual. Indeed, this vitriol so preoccupies some writers that it appears to be the only thing they can say on the topic (e.g., Daniel J. Boorstin, *The Americans: The Democratic Experience* [New York: Random House, 1973], 147). But we have been capable of better than this since Durkheim, about whom I will say more in the conclusion.

61. Bharati Mukherjee, "American Dreamer," *Mother Jones* 22, no. 1 (1997): 32.

62. Richard M. Merelman, *Making Something of Ourselves: On Culture and Politics in the United States* (Berkeley: University of California Press, 1984), 30. See also the older but still serviceable remark from Linton: "Group characteristics no longer inform people about what to expect of others, what they can legitimately require of another, what to fear about each other, how far they can advance with another, or how they can be protected from each other. Each new person is 'special,' and each such person must be met anew." Ralph Linton, *The Study of Man* (New York: Appleton-Century, 1936).

63. Richard A. Shweder and Edmund J. Bourne, "Does the Concept of the Person Vary Cross-Culturally?" in *Culture Theory: Essays on Mind, Self, and Emotion,* ed. Richard A. Shweder and Robert A. LeVine (New York: Cambridge University Press, 1984), 190; and Louis Dumont, *Essays on Individualism* (Chicago: University of Chicago Press, 1986) and "Christian Beginnings of Modern Individualism," in Carrithers, Collins, and Lukes, *The Category of the Person,* 93–122.

64. Clifford Geertz, "'From the Native's Point of View': On the Nature of Anthropological Understanding," in Shweder and LeVine, *Culture Theory,* 126.

65. These few remarks are speculative in nature and they engage a topic in which I am no expert. Still, there is something suggestive here, as I think the evidence will show. My larger argument does not depend upon what I argue here. I offer these remarks as a provocation more than as the rehearsal of well-established fact. For a more balanced view of one aspect of this debate in anthropological circles, especially the Boasian contribution, see Richard G. Fox, "For a Nearly New Culture History," in *Recapturing Anthropology: Working in the Present,* ed. Richard G. Fox (Santa Fe, N.M.: School of American Research Press, 1991), 104–109. (I would note in passing that Ricoeur's theory of the individual's constitution of culture, as well as Fox's own, appears useful, indeed illuminating, for modern and postmodern cultures, and less so for traditional ones. The data Fox cites from Lesser on the Pawnee is postcontact and therefore moot.)

66. Richard B. Lee and Irven Devore, "Problems in the Study of Hunters and Gatherers," in *Man the Hunter*, ed. Richard B. Lee and Irven Devore (Chicago: Aldine, 1968), 3.

67. I have neglected one or two changes: the domestication of the dog, the invention of bows and boats, a new complexity to hunting and food preparation. But it is worth pointing out that these took place "in the *last few thousand* years before agriculture," which is to say, exceedingly late in the 2-million-year scheme of things. Sherwood L. Washburn and C. S. Lancaster, "The Evolution of Hunting," in Lee and Devore, *Man the Hunter*, 295, emphasis added. This is not to say there was no transformational activity taking place, merely that it was not transformational activity performed upon the outward face of the world.

68. Marshall Sahlins, *Stone Age Economics* (Chicago: Aldine, 1972), 1–39. For a review of the more recent archaeological literature on what remains "the mystery of how, let alone why, prehistorical people ceased to forage and turned to farming," see David R. Harris, *Settling Down and Breaking Ground: Rethinking the Neolithic Revolution* (Amsterdam: Twaalfde Kroon-Voordracht, 1990), 29.

69. See Robert Nisbet, *Social Change and History: Aspects of the Western Theory of Development* (New York: Oxford University Press, 1969) for a review of the many ideas of change cultivated in the Western tradition.

70. Fernand Braudel, *Afterthoughts on Material Civilization and Capitalism*, translated by Patricia M. Ranum (Baltimore: Johns Hopkins University Press, 1977), 7.

71. "[T]he important thing the Agricultural Revolution [of the seventeenth century] brought in was not any specific method but an idea—the idea that all methods of agriculture could be studied and improved, the idea of a rational agriculture. This idea was new in Europe, at least since Roman times. In the Middle Ages, agriculture was customary. Men farmed as their fathers had farmed and did not dream of anything better." George C. Homans, *English Villagers of the Thirteenth Century* (New York: W. W. Norton, 1941), 41.

72. Hugh Trevor-Roper, "The Invention of Tradition: The Highland Tradition of Scotland," in *The Invention of Tradition*, ed. Eric Hobsbawm and Terence Ranger (Cambridge: Cambridge University Press, 1983), 15–41.

73. Ernest Gellner, *Nations and Nationalism* (Oxford: Basil Blackwell, 1983). Silverman is particularly good on how deliberate and policy-driven was the French definition of national identity. Debora Silverman, *Art Nouveau in Fin-de-Siècle France: Politics, Psychology, and Style* (Berkeley: University of California Press, 1989).

74. Eric Hobsbawm, "Introduction: Inventing Traditions," in Hobsbawm and Ranger, *The Invention of Tradition*, 2.

75. I got to see this inclination firsthand when I was in the United Kingdom touring one of Britain's great educational institutions with its chief executive officer. I said casually that the institution was a repository of the nation's understanding of itself and that a change in the institution might work a change in the nation. (Change the image to change the reality, as it were.) He looked at me, and said with some exasperation, "Goodness, no, change is always made to seem continuous with the past." I guessed he was exasperated not only with a clueless foreigner who could not see the obvious, but also with a nation that had made it so.

Section 3. Status Transformations

1. Upward transformation is an important motif of religious experience in the West. Indeed, before the Reformation the worldly hierarchy was continuous with a greater, higher chain of beings. This section is devoted to social transformation only.

2. There are surprisingly few ethnographically substantial treatments of status and status mobility. Some of this is no doubt due to how badly Veblen misrepresented the matter (Thorstein Veblen, *Theory of the Leisure Class* [New York: Mentor, 1953]). But a childhood in an isolated Scandinavian community in the American Midwest can't have prepared him very well. This is perhaps the same difficulty that frustrated Martin Scorsese in making *The Age of Innocence* (1993). Neither had a fine control of what Goffman calls "social style," the "matters of etiquette, dress, deportment, gesture, intonation, dialect, vocabulary, small bodily movements" (Erving Goffman, "Symbols of Class Status," *British Journal of Sociology* 2, no. 4 [December 1951]: 300). Edward Shils's study is useful ("Deference," in *The Logic of Social Hierarchies*, ed. Edward O. Laumann, Paul M. Siegel, and Robert W. Hodge [Chicago: Markham, 1970], 420–48); and Georg Simmel's is particularly illuminating ("Fashion," in *On Individuality and Social Forms: Selected Writings* [Chicago: University of Chicago Press, 1971], 294–323). There is a fleeting reference to the directionality of status space in George Lakoff and Mark Johnson, *Metaphors We Live By* (Chicago: University of Chicago Press, 1980), 16.

3. For the individual, Bourdieu notes, "Taste classifies, and it classifies the classifier. Social subjects, classified by their classifications, distinguish themselves by the distinctions they make, between the beautiful and the ugly, the distinguished and the vulgar, in which their position in the objective classifications is expressed or betrayed." Pierre Bourdieu, *Distinction: A Social Critique of the Judgement of Taste*, translated by Richard Nice (Cambridge, Mass.: Harvard University Press, 1984), 6.

4. See the IMDB entry for this film at http://us.imdb.com/Title?0058578. For more on Estuary English, see the useful website maintained by University College London's Department of Phonetics and Linguistics at http://www.phon.ucl.ac.uk/home/estuary/home.htm. The term was introduced by David Rosewarne in "Estuary English," *Times Educational Supplement* 19 (October 1984), http://www.phon.ucl.ac.uk/home/estuary/rosew.htm.

5. Bourdieu is particularly good on the natural appearance of status. Pierre Bourdieu, *In Other Words: Essays toward a Reflexive Sociology* (Oxford: Polity, 1990), 10.

6. Found and then, typically, concealed. It is usual for elites to deny that movement happens and to seek to conceal it when it does.

7. Simmel, "Fashion"; and Grant McCracken, "'Ever Dearer in Our Thoughts': Patina and the Representation of Status before and after the Eighteenth Century," in *Culture and Consumption: New Approaches to the Symbolic Character of Consumer Goods and Activities* (Bloomington: Indiana University Press, 1988), 31–43. For more on Simmel and the diffusion of innovations, see the essay called "Fashion, Designers, and Trends (and collective transformations)" in section 5.

8. The sixteenth-century courtier Stephan Guazzo watched the ritualized performance of social distinction with amusement. From a distance, he said, it appeared as if everyone at court were "skipping, leaping, and dauncing." Predictably, he was

less amused by his own part in the performance of these social duties, calling it "nothing else but a paine and subjection." Stephan Guazzo, *The Civile Conversation of M. Stephen Guazzo* (London, 1586), 77r, 3r. His contemporary Thomas Churchyard referred wearily to the courtier's constant "creeping and crouching to keepe that [which] we have and winne that [which] we wish." "A Sparke of Friendship and Warme Goodwill," in *The Progresses and Public Processions of Queen Elizabeth*, ed. John Nichols (London, 1923), 2:586.

9. Plainly, the transparency of role and the opportunity to glimpse the parts of the self it left out of account were to be fertile ground for the cultivation of new ideas of individualism and the investigation of interior life. See Marshall Berman's treatment of Pascal's investigation of "insincerity": *The Politics of Authenticity: Radical Individualism and the Emergence of Modern Society* (New York: Atheneum, 1980), 58.

10. Sylvia Lettice Thrupp, *The Merchant Class of Medieval England* (Ann Arbor: University of Michigan Press, 1948). I have drawn heavily upon this book.

11. Ibid., 280.

12. Ibid., 308.

13. It occurs to me that some readers will object to this point on the grounds that it appears to argue that social rank is merely a matter of make-believe and that it is entirely divorced from the real material conditions on which gentle standing stood. I take this point and wish to emphasize here that there can be no successful imitation of the gentle style of life without possession of very material conditions, not least wealth and power. I do not think that this is necessarily what J. L. Austin had in mind when he introduced us to the "felicity conditions" of the performative act, but it does no violence to his theory to insist that we broaden the term in this way. J. L. Austin, *How to Do Things with Words* (New York: Oxford University Press, 1965).

14. Thomas Fuller, *The Holy State and the Profane State*, ed. Maximilian Graff Walten (1642; New York: Columbia University Press, 1938), 2:106.

15. Lawrence Stone, *The Crisis of the Aristocracy, 1558–1641* (Oxford: Oxford University Press, 1965), 23. For more on English mobility in the early modern period, see Anthony Esler, *The Aspiring Mind of the Elizabethan Younger Generation* (Durham, N.C.: Duke University Press, 1966), 34–37; and J. H. Hexter, "The Myth of the Middle Class in Tudor England," in *Reappraisals in History* (London: Longmans, 1961), 71–116. For a controversial account of the medieval precedents of this mobility, see Alan Macfarlane, *The Origins of English Individualism* (Oxford: Basil Blackwell, 1978).

16. Mildred Campbell, *The English Yeoman under Elizabeth and the Early Stuarts* (New Haven, Conn.: Yale University Press, 1942), 379; and Albert J. Schmidt, *The Yeoman in Tudor and Stuart England* (Washington, D.C.: Folger Shakespeare Library, 1961).

17. By the end of Elizabeth's reign, fashions in men's hats were changing several times a decade. F. W. Fairholt, *Costume in England: A History of Dress to the End of the Eighteenth Century*, enlarged and revised by H. A. Dillon (London: George Bell, 1885), vol. 2. The Houses of Parliament required rebuilding to accommodate gentlemen in their newly expansive leggings.

18. Raphaell Holinshed, *The Firste Volume of the Chronicle of England, Scotlande, and Ireland . . .* (London: Iohn Hunne, 1577), book 3, chapter 1.

19. Old Strowd: "your bought gentility that sits on thee, like peacock's feathres cocked upon a raven," in John Day, *The Blind Beggar of Bednall Green*, Materialien zur Kunde des älteren englischen Dramas (Louvain: Uystpruyst, 1902), 39.

20. Thomas Fuller, *The Holy State and the Profane State*, edited with notes by James Nichols (London: Thomas Tegg, 1841), 106.

21. I am simplifying for the sake of exposition. The transition to gentility was a complicated business and many things contributed to it, including connections established through marriage, locality, political conduct, and social interaction. But none of these would serve the aspirant gentleman if he got the amateur dramatics wrong.

22. I have been unable to find an Elizabethan account of the transformation of culture into nature. Elizabethans appear to have believed that it was possible, that it happened, but nowhere supplied an explanation of how it happened. The contention that it does happen is, of course, the last recourse of the snob. It is said that ancient New England families believed that real connoisseurship was impossible for someone who was not born into the right family, that acts of discernment were literally impossible unless the individual had the right genes. Less dramatically, this assumption underlies the famous (and hegemonically most useful) contention that the wellborn "just know what to do," that they are naturally and effortlessly the masters of social situations that test (and discover) the newly arrived.

Certainly, there were many other kinds of transformation in the Elizabethan period. Many rituals of birth, marriage, and death were available (David Cressy, *Birth, Marriage, and Death: Ritual, Religion, and the Life-Cycle in Tudor and Stuart England* [New York: Oxford University Press, 1997]). Elizabeth was a monarch created out of transformational objects and events, including the precoronation progress, her coronation, her portraiture, her wardrobe, her Tillsbury speech, and many other state events. On her summer progresses, she was sometimes met in the garden of a stately home by a howling wild man (a gardener dressed and coached for the occasion), whom she would civilize at a stroke. The contemporary term for some social transformations was *preferment*, defined by the OED as "the advancement or promotion in condition, status, or position in life." Sixteenth-century England used the term for all kinds of advancement: through age-grades, occupations, offices, or ranks in the hierarchy. "Gravitie is assumed . . . upon notable changes: as when a Courtier is *preferred* to be a Chancellor; and a Chaplen to be a Bishop; a servant a master; a young Gentleman a Justice; a Merchant an Alderman and such like." Thomas Gainsford, *The Rich Cabinet* (London, 1616), 62v, emphasis added. Humanist scholars were arguing for the transformational powers of education. Virtue, they argued, could promote someone in the social hierarchy more surely than the advantages of birth. Several magical and alchemical traditions were at work. The theater of the day was robust, even without the achievements of the master of transformation. It is no surprise that Ovid was so loved by Elizabethans. They lived in a transformational age.

23. The word "imitation" has a pejorative overtone in the contemporary world. As a society preoccupied with authenticity, we are inclined to regard imitation as discreditable behavior. The classical world had another view, seeing imitation as an opportunity for learning and illumination. Marion Trousdale, "Recurrence and Renaissance: Rhetorical Imitation in Ascham and Sturm," *English Literary Renaissance* 6, no. 2 (1976): 156–79. Another way to talk about the appro-

priation of these status markers is to call them acts of identification. In this language, the actor claims a similarity with the superordinate and constructs him- or herself accordingly. So much appropriation is undertaken idly or playfully, however, that "identification" seems too strong a term. It would, though, solve the pejorative problem. The third choice might be "occupation." We will return to this issue in the essay called "Shakespeare-in-the-Park Transformations (free transformations)" in section 5.

24. There is much more to say here, especially on the topic of the "accidental" appropriation. How do things find their way through the aquifer, later to return as "spontaneous" and "natural" expressions of the self? We have been so busy protesting appropriations that we have not bothered to consider how they happen.

25. Frances Trollope, *Domestic Manners of the Americans,* 5th ed. (New York: Dodd, Mead, 1839), 205. Notice the reference here to novels as a template for behavior undertaken in the hope of upward transformation.

26. Modern and postmodern societies harbor a strong dislike of status transformation. Our concern for authenticity obliges us to suppose that such transformation is a falsehood, or a dream from which the individual eventually wakes up. This storyline is a Hollywood cliché. See, for example, *Curly Sue* (1991, dir. John Hughes), in which Grey Ellison (Kelly Lynch) begins as an upwardly mobile corporate executive who eventually comes to her senses and gives up the hollow pleasures of her Yuppie world for something "real" and "authentic." But it is probably true that even in unambiguously hierarchical societies some status transformations must have felt wrong or fraudulent, and failed to persuade the internal audience.

27. Austin, *How to Do Things with Words,* 15–24.

28. Here too audiences make a difference. The status credentials that enable a transformation before one audience will not do so before another.

29. James Kernan, *Perfect Etiquette: or, How to Behave in Society. A Complete Manual for Ladies and Gentlemen . . . with Suggestions How to Dress Tastefully* (New York: Albert Cogswell, 1877). The details of social transformation are many and exacting. In the words of Goffman, to recite them once more, they consist of "matters of etiquette, dress, deportment, gesture, intonation, dialect, vocabulary, [and] small bodily movements. . . . In a manner of speaking . . . a social style." Goffman, "Symbols of Class Status," 300.

30. Richard Braithwait, *The English Gentleman and the English Gentlewoman,* 3rd ed. (London, 1641), 34–35.

31. This view of the hierarchy comes mostly from Edward Sapir, for whom every social order is a perishable, fragile arrangement which depends for its survival on daily acts of confirmation and recreation. *Encyclopedia of the Social Sciences.* s.v. "Communication," by Edward Sapir.

32. Kevin M. Sweeney, "High-Style Vernacular: Lifestyles of the Colonial Elite," in *Of Consuming Interests: The Style of Life in the Eighteenth Century,* ed. Cary Carson, Ronald Hoffman, and Peter J. Albert (Charlottesville: University Press of Virginia, 1994), 9–10.

33. Abraham H. Maslow, *Motivation and Personality* (New York: Harper & Row, 1970).

34. Richard L. Bushman, *The Refinement of America: Persons, Houses, Cities* (New York: Alfred A. Knopf, 1992), 79–80.

35. Ibid., 61–99.

36. Karin Calvert, "The Function of Fashion in Eighteenth-Century America," in Carson, Hoffman, and Albert, *Of Consuming Interests*, 272–73. Note that Bourdieu makes a point very like this one: Bourdieu, *In Other Words*, 10–11.

37. Baldassarre Castiglione, *The Book of the Courtier from the Italian, Done into English by Sir Thomas Hoby, Anno 1561, with an Introduction by Walter Raleigh*, Tudor Translations 23 (New York: AMS Press, 1967).

38. A couple of readers have queried my use here of this famous phrase, which I have by way of Clifford Geertz from T. S. Eliot and *The Sacred Wood*. I have used Geertz's phrasing and not Eliot's, which is "immature poets imitate; mature poets steal." I mean simply that the imitative behavior of an aspirant is almost always characterized by an anxious, too-perfect performance while the *sprezzatura* rule encourages the actor to make things her own, not to imitate but to appropriate.

39. Ruth Kelso, *The Doctrine of the English Gentleman in the Sixteenth Century, with a Bibliographical List of Treatises on the Gentleman and Related Subjects Published in Europe to 1625* (Urbana: University of Illinois Press, 1929), 89; M. E. James, *A Tudor Magnate and the Tudor State* (New York: St. Anthony's, 1966), 8; and Jules Lubbock, *The Tyranny of Taste: The Politics of Architecture and Design in Britain, 1550–1960* (New Haven, Conn.: Yale University Press, 1995).

40. Sir Thomas Elyot, *The Boke Named the Governour* (1531; London: J. M. Dent, 1907), 5; and John M. Major, *Sir Thomas Elyot and Renaissance Humanism* (Lincoln: University of Nebraska Press, 1964), 22.

41. Matthew Arnold, *Culture and Anarchy and Other Writings*, ed. Stefan Collini (Cambridge: Cambridge University Press, 1993), 62.

42. The phrase "culturally constituted" is from Marshall Sahlins, *Culture and Practical Reason* (Chicago: University of Chicago Press, 1976). It is also to be found in Bernard Cohn, "History and Anthropology: The State of Play," *Comparative Studies in Society and History* 22, no. 2 (1980): 220.

43. There is a third category: those who move upward and protest continuities of self and social style. One such person is the respondent Lamont calls Willy Pacino, child of parents who left Italy for Pennsylvania coal mines. Pacino rails against "pseudosophisticates" and insists that he and his friends are "real people." This is a defensive posture but it is not clear that it is an anti-transformational one. When Pacino insists on certain attitudes and behaviors, especially for this aggressively expressive purpose, we might be obliged to say that he is engaged in a transformational activity. Sometimes "being yourself" is a deliberate act of construction. Michèle Lamont, *Money, Morals and Manners: The Culture of the French and the American Upper-Middle Class* (Chicago: University of Chicago Press, 1992), xxvi.

There is a fourth category: those who conform outwardly. They make exterior changes as a way of accommodating to their new social location, but refuse to make interior ones. Strictly speaking, they should be excluded from the argument, except among them too there is a fair amount of "drift," as a result of which the individual discovers he or she "can't go home again," or at least can't go home except with discomfort.

44. Thanks to Hargurchet Bhabra for this.

45. This remark is quoted from memory and probably inaccurate in some of its details. I believe the documentary was *The Magic Season of Robertson Davies*, directed by Harry Rasky and broadcast on CBC Television, December 27, 1990.

46. The words "thick," "heavy," "perfect," and "standard" should really all be in quotation marks.

47. Plainly there have been other important movements. In the American case, when the Northeast held sway, these included from west and mid-west to east coast and from south to north.

48. Arthur J. Vidich and Joseph Bensman, *Small Town in Mass Society: Class, Power and Religion in a Rural Community*, rev. ed. (Princeton, N.J.: Princeton University Press, 1968).

49. Theodore Dreiser, *Sister Carrie* (1900; New York: The Modern Library, 1997), 89.

50. For a different account of Dreiser's interest in these details, see Rachel Bowlby, *Just Looking: Consumer Culture in Dreiser, Gissing and Zola* (New York: Methuen, 1985).

51. We might say that Carrie takes advantage of the Diderot effect the city makes available to her. Grant McCracken, "Diderot Unities and the Diderot Effect," in *Culture and Consumption: New Approaches to the Symbolic Character of Consumer Goods and Activities* (Bloomington: Indiana University Press, 1988), 118–29.

52. Milton M. Gordon, *Assimilation in American Life: The Role of Race, Religion, and National Origins* (New York: Oxford University Press, 1964), 70, 112.

53. Karal A. Marling, *As Seen on TV: The Visual Culture of Everyday Life in the 1950s* (Cambridge, Mass.: Harvard University Press, 1994).

54. David L. Cohn, *The Good Old Days: A History of American Morals and Manners as Seen through the Sears, Roebuck Catalogues, 1905 to the Present* (New York: Simon and Schuster, 1940). See Cohn's introduction for an impassioned defense of the significance of material culture and a really embarrassing preface from Sinclair Lewis that misses the point altogether. For more on the Sears genre, see Jennifer Scanlon, *Inarticulate Longings: The Ladies' Home Journal, Gender, and the Promises of Consumer Culture* (New York: Routledge, 1995).

55. In his majestic study of the immigrant experience, Daniel Boorstin weaves what he takes to be a tragic tale. Immigrants in America, he says, became the dupes of advertising. They were persuaded to care about consumer goods— things they did not need. In an unguarded moment, he observes that ready-made clothing "instantly Americanized" the immigrant. Was this a market-made delirium, or was there something more systematic and purposeful at work? Daniel J. Boorstin, *The Americans: The Democratic Experience* (New York: Random House, 1973), 100.

56. For a review of trickle-down diffusion theory, see Grant McCracken, "Consumer Goods, Gender Construction, and a Rehabilitated Trickle-Down Theory," in *Culture and Consumption*, 93–103.

57. See, for instance, Steven Watson, *The Harlem Renaissance: Hub of African-American Culture, 1920–1930* (New York: Pantheon, 1995).

58. This ignores the example of Michael Jackson, who has apparently lightened the tone of his skin. As we assume more control over DNA and the appearance of

the social self, the issue that Jackson presents, someone who passes by undertaking a physical change, will move from the celebrity world to the everyday one.

59. Nella Larsen, *Quicksand and Passing* (New Brunswick, N.J.: Rutgers University Press, 1986), 150, 158.

60. This is true until the individual in question distinguishes him- or herself, at which point even one drop of non–African American blood is remembered. Thus did the popular media suddenly recall the Latin heritage of Reggie Jackson, the Irish heritage of Muhammad Ali, the Thai heritage of Tiger Woods.

61. F. James Davis, *Who Is African-American? One Nation's Definition* (University Park: Pennsylvania State University Press, 1991), 13–14. The issue of race, especially the notion that social and cultural characteristics have some biological foundations, is deeply problematical. Gates suggests we think of race as metaphor. Henry L. Gates, *"Race," Writing, and Difference* (Chicago: University of Chicago Press, 1986). This is right, but we must sometimes engage in more essentialist treatments when they are the language and logic of our respondents. It is an interesting empirical question how many North Americans are prepared to see race as metaphor. I suspect the number is still quite small.

62. I have made status and race appear more mutually exclusive than they really are. In our worst moments, we like to suppose that status is a matter of birth. Certain sensibilities come only, it is supposed, from high birth. We say, "You can take the boy out of poverty, but not poverty out of the boy."

63. Matthew Wilson, introduction to *Paul Marchand, F.M.C.*, by Charles W. Chesnutt (Jackson: University Press of Mississippi, 1998), xxxi.

64. Quoted in Judith R. Berzon, *Neither White nor African-American: The Mulatto Character in American Fiction* (New York: New York University Press, 1978), 231. The notion of passing, its cultural artifacts, and even some of its scholarship presume that selves, like races, are somehow real. And because they are real, they can be appropriated, lost, regained. As we shall see, this is very much in the modernist tradition.

65. "Stonewall" is the short-hand term for an event that took place in Greenwich Village, New York City, June 28, 1969, when a gay bar called the Stonewall Inn was raided by the police and its patrons and others rioted in response. A description of the event appears in Robert Amsel, "Back to Our Future? A Walk on the Wild Side of Stonewall," *The Advocate*, September 15, 1987, http://www.cs.cmu.edu/afs/cs/user/scotts/ftp/bulgarians/stonewall.txt. This event marked the beginning of a new period of activism and militancy for the gay community, and indeed the history of the gay community is sometimes divided into "pre-Stonewall" and "post-Stonewall" periods.

66. "Gaydar" is a good metaphor, and a successful pun, but the term seems to me to concentrate our attention on the act of deciding who is and isn't gay, when there is a much richer, more nuanced semiotic activity.

67. Richard Dyer, "Fashioning Change: Gay Men's Style," in *Stonewall 25: The Making of the Lesbian and Gay Community in Britain*, ed. Emma Healy and Angela Mason (London: Virago, 1994), 179.

68. This is all rank speculation on my part. Not only am I not African American or gay, I have done no sustained research in these communities.

69. Roberta Best, "Drag Kings: Chicks with Dicks," *Canadian Woman Studies* 16, no. 2 (spring 1996): 58–59.

70. Royal Commission on Aboriginal Peoples, "Looking Forward, Looking Back," in *Highlights from the Report of the Royal Commission on Aboriginal Peoples* (Ottawa: Government of Canada, 1996), http://www.ainc-inac.gc.ca/ch/rcap/rpt/index_e.html. U.S. government policy was equally coercive. For details, see "Federal Education Policy and Off-Reservation Schools, 1870–1933," a website by the Clarke Historical Library, Central Michigan University, http://clarke.cmich.edu/indian/treatyeducation.htm.

71. Lynda Powless, "Mush-Hole: $900 Million Survivor Suit Sparks Memories," *Turtle Island* 4, no. 44 (1998): 3.

72. Mary C. Waters, *Ethnic Options: Choosing Identities in America* (Berkeley: University of California Press, 1990).

73. Eric Liu, *The Accidental Asian: Notes of a Native Speaker* (New York: Random House, 1998), 46, 35.

74. Ray Chang, "Give Me a Punkin' Job," *Yolk* 2, no. 1 (1995): 14.

75. I have explored this point in Grant McCracken, *Plenitude 2.0*, 2nd ed. (Toronto: Periph. Fluide, 1998).

76. Melanie McGrath, *Motel Nirvana: Dreaming of the New Age in the American Desert* (New York: HarperCollins, 1995), 22.

Section 4. Modern Transformations

1. For the early modern beginnings of this individualism, see Roy F. Baumeister, *Identity: Cultural Change and the Struggle for Self* (New York: Oxford University Press, 1986), 35–42.

2. Richard M. Merelman, *Making Something of Ourselves: On Culture and Politics in the United States* (Berkeley: University of California Press, 1984), 30. See also Ralph Linton, *The Study of Man* (New York: Appleton-Century, 1936). A founding statement of the individual released from historical and cultural definitions appears in Immanuel Kant's essay "An Answer to the Question: What Is Enlightenment," in *Foundations of the Metaphysics of Morals and What Is Enlightenment?* (New York: Macmillan, 1990).

3. Saul Bellow, foreword to *The Closing of the American Mind*, by Allan Bloom (New York: Simon and Schuster, 1987), 13.

4. Virginia Satir, *Self Esteem*, text on poster, publisher unknown. (Even the name seems to me doubtful. Are we to suppose this passage was written by a virgin satyr?) Could C. B. Macpherson have imagined such a thing when he coined the term "possessive individualism"? See his *The Political Theory of Possessive Individualism* (Oxford: Clarendon, 1962). However, I now stand corrected. Virginia Satir, now deceased, was a real and influential person. For more details, see http://www.satir.org/.

5. Richard A. Shweder and Edmund J. Bourne, "Does the Concept of the Person Vary Cross-Culturally?" in *Culture Theory: Essays on Mind, Self, and Emotion*, ed. Richard A. Shweder and Robert A. LeVine (New York: Cambridge University Press, 1984), 190.

6. Frederic Jameson, "Postmodernism and Consumer Society," in *The Antiaesthetic: Essays on Postmodern Culture*, ed. Hal Foster (Port Townsend, Wash.: Bay Press, 1983), 114.

7. Lionel Trilling, *Sincerity and Authenticity* (Cambridge, Mass.: Harvard University Press, 1971). Berman's treatment of Montesquieu's treatment of Usbek's unhappiness with the role of master, while different in some particulars, captures what is, from a modernist point of view, the emptiness of performances and relationships defined by roles. Marshall Berman, *The Politics of Authenticity: Radical Individualism and the Emergence of Modern Society* (New York: Atheneum, 1980), 24–25.

8. John G. Cawelti, *Apostles of the Self-Made Man: Changing Concepts of Success in America* (Chicago: University of Chicago Press, 1965), 12.

9. As an academic topic, individualism has been so fiercely politicized that a balanced, a cultural treatment is hard to find. The most anthropological treatment has come, interestingly, from the sociologist Herbert Gans. See his *The Levittowners: Ways of Life and Politics in a New Suburban Community* (New York: Vintage, 1967) and *Popular Culture and High Culture: An Analysis and Evaluation of Taste* (New York: Basic Books, 1974). He discusses the "ecumenical" politicization of individualism in *Middle American Individualism: The Future of Liberal Democracy* (New York: Free Press, 1988), 98–120.

10. M. P. Baumgartner, *The Moral Order of a Suburb* (New York: Oxford University Press, 1988), 9, 17.

11. I thank Michael Valdez Moses, Johanne Lamoureux, and Johanne Sloan for alerting me to the issues here. As an anthropologist, I am self-taught in these matters and inclined to go off course.

12. Malcolm Bradbury and James Walter McFarlane, "The Name and Nature of Modernism," in *Modernism: A Guide to European Literature, 1890–1930*, ed. Malcolm Bradbury and James Walter McFarlane (London: Penguin, 1991), 46.

13. Jim Finnegan of the University of Illinois offers this treatment of the difference between modernism and modernity: "The term *modernity*, more recent critics now suggest, should be used to distinguish between the historical, cultural, economic and political conditions of the time and *modernism*, which signifies the literary and aesthetic representations of (or responses to) those historical conditions. Modernity defined in this way becomes the historical and cultural conditions of possibility that make modernism both necessary and possible in the first place. One way to think about it would be to say that the mass availability and rising popularity of the automobile from the 1910s through the 1920s is a condition of modernity, whereas car metaphors and the use of the automobile as a symbol of mechanical reproduction frequently appear as tropes in *modernist* writing. If, however, you allow that authors and artists (like everyone else) must to some degree be the product of the historical and cultural conditions of their own times, then you can see that this distinction between modernity and modernism is partly a rhetorical abstraction full of inevitable slippages and gray areas." Handout for English 251: American Novels after 1914, http://www2.english.uiuc.edu/finnegan/English %20251/251_Fall01.htm, emphasis in original.

14. Eric Homberger, "Chicago and New York: Two Versions of American Modernism," in Bradbury and McFarlane, *Modernism*, 158–59.

15. Renato Poggioli, *The Theory of the Avant-Garde* (Cambridge, Mass.: Harvard University Press, 1968), 50.

16. For one of the most sustained treatments of this argument, see ibid., 30–40.

17. What I am not prepared to do is to apply Poggioli's otherwise inspirational notion and treat brightwork as modernism become stereotype (ibid., 83). This modernism is, as I will try to show, exceedingly robust. Marshall Berman sometimes appears prepared to accept Poggioli's approach. Marshall Berman, *All That Is Solid Melts into Air: The Experience of Modernity* (New York: Simon and Schuster, 1982). See, for instance, his treatment of Jones Beach (297–98).

18. I appreciate that this is a long-standing distinction in Western discourse, and that it was sharpened and given new purpose by the modernist enterprise. I am, in the anthropological lingo, taking issue with the "native's point of view," even as I am seeking to understand and represent it.

19. Charles Taylor, "Two Theories of Modernity," *Hastings Center Report* 25, no. 2 (March–April 1995): 24–33.

20. Interestingly, there isn't very much in the recent collection by Harrison and Huntington that examines "progress" with the ethnographic specificity that is required to let us see what besides beats and brightwork will serve the cause of modernity in other cultural contexts. Samuel P. Huntington and Lawrence E. Harrison, eds., *Culture Matters: How Values Shape Human Progress* (New York: Basic Books, 2000).

21. Ginsberg's *Howl* was given its influential public reading in 1955 and was published by City Lights in 1956. Kerouac's *On the Road* appeared in 1957. Burroughs's *Junky* appeared in 1953 and *Naked Lunch* was excerpted in 1957 and published in 1959.

22. Steven Watson, *The Birth of the Beat Generation: Visionaries, Rebels and Hipsters, 1944–1960* (New York: Pantheon, 1995), 3, 75–76. See Watson's illuminating chapter "Beat to Beatnik," 249–84. My account of the beats is deeply indebted to this book. Burroughs was later to complain that Huncke could be relied on to steal most from those to whom he owed most, and the title of Huncke's autobiography appears to accept the judgment: Herbert Huncke, *Guilty of Everything* (New York: Paragon House, 1990). For more on the notion of "beat," see Norman Mailer, *The White Negro: Superficial Reflections on the Hipster* (San Francisco: City Lights, 1957).

23. Watson, *Birth of the Beat Generation*, 246. For more on the beat adoration of the anti-hero, see William Plummer, *The Holy Goof: A Biography of Neal Cassady* (New York: Paragon House, 1981). The ingenuous quality of the beats was one of the several things that differentiated them from the "angry young men" who had such cultural and literary influence in Britain, and who were known for their "irreverence, stridency, impatience with tradition, vigor, vulgarity, sulky resentment against the cultivated, [and] intellectual nihilism." Kenneth Allsop, *The Angry Decade: A Survey of the Cultural Revolt of the Nineteen-Fifties* (London: Peter Owen, 1964), 18.

24. Watson, *Birth of the Beat Generation*, 56. Heroin may have made some contribution to Burroughs's WASP style. Heroin, he said, "blunts emotional reactions to the vanishing point." Ibid., 148.

25. Ibid., 60–61.

26. Ibid., 15, 16. I think it's possible that when the beats appropriated the cultural inventions and liberties of a marginal community, they were not merely taking advantage of an outsider's perspective, they were drawing upon a deliberate redefinition of the self that sought out spontaneity. See Harold Finestone's brilliant and odd article "Cats, Kicks and Color," in *Identity and Anxiety: Survival of the*

Person in Mass Society, ed. Maurice R. Stein, Arthur J. Vidich, and David M. White (Glencoe, Ill.: Free Press, 1960), 435–48.

27. Ted Morgan, *Literary Outlaw: The Life and Times of William S. Burroughs* (New York: Holt, 1988), 173. It may be that Vollmer used "lay terms" to let Ginsberg know that she did not feel qualified to use a more technical language.

28. Watson, *Birth of the Beat Generation*, 51. It is astonishing now to hear the certainty with which Ginsberg and others mocked the middle class. I'm not sure alternative perspectives can still muster this conviction.

29. Wallace Fowlie, *Rimbaud, the Myth of Childhood* (New York: D. Dobson, 1946), 35. This is, from an anthropological point of view, an interesting cultural construct. It assumes that there are truths out there, that it is artists who must go after them, and that they can be got at only by breaking through the constraints of mainstream society.

30. Watson, *Birth of the Beat Generation*, 39.

31. Donald B. Kuspit, *The Cult of the Avant-Garde Artist* (Cambridge: Cambridge University Press, 1993), 7–8.

32. Watson, *Birth of the Beat Generation*, 138.

33. Ibid., 98, 127, 128. Anthropologists are, of course, a little uncomfortable with talk like this, inclined as they are to believe that there is no "percept" without "concept": in this case, no experience that is not instantaneously constituted by culture. This allows them to see and account for the role of culture, but it also means they are not very good at distinguishing between cultural acts that are, to use Silverstein's terms with some liberty, presupposing and those that are relatively creative. There can't be any question that the beats were not wrong. Even when merely substituting one set of rules of sensation and writing for another, they had broken with what Sahlins calls the regnant culture. Even when rule-bound, they were, in the 1990s phrase, "out there." For an indication of a shift in the anthropological paradigm, see Richard G. Fox, "For a Nearly New Culture History," in *Recapturing Anthropology: Working in the Present*, ed. Richard G. Fox (Santa Fe, N.M.: School of American Research Press, 1991), 93–113.

34. Watson, *Birth of the Beat Generation*, 21–22.

35. Gerald Nicosia, *Memory Babe: A Critical Biography of Jack Kerouac* (New York: Grove, 1983), 116, quoted in Watson, *Birth of the Beat Generation*, 37.

36. William S. Burroughs, *Interzone*, ed. James Grauerholz (New York: Viking, 1989), 128, quoted in Watson, *Birth of the Beat Generation*, 244.

37. Watson, *Birth of the Beat Generation*, 258.

38. Ibid., 236. Watson suggests that this remark may have been motivated by Kerouac's apparent role in the affair between Robert Creeley and Rexroth's wife, Marthe.

39. Ibid., 78. It is hard to know what to make of Solomon's gesture. It has an irresistibly parodic feeling to it. But it is also true that Solomon was a genuinely tragic figure in a community filled with people aching to be tragic figures. At times he seems desperately out of step with the objectives of beats. At times he appears to be the only one with wit enough to turn the self-consciously "disturbational" reflex of the movement against itself. On the issue of the beat attitude toward the middle class, it may be worth recalling the famous moment in *On the Road* when Paradise and Moriarty return the Cadillac they have been driving. It is so misshapen that the mechanic

does not recognize it. Instead of taunting the Chicago baron who owns the car for his pompous materialism (as a hippie surely would have done), Paradise frets that they know his address. Jack Kerouac, *On the Road* (1957; New York: Penguin, 1991), 243.

40. Watson, *Birth of the Beat Generation*, 53.

41. Ibid., 34, 42, 53.

42. Ibid., 65.

43. Ibid., 246.

44. Françoise Sagan, *Bonjour Tristesse* (New York: Dutton, 1955). This book was a literary sensation and a best-seller. It was written by a moody Paris teenager and begins, "A strange melancholy pervades me to which I hesitate to give the grave and beautiful name of sorrow."

45. The hoodlum-beat comparison is also drawn out in Francis Ford Coppola's film *Rumble Fish* (1983) and in the novel by S. E. Hinton on which the film was based.

46. Quoted in John L. Caughey, *Imaginary Social Worlds: A Cultural Approach* (Lincoln: University of Nebraska Press, 1984), 68.

47. Brooks may be wrong to suppose that the "bourgeoisie" and "bohemians" were mutually exclusive communities in post–World War II America. There is evidence of interpenetration from the 1950s onward. This may indeed have been the bobo's ("bourgeois bohemian's") childhood training. David Brooks, *Bobos in Paradise: The New Upper Class and How They Got There* (New York: Touchstone, 2000).

48. David Halle has given us a glimpse of the motives of latter-day owners of modernist art. His respondents appear to say that it was precisely the ill-definedness of the art that appealed to them. Abstract art permitted the imagination to wander and provoked creativity. Abstract art, they said, took you somewhere, away from received categories and conventions. This may have been the beat ideology at work. David Halle, *Inside Culture: Art and Class in the American Home* (Chicago: University of Chicago Press, 1993), 132, 133. For another view of art in the home, see Gerry Pratt, "The House as an Expression of Social Worlds," in *Housing and Identity: Cross-Cultural Perspectives*, ed. James S. Duncan (London: Croom Helm., 1981), 135–80.

49. I thank John Galvin for suggesting that I look at this documentary. There is also a book: D. A. Pennebaker, *Bob Dylan: Don't Look Back* (New York: Ballantine, 1968).

50. I realize that the reporter does appear to encourage Dylan's reading of his motivation by replying to his outburst with "I have to ask you that because you have the nerve to question whether I can." It's possible that this is merely his response to the outburst, and that it represents a change in his motive that results from the heat and indignation of Dylan's reply.

51. Martin points out that many of the values of the hippie were continuous with those of the beat. Bernice Martin, *A Sociology of Contemporary Cultural Change* (Oxford: Basil Blackwell, 1981).

52. To call brightwork any kind of modernism is, I now see, to defy convention. Bradbury and McFarlane wish to distinguish the modern from the modernist, and they would almost certainly place the brightwork constellation in the first category, not the second. By this rendering, brightwork is not only not modernist, it is anti-modernist. I will use as my defense the observation that my notion of modernism was, at the time this essay was written, mostly informed by modernism in the

built form and architectural literature, where it seems to me that Bradbury and McFarlane's distinction breaks down. Bradbury and McFarlane, "The Name and Nature of Modernism," 41–50, esp. 49–50.

53. I have come to think of these cars and the ads that promoted them as Poggioli thinks of the publications so "highly characteristic" of the avant-garde: as "proclamations and programs or a series of manifestos, announcing the foundation of a new movement, explicating and elaborating its doctrine, categorically and polemically." Poggioli, *Theory of the Avant-Garde*, 22.

54. Vance Oakley Packard, *The Status Seekers: An Exploration of Class Behavior in America and the Hidden Barriers That Affect You, Your Community, Your Future* (New York: D. McKay, 1959).

55. Neil McKendrick, John Brewer, and J. H. Plumb, *The Birth of a Consumer Society: The Commercialization of Eighteenth-Century England* (Bloomington: Indiana University Press, 1982); "Even the Swing of the Doors Is New," Buick ad in *Life* 36, no. 19 (1954): 13; "Worth Its Price in PRESTIGE," Cadillac ad in *Life* 36, no. 11 (1954): 6–7; "Elegance in Action," Dodge ad in *Life* 36, no. 3 (1954): inside front cover; Pierre Martineau, "Snob Appeal Losing Ground," *Advertising Age* 25, no. 43 (1954): 12; and "Notice How Many More People Are Arriving in Lincolns?" ad in *Life* 36, no. 22 (1954): 42–43. Note that I am citing these advertisements in the bibliographic form normally reserved for anonymously written articles. I hope that when the history of the advertising agency is undertaken in a more substantial way, it will be possible to specify the authors of advertisements (at least the creative director and copy writer) and the agency from which they came. As it is, I am able to supply the name of the agency in only a couple of cases, and never the names of the creative team.

56. "You're Fashion First—With the Last Word in Cars," Buick ad in *Life* 36, no. 14 (1954): 154; "Here's Wonderful Inside News for You," Chrysler ad in *Life* 36, no. 18 (1954): 46–47; "High Fashion Note All over America This Year!" Fisher ad in *Life* 36, no. 9 (1954): 6–7; "New '54 Plymouth: Under the Beauty, Solid Value," ad in *Life* 36, no. 7 (1954): 55; "This Year Buy a '54 Studebaker," ad in *Life* 36, no. 2 (1954): 2; "What Kind of 'Hat' Does Your Horsepower Wear?" Chrysler ad in *Life* 36, no. 22 (1954): 34–35; and "Presenting the Beautiful New Packards for '54," ad in *Life* 36, no. 16 (1954): 18–19. For an advertisement that manages to combine the fashion theme with emphasis on the future, see "General Motors: Way, Way Ahead!" *Life* 36, no. 10 (1954): 100–101. For an advertisement that combines the status and fashion themes, see "Night Scene by '21,'" Fisher ad in *Life* 36, no. 21 (1954): 64–65.

57. "Moonlit Drive," Pontiac ad in *Time* (Canadian edition) 68, no. 32 (1956); "Announcing the Hudson Hornet Special," ad in *Life* 36, no. 22 (1954): 110; "Extra Dividends at No Extra Cost in the '54 Ford," ad in *Life* 36, no. 9 (1954): 114; and "Some Sensible Reasons Why It's Still More Fun to Own a Chevrolet," ad in *Life* 36, no. 22 (1954): 49.

58. "Lincoln Shows How New Your Car Should Be," ad in *Life* 36, no. 9 (1954): 42–43; "Let Lincoln Show You What Modern Driving Means," ad in *Life* 36, no. 16 (1954): 94–95; "DeSoto Automatic," ad in *Life* 36, no. 11 (1954): 88; and "The Thrifty '54 Studebakers Are the Only Really Modern Cars in America," ad in *Life* 36, no. 11 (1954): inside front cover.

59. Richard Horn, *Fifties Style: Then and Now* (Harmondsworth: Penguin, 1985), 12.

60. "Sales Acceleration Leaves Detroit Auto Men Breathless," *Advertising Age* 25, no. 1 (1954): 3, 46; Herbert Brean, "'54 Car: 3 Years Old at Birth," *Life* 36, no. 3 (1954): 80–92; Anonymous, 1955; John B. Rae, *The American Automobile: A Brief History* (Chicago: University of Chicago Press, 1965), 199; and "Ford's '55 Nine-Month Profits Top Those of Any Prior Full Year: Breech," *Advertising Age* 26, no. 45 (1955): 3.

61. "Autos: Step to the Rear," *Time* 66, no. 22 (1955): 82.

62. "Flight into Anywhere," Buick ad in *Time* 68 (1956): 29; "Oldsmobile 'Dream Car,'" ad in *Life* 36, no. 8 (1954): 42–43; "Thrill of the Year Is Buick," ad in *Maclean's* 68, no. 6 (1955): 37; Benton and Bowes Agency, "Craftsmanship with a Flair," Studebaker ad in *Time* 66, no. 22 (1955): 8; and "Plymouth Hikes '56 Ad Budget 18%; Seeks to Garner 11½% of Market," *Advertising Age* 26, no. 41 (1955): 2, 114.

63. "GM's Motorama to Be Lavish Spectacle; Will Also Show Cars," *Advertising Age* 26, no. 2 (1955): 96; Benton and Bowes Agency, "Craftsmanship with a Flair"; and "General Motors Wages Record Ad and Promotion Drive for Powerama Show," *Advertising Age* 26, no. 36 (1955): 4, 68. Notice that the General Motors Motorama of 1956 offered the "Kitchen of Tomorrow," which featured the "sheer look." This look "discarded the clutter of applied baroque decoration on appliances and virtually eliminated the use of metal stampings and glass enamel." Arthur J. Pulos, *The American Design Adventure, 1940–1975* (Cambridge, Mass.: MIT Press, 1988), 138 (with a photo of the kitchen). In this case, the material culture and built form of the period are truer to the modernist aesthetic than cars proved to be. For photographs of the Futura and the Firebird, see Pulos, *The American Design Adventure*, 373, 374. Karal Marling touches on the "forward look" in "Autoeroticism: America's Love Affair with the Car in the Television Age," chapter 4 of her *As Seen on TV: The Visual Culture of Everyday Life in the 1950s* (Cambridge, Mass.: Harvard University Press, 1994), 129–62.

64. "B&B Revives 'Craft' Motif in 1st Drive for Studebaker," *Advertising Age* 26, no. 48 (1955): 8. The advertising industry played a double game. It moved away from modernism when it was clear that there was another, more profitable way to sell automobiles, but it was prepared to insist that its grinning brightwork was still modernist, at least when it was advantageous to do so. Consider this copy text from an odd little ad for a television set: "The 'Capri' was created for Westinghouse by Harley Earl, internationally famous designer of Le Sabre, 'the car of the future.' Mr. Earl has won wide acclaim for his 'form follows function' styling for contemporary living." "Introducing the New TV Design Sensation," Westinghouse ad in *Life* 36, no. 7 (1954): 47. See also "Studebaker Plans $8,000,000 Budget, up 3% from 1954," *Advertising Age* 26, no. 19 (1955): 34.

65. Dan Guillory, "Star Wars Style and American Automobiles," in *The Automobile and American Culture*, ed. Laurence Goldstein and David Lanier Lewis (Ann Arbor: University of Michigan Press, 1983), 392. Thanks to Lonnie Weatherby of the McGill University Libraries for finding this reference when it went astray.

66. John B. Rae, *The American Automobile: A Brief History* (Chicago: University of Chicago Press, 1965), 209.

67. That this cultural phenomenon was Western, or at least North American, is suggested by an ad that appeared in the Canadian popular press: "Men Who Guide Canada's Advance Wear Rolex Watches," ad in *Time* (Canadian edition) 66, no. 22 (1955): 39.

68. Mircea Eliade, *The Myth of the Eternal Return*, translated by Willard R. Trask (New York: Pantheon, 1954); and J. B. Priestly, *Man and Time* (Garden City, N.J.: Doubleday, 1964). For useful looks at how the West constructed its peculiar sense of time, see Ricardo J. Quinones, *The Renaissance Discovery of Time* (Cambridge, Mass.: Harvard University Press, 1972); and Daniel J. Boorstin, *The Republic of Technology: Reflections on Our Future Community* (New York: Harper & Row, 1978).

69. Yehoshua Ariely, *The Future-Directed Character of the American Experience* (Jerusalem: Magnes Press, Hebrew University, 1966); and Clyde Kluckhohn and Florence R. Kluckhohn, "American Culture: Generalized Orientations and Class Patterns," in *Conflicts of Power in Modern Culture*, ed. Lyman L. F. Bryson, Louis Finkelstein, and R. M. MacIver (1947; New York: Cooper Square, 1964), 111. The American world fairs may be treated as studies in America's passion for progress and concern for the future. Robert W. Rydell, *World of Fairs: The Century-of-Progress Expositions* (Chicago: University of Chicago Press, 1993). The Disneyland pavilion devoted to the future is perhaps another case in point. Seth Schiesel, "New Disney Vision Making the Future a Thing of the Past," *New York Times*, February 23, 1997: 1, 24; and Alan Dundes, "Thinking Ahead: A Folkloristic Reflection of the Future Orientation in American Worldview," in *Interpreting Folklore* (Bloomington: Indiana University Press, 1980), 69–85.

70. The extremely interesting period caricature of the "egghead" captures the contempt and the regard the period felt for those who could traverse this domain. To my knowledge we have no study of this cultural artifact.

71. Julian Marias, *America in the Fifties and Sixties*, translated by Blanche de Puy and Harold C. Raley (University Park: Pennsylvania State University Press, 1972), 35. See the reference to gadgets in "The New American Domesticated Male," *Life* 36, no. 1 (1954): 42–45. See Siegfried Giedion, *Mechanization Takes Command: A Contribution to Anonymous History* (New York: Oxford University Press, 1948) for useful comments on the relationship between culture and technology in general and gadgets in particular. This book treats the period from the 1930s to the middle 1940s, too early, strictly speaking, for our purposes. There is a nice reference to the "push-button future" in *This Island Earth* (1955, dir. Joseph M. Newman), the science fiction film mocked in *Mystery Science Theatre 3000: The Movie* (1996, dir. Jim Mallon). The "push-button" was indeed everywhere in the 1950s. This and the "atomic," "ball," or "starburst" clock that graced many modernist kitchens would both appear to be instances of material culture into which more research would be promising. One captures an interesting attitude toward technology, the other an interesting attitude toward time. The other topic that calls out for further study in this connection is the delta shape that invaded the material culture and interior design of the modernist world. The deltoid shape and the delta name were everywhere in the constellation under study here. See for instance, "Pratt and Whitney Aircraft: Power," *Time* 67, no. 8 (1956): 81.

72. Horn, *Fifties Style*, 34.

73. "Billions for Defense Build Wondrous Weapons," *Life* 36, no. 1 (1954): 12–19; and "The U.S. Air Force: The Nation's Youngest Service Has Entered the Supersonic Age," *Time* 67, no. 10 (1956): 42–51.

74. A visiting anthropologist in the 1950s might have remarked upon the fact that Americans talked about their national and their personal aspirations in almost

precisely the same language. They spoke of themselves as "getting ahead," "really going somewhere," "traveling in the fast lane," "making it to the top." In a time of class mobility, the theme was as important for individual reasons as for collective ones. W. L. Warner and James C. Abegglen, *Occupational Mobility in American Business and Industry, 1928–1952* (Minneapolis: University of Minnesota Press, 1955); Seymour M. Lipset and Reinhard Bendix, *Social Mobility in Industrial Society* (Berkeley: University of California Press, 1959); Thomas Luckmann and Peter Berger, "Social Mobility and Personal Identity," *Archives européennes de sociologie* 5 (1964): 331–43; Richard M. Huber, *The American Idea of Success* (New York: McGraw-Hill, 1971); David K. McClelland, *The Achieving Society* (New York: Nostrand, 1961); Kluckhohn and Kluckhohn, "American Culture"; and Neil L. Shumsky, *Social Structure and Social Mobility* (New York: Garland, 1996).

75. Raymond Loewy, "Jukebox on Wheels," *Atlantic Monthly* 195, no. 4 (1955): 36–37.

76. Warren I. Susman, "Culture and Communications," in *Culture as History: The Transformation of American Society in the Twentieth Century* (New York: Pantheon, 1984), 263.

77. I am suspicious of this argument. Surely, it's unlikely that the Victorians created decoration for the sake of it.

78. This paragraph draws on several conversations with Annie Pedret. I think it is unlikely that she would agree with my conclusion, but I am grateful for her observations. For more on how material culture makes cultural material, see Kenneth L. Ames, "Meaning in Artifacts: Hall Furnishings in Victorian America," in *Common Places: Readings in American Vernacular Architecture*, ed. Del Upton and John M. Vlach (Athens: University of Georgia Press, 1986), 240–60; and Jules D. Prown, "Mind in Matter: An Introduction to Material Culture Theory and Method," *Winterthur Portfolio* 17, no. 1 (1982): 1–19.

79. Jean Baudrillard, *America*, translated by Chris Turner (New York: Verso, 1989), 10. For more on Baudrillard, see Sarah Zupko's website on popular culture at http://www.popcultures.com/theorists/baudrillard.html. See also Alan Taylor's webpage, Baudrillard on the Web, at http://www.uta.edu/english/apt/collab/baudweb.html. For an interesting view of the significance of the automobile windshield, see the work of Kristin Ross, who compares it to a movie screen: Kristin Ross, *Fast Cars, Clean Bodies: Decolonization and the Reordering of French Culture* (Cambridge, Mass.: MIT Press, 1995).

80. Jurgen Habermas, "Modernity—An Incomplete Project," in *The Antiaesthetic: Essays on Postmodern Culture*, ed. Hal Foster (Port Townsend, Wash.: Bay Press, 1983), 3–15.

81. Matei Calinescu, *Five Faces of Modernity* (Durham, N.C.: Duke University Press, 1987), 66.

82. Matei Calinescu, "From the One to the Many: Pluralism in Today's Thought," in *Innovation/Renovation: New Perspectives on the Humanities*, ed. Ihab Hassan and Sally Hassan (Madison: University of Wisconsin Press, 1983), 263–88.

83. Peter Osborne, introduction to *The Politics of Time: Modernity and Avant-Garde* (New York: Verso, 1995), xii.

84. Jameson, "Postmoderism and Consumer Society," 125. For a detailed study of the idea of amnesia as a cultural reflex, see Andreas Huyssen, *Twilight Memories:*

Marking Time in a Culture of Amnesia (New York: Routledge, 1995). All of the sources cited in this paragraph identify modernism as a temporal orientation that becomes, finally, a cultural value. But many observers see this notion of time as the problem that modernity creates for modernism. Thus Octavio Paz says that modernity is "cut off from the past and continually hurtling forward at such a dizzy pace that it cannot take root, that it merely survives from one day to the next: it is unable to return to its beginnings and thus recover its powers of renewal." Quoted in Berman, *All That Is Solid Melts into Air,* 35.

85. "You're Fashion First—With the Last Word in Cars," Buick ad in *Life* 36, no. 14 (1954): 154; "Car of the Future: Styling Comes True in Five General Motors Cars You Can Buy Today," ad in *Life* 36, no. 5 (1954): 22–23; "Here the Stylists Went All Out," Buick ad in *Life* 36, no. 2 (1954): 46–47; Pulos, *The American Design Adventure,* 373; and "Oldsmobile 'Dream Car,' " ad in *Life* 36, no. 8 (1954): 42–43. The Bel Geddes exhibit called "Futurama" was constructed inside the General Motors building, a pitch for superhighways that was also a picture of the future delivered to visitors, who were whisked above the exhibit in overstuffed chairs. Rydell, *World of Fairs.*

86. Here is Le Corbusier on modernism as material culture. "Our modern life, when we are active and about (leaving out the moments when we fly to gruel and aspirin) has created its own objects: its costume, its fountain pen, its eversharp pencil, its typewriter, its telephone, its admirable office furniture, its plate-glass and its 'Innovation' trunks, . . . the limousine, the steamship and the airplane. Our epoch is fixing its own style day by day. It is there under our eyes." John Docker, *Postmodernism and Popular Culture: A Cultural History* (Cambridge: Cambridge University Press, 1994), 2.

87. Examples of these spaces may be found in Horn, *Fifties Style.* See particularly the photographs on pages 106 and 107.

Section 5. Postmodern Transformations

1. Denise Linn, *Sacred Space: Clearing and Enhancing the Energy of Your Home* (New York: Ballantine, 1995), 229. I should note that this statement is less capricious than an uncontextualized quotation makes it sound. This is because her "intuition" is a particular, disciplined instrument of knowing.

2. How can intuition be its own guarantor? The notion of self-supplied authority is one of the chief puzzles that must be solved if anthropology is to make sense of contemporary culture. Charles Taylor has explored this idea in chapter 15 of his *Sources of the Self: The Making of the Modern Identity* (Cambridge, Mass.: Harvard University Press, 1989).

3. Marion Weinstein, *Earth Magic: A Dianic Book of Shadows: A Guide for Witches,* 4th ed. (New York: Earth Magic Productions, 1998), 84.

4. There is also a slightly eerie conflation of witchcraft magic and Hollywood "magic" when demons are said to be "full of special effects." It's interesting to think about the unsuspected harmonies that may exist between these two traditions, and the extent to which these harmonies have been encouraged by the steady attention Hollywood and television have recently paid to the witchcraft tradition (e.g., *The*

Witches of Eastwick, 1987, dir. George Miller; *The Craft*, 1996, dir. Andrew Fleming; *Practical Magic*, 1998, dir. Griffin Dunne). This attention dates back to the television show *Bewitched*, which aired from 1964 to 1972.

5. Carole Kammen and Jodie Gold, *Call to Connection: Bringing Sacred Tribal Values into Modern Life* (Salt Lake City, Utah: Commune-A-Key Publishing, 1998), 198.

6. Quoted in Sera L. Tank, "Personalized Vows Provide a Break from Traditional Formula." http://www.spub.ksu.edu/issues/v100/sp/n099/feab-vows-tank.html. Unfortunately, this website is defunct.

7. Kath Weston, *Families We Choose: Lesbians, Gays, Kinship* (New York: Columbia University Press, 1991), 4.

8. My thanks to Dave Lakata for his help in locating this scene.

9. Language can make a marriage ("I now pronounce you . . ."), but we insist it cannot make a mother-daughter relationship. See David Schneider, *American Kinship: A Cultural Account* (Chicago: University of Chicago Press, 1968).

10. Hollywood films are littered with studies of ordinary and extraordinary kinship. In *Raising Arizona* (1987, dir. Joel Coen), H.I. (Nicolas Cage) and Ed (Holly Hunter) steal a child. They stare in wonder at their new "son" and H.I. exclaims, "Hey, we got ourselves a family here!" This amuses viewers because families do not normally begin with kidnap, but part of us is inclined to say, "Well, if they say so." That there is not an authoritative study of kinship in the movies is a mystery of the academic world.

11. David I. Kertzer, *Rituals, Politics, and Power* (New Haven, Conn.: Yale University Press, 1988); and John J. MacAloon, "Sociation and Sociability in Political Celebrations," in *Celebration: Studies in Festivity and Ritual*, ed. Victor W. Turner (Washington, D.C.: Smithsonian Institution Press, 1982), 255–71.

12. James H. Barnett, *The American Christmas: A Study in National Character* (New York: Macmillan, 1954); Daniel Miller, ed., *Unwrapping Christmas* (Oxford: Clarendon, 1993); William B. Waits, *The Modern Christmas in America: A Cultural History of Gift Giving* (New York: New York University Press, 1993); and Leigh E. Schmidt, *Consumer Rites: The Buying and Selling of American Holidays* (Princeton, N.J.: Princeton University Press, 1995).

13. "Coca-Cola . . . has directly shaped the way we think of Santa. Prior to the Sundblom illustrations, the Christmas saint had been variously illustrated wearing blue, yellow, green, or red. In European art, he was usually tall and gaunt, whereas Clement Moore had depicted him as an elf in 'A Visit from St. Nicholas.' After the soft drink ads, Santa would forever more be a huge, fat, relentlessly happy man with broad belt and black hip boots—and he would wear Coca-Cola red." Mark Pendergrast, *For God, Country and Coca-Cola: The Unauthorized History of the Great American Soft Drink and the Company That Makes It* (New York: Macmillan, 1993), 181. Daniel Boorstin suggests that it is Thomas Nast to whom the honor should go: "The American Santa Claus's rotund figure, jolly mien, and white beard were conferred on him by Thomas Nast in his series of Christmas drawing for *Harper's Weekly* beginning in 1863. By the late nineteenth century, 'belief' in Nast's Santa Claus had become a symbol of childhood innocence and adult warm-heartedness." Daniel J. Boorstin, *The Americans: The Democratic Experience* (New York: Random House, 1973), 161. We are alarmed by both possibilities, but they do suggest that folk heroes like Santa (and many cartoon characters

and Hollywood stars) may be shaped by the marketplace without being disqualified as folk heroes. Or, in Boorstin's language, that Santa has commercial origins does not prevent him from being a symbol of childhood innocence. For more on this theme, see Tyler Cowen, *In Praise of Commercial Culture* (Cambridge, Mass.: Harvard University Press, 1998); John Docker, *Postmodernism and Popular Culture: A Cultural History* (Cambridge: Cambridge University Press, 1994); Daniel Miller, *Material Culture and Mass Consumption* (Oxford: Basil Blackwell, 1987); and Russell Belk, "A Child's Christmas in America: Santa Claus as Deity, Consumption as Religion," *Journal of American Culture* 10, no. 1 (1987): 87–100.

14. In his review of this film, Roger Ebert asks, "Have we not all, on our ways to family gatherings, parked the car a block away, taken several deep breaths, rubbed our eyes and massaged our temples, and driven on, gritting our teeth?" http://rogerebert.suntimes.com, review dated November 3, 1995.

15. This holiday too is under-studied. One of the very few studies is Jack Santino, *Halloween and Other Festivals of Death and Life* (Knoxville: University of Tennessee Press, 1994).

16. These and other urban legends sometimes do as much to confirm the liminal character of the event as to discourage its practice.

17. Jack Kugelmass and Mariette P. Allen, *Masked Culture: The Greenwich Village Halloween Parade* (New York: Columbia University Press, 1994). This is a remarkable study.

18. One of the innovations of Halloween is the new pumpkin. The pumpkins of the 1950s and early '60s were relatively standard: triangles for the eyes and nose, crenellation to mark the mouth. The pumpkins of Halloween 1998 in Toronto showed a marked decline in this pattern. Indeed I was hard pressed to find many of this form, or even two pumpkins that looked alike, despite the considerable constraints imposed by the size and texture of a pumpkin and the relative crudity of cutting instruments and cutters' skill. My data was collected in the three days leading up to Halloween 1998 on my walk home. This took me from the Royal Ontario Museum a couple of miles eastward across the city, through a variety of neighborhoods (including, on one route, Rosedale; on another, a housing project; and on a third, Cabbagetown), and finally to, and through, Riverdale—a relatively good socioeconomic range. In a total of three hours of walking, I passed roughly five hundred pumpkins.

19. Perry Miller gives voice to radical Protestant skepticism: "By rituals men charm their consciences and then imagine that God is pacified." Perry Miller, *The New England Mind* (Boston: Beacon, 1939), 46.

20. Charles Taylor, *Sources of the Self: The Making of the Modern Identity* (Cambridge, Mass.: Harvard University Press, 1989), 209–302.

21. Lionel Trilling, preface to *Beyond Culture: Essays on Literature and Learning* (New York: Penguin, 1965), 12. For a postmodernist version of the Trilling agenda, see the treatment in Peter Dews, *The Limits of Disenchantment: Essays on Contemporary European Philosophy* (London: Verso, 1995).

22. This is one of the things that may have helped make the defection of T. S. Eliot and other writers to the Catholic Church so stunning in its time.

23. Michèle Lamont, *Money, Morals and Manners: The Culture of the French and the American Upper-Middle Class* (Chicago: University of Chicago Press, 1992), 116.

24. This is one of the key issues at work in laws that impose dress and grooming standards. John D. Ingram and Ellen R. Domph, "The Right to Govern One's Personal Appearance," *Oklahoma City University Law Review* 6, no. 2 (1981): 339–72.

25. Elizabeth Colson, "The Least Common Denominator," in *Secular Ritual*, ed. Sally F. Moore and Barbara G. Myerhoff (Amsterdam: Van Gorcum, 1977), 190. For more on what Robert Bocock calls "life-cycle rituals," see Robert Bocock, *Ritual in Industrial Society: A Sociological Analysis of Ritualism in Modern England* (London: Allen & Unwin, 1974), 118–46. See also Mary Jo Deegan, *American Ritual Dramas: Social Rules and Cultural Meanings* (Westport, Conn.: Greenwood, 1988); and Michael Thurgood Haynes, "Coronation in San Antonio: Class, Family and the Individual," in *Celebrations of Identity: Multiple Voices in American Ritual Performance*, ed. Pamela R. Frese (Westport, Conn.: Bergin and Garvey, 1993), 177–94.

26. Grant McCracken, *Plenitude 2.0*, 2nd ed. (Toronto: Periph. Fluide, 1998), 18.

27. Barbara Lippert, "Our Martha, Ourselves," *New York Magazine*, May 15, 1995: 32. The New Age community is constantly creating new rituals, and I discuss these activities further in the essay entitled "New Age, British Columbia" in this section.

28. McCracken, *Plenitude 2.0*. Max Gluckman observes, somewhat clumsily, "There are tensions between too many diverse political and other groups in our society to be dramatized simply, and, paradoxically, because of the very fragmentation of our social relationships we do not have as well-developed or as frequent rituals which involve the appearance of persons according to their social roles." Max Gluckman, *Order and Rebellion in Tribal Africa* (London: Cohen and West, 1963), 126.

29. Robert Bly, *Iron John: A Book about Men* (New York: Vintage, 1992), 182. Bly's book is somewhat ambiguous about the Wild Man. Strictly speaking, he is the guide, the ritual officer, who conducts young men through their development. But he is occasionally held up as the essential self to which all men should aspire.

30. To be fair, this is not just Bly's problem. Series like this one put anthropology on notice. The field can understand any one of these items, but when the object of analysis is all of them together, you can hear the mind reel and the categories tear.

31. Joseph Campbell, with Bill Moyers, *The Power of Myth* (New York: Doubleday, 1988), 8. I know this is going to offend people. I know that the world has learned more about myth from Joseph Campbell than from all anthropologists combined. To give him his due, he was an intelligent man and a gifted communicator. But I am obliged to say his work is deeply flawed. I will take as one example his comments on female initiation in "primary cultures," as he calls them. "She is now a woman. And what is a woman? A woman is a vehicle of life. . . . Woman is what it is all about—the giving of birth and the giving of nourishment" (83). Interestingly, an earlier Campbell seems more sensitive to the possibility that the myth and ritual of traditional society cannot be transferred so crudely to Western developed societies. In *Myths to Live By*, he says, "And the first function of the rites of puberty, accordingly, must be to establish in the individual a system of sentiments that will be

appropriate to the society in which he is to live, and on which that society itself must depend for its existence. . . . In a modern Western world . . . there is an additional complication. [We want] independent, observant, free-thinking individuals . . . [each] not simply reproducing inherited patterns of thought and action but becoming himself an innovating center, an active creative center of the life process." Joseph Campbell, *Myths to Live By* (New York: Viking, 1972), 47.

32. Bill Buford, *Among the Thugs* (London: Secker and Warburg, 1991).

33. William Arens, "Professional Football: An American Symbol and Ritual," in *The American Dimension,* ed. Susan Montague and William Arens (Port Washington, N.Y.: Alfred, 1976), 3–14.

34. George Gmelch, "Baseball Magic," in *Conformity and Conflict: Readings in Cultural Anthropology,* 6th ed., ed. David W. McCurdy and James P. Spradley (Boston: Little, Brown, 1987), 344.

35. Claude Lévi-Strauss, *The Savage Mind* (Chicago: University of Chicago Press, 1966), 32.

36. Campbell and Moyers, *The Power of Myth,* 82. This tells us that Campbell subscribed to one of our own myths: that culture that comes from commerce cannot be culture. There are less "mythic" accounts.

37. John L. Caughey, *Imaginary Social Worlds: A Cultural Approach* (Lincoln: University of Nebraska Press, 1984). See also Kristin Ross, *Fast Cars, Clean Bodies: Decolonization and the Reordering of French Culture* (Cambridge, Mass.: MIT Press, 1995), but Ross makes the argument more from a collective than from an individual point of view. There is some treatment of the latter in Tessa Perkins's interesting essay "The Politics of Jane Fonda," in *Stardom: Industry of Desire,* ed. Christine Gledhill (London: Routledge, 1991), 237–50. Lee Drummond investigates the connection between movies and viewers, but concentrates too much on the movies as displaced and compensatory opportunities for self-invention, in *American Dreamtime: A Cultural Analysis of Popular Movies and Their Implications for a Science of Humanity* (Lanham, Md.: Littlefield Adams, 1996).

One of the reasons that we have been slow to admit to the role of Hollywood in shaping the self is because we so often think about movies as "away" worlds, fantastic departures from the here and now. This construction is circulated even by Hollywood insiders. Here is the American director Martin Scorsese: "Movies can transport you to another place in time. And that's magic. They take you away to another world. It's like a dream state." Advertisement for U.S. Satellite Broadcasting, *Movieline* 10, no. 2 (October 1998): 31. This is, I think, the single most destructive figure of speech at work in the popular understanding of Hollywood. We may enter the world of a film, but what is equally interesting is what we bring back with us for deployment in everyday life and the construction of a quotidian self.

38. Eric Hobsbawm, "Introduction: Inventing Traditions," in *The Invention of Tradition,* ed. Eric Hobsbawm and Terence Ranger (New York: Cambridge University Press, 1984), 10.

39. Sheldon Wolin, "Postmodern Politics and the Absence of Myth," *Social Research* 52, no. 2 (summer 1985): 218, 217, 221. For another reference to the "paradox of self-conscious mythmaking," see David E. Cooper, "Modern Mythology: The Case of 'Reactionary Modernism,'" *History of the Human Sciences* 9, no. 2 (1996): 26.

40. Marjorie H. Nicolson, *The Breaking of the Circle: Studies in the Effect of the "New Science" upon Seventeenth-Century Poetry* (New York: Columbia University Press, 1960).

41. Max Weber, "Science as a Vocation," in *From Max Weber*, ed. H. H. Gerth and C. Wright Mills (New York: Oxford University Press, 1946), 148, 155.

42. See notes on the "myth of mythlessness" in Robert Jewett and John S. Lawrence, *The American Monomyth* (Garden City, N.J.: Anchor, 1977); and William G. Doty, *Mythography: The Study of Myths and Rituals* (University: University of Alabama Press, 1986).

43. Barry A. Shain, *The Myth of American Individualism: The Protestant Origins of American Political Thought* (Princeton, N.J.: Princeton University Press, 1994).

44. David Abram, *The Spell of the Sensuous: Perception and Language in a More-Than-Human World* (New York: Pantheon, 1996).

45. I owe this understanding of rock climbing to Miklos Sarvary. He is not responsible for my treatment of the data.

46. Extreme sports include rock climbing, mountain biking, motor biking, skiing, white-water rafting, surfing, bodyboarding, skateboarding, street luge, sky-diving, and snowboarding, among others. I have also seen these referred to as "gravity sports." As I will argue here, extreme sports are defined by their working at the edge of the individual's athletic competence. The account that appears in these pages is not exhaustive. I am told that the community of athletes in these sports now resents the term "extreme" and refuses to use it. It is now the term of choice among TV programmers and marketers. Thanks to Wade Nelson for this observation.

47. Mihaly Csikszentmihalyi, *Flow: The Psychology of Optimal Experience* (New York: Harper & Row, 1990).

48. This may be why injuries are not just the usual sportsman's badge of courage, but proof that the player was "out there on the edge."

49. I am grateful to Suzanne Stein for helping me see this connection.

50. Michael Lewis, *The New New Thing: A Silicon Valley Story* (New York: W. W. Norton, 2000), 35. This is a very interesting ethnography.

51. According to its 1999 annual report, Oracle Corporation is the world's largest supplier of database software and the second largest supplier of application software.

52. What Clark and Ellison do is now relatively commonplace in Silicon Valley. Carol Hymowitz, "New Economy Chiefs, Seeking Stress at Play, Find Golf Too Stodgy," *Wall Street Journal*, June 27, 2000: B1. Ellison is trading on the male notion of heroism in his account, apparently betting that understanding the peril will make him appear all the more heroic. But what he is not doing, and this is the point at issue, is claiming to have engaged in extreme sports as a reflection of his professional life in extreme business.

53. I am using the term "self" as if it were something that exists, that we understand, that is possible. All of these notions have been thrown into question by the theoretical developments of the last twenty years. We will have a chance to return to the notion of the self. Let me say here only that the illusion of self-hood, if that's what it is, is very strong in those who possess swift selves.

54. John G. Cawelti, *Apostles of the Self-Made Man: Changing Concepts of Success in America* (Chicago: University of Chicago Press, 1965), 12.

55. Daniel Bell, *The Cultural Contradictions of Capitalism* (New York: Basic Books, 1976).

56. I am generalizing dangerously. It is simply true that even the most instrumental member of the corporation forms deeper emotional and social ties to the organization. The field of organizational behavior takes as its subject these ties and especially the institutional puzzles that emerge when organizations that pretend perfect rationality find themselves complicated by extra-rational considerations. But it remains relatively true that the organizations to which the swift self is drawn are often, by the standard of other enduring affiliations, relatively bloodless. This is why they can devote themselves with ferocious intensity to "winning one" for IBM, and some months later, with no sense of contradiction, transfer their loyalty and passion to Compaq.

57. Max Weber, *Economy and Society*, ed. Guenther Roth and Claus Wittich (Los Angeles: University of California Press, 1978), 2:959.

58. It is also true that many moments in the history of capitalism discouraged the participation of swift selves. Managerial capitalism, for instance, defined as it was by bureaucratic requirements, looked for functionaries instead. It is only the relatively recent shift to entrepreneurial capitalism that has let the swift self in.

59. Clayton M. Christensen, *The Innovator's Dilemma: When New Technologies Cause Great Firms to Fail* (Boston: Harvard Business School Press, 1997); and Geoffrey A. Moore, *Crossing the Chasm: Marketing and Selling Technology Products to Mainstream Customers* (New York: HarperBusiness, 1991). Both these books exercised great influence at Harvard Business School in 1999.

60. Thomas J. Peters, *Thriving on Chaos: Handbook for a Management Revolution* (New York: Knopf, 1987) and *Liberation Management: Necessary Disorganization for the Nanosecond Nineties* (New York: Knopf, 1992).

61. One case in point: *Doc Hollywood* (1991, dir. Michael Caton-Jones). Here a young doctor (Michael J. Fox) destined for a lucrative, upwardly mobile career as a plaster surgeon to the stars discovers that the more honest and substantial choice is life in a small town as a general practitioner. See also *Baby Boom* (1987, dir. Charles Shyer), *Backbeat* (1993, dir. Iain Softley), and *That Thing You Do* (1996, dir. Tom Hanks). Thanks are due to Jacqueline Majers for these last three references.

62. My assignment, for the Capital Markets Company, was to interview people with wealth in Boston and San Francisco. I did ethnographic interviews with twenty people, ten on each coast, in May of 2000.

63. I am overstating a little for the sake of exposition. Many people find a way out of swiftness. I believe that many more are driven out and that they survive only because they succeed in accommodating themselves, abruptly, to another modality. Their powers of adaptation now serve them well. The question is finding something that will take.

64. Susman is useful in showing a connection between modernism and the swift self. Warren I. Susman, "'Personality' and the Making of Twentieth-Century Culture," in *Culture as History: The Transformation of American Society in the Twentieth Century* (New York: Pantheon, 1984), 271–85.

65. De Man is talking about Nietzsche. Paul de Man, "Literary History and Literary Modernity," in *Blindness and Insight* (New York: Oxford University Press, 1971), 147.

66. Richard A. Shweder and Edmund J. Bourne, "Does the Concept of the Person Vary Cross-Culturally?" in *Culture Theory: Essays on Mind, Self, and Emotion,* ed. Richard A. Shweder and Robert A. LeVine (New York: Cambridge University Press, 1984), 190.

67. One opportunity to study this delight is in swift adoration for the fictional character James Bond. The Bond character is swift in several respects. He has no enduring family or community connections. He is a creature of perpetual motion. He glitters with mechanical additions that extend his powers. He need only observe a social or practical problem to make himself the master of it.

68. I wonder whether this is one of the ways David Cronenberg means us to understand his movie *Crash* (1996), in which people seek to make themselves the victims of automobile accidents in order to qualify for new prosthetic implants. Toward the end of the film, James Ballard (James Spader) and Helen Remington (Holly Hunter) stage a traffic accident and Remington is trapped in the wreckage. Ballard embraces her and asks, "Are you hurt?" She replies, "No, I'm all right." Ballard sympathizes, "Too bad," as if to say, "No prosthetics, this time." It's as if Cronenberg is observing the last moments in which prosthetic extension comes from automobiles. As we prepare ourselves for cyberextensions, this is a farewell.

69. Susman was particularly interesting in this connection. He proposed that a culture of personality began to supplant the culture of character sometime in the early twentieth century. And he proposed that this cultural shift was driven in part by the self-help literature of the period. Susman sounded at times as if he was proposing the emergence of a culture that is bound to domesticate the self. The new literature encourages the individual to "master" and "develop" the self. If Susman is right, my supposition that a key development occurs in the transition from Peale to Robbins must be wrong. Susman, "Personality."

70. A recent example of this pattern is Wendy Kaminer's *I'm Dysfunctional, You're Dysfunctional: The Recovery Movement and Other Self-Help Fashions* (New York: Random House, 1992). This is a very funny book. But all too often, it goes for the joke and refuses larger and more interesting possibilities. As long as observers like Kaminer are allowed to indulge their loathing for these therapies, we will never see their larger cultural significance. Anthony Robbins is an entrepreneur, a "peak performance" consultant, and the author of *Awaken the Giant Within: How to Take Immediate Control of Your Mental, Emotional, Physical, and Financial Destiny!* (New York: Simon and Schuster, 1991).

71. Norman Vincent Peale, *The Power of Positive Thinking* (1952; New York: Random House, 1963), 108. See *Gates of Heaven* (1978, dir. Errol Morris) and the case of Philip Harberts, who compares himself to a computer. This is precisely the vision of the swift self intellectuals like to mock. On the issue of the mechanistic self proposed by Peale, I think the section above on 1950s automobiles suggests that the comparison was in this decade conventional and compelling.

72. Norman Vincent Peale, *Have a Great Day* (New York: Ballantine, 1985), 6.

73. There is an odd tension in our culture on this score. On the one hand, there are the tough-minded pragmatists who argue that people never change, that the world never bends, that wishing never makes it so. And the world obliges with countless stories of how it has "corrected" failure and naïveté in its heartless, humorless way. On the other hand, there are stories of people who do triumph or

at least survive in the face of astonishing odds, and these are often stories in which a brute optimism plays a part. Sometimes wishing (together with hard work) does make it so. Hollywood is a champion of this belief, and movies like *Rudy* (1993, dir. David Anspaugh) are examples. It will not do to dismiss them merely as instances of feel-good wishful thinking, for the movies speak to something in the world and inspire many personal aspirations and life-changing decisions.

74. But self-help theorists like Robbins rarely have a "Durkheimian" moment. They do not appear to think about the social and cultural context in which the self must operate. Durkheim helped "discover" the collectivity of culture and society obscured by the Western myth of individualism, even as he sought to understand this individualism. Steven Lukes, *Emile Durkheim, His Life and Work: A Historical and Critical Study* (Harmondsworth: Penguin, 1973), 19.

75. Robbins, *Awaken the Giant Within*, 7.

76. Ibid., 19. This is in fact the first line of the book's main text.

77. There may be a way out of this paradox if it's the case that the road to discovering one's uniqueness runs through a brief period of being more like Robbins. On the other hand, Robbins may only care to claim that individual variation serves as a better means to the end of instrumentality, itself a means to activity in the world.

78. Ibid., 316, emphasis added.

79. I do not mean to attribute this development only to Robbins. It is evident throughout the self-help literature.

80. This argument is not peculiar to Robbins. Indeed, it is one of the great themes of the therapeutic literature. Many writers now insist that the only reliable or telling judge of the self and its accomplishments is the self. "Only you can decide what's right for you!" is a ubiquitous phrase.

81. Stephen R. Covey, *The Seven Habits of Highly Effective People: Restoring the Character Ethic* (New York: Simon and Schuster, 1989).

82. I am told that one of the best representations of this protest and movement is the video entitled *This Is What Democracy Looks Like* (2000, dir. Jill Freidberg and Rick Rowley), more information on which can be found at http://www.thisisdemocracy.org.

83. In the spring of 2000 an applicant to Harvard Business School sent a letter to each member of the teaching staff that showed a portrait of the applicant and the HBS shield joined by an equals sign. Beneath, a slogan read "A great team together." Faculty members came out of their offices and stared at one another in wonder.

84. To pink, as with pinking shears, is to decorate with perforations or a zigzag cut.

85. The most baffling example I have encountered occurred in a telephone conversation. I surprised my conversational partner, and he said, "Let me drop back ten yards on that one." There is a lot of work to be done here, and I do not intend my summary treatment to serve as anything but an indication of the scholarly opportunities that exist.

86. For computer metaphors, see "Tom Davis's Buzzword Bingo" at http://lurkertech.com/chris/bingo/index.html, a website that will generate bingo cards. See also "The Microsoft Lexicon, or Microspeak Made Easier," compiled and

edited by Ken Barnes, at http://cinepad.com/mslex.html. I thank Leora Kornfeld for both references. It was striking how little figurative language, outside the buzz-word category, actually occurs in some business settings. I remember remarking to one of my colleagues that no one seemed to use figurative language at Harvard Business School. In his thoughtful way, he kept watch for several days. In our next conversation, he agreed that HBS was virtually "metaphor-free." I am saying three things. First, that swift selves use lots of prefabricated metaphors of the muscular type described here. Second, that it is permissible to invent one's own metaphors, but these are often muscular as well. Third, that truly freeform metaphors are not much heard and, as I recall from my own experience, not always entirely welcome. I remember one or two of my colleagues responding with looks of surprise or puzzlement when I would try one out.

87. This research was the basis for an exhibit at the Royal Ontario Museum entitled "Toronto Teens: Coming of Age in the 1990s."

88. Alex Keaton was the lead character of the television series *Family Ties*. He was played by Michael J. Fox.

89. Billy Kluver, *A Day with Picasso: Twenty-four Photographs by Jean Cocteau* (Cambridge, Mass.: MIT Press, 1997), 22.

90. There is a third, economic question: "Can this create value?" But it is interesting how often this is a distant, indifferent third for many of the key players.

91. I worked with someone in the telecommunications industry, a woman frustrated with the male engineers on whom she was obliged to impress the consumer's point of view. "If I leave them alone in a room for even fifteen minutes, when I get back they're designing a machine!"

92. My friend Victor Li once told me about a physicist he would pass in the Wren Library of Trinity College, Cambridge, sometime around 1980. Working at his calculator, his gaze turned inward, this man had slipped out of his body and was now living in mental space. Thinking made him drool, and so great was his concentration that the front of his shirt was usually soaked through. My reference to IBM is based on a single visit there in April of 2000. I saw perhaps thirty offices and no more than two images.

93. Lévi-Strauss, *The Savage Mind*, 19.

94. Barry Diller was the president of Paramount in his mid-thirties. He now runs USA Networks, which owns several cable television stations and produces films and television programs. He has increased the market capitalization of his company from $250 million to $15 billion. He founded the Fox Network. For more, see Peter Bart, "The Oddest Couple," *GQ*, October 2000: 166–70.

95. Caroline Chauncey, "Going for the Summit," interview with Candice Carpenter, *HBS Bulletin Online* (Harvard Business School alumni magazine), April 1998, http://www.alumni.hbs.edu/bulletin/1998/april/carpenter.html.

96. Andrea Petersen, "IVillage's CEO Is Stepping Down; Net Loss Widens," *Wall Street Journal*, July 28, 2000: B2.

97. This is an important topic. One feminist goal was to give women access to the swiftness that had been denied them.

98. Candice Carpenter, address to the Harvard Business School Women's Student Association Conference, January 22, 2000.

99. Ibid.

100. Quim Cardona, "A Conversation with Matt Field," *Thrasher* 17, no. 11 (1997): 56, 61. All the quotations from Field in this and the next paragraph are taken from this article.

101. Needless to say, I am uncomfortable saying this about Field, not least because it breaks the first rule of anthropology. But there is, I think, something self-indulgent in what Field says here, and not to say so is to risk antagonizing a great many readers. On the other hand, we are always tempted to ridicule radiant selves, and it is some measure of their courage that they accept this punishment as one of the costs of knowledge. The only way to put this right, perhaps, is to open myself to this punishment and to recount one of my own radiant experiences. It was in the late '70s. I was sitting in the Rare Books Room of the Cambridge University Library, reading a book from the sixteenth century. It was after lunch and I was drowsy. For what we usually call a split second, I had the overpowering sensation that I was extremely fat, covered in grease, breathing noisily, rocking unsteadily in a wooden chair or bench, and slipping in and out of consciousness as I struggled to read the delicate book in my now meaty hands. And then the moment passed. Fifty years ago, I would have dismissed this as a dream state. Now, in a radiant age, I am prepared to think, "Well, maybe, who knows?" I have a friend who says that everything one sees in one's peripheral vision is a glimpse into reality that counts. Fifty years ago, I would have dismissed this statement as ludicrous. Now I'm like, "Could be."

102. Al Franken, *Rush Limbaugh Is a Big Fat Idiot, and Other Observations* (New York: Delacorte, 1996).

103. Deepak Chopra, *Ageless Body, Timeless Mind: The Quantum Alternative to Growing Old* (New York: Harmony, 1993), 6.

104. Clifford Geertz, "'From the Native's Point of View': On the Nature of Anthropological Understanding," in Shweder and LeVine, *Culture Theory*, 126.

105. W. P. Kinsella, *Shoeless Joe* (Boston: Houghton, Mifflin, 1982).

106. See the popular TV shows *Buffy the Vampire Slayer, Angel, Charmed, Highway to Heaven,* and *Touched by an Angel.* We might add to this list the TV situation comedy *Ally McBeal,* on which supernatural, or at least super-realistic, events were common. This is not mythic content, but it certainly explodes the naturalistic conventions that govern most television. Similarly, the TV show *Due South* featured the ghosts of two dead fathers, who were visible, without explanation, to their sons and no one else. "Real-life angel encounters" were at one time documented at http://www.netangel.com/doc8.htm, but the website is now defunct.

107. See the Wikipedia article on "New Age," under "Beliefs": http://en .wikipedia.org/wiki/New_age#Beliefs (accessed June 27, 2007).

108. Jeremiah Creedon, "God with a Million Faces," *Utne Reader* 88 (July–August 1998): 47. I think it was while listening to my Toronto dentist tell me that he spent the weekend with his kids "burying crystals in the yard to balance the harmonics of the house" that I first glimpsed how far some New Age assumptions were beginning to penetrate the mainstream.

109. The term "magical comedy" is from Lisa Schwarzbaum, "In Living Color," *Entertainment Weekly,* October 30, 1998: 78. For Weber's notion of disenchantment, see Weber, "Science as a Vocation." For a broader view, see Stanley

J. Tambiah, *Magic, Science, Religion, and the Scope of Rationality* (Cambridge: Cambridge University Press, 1990).

110. This might be a good place to acknowledge my debt to the Internet Movie Database (http://www.imdb.com). This is an extremely useful resource, a must-have for anyone interested in the study of contemporary culture, and particularly welcome because it covers television as well as it does movies, a great deficit in other databases.

111. James Redfield and Carol Adrienne, *The Celestine Prophecy* (New York: Warner, 1995).

112. Weber, "Science as a Vocation."

113. In the Weberian view, rationalism was extraordinarily powerful and invasive, insinuating itself into "everything from the development of a fixed perspective in painting and architecture, to the institutionalization of art in theatres and museums and the development of tempered keyboard instruments." Anthony J. Cascardi, *The Subject of Modernity* (Cambridge: Cambridge University Press, 1992), 17.

114. Ibid., 24. See Cascardi's interesting discussion of disenchantment, 16–71.

115. Iridology is a system of diagnosis by a close reading of the condition of the iris.

116. I discuss this development in more detail in McCracken, *Plenitude 2.0*.

117. Keith Thomas, *Religion and the Decline of Magic* (London: Weidenfeld and Nicolson, 1971). Thomas paints a more complicated picture, one in which religion and magic coexisted before the former's triumph.

118. Creedon, "God with a Million Faces." Note that the new freedom of choice also allows the choice of ethnicity: Mary C. Waters, *Ethnic Options: Choosing Identities in America* (Berkeley: University of California Press, 1990). Governments, political parties, corporations, churches, elites have all discovered a newly fractious individualism in the world. Individuals are less likely to be passive, accepting, credulous, and obedient. In a sense, it's merely culture's turn. We could argue that reenchantment was a refusal of two authorities: reason and the old systems now in the process of being restored. The new individual welcomed the old systems, if only as a way to dispose of the authority of reason, but was not prepared to pay this newcomer in the old deference.

119. Quoted in Debora L. Silverman, *Art Nouveau in Fin-de-Siècle France: Politics, Psychology, and Style* (Los Angeles: University of California Press, 1989), 314. See also Gerald N. Izenberg, *Impossible Individuality: Romanticism, Revolution, and the Origins of Modern Selfhood, 1787–1802* (Princeton, N.J.: Princeton University Press, 1992).

120. This description is taken from the Hollyhock website at http://www.hollyhock.bc.ca.

121. This radiance is not unprecedented. But it departs from the traditional Western version, in which radiant selves move *en masse*, to emulate something from another culture (chinoiserie, for instance). Radiant selves are prepared to establish their own warrants, proceed by their own efforts, work by their own lights. What cultures did mostly as collectivities, radiant individuals presume to do for themselves. Carl L. Becker, *The Heavenly City of the Eighteenth-Century Philosophers* (New Haven, Conn.: Yale University Press, 1932), 150; Gustave E. Von Grunebaum, *Modern Islam: The Search for Cultural Identity* (Berkeley: University of California

Press, 1962); Robert A. Nisbet, *Social Change and History: Aspects of the Western Theory of Development* (New York: Oxford University Press, 1969), 51; and Ovid (Publius Ovidus Naso), *Metamorphoses*, translated by Mary M. Innes (London: Penguin, 1955). It may be true that radiant selves take up residence more securely than radiant cultures do. Radiant cultures sometimes (though not always) use the cultural exemplar for purposes of displacement or distortion. In other cases, the act of admiration results in not much more than small acts of stylistic deference played out in material culture or built form. Certainly, many radiant selves touch down lightly, as we will observe below, but most take up residence in a more substantial way. Matt Field may be an idiot, but he is a relatively well transformed idiot. His clothing, his language, his cuisine, his most fundamental beliefs and aspirations, all are different because of his emulation of things Caribbean. Chinoiserie was for many English men and women in the eighteenth century less transformational. Edward Said, *Orientalism* (New York: Pantheon, 1978); and Grant McCracken, "The Evocative Power of Things," in *Culture and Consumption: New Approaches to the Symbolic Character of Consumer Goods and Activities* (Bloomington: Indiana University Press, 1988), 104–17.

122. We might call this the "Chief Seattle" stereotype, named for the aboriginal who figured in ads about the tragedy of highway littering. The stereotype was put to the test recently when the national chief of the Assembly of First Nations asked the Canadian government to give aboriginals the right to hunt endangered animals. Andrew Duffy, "Chief Wants Right to Hunt Endangered Animals," *National Post*, August 16, 2000: A7. Still, the sentimentalized image of Chief Seattle is a better stereotype than the earlier Hollywood image of Indians as bloodthirsty creatures bound to provoke simple, good-hearted European homesteaders to acts of slaughter. Dr. Trudy Nicks of the Royal Ontario Museum, curator of a large aboriginal collection there, told me she once surprised a group of nonnative visitors running their hands over objects in the collection. When she asked what they were doing, they explained they were "hoovering [vacuuming] up the vibes." For a study of a more sustained and substantial imitation of an aboriginal culture, see Riku Hamalainen, "We Are the Mystic Warriors of Finland: Finnish Indianism," *European Review of Native American Studies* 12, no. 1 (1998): 13–18. Thanks to Arnie Brownstone of the Royal Ontario Museum for this reference.

123. *Teen Wolf* (1985, dir. Rod Daniel); *American Werewolf in London* (1981, dir. John Landis); *Wolf* (1994, dir. Mike Nicols); and *Bad Moon* (1996, dir. James G. Robinson).

124. Matt Tyrnauer, "Married, with Tigers," *Vanity Fair*, August 1999: 170–81.

125. Clarissa Pinkola Estés, *Women Who Run with the Wolves* (New York: Ballantine, 1992). There is an unverified story circulating in British Columbia that, during the late 1960s, a member of a hippie commune decided to live like a wolf, which, for him, meant moving around constantly, sleeping infrequently and only briefly, and living off the land. It was reported, with an air of scholarly interest, that he was shortly reduced to incoherence. That there could have been a time when this was regarded as something worth doing, and something worth reporting, is a measure of the extent to which radiant selves made a place for their ideas in our culture.

126. Peg McNabb wrote this description on the IMDB website for the show: http://us.imdb.com/Plot?0092319.

127. http://us.imdb.com/Title?0154147.

128. Mark Van Proyen, "Matthew Barney's Blarney: Sartoriasis and Self-Spectacle in Contemporary Art," *Bad Subjects*, no. 38 (May 1998), http://bad.eserver .org/issues/1998/38/vanproyen.html. I am told Trevor Gould has also done work in this area. Thanks are due to Peter White and Gisele Amantea for these references.

129. Sprague has had more than 450 hours of tattooing to give his skin the appearance of scales. He has had plastic surgery to install Teflon bumps in his forehead and to bifurcate his tongue. He has had his teeth filed to make them look like fangs. Thanks to Martin Weigel for telling me about Sprague. See the LizardMan website at http://www.TheLizardMan.com for more information. There is also a useful and thoughtful interview with Sprague by Michael Williams at http://gmwc .netfirms.com/lizardman/TheLizardman.html.

130. For an extraordinarily full documentation of this theme in popular culture, see Phaedrus's Transformation Stories List at http://www.transformationlist.com. "This list includes books, short stories, movies, web sites, and other works that feature physical shapeshifting. All methods of transformation are covered; werewolves and other animal shapeshifters, nanotechnology, magic spells, etc."

131. Bjork, "Hunter," *Homogenic* (One Little Indian/Elektra, 1997). The video was directed by Paul White of Me Company and can be found at http://www.bjork .com/videogallery.

132. Ironically, Snoop Dogg was named for his childhood resemblance to Snoopy, the cartoon character invented by Charles Schulz. For the men as dogs theme, see also the album by Baha Men called *Who Let the Dogs Out?*

133. Donna J. Haraway, "A Cyborg Manifesto: Science, Technology and Socialist-Feminism in the Late Twentieth Century," in *Simians, Cyborgs, and Women: The Reinvention of Nature* (New York: Routledge, 1991), 151–52.

134. E. M. W. Tillyard, *The Elizabethan World Picture* (London: Chatto & Windus, 1943).

135. For the wheel of fortune that shows the transformation of men into beasts and beast into men, see Ruth Mohl, *The Three Estates in Medieval and Renaissance Literature* (New York: F. Ungar, 1962), 118. A seventeenth-century writer noted that "men were turned into brute beasts, and into trees; to signify under that fiction . . . [that they] had lost the excellent shape and forme of men." Lodowick Bryskett, *A Discourse of Civill Life* (London, 1606), 189. For Robert Dudley's statement of the great chain of being, see Christopher Morris, *Political Thought in England: Tyndale to Hooker* (Westport, Conn.: Hyperion, 1980), 16–17.

136. Radiant selves refuse the great chain of being for some purposes, but not for all. It is odd to find them wishing to take on the properties of plant life or inanimate objects. But the reverse is not also true. Radiant scholars are prepared to suggest that the plants and objects are better thought of as creatures, and the planet as "Gaia." McCracken, *Plenitude 2.0*, 115. See Abram, *The Spell of the Sensuous*.

137. It is not hard to see how we construct this myth. We can spend a week in a North American city without seeing anyone wearing the same shirt we are. But we know such articles of clothing must begin as multiples from the same job lot.

There is merely enough difference to obscure substantial commonalities. We participate in the myth by refusing to see that when we respond to a new TV show, we join, and affirm our commonality with, millions of others who do the same. Or perhaps it is merely that this shadow of suspicion falls so rarely, it is easy to overlook or dismiss it.

138. I do not mean to belittle the discovery of childhood trauma, only to observe that it sometimes has definitional consequences.

139. Linn, *Sacred Space*, 18. See also Carole Kammen and Jodie Gold, *Call to Connection: Bringing Sacred Tribal Values into Modern Life* (Salt Lake City, Utah: Commune-A-Key, 1998).

140. The holodeck appeared in several of the Star Trek television series and movies. I am told that Star Trek fans interpret the holodeck in several ways. An official Star Trek website defines "holodeck" (without quite satisfying the point at issue) as "[t]he generic name, especially in use aboard Federation starships, for the 'smart' virtual reality system as evolved by the 2360s—a technology that combines transporter, replicator, and holographic systems. The programs, projected via emitters within a specially outfitted but otherwise empty room, can create both 'solid' props and characters as well as holographic background to evoke any vista, any scenario, and any personality—all based on whatever real or fictional parameters are programmed. While personal holoprograms relieve the stress and isolation of shipboard life for crew personnel, holodecks are also used for tasks ranging from scientific simulation to tactical or even covert training. Off starships, many commercial users have equipped facilities with so-called Holosuites." http://www .startrek.com/startrek/view/library/technology/article/105222.html.

141. Quoted in Kate Taylor, "A Juno Loss Is in Their Prayers: Non-native Nominee Criticized for Recording Sacred Family Song," *Globe and Mail*, March 19, 1994: C6.

142. Some will object to the suggestion that Jarmusch and Costner can have anything filmic in common, but I think there is not much to choose between these two films so far as their Orientalism is concerned.

143. Quoted in Linda Weintraub, "James Luna: A Native American Man," in *Art on the Edge and Over: Searching for Art's Meaning in Contemporary Society* (Litchfield, Conn.: Art Insights, 1996), 102. The practice of pretending to be Indian has a long tradition. Lewis Henry Morgan, founder of American anthropology, insisted that his nineteenth-century men's club give up a classical inspiration to model itself after the Iroquois. For an interesting treatment of the way in which the image of the "Indian" has been used to define the non-Indian North American, see James A. Clifton, "Alternate Identities and Cultural Frontiers," in *Being and Becoming Indian: Biographical Studies of North American Frontiers*, ed. James A. Clifton (Chicago: Dorsey, 1989), 1–38.

144. Creedon refers to a smorgasbord spirituality in "God with a Million Faces."

145. This "quotation" is entirely invented, except for the startling last phrase ("i.e., whatever"), which I heard from a middle-ranked administrator of a Canadian museum, and which I am pleased finally to be able to read into the ethnographic record. (It was a terrible burden.)

146. I am grateful to Paula Rosch for the opportunity to attend this conference.

147. This story is vaguely reminiscent of the one in which someone reacted to the famous declaration "I accept the universe" with "She damn well better."

148. One of the few places a counter-trend is visible is in extreme sports and the new taste for stories of risk and adventure like Sebastian Junger's *The Perfect Storm* (New York: Norton, 1997) and Jon Krakauer's *Into Thin Air* (New York: Villard, 1997). Nature is being reinvested with menace. There is a rustling here that deserves more careful study. The culture of commotion is beginning to suppose that the natural world has outsized and uncontrollable properties, and this supposition may reflect the new structural properties that we are beginning to suspect exist in the social world. Another challenge to the centrality of nature in the Western scheme of things comes in the rave, dance, and club cultures where artifice is cultivated and embraced. (I offer as evidence the name of a Montreal dance club: Polly Esthers.)

149. Wolin, "Postmodern Politics," 218. For another reference to the "paradox of self-conscious mythmaking," see Cooper, "Modern Mythology," 26.

150. Some of these are relatively recent fears. During the cultural revolution of the 1960s, there was an impatient confidence that we needed merely to master the liberties of radiance (to participate in other cultures, to open ourselves to the world) to gain the unalloyed advantages that would follow. It was believed that this new modality could only bring good.

151. *Being John Malkovich* can be read as a morality play about the porous self. I believe this is why it is about an actor (actors are, famously, our most porous selves outside the radiant community) and, in fact, a real actor who has opened himself up to many, many selves (read "roles"). Over the many years of his career in Hollywood, we have watched Malkovich pour himself into roles as various as the Vicomte de Valmont (*Dangerous Liaisons*, 1988, dir. Stephen Frears) and Lennie Small (*Of Mice and Men*, 1992, dir. Gary Sinise), and this makes more plausible the idea that connection and porousness could run in the other direction. (The movie could have been about a fictional actor, but we would then have no evidence of porousness in one direction opening up porousness in the other.)

152. If this were not so early and so general a survey of the theme, I would stop to contemplate how this aspect of the transformational self suggests a new reading of Macpherson's notion of possessive individualism. C. B. Macpherson, *The Political Theory of Possessive Individualism* (Oxford: Clarendon, 1962). Claims of ownership now seem thrown into question. The very thing that gives the self new mobility, new transformational power, exposes it to risk. It is almost as if our individualism is so voracious that it is now prepared to pursue definitional opportunities that put its individualism (if by this we mean the distinctness of the individual) at risk. It is worth pointing out, perhaps, that we have some very unofficial and grim evidence of this now alienable character of the self. Do not stalkers, a growing and vexing problem in the contemporary world, appear to be driven by the assumption that they can take possession of the other's self? The theme of a stealable self appears also in *Single White Female* (1992, dir. Barbet Schroeder), *The Sixth Day* (2000, dir. Roger Spottiswoode), *All of Me* (1984, dir. Carl Reiner), and *Basic Instinct* (1992, dir. Paul Verhoeven).

153. Irving Howe, "The Self in Literature," in *Constructions of the Self*, ed. George Levine (New Brunswick, N.J.: Rutgers University Press, 1992), 251.

154. Kaminer, *I'm Dysfunctional; You're Dysfunctional;* and Melanie McGrath, *Motel Nirvana: Dreaming of the New Age in the American Desert* (New York: HarperCollins, 1995).

155. The show's website tells us that Otto remains true to the Bus Driver's Pledge: "never crash the bus on purpose." http://www.thesimpsons.com/characters/home.htm.

156. Michael Hot, *Holding the Lotus to the Rock: The Autobiography of Skokie-an, America's First Zen Master* (New York: Four Walls Eight Windows, 1982), 165.

157. This is brilliantly captured in "Stoner Regales Friends with Tale of This One Bong He Saw in Iowa City Once," *The Onion* 35, no. 12 (March 31, 1999), http://www.theonion.com/content/node/39096.

158. Douglas Rushkoff, "Playing Undead," *Swing* 1, no. 5 (April 1995): 34–43. Thomas Frank has taken me to task for observations of this kind. My response is that Mr. Frank might wish to take an undergraduate course in anthropology. Usually, his work is what we might call "ethnographically insensate," so persuaded of its rightness that it neglects to ask the parties concerned.

159. Aileen Ribeiro, *The Dress Worn at Masquerades in England, 1730 to 1790, and Its Relation to Fancy Dress in Portraiture* (New York: Garland, 1984); and Sara Stevenson and Helen Bennett, *Van Dyck in Check Trousers: Fancy Dress in Art and Life, 1700–1900* (Edinburgh: Scottish National Portrait Gallery, 1978).

160. Andrew Ballantyne, "Becoming Ancient," *Times Literary Supplement,* August 18, 1995: 11.

161. Is this a minority interest? Colonial Williamsburg says it gets 4 million visitors a year: http://www.williamsburg.com.

162. There is an interesting research project here: to interview the actors who are routinely called upon to be someone else. What happens when someone is two ones in this systematic, enduring way? Some of the secrets of transformation are to be discovered here.

163. It is worth pointing out that the question of who is authentic is enormously preoccupying in some subcultures, and that it becomes a chief occasion for self-definition and identity formation. This is to say, in a way, that dubiety about the claims of some members of the community is crucial to the formation of the claims of others. Calculations of and tests for authenticity are a crucial device by which claims to membership are constructed.

164. Jerome S. Bruner, "Myth and Identity," in *Myth and Mythmaking,* ed. Henry Alexander Murray (New York: G. Braziller, 1960), 284.

165. I am grateful to Nick Hahn and to Lisa Werenko for a glimpse of Santa Fe life.

166. I have previously avoided the term "self-actualizing" precisely because it assumes the essentialist position that change is a matter of bringing forward what is already there in the individual. The idea of radiance is obscured.

167. Ron Popeil is a man who sells things on TV. I must ask you to do your own ethnography: http://www.ronco.com.

168. Johan Huizinga, *Homo Ludens: A Study of the Play Element in Culture* (Boston: Beacon, 1955), 7.

169. Todd Gitlin, *The Sixties: Years of Hope, Days of Rage* (New York: Bantam, 1987), 209.

170. I have lost touch with the person who told me this story, and since he has not given me permission to use it, I have given his son a pseudonym. In this essay I treat masculinity as something culturally constituted, or, in the more popular phrase, "socially constructed." Kimmel and Messner define this approach this way: "The social constructionist perspective argues that the meaning of masculinity is neither transhistorical nor culturally universal, but rather varies from culture to culture and within any one culture over time. Thus, males become men in the United States in the late twentieth century in a way that is very different from men in Southeast Asia, or Kenya, or Sri Lanka. The meaning of masculinity varies from culture to culture." Michael S. Kimmel and Michael A. Messner, introduction to *Men's Lives*, 5th ed. (Boston: Allyn and Bacon, 2001), xvi.

171. Fred Biletnikoff played wide receiver for the Oakland Raiders from 1965 to 1975. He was voted Most Valuable Player in Super Bowl XI.

172. Too much cultural commentary devotes itself to decrying the phenomenon under study, and I must confess I feel this temptation powerfully here. But this is precisely where anthropology slants abruptly into polemics. Something more dispassionate is called for. The reader will detect ambivalence throughout this account.

173. Goffman makes roughly the same point, but a good deal more broadly. "In an important sense there is only one completely unblushing male in America: a young, married, white, urban, northern, heterosexual Protestant father of college education, fully employed, of good complexion, weight, and height, and a recent record in sports. Every American male tends to look out upon the world from this perspective, this constituting one sense in which one can speak of a common value system in America. Any male who fails to qualify in any one of these ways is likely to view himself—during moments at least—as unworthy, incomplete, and inferior." Erving Goffman, *Stigma* (New York: Doubleday, 1963).

174. For more on the feminization of intellectual labor, see James Eli Adams, *Dandies and Desert Saints: Styles of Victorian Manhood* (Ithaca, N.Y.: Cornell University Press, 1995).

175. For an excellent bibliography of readings in this area, see Michael Flood, *The Men's Bibliography: A Comprehensive Bibliography of Writing on Men, Masculinities, Gender, and Sexualities*, 15th ed. (2006), http://mensbiblio.xyonline.net/. The discussion concentrates on definitions of maleness in the straight and white community. I will refer to gay and African American definitions of maleness, but only as they have helped modify the straight, white definition.

176. Ovid, *Metamorphoses*, line 1.

177. This is marked variously in our culture. Any time there is a choice between the deliberate and the haphazard, the first is marked as female and the second as male. Thus, women make themselves a meal and eat it at a well-appointed table. Men eat two-day-old pizza directly from a box in the fridge. It is a robust operator. What follows draws mostly on my own experience. I was born in 1951 and raised in Vancouver, British Columbia. I came of age in an era still very much in the thrall of a relatively violent gang culture, where fighting was commonplace, but, one could not help noticing, more a matter of show than of contact. At the age of nine, I was recruited into a Vancouver gang. This chiefly meant carrying beer out to the woods so that senior members of the gang could continue their binge drinking without interruption. By my early teens, "cliquers" had established themselves, and

I now delighted in baiting "greasers" with athletic acts of mischief. The cliquer era was supplanted by the hippie movement, which I joined at about fifteen. I had played organized and casual sports throughout my childhood, especially baseball and football. I gave these up upon becoming a hippie. These three vantage points gave me the chance to see several variations on maleness. Whether they allow me to generalize as I have here is another question. I make no special claims to the veracity of this treatment. I have attempted to root the discussion in popular culture. I believe this helps a little to substantiate the argument.

178. The Riggins male appears everywhere in popular culture. In an ad for a long-distance carrier starring Terry Bradshaw and Doug Flutie. Bradshaw is offered a plate of sushi. "Suchi?" he mispronounces it. "Where I'm from, we call that bait." We are meant to find this endearing. This spot may be seen at http://www.adcritic.com/content/10-10-220-sushi.html. Some Mountain Dew advertisements also feature the Riggins male.

179. One of Belushi's successors on *Saturday Night Live*, Chris Farley (1964–1997), belongs in this category, too.

180. There is an intricate relationship between the putative lead male of the group and the Riggins companion. The leader will give the Riggins male license to proceed with his mischief, and then issue a cease and desist order when things threaten to get out of hand. In a sense, this collaboration says merely that the Riggins male uses the leader of the group as a kind of executive function he cannot manage for himself. But it also suggests how much of the Riggins role is performed and not spontaneous.

181. Zahn's most recent version of this role is in *Saving Silverman* (2001, dir. Dennis Dugan). Brendan Fraser played one in *Encino Man* (1992, dir. Les Mayfield). See also Jay (Jason Mewes) and Silent Bob (Kevin Smith) in the movies directed by Kevin Smith: *Clerks* (1994), *Mallrats* (1995), *Chasing Amy* (1997), and *Jay and Silent Bob Strike Back* (2001). There are new Zahns coming up. See the characters played by Seann William Scott in *American Pie* (1999, dir. Paul Weitz) and *Dude, Where's My Car?* (2000, dir. Danny Leiner) and by David Arquette in *See Spot Run* (2001, dir. John Whitesell).

182. I have quoted this line from memory. I searched the *Saturday Night Live* website to see if I could locate the show and identify its writers, but could not. This is a disappointing website. Note to Lorne Michaels: Congratulations on creating a cultural institution. Is there any chance you could act like one?

183. Bly, *Iron John*, 6, 8.

184. Philip Jackman, "Spike Lee Accuses Tarantino of Doing the Wrong Thing," *Globe and Mail*, December 19, 1997: C10. How Mr. Jackman, a middle-class Canadian, would know what is and what is not a "bad approximation of African-American slang" is not clear. Does Jackman's criticism not reproduce the behavior it wishes to criticize? For Spike Lee's own investigation of the issue, see his film *Bamboozled* (2000), in which he has a white TV producer named Dunwitty, skin-crawlingly played by Michael Rapaport, say, "I don't give a damn what Spike says, Tarantino is right. 'Nigger' is just a word." That Lee was able to make this film contradicts one of its tenets, that African Americans are allowed to participate in mainstream culture only if they are prepared to stick to the stereotypes. It also suggests that Lee himself wonders whether he has not been caught in this contradiction.

This would put caution in place of his customary courage and it would represent a terrible loss.

185. To those who accuse wiggers of pretending to be black, the author replies, "I dont want to be black (much love to my black homies [name removed] and [name removed]) but just give props to my black brothers and sisters." This webpage has disappeared. I have removed the author's name and identifying details to protect his privacy. (If he wishes to be acknowledged, I will happily do so.)

186. Quoted in William Finnegan, "A Reporter at Large: The Unwanted," *New Yorker*, December 1, 1997: 63, emphasis added to indicate the borrowed phrase.

187. For other instances, see the character of Kenny (Seth Green) in *Can't Hardly Wait* (1998, dir. Harry Elfont and Deborah Kaplan) and "Fresh like a Can of Picante," a 2001 ad for Fox Sports by the ad agency Propaganda (Eric Silver, creative director; Rees Collins, art director and copy writer), http://www.adcritic.com/content/fox-sports-nba-lakers.html.

188. Neil Strauss, "The Hip-Hop Nation: Whose Is It?" *New York Times*, August 22, 1999, section 2, p. 1. What's odd about this list is that it repeats the pattern seen in rock and roll in which white kids prefer to get African American music and style from white artists.

189. For the origins of cool as a discipline of the body to show distance from a slave status, see Shane White and Graham White, *Stylin': African American Expressive Culture from Its Beginnings to the Zoot Suit* (Ithaca, N.Y.: Cornell University Press, 1998), 63–84. In this valuable book, White and White are most interested in the dancer as a "powerful counter-image" with which African Americans resisted the racist regime. They do not refer to gestures of greeting or other expressive acts of nonverbal community, preferring to suppose that the body outside of dance was constrained.

For a surprisingly lazy treatment of cool, see Marcel Danesi, *Cool: The Signs and Meanings of Adolescence* (Toronto: University of Toronto Press, 1994). For a definition of cool that resembles the present one, see Geneva Smitherman, *African-American Talk* (New York: Houghton Mifflin, 1994); and Donnell Alexander, "Are African-American People Cooler than White People?" *Utne Reader* 84 (November–December 1997): 51–53. For a historical study of cool that makes distressingly little reference to the cultural category itself, see Peter N. Stearns, *American Cool: Constructing a Twentieth-Century Emotional Style* (New York: New York University Press, 1994). For the 1950s construction of cool, see Norman Mailer, *The White Negro: Superficial Reflections on the Hipster* (San Francisco: City Lights, 1957).

I think we might see the success of movies like *Men in Black* (1997, dir. Barry Sonnenfeld) and *Nothing to Lose* (1997, dir. Steve Oedekerk) as reflections of a white interest in reappropriating cool. In the first movie, it is the old white guys who are worldly and knowing, and the young, street-savvy, black one who is stumbling and naïve. A key scene has Agent J (Will Smith) offering to sort out a pawn shop with ghetto know-how: "I'm going to go in there and lay my thing down." Agent K (Tommy Lee Jones) indulges him wearily—"You go in there and lay your thing down"—because he knows that Agent J will be astonished and undone by the alien technology he encounters there. And, indeed, Agent J returns from the pawn shop speechless and without cool. In the second movie, Nick Beam (Tim Robbins) is suffering a career meltdown, and when his car is jacked by T. Paul (Martin Lawrence) he responds by kidnapping his carjacker and going on a rampage. He is now the dangerous, powerful, lawless party because he has nothing to lose.

190. Tarantino is so manifestly gifted as a filmmaker and creator of popular culture that it might seem a mystery why he should believe himself in need of additional credentials. But being a Hollywood filmmaker does not confer street credibility. I hope that it does not need to be said that when white teenagers and filmmakers believe that black style gives them street credibility they are engaged in a construction of the African American that is as racist in its way as the suburban imputation of criminality. Ironically, they feel their imitation to be an act of homage, but it helps reinforce a notion of blackness that is defined by its criminality.

191. *Chris Rock: Bring the Pain* (1997, dir. Keith Truesdell).

192. The black appropriation of cultural forms associated with the white community is another important transformational activity. I give it only fleeting reference here. The movies *Chameleon Street* (1991, dir. Wendell B. Harris, Jr.) and *Six Degrees of Separation* (1993, dir. Fred Schepsi) explore the explicit appropriation of white selves by African Americans. This is a form of "passing" informed by the efforts of a con to deceive particular parties for particular benefits. *Trading Places* (1983, dir. John Landis) and *Down to Earth* (2001, dir. Chris Weitz and Paul Weitz) offer something more like an exercise in involuntary improv (see below) in which Eddie Murphy and Chris Rock, respectively, find themselves catapulted into white selves. *Double Take* (2001, dir. George Gallo) might be taken as a repeat of *Trading Places* except that, happily, both the high- and the low-standing roles are occupied by African Americans. Daryl Chase (Orlando Jones) is a banking executive and Freddy Tiffany (Eddie Griffin) is, apparently, a street hustler. Still more refreshing, Chase and Tiffany are obliged to swap roles with one another on several occasions, each time demonstrating the arbitrariness and the fluidity of their performances. There is work here that departs from the genre. In one case, Tiffany complains that Chase's performance of the street persona is so bad, it looks stolen from the movie *Car Wash* (1976, dir. Michael Schultz). In another, Chase responds to Tiffany's claim that he is engaged in rogue behavior simply by incredulously repeating the word "rogue." This performance of African Americanness no longer trades away transformational nuance to obtain elemental menace. Orlando Jones is on record as having sought out roles in movies that similarly avoid such a trade. See his remarks on role models in his interview with Cynthia Fuchs at Pop Matters, http://www.popmatters.com/film/interviews/jones-orlando.shtml. In a truly genre-busting gesture, his character, Daryl Chase, actually cries with relief at the end of *Double Take*. The question of whether and to what extent the selves crafted by African Americans, and especially the stereotypes fashioned for African Americans, can take the individual hostage, forcing him or her to give up transformational versatility, is now being addressed by the community. Ironically, some members of the new black middle class are said to be trading the old confinement for the one created by upward transformation. *Double Take* suggests a new freedom, newly created or perhaps proclaimed.

193. It's important to see this movement from the native's point of view. Certainly, some of hip hop comes to a teenager through music videos, movies, the behavior of friends, and so on, seeping down through ground cover and aquifers and returning as if from within, as if new, as if original. Suddenly, we are just using

the phrase of the moment, and although we must have got it from somewhere, we don't feel like we are engaging in rank imitation. But I do not think all of the style, certainly not a style so slavishly copied by a teen from Long Island, can come this way. Some of it has to the result of careful observation, trial and error, and practical effort.

194. "Irresponsible: There's no other word for Limp Bizkit front man Fred Durst. He's goading the crowd, pumping them up, higher and higher. It's beyond working them into enjoying the show. He's encouraging the pit, working them into a frenzy. He wants people to 'smash stuff.' 'C'mon y'all, c'mon y'all,' he shouts. Below him, the pit is a war zone, a sweaty, dirty, roiling mass of vicious guys knocking the fuck out of one another. It's not a fun scene. It's nasty, and people are getting hurt—bad. Bodies on cardboard stretchers emerge from the audience a couple of times per song." Jeff Stark, "What a Riot: Diary of a Woodstock 99 Survivor," *Salon*, July 27, 1999, http://www.salon.com/ent/music/feature/1999/07/27/woodstock/index.html. That this behavior is not restricted to Durst or to men is suggested by a firsthand account of the mosh pit at a Courtney Love performance in 1999. "Come On, Courtney, Be a Man," http://www.vintagestars.com/river/ChaosLilly.html.

195. This data was collected haphazardly. I was teaching in Cambridge (actually, just south of Cambridge; Harvard Business School is on the far side of the Charles River and therefore, strictly speaking, in Boston). And I was living in downtown Boston (very near the New England Aquarium). I would sometimes walk the whole distance, meaning I was in the street for about an hour and a half. More often, I would walk to the Kendall Square subway station and take the subway to Park Street. This would leave me walking for about thirty minutes. This was my pattern from September 1999 to July 2000. In this period I found myself involved in five confrontations that threatened bodily harm, one at gunpoint. In all cases but one, I was dealing with a white male in his twenties. (The exception was a white male in his late thirties.) I understand that I am, in a sense, the person most likely to be affronted by a mook. I am a middle-aged male, increasingly abandoned by physical prowess (what there was of that) and the self-confidence of youth, and therefore just beginning to feel a new, and disconcerting, vulnerability in the street. Perhaps worse, I am from Canada, a country where strangers still say "excuse me" to one another. This is to say that I may have imagined a threat to civil order in mooks that does not exist. It is also true that Boston is a town where bad temper and bad manners are sometimes regarded as a civic accomplishment. (And all these years we Canadians thought it was "Beantown.") I was interested in the response of my Harvard colleagues when I told them of their mean streets. They seemed to agree that if I was going to insist on walking everywhere, I was going to have to expect this sort of thing.

196. R. J. Smith, "Among the Mooks," *New York Times Sunday Magazine*, August 6, 2000. Thanks to Leora Kornfeld for bringing this to my attention. For a good treatment of Fred Durst of Limp Bizkit and the "neo-cracker elite," see Steve Dollar, "Cracker-Rap Losers," *Salon*, November 7, 2000, http://www.salon.com/ent/music/feature/2000/11/07/bizkit/index.html.

197. Bill Murray (1950–), born in Chicago, was a member of Chicago's comedy troupe *Second City*, and later a star of the television comedy series *Saturday Night*

Live. Murray specializes in two quite different character types. In the first he is a self-adoring but spectacularly untalented lounge singer (*Saturday Night Live*) or an equally irritating and incompetent passive-aggressive whiner (*What about Bob?* 1991, dir. Frank Oz). In the second, he is a self-possessed, ironic, mocking smart aleck (*Stripes,* 1981, dir. Ivan Reitman; *Ghostbusters,* 1984, dir. Ivan Reitman; *Quick Change,* 1990, dir. Howard Franklin and Bill Murray). This second is an instance of the deeply cynical frat-boy tradition that emerged as one of the defining motifs of the 1980s and included David Letterman and writer P. J. O'Rourke. (For more on this, see the essay "Martha Stewart (and status transformations)" in this section.) In the 1990s, Murray developed a third persona: a character without irritation or irony (e.g., in *Mad Dog and Glory,* 1993, dir. John McNaughton; *Ed Wood,* 1994, dir. Tim Burton).

For more on Bond, see Lee Drummond, "The Story of Bond," in *Symbolizing America,* ed. Herve Varenne (Lincoln: University of Nebraska Press, 1986), 66–89. See also Drummond, *American Dreamtime;* and Tony Bennett and Janet Woollacott, *Bond and Beyond: The Political Career of a Popular Hero* (London: Methuen, 1987).

198. Some months later it become clear this performance had been a dress rehearsal for the movie *The Man Who Knew Too Little* (1997, dir. Jon Amiel), in which Murray (as Wallace Richie) plays an inadvertent spy.

199. There is some evidence of a shift. In *Tomorrow Never Dies* (1997, dir. Roger Spottiswoode), there are no bimbos and Bond is teamed with a Chinese spy (Michelle Yeoh) who is no less capable and no more vacuous than he.

200. The *Austin Powers* movies (1997 and 1999, dir. Jay Roach) appear to represent another satiric attack on the Bond legacy. I say this with the knowledge that the traditional notion of Bond is not only not going away but appears to be flourishing, with new Bond films appearing and the old ones still popular. I have the uneasy feeling this is plenitude in action. Bondness will be repudiated in some circles even as it is celebrated in others. On the other hand, it is tempting to think that Bill Murray and Mike Myers are Don Quixotes, helping to demolish cultural forms (chivalric in both cases) that have outlived their relevance.

201. After all, this is a world of plenitude—so the old and, in some circles, discredited will remain in circulation. Murray can discredit the Bond persona for some, but not all.

202. There is a further irony here to the extent that Murray is engaged in a widespread practice in our culture: the hijacking of a celebrity self for definitional purposes. We are amused to see a celebrity do it too.

203. There is a parodic response at work in contemporary culture, constantly undoing conventional notions of gender. The Wazzup campaign with which Budweiser inspired imitation and endless repetition was harpooned by "Loser" and the team at http://www.tinyriot.com. See the original Wazzup ads and the "Loser" response at http://www.adcritic.com/content/budweiser-true-wazzup.html. See also " '88 Dodge Aries," the exemplary spoof ad by Tim McAuliffe and Brendan Peltier at http://www.adcritic.com/content/spoof-dodge-88-dodge-aries-k-car.html. Notice that the "Fresh like a Can of Picante" ad appears to take aim at Eminem.

204. The *Saturday Night Live* routine "Hans and Franz" is a nice study in the anxieties expressed by males who embrace the overdetermination of gender that

weightlifting sometimes represents. I have given this topic much less attention than it deserves. For more on the topic, see Alan M. Klein, *Little Big Men: Bodybuilding, Subculture and Gender Construction* (Albany: State University of New York Press, 1993).

205. It is not clear how much effect gay culture has had on the new fashion sensitivity of straight males, but it is pretty clear that it has had some. It is probably true, for instance, that some parts of the gay community embrace contrivance as an ordinary, necessary device in the act of self-construction. It is also probably true that this community is an early adopter of fashions that the straight community later takes up. (It is said, for instance, that the preppie look that so dominated the mainstream in the 1980s was first cultivated by a gay community in Florida.) It may be true that one of the sources of the straight community's interest in contrivance was the gay community.

206. I think we may be seeing a change in the "great white hope." The innovations and accomplishments of a black community no longer require racial transposition quite as much as they did in Elvis Presley's era.

207. Quoted in Arlene Dahl, *Always Ask a Man: The Key to Femininity* (New York: Pocket, 1965), 8. I thank Dayna McLeod for pointing out the importance of Dahl's work in this connection.

208. The phrase "snooty society beauty" appeared on the poster for the film, which can be seen accompanying a review of it by Tim Dirks at http://www.filmsite .org/phil.html.

209. I have taken this and the following dialogue from Tim Dirk's impressively detailed account of the film at http://www.filmsite.org/phil.html.

210. I appreciate that it is more usual to see Cukor as a director with feminist sympathies.

211. I believe the movie *Bell, Book and Candle* (1958, dir. Richard Quine) turns on this theme as well. Gillian Holroyd (Kim Novak) must give up her powers as a witch to make herself ready for love and marriage.

212. "This is the year of Women's Liberation. Or at least, it's the year the press has discovered a movement that has been strong for several years now." Gloria Steinem, "Women's Liberation Aims to Free Men, Too," *Washington Post*, June 7, 1970, http://scriptorium.lib.duke.edu/wlm/aims/. I have drawn heavily on a magnificent Internet resource: Documents from the Women's Liberation Movement: An On-Line Archival Collection, held at the Special Collections Library at Duke University and available at http://scriptorium.lib.duke.edu/wlm. See particularly Shulamith Firestone, "Women Rap about Sex," a set of remarks collected from consciousness-raising groups, in New York Radical Women, *Notes from the First Year* (New York, 1968), http://scriptorium.lib.duke.edu/wlm/notes/#sexrap. This is an illuminating ethnographic glimpse of how women thought about themselves, their bodies, and their relationships.

213. Kathy Amatniek, "Funeral Oration Given for the Burial of Traditional Womanhood," a speech given in Washington, D.C. to the main assembly of the Jeannette Rankin Brigade on January 15, 1968, in New York Radical Women, *Notes from the First Year,* http://scriptorium.lib.duke.edu/wlm/notes/#funeral.

214. Shirley Chisholm, "Equal Rights for Women," a speech read in the U.S. House of Representatives, May 21, 1969, http://scriptorium.lib.duke.edu/wlm/ equal/.

215. Women began to glimpse the possibilities of liberation in large and growing numbers. Men helped by responding with belligerence and hostility. Even "progressive" men made a contribution. Judith Gabree said, "We have watched men organize, speak, conduct workshops and write about the movement for us for years; we watched while we organized (the food, papers), spoke (answering the phones, and sometimes to each other—but not often enough) and sat in workshops and maybe read articles (though men usually didn't know what we thought about all that). But our time was not lost. We learned that we must organize for our own liberation." Judith Gabree, "On Staughton Lynd's 'Good Society,' " in New York Radical Women, *Notes from the First Year*, http://scriptorium.lib.duke.edu/wlm/notes/#lynd.

Popular culture made an odd and unexpected contribution of its own. The women who attended the first Michigan Womyn's Music Festival in 1976 eschewed hairdressing, makeup, and sexualizing clothing as a collaboration with the enemy (http://www.michfest.com/). When Studio 54 opened in 1977, men came in shiny fitted shirts, gold chains, and sculpted hairdos. *Saturday Night Fever* (1977, dir. John Badham) introduced a strutting peacock, Tony (John Travolta), a man who had found a new power and was using it. "You make it with some of these chicks, they think you gotta dance with them." (I have taken this quotation from the film's page at the Internet Movie Database, http://us.imdb.com/Title ?0076666, and cannot vouch for its accuracy.) I realize it is customary to think of Tony and of the young men who danced at Studio 54 as "little guys" who used disco as an opportunity for class mobility, a way to escape a working-class existence. This is indeed the theme of the movie *Studio 54* (1998, dir. Mark Christopher). Class no doubt had a role to play, but gender appears to have been at work as well.

216. This paragraph is a selective summary of National Women's History Project, "Timeline of Legal History of Women in the United States: A Timeline of the Women's Rights Movement, 1848–1998," which appears at http://www .legacy98.org/timeline.html. The book titles do not appear in the timeline and appear here out of chronological order.

217. Fred Durst is the lead singer for Limp Bizkit. There is more on Mr. Durst below. Jenny McCarthy was Playboy's Miss October 1993 and then Playmate of the Year. She has appeared on a number of TV shows, including *Singled Out* and *The Jenny McCarthy Show*, and in movies, including *The Stupids* (1996, dir. John Landis), *BASEketball* (1998, dir. David Zucker), and *Scream 3* (2000, dir. Wes Craven). This career was apparently guided by her mother's advice: "Be like Vanna White."

218. There was an interesting commonality of objective between feminists and anthropologists and historians. The political and the academic were eventually to cross. Victoria De Grazia and Ellen Furlough, *The Sex of Things: Gender and Consumption in Historical Perspective* (Berkeley: University of California Press, 1996); and Katharine Martinez and Kenneth L. Ames, eds., *The Material Culture of Gender, the Gender of Material Culture* (Winterthur, Del.: The Henry Francis du Pont Winterthur Museum, 1997).

219. I take this quotation from the documentary *From the Journals of Jean Seberg* (1995, dir. Mark Rappaport). My memory tells me that it was attributed there to Jean Seberg. Readers with more reliable memories tell me it was said by Jean-Luc Godard, but cannot supply its source. Godard's remark is so close to the

one by George Hamilton quoted at the beginning of this essay that I wonder if he did not intend an homage of some kind.

220. Nancy Friday, *The Power of Beauty* (New York: HarperCollins, 1996), 1.

221. The interrogative lilt turns the statement "I was going into university" into a kind of question—"I was going into university?"—by "lifting" the last three syllables of the word "university." The interrogative lilt turns statements into questions, speakers into supplicants, listeners into authorities, and it helps mark and construct a power difference between the two conversational partners. The technical term for this practice is "uptalk." Thanks to Leora Kornfeld for finding this name.

222. Dana Kennedy, "Jane Fonda: An Unscripted Life Starring Herself," *New York Times*, May 6, 2001, http://www.nytimes.com/2001/05/06/arts/06KENN .html?pagewanted=2. Fonda understands this development according to the theories of Carol Gilligan. "She [Gilligan] talks about women losing their voices, and sometimes it's actually physiological. The throat narrows and the breath goes high in the head, where no human emotions can be heard. I went back and looked at some of those movies. And my voice is way up there. It's like there was nothing of me." Sometime after embracing feminism and doing the film *Klute* (1971, dir. Alan Pakula), her voice fell. "I didn't do it on purpose. It just dropped. It was because I was tapping into something in my solar plexus. It wasn't all from the mouth up."

223. Who are the other women who helped reshape our understanding by breaking the rules of femaleness on the public stage? Everyone has their own list. Mine includes Sandra Bernhard, Christiane Amanpour, Liz Phair, Roseanne Barr, Janeane Garofalo, Kimberly Peirce, and probably Courtney Love. Friends suggested other candidates, including Sinead O'Connor, Madonna, and two fictional characters, Lisa Simpson of *The Simpsons* and Dana Scully of *The X-Files*. Thanks to Jo-Anne Balcaen, Dayna McLeod, and Naomi Potter for these suggestions.

224. Some readers have objected that this statement is "extreme" or "hyperbolic." But isn't it true that in most North American cities women cannot walk outside at night? We may be so habituated to this condition that we no longer think of it, but it represents, I think, a kind of *de facto* house arrest and one proof of the constant threat of exploitation and abuse.

225. My favorite example of this is the Victorian belief that the contemporary passion for natural history was a good thing because it gave gentlemen an excuse to shoot things. Lynn Barber, *The Heyday of Natural History, 1820–1870* (London: Jonathan Cape, 1980).

226. Sarah Stickney Ellis, *The Daughters of England* (London: Charles Griffin, 1842), 147, 148.

227. "I really liked Ani's music when I first heard her two years ago at a folk festival, but I stayed with my 'safe' folk music. Last month, I saw her again in concert and said 'To hell with it. It's time to break free.'" Shawn Linderman, review of *Dilate* for the *Folk and Acoustic Music Exchange*, http://www.acousticmusic.com/ fame/p00308.html.

228. Quoted in J. Poet, "Ani DiFranco: Independent as She Wants to Be," *Pulse*, September 1996: 5.

229. Once more, I am giving DiFranco too much credit. A generation of women in the 1990s—anyone, in any case, hip enough to be alternative—undertook a de-

tailed and sustained exploration of "ugliness" in clothing, hair care, and makeup, so breaking the conventional rules of beauty that the fashion world was, eventually, obliged to revise its own.

230. Some people will ask why it is necessary to depart from the usual terms for diffusion players ("early adopter," etc.) Those terms do not capture the elements of risk and persuasion on which cultural diffusion depends. I am grateful to Paula Rosch, Lanny Vincent, and Gil McWilliam for the opportunity to discuss diffusion. (Rosch uses a different metaphor, preferring to speak of "scouts" and "homesteaders" and to emphasize the elements of discovery and habitation.)

231. Quoted in Poet, "Ani DiFranco," 5.

232. Quoted in Brantley Bardin, "Ani DiFranco: Taking Me Seriously Is a Big Mistake. I Certainly Wouldn't," *Details* 12, no. 2 (1997): 130.

233. Ibid., 130. *Spin* offers a dramatic account of DiFranco's stopping a concert to take exception to fans who want to tell her who she is and what she believes. Ani DiFranco, interview by Jonathan Van Meter, *Spin* 13, no. 5 (1997): 56.

234. Quoted in Lorraine Ali, "Ani DiFranco," *Rolling Stone*, no. 753 (1997): 20.

235. Michael Silverstein, "Shifters, Linguistic Categories, and Cultural Description," in *Meaning in Anthropology*, ed. Keith H. Basso and Henry A. Selby (Albuquerque: University of New Mexico Press, 1976), 11–55.

236. The term "identity politics" was invented, I think, by Todd Gitlin ("The Rise of Identity Politics," *Dissent* 40 [spring 1993]: 172–77). My treatment of "players" is more sympathetic and I think anthropologically canny than Gitlin's.

237. "As we near the end of the 20th century, we are at a point where we can speak of at least two feminist generations coexisting simultaneously: the second-wave feminists of the 1970s and a new generation of feminists—women who have grown up with feminism—who are being called the third wave." Anonymous (possibly Astrid Henry, Jennifer Mahler, and/or Joan Ruffino) from the description of a session called *Just a Stage: The Rhetoric of Third Wave Feminism* from the conference called *Challenging Rhetorics: Cross-Disciplinary Sites of Feminist Discourse* held in Minneapolis in 1999.

238. John Gray, *Men Are from Mars, Women Are from Venus: A Practical Guide for Improving Communication and Getting What You Want in Your Relationships* (New York: HarperCollins, 1992). The Mars Venus institute (http://www.marsvenusinstitute.com) calls Gray an "internationally recognized expert in the fields of communication and relationships," which makes it especially interesting that he cannot write to save his life.

239. A. Justin Sterling, *What Really Works with Men: Solve 95% of Your Relationship Problems and Cope with the Rest* (New York: Warner, 1992), 86, 88. I owe this reference to Dayna McLeod. The notion that men and women were essentially different was a theme of stand-up comedy in the 1990s. "The reaction is really against the guy we kept seeing on cable, the guy with the tie and the tan who talked for 10 minutes about airline food and the difference between men and women and how horrible his wife is." Beth Lapides, owner of the Un-Cabaret in Los Angeles, in Bernard Weinraub, "A Trend toward Personal, Off-Beat Comedy at Aspen Festival," *New York Times*, March 5, 2001, http://www.nytimes.com/2001/03/05/arts/05COME.html.

240. Johanna Schneller, "Long Cool Daddy," *Premier* 12, no. 5 (1999): 72, 76, 72, 96, 75. What is surprising about this article that it includes Janeane Garofalo's endorsement of Vaughn: "He's got charisma like no one else."

241. Manohla Dargis, "Russell Crowe's Special Brand of Masculinity," *New York Times*, March 4, 2001.

242. The *Material Girl* video made its MTV debut on February 1, 1985. Thanks to Luis Puente of Allexperts.com for this information.

243. The girl band Atomic Kitten captures the new duality. Post-Madonna, women may return to the kittenish representation of femininity, because they are assured that the world has been put on notice. They are *Atomic* Kitten. On the other hand, they can perform the atomic part because, after all, they are really kittens. It is not clear whether this strategy stretches out the space these women inhabit or cancels it out. On "boy toy," see Denise Worrell, "Now: Madonna on Madonna," *Time*, May 27, 1985.

244. Jedediah Purdy, *For Common Things: Irony, Trust, and Commitment in America Today* (New York: A. A. Knopf, 1999).

245. Kate Davy, "Fe/Male Impersonation: The Discourse of Camp," in *Critical Theory and Performance*, ed. Jannelle G. Reinelt and Joseph R. Roach (Ann Arbor: University of Michigan Press, 1992), 231–47; and Susan Sontag, "Notes on Camp," in *Against Interpretation, and Other Essays* (New York: Farrar, Straus and Giroux, 1966), 275–92.

246. Here is Traci Vogel on the "girlie style": "Stretch 'Foxy' across your chest in glitter letters, and sexism becomes a stupid construction held up to ridicule." Traci Vogel, "Is Outrage Dated?" *The Stranger* 10, no. 28 (March 29–April 4, 2001), http://www.thestranger.com/seattle/Content?oid=6881. Thanks to Leora Kornfeld for this reference.

247. "Rat-pack masculinity" refers to the style cultivated in the postwar period by the entertainers and film stars Frank Sinatra, Dean Martin, and Sammy Davis, Jr., men famous for their self-confidence, irreverent attitude, and flammable personalities. They were featured in *Ocean's Eleven* (1960, dir. Lewis Milestone) and *Robin and the Seven Hoods* (1964, dir. Gordon Douglas). Between 1993 and 1997, the number of cigar smokers in the United States rose by nearly 50 percent, and the annual consumption of large cigars increased 66 percent, to an estimated 3.55 billion. Celebrities (shades of the rat pack) posed for the cover of the newly influential *Cigar Aficionado* magazine, the circulation of which rose from 141,000 in 1994 to nearly 400,000 in 1996. For details of the scotch revival, see Marc Spiegler, "The Cocktail Nation," *American Demographics*, July 1998: 43.

248. David Stowe defines swing as "a stage in the development of jazz characterized by written arrangements and performed by big bands—or small ensembles culled from those bands—during the 1930s and 1940s." David W. Stowe, *Swing Changes: Big-Band Jazz in New Deal America* (Cambridge, Mass.: Harvard University Press, 1994), 5. Swing, represented by the likes of Cab Calloway, Gene Krupa, Duke Ellington, Glenn Miller, and the so-called "King of Swing," Benny Goodman, achieved national visibility in the summer of 1935 and became a national fad in 1938. Swing owed a heavy debt to African American culture, and Stowe calls it "the preeminent musical expression of the New Deal: A cultural form of 'the people,' accessible,

inclusive, distinctively democratic, and thus distinctively American" (13). Swing was popular culture, unabashedly commercial. As Krupa put it, "I get paid for dance music, the art's thrown in extra" (36). Many observers believed swing was gone for good when it suddenly reappeared in Los Angeles and San Francisco in the late 1980s. In 1989, attendance at the Midsummer Night Swing series at Lincoln Center was around 8,000 people. By 1997, this figure had grown to 96,000. The album *Zoot Suit Riot* by the Cherry Poppin' Daddies sold 1.3 million copies in little over a year. Steve Graybow, "Swing Revival Could Stay Awhile," *Billboard*, August 1, 1998: 47–48.

249. Abigail M. Wolfe, "The Politics of Dancing: The Bay Area's Exploding Swing Scene," *Left Coast Art Magazine*, 1999, http://mag.leftcoastart.com/html/cult_of_swing.html.

250. With thanks for a brief discussion on this phenomenon with author and *Toronto Life* restaurant critic James Chatto.

251. "At modern swing clubs, you can find people dressed in vintage garb like dresses, zoot suits, skinny ties and fedoras, doing the same dances that the young and stylish did 60 years ago." Jennifer Christman, "That Swing Thing: Don't Call It Big Band, Just Call It BIG," *Arkansas Democrat-Gazette*, August 11, 1998.

252. Consider the *Maxim* website at http://www.maximonline.com/.

253. See Home Improvement Cyberfans, the website of the *Home Improvement* International Online Fan Club, http://www.morepower.com, for details on *Home Improvement*. Note that in the pilot, Allen threatens to rewire the dishwasher to make it more "powerful" and "masculine."

254. For more biographical details on Eminem, see the account by Jason Ankeny and Bradley Torreano at http://www.allmusic.com/cg/amg.dll?p=amg&sql=11:0xfpxqyjldke. This essay is my source for the first week of album sales. See also Marshall Mathers, *Angry Blonde* (New York: HarperCollins, 2000). *Billboard* (http://www.billboard.com) was my source for record sales to date.

255. Andrew Dice Clay, also known as "the Diceman," was born Andrew Clay Silverstein in 1957. He appeared in several Rodney Dangerfield projects and several of his own movies. He fell from grace in the 1990s but continues to appear at Bally's in Las Vegas. See his website at http://www.andrewdiceclay.com.

Here is the film critic Roger Ebert on one of Clay's films: "*Dice Rules* is one of the most appalling movies I have ever seen. It could not be more damaging to the career of Andrew Dice Clay if it had been made as a documentary by someone who hated him. The fact that Clay apparently thinks this movie is worth seeing is revealing and sad, indicating that he not only lacks a sense of humor, but also ordinary human decency. . . . He has many other targets. The handicapped. The ill. Minorities. Women. Homosexuals. Anyone, in fact, who is not exactly like Andrew Dice Clay is fair game for his cruel attacks. His material about women constitutes verbal rape, as far as I'm concerned. Using obscenity as punctuation, he describes women as essentially things to masturbate with." Review dated May 17, 1991, http://rogerebert.suntimes.com. I thank Dayna McLeod for the suggestion that *Married with Children*, the situation comedy from the Fox Network (1987–1997), should be regarded as one of the ways Clay's cultural mission was sustained. For more on this show, see its page at the Internet Movie Database, http://us.imdb.com/Title?0092400.

256. I thank Denise Fernandes of McGill University for testing me on my reading of Eminem. I had failed to see how transformational he is.

257. Dollar, "Cracker-Rap Losers."

258. Smith, "Among the Mooks."

259. This is the number of times the word "ho" was returned by a search of the website at http://www.hiphoparchives.com/. Unfortunately, this website is now defunct.

260. With thanks to Bree Short and Meagan Mays.

261. She names Eric Boehlert of *Salon Magazine* as an exception. DeSantis, "Eminem and His Message of Hate," 5. See also Eric Boehlert, "Helping Eminem Sell Records," *Salon*, September 14, 2000, http://archive.salon.com/politics/feature/2000/09/14/eminem_react/index.html.

262. Some mook rage may come from the fact that these young men are the first generation of males to be seen explicitly as sexual objects and judged as sexual performers. As it turns out, the gender revolution established equity not by desexualizing women but by sexualizing men.

263. *Sex and the City* was an HBO production. It aired from 1998 to 2004. See http://www.hbo.com/city for more details.

264. This quotation is from HBO's summary of the first episode, at http://www.hbo.com/city/episode/season1/episode01.shtml.

265. This line is quoted by Simran Khurana on About.com's website for *Sex and the City* quotations: http://quotations.about.com/cs/tvquotes/a/sex_city_quotes_3.htm.

266. This line is quoted by RiotGrrlie01 on ThinkExist.com: http://thinkexist.com/quotation/maybe_some_women_aren-t_meant_to_be_tamed-maybe/258229.html.

267. A sexist society is productive of transformational activity. This is clear in the Western tradition when men insist that a woman be both a Madonna and a whore. One of the ways to negotiate a sexist world is to cultivate selves that can endure constraint and those that overthrow it. See the multiplicity of selves recounted in Kali A. K. Israel, "Style, Strategy, and Self-Creation in the Life of Emilia Dilke," in Levine, *Constructions of the Self*, 191–212.

268. John Ellis, *Visible Fictions: Cinema, Television, Video* (London: Routledge & Kegan Paul, 1982), 43. This argument is developed in Leon Rappoport, Steve Baumgardner, and George Boone, "Postmodern Culture and the Plural Self," in *The Plural Self: Multiplicity in Everyday Life*, ed. John Rowan and Mick Cooper (London: Sage, 1999), 93–106. "[I]nsofar as personality development is concerned, the difference between the modern and postmodern eras may be epitomized as the distinction between serial and simultaneous pluralism [of the self]" (99).

269. I have transcribed this dialogue from a DVD of the film.

270. B-movies have a weakness for physical gestures of superordination, including flicking a cigarette at the vanquished, and even (though this may be the preserve of the C-movie) spitting on him. Thanks are due to Jeff Brown of Bowling Green State University for alerting me to the generic properties of the action adventure movie and particularly the use of triumphant language and gestures. In *Charlie's Angels* (2000, dir. McG), Dylan Sanders (Drew Barrymore) concludes a fight scene with the line "And that's kicking your ass." This might be an exercise in the traditional idiom, or it might be a departure that suggests a feminist difference.

271. To be precise, when Ali beat Liston on February 25, 1964, he was still using the name "Cassius Clay." He changed his name to "Muhammad Ali" two days later. The official Muhammad Ali website is at http://www.ali.com.

272. This is roughly the equivalent of the effect that women achieve when wearing male clothing. Instead of making them look like men, it serves to emphasize their femaleness. I believe that this effect is often at work in the notion of the "cute." Cuteness is often little and unthreatening. As far as I know, there is no cultural account of cuteness.

273. Meg Ryan understands that her stage persona is deeply wedded to conventional notions of femaleness. In the voice-over track for the DVD of *City of Angels* (1998, dir. Brad Silberling), she says she was nervous that her audience would have trouble accepting her as a surgeon.

274. For a glimpse of the range of products Stewart sells at Kmart, see the Kmart website, http://www.kmart.com.

275. The phrase "hick town" is Kid Rock's own and it appears in the *Rolling Stone* biography by Lana Fanelli, which I found at http://www.rollingstone.com/sections/artists/text/bio.asp?afl=rsn&LookUpString=6047; unfortunately the website is defunct. Kid Rock appeared on the VH-1 Vogue fashion awards in 2000. All the members of the band wore t-shirts identifying downmarket department stores: Target, Kmart, Wal-Mart, Home Depot.

276. Quoted in Diane Brady, "Martha: Inside the Growing Empire of America's Lifestyle Queen," *Business Week*, January 17, 2000: 72.

277. As I suggested in the opening essay, Stewart has several audiences. I am referring here to only one of them. Martha Stewart's following in the gay community demands other models of explanation. One of them is that of transgressive appropriation.

278. What this statement excludes, and means to exclude, are all the "sociological" exertions that also make up an individual's preparation for upward mobility: the pursuit of education, a better job, and so on. Marriage undertaken for status purposes (i.e., marrying someone for their membership in one's own or a higher class) is a matter of upward transformation when it results in a change in the individual's experience of, or performance in, the world. It is judged a sociological exertion when it is merely a matter of "credentialing" and networking. This statement also excludes notions of status that are established by birth. Some condition of this kind is almost always in place as one of the "felicity" conditions on which claims to status depend. But no claim to status based on birth is strong enough to withstand a refusal of other transformational cultivations. Certainly, a prince would remain a prince of some kind even if he lived as a messenger boy. Certainly, he could be recalled to monarchical duties. But he might insist on living as a messenger boy. On another topic, speech is plainly both an interior and an exterior matter. A story circulates at Cambridge about the don who spoke with a northern accent until coming to study at Cambridge, where he learned the middle-class accent often used there. Now when he returns to Durham for the holidays, he reverts to his original accent. Sometime during the drive back to Cambridge the middle-class accent returns, but when he stops for gas on the way, he never knows which accent he will use to ask for service.

279. Beatrix Le Wita is particularly good on this part of the status system. See her *French Bourgeois Culture* (New York: Cambridge University Press, 1994).

280. This must be why connoisseurship is so important to, so celebrated by, status communities, and why museum curators who have no other claim to standing are given honorary status. Connoisseurship is a formalization of the first round with which all status advancement begins. And this would also explain why the American eastern seaboard likes to suppose that the best connoisseurs must have some claim to status by birth. I thank Adrienne Hood for pointing out this last ethnographic particular.

281. These are arbitrary distinctions, in one sense. There is nothing inevitable or necessary about them. But they are mandated in another, for they are always about distinction. Thus a diphthong will be endured or perhaps embraced by a low-standing community precisely because it elides distinction. A high-standing community, on the other hand, will search out differences, the finer the better, to make the rest of the world look like it is eliding distinctions.

282. The phrase "One doesn't" indicates the power of the ideology. Note the way it makes interchangeable the personal, the collective, and the abstract.

283. Code bearers are a little like teens. They constantly survey the social world, with a fine eye to details that others do not observe or care about. The difference is that teens are often highly self-conscious about the process of observation and judgment, whereas the code bearers we are talking about here are often more self-confident and operate by rote.

284. Laura Mulvey, *Visual and Other Pleasures*, Theories of Representation and Difference (Bloomington: Indiana University Press, 1989).

285. This may be why, in some communities, two high-standing individuals in the presence of a middle-standing individual will decline to acknowledge the status misdemeanors of this third individual. Nothing will be said to the third individual, and, more important, no hint of it, verbal or otherwise, will pass between the high-standing individuals. This is not just because they already know they know, but because it is the very fact that they are noticing misbehavior that confirms their status. That they are not "noticing" this misbehavior confirms it further.

286. Every cultural world forms and directs the act of noticing, but some depend on "hypernoticing."

287. I have simplified for the sake of clarity. The two may interact, as when experience and performance become an opportunity for engagement, play, amusement, provocation, generosity, misdirection, competition, and hostility. Fine differences in choice and performance carry meaning and produce results.

288. There is a model within the model. Let's call it a "patrician" position. In some communities, it matters a great deal that the individual search for signs in order to cultivate the spiritual, aesthetic, or emotional domains of the self. What is sought is the ability to detect interior events, to reflect on them, to cultivate them. What is sought is the domains of the self and their cultivation, so that the self becomes a richer, more various, more complicated, more cultivated thing. Some of this search will show, and some of it the individual will demonstrate, in order to claim the status that belongs to those so cultivated, but some of it will be a purely private accomplishment that has only intrinsic qualities.

289. Paul Myer Mazur, *American Prosperity: Its Causes and Consequences* (New York: Viking, 1928), 24; John O'Neill, "The Productive Body: An Essay on the Work of Consumption," *Queen's Quarterly* 85, no. 2 (1978): 224; and William R.

Leach, "Transformations in a Culture of Consumption: Women and Department Stores, 1890–1925," *Journal of American History* 71 (September 1984): 319–342.

290. "At bottom the key to the Industrial Revolution was the infinitely elastic home demand for mass consumer goods. And the key to that demand was social emulation, 'keeping up with the Joneses,' the compulsive urge for imitating the spending habits of one's betters, which sprang from an open aristocracy in which every member from top to bottom of society trod closely on the heels of the next above." Harold James Perkin, "The Social Causes of the Industrial Revolution," in *The Structured Crowd: Essays in English Social History* (Totowa, N.J.: Barnes & Noble, 1981), 41. This is an ancient argument and an insufficient one. But what is wrong with it is not, as I once thought, that it narrows our understanding of the motives and objectives of "emulative spending," but that it fails to see that this was a transformative, not a mechanical, exercise.

291. Fernand Braudel, *Capitalism and Material Life, 1400–1800*, translated by Miriam Kochan (New York: Harper and Row, 1973).

292. Lamont, *Money, Morals and Manners*, 145.

293. "Movement to upper-middle or intermediate positions or from working class to middle class, or from the slums to the suburbs in one generation [was] attainable for millions." Neil J. Smelser and Seymour M. Lipset, *Social Structure and Mobility in Economic Development* (Chicago: Aldine, 1966), 278.

294. Ross, *Fast Cars, Clean Bodies*.

295. "American culture encourages men to seek both occupational advancement and the acquisition of material possessions. But workers who respond to both of these admonitions use the second to rationalize their failure to achieve the first. As long as possessions continue to pile up, the worker can feel that he is moving forward; as long as his wants do not give out, he can feel that he is ambitious." Ely Chinoy, *Automobile Workers and the American Dream* (Garden City, N.Y.: Doubleday, 1955), 126.

296. Cawelti, *Apostles of the Self-Made Man*, 61, 80–98.

297. The classical pattern of upward transformation has been observed in the life of Abraham Lincoln. As Lincoln moved upward occupationally and economically, he undertook a series of other, smaller changes. "He changed his speech and his dress, the houses he lived in and their location, modified his manners and some of his values." As Warner says, Lincoln did not conceive of mobility in "purely economic terms." W. Lloyd Warner, *The Living and the Dead: A Study of the Symbolic Life of Americans* (New Haven, Conn.: Yale University Press, 1959), 93.

298. I do not suppose that there is a developmental, evolutionary, or graduated change between these two historical moments. For all I know—and, as my historical colleagues do not hesitate to tell me, I know very little—the status system shifted frequently between organization and disorganization. There is precedent for such shifts in the ethnographic record. See, for instance, Edmund Leach, *Political Systems of Highland Burma* (London: Athlone, 1964).

299. "If and when her ambition is realized, she quite naturally slips into the roles pre-defined in this imagery, not only in her actions but in her tastes, opinions, attitudes and even emotions—in sum, she acquires a pre-fabricated identity, advertised, marketed and guaranteed by the identity-producing agencies. The identity thus acquired, however, has a peculiar second-hand quality, not only because of its

mass-communicated stereotypes, but because it remains anticipatory even when mobility has taken place." Thomas Luckmann and Peter Berger, "Social Mobility and Personal Identity," *Archives européennes de sociologie* 5 (1964): 338.

300. There is an interesting paper to be written about the role of Hollywood in the relative decline of the influence of so-called "polite society." In the early days of Hollywood, polite society is revered and admired. In *Platinum Blonde* (1931, dir. Frank Capra), Jean Harlow, of all people, plays a member of high society without reproach. As we have seen, things move swiftly. In *The Philadelphia Story* (1940, dir. George Cukor), Katharine Hepburn is as much mocked as admired for her high-society standing. Kidwell and Christman are good on this theme: Claudia B. Kidwell and Margaret C. Christman, *Suiting Everyone: The Democratization of Clothing in America* (Washington, D.C.: Smithsonian Institution Press, 1974).

301. There is no firm evidence that this "discovery" actually took place. According to the myth, it happened in 1936 and the discoverer was a Hollywood film journalist.

302. Cara Greenberg, *Mid-century Modern: Furniture of the 1950s* (New York: Harmony, 1984); and Lesley Jackson, *The New Look: Design in the Fifties* (London: Thames and Hudson, 1991).

303. Gerry Pratt, "The House as an Expression of Social Worlds," in *Housing and Identity: Cross-Cultural Perspectives*, ed. James S. Duncan (London: Croom Helm, 1981), 135–80. For modernism that takes the form of primitive art, see David Halle, *Inside Culture: Art and Class in the American Home* (Chicago: University of Chicago Press, 1993).

304. This is a line from the song "My Way," made famous by Frank Sinatra.

305. David Riesman, with Nathan Glazer and Reuel Denney, *The Lonely Crowd: A Study of the Changing American Character* (New Haven, Conn.: Yale University Press, 1961), esp. 37–38. For comments on this approach to the study of contemporary culture, see McCracken, *Plenitude 2.0*; Andrew Ross, *No Respect: Intellectuals and Popular Culture* (New York: Routledge, 1989); and Samuel G. Freedman, "Suburbia Outgrows Its Image in the Arts," *New York Times*, February 28, 1999, section 2, p. 1. This is a good article. There is some question about the depth of John Cheever's hostility to the suburb. See, for instance, his fond treatment of Eliot and Nellie Nailles in *Bullet Park*, and his damning parody of the Riesman school of criticism, which he dismisses as "adolescent." Eliot Nailles begins his subtle and thoroughly ambivalent defense of the suburb with a burst of indignation: "it makes me sore to have people always chopping at the suburbs." John Cheever, *Bullet Park: A Novel* (New York: Knopf, 1969), 5–6, 66–67. More sophisticated treatments of the suburbs are now beginning to emerge. See particularly Rosalyn Baxandall and Elizabeth Ewen, *Picture Windows: How the Suburbs Happened* (New York: Basic, 2000).

306. David Riesman, "The Suburban Dislocation," in *Abundance for What? and Other Essays* (1957; Garden City, N.Y.: Doubleday, 1964), 242. Why a "small" college, exactly?

307. McCracken, *Plenitude 2.0*, 105–106.

308. The theory of upward transformation distinguishes itself from Veblen's in the following way. Status competition is not a matter of spending more but of choosing well (i.e., according to the code). Perhaps we should call consumption "conspicuous" when it is used for upward mobility and "constructive" when it is

undertaken for upward transformation. Veblen's ideas continued to hold sway for many social scientists. For a rare dissenting voice, see Jules Lubbock, *The Tyranny of Taste: The Politics of Architecture and Design in Britain, 1550–1960* (New Haven, Conn.: Yale University Press, 1995).

309. John R. Seeley, R. Alexander Sim, and E. W. Loosley, *Crestwood Heights: A Study of the Culture of Suburban Life* (Toronto: University of Toronto Press, 1956), 7.

310. Ibid., 7, 52. One can't help wondering why this complexity did not serve as a Kuhnian "anomaly" encouraging theoretical accommodation. Indeed, it was fashionable for sociologists mesmerized by Veblen to admit to their limitations. Felson, in his study of the status and the homes of postwar Detroit, said that the "Bric-A-Brac factor" was "beyond the reach of this writer's sociological imagination." Marcus Felson, "The Differentiation of Material Life Styles, 1925–1966," *Social Indicators Research* 3 (1976): 414. Laumann and House, in their study of living room furnishings, acknowledged "distinction beyond the untutored grasp of our interviewers." Edward O. Laumann and James S. House, "Living Room Styles and Social Attributes: The Patterning of Material Artifacts in a Modern Urban Community," *Sociology and Social Research* 54, no. 3 (1970): 338. There is something almost coy about this admission, as if the sociologists are admitting, with theatrical chagrin, "Well, there's just no accounting for taste, is there?" But when one has embarked upon the study of the status encoded in living spaces, is "accounting for taste" not precisely the scholarly charge? It is a mystery why these sociologists, members of a discipline and a profession not famous for admitting its limitations, should have found this particular admission acceptable, perhaps even somehow becoming. What was the rhetorical objective here?

311. I owe this reminder to Jim Gough.

312. Seeley, Sim, and Loosley, *Crestwood Heights*, 7, 52. It is true that Forest Hill attracted some individuals so desperate for status elevation and so "codeless" that they were blindly imitating the behavior of people they saw around them. But to proceed as if this were true of everyone who lived there suggests a failure of the sociological eye and the anthropological imagination. A thoughtful conversation with any relatively sophisticated inhabitant of the neighborhood would have demonstrated the limits of the Veblenian view.

313. W. L. Warner and Paul S. Lunt, *The Social Life of a Modern Community* (New Haven, Conn.: Yale University Press, 1941), 108.

314. Veblen was the product of an immigrant community in Minnesota and, despite his upbringing in the United States, spoke English as a second language. It is also true that he was an economist. Somewhere it is said that he saw the world as if through the eyes of a Martian. The text of his *The Theory of the Leisure Class*, and several articles on him, can be found at the Thorstein Veblen Linkpage, part of the Great Norwegians website, at http://www.mnc.net/norway/veblen.html.

315. Warner, *The Living and the Dead*, 97, 45. Jessie Ventura, the Minnesota governor, is the public figure closest to Muldoon now. That Muldoon should have succeeded so well in his attack on the elite makes him, one can't help feeling, a better social scientist than Veblen, Packard, or Seeley. I developed this view of Warner for a conference organized by Noel Salinger and Andrew Abbott at the University

of Chicago, and I thank them for including me. Grant McCracken, "Resuming Social Science" (paper presented at Consuming Social Science, a conference at the University of Chicago, November 11, 2000).

316. Warner, *The Living and the Dead*, 47. Warner was not interested only in the behavior of upper-class Americans. He and Lunt noted that the striving Starr family was not above buying up the status trophies of an old family and using them for their own status aggrandizement. Warner, and Lunt, *The Status System of a Modern Community*, 107, 131.

317. Warner, *The Living and the Dead*, 47.

318. Nelson W. Aldrich, Jr., *Old Money: The Mythology of America's Upper Class* (New York: Vintage, 1988), 38–39.

319. Ibid., 47.

320. Paul Fussell, *Class: A Guide through the American Status System* (New York: Summit, 1983). This strategy of giving away status information while pretending not to is particularly necessary in a society that has abolished envy as an acceptable motive for the middle class. I will admit to playing Fussell's own game with this observation. I am spotting him spotting status, and in this game the last spotter wins. But two things should be noted. The first is how really nasty this book is. (See for instance Fussell's treatment of the "poor chap" on p. 62.) For all of his intellectual distance, Fussell is a player, and a mean-spirited one at that. The second is that the popularity of this book is some measure of how keenly interested the middle class was in upward transformation even in this period of relative eclipse.

321. Aldrich, *Old Money*, 269.

322. Ron Chernow, *The Death of the Banker* (New York: Vintage, 1997), 32, 33. Thanks to Nick Hahn for this reference.

323. The first of these phrases eventually became the title of a television show starring Chris Elliott. Parts of this short-lived production were meant to satirize the preppy era, with Elliott serving as the anti-prep. See Joyce Millman, "Get an Afterlife," *Salon*, February 5, 1999, http://www.salon.com/ent/tv/feature/1999/02/05feature.html. The accusation "Loser!" was sometimes accompanied by making an "L" with the thumb and first finger of one hand held against the forehead. I believe this gesture emerged in the 1980s.

324. This account is indebted to Mark Simonson and his Very Large National Lampoon Site at http://www.marksverylarge.com, which recounts the history of the *National Lampoon*. One or two articles from the *National Lampoon* may be found at http://www.nationallampoon.com.

325. The circulation figure is from the May 1997 issue of the *Las Vegas Review-Journal*. I found it at http://www.lvrj.com/lvrj_home/1997/May-30-Fri-1997/business/5463188.html, but this website is defunct.

326. When the history of the discovery of irony by popular culture is written, the movement of the *Lampoon* from Cambridge enthusiasm to national institution will loom large.

327. This creature was very specifically gendered. In the gender notions of the day, women were insufficiently cruel to participate.

328. Letterman was to specialize in the new and peculiar combination of wit and loutishness, standing in a window of Rockefeller Center and declaring with a

bullhorn, "I am not wearing any pants." Inevitably, there were also anti-preppies, including Donald Trump, the man *Spy Magazine* loved to excoriate as a "short-fingered vulgarian."

329. This is why the early Letterman interviews were always so painful. The talk-show format called for interaction, an expression of interest, something like curiosity on the part of the host. But Letterman's private-school boy was only really comfortable when engaged in pranks and scorn. To take an active interest in the world would betray both the code and the pose.

330. It is worthwhile thinking about the differences between Alex Keaton, Michael J. Fox's character on the NBC comedy *Family Ties*, and the frat crew of *Animal House*. The frat boys were, as we have noted, reckless, overweening, and crude. Alex Keaton was a different creature. He was much more concerned with making the right impressions, going to the right schools, crafting the right career path. He showed an attention to form, an anxiety about performance, an eagerness to get ahead that were more genuinely middle-class even as he aspired to something more elevated than this.

331. It is odd to write a book about transformation and contemporary culture, and to acknowledge Tom Wolfe's influence as late as this. If there is a transformational journalist, it is Wolfe. His early work for *Rolling Stone* helped to shape the counter-culture of the 1960s and 1970s and his later work, especially "The 'Me' Decade and the Third Great Awakening" (*New York*, August 23, 1976: 26–40) helped bring it to a close. The pattern was to repeat itself with the publication of *The Right Stuff*, which, as we have just noted, was key to the creation of the culture of the 1980s. Wolfe then helped dismantle this cultural moment with the publication of *The Bonfire of the Vanities* in 1987. Now that the sheer pluralism of contemporary culture threatens to frustrate the creation of decade cultures, Wolfe writes novels (such as his 1998 *A Man in Full*) that suggest he is one of the few writers, perhaps the only writer, with sufficient ethnographic breadth and touch to work with this diversity.

332. Cader Books, "1980s Bestsellers," http://www.caderbooks.com/best80.html.

333. The phrase appeared at http://www.americanpresident.org/KoTrain/Courses/RR/RR_The_First_Lady.htm; unfortunately the website is defunct.

334. Both the Friedmans' book and Nancy Reagan's expenditures are, in a way, antithetical to the upward transformation modality. The Friedmans' position would be regarded by some as a mandate to refuse the social responsibilities that are essential to certain status performances. But it allowed individuals to move away from the various solidarities created in the 1960s and 1970s, to imagine a status hierarchy, and even to imagine the possibility of admiring those who ranked high. The display of wealth in the Reagan era was vulgar and noisy. And this opened up the possibility of "noticing" on which so much depends, and directed attention to relatively fine objects and their properties. Here the first fineness demands the second, and so the upward transformation succeeds in demanding and creating attention to the telling detail.

335. For more on the importance of the telling detail, see Le Wita, *French Bourgeois Culture*. I am a great admirer of this book, but I am uncomfortable with its suggestion that attention to detail, self-control, and the ritualization of life are

the key markers of this style of life (71–73). Are there any social groups of whom this is not true?

336. "Go to hell" pants had a double significance. They were booby traps that tested the pretender's knowledge of the status code. Not to wear them would leave the individual looking earnest, humorless, and rather too Eddie Bauer. To wear them and get them wrong would immediately reveal the pretender. But learning how to wear them without error (i.e., to combine them correctly with other clothing) was impossible for anyone who had merely a mechanical or imitative knowledge of the code. The pants also offered a release from the rigidity and conformity of the preppy look. Not to wear them was to sacrifice the opportunity for frat-boy abandon that was for some the point of the exercise.

337. I think the elephant may have been a reference to English colonialism in India, regarded by some as the breeziest face of the English status system.

338. There is a little literature on this creature. "Hooray Henrys" are described in Ann Barr and Peter York, *The Official Sloane Ranger Handbook: The First Guide to What Really Matters in Life* (London: Ebury, 1982). "Gay table" types are described in Aldrich, *Old Money*.

339. There was in fact a double message at work. The *Handbook* made preppies look like idiots, but it was written in a voice that was witty, restrained, and mocking. This voice was more becoming and attractive than the preppies it described.

340. Ann Stroh, "The Preppy Handbook and Other Myths." I found this important document at http://www.sit.wisc.edu/%7Exanadu/preppy_handbook.html; unfortunately, it has since disappeared.

341. No trend or lifestyle ever wins the day and establishes hegemony. Cultural innovation in the 1980s carried on. One particularly interesting variation was the "straight-edge" movement, a punk refusal of drugs, alcohol, and other kinds of indulgence. This reflects some of the things at work in the "aboveground" 1980s, particularly "get a life" clarity and impatience, even as it makes frat-boy self-indulgence look particularly offensive and dissolute. One of the symbols of straight-edge was a large X on the back of the hand. This was taken from the symbol used by club and event promoters to signify that the bearer was to be sold no alcohol. Thanks to Wade Nelson for an explanation of the X on the hand.

342. This writer is documenting his transformation from "slacker guy to working stiff." I found this account at http://www.widomaker.com/~xiled/journal/121497.html; unfortunately, it has since disappeared.

343. As always, the Internet Movie Database is illuminating: see its page for *Cheers* at http://us.imdb.com/Title?0083399. *Cheers* opened the way for shows of a similar theme. *Night Court*, a series that ran on NBC from 1984 to 1992, has a very similar structure. It centers on a fallen male lead (Harry the magician), and surrounds him with lawyers and court personnel with robust personality flaws and no evidence of personal ambition. All are apparently indifferent to their downward mobility. (I am assuming, perhaps wrongly, that a New York City night court in the 1980s was a deeply depressing place, a place that legal careers went to die.) The important difference is that the bit players on *Cheers* were creatures of a middle-class Boston bar, but on *Night Court* they were often the homeless and wretched of New York City. This was real downward mobility, which the series was obliged to show but then fastidiously ignored. See its page

in the Internet Movie Database at http://us.imdb.com/Title?0086770. If people took comfort in the notion of a life that did not require the exertions of upward transformation, or one that offered a momentary respite therefrom, they lived in fear of sudden status demotion. This was the theme of several Hollywood films, particularly *Trading Places* (1983, dir. John Landis) and *Maid to Order* (1987, dir. Amy Holden Jones).

344. I have the "tie salesman" remark from a man of some standing in the world of Canadian fashion. He must remain nameless.

345. Ralph Lauren Media, "1972," http://about.polo.com/history/history.asp ?year=1972. If this record is accurate, Lauren was well ahead of the trend.

346. I thank Joan Kron for having made this conversation possible.

347. Caughey, *Imaginary Social Worlds*.

348. I believe we can go further than this, but without evidence I cannot prove it. Many of the shifts in boomer taste, and especially the shifts to country homes, four-wheel-drive vehicles, wine and food connoisseurship, riding, opera, and the arts, to name a few, may be taken as evidence of some version of the upward trans- formational modality. I believe the people who achieved round 3 transformation are more numerous than we are inclined to suppose.

349. David Brooks, *Bobos in Paradise: The New Upper Class and How They Got There* (New York: Simon and Schuster, 2000).

350. If anyone knows of the origins of this phrase, I would be grateful to hear of it. Yuppie bashing became a fashion at some point.

351. Ebert's review can be found at http://rogerebert.suntimes.com, dated De- cember 11, 1987.

352. To be fair, preps had been favorite villains throughout the '80s. This was presumably because, from the Hollywood point of view, there were good preps and evil ones. This is the case even in *Animal House*. It was also because Hollywood was uncomfortable with, and, in its way, critical of, the '80s cultural moment. (I think this discomfort was due to Hollywood's commitment to a Frank Capra–esque pop- ulism.) See, for instance, the ambivalence toward preppies exhibited in the influen- tial movies of John Hughes: *Sixteen Candles* (1984), *Pretty in Pink* (1985), and *The Breakfast Club* (1986).

353. It is possible that the movie *Wall Street* (1987, dir. Oliver Stone) should be added to this list. *American Psycho* and the movie have a lot in common.

354. This research was performed for the Institute of Contemporary Culture at the Royal Ontario Museum and resulted in an exhibit called "Toronto Teenagers: Coming of Age in the 1990s."

355. I cannot remember where Deal made this observation. Details of her influential career in rock are noted at a fan website for the Breeders at http://www .noaloha.com/, and the interviews with her that were once posted there offered an illuminating window on the 1990s.

356. The British literary magazine *Granta* dedicated its spring 1994 issue to the theme "loser." For an excellent account of the "loser" self-definition, see Stephen Duncombe, *Notes from Underground: Zines and the Politics of Alternative Culture* (London: Verso, 1997), 17–21. Another way to mark the change between the 1980s and the 1990s is to compare the character of Woody (Woody Harrelson) on *Cheers* (NBC, 1984–1992) with that of Matthew (Andy Dick) on *Newsradio*

(NBC, 1995–1999). Both are dim and clueless, but Matthew is dramatically odder, manifestly a "loser" in the new sense of the term.

Another measure of how hostile this trend was to upward transformation is the new affection for things that were "cheesy." Cheesy things were scorned by, and a threat to, all status claims, and embraced by this generation. Here, too, we need a thorough cultural account.

The preppy look was to enjoy one more revival in the twentieth century. It was briefly preferred by some rappers and helped to make a fortune for the Ralph Lauren of the moment, Tommy Hilfiger. McCracken, *Plenitude 2.0*, 190. For more on Hilfiger, see Lou Taylor, "The Hilfiger Factor and the Flexible Commercial World of Couture," in *The Fashion Business: Theory, Practice, Image*, ed. Nicola White and Ian Griffiths (New York: New York University Press, 2000). Thanks to Jeff Brown for this reference.

357. Gretchen Voss, "The Vineyard," *Boston Magazine*, July 1999, http://www .bostonmagazine.com. To be fair to Mr. Boch, nothing in Fussell warns against the status loss that can result from the ownership of a herd of llamas.

358. This line was not uttered by Mr. Boch. I made it up.

359. Quoted in Brady, "Martha," 66.

360. Bill Geist, "It's a Good Thing," *CBS News Sunday Morning*, broadcast on December 19, 1999.

361. Geist used a test for sexism. To see if a word, phrase, or phrasing is gender-specific it is put in the mouth of a speaker of the opposite sex. If it does not change in meaning, it is judged to be not gender-specific.

362. I believe Joan Kron deserves the honor of first noting this phenomenon. Joan Kron, *Home-Psych: The Social Psychology of Home and Decoration* (New York: Clarkson N. Potter, 1983).

363. In a well-organized status hierarchy, there are as few elites as possible. If there must be several, they are clearly differentiated (e.g., military, church, society). A plethora of elites makes the social world problematic. It encourages the development of multiple ways to produce and evaluate standing. And such a multiplicity undermines the authority of each. Good hierarchical operators, to use James Boon's language, obliterate the possibility, the very thought, of other hierarchies. This is where their power to control consciousness comes from. To reduce them from "one and only" to "one of several" is to mortally wound them. James A. Boon, "Further Operations of Culture in Anthropology: A Synthesis of and for Debate," in *The Idea of Culture in the Social Sciences*, ed. Louis Schneider and Charles Bonjean (Cambridge: Cambridge University Press, 1973), 1–32.

364. In most well-organized status hierarchies a handful of people enjoy special powers of observation. Well born, well placed, gifted as observers, indefatigable as participants, they know everyone and, for status purposes, everything. They can predict who is going to marry whom—while the bride and groom are still children. They comprehend all from a single vantage point. I believe such people no longer exist. The vista of a kind created by Edith Wharton is no longer impossible. There are too many landscapes.

365. There are three measures of a decline of status. One is the decline and disorganization of philanthropy among the upper classes. Many families now refuse to participate in this crucial way of manufacturing status. The second is the

failure of elites to recruit new wealth. More and more people accumulate wealth but do not join the existing elites. Celebrities, as a new elite, have always been reluctant to join the old elite. And some of the individuals made wealthy in the 1990s by Silicon Valley saw themselves as too revolutionary, or merely too youthful, to want to join. Status elites cannot maintain their place and their power as social arbiters in the face of refusals of this kind. The third is our ban on envy. Many people suppose (often encouraged by Hollywood) that individuals of high standing must live lives of emotional aridity and dishonesty.

366. This is sometimes called a "trickle-up" diffusion pattern, and it has been observed in several places in the literature. George A. Field, "The Status Float Phenomenon: The Upward Diffusion of Innovation," *Business Horizons* 13, no. 4 (August 1970): 45–52; and Paul Blumberg, "The Decline and Fall of the Status Symbol: Some Thoughts on Status in a Post-industrial Society," *Social Problems* 21, no. 4 (April 1974): 480–98.

367. John Carey, *The Intellectuals and the Masses: Pride and Prejudice among the Literary Intelligentsia, 1880–1939* (London: Faber and Faber, 1992), 205.

368. Tom Wolfe, *Radical Chic & Mau-Mauing the Flak Catchers* (New York: Farrar, Straus and Giroux, 1970). The status hierarchy of the 1960s was so turned upside down that it is possible that Bernstein was flattered by this stinging examination when it appeared in *New York Magazine*.

369. Ellen Moers, *The Dandy: Brummell to Beerbohm* (New York: Viking, 1960); Sontag, "Notes on Camp"; Martin Burgess Green, *Children of the Sun: A Narrative of "Decadence" in England after 1918* (New York: Basic Books, 1976); Joris-Karl Huysmans, *Against Nature*, translated by Robert Baldick (Harmondsworth: Penguin, 1971); and Domna C. Stanton, *The Aristocrat as Art: A Study of the Honnête Homme and the Dandy in Seventeenth- and Nineteenth-Century French Literature* (New York: Columbia University Press, 1980). I am grateful to Johanne Sloan and Alison Matthews for several of these references.

370. Artfulness truly is the last line of defense for a status system that depends as heavily as the Western one has always done on the element of performance. It must protect itself from the pretender who is note-perfect. It must have ready, and Western societies have failed to use, the paradoxical accusation that someone is too perfect. Now the closer offenders get to perfection, the more they open themselves to this accusation. Yes, it's a contradiction, but it gets the job done. Very particular in some things, the status system can't afford to be very particular here.

371. The current interest in the television show *Antiques Roadshow* is an interesting case in point here. The show begins with a classic encounter between status supplicant and status keeper. We listen raptly to see who will prove to be whom. This is determined by how the two parties handle the proceedings, and of course by the value and standing of the object in question.

372. Lamont, *Money, Morals and Manners*, 116.

373. Braudel, *Capitalism and Material Life*, 235–36.

374. "Roman fashions did not change much over the centuries." SPQR Online, "Daily Life: Roman Fashions," http://library.thinkquest.org/26602/fashions.htm. The Egyptian case is still more striking and helps to shake us out of our presumption that fashion has always proved a transformational force. "During the 3,000 years of

the Egyptian culture, costume changed comparatively little and very slowly. . . . This draped type of dress conformed to that of other civilizations in the Mediterranean and Middle Eastern region such as Greece, Rome, and Mesopotamia but differed from the more Oriental styles of Persia, India, and China, where people wore more fitted, sewn garments based upon coats, tunics, and trousers." Encyclopedia Britannica Online, http://www.britannica.com/eb/article-9106185/dress.

375. There is another way to put this: had Ovid moved two thousand years backward in time, not, courtesy of this experiment, two thousand years forward, he would have been very much less out of step with fashion.

376. Braudel, *Capitalism and Material Life*, 231. There are grounds to doubt Braudel's timing. The Elizabethan period, for instance, saw a great deal of change in fashion.

377. It was, in fact, a double penalty. Sovereigns would have to give up power to fashion. And they would have to give up fashion as a source of power. In fact, fashion had been a royal prerogative. Elizabeth I, for instance, used it as an instrument of government to help establish her court, her hegemony, her reign. Roy C. Strong, *The Cult of Elizabeth: Elizabethan Portraiture and Pageantry* (London: Thames and Hudson, 1977).

378. Moers, *The Dandy*, 26, 28.

379. For more on the rise of fashion and its social consequences, see Grant McCracken, "'Ever Dearer in Our Thoughts': Patina and the Representation of Status before and after the Eighteenth Century," in *Culture and Consumption: New Approaches to the Symbolic Character of Consumer Goods and Activities* (Bloomington: Indiana University Press, 1988), 31–43.

380. Frederic J. Schwartz, "Cathedrals and Shoes: Concepts of Style in Wolfflin and Adorno," *New German Critique* 76 (winter 1999): 16, 17. Thanks to Johanne Sloan for this reference.

381. "Color was often the easiest and most advertisable way of converting staple products into fashion goods." Roland Marchand, *Advertising the American Dream: Making Way for Modernity, 1920–1940* (Berkeley: University of California Press, 1985), 127.

382. Quoted in Susan Strasser, *Waste and Want: A Social History of Trash* (New York: Metropolitan Books, 1999), 189. The intrusion of fashion into new product and cultural categories continues apace. Its hold on children's clothing is relatively recent. It now has an influence on body shapes. In the movie *Terminator 2: Judgment Day* (1991, dir. James Cameron), Linda Hamilton appeared in a body shape that she was to later complain became "the body" of the early 1990s. Jeffrey Brown, "Gender and the Action Heroine: Hardbodies and the Point of No Return," *Cinema Journal* 35, no. 2 (1996): 52–71.

383. It is very late in the game, only in the last thirty years, that we have seen that the so-called "industrial revolution" must necessarily have been accompanied by a consumer revolution. This realization has caused a small revolution in the field of history. See particularly Neil McKendrick, John Brewer, and J. H. Plumb, *The Birth of a Consumer Society: The Commercialization of Eighteenth-Century England* (Bloomington: Indiana University Press, 1982).

384. For more on superficiality, see Mariana Valverde, "The Love of Finery: Fashion and the Fallen Woman in Nineteenth-Century Social Discourse," *Victorian*

Studies 32, no. 2 (winter 1989): 169–88; and Helene E. Roberts, "The Exquisite Slave: The Role of Clothes in the Making of the Victorian Woman," *Signs* 2, no. 3 (spring 1977): 554–69. For a discussion of how this circularity was taken up by in the voting rights controversy, see Jeanette C. Lauer and Robert H. Lauer, *Fashion Power: The Meaning of Fashion in American Society* (Englewood Cliffs, N.J.: Prentice-Hall, 1981). Thanks to Beverly Lemire for the first two references.

385. The *Oxford English Dictionary* defines "superficial" as "Of or pertaining to the surface; that is, lies, or is found at or on the surface." I thank George Anastapolo for pointing this out to me.

386. The obsolescence-creation theory appears in Annette B. Weiner and Jane Schneider, eds., *Cloth and the Human Experience* (Washington, D.C.: Smithsonian Institution Press, 1989); and Roland Barthes, *The Fashion System*, translated by Mathew Ward and Richard Howard (Berkeley: University of California Press, 1990). The notion of a conspiracy may be found in several places, especially Nicolas Coleridge, *Fashion Conspiracy* (New York: Harper & Row, 1988). For the argument against seeing the consumer as a dupe, see John Fiske, *Reading the Popular* (Boston: Unwin Hyman, 1989).

387. Shaw's characterization of fashion as an "induced epidemic" is in James B. Simpson, comp., *Simpson's Contemporary Quotations* (Boston: Houghton Mifflin, 1988), excerpted online by Bartleby.com at http://www.bartleby.com/63/75/6075 .html. The roller coaster image is from Northrop Frye, *The Modern Century* (Toronto: Oxford University Press, 1967), 21. The Lynds' reference to "rouged clerks" is in Robert Lynd and Helen Lynd, *Middletown: A Study in Modern American Culture* (New York: Harcourt, Brace and World, 1956), 82. The Vatican epithet is in Peter York, *Modern Times* (London: Heinemann, 1984), 10. (To be fair, it was probably not meant pejoratively.) For a less anxious view of fashion, see Gilles Lipovetsky, *The Empire of Fashion: Dressing Modern Democracy*, translated by Catherine Porter (Princeton, N.J.: Princeton University Press, 1994); McKendrick, Brewer, and Plumb, *The Birth of A Consumer Society;* Fred Davis, *Fashion, Culture, and Identity* (Chicago: University of Chicago Press, 1992); and Jennifer Craik, *The Face of Fashion: Cultural Studies in Fashion* (London: Routledge, 1993).

388. An examination of Braudel's question begins to look like one of those old-fashioned exercises in anthropology that searched for "latent functions." But I do not care about discovering the secret of fashion, the thing that makes it so. This would be another way of diminishing it. And I do not think of my account of it as exhaustive, by any means. I am merely keen to try to think about how it is fashion enables us to engage in transformation as collectivities. For an account of Bronislaw Malinowski's version of the search for a latent function, see Audrey I. Richard, "The Concept of Culture in Malinowski's Work," in *Man and Culture: An Evaluation of the Work of Bronislaw Malinowski*, ed. Raymond Firth (London: Routledge & Kegan Paul, 1957), 19.

389. For more on this theme, see the "Anti-transformation" essay at the end of section 2 of this book.

390. Pierre Bourdieu, *The Logic of Practice*, translated by Richard Nice (Stanford, Calif.: Stanford University Press, 1990), 54.

391. "Narc" is short for "narcotics officer" and a slang term for a square, one who might turn people in to the cops.

392. Frank Zappa and the Mothers of Invention, "Who Needs the Peace Corps?" *We're Only in It for the Money* (1968). So earnest was this period, Zappa was one of its few satirical voices.

393. Some readers will mock this suggestion. But I hope I have said enough to suggest that their mockery is a cultural reflex and that it is incumbent upon them to show why this possibility should be risible.

394. The wave metaphor is especially useful here. Picture three birds in the water. All rise and fall with the wave but their relative locations remain the same.

395. See a biography of Georg Simmel excerpted from Lewis A. Coser's *Masters of Sociological Thought: Ideas in Historical and Social Context*, 2nd ed. (New York: Harcourt Brace Jovanovich, 1977) by Sociology in Switzerland, at http://www.socio.ch/sim/bio.htm.

396. Georg Simmel, "Fashion," in *On Individuality and Social Forms: Selected Writings* (Chicago: University of Chicago Press, 1971), 294–323. The essay was originally published in *International Quarterly* 10 (October 1904): 130–55 and reprinted in *American Journal of Sociology* 62, no. 6 (May 1957): 541–58. For a more detailed treatment of Simmel's theory, see Grant McCracken, "Consumer Goods, Gender Construction, and a Rehabilitated Trickle-Down Theory," in *Culture and Consumption: New Approaches to the Symbolic Character of Consumer Goods and Activities* (Bloomington: Indiana University Press, 1988), 93–103. In the discussion that follows, I will never refer to more than three waves. This simplifies exposition (it is all the theory requires) but a diffusion chain may have many more waves than this.

397. Nancy F. Koehn, *Brand New: How Entrepreneurs Earned Consumers' Trust from Wedgwood to Dell* (Boston, Mass.: Harvard Business School Press, 2001), 34. For more on the colonial case, see Kevin M. Sweeney, "High-Style Vernacular: Lifestyles of the Colonial Elite," in *Of Consuming Interests: The Style of Life in the Eighteenth Century*, ed. Cary Carson, Ronald Hoffman, and Peter J. Albert (Charlottesville: University Press of Virginia, 1994), 30.

398. Charles W. King, "Fashion Adoption: A Rebuttal to the 'Trickle-Down' Theory," in *Toward Scientific Marketing*, ed. Stephen A. Greyser (Chicago: American Marketing Association, 1963), 108–25. See also R. Tamar Horowitz, "From Elite Fashion to Mass Fashion," *Archives européennes de sociologie* 16, no. 2 (1975): 283–95.

399. For our purposes, it is enough to say that "disintermediation" is the process by which a channel that brings goods to market (from manufacturer to wholesaler, retailer, and customer) is collapsed by a new technology. The classic example is the Dell Computer Company, which moves computers from the manufacturer directly to the customer.

400. See the website of *Fashion Television* at http://www.fashiontelevision.com/. I had an interesting conversation in 1996 with a New York publisher who snorted when Jeannie Beker's name came up in conversation. When I asked her to explain, she sniffed, "Well, New Yorkers are unaccustomed to learning things about fashion from a Canadian." *Fashion Television* had so disintermediated the fashion system that the publisher no longer enjoyed the traditional New York advantage of being several months ahead of the rest of the country. Naturally, she was taking it with a New Yorker's good grace. (It remains to say that New Yorkers still have the advantage of

seeing what the many "early adopters" in the city choose from the stream of the new, and this still gives them an advantage.)

401. "Currency" is a lively word, applying, as it does, to money, water, and electricity, all things that come in waves.

402. The dean of fashion history, James Laver, has an account of the way things cycle in and out of fashion. James Laver, *Costume and Fashion: A Concise History* (London: Thames and Hudson, 1996).

403. I have two complaints to make about Thornton. She accepts Bourdieu's lead, and treats something like a dance style as a marker of subcultural capital when it *is* this capital. Second, there is no sense in Thornton's work (or in Bourdieu's) that individuals are crafting themselves, performing themselves, that cultural capital is not merely knowledge but action, and not merely action but a continuous outcome. There is a still more general complaint to make of them both. The use of the notion "capital" represents an effort to see how successfully an economic model can capture things that are normally considered outside its purview. In some ways it is bracing to think of cultural competence or knowledge as a "good." This allows us to think about how it serves the stuff of distinction ("class" in Bourdieu's case, "hipness" in Thornton's) and to think about it as a tangible, fungible, value these have in the world. (This is the place to note the difference between Bourdieu and Thornton: that the former looks at influence that works from the top down and the bottom out, while Thornton looks at influence that works from the margin in toward the mainstream.) But we may ask whether the intellectual strategy is well advised, especially when so much of what distinguishes the cultural undertakings that surround fashion or style have no correlate in (and indeed are systematically unanticipated by) the economic model. This feels like the post-Kantian contest between scientific and interpretive approaches to the understanding of social behavior. The economic model may have one insight into the world of meanings, and to be sure it is sometimes a vast and telling insight, but that's all it has, and, as we have already seen, fashion is the last place the model seems apt. See Sarah Thornton, *Club Cultures: Music, Media, and Subcultural Capital* (Middletown, Conn.: Wesleyan University Press, 1996); Pierre Bourdieu, *Distinction: A Social Critique of the Judgement of Taste*, trans. Richard Nice (Cambridge, Mass.: Harvard University Press, 1984).

404. I don't mean to pick on dentists here but, structurally, they are perfectly positioned to be gulled. Nothing in their professional experience gives them the chance to stay current with contemporary culture. (All that easy-listening music must finally tell.) But they are of course liquid in another sense.

405. Strawberry Saroyan and Michelle Goldberg, "What's Up with Madonna?" *Salon*, October 10, 2000, http://www.salon.com/ent/music/feature/2000/10/10/madonna/index.html.

406. Malcolm Gladwell, "The Coolhunt," *New Yorker*, March 17, 1997: 78–88.

407. This passage owes a great deal to Gil McWilliam, with whom I discussed the topic at length in the fall of 2000. On the other hand, she is not to be held accountable for the breezy way in which I treat it here. For more on the "critical mass" thesis, see Thomas C. Schelling, *Micromotives and Macrobehavior* (New York: Norton, 1978).

408. For present purposes, I am ignoring the fact that things thrill by terrifying and that what we are talking about here is a system in which the thrilling consists of

some combination of the familiar and the strange, a different balance for each wave. I remember hitchhiking on a street corner in Vancouver in 1965 in my new, extravagantly odd "mod" shirt, gray with enormous white collar and cuffs. Mod was likely already dead in London by this time. It was probably already repudiated in Vancouver by anyone with real fashion sense. But for me it represented a stepping off into a grand adventure. The new promised . . . well, it wasn't clear what it promised, and this is part of why the new can be thrilling. We know something's coming but we can't say what. Risk promises the new without threatening to be irrevocable.

409. Malcolm Gladwell, *The Tipping Point* (Boston, Mass.: Little, Brown, 2000).

410. Gladwell uses the contagion model, and the meme theory is from Richard Dawkins, *The Selfish Gene*, new ed. (New York: Oxford University Press, 1989), 196. I have worked up a more detailed criticism of meme theory in McCracken, *Plenitude 2.0.*

411. One example of the freedom with which the mullet is ridiculed may be found at Mullet Madness, http://www.mulletmadness.com/. The reader who searches the Internet for "mullet" will discover how popular and how vicious mullet ridicule on the net can be. See Scott Morrow, "Truth or Hair: How Do You Say Moo-lay?" review of *The Mullet: Hairstyle of the Gods* by Mark Larson and Barney Hoskyns, *L.A. Weekly*, March 29, 2000, http://www.laweekly.com/music/music-reviews/truth-or-hair/11517/. Morrow suggests that the term "mullet" was coined by the Beastie Boys. Thanks to Leora Kornfeld for pointing me to this review.

412. Herbert Blumer, "Fashion: From Class Differentiation to Collective Selection," *Sociological Quarterly* 10, no. 3 (1969): 275–91.

413. I am grateful to Joan Kron for several conversations on the fashion industry, and especially for her observations on how vague members of the industry are when talking about the creative and selection processes.

414. "No American transformation was more remarkable than these new American ways of changing things from objects of possession and envy into vehicles of community. . . . Nearly all objects . . . became symbols and instruments of novel communities." Boorstin, *The Americans*, 89.

415. Albert O. Hirschman, *Rival Views of Market Society and Other Recent Essays* (Cambridge, Mass.: Harvard University Press, 1992), 78.

416. Hirschman's theory allows for only exit and loyalty. The clique theory of sociology captured a third, intermediate category, one in which individuals stayed within the organization but created values that mocked and diminished it.

417. It may prove that clothing fashion is a leading edge for the other agents of transformation. And there would be simple economic reasons for this. After all, the designer can mount a season of innovation at a fraction of the cost of a television series or a Hollywood movie.

418. I am using the term "script" here as it is used by the field of information processing, to describe the intellectual and practical routines that allow us to identify and solve problems without consciously considering them. Lawrence A. Hirschfeld and Susan A. Gelman, *Mapping the Mind: Domain Specificity in Cognition and Culture* (Cambridge: Cambridge University Press, 1994). Bateson was particularly good on this aspect of cognition: Gregory Bateson, *Steps to an Ecology of Mind: Collected Essays in Anthropology, Psychiatry, Evolution, and Epistemology* (San Francisco: Chandler, 1972).

419. Clearly, involuntary improv is a necessary feature of every human life. There will always be something (if only the individual's movement through the developmental arc) that creates novelty and the need for improvisation. There will always be moments of crisis in which novelty overwhelms tradition, forcing individual and community to improvise for some time. The question is this: do we find ourselves in a world in which involuntary improv is more conspicuous, more active, more demanding of us, less the exception and more the rule . . . a world, that is to say, in which the exception is the rule? Have we created a world in which scripts for problem solving are routinely found wanting, a world in which improvisation is becoming the order of the day?

420. The Western historical tradition is filled with extraordinary moments in which individuals are faced with enduring religious, economic, or social change. If there is something uncommon about the present day (and there may not be), it could be that extraordinary change is happening on all dimensions at once. English men and women of the sixteenth century watched as religious ceremonies were reworked, but there were other aspects of their very dynamic lives that were somewhat more steady.

421. Marshall David Sahlins, *Culture and Practical Reason* (Chicago: University of Chicago Press, 1976).

422. Henry Adams, *The Education of Henry Adams* (New York: Penguin, 1995), 346.

423. I watched this happen recently, as a friend contemplated the loss of her life partner. One nasty domestic argument, and once-distant questions were suddenly pressing. Would she have to sell the house, change jobs, change cities, change her daughter's school, change how she thought of herself in the world? Fifteen years of relative stasis were thrown into question.

424. The following discussion relies heavily on movies as illustrations. I believe popular culture is warming to the transformational theme. But I am also convinced that Hollywood is a particularly good window through which to observe contemporary culture.

425. This treatment appears also, in a way, in the Jim Carrey movie *Me, Myself, and Irene* (2000, dir. Bobby Farrelly and Peter Farrelly). Its execution there is somewhat different.

426. "Julie" is a composite created out of stories I heard during and after a visit to Silicon Valley in February of 2001.

427. Around twenty thousand Internet jobs were lost in January and February of 2001. Judith Lewis, "404, Host Not Found," *L. A. Weekly*, February 28, 2001, http://www.laweekly.com/general/features/404-host-not-found/5005/. See also the story of Freddy Nager in Michelle Goldberg, "Welcome to the Real World," *The Industry Standard*, December 11, 2000, http://www.thestandard.com/article/o ,1902,20648,00.html. For an account that captures the suddenness of the dot.com layoffs, see Jennifer Lee, "Management: Discarded Dreams of Dot-Com Rejects," *New York Times*, February 21, 2001, http://www.nytimes.com/2001/02/21/ technology/21DOTC.html. Lee notes that the dot.coms tend to lay off employees the way they hired them, with "seat of the pants" spontaneity. The question is whether this is an historical accident or the way a freeform capitalism is now practiced. For a running account of the dot.com meltdown, see the stories posted at

Fucked Company, http://www.fuckedcompany.com. Thanks to Leora Kornfeld for several of these references.

428. Something like this is proposed in Jeremy Rifkin, *The End of Work* (New York: Putnam, 1995).

429. For more on this theme, see Marcelle Clements, *The Improvised Woman: Single Women Reinventing Single Life* (New York: Norton, 1998).

Sometimes the change is driven by a resolution of the kind voiced by Peter Finch in *Network* (1976, dir. Sidney Lumet): "I'm mad as hell, and I'm not going to take it anymore!" More often it comes as an accumulation of unhappiness, a quiet, insistent voice warning that things are not OK. Here's how Jane Christmas described the revelation. "I've had it with the relentless hustle, with feeling as if I'm competing in an urban triathlon. I'm tired of stretching my energies and loyalties to the limit. I'm tired of short-changing my children on affection and help with their homework because I'm drained by the end of a weekday. . . . I have tried to regain some balance in my life, but no matter how many neat little schedules I draw up, I can never find the time to put them into practice." Christmas's solution was to move to a small town and a simpler life. She is recording her experience, presumably, because many readers would like to do the same. Few people have the resources to indulge this wish, but the hydraulic pressure is plainly there. Jane Christmas, "I Need to Get Away," *National Post*, February 17, 2001: A16.

I hope that readers of the book will email me stories of their own transformations; I can be reached at grant27@gmail.com.

430. Does NBC have a special passion for this theme? As we shall see, it is responsible for several series that make transformation their theme, especially *The Pretender* and *The Profiler*. In the first case, the protagonist moves deliberately from one manifestation to another and adapts quickly and well. In the second, the protagonist finds herself suddenly and only briefly dropped into the experience of someone else, the person who committed the crime under investigation. The television series *Sliders* (1995–2000, Fox and Sci-Fi Channel) had a group "sliding" from one parallel universe to another, unable to find its way back home. This, too, is a lesser form of challenge, since the players remain the same. It is only the world that is novel and unknown.

431. Some will complain that the quality of these films is not particularly high. I would argue that this increases the likelihood of their cultural veracity, because, as we know, good poets steal and bad poets borrow.

432. This example will help illustrate, I hope, that we are not always heroic in our involuntary improv. Sometimes, the problem is simply that the world has changed and we have not.

433. *Whose Line Is It Anyway?* (Hat Trick Productions) is a television series that ran first in Britain, from 1988 to 1998 (http://us.imdb.com/Title?0094580), and then in the U.S., from 1998 to 2006 (ABC and Warner Brothers) (http://us.imdb .com/Title?0163507). It consists of four improv players responding to the prompts of a genial host sitting behind a desk (Clive Anderson in the British case, Drew Carey in the American one).

434. Jeffrey Sweet, *Something Wonderful Right Away: An Oral History of the Second City and the Compass Players* (New York: Avon, 1978).

435. The credit for this speech belongs to the screenwriter, Robert King, and perhaps also to Dana Carvey. The copyright belongs to MGM.

436. John Lahr, "Making It Real: Mike Nichols' Improvised Life," *New Yorker*, February 21 and 28, 2000: 202.

437. Ibid., 205. The speaker is Elaine May, and it's interesting to think that her impromptu remark should have become a staple of self-help books and those "inspirational message" shops that are now appearing in malls and airports. See in particular the chain called Successories.

438. Ibid., 204.

439. Viola Spolin, *Improvisation for the Theater: A Handbook of Teaching and Directing Techniques* (Evanston, Ill.: Northwestern University Press, 1963). For more detail, see the Spolin Center's website at http://www.spolin.com/.

440. You may well ask what makes me think I have anything useful to say on the topic. In fact, I have done quite a lot of improv in the private sector, chiefly in problem-solving sessions. It is also true that my biographical arc has taken me from the public to the private sector and back again, from a museum to a corporation to a business school to a liberal arts program, from solitary work in a university archive to the sometimes solitary, sometimes gregarious but still private status of a consultant, to the more public status of an arts administrator, to the still more public status of a "talking head," and back to the isolation of a private scholar scratching out this book. More particularly, I taught for several years in what had been a school of home economics (University of Guelph), served as the director of the Institute of Contemporary Culture at the Royal Ontario Museum, worked as a consultant on a variety of projects in the private sector (chiefly for Kodak, Chrysler, the Coca-Cola Company, and the Capital Markets Company), taught at Harvard Business School, and taught in the Department of Art History and Communications Studies at McGill University. The "talking head" stage of my career reached its crescendo when I appeared on the Oprah Winfrey Show.

441. I am indebted to the following books for my understanding of blocking: Keith Johnstone, *Impro: Improvisation and the Theatre* (Boston, Mass.: Faber and Faber, 1979); and Kathleen Foreman and Clem Martini, *Something like a Drug: An Unauthorized Oral History of Theatresports* (Red Deer, Alberta: Red Deer College Press, 1995). Here is Johnstone on blocking: "Each actor tends to resist the invention of the other actor, playing for time, until he can think up a 'good' idea, and then he'll try to make his partner follow it. The motto of scared improvisers is 'when in doubt, say 'NO' " (94).

442. Zyman has left the Coca-Cola Company and now runs his own management consulting company, the Zyman Group (http://www.zyman.com).

443. Zyman is famous for his impatience. I saw this once in his boardroom at Coca-Cola. There were nine of us at the table. Zyman sat at its head. At the far end sat four guys, all of them high-ranking executives at the corporation, all of them so well dressed, handsome, and presentable, I thought of them as the "four quarterbacks." Between these four people and Zyman sat four more, somewhat less presentable creatures, of whom I was one. As it turned out, the day belonged to the nonquarterbacks. About halfway through the proceedings an idea took shape among the nonquarterbacks with such speed and force that it felt as if five heads were joined in a single synaptic connection. (Lest it sound like I am making a claim about corporations, Zyman, or myself, I should say this was a freak intellectual event that I have never seen in any circumstances before or since.) Everyone at the

table whistled silently at what had just happened. Zyman turned a cool eye on the four quarterbacks and said, "I hope at least you're keeping notes."

444. Johnstone, *Impro*, 79.

445. Sweet, *Something Wonderful Right Away*, 78.

446. The process of invention was haphazard, but the process of evaluation is not. Good patterns are good for very particular reasons, and especially because they are exact, economical, internally consistent, externally consistent, unified, powerful, and fertile. These conditions are discussed in Grant McCracken, *The Long Interview* (Thousand Oaks, Calif.: Sage, 1988), 50.

447. Foreman and Martini, *Something like a Drug*, 183.

448. This is, perhaps not incidentally, precisely the difference between quantitative and qualitative research methodologies. In the quantitative case, the process of inquiry is broken down into discrete stages that unfold strictly linearly. Literature is consulted, terms defined, questions posed and formulated, methods interrogated and applied, tests performed. In the qualitative case, everything is happening at once.

449. In the world of improv, these are called exercises in "pointless originality," "an idea that comes out of nowhere and is so farfetched that it has no grounding in the reality of the story." Foreman and Martini, *Something like a Drug*, 183. This helps emphasize that offers must be grounded. Those who come to involuntary improv with wild and crazy ideas that celebrate their sheer creativity are not useful. At the opposite extreme are ideas that do not have any real imaginative reach. They are too immobile and inert. Interestingly, the individuals who produce ideas of these types eventually withdraw from the proceedings, driven into a kind of exile by the periods of silence that follow their contributions. The group has not made an obvious choice. No real wounds are inflicted. Who will play and who will not is, like so much about this exercise, emergent.

450. Sometimes this is insisted on in a policy called "no nos." I watched as Denise Fonseca, then director of advertising planning at Coca-Cola, spent the first thirty minutes of a brainstorming session pelting anyone (including me) who said "no" to anyone else's suggestions.

451. Engaging in involuntary improv in a group is fraught with peril. Pointless originality is one such peril. I had a chance to see this too at Coca-Cola. An outside consultant began declaiming and held forth with passion for some time. I couldn't quite make out what he was saying, but I thought the problem might be with me. When the oration was over, a Coca-Cola executive leaned over and said quietly in my ear, " 'Brainstorm,' indeed."

452. There are interesting rules of courtesy at work here. When you offer a combination of previous offerings, you are obliged to name, look at, and sometimes point to the people whose offerings you're using. This suggests that the consensus does not blur the work of individuals even in the most syncretic moments.

453. Just a reminder from the opening essay: this is invented speech. I wrote it originally as "And he's like all mad and stuff and walking around and everything." But my advisor, Bree Short, insisted that "all like mad" was better. My ear tells me this is wrong, but I defer to her knowledge of the ethnographic particulars. This section is, incidentally, a very partial treatment of the functions of the term "like." I am mystified by the term "all" and, for that matter, "everything," though both

may serve as a kind of "you can imagine, and I ask you to fill in, the other details that apply here."

454. Despite its name, Valley talk is widespread. I have heard it throughout Canada and the United States. To the extent that its widespread diffusion is the result of movies like *Clueless* (1995, dir. Amy Heckerling), this is another example in our culture of satire inspiring adoption. If there is a useful piece of academic literature on the subject, I would be grateful to hear of it. I would have thought the sociolinguists would find this topic irresistible.

455. Some unstaged air guitar can be seen in the documentary Jeff Krulick shot in the parking lot outside a Judas Priest concert sometime in the mid-1980s. Jeff Krulick and Jeff Heyn, *Heavy Metal Parking Lot* (Jeff Krulick Productions, 1986), http://www.planetkrulik.com/filmpages/parkinglots/hmpl.htm. Thanks to Leora Kornfeld for this reference. There is a website dedicated to helping people learn how to play air guitar: the Air Guitar Home Page at http://www.mirrorimage.com/air/index.html. I am told that air guitar was in evidence at a heavy metal concert held in Montreal, March 12, 2001. Thanks to Will Straw for this observation.

456. A small cult surrounds the air drumming work of Kevin Dabbs. Dabbs air-drums to Metallica songs. A home video of one of his performances found its way into circulation in Alberta and then San Francisco. Copies began to circulate there under the title "Metallica Drummer." Dabbs had no idea his work was circulating this way until he got a call from the *S.F. Weekly*. Mark Athitakis, "Air Canada," *S.F. Weekly*, January 27, 1999, http://www.sfweekly.com/1999-01-27/music/air-canada/. Thanks to Leora Kornfeld for this reference and the URL.

457. At a performance of the Chicago Symphony in the middle 1970s, I had the bad fortune to sit near a large white male who, five seats from me, accompanied the whole of Beethoven's Fifth by whistling along, badly, throughout—my opportunity to hear some of the great musicians of our time and an idiot without a trace of talent. When I confronted him afterward, he looked at me with astonishment. I could not tell (why didn't I ask?) whether this was because he did not know he had been whistling or because he was astonished that anyone should mind.

458. One of the songs most often lip-synced is "Bohemian Rhapsody," by Queen. It has been used in several advertisements, one of them the Mountain Dew ad by Samuel Bayer at http://www.adcritic.com/content/mountain-dew-bohemian-rhapsody.html.

459. See the documentary by Jennifer Livingston, *Paris Is Burning* (1990), and *Wigstock: The Movie* (1995, dir. Barry Shils). The latter includes a character called Lypsinka.

460. See the documentary by Colleen Ayoup, *Kings* (2001), and Roberta Best, "Drag Kings: Chicks with Dicks," *Canadian Woman Studies* 16, no. 2 (spring 1996): 58–59. As Best puts it, "The aim [of drag] is not to replicate, to 'pass' as another gender, but . . . to question the . . . notion of gender . . . by exposing its . . . fluidity" (58). For the element of ridicule, see the drag king representation of the "geezer" in Del Lagrace Volcano and Judith Halberstam, *The Drag King Book* (London: Serpent's Tail, 1999), 68–71. Halberstam describes a themed evening, one that examines the most disagreeable characteristics of a particularly disagreeable British male, and notes, "If you didn't know what a geezer was at the beginning of the evening, by its end you wished you still didn't" (71).

461. I attended a karaoke night at a bar in Toronto in 1996 and I was impressed by how competitive it was, and how grudging was the approval that greeted good performances. I even thought I detected an interesting ambivalence to the guy scribbling notes in the corner (me), something on the order of "how dare you judge me" mixed with "well, finally someone's taking notice."

462. "Killer app" is a term for a piece of software so interesting and widely adopted that it sells not just itself but computers, operating systems, peripherals, memory upgrades. (Some small part of the present malaise in the general economy and the computer business at the moment comes from the fact that wireless Internet access did not prove to be the killer app the industry hoped it would be.) Two killer apps emerged to help sell the personal computer: VisiCalc, the spreadsheet program, and the Microsoft Flight Simulator. Information on the first can be found at http://www.bricklin.com/visicalc.htm, and on the second at http://www.microsoft.com. More detail on the killer app can be found in Larry Downes and Chunka Mui, *Unleashing the Killer App: Digital Strategies for Market Dominance* (Boston, Mass.: Harvard Business School Press, 1998).

463. But this is of course Toronto's problem. It is merely well rendered.

464. Woody Allen is of course many personae. I am thinking particularly of the one who struggles with lobsters in *Annie Hall* (1977, dir. Woody Allen).

465. Thanks to Christopher Dingwall and his dad, Jim, for permission to tell this story. Jim Dingwall played a part in this book. I wrote a piece about Michael Jackson and transformation ("Seeing the Future in Black and White," *Globe and Mail*, November 21, 1991), and Jim said he thought the theme was worth pursuing.

466. The game's website is at http://thesims.ea.com/.

467. Many sites sprang up in support of the Sim community, including http://www.disturbedsims.com; htp://www.simzonline.com; http://www.7deadlysims.com; http://www.welldressedsim.com; and http://www.homesims.com.

468. "In some ways, the Web has made the mainstream more like a nation of cultural undergrounds—more participatory, less monolithic. Writing your own episode of 'Buffy' isn't that different from picking up a guitar and joining a punk band. Underground culture's openness to networking and fan participation offers hints at what might happen on a grand scale if legal regulation fails to stop technology." Ann Powers, "Fans Go Interactive, and Popular Culture Feels the Tremors," *New York Times*, September 20, 2000.

469. This passage was at http://xfiles.about.com/mbody.htm on July 22, 2001, but the subdomain has since been discontinued.

The website at http://www.x-philes.com hosts what is, by its own estimation, "the first and . . . still the largest automated mailing list for X-Files fan fiction on the Internet. . . . This list exists to allow anyone with an email account to read and write fan fiction based upon the series The X-Files." For more fanfic, see http://www.gossamer.org/.

470. "Majestic [a computer game] is best described as an interactive, immersive and invasive online mystery that combines fiction with (debatable) reality in a very Webby way. For $10 a month, you too can receive mysterious midnight phone calls, anonymous e-mails and tips about a boggling number of surreal goings-on for the next six months of your life." Janelle Brown, "Paranoia for Fun and Profit," *Salon*, August 10, 2001, http://www.salon.com/tech/feature/2001/08/10/majestic/index.html.

471. "Talking to the screen" is my name for this activity.

472. Caughey, *Imaginary Social Worlds*, 38.

473. "Based in Vancouver, British Columbia, Canada, *Adbusters* is a not-for-profit, reader-supported, 85,000-circulation magazine concerned about the erosion of our physical and cultural environments by commercial forces." Adbusters website at http://adbusters.org. See particularly the page of "spoof ads," http://adbusters.org/spoofads/index.php.

474. Am I giving too much away?

475. Janet Horowitz Murray, *Hamlet on the Holodeck: The Future of Narrative in Cyberspace* (New York: Free Press, 1997).

476. My account of this game comes from a remarkable article by Douglas Rushkoff: "Playing Undead," *Swing* 1, no. 5 (April 1995): 34–43. *Swing* is now defunct, but the full text of this article can be found at http://www.rushkoff.com/features/undead.html. Rushkoff refers to an "arts pavilion," by which I think he must mean the Palace of Fine Arts.

477. For commentary on vampires, see Nina Auerbach, *Our Vampires, Ourselves* (Chicago: University of Chicago Press, 1995).

478. Rushkoff, "Playing Undead."

479. Don Steinberg, "Inside the Noisy World of Online Chat," *VirtualCity* 1, no. 2 (winter 1996): 35–42; and Robert Rossney, "Metaworlds," *Wired*, June 1996: 140–46, 202–12. See also Bernie Roehl's illuminating *Playing God: Building Virtual Worlds* (Corte Madera, Calif.: Waite Group, 1994). For Magic: The Gathering, see the game's website at http://www.wizards.com/magic/ and Darcy Steinke, "Masters of Their Domain," *Spin* 13, no. 5 (1997): 102–106.

480. Rushkoff, "Playing Undead." When this article was written, Craig was twenty-three and, according to Rushkoff, the "center of gameplaying in San Francisco." He had a connection to a San Francisco institution called Gamescape (http://www.gamescape.com/). I would be most grateful to hear of his present whereabouts. In this quotation, Craig refers to the Elysium. I gather that this is sometimes the name given to the Arts Pavilion but that it is also an otherworldly realm. Elysium is also the paradise of ancient Greek mythology.

481. Tony Horwitz, "In Virtual Mudville, Outlook Is Joyless as Rotisseries Halt," *Wall Street Journal*, August 11, 1994: A1. Horwitz says that the league is named for the now defunct Manhattan restaurant in which it was founded in 1980.

482. The Hollywood Stock Exchange can be found at http://www.hsx.com.

483. It might have been his film *Mission to Mars* (2000, dir. Brian De Palma).

484. Karen Wendel, formerly of the Capital Markets Company, believes we will see liquidity of this kind come even to Hollywood.

485. See Alexandra Artley and John Martin Robinson, *The New Georgian Handbook* (London: Ebury, 1985). Thanks to Charles Saumerez Smith for this reference.

486. Rushkoff makes the link still more particularly. "Each of [the] clans appears to be based on one of the vampire film traditions. Nosferatus are from the old silent horror movie, Tremere are Lugosi-style scientists, Toreadors are the guilt-stricken romantics of Ann [*sic*] Rice's Interview, and Brujahs are the punkish Lost Boys. Each clan of vampires appears to be fighting for the value of their own aesthetic." Rushkoff, "Playing Undead."

487. This was actually my starting point for this essay. I attended a wedding in Canada. Almost everyone who stood up to offer their congratulations did so in the voice, and with the skill, of a stand-up comedian. Certainly, these were smart people, but they were not, in this moment, exceptional ones. We have now watched so much stand-up and situation comedy that we can reproduce it.

488. See http://www.murdermystery.com/ for events of this kind.

489. For more on *Tony n' Tina's Wedding*, see the show's official website at http://www.tonylovestina.com.

490. *The Man Who Knew Too Little* (1997, dir. Jon Amiel), a film staring Bill Murray, turns on the notion of a man who enters a dangerous reality believing that it is a managed reality. The movie uses the predictable device, that Murray is protected by this innocence, and the audience is left to gasp at his stupidity and self-congratulation, and his repeated brushes with disaster.

491. See the Club Med website at http://www.clubmed.com.

492. "Celebration, which now has 2,500 residents, was built on 4,900 acres of land in Osceola County by top American architects. The town has many trademarks of the new urban style: large porches, back alleys, and a vibrant town centre that is meant to encourage people to talk to their neighbours and walk to the shops. The town is a throwback to turn of the century neighbourliness, orderliness and charm." Marina Jimenez, "In Celebration of the Unplanned Community," *National Post*, February 20, 1999: B11. For more on this Disney experiment, see Andrew Ross, *The Celebration Chronicles: Life, Liberty and the Pursuit of Property Value in Disney's New Town* (New York: Ballantine, 1999); and Douglas Frantz and Catherine Collins, *Celebration, U.S.A.: Living in Disney's Brave New Town* (New York: Henry Holt, 1999).

493. B. Joseph Pine and James H. Gilmore, *The Experience Economy: Work Is Theatre and Every Business A Stage* (Boston, Mass.: Harvard Business School Press, 1999).

494. Restoration Hardware is a retail operation that sells an interesting mix of goods: home hardware, furniture, art, decorations, kitchen appliances, and books. The only thing that makes this mix makes sense is that all the pieces carry the same narrative objective, to create and then summon a nostalgic past. For more information, see the store's website at http://www.restorationhardware.com.

495. On the "Rembrandt/Not Rembrandt" exhibit at the Metropolitan Museum, see Simon Schama, "Did He Do It? Sleuthing at the Met's Rembrandt Show," *New Yorker*, November 13, 1995: 114.

496. "Sharks! Fact and Fantasy" was at the Natural History Museum of Los Angeles County July 1 to September 23, 1990, and at the Royal Ontario Museum in Toronto February 6 to May 2, 1993. This show was funded by the National Science Foundation, and promotional literature from the Natural History Museum calls it "the largest, most comprehensive exhibition about sharks ever mounted." The show drew large audiences everywhere it was exhibited.

497. I spent many hours interviewing visitors to the shark show when it was mounted at the Royal Ontario Museum. The result was a paper available on request: Grant McCracken, "Culture and Culture at the Royal Ontario Museum," working paper presented at Harvard Business School on May 13, 1998.

498. I apologize for how maudlin my examples are. But if we can breathe life into even these, the chances of adoption of this game are good. I was interested to

see that the science fiction writer Dan Simmons, in his novel *Hyperion* (New York: Doubleday, 1989), has one of his characters engage in a "stimsim" that is bloody, terrifying, and unheroic. This is, of course, no proof that this is what we can look forward to, but it is interesting to see that in these pages it rings true.

499. Goffman was the great student of the strategies of self-presentation. Erving Goffman, *The Presentation of Self in Everyday Life* (Harmondsworth: Penguin, 1959).

500. The double movement is particularly evident in the English reaction to Basil Fawlty (John Cleese), the lead character in the BBC series *Fawlty Towers*. (See The Unofficial Guide to *Fawlty Towers*, http://www.btinternet.com/~c.tomlinson/fawlty1.html.) Basil offers both a holiday from the strict rules of politeness that govern most of English life and a chance to repudiate the man who violates them. Something like this doubleness was at work in the deep ambivalence that the American audience felt for Archie Bunker in *All in the Family*.

501. I thank Wade Nelson for suggesting this example.

502. For an excellent review of the connection between celebrities and fans, see Jackie Stacey, "Feminine Fascinations: Forms of Identification in Star-Audience Relations," in Gledhill, *Stardom*, 141–63.

503. I believe this observation may help explain the mystery of the film *Wonder Boys* (2000, dir. Curtis Hanson). This film seemed to have everything going for it, including origin in a novel by Michael Chabon, direction by Curtis Hanson, a screenplay by Steve Kloves, performances by Michael Douglas, Tobey Maguire, Frances McDormand, Robert Downey, Jr., and Katie Holmes, and enthusiastic critical acclaim, including a place on several Top 10 lists, including that of Roger Ebert, who called it "one of the great movies of the year." Its first release earned disappointing returns (see the figures at http://www.boxofficemojo.com/movies/?id=wonderboys .htm), and it was rereleased on the theory that the popular response was somehow due to bad luck or bad timing. But, mysteriously, the second release proved as unsuccessful as the first. The world really didn't like, or get, something about this film. I think it may be because Mike Douglas insisted on stepping out of the Robert Wagner/Warren Beatty/Harrison Ford model of stardom—the one Douglas assumes in the more recent movie *Traffic* (2000, dir. Steven Soderbergh)—and disappeared into his role as Professor Tripp: out of celebrity, that is to say, into uncharacteristically nuanced acting. The filmgoing audience is eager for nuanced acting, but not when it comes from someone who is iconic, more important for the celebrity the actor carries from role to role than for the persona occupied in any particular role.

504. I do understand that this date is controversial, with some parties insisting that punk began in the 1960s. I am merely erring on the side of caution.

505. Quoted in Greil Marcus, *Lipstick Traces: A Secret History of the Twentieth Century* (Cambridge, Mass.: Harvard University Press, 1989), 7. For more on punks, see Jon Savage, *England's Dreaming: Sex Pistols and Punk Rock* (London: Faber and Faber, 1991).

506. This punk fondness for imperfection carried over into the alternative music of the 1990s it helped create. I talked to someone in an Austin band in 1994. He was troubled about the most unexpected thing. "The trouble is," he said, "we're getting too good." Contemporary artists like the postmodernist Joseph Beuys (1921–1986) insisted that everyone was an artist. I leave this aspect of the participatory turn to someone else.

507. I worked as a chauffeur for Julie Christie during the filming of *McCabe and Mrs. Miller* (1971, dir. Robert Altman).

508. I don't know what evidence I can supply for this shift beyond my say-so. The number of films that now examine Hollywood from the inside might serve as a kind of indicator: *The Player* (1992, dir. Robert Altman), *Swimming with Sharks* (1994, dir. George Huang), *Living in Oblivion* (1995, dir. Tom DiCillo), *Soapdish* (1991, dir. Michael Hoffman), *The Big Picture* (1989, dir. Christopher Guest), and *The Newsroom* (1996, dir. Ken Finkleman). There is also the HBO series *The Larry Sanders Show*, which ran from 1992 to 1998.

This project produced a second body of evidence in illustration of the participatory turn. We designed the exhibit that sprang from this research, "Toronto Teenagers: Coming of Age in the 1990s," to include a last section in which people could leave comments on the walls. We put up boards and covered about 440 square feet. We naively thought this would be sufficient to accommodate all the comments made by visitors over the run of the show. As it turned out, the boards had to be replaced once and sometimes twice a day.

509. Duncombe, *Notes from Underground*, 14. A publication called *Factsheet Five* was once a clearing house for zine information. It has suspended publication, but maintains a website at http://www.factsheet5.org.

510. For a treatment of this phenomenon, see Jon Katz, "The Netizen: The Digital Citizen," *Wired* 5, no. 12 (1997): 68–82, 274–75. Katz talks more about the Internet as an opportunity for political participation, but a good deal of what he says applies to those who participate in culture.

511. Henry Jenkins, *Textual Poachers: Television Fans and Participatory Culture* (New York: Routledge, 1992). See the excellent chapter "Participatory Culture" in Duncombe, *Notes from Underground*.

512. The rhythm of *Law and Order*: victim discovered in opening seconds, detectives hand over to lawyers at the half-hour mark, final court engagement begins at the forty-five-minute mark. I thank Dayna McLeod for pointing this out to me.

513. Norbert Elias, *The History of Manners*, translated by Edmund Jephcott (New York: Pantheon, 1978).

514. Lionel Trilling, *Sincerity and Authenticity* (Cambridge, Mass.: Harvard University Press, 1971).

515. Claude Lévi-Strauss's *La pensée sauvage* appeared in English as *The Savage Mind* (London: Weidenfeld and Nicolson, 1966). The title might have been translated as "wild thought," and it represented Lévi-Strauss's attempt to capture the logic of investigation, or, as he calls it, the "science of the concrete," in traditional societies. For more on "shamanic liberty," see the sixth paragraph of the essay above called "New Age, British Columbia (and radiant selves)." The maps of early modern Europe sometimes marked terra incognita with the phrase "here lie wilde beasties." Gamelan orchestras date from at least the fourteenth century. Echinacea is now a fixture in the cold-fighting regime of many Westerners. It was adopted by millions of users on the strength of hearsay, and without the benefit of scientific tests. Our adoption of this substance is some measure of the rise of the authority of alternative medicines.

516. Many episodes of *Frasier* will illustrate this point, but "A Tsar Is Born" (episode 7 of season 7), the one that concerns an antique clock from the Russian court, is particularly apt. Frasier and Niles hope that it will serve as proof of the

family's aristocratic origins and they are eager to use it in this capacity. They are horrified when it proves, instead, that one of their ancestors was a prostitute.

517. Camille Paglia, "How the Demos Lost the White House in Seattle," *Salon*, December 8, 1999, http://www.salon.com/people/col/pagl/1999/12/08/cp1208/index2.html. See also the still more damning treatment in Arlene Vigoda, "Brits Embrace Madonna, Even the Accent," *USA Today*, December 15, 2000, http://www.usatoday.com/life/music/music413.htm.

518. Thanks to Leora Kornfeld for encouraging me to think about Madonna's latest manifestation.

519. It's as if we are caught in an endless movement between sincerity and authenticity, to use Trilling's terms. And this must mean victory goes to the latter and away from upward transformation. Authenticity is embarrassed by the memory of sincerity but it can endure it—as long as we *meant* it. The reverse is not also true. To recall authenticity is to surrender.

520. Ted Morgan, *Literary Outlaw: The Life and Times of William S. Burroughs* (New York: Holt, 1988), 173.

521. "Retrofit" is machine language and refers to the practice of giving early models of a product the advancements characteristic of later ones. This is a favorite term in the swift vocabulary. According to the *Oxford English Dictionary*, it did not achieve currency until the late 1950s.

522. Christopher Dewdney, *Last Flesh: Life in the Transhuman Era* (Toronto: HarperCollins, 1998), 24. Haraway says that the combination of human and machine has already been accomplished. Haraway, "A Cyborg Manifesto," 150.

523. "Our consciousness of the self will have to undergo a profound change as we continue to embrace the transforming advances in biological and communications technologies. A new construction of the self will inevitably take hold as ever more powerful body-altering techniques become commonplace." Jeffrey Deitch, *Post Human* (New York: Distributed Art Publishers, 1992), 29.

524. William Gibson, *Mona Lisa Overdrive* (New York: Bantam, 1988).

525. Burning Man is a festival that takes place each year in the Nevada desert. For more, see the official website at http://www.burningman.com/whatisburningman/.

526. Jean Baudrillard, *Simulacra and Simulation*, translated by Sheila Glaser (Ann Arbor: University of Michigan Press, 1994).

527. I have developed this argument in a treatment of what I take to be the inability of postmodernists to account for "turn-taking" in conversation. McCracken, *Plenitude 2.0*, 123.

528. Homa Bahrami and Stuart Evans, "Flexible Re-Cycling and High-Technology Entrepreneurship," *California Management Review* 37, no. 3 (spring 1995): 71.

529. Emile Durkheim, *The Division of Labor in Society*, translated by George Simpson (New York: Free Press, 1933).

530. Stanley M. Davis and Christopher Meyer, *Blur: The Speed of Change in the Connected Economy* (Reading: Addison-Wesley, 1998); James Gleick, *Faster: The Acceleration of Just About Everything* (New York: Pantheon, 1999); and Paul Virilio and James Der Derian, *The Virilio Reader* (Malden, Mass.: Blackwell, 1998).

531. "In general, people neither insist on naming all of their ancestries nor just call themselves American. Most pick and choose. And the trend is apparently

toward more and more people making choices about their ethnic ancestry." Waters, *Ethnic Options*, 20. Waters is concerned with understanding how people answer questions about ethnicity for the census. She gives relatively little attention to outright invention of ancestors or origins.

532. "[M]any of the American men I talked with often expressed their belief in the cultural sovereignty of the individual. They argued that 'the way you choose to dress and spend your money is your business,' that 'the way you feel comfortable with it, that's fine,' and that it is wrong to be judgmental regarding other people's lifestyles and tastes ('If that's what they want that's what they want')." Lamont, *Money, Morals and Manners*, 116.

533. John Lahr, "The Izzard King," *New Yorker*, April 6, 1998: 82.

534. Geertz, "From the Native's Point of View," 126.

535. So there is a naturally occurring (i.e., extra-political) constraint, and this needs investigating. Such a constraint means that not everyone has the right to change cultural categories. Or it might mean that everyone has the right, but only some have the qualities necessary to exercise it.

536. Margo Jefferson, "Dennis Rodman: Bad Boy as Man of the Moment," *New York Times*, January 30, 1997: C13.

537. Elias Canetti, *Crowds and Power*, translated by Carol Stewart (London: Penguin, 1992), 438.

538. Henry Louis Gates, Jr., *Loose Canons: Notes on the Culture Wars* (New York: Oxford University Press, 1992).

539. I have tried to address this question in the first book in the Culture by Commotion series, *Plenitude*.

540. Farrah Fawcett, interview by Matt Lauer on *The Today Show*, NBC, October 6, 2000, when asked to account for her behavior on the *David Letterman Show*.

541. The year 1972 is a rough marker, an arbitrary date that stands somewhere between the first appearance of the work of these three authors and the dates their work found its way into currency, translation, and general acceptance (i.e., the late 1960s and the middle 1970s). Michel Foucault's *L'archeologie du savoir* was published in 1969, with the English translation, *The Archaeology of Knowledge*, appearing in 1972. Jacques Lacan's *Écrits* appeared in 1966, with the English translation following in 1977. Jacques Derrida's *De la grammatologie* appeared in 1967, with the English translation, *Of Grammatology*, following in 1976. His *L'écriture et différence* also appeared in 1967, with the English translation, *Writing and Difference*, following in 1978. For an overview of this literature, see Levine, *Constructions of the Self*, and Charles Taylor, *Hegel* (Cambridge: Cambridge University Press, 1975).

542. See "Central Park: The Complete Guide," http://www.centralpark.org/home.html.

543. There are a couple of interesting excursions in this area: Kenneth J. Gergen, *The Saturated Self: Dilemmas of Identity in Contemporary Life* (New York: Basic Books, 1991); and Robert Jay Lifton, *The Protean Self: Human Resilience in an Age of Fragmentation* (New York: Basic Books, 1993).

544. Halberstam handles with intelligence this distinction between those who pursue fluidity and those for whom it is merely the transition that takes them to a new, stable, and "real" destination. Volcano and Halberstam, *The Drag King Book*, 41.

545. "A *bot* is a software tool for digging through data [on the Internet]. You give a bot directions and it brings back answers. The word is short for *robot* of course, which is derived from the Czech word *robota* meaning *work*." Botspot, "What's a Bot," http://www.botspot.com/bot/what_is_a_bot.html.

546. Geertz, "From the Native's Point of View," 126.

Conclusion

1. Ingrid Hein, "The Payphone Project," *Shift* 9, no. 2 (2001): 38. See the Payphone Project website for more information: http://www.payphone-project .com/. I think the global self is also in evidence in the scene in *Being John Malkovich* (1999, dir. Spike Jonze) in which everyone looks like John Malkovich. The multiple self appears in recent music videos, which, it should be noted, have almost nothing else in common. See the video for "ILuvIt" from the album *Duces N' Trays: The Old Fashioned Way*, by Snoop Dogg and Tha Eastsidaz, and the one for "Rockin' the Suburbs" from the eponymous album by Ben Folds.

2. And here the enduring feature and theme of the film, the stupendous fatness of the Klumps, plays out in an interesting way. It is both a statement of how capacious Klump, and Murphy, must be, and of how large is the territory that is allowed to exist in any one character despite its impending "incorporation." One measure of the film's success is its success at the box office. According to the Internet Movie Database (http://us.imdb.com/Business?0117218), it earned a $300 million gross on the theatrical release and rentals, on an investment of $54 million.

3. Peter Travers, review of *The Nutty Professor*, *Rolling Stone*, nos. 738–739 (December 8, 2000), http://www.rollingstone.com/reviews/movie/5948937/ review/5948938/the_nutty_professor.

4. *Possible Worlds* is perhaps less well known than the others. See the interesting review by Jason Anderson: "From the Page to Lepage," *Eye Magazine*, January 18, 2001, http://www.eye.net/eye/issue/issue_01.18.01/film/possibleworlds.html. The movie was based on John Mighton's remarkable play *Possible Worlds*, 2nd rev. ed. (Toronto: Playwrights Canada Press, 1997).

5. The total known to have been spent on these films is actually $327 million. Figures for this calculation come from the Internet Movie Database (http:// www.imdb.com) and from *Variety* (http://www.variety.com) for *Possible Worlds*. It was necessary to estimate the costs of *Sliding Doors*, *Passion of Mind*, and *Me Myself I* (which I did as $10 million, $10 million, and $2 million, respectively).

6. John Ellis, *Visible Fictions: Cinema, Television, Video* (London: Routledge & Kegan Paul, 1982), 43.

7. As the life of North Americans grows more fragmented and transformational, the career of the celebrity finds a parallel in the life of the fan.

8. Ernst Hartwig Kantorowicz, *The King's Two Bodies: A Study in Mediaeval Political Theology* (Princeton, N.J.: Princeton University Press, 1957).

9. This frontispiece is reproduced on the cover of Thomas Hobbes, *Leviathan* (1651; New York: Oxford University Press, 1996).

10. We might go so far as to say the celebrity has a third body, composed of all those fans who construct themselves out of materials from the star and, so constructing themselves, make the star a star.

11. Ellis, *Visible Fictions*, 43.

12. Simon Frith, "Beggars Banquet," in *Stranded: Rock and Roll for a Desert Island*, ed. Greil Marcus (New York: Knopf, 1979), 30.

13. This quotation is recalled from memory and may be inaccurate. Soderbergh said it while being interviewed by Mitchell on an episode of the Independent Film Channel program *IFC Focus*, for more on which see http://www.ifctv.com.

14. I do not mean to imply that Soderbergh acts in a manner that is cavalier. The fact that a great many filmmakers continue to agonize over the choice tells us that dismissing this boundary is not something Soderbergh can do just because he wants to, and more to the point, that doing so is a DiFranco-like innovation and accomplishment. How far Soderbergh is prepared to go to investigate the theme of an expansionary individualism may be seen in his 1999 film *Schizopolis*, in which he plays Fletcher Munson and Dr. Jeffrey Korchek. See the film's page at the Internet Movie Database at http://us.imdb.com/Title?0117561.

15. Shep Steiner, "Rodney Graham: Au dèla des principes de la blague," *Last Call* 1, no. 1 (2001): 1-2. Thanks to Leora Kornfeld for this article. For more on Graham and his art, see the Lisson Gallery website at http://www.lissongallery.com. For more on Cindy Sherman, see remarks by Peter Galassi at http://csw.art.pl/new/98/shermeg.html.

16. Jamie James, "Yo-Yo Ma May Be a National Institution, but He Continues to Reinvent Himself," *New York Times*, December 31, 1995: H32.

17. This quotation is from Chris Hilker's webpage, which appears now to be defunct: http://www.hyperreal.com/raves/altraveFAQ.html. It may have appeared in the liner notes of Eno's album *Ambient 4: On Land* (1986): http://music.hyperreal.org/artists/brian_eno/onland-tet.html. This quotation reads as a kind of mandate for several of the Hollywood pictures referred to above. It appears to explain, for instance, *Sliding Doors* (1998, dir. Peter Howitt), *Fight Club* (1999, dir. David Fincher), *Passion of the Mind* (2000, dir. Alain Berliner), *The Family Man* (2000, dir. Brett Ratner), *Me Myself I* (1999, dir. Pip Karmel), and *Possible Worlds* (2000, dir. Robert Lepage).

18. David Brooks, *Bobos in Paradise: The New Upper Class and How They Got There* (New York: Simon and Schuster, 2000).

19. I believe that the term "Generation X" was originated by Douglas Coupland in his book *Generation X: Tales for an Accelerated Culture* (New York: St. Martin's, 1993). It identifies the generation that entered their late teens and twenties in the 1990s. Subsequent generations are now designated "Y" and "Z."

20. David Denby, "Buried Alive: Our Children and the Avalanche of Crud," *New Yorker* 72, no. 19 (1996): 50–51. I have reversed the halves of this quotation. In the original, everything before the phrase "crashing into the kitchen" appears after the phrase "and other Jim Carrey movies." The real measure of Denby's failure to grasp what is going on here is his use of the term "private languages." These are anything but private—as he acknowledges.

21. Joshua Meyrowitz, *No Sense of Place: The Impact of Electronic Media on Social Behavior* (New York: Oxford University Press, 1985), 227. Meyrowitz is so struck by

the crossover happening here that he does not remark sufficiently on the second, and equally striking, feature of this development: that each party is prepared to appropriate the definitions of the other, but wishes to keep, and to exercise, the definitions with which it began. Both parties are adding selves, not trading them.

22. Calvin O. Schrag, *The Self after Postmodernity* (New Haven, Conn.: Yale University Press, 1997), 8, emphasis in the original.

23. Quoted in Malcolm Bradbury and James Walter McFarlane, "The Name and Nature of Modernism," in *Modernism: A Guide to European Literature, 1890–1930*, ed. Malcolm Bradbury and James Walter McFarlane (London: Penguin, 1991), 47.

24. Berman describes Montesquieu's description of the authenticity accomplished through Western urban life this way: "[These Parisians] are remarkably flexible, sensitized to a life of perpetual change and mobility; on the other hand, for all the metamorphoses they go through, their underlying sense of self remains intact." Marshall Berman, *The Politics of Authenticity: Radical Individualism and the Emergence of Modern Society* (New York: Atheneum, 1980), 53. Taylor, too, talks about the self sought through the pursuit of authenticity as a singular self. "Being true to myself means being true to my own originality, and that is something only I can articulate and discover. In articulating it, I am also defining myself. I am realizing a potentiality that is properly my own. This is the background understanding to the modern ideal of authenticity." Charles Taylor, *The Malaise of Modernity* (Concord, Ontario: Anansi, 1991), 29.

25. Daniel Bell, *The Cultural Contradictions of Capitalism* (New York: Basic Books, 1976), 53–54.

26. Plato, quoted in Arthur O. Lovejoy, *The Great Chain of Being: A Study of the History of an Idea* (Cambridge, Mass.: Harvard University Press, 1950), 52. It should be pointed out that Plato was referring to the natural world, not the social one.

27. Steven Lukes, "Durkheim's 'Individualism and the Intellectuals,'" *Political Studies* 17, no. 1 (1969): 26.

28. Ibid.

Acknowledgments

This book was started when I was working at the Royal Ontario Museum in Toronto. Thanks are due to Adrienne Hood, Suzanne Stein, and Wentworth Walker, all long-term supporters of this project, and especially to Hargurchet Bhabra, a friend now deceased, to whom this book is dedicated. Thanks are also due to the Saturday afternoon group, Gloria Bishop, Gilbert Reid, John Roberts, and Bhabra, the leader of those proceedings, and to the Friday lunchtime group, particularly Jim Dingwall, Alan Middleton, Lee Simpson, and Jim Stacey. Particular thanks are due to Dave Dyment, Leora Kornfeld, Rikk Villa, and Lisa V. Werenko for impromptu instruction in contemporary art, music, and culture. Thanks are due to friends at the Royal Ontario Museum, particularly Lindsay Sharp, Margo Welch, Trudy Nicks, Jeff Brown, Nick Harney, Cathy Logan, Ronnie Burbank, Angela Raljic, and Julia Matthews, and to other friends and colleagues in and out of Toronto, particularly Bree Short, Nick Hahn, Charlotte Oades, Martin Weigel, Denise Fonseca, Michael Stoner, Evan Solomon, Ken Ames, Patrick Crane, Ben Stone, Rita Rayman, Kevin Clark, Shaista Justin, Sheri Roder, Mark NcNeilly, Meg Beckle, Leo Suarez, Rae Burdon, Kimberley Van Der Zon, John Sherry, Harry Roth, Beverly Lemire, David Mick, Rick McGee, Peter Grossman, Mary Mills, Noel Marts, Murray Belzberg, Rick Sterling, Paula Rosch, Tess Resman, Myra Stark, John Prevost, Kenelm Burridge, Marilyn Zavitz, Wodek Szemberg, Linda Scott, Matthew Ariker, Russ Belk, Sarah Fitzharding, Bill O'Connor, Elvi Whitaker, Rich Lutz, Chris Commins, Jeannie Beker, Khalil Younes, Elizabeth Torlée, Jackie Kaiser, Melanie Wallendorf, Joan Adelman, Vic Roth, Donna Woolcott, Claire Quinn, Karen Wendel, Heather Monroe-Blum, Mike Lotti, Joan Kron, Anat Shavit, Michel Blondeau, Virginia Postrel, Stephanie Handcock, Sergio Zyman, and Montrose Sommers.

It was written in part while I was teaching at Harvard Business School. Thanks are due to the students of Section D, MBA 2001, and especially Charles Hale, Patrick Killick, Wui-Yen Liow, Shaka Rasheed, Christina Ehrenberg, Neil Houghton, William Nolan, Courtney Swerdloff, John

Lippman, Daniel Allen, Monisha Saldanha, Aaron Benway, Naomi Weinberg, Pryce Greennow, Tayfun Umer, Bryn Zeckhauser, Zulfiqar Khan, Ted Berk, Omar Lodhi, Weigang Ye, David DeGiralamo, Jesse Hsu, Farouk Ladha, Roberto Figueroa, Margaret Woolley, Sonia Alcantarilla, Jennifer Duong, Marc Durance, Robert Murdocca, Dawn Landry, Ness Okonkwo, John Multhauf, Vittorio Ragazzini, Michael East, Charles Warner, Sacha Ghai, Dessi Donkova, and, of course, Krylov Dimitri, and to other members of the HBS community, particularly John Deighton, and to Susan Fournier, Kay Lemon, Sam Chun, Gil McWilliam, Bob Dolan, Tiziana Casciaro, Kash Rangan, Kerry Herman, Rohit Deshpandé, Youngme Moon, Gerry Zaltman, Natalie Zakarian, Jed Emerson, Rajiv Lal, David Arnold, Andrea Wojnicki, John Gourville, Kip King, Luc Wathieu, Steve Greyser, Miklos Savary, and Alvin Silk, and to other friends in Cambridge and Boston, particularly Amy Domini, George Anastapolo, Stanford Anderson, Nancy Royal, Renata Simon, David Fanning, Glorianna Davenport, Deborah Cohen, and Annie Pedret.

I continued writing while living in Montreal. Thanks are due to Jim Gough, Margaret van Nooten, Peter White, Giselle Amantea, Lise Ouimet, Michel Verdon, Heather Juby, Maggie Fadoul, Dayna McLeod, Johanne Lamoureux, Christine Ross, Johanne Sloan, Karl Moore, Jim Drobnick, Marlene Gauthier, Don McGregor, Alain Lapointe, Jennifer Fisher, Daniel Langlois, France De Palma, Normand Blouin, Alan Blum, Elke Grenzer, and the participants in a course taught at McGill in the winters of 2001–2002 and 2002–2003. Particular thanks are due to Will Straw for the opportunity to participate in the remarkably interesting life of the Department of Art History and Communications Studies at McGill University.

I finished the book while living outside New York City. Thanks are due to Richard and Pam Shear, Joe and Christine Melchione, Andrew Zolli, Tom Guarriello, Mark Murray, Tom Asacker, Bob Woodard, Pip Corburn, Lee Green, Dave Bujnowski, Debbie Millman, Lynne Kiesling, Margaret Mark, Jerry Kathman, Cheryl Swanson, Ron Smith, Chuck Freund, James Cerrutti, John Winsor, Stewart Owen, Craig Swanson, Russell Davies, Tyler Cowen, Piers Fawkes, Marc Babej, Erich Joachimsthaler, Tom Neilssen, Rob Wallace, Ricardo Sapiro, J. Duncan Berry, Nancy White, John Fledtmose, Winnie Klotz, Paul Hutton, Les Tuerk, Susan Royer, Joe Plummer, and Peter Ellis. Special thanks are due to Henry Jenkins, William Uricchio, Sam Ford, Ivan Askwith, Parmesh Shahani, David Edery, Generoso Fierro, and Joel Greenberg.

The manuscript has had the benefit of comments and suggestions from several readers. Thanks are called for here to Mish Vadasz, Will

Straw, Leora Kornfeld, Jim Dingwall, Lise Ouimet, Christopher Dingwall, Amy Domini, Don McGregor, Ken Ames, Wodek Szemberg, Johanne Lamoureux, Mary Mills, Martin Weigel, Guy Lanoue, Herbert Gans, Suzanne Stein, Wentworth Walker, Annie Pedret, Kenelm Burridge, and William Morrison. Special thanks are due to Robert Sloan and the editorial team at Indiana University Press.

Finally, my deepest thanks to my wife, Pamela DeCesare, and our Molly.

Index

Grant McCracken is a research affiliate of the Comparative Media Department at MIT. Born and raised in Vancouver, he holds a Ph.D. from the University of Chicago in cultural anthropology. He has taught at the University of Cambridge and Harvard Business School. He is the author of several books, including *Culture and Consumption, Culture and Consumption II, Flock and Flow* (all three published by Indiana University Press), *The Long Interview*, and *Plenitude*. He has consulted widely in the corporate world, with organizations including the Coca-Cola Company, IBM, and Chrysler.